Social Fabric or Patchwork Quilt

Social Fabric or Patchwork Quilt

THE DEVELOPMENT OF SOCIAL POLICY IN CANADA

edited by

Raymond B. Blake and Jeffrey A. Keshen

University of Toronto Press

Previously published by Broadview Press, 2006 © the authors

Library and Archives Canada Cataloguing in Publication

Social fabric or patchwork quilt : the development of social policy in
Canada / edited by Raymond B. Blake and Jeff rey A. Keshen.
Includes bibliographical references.

ISBN 978-1-55111-544-3

1. Canada—Social policy. 2. Public welfare—Canada—History. 3. Welfare state—Canada—History. I. Blake, Raymond B. (Raymond Benjamin) II. Keshen, Jeff , 1962–.

HV108.S62   2006   361.6'10971   C2006-901266-0

We welcome comments and suggestions regarding any aspect of our publications—please feel free to contact us at news@utphighereducation.com or visit our Internet site at www.utphighereducation.com.

North America
5201 Dufferin Street
North York, Ontario, Canada, M3H 5T8

2250 Military Road
Tonawanda, New York, USA, 14150

ORDERS PHONE: 1-800-565-9523
ORDERS FAX: 1-800-221-9985
ORDERS E-MAIL: utpbooks@utpress.utoronto.ca

UK, Ireland, and continental Europe
NBN International
Estover Road, Plymouth, PL6 7PY, UK
ORDERS PHONE: 44 (0) 1752 202301
ORDERS FAX: 44 (0) 1752 202333
ORDERS E-MAIL: enquiries@nbninternational.com

The University of Toronto Press acknowledges the financial support for its publishing activities of the Government of Canada through the Canada Book Fund.

Printed in Canada

Contents

6

II: Triumph to Reform 171

III: New Realities in Social Security 339

Introduction

PERHAPS IT IS ONLY IN CANADA that the social welfare system is seen as a defining national characteristic. Yet, Canadians continue to tell those who take the national pulse in the various annual surveys that their identity is defined, in part, through Canada's various social security programs.[1] Although the social welfare system has taken shape over several generations—and many would in fact quarrel with calling it a "system"—there has emerged in Canada, over the past century or so, a series of social policies that cumulatively have become a part of the nation's social fabric; this is so even if, collectively, the various pieces of social welfare legislation resemble a patchwork quilt.

There are many elements to the welfare state and many participants in the creation of social policy. Perhaps key among them are the various levels of government—federal, provincial, municipal, and First Nations—that provide publicly funded programs to address a particular problem or issue. The creation of social policy is not limited, however, to the state powers to provide programs: increasingly, the tax system is being used to address particular concerns, such as child poverty. Moreover, the voluntary sector continues to play an important role in the provision of social welfare services, and even the courts have been an actor in social policy; and they may well play an even greater role in the future.

This collection seeks to examine many of the actors involved in the creation and implementation of social policy in Canada. For our purposes here, we have taken social policy to mean not simply the policies that governments use for welfare and social protection, but the ways in which Canadian society has come to share the risks of unemployment, ill health, poverty, and other social ills.[2] While social policy is often concerned with the delivery of social services and the instruments of the welfare state, this collection deals with a range of issues that extend far beyond the actions of various levels of government to deliver programs. Here, we will consider how the social, political, and economic conditions helped shape the development of social policy in Canada since Confederation in 1867.

Canada's social welfare system has emerged slowly since Confederation. While there was nothing akin in 1867 to the social security programs that would emerge in the middle of the twentieth century, there was, nonetheless, a clearly articulated philosophy towards the poor and a rudimentary manner for dealing with the destitute, even if the primary responsibility fell to either the church or the local community. Regardless of where any destitute or needy person lived in Canada around the time of Confederation, they were usually regarded as personal failures. In a largely rural and agrarian society, the belief in individual responsibility was dominant, and most Canadians believed that any assistance rendered to the poor, either by the state or private charity, had to be demeaning and insufficient so as not to destroy the incentive to work. Consequently, there was little sharing of the risk when citizens found themselves out of work because of ill health and injury, unemployment, or any other misfortunes that life invariably brought to people.

There had emerged in early Canada a clear distinction between the deserving and the undeserving poor. Children, women, and the disabled, for instance, who did not participate in the labour economy, were considered to be the "deserving" poor, but they had to rely on family or voluntary organizations for any help against the vicissitudes of life. Able-bodied men who found themselves destitute, on the other hand, were clearly deemed undeserving of assistance. The most common mode of dispensing charity, especially in the urban centres, was in the poorhouse, or Houses of Industry, as they were frequently called. Like the early prisons, they housed the physically and mentally challenged, the sick, the elderly, orphans, and all other charity cases. Such institutions not only fulfilled basic sustenance but also sought to encourage desirable work habits, foster discipline, and promote morality. The situation for the poor was not much better in rural areas, where cash-strapped local communities and voluntary organizations were left to deal with the poor and destitute. All told, the colonies allocated about 3 percent of their total expenditures to public welfare in 1866.

Not much changed in social policy legislation with Confederation in 1867. The federal government was simply not interested in any of the instruments of social policy such as hospitals, charities, asylums, schools, and other related institutions, as it saw social welfare as primarily a local concern. Responsibility for social welfare fell to the provinces, and only later would the jurisdictional question emerge as an important one in Canadian social policy.[3]

Even so, one could argue that the foundations of modern social security were laid in the years immediately following Confederation, when governments had to deal with the realities of the new industrial order. As Elizabeth Wallace has argued, "at no time since 1867 were laissez-faire theories consistently practised or government intervention in economic or social matters considered inappropriate."[4] During the latter decades of the nineteenth century and the first decades of the twentieth, when Canada's rate of economic growth surpassed that of much of the industrializing world, the nation experienced a period of considerable change. With industrialization came the first major wave of urbanization, and large number of Canadians became wage earners, dependent upon a steady job and a regular income. Yet, it was still widely accepted that if a citizen was poor or unemployed it was not a systemic problem with industrial capitalism or the market economy, but a moral flaw with the individual.

Still, many Canadians, especially women and members of various religious and civic-minded groups, became concerned with the increasing incidence of poverty, industrial accidents, child labour, prostitution, and other social problems associated with the new economy.[5] They did much to spark inquiries into the most visible social problems, which often resulted in calls for government intervention, especially in the form of increased regulation of the workplace and further restrictions on the use of alcohol.[6] By the end of the nineteenth century, it was clear that municipal and provincial governments, especially, were prepared to become involved in the social sphere, given that many of the support mechanisms associated with rural and farming communities were being lost, as Canada became increasingly urban.[7] Still, building a social security system was not an easy feat as the old myths surrounding public assistance proved to be quite enduring.

The early social reform movement was directed primarily at municipal and provincial governments, and it was at these levels that the first social security programmes emerged. Following similar trends in Europe, Ontario introduced a *Workman's Compensation Act* in 1914 that allowed workers a regular cash income while they recovered from injuries sustained on the job, but prevented them from suing their employers in court.[8] Mother's Allowances followed, first in Manitoba in 1916, to assist women who faced difficulty in raising their families without the father who had gone to fight in World War I, never to return.[9] The First World War also created an activism government in Ottawa that was primarily interested in mobilizing the nation's resources to win the war, but many social reformers hoped that it would also signal the beginning of an interventionist federal government to address some of their concerns about ills associated with the times. The federal government did, however, assume much of the responsibility for war pensions and the rehabilitation of veterans.[10] In 1921 many expressed the hope that the election of William Lyon Mackenzie King as prime minister would translate into new initiatives in social policy, as in his earlier years he was a noted social scientist who had spelled out a vision of a new social order for Canada. Also, he had been elected on a platform that promised old-age pensions, as well as health and unemployment insurance. However, during his first ten years in office, his accomplishments did not come close to meeting such expectations. While King delivered Canada's first old-age pension program in 1927, it was cost-shared by the federal and provincial governments, and paid a paltry $20 per month to needy Canadians over 70, who had to first pass a humiliating means test. It was, nonetheless, an important step forward, and a recognition by Ottawa that it had some responsibility towards the poor.[11] The initiative was also important as it set the pattern for later cost-shared programs between the federal and provincial governments, and was designed to achieve national standards in policy areas that fell under provincial jurisdiction.

King lost the 1930 federal election just as the Great Depression was beginning, a catastrophe that Canadian governments were woefully unprepared to fight. As unemployment rates rose rapidly in the early 1930s, governments at all levels adhered to the nineteenth-century model of poor relief, supplemented with a growing dependency on voluntary charity. The federal government maintained that relief was a local responsibility, even though R.B. Bennett, the Conservative Prime Minister, realized that the sheer volume of Canadians out of work made the issue a national one. As a "temporary" measure, the federal government made modest payments to the provinces each year from 1930 to 1939, to allow them to provide relief to the unemployed. Even Bennett had to admit that the capitalist system had to be reformed, and introduced a series of measures, including unemployment insurance, in his "New Deal," to save the system just before the 1935 federal election; the courts, however, ruled that the federal government had exceeded its authority, and struck down the legislation.[12] The voters returned King, who still refused to accept the need for decisive government intervention. Yet, even if political leaders were slow to recognize the need for new approaches to social welfare, the decade ended with many of the old myths governing unemployment and poverty severely shaken. It had become clear that local communities—and even some of the provinces—simply did not have the financial resources to cope with relief during severe economic downturns, and charity and voluntary aid could not be expected to fill the gap. The period marked an important shift in Canadian thinking about both economics and social welfare.[13] No longer did most people believe that all types of social welfare for their fellow citizens should be demeaning and limited, a point made in the Rowell-Sirois Commission that King had appointed in 1937 to study dominion–provincial relations.

It took war in 1939 to put Canadians back to work and bring major improvements in Canada's social welfare system. The industrial and military mobilization in Canada created full employment, but from the outset of hostilities, Canada's leaders—as well as those of other countries—were concerned about the postwar period. The immediate aftermath of the First World War had been extremely difficult for many Canadians, and governments wanted to avoid similar problems this time.[14] Consequently, governments knew that the transition from war to peace had to be managed better than in the past. These concerns were reflected in the Atlantic Charter, signed on 14 August 1941, when British Prime Minister Winston Churchill and American President Franklin Roosevelt announced their desire "to bring about the fullest collaboration between all nations in the economic field with the object of securing, for all, improved labour standards, economic adjustment and social security." Moreover, more than twenty countries from North and South America agreed at a conference held in Chile in 1942 that social security would be one of their prime objectives in the post-war period. As Leonard Marsh remarked years later, "by 1943 social security was in the air as never before," as discussion about a new social order was as persuasive in Ottawa as elsewhere.[15]

Many of Canada's current social welfare programs had their genesis in the planning for the postwar period, though it would be several decades (if at all) before all the measures discussed were fully implemented. In 1940, following a constitutional amendment, the federal government introduced unemployment insurance, in part, as a way to deal with the problems created by the Great Depression.[16] Ottawa also appointed an Advisory Committee on Reconstruction, known as the James Committee (after its chair, Dr. Cyril James), to offer advice to the government. Leonard Marsh was appointed the Committee's research director and his *Report on Social Security for Canada* created considerable interest throughout Canada, following as it did the British report on reconstruction, *Social Insurance and Allied Services*, better known as the Beveridge Report. Marsh proposed a "comprehensive and integrated social security system for Canada." In fact, it was a plan for freedom from want for every Canadian from the cradle to the grave. He proposed maternity benefits and children's allowances to cover the child until reaching working age. Also part of his proposed comprehensive, integrated, social security system was unemployment insurance, sickness benefits, free medical insurance, pensions for the permanently disabled and widows, old age pensions, and, finally, funeral benefits.[17]

The federal government had its own plans for the postwar period, and it ignored much of Marsh's advice. It introduced a series of programs, beginning with a universal system of family allowances in July 1945 that paid an allowance, usually to mothers, for all children under the age of 17. Ottawa followed in 1945 with a proposal to the provinces for a cost-shared medical and hospital insurance plan, sole federal responsibility for old-age pensions for citizens over 70, a shared pension scheme for those between 65–69, and other social security measures. Despite considerable discussion over the proposals at several Dominion–Provincial conferences (known today as "First Ministers' Conferences"), the initiatives collapsed when the provinces and Ottawa failed to reach an agreement on revenue sharing. Despite the apparent failure at the time, over the following two decades, many of the programs discussed in 1945 were implemented, including, in 1951, a universal old-age pension plan for Canadians over 70 (and means tested for ages 65 to 69), a cost-shared arrangement in 1954 between Ottawa and the provinces to assist the blind, and, two years later, an *Unemployment Assistance Act* to help finance provincial social assistance for the longer-term and seasonally unemployed.

Between 1956 and 1959, Ottawa negotiated agreements with each of the provinces to reimburse them for half their expenditures on those who were able-bodied but unemployed. This arrangement established several principles for social welfare in Canada. First, it set no ceiling on individual benefits or federal expenditures under the arrangement. Second, the needy unemployed who lived in homes for special care were eligible for assistance. Third, the means test based on income and assets was replaced by a needs test, which assessed each applicant's need, and awarded assistance to fill the gap between need and resources. Finally, the residency eligibility was changed from individual provinces to the nation. Previously, provinces had been known to encourage the movement of individuals in need of assistance out of the province rather than provide them with assistance, but under the *Unemployment Assistance Act*, the definition of residence was changed to mean residence in Canada.[18] The eligibility rules for all of these programs under the *Act* were stringent, however, to ensure that only the "deserving" poor qualified, which, in effect, excluded many of the needy. Moreover, the allowance paid took no account of family needs, and the dollar-for-dollar reduction for any wages earned meant that recipients had no incentive to augment their income. Yet, through the *Unemployment Assistance Act*, the federal government intervened, once again, in an area of provincial jurisdiction and made it clear that it considered social welfare a national priority.

In the area of health policy, the provinces (particularly Saskatchewan) usually led by example. In 1947, when Premier Tommy Douglas and his Co-operative Commonwealth Federation (CCF) Government introduced the first hospital insurance plan, people in the other provinces clamoured for a similar program. The federal government responded, and in 1957, it promised that it would share with all provinces the cost of hospital insurance and diagnostic services. Within four years, all provincial legislatures had introduced legislation to implement such a program. Saskatchewan also led the way in 1962 with "Medicare," a universal, publicly supported, medical-care insurance plan covering visits to physicians and most specialists. In 1966, with the success of Saskatchewan initiative fully established, Ottawa passed the *Medical Care Act*, promising to contribute to provincial plans that met with federal objectives of covering all citizens for a wide range of medical services. It took until 1968 before all provinces and territories finalized cost-sharing agreements with Ottawa, and another three years for all provinces to launch their medical-care insurance plans.[19]

The 1960s saw four major, and national, additions to social policy legislation. The Canada and Quebec Pension Plans were designed to meet two objectives: to improve the standard of living for old age pensioners, nearly half of whom lived in poverty without any occupational pension plans; and to allow Canadians to remain in the plan even if they changed jobs or moved from one part of the country to another. In 1964, Youth Allowances extended children's benefits to those aged 16 and 17 who remained in educational institutions. In 1966, the federal government also improved pensions for the elderly, when it enacted a Guaranteed Income Supplement for recipients with little or no other income. Another major federal initiative came in 1966, when Ottawa introduced, at the insistence of the provinces, the Canada Assistance Plan (CAP) that saw it share the cost for provincial social-assistance programmes.[20]

Despite the increased level of social security, the country was shocked to learn in 1970 that 1 in 4 of all Canadians, including two million who were actually in the labour force, lived in poverty. The welfare state had obviously failed to provide all Canadians with a decent standard of living. Several provinces responded by introducing measures to supplement the incomes of working-poor families. The Department of National Health and Welfare released a *White Paper on Income Security* that called for a guaranteed annual income for families. Despite considerable debate and a lengthy federal-provincial review of the social security system, Ottawa finally dropped this plan, given the considerable provincial opposition resulting from the costs that would have been involved. However, in 1974, Ottawa enacted a new *Family Allowances Act*, which virtually tripled monthly payments to an average of $20 per child, and four years later, to redistribute income, added a tax credit of $200 per child for families with income below $18,000.

Yet, even as governments demonstrated greater willingness to use social welfare legislation to address problems such as poverty, serious rumblings of opposition could be heard. In the federal treasury pressure mounted to control spending on such programs as CAP, and some suspicion was expressed that the provinces were more interested in getting revenue from the federal government than in solving the social problems confronting the nation.[21] The criticism of the social security system grew in the mid-1970s and continued for much of the next two decades, as Canada faced various economic problems, including double-digit inflation, a serious economic recession, and a burgeoning debt crisis. At the same time, globalization, deregulated markets and the changing demographic composition of Canada also posed challenges to Canada's welfare state.

The past two decades have seen governments at both the federal and provincial levels preoccupied with controlling spending to eliminate deficits and manage the debt. Ottawa had enjoyed surpluses for much of the period between 1946 and 1974, and seemed to exude the message that governments could solve any problem. However, when governments found themselves in a deficit position between 1975 and 1997,[22] and turned their focus on economic performance, social welfare came in for serious scrutiny and cuts. The preoccupation with "balancing the books" has been most evident in the way that the federal government has reduced the funds transferred to the province to provide for a variety of social programs. In 1977 Ottawa introduced the Established Program Financing (EPF), combining tax and cash transfers to the provinces to replace cost-sharing programs for health and post-secondary education. This allowed the federal government to set spending limits on certain social policies unilaterally, even though it usually engaged in discussion with the provinces first. When EPF was established, the value of the tax points was to grow as the economy expanded and the cash transfer was to increase by the growth rate of per capita GNP. However, beginning in 1982, Ottawa announced measures to control expenditures through the program, and in the 1990 budget it imposed a limit on federal cost-sharing under the CAP.

In the 1995 budget Ottawa replaced EPF and the CAP with a Canada Health and Social Transfer (CHST) block fund to the provinces in support of health care, post-secondary education, social assistance, and social services. This further reduced federal expenditures and removed many of the conditions that Ottawa had placed on the transfers, though Ottawa insisted that the provinces refrain from creating a residency requirement for eligibility. The introduction of the CHST signalled that Ottawa wished to reduce its share of the cost for some social policies as it attempted to control federal spending; the CHST also ended the cost-sharing arrangement with the provinces and set ceilings on

Ottawa's contribution far below the level to which the provinces had grown accustomed. This new arrangement effectively downloaded the cost of many existing social programs to the provinces. Since then, Ottawa has periodically increased its contributions under the CHST, but much of the new monies have been for mushrooming health care costs. However, Ottawa promised the provinces $900 million over five years in federal support for early learning and child care in the 2003 budget. This might be an indication that with a series of balanced budgets and a growing federal surplus, the federal government was trying to re-establish itself in the some areas of social policy, but only in those areas that Ottawa considered priorities, such as health care, child policy, and post-secondary education. Indeed, as part of the 2003 funding agreement with the provinces for health, the CHST was restructured with a separate transfer for health (Canada Health Transfer). In April 2004, Ottawa introduced the Canada Social Transfer (CST) that provided a federal block transfer to the provinces and territories to support post-secondary education, social assistance, and social services, including early childhood development and early learning and childcare. However, the provinces are free to allocate the CST between their priorities in post-secondary education, social assistance, and social services. The First Ministers also signed a health accord in October 2004 that saw the federal government contribute $21.8 billion to the provinces in fiscal 2004 to support health services and health reform, a figure that was scheduled to rise to $30.1 billion in 2007–2008.

The federal government has increasingly relied on the tax system as a primary means of funnelling money directly into the hands of individual citizens. This has been evident particularly in the area of support for children where Ottawa has transferred financial resources to families rather than to the provinces. Although the Liberal government said in 1993 that it wished to expand child care and eliminate child poverty in Canada, it was not until 1997 that it announced the National Children's Agenda. The goal of the NCA is to reduce child poverty through the National Child Benefit, which pays a cash supplement to poor families (in addition to the Child Tax Credit), which is received by 80 percent of Canadian families with children. Under the NCB, provinces may reduce the amount they pay in social assistance up to the amount that Ottawa contributes under the program, though any savings to the province must be re-directed to programs aimed at children. Moreover, Ottawa demanded that the provinces report on the programs (i.e., NCB) that it helps fund, and thus be accountable for federal transfers, though, in fact, under Prime Minister Paul Martin's leadership, the provinces have been given considerable autonomy.

The last decades of the twentieth century witnessed a dramatic upheaval in Canada's system of social welfare. Governments had committed themselves to building a social security system for Canada during the Second World War. By the end of the 1970s, social security spending consumed more than 53 percent of all government expenditures.[23] Not surprisingly then, during the 1980s and especially during the 1990s, when governments attempted to deal with the burgeoning deficits and the debt, social security spending came in for considerable scrutiny. Yet, even after all the rhetoric about the dismantling of the social welfare system, after all the cuts, and the dire warnings from those who attempted to defend Canada's social programs, social security spending in Canada remained relatively constant throughout the period. By 2002, governments spent more than $219.7 billion on Canada's social welfare system, which accounted for 52.83 percent of all government expenditures.[24]

Even though the level of expenditure in social policy has remained relatively constant, there have been marked changes in the social welfare system in recent years. One of the most noticeable shifts has been the drop in the expenditure on welfare recipients, with the introduction of more stringent eligibility rules and lower benefits across all provinces. In 1993, 10.4 percent of the Canadian population received social assistance; by 2003 that number had declined to 5.5 percent. Social assistance rates also declined in every province over that period, but were most dramatic in Alberta and Ontario, where they fell by 70.5 and 50 percent for individual recipients, respectively. These provinces enjoyed periods of strong economic growth, but in Ontario, for instance, couples with two children on social assistance saw their benefits fall by 45 percent between 1993 and 2003.[25] There have been similar changes for the unemployed through the Employment Insurance program. Another major change in social policy spending has been the share taken by health care. In 1994–95, health care expenditures represented 26.3 percent of all spending on social security, but reached 29.4 percent just four years later, with every indication being that the trend will not abate.

What is clear from the essays in this collection is that social policy in Canada is never stable or fixed. Over the past century, all levels of government in Canada have strived to deal with a variety of social problems in many different ways. Until the Great Depression in the 1930s, governments looked primarily to the community to deal with unemployment, poverty, and other social ills. By the middle of the twentieth century, governments came to believe that they could solve many of society's problems. The belief in the efficacy of government was so strong that the 1960s witnessed the birth of what some have called the Canada's *social service state*. However within a generation, governments were eager to diminish expectations of what the state could deliver, as they directed increased efforts into controlling debt and fostering stronger economic growth.

Where is social policy headed in Canada? To that question there is no easy answer. It has been clear in the past, however, that Canada's social policy has been a reflection of the ideology and philosophy of the times. As one looks ahead and ponders the next steps in the evolution and development of the welfare state in Canada under a new Conservative Government led by Stephen Harper, we think this book will provide some guidance. The essays that follow examine the development of social welfare policy in Canada historically and regionally, and from different disciplinary approaches and ideological perspectives. Readers will find in this collection essays written by historians, sociologists, social workers, public policy experts, and political scientists, all of whom help us understand the complex past and remind of the wide variety of actors and philosophies at work as social policy continues to evolve in Canada.

Notes

1. Michael Adams, *Fire and Ice: The United States, Canada and the Myth of Converging Values* (Toronto: Penguin, 2003), 58.
2. For a good discussion of social policy, see www.rgu.ac.uk/publicpolicy/introduction/policy.htm.
3. See Leslie A. Pal, "Federalism, Social Policy and the Constitution," in Jacqueline S. Ismael, ed., *Canadian Social Welfare Policy: Federal and Provincial Dimensions* (Kingston and Montreal: McGill-Queen's University Press, 1985).

4. Elizabeth Wallace, "The Origin of the Social Welfare State in Canada, 1867–1900," in *Canadian Journal of* Economics *and Political Science* 16, 3 (August 1950): 383–93.

5. See R.C. Brown and Ramsay Cook, *Canada, 1896–1921: A Nation Transformed* (Toronto: McClelland and Stewart, 1974), and Richard Allen, *The Social Passion: Religion and Social Reform in Canada, 1914–28* (Toronto: University of Toronto Press, 1971).

6. See Herbert Brown Ames, *The City Below the Hill* (Toronto: University of Toronto Press, 1972).

7. Elizabeth Wallace, "The Origin of the Social Welfare State in Canada, 1867–1900," in *Canadian Journal of Economics* and *Political Science* 16, 3 (August 1950): 383–93.

8. R.C.B. Risk, "'This Nuisance of Litigation': The Origins of Workers' Compensation in Ontario," in David H. Flaherty, ed., *Essays in the History of Canadian Law* 2 (Toronto: University of Toronto Press, 1983).

9. Veronica Strong-Boag, "Mother's Allowances and the Beginnings of Social Security in Canada," *Journal of Canadian Studies* 14, 1 (Spring 1974): 24–34.

10. See Desmond Morton and Glenn Wright, *Winning the Second Battle: Canadians and the Return to Civilian Life, 1915–1930* (Toronto: University of Toronto Press, 1987).

11. See Kenneth Bryden, *Old Age Pensions and Policy-Making in Canada* (Montreal: McGill-Queen's University Press, 1974).

12. See Larry A. Glassford, *Reaction and Reform: The Politics of the Conservative Party under R.B. Bennett, 1927–1938* (Toronto: University of Toronto Press, 1992).

13. On changes in economic thinking in the period, see Doug Owram, "Economic Thought in the 1930s: The Prelude to Keynesianism," *Canadian Historical Review* 66, 3 (1985).

14. See David Bercuson, *Confrontation at Winnipeg: Labour, Industrial Relations and the General Strike* (Montreal: McGill-Queen's University Press, 1974).

15. Leonard Marsh, *Report on Social Security for Canada* (Toronto: University of Toronto Press, 1975), xvii.

16. See James Struthers, *"No Fault of Their Own": Unemployment and the Canadian Welfare State, 1914–1941* (Toronto: University of Toronto Press, 1983).

17. See Marsh, *Report on Social Security for Canada 1943.*

18. John E. Osborne, "The Evolution of the Canada Assistance Plan." Published as an appendix for the Task Force on Program Review, known as the Nielsen Task Force, Ottawa, 1985.

19. See Gwendolyn Gray, *Federalism and Health Policy: The Development of Health Systems in Canada and* Australia (Toronto: University of Toronto Press, 1991).

20. See Rand Dyck, "The Canada Assistance Plan: The Ultimate in Cooperative Federalism," *Canadian Public Administration* 19 (Winter 1976).

21. Osborne, "The Evolution of the Canada Assistance Plan."

22. Stephen Laurent and François Vaillancourt, *Federal-Provincial Transfers for Social Programs in Canada: Their Status in May 2004.* IRPP Working Paper Series. No 2004-07.

23. Statistics Canada. Social Security Statistics and Provinces. www11.*sdc*.gc.ca/en/cs/sp/socpol/publications/statistics/9999-000096/table3c.shtml.

24. Statistics Canada. Social Security Statistics and Provinces. www11.sdc.gc.ca/en/cs/sp/socpol/publications/statistics/9999-000096/table3.shtml.

25. Statistics Canada. *Canadian Economic Observer* (November 2004).

I

BEGINNINGS

Beginnings

PRIOR TO THE SECOND WORLD WAR, one would be hard-pressed to speak of a Canadian social security system. Programs were ad hoc, rudimentary, and miserly. In 1867, under the *British North America Act*, responsibility for providing social welfare was placed with the provinces in large part because the amounts spent were so small. The provinces, in turn, passed responsibilities to local governments that struggled to provide even the most basic of services, and great reliance was placed on philanthropists and churches, to carry the load.

Helping to keep costs down was the widespread image of social welfare as being linked to indolence and personal failure. The wisdom of the day also held that too generous an approach would discourage people from work; and moreover, work—aside from being essential for sustenance—was a moral and social good that built self-reliance, self-discipline, and thrift, and discouraged sloth, vice, and an ungodly lifestyle. Directors and administrators of social welfare programs regularly distinguished between "deserving" and "undeserving" poor, the former being those unable to help themselves; the latter, by contrast, were expected to provide something in exchange (such as breaking rocks for roads) to obtain a meager assistance.

While Canada remained mostly rural, the belief was that the destitute could always live off the land. But this was not possible in emerging industrial cities. Late nineteenth and early twentieth century Canadian cities also faced problems that included shortages of decent housing, growing disease rates, corporate concentration, more evident bifurcation of wealth, labour unrest, and what was perceived as brazen displays of intemperance and prostitution, trends that many "respectable" citizens warned portended social chaos and decay.

The selections that follow exemplify many of the characteristics of early social welfare. Denis Guest contrasts the often widespread and desperate need in the population against the inadequacy of early policies. He also identifies the principal groups advocating reforms and their often conflicting agendas, ranging from advancing social justice to seeking social control. Robert Babcock focuses on the movement in the United States and Canada during the late nineteenth and early twentieth centuries for Workers' Compensation legislation. Few labourers had private insurance, thus leaving many who were injured dependent on local charities. Suing the boss was difficult and costly, especially given the Common Law tradition of "voluntary assumption of risk" in taking a job. Yet, Babcock notes successful lawsuits were growing, and that more employers came to view the new legislation as controlling their costs because the injured party—by claiming from the Workers' Compensation fund—relinquished their right to sue.

Early social policy also focused on women and children: the message here was the imperative to protect the weak and innocent. Yet, early measures harboured a strong, and arguably repressive, moral quality, namely by enforcing traditional gender roles. James Struthers makes this point with respect to Mother's Allowances, an initiative viewed by many as especially important in light of the increasing number of fatherless families created by World War I. With children of working mothers often found in orphanages, the

Mother's Allowance was touted as enabling full-time maternal care. But the program was means tested, stipulated minimum residency requirements, available only to British subjects, and paid out only half the amount that had been provided through the Canadian Patriotic Fund. Particular conduct was also demanded of recipients. A dirty home, the use of foul language, flirtatious behaviour, or purchases that conflicted with the image of frugality were all grounds for losing the funding. While widows were considered worthy of financial support, women who had been deserted, separated, or divorced were generally disqualified for being morally suspect. Similar themes appear in Karen Balcolm's piece, set a generation later on adoption in Nova Scotia. Because of the shame surrounding children born out of wedlock, and virtually non-existent provincial Child Welfare services, the privately run Ideal Maternity Home was able to ruthlessly exploit pregnant single women, provide much-wanting facilities that added to the infant mortality rate, and sell babies across North America for profit.

Other articles in this section, however, provide something of a counterweight to the traditional scholarly depiction of the pre-World War II period as being akin to the Dark Ages when it came to social welfare. Dawn Bowen examines efforts in Saskatchewan during the Depression to encourage a "back to the land" movement among the urban poor. Although cataloguing many shortcomings, she also notes that the failure rate among those selected to participate was not significantly different from long-established patterns among new settlers in the rural West. B.L. Vigod challenges the conventional depiction of pre-Quiet Revolution Quebec as especially backwards when it came to state welfare; he contends, for instance, that had the Godbout government been re-elected, some of the province's most substantial social initiatives passed after 1960 would have appeared a generation earlier. Finally, Shirley Tillotson reveals that even as the modern social welfare system came into being, private charity continued to play a seminal role; indeed, people increased their charitable donations despite governments taking on more responsibility to assist the needy. While by no means promoting the private over the public, Tillotson's analysis demonstrates that local Community Chests grew far more effective in widening their base of support, in large part by convincing donors that the money raised would not be wasted. Still, increasingly, the funds dispensed by private sources were dwarfed by government social welfare programs. By the end of the Great Depression, Canadians were more convinced than ever that old approaches were woefully inadequate; that a bolder, more compassionate, direction was essential; and that, if necessary, Canada's federal system be overhauled to provide some security for all.

Further Reading

Allen, Richard, *The Social Passion: Religion and Social Reform in Canada, 1914–28*. Toronto: University of Toronto Press, 1971.

Burke, Sara Z., *Seeking the Highest Good: Social Service and Gender at the University of Toronto, 1888–1937*. Toronto: University of Toronto Press, 1996.

Christie, Nancy and Michael Gauvreau, *A Full-Orbed Christianity: The Protestant Churches and Social Welfare in Canada, 1900–1940*. Kingston and Montreal: McGill-Queen's University Press, 1996.

Chunn, Dorothy E., *From Punishment to Doing Good: Family Courts and Socialized Justice in Ontario, 1880–1940*. Toronto: University of Toronto Press, 1992.

Comacchio, Cynthia R. *Nations Are Built of Babies: Saving Ontario's Mothers and Children, 1900–1940*. Kingston and Montreal: McGill-Queen's University Press, 1993.

Cook, Ramsay, *The Regenerators: Social Criticism in Late Victorian English Canada*. Toronto: University of Toronto Press, 1985.

Copp, Terry, *The Anatomy of Poverty: The Condition of the Working Class in Montreal 1897–1929*. Toronto: McClelland and Stewart, 1974.

Craven, Paul, *An Impartial Umpire: Industrial Relations and the Canadian State, 1900–1911*. Toronto: University of Toronto Press, 1980.

Kealey, Gregory, ed., *Canada Investigates Industrialism: The Royal Commission on the Relations of Labor and Capital, 1889*. Toronto: University of Toronto Press, 1973.

Minville, Esdras, *Syndicalisme, Législation Ouvrière et Régime Social au Québec avant 1940*. Montréal: Fides, 1987.

Montigny, Edgar-André, *Foisted Upon the Government?: State Responsibilities, Family Obligations, and the Care of the Dependent Aged in Late Nineteenth-Century Ontario*. Kingston and Montreal: McGill-Queen's University Press, 1997.

Moran, James E., *Committed to the State Asylum: Insanity and Society in Nineteenth-Century Quebec and Ontario*. Kingston and Montreal: McGill-Queen's University Press, 2000.

Morton, Desmond and Glenn Wright, *Winning the Second Battle: Canadian Veterans and the Return to Civilian Life, 1915–1930*. Toronto: University of Toronto Press, 1987.

Morton, Desmond, *Fight or Pay: Soldiers' Families in the Great War*. Vancouver: University of British Columbia Press, 2004.

Orloff, Ann Shola, *The Politics of Pensions: A Comparative Analysis of Britain, Canada, and the United States, 1880–1940*. Madison: University of Wisconsin Press, 1993.

Piva, Michael J., *The Condition of the Working Class in Toronto, 1900–1921*. Ottawa: University of Ottawa Press, 1979.

Raymond, Jocelyn Moyter, *The Nursery World of Dr. Blatz*. Toronto: University of Toronto Press, 1991.

Snell, James G., *The Citizen's Wage: The State and the Elderly in Canada, 1900–1951*. Toronto: University of Toronto Press, 1996.

Struthers, James, *No Fault of their Own: Unemployment and the Canadian Welfare State, 1914–1941*. Toronto: University of Toronto Press, 1983.

Valverde, Mariana, *The Age of Light, Soap, and Water: Moral Reform in English Canada, 1885–1925*. Toronto: McClelland and Stewart, 1991.

Wade, Jill, *Houses for All: The Struggle for Social Housing in Vancouver, 1919–50*. Vancouver: University of British Columbia Press, 1994.

Wills, Gale, *A Marriage of Convenience: Business and Social Work in Toronto, 1918–1957*. Toronto: University of Toronto Press, 1995.

1

Saving for a Rainy Day

Social Security in Late Nineteenth-Century and Early Twentieth-Century Canada*

DENNIS T. GUEST

THE FIRST THIRTY YEARS OF CONFEDERATION, up to the end of the nineteenth century, witnessed the completion of an all-Canadian transcontinental railway, the promotion of large-scale immigration, the opening of western Canada to settlement, and the fostering of Canadian industry by means of protective tariffs. These developments reflected three goals generally recognized and accepted by Canadians of the time: to settle the country's vast and sparsely inhabited western regions; to promote a strong, integrated, and varied economy; and to make Canada "the homeland of a prosperous and contented people."[1]

The progress of this "National Policy," as it was termed, was initially slowed by an economic depression that lasted, with only brief periods of respite, from 1873 until the end of the century. Despite the economic setbacks, the processes of urbanization and industrialization began to accelerate, and the face of Canada was changed, unalterably, within a few years. The imposition in 1879 of a series of protective tariffs by the federal government to protect and stimulate the development of secondary industry set the stage for a rapid growth of towns and cities.[2] The factory system in Canada, according to contemporary observers, "sprang into existence almost at one bound" as a result of the 1879 legislation.[3]

A statement made by J.S. Woodsworth in 1908 succinctly described the rapid urbanization that had taken place in Canada and that was continuing even more rapidly in the first decade of the twentieth century: "Canada is leaving the country for the city.... The population of Ontario more than doubled from 1851 to 1901, but the population of Toronto increased over six times during the same period. The population of the Province of Quebec was almost twice as large in 1901 as in 1851, but that of Montreal was over four and one-half times as large. Manitoba is an agricultural Province, and yet one-quarter of the entire population is resident in the city of Winnipeg alone."[4]

By the 1880s the social and economic consequences of rapid industrialization in a competitive, free enterprise economy began to accumulate, most noticeably in the towns and cities. The working and living conditions of the industrial worker became an early focus of attention spurred on by an increasingly militant and articulate labour movement.

---

* This chapter was first published as "Saving for a Rainy Day: Social Security in Late-Nineteenth-Century and Early-Twentieth Canada," in Dennis Guest, *The Emergence of Social Security in Canada*, 3rd edn. Vancouver, University of British Columbia Press, 1997: 20–39.

Royal Commission on the Relations of Labour and Capital, 1887

A series of federal investigations into industrial conditions in 1882 and again in 1885 reported the exploitation of children in factories and the unsanitary and dangerous working conditions for many workers.[5] Prime Minister John A. Macdonald, faced with an election in 1887 and anxious to maintain the working-class support that he had won in 1872 with the passage of the *Canada Trade Unions Act*,[6] appointed a royal commission "to enquire into and report on all questions arising out of the conflict of labor and capital."[7] The commissioners were, almost to a man, supporters of Macdonald's Conservative Party, but this did not prevent a split from developing along class lines within the commission between the labour representatives and those who took a more paternalistic and conservative view. The result of the split was the publication of two reports, the *First Report*, the more conservative of the two, and the *Second Report*, reflecting a pro-labour, albeit conservative, viewpoint. Both reports were unanimous in their condemnation of certain aspects of the factory system; both urged repeal of, or change in, certain laws that oppressed the working man, woman, and child; and both acknowledged, although with differing degrees of emphasis, that labour organizations had a legitimate role to play in society. As Greg Kealey notes, it takes a close examination of the two reports to observe the differences.[8]

The "Labour Commission," as it came to be known, travelled extensively through eastern Canada over a period of seven months and heard testimony from nearly 1,800 witnesses representing both workers and management. Of interest to the student of Canadian social security programs is the evidence presented as to how people coped with the common exigencies of life in an urban, industrial society, given the almost total absence of social security programs. The record reveals for the most part a pattern of grim exploitation of men, women, and children: long hours of work (fifty-four to sixty hours a week was commonplace), low pay (which was quite callously reduced in winter months by many manufacturers), dangerous and unhealthy workplaces, and chronic unemployment and underemployment for many as trade recessions and the immutable law of supply and demand worked through the economic system.

From a twentieth-century perspective, the most striking impression received from reading the testimony of workers and employers, apart from the absence of social security protection, is the powerlessness of the working classes. Factories and workplaces as described by witnesses read more like places of detention than employment. It was not uncommon for factory hands to be locked into their factories during working hours—one consequence, perhaps, of the many young children employed.[9] Employers and their supervisors acted like martinets. Many physically disciplined their child employees, some to an extent that shocked the commissioners and earned their strong condemnation. Employers imposed fines for being late, for breakage, for substandard work, and in some concerns, for laughing and talking. The *Second Report* commented: "Of all the mean pitiless exactions which labor has to suffer from, this is the vilest. A young woman will work hard from Monday morning until Saturday evening for a paltry pittance of three or four dollars, and when pay day comes find that the sum of 25 or 50 cents, or even one dollar, has been deducted for some trifling breach of rules, or because of the petty spite of the overseer."[10]

This practice was generally imposed upon women and children, as they were said to be more passive in their acceptance of these impositions than men. However, evidence taken in Nova Scotia from miners indicated that their pay was unfairly docked for short weight, and the practice of docking men's pay for being late for work was common in many industries.[11]

Attempts by workers to redress the imbalance of power by forming unions were met with intimidation and blacklisting. The typical attitude of management of the day toward unions is revealed in the following exchange between the superintendent of the Toronto Street Railway and a commissioner:

Q. Is there any objection on the part of the street railway company to men belonging to a secret society of any kind?

A. We have no objection to men belonging to anything except labor organizations.

Q. Are the men in your employ required to sign a paper previous to entering your employment?

A. They are.

Q. What is the nature of that agreement?

A. That they will not join any labor organization while in the employ of the company.

Q. And if a man joins such an organization, what is the result?

A. It is optional with us whether we keep him on or not.[12]

With respect to the adequacy of wages, the commissioners noted that "the testimony taken sustains a belief that wages in Canada are generally higher than at any previous time, while hours of labor have been somewhat reduced. At the same time, the necessaries and ordinary comforts of life are lower in price than ever before, so that the material condition of the working people who exercise reasonable prudence and economy has been greatly bettered, especially during the past ten years."[13]

The *Second Report*, from the labour faction, repeated this testimonial to Macdonald's administration almost word for word.[14] No attempt was made to relate wages paid to the cost of living except to note that women's wages, which were generally set at half that paid to a man, were not high enough to enable a young woman to live independently from her family. The *Second Report* contained the general comment that "all wage earners in subordinate positions" earn "barely enough to supply sufficient of the necessaries of life for the proper maintenance of wife and family."[15]

Both reports mentioned the high cost of rental accommodation and noted that yearly increases in rents, common at the time, imposed "a serious burden on ... people struggling for a living."[16] The *Second Report* added: "No matter how great the increase, how serious the exaction, the landlord is all powerful; there is no appeal from his decision."[17] The answer to the housing problem, according to the *First Report*, was for the worker to own his own home. In view of the low level of wages and the rising costs of land in cities, this was a naive recommendation. Even with home ownership, the worker was still at a disadvantage in many communities. The *First Report* noted that "in most cities, if not all, the homes of the comparatively poor are, in proportion to their value, more highly taxed for municipal purposes than those of wealthy people."[18] Both reports observed that the blight of over-crowded tenements, which had so disfigured large American and European cities by this time, "was only found in a few instances" in Canada. Given less prominence, however, in an appendix to the *First Report* was the following statement: "It is undeniable that workers are badly lodged in houses badly built, unhealthy and rented at exorbitant prices."[19] The sanitary condition of workers' dwellings led the commissioners to recommend a general tightening of municipal sanitation laws, which were found to be "in large measure inoperative" owing to "their indefiniteness, the apathy of inspectors, the influence of landlords, or the helplessness of the tenant."[20]

The evidence presented to the commission vividly illustrated the need for a law covering compensation for work-related injuries or death (not to mention regulations pertaining to industrial safety).[21] The following exchange between a commissioner and an official of a cotton mill in Cornwall, Ontario, is one example:

Q. Have you had any accidents in the mill?
A. We have.
Q. Would you state the nature of the accidents?
A. Well the only thing that I remember was a man falling into the vat; that was on account of a staging of his own putting-up falling into the vat.
Q. He lost his life?
A. He died a few days afterwards.
Q. Is any provision made by the company to aid the families of operatives who are injured or lose their lives—was any recompense made to the widow of this man?
A. Yes; we recompensed her considerably.... We gave her one month's pay, and paid the funeral expenses—in fact, I believe we gave her $100—paid the doctor's bill; paid everything of that sort—the grocer's bill, even.[22]

Evidence was taken as well from several youngsters who testified they had lost fingers, arms, and legs working with dangerous machinery. The following testimony of a former employee of a mill in Ottawa reports the results of a serious accident and the discretionary nature of any help offered the injured worker:

Q. Did you lose your arm and leg in the same accident?
A. Yes sir; I fell in a hole, and the axle of the wheel crushed my arm and leg.
Q. How old were you?
A. Twelve years—going on thirteen.
Q. How old are you now?
A. I am going on nineteen years.
Q. What is your business now?
A. I have none at all.
Q. Did your boss do anything for you?
A. Well, he gave me $10 over and above the wages he owed me, and then they got up a collection and raised $25 for me.
Q. Was the subscription made up among the workingmen?

A. Yes, sir.

Q. Who paid for the medicines and the doctor's fees?

A. I did, sir, but I rather think that the boss paid the hospital dues for the time
I was there. I was sixteen days in hospital.[23]

The following evidence was taken from an Ottawa logger, known in the nineteenth
century as a "shanty-man":

Q. Are any precautions taken by these men or their employers while they are
in the shanties in case of accident? Suppose a man is cut—supposing he
receives a severe cut, is anybody there to attend his wounds?

A. Yes; it is done this way. One man has to dress the other, and the man that is
cut or is sick is charged for his time and he loses his pay.

Q. Supposing you are injured, supposing you receive a severe cut in the middle
of the month, is your time stopped at once?

A. Yes; the moment that you are wounded your time is stopped.[24]

A Nova Scotia miner was asked: "In the case of sickness or in the case of the death of
a cutter or a laborer, would any assistance be rendered by the mining company except the
doctor's attendance? A. Not as I know of; they are not in the habit of doing anything like
that."[25]

The only form of income protection that a worker had would be from membership
in a union or some type of fraternal organization or benefit society (the latter two types
of organizations proliferated in the latter part of the nineteenth century). Only the most
stable members of the working class would be able to take advantage of these forms of help
since membership in a union at this time was restricted to a few skilled trades, and regular
premium payments to a fraternal organization or benefit society were difficult to maintain
for workers in low-paid, unskilled, or seasonal work. Members of the cigar makers union,
for example, were paid $5 per week for sixteen weeks in case of sickness or injury (average
earnings of cigar makers at this time being about $8 or $9 per week). If the worker was still
unable to work after sixteen weeks, his benefit was reduced to $3 and then finally to $2.
When a member died, a lump sum benefit was paid, ranging from $200 to $500, depending
upon the length of time he had been a member.

If a worker could not call upon a benefit society in time of need, there was nothing to
stave off complete destitution except municipal poor relief, where it existed, or emergency
aid from a church or voluntary charitable agency. The *Second Report*, in commenting
on the value of trade unions, said: "In nearly all of these societies benevolence forms a
prominent part of their work—the caring for the sick and injured, and the providing for
the families of deceased members by their insurance departments."[26]

Some companies assisted their employees in forming and operating benefit plans. The
Springhill Mine in Nova Scotia, for example, contributed to a benefit fund as well as arranging for a check-off system for members' contributions. At Springhill the minimum
contribution was 30 cents a month, for which a worker would be eligible, in the case of sickness or injury, to receive $2.50 a week for twenty-six weeks (a miner's rate of pay averaged
from $1.40 to $1.65 per day). If a miner wished to contribute a higher premium of 50 cents

a month, he could qualify for benefits of $4 a week. In the case of death of a member, a lump sum benefit of $60 was paid.[27] These benefit schemes covered a worker whether or not his sickness or injury was work related. When workers' compensation laws did arrive, they covered only work-related injury, disease, or death—a much narrower range of protection.

Some companies required their workers to join a company benefit scheme through which the employees were forced to pay the costs of expensive private insurance against sickness, accident, or death. The commissioners were particularly critical of the Grand Trunk Railway, which, in addition to compelling its employees to pay 80 per cent of the cost of their own benefit scheme, required that they waive any rights to sue the company for compensation in cases of injury or death due to company negligence.[28] This was at a time when railroads were coming under increased criticism for their poor industrial safety record.

The commissioners who signed the *First Report* recommended that the federal government establish an annuity system that would enable Canadian workers to save for their old age. This would "remove from many the fear of dependence upon relatives or upon charity in their declining years."[29] Such a scheme, they maintained, could be operated without expense to the government. This recommendation was predicated on one of the most cherished beliefs of those nineteenth-century Canadians who lived well above the poverty line—that much poverty in old age, or at any other time of life, could be avoided by application of thrift. But the possibility of saving for one's old age, given the low wages and the unemployment, particularly during the winter months, was an illusion that would impede progress toward old age pension legislation for years to come.

The Labour Commission made a number of recommendations to improve the lot of the average industrial worker in Canada. But the sense of urgency that should have animated its report was muted by preliminary comments that cast an unwarranted rosy glow over industrial conditions generally. Of all the recommendations made touching on issues that cried out for change, only one was acted upon—the proclamation of Labour Day as a national holiday in 1894. Kealey suggests that the Macdonald government used the question of possible infringement on provincial jurisdiction as a convenient excuse for its failure to take action on the report's recommendations.[30]

Added to the problems of the industrial worker in Canada were the social problems created by the neglected child, the delinquent, the mentally ill and mentally disabled, the growth of slums, the incidence of poverty, crime, disease, and infant mortality. These and other social ills generated "a great outpouring of concern" as the nineteenth century drew to a close.[31] The public discussion that took place at this time had as its theme the proper relationship between government and the citizen. In the latter part of the nineteenth century, Canadian public opinion underwent "a rapid and marked transformation." The doctrines of laissez faire and of individualism were being challenged by notions of social justice, by a concern for the well-being of the group and of the wider interests of the community as a whole.

The Establishment of Social Minima

One aspect of this shift of opinion was an attempt, however ill-defined, to establish some concept of a social minimum for Canadians living in a society where they were virtually unprotected from the effects of rapid social change and the costs of industrial progress. Efforts to establish social minima invariably spring from a variety of motives. The agitation for free public schools, for example, was supported by those whose strongest motivation was the belief that education was of value for all children and should be their right.[32] But public education, as far back as the colonial period, had been advocated on the grounds that providing a minimum of education for all would increase law and order in the community—an argument judged to have more general appeal than one based on purely religious or moral views.[33] Moving children off the streets and into schools was also seen as a measure of social control—a means of combating juvenile delinquency. But it was the industrial revolution that most propelled the notion of compulsory education for all children into action. Industry came to recognize that it not only required a work-force with a minimum of education but that the school experience prepared the child for the discipline of the factory. "By the end of the nineteenth century," according to Anthony Platt, "the working class had imposed upon them a sterile, authoritarian education system which mirrored the ethics of the corporate workplace and was designed to provide an increasingly refined training and selection mechanism for the labor force."[34]

In the 1870s, primary schooling became free in Ontario, British Columbia, and Manitoba. Prince Edward Island had free education in 1852. Nova Scotia provided elementary and secondary education as early as 1864. But in each of these provinces the opportunity afforded by free schools was not fully realized until attendance was made compulsory some years later. Free public libraries, an informal extension of public education, began to be established in Canada in the 1880s; by 1900 they were fairly common in the larger Canadian cities and towns.

The idea of a social minimum in health began with the entry of governments into the field of public health, initially at the municipal level on an ad hoc basis to combat outbreaks of cholera, smallpox, and typhoid, followed by the development of provincial boards of health over the opposition of tax-conscious citizens and those who believed that death rates were fixed by God. One of the first provincial boards of health was set up in Ontario in 1882. In Nova Scotia, a Department of Public Health, succeeding an earlier Central Board of Health, was established in 1904. New Brunswick created a full-time cabinet post for health in 1918, and this example was followed by several other provinces. After pressure from the provincial governments, a federal Department of Health was established in 1919.

In an attempt to establish certain socially desirable minima for factory workers, seven bills were introduced into the federal parliament between 1880 and 1886 aimed at regulating working conditions. The need for such regulation was undeniable, and considerable public support was created. But none of the bills passed, some having been withdrawn under pressure from employers' groups (although they were supported by manufacturers who wished to eliminate the competition of the sweatshops). Other bills were successfully challenged on the ground that they were beyond the constitutional powers of the federal government.[35]

The extension of the franchise can be seen as another aspect of the social minimum—a minimum of political democracy and power-sharing. In 1867 the newly formed Dominion of Canada began by using the provincial franchises for federal elections, which, by and large, linked voting rights to the ownership of property. This effectively disenfranchised a sizeable segment of the population. In the 1850s, for example, fewer than half of the adult males in Hamilton, Ontario, owned or rented enough property to vote in elections for the legislative assembly.[36] Women were denied the right to vote even if they met the property qualifications.[37] The discrimination against women voting was partially rectified during the First World War when Manitoba became the first province to grant them a vote in provincial elections. Other provinces quickly followed; by 1919 all except Prince Edward Island and Quebec had granted women the right to vote provincially.[38] The federal government moved toward giving women the vote when, in 1917, it enfranchised women members of the armed forces, notably nurses, along with all other serving members. Later that same year, close female relatives of men serving in the armed forces overseas were permitted to vote federally. Finally, in 1920, the federal government passed the *Dominion Elections Act* that established universal suffrage for men and women in federal elections, though it still excluded significant groups of Canadians—registered Natives, Canadians of Chinese, Japanese, and East Indian parentage (unless they had served in the armed forces), and members of certain religious sects who were exempt from military service.

Extending the franchise to women was more than a matter of simple social justice. It was also part of the strategy of the prohibitionists, who, realizing the close relationship between the women's suffrage and the prohibition movements, assumed that if women were given the vote they would overwhelmingly endorse prohibition. At the federal level, the government, by extending the vote to close female relatives of men serving overseas in 1917, hoped to win their electoral support for its controversial conscription policy. Somewhat the same mixture of expediency and principle was evident in trade union pressure to prohibit child labour and thereby eliminate a source of downward pressure on wages.

Having secured the vote, even in a restricted form, it was possible for most skilled workers to press for recognition of their right to unionize. Until 1872, when unions were legalized, breaking an employment contract was a criminal conspiracy. Between that date and 1900, industrial workers became free of many legal restraints on union activity, although in disputes involving management and labour the application of the law was said to have had a "peculiarly one-sided impact."[39] At the turn of the century, as Canadian unions slowly gained strength, they agitated for legislation that had a wider application than the issue of wages and working conditions and that expressed a social minimum concept. Thus, in 1898 the Trades and Labour Congress of Canada passed resolutions in favour of free compulsory education, the reduction of the working day to eight hours, six days a week, the government inspection of all industries, minimum wages based on local conditions, public ownership of all utilities, and the abolition of child labour for children under fourteen. The impact of these resolutions was negligible; prior to the First World War Canadian unions were weak and few in number, owing to the mobility of labour, its heterogeneous nature, and the active resistance of employers.[40]

Herbert Ames: Pioneer Social Researcher

By the 1890s social reform had become a multifaceted public issue. Proposals for reform in the field of housing, sanitation, town planning, public health, factory legislation, child welfare, corrections, civic politics, and a host of other related subjects were brought to the public's attention by the press, the work of concerned individuals, voluntary organizations, and social movements.

A leading example of individual effort was the work of Sir Herbert Brown Ames, a well-to-do Montreal manufacturer who typifies the "tory touch" in Canada's ideological development.[41] As a member of Montreal's social and business establishment, he accepted the class divisions that existed but felt that his position in society carried with it a responsibility for the welfare of the industrial classes. With an enlightened self-interest, he viewed society as an organic whole, noting that "honest thinkers in every land are coming more and more to realize what is meant by the interdependence of society, when those who study city life are each day more fully persuaded that ordinary urban conditions are demoralizing and that no portion of the community can be allowed to deteriorate without danger to the whole."[42]

During the autumn and early winter of 1896, Ames launched a study of the "ordinary urban conditions" to be found in a square mile of Montreal's working-class district, containing 38,000 homes as well as factories and other working establishments. He organized a house-to-house survey, modelled on the pioneering work of Charles Booth in London,[43] gathering information on employment and family incomes, with a particular focus on housing conditions—the degree of overcrowding, sanitary arrangements, and rentals charged.

His work, published in 1897, provides an invaluable glimpse into the life of a representative segment of Montreal's working class just before the turn of the century. The information gleaned from the survey permitted Ames to challenge some of the conventional attitudes toward poverty and its causation: "As to the causes of poverty, chief among them is insufficient employment. Few are the families where nothing is earned, although there are such subsisting more or less worthily upon charity. Almost without exception each family has its wage earner, often more than one, and upon the regularity with which the wage earner secures employment depends the scale of living for the family."[44]

Ames then proceeded to deal with the argument that he knew his readers would raise: that the effects of irregularity of employment could be met by the worker practising thrift and "saving for a rainy day" while employed. Referring to some of the poorer families in his survey, he wrote: "With most of the wage-earners of these families the program for the year is as follows: Work upon the wharves in summer and odd jobs of any sort during five long winter months. When spring arrives, overdue rent and debt at the corner grocery have so mortgaged the coming summer's earnings that saving becomes impossible."[45]

This view, backed up by his research, served to refute the complacent attitude of another member of Montreal's establishment, William C. Macdonald, the tobacco manufacturer, who ten years previously in an appearance before the Labour Commission was asked about his company's policy of reducing wages in the winter:

Q. Does not the cost of living, to working people, increase during the winter? Do they not have to pay much larger sums in the winter than in the summer season?

A. Oh, yes.

Q. Is it not a hardship to them to have their wages reduced at the time they need it more than in summer?

A. That will depend on how they provide for rainy days. When they have good
wages they should save for the short period.[46]

Ames selected a smaller sample of 323 families classified as "the poorest of the poor"
for closer examination. One of his areas of inquiry involved asking the poor families to
assign a cause for their poverty:

> With 109 families, or 34 per cent the reply was "irregularity of work." The
> wage earners were not without vocations but their employment was inter-
> mittent and often work ceased altogether for considerable periods. With 87
> families or 28 per cent the answer was that the wage earners had no work
> whatsoever, nor did there seem to be any immediate prospect of getting any.
> With 27 families, or 9 per cent, old age had unfitted and with a like number
> sickness had prevented the workers from earning the requisite support. Out
> of these 323 families, among the poorest of the poor, 62 per cent claimed to
> be able to better their condition were employment regular and abundant.
> That a certain percentage of the answers given did not state the real facts of
> the case is quite probable. Few are the families that will admit to a stranger
> that drink, crime or voluntary idleness is the cause of their misery, though in
> 7 per cent of the cases visited drunkenness was clearly at the bottom of the
> trouble. Still it is the belief of the investigator that the undeserving among
> the poor form a far smaller proportion than is generally imagined.[47]

Here again, Ames was questioning the conventional wisdom that defined poverty
very largely in terms of personal inadequacy. As if anticipating a chorus of protest from
his readers, he supported his findings by quoting similar studies from the United States,
where, in Ames's words, "want of employment was believed to be the cause of distress in
as many cases as sickness, intemperance, and shiftlessness combined."[48]

Ames helped Canadians to redefine the causes of poverty. His research demonstrated that the problem was very largely rooted in economic and social arrangements. His
proposals for remedying the problems he uncovered included winter works programs
at minimum wages for those who could work,[49] the enforcement of higher standards in
housing construction, sanitation, and town planning,[50] as well as the building of low-
rental accommodation under private, philanthropic auspices.[51] The very poor, those
whom Ames called "the submerged tenth," who were unable to work through illness, old
age, or for other reasons, could, he thought, be left to private charity.

Ames's research is remarkable for its early attempt to define a poverty line (another
expression of the social minimum) and to estimate the incidence of poverty existing in
Montreal in 1897. Ames estimated that families with less than $5 per week of income could
not make proper provision for a growing family. Families below this level he classified as
"poor," and they comprised between 11 and 12 per cent of the population surveyed.[52] At
the other end of the economic spectrum were the families with incomes of not less than
$20 per week or $1,000 a year. These were the "well to do" of the area, comprising 15 per
cent of the total sample, made up of proprietors, managers, professionals, storekeepers,
and a few families where the combined income of several workers produced this standard

of living.[53] The remaining 73 per cent of the population, comprising the "real industrial class," had family incomes averaging $10 per week.[54]

Ames's poverty line of $5 per week for a family of five was not supported by any survey of average family expenditure; but modern investigators, using the Department of Labour's family budget survey developed in 1926 and calculating back to 1900, have estimated that basic necessities for a family of five at that time would have cost $9.64 per week, and the cost for the total needs of the same family would have been $13.77.[55] Using the figure of $9.64 as the poverty line for a family of five, a recent investigator, Terry Copp, suggests that the great majority of Montreal's working-class population—the 73 per cent that made up what Ames called the "real industrial class"—lived at the poverty level or fractionally above it. Many families at this level of income would have had little or no margin of income left for savings, unforeseen expenditures, or investment in personal development.

The Urban Reform Movement

The work of Ames was part of a larger movement of urban reform that developed in Canada in the 1880s.[56] Initially, the movement was sparked by newspapers known as "the peoples' journals," which published articles and stories on the social pathology of city life in the United States, Britain, and Canada, in all its fascinating and sometimes lurid manifestations. These reports so magnetized the reading public that by the end of the century, any paper that had a regard for its circulation had to "pay at least lip service to the cause of urban reform."

The urban reform movement in Canada, with theoretical and practical underpinnings derived from both European and American experience, encompassed a bewildering variety of causes: public control of utilities, including street railways; improvements in the health and moral character of cities; the promotion of a larger measure of social justice; campaigns for town planning, the provision of parks and playgrounds, and other public amenities; and pleas for "purity in government," a reference to corruption in the political arena.

Running through the spirited public debates that the movement stimulated was the common theme of the interdependence of city people and the organic nature of the urban community—arguments that nourished collective solutions to social problems. Prior to the turn of the century, however, voluntary effort in dealing with social problems was still preferred to encouraging a public response, particularly by the more conservative and influential segment of the community. Consequently, voluntary organizations to combat a wide variety of social ills sprang up on every side. The founding of the Toronto Humane Society in 1887 is a case in point. It evolved out of a series of articles written by Joseph J. Kelso, a young court reporter for the Toronto *Globe*, on the plight of neglected, abused, and delinquent children and on cruelty to animals in that city. The society, pledged to protect both animals and children from cruelty, soon found that it could not operate on behalf of children without the legal authority to do so and without some public financial commitment. They obtained both by successfully petitioning the Ontario provincial legislature to pass An *Act for the Protection and Reformation of Neglected Children* (1888), and later, in 1893, to pass a more advanced piece of child welfare legislation that emphasized even more strongly a public responsibility and a public role through the appointment of a superintendent of neglected and dependent children. However, this public concern for the welfare of neglected children was to be expressed through the use of voluntary children's aid societies, the first of which had been formed in Toronto in 1891. Thus, voluntarism and collectivism were combined to provide what Kelso and his friends hoped would be an effective as well as an economical service for neglected and dependent children.[57]

The urban reform movement signalled the growing strength of collectivist thought in Canada and the ebbing of the laissez-faire tide. This trend was reflected in an address given to the Canadian Club of Ottawa in 1914 by the mayor of Toronto, H.C. Hocken.[58] He spoke of "a new Spirit in municipal government" that involved a growing public responsibility for a variety of human services and regulatory agencies. He noted "with astonishment" the increases in public expenditure by his city over the five-year period from 1909 to 1913 and cited a number of municipal services operating in 1913 that had not existed five years earlier. They included public health nurses to combat the infant mortality rate, inspection of milk supplies, food outlets, and food processors, and dental clinics for poor children. The city had also established a minimum wage for civic employees and had instituted a number of programs to deal with the unemployment situation, which was particularly bad in the years 1913 and 1914. Municipal government, the mayor said, had ceased to be a matter of construction and maintenance of sewers, sidewalks, and roads: "the problems we have to deal with now are problems affecting human welfare, problems of prevention, the problems looking to the betterment of the people of cities."

The Social Gospel Movement

Coinciding with the urban reform movement was the social gospel movement, strongly influenced by American and British examples, which surfaced in Canada in the 1890s. It represented an attempt by the Protestant religions, principally the Methodists, Presbyterians, and Anglicans, to apply the teachings of Christ to the economic and social problems of the day.[59] This appealing and apparently simple idea had its radical, conservative, and middle-of-the-road adherents. The conservatives tended to support government legislation to promote the good of society by suppressing evil, specifically by campaigning for prohibition, Sunday blue laws, and the repression of prostitution and gambling. The more radical element saw an affinity between Christianity and socialism and were prepared to support the implications of this linkage. They urged that cooperation replace competition as a motivating force in society, in effect advocating an overturning of the capitalist system. A majority took a middle road, favouring a broad program of liberal reform measures, leading ultimately to the welfare state.

Canadians had attended three notable interdenominational conferences in the United States on social problems in 1887, 1889, and 1893. In 1902 the Methodist Church in Canada set up a standing committee to deal with social problems. In its policy statements, the church became increasingly critical of the social and economic system, and in 1906, at its Seventh General Conference, it issued a strong denunciation of capitalism, denouncing it for its vast private fortunes coexisting with poverty wages, sweated labour, and child labour. It called for the regulation of the economic system according to the principles expressed in the Golden Rule and the Sermon on the Mount.[60]

In 1907 the Moral and Social Reform Council of Canada was organized, including representatives of the Anglican, Methodist, Presbyterian, and Baptist Churches as well as the Trades and Labour Congress of Canada. It was this alliance that succeeded in having the federal government enact the *Lord's Day Act* in 1906, which prohibited the sale of articles and the employment of persons in industrial and commercial work on Sunday (works of necessity and mercy were excepted). From labour's point of view, this act was an expression of one type of social minimum—that of restricting weekly hours of labour.

As the churches became more active in programs of social reform and community action, they set up departments of social service to run and coordinate their expanding social welfare and social reform activities.[61] The secretaries and other personnel of these departments invariably spearheaded the more radical thrusts of the social gospel movement that developed in the first two decades of the twentieth century. In 1913 the Moral and Reform Council of Canada changed its name to the Social Service Council of Canada. In March of 1914, five months before the outbreak of the First World War, the council called its first national congress on social problems.

The Social Service Congress, 1914

Delegates from all parts of the country, including representatives from the three levels of government, but lacking any representation from business or industry, assembled in Ottawa to hear speakers on a wide selection of topics. They included, among others, the relationship of the church to industrial life, child welfare, the problems of the city and the country, commercialized vice and the white slave traffic, immigration, political purity, and temperance.

The right, centre, and left wings of the social gospel movement were each represented from the speaker's platform. However, the enthusiasm for this first large and impressive gathering cast a patina of unity over the congress. Those on the left denounced capitalism, referring to it as "an evil tree that bears evil fruit";[62] they urged closer links between labour and the church[63] and called for a more equitable distribution of wealth.[64] Speakers on the right took more traditional positions on such issues as the weekly day of rest and "the fitting employment of its hours," and the problems of prostitution, drinking, and gambling.[65] It is important to note, however, that many prohibitionists were in the vanguard of social reform. The elimination of the sale of liquor was, for many of them, a first step in a broad program of social reconstruction. The mainstream of the movement was well represented by those calling for measures of reform and regulation in aid of various categories of people or for the extension of existing social services.[66]

The 1914 congress is noteworthy for its evidence of a growing appreciation for social security programs, specifically the use of social insurance to protect people against work injury, old age, and unemployment. Proponents of these measures displayed a knowledge of European and American developments in this field, and they were considerably less tolerant of the conventional objections to providing an income to people in need. Speaking on pensions for widows left with the care of children, Rose Henderson, a Montreal delegate, made the point in these terms:

"We must be careful not to pauperize," say some comfortable wiseacres. We pension Royalty, noblemen, statesmen, judges, civil servants, industrial magnates, army and naval officers, all in receipt of good salaries during their lives. Is there any reason why our widowed mothers with young children should not be pensioned? Thirty-three bishops and archbishops in the House of Lords in England draw large pensions for practically doing nothing but opposing progressive measures introduced for the amelioration of the lot of the poor. Would anyone suggest that these noble lords were being pauperized by their pensions?[67]

The 1914 congress was a display case of religiously motivated social reform thought in Canada, just prior to the First World War. It was part of the great "outpouring of concern" by Canadians in reaction to the social disorganization, the squalor, the poverty, and the oppression of labour that accompanied Canada's move into the industrial age. The delegates left the congress more confident than ever that it was possible to reconstruct Canadian society on Christian principles. The social gospel movement was in the ascendancy. But, five months away, the horror of the First World War was waiting to shatter its dreams and aspirations.

Government Annuities Act of 1908

One of the resolutions passed at the Social Service Congress of 1914 was a request to the federal government to institute a system of old age pensions. This action reflected the growing concern for the elderly in Canada, which had been raised periodically from various public forums from the 1880s on.[68] In 1886 the Royal Commission on the Relations of Labour and Capital had congratulated the federal government on encouraging working people to save from their surplus earnings in post office and government savings banks but went on to urge the creation of a government annuity system, "under which working people and others might make provision for old age by periodical or occasional payments of small sums."[69] In 1891 an Ontario Royal Commission on the Prison and Reformatory System decried the numbers of homeless elderly who were lodged in local jails on charges of vagrancy because there was no other place for them. It was recommended that each county in Ontario be required to operate a poorhouse for the reception and care of homeless people. This view of how poor, elderly people should be treated would be deemed archaic within the next decade.[70] At the beginning of the century, the Canadian trade union movement was asking for public pensions in line with programs adopted by other industrialized nations, notably Germany (1889), Denmark (1891), New Zealand (1898), Australia (1901 and 1908), and Britain (1908). By 1900 the only initiative taken by the federal government was to extend the hours of post office savings departments on Saturday evenings from 7:30 to 9:00 pm.[71] The question of pensions for cabinet ministers received more prompt attention. In 1905 privy councillors who had been head of a department for five years or over were granted a retirement pension of $3,500 per annum, and this legislation was made retroactive to include all former cabinet ministers with the required years in office.[72] This action may have helped to prompt the Trades and Labour Congress of Canada to call for a system of public pensions at its annual convention in 1905. The issue of old age pensions was first raised in the House of Commons in 1906; between that date and 1914, when the war's emergency deflected parliamentary energies, two special committees of the House studied the question, but the federal government was not sympathetic to the idea. Pensions for cabinet ministers were condoned, but pensions for average Canadians were characterized as a "socialist experiment."[73] To forestall such experiments, the federal government introduced a system of government annuities in 1908.

In an era in which the residual concept of social welfare was dominant, one might have expected the government to call for tenders from the private market in setting up such a scheme. However, it was widely appreciated that premiums for endowment policies offered by private insurance companies were beyond the financial means of most working-class Canadians. In any case, the government was in a poor position at this time to recommend that Canadian workers seek income protection for their old age from the private sector. In 1906 a federal Royal Commission on Life Insurance, sparked by a similar investigation of irregularities in the insurance business in New York state, revealed instances of mismanagement of funds, financial irregularities, and what one Toronto newspaper called "disclosures of the most barefaced and brazen dishonesty."[74] The result of the commission's hearings and report was a considerable fall in public confidence in private insurance companies. Thus, a compromise between public and private provision emerged: a scheme of government-operated annuities was offered to the public as a means of overcoming the deficiencies in the private market. Individual contracts could be started with an initial premium of $10. Payments did not have to be made monthly or yearly, although regular contributions were encouraged. There was no cancellation of the contract because of failure to keep up with payments. One source of serious criticism of private insurance that had come to light was the millions of dollars in unearned profit that had accrued from lapsed policies. It was recognized, however, that failure to make regular payments to the government annuity would result in very small pension incomes.

A Canadian researcher who made a detailed study of the *Government Annuities Act* of 1908 concluded that

> this Act had many excellent features. Public administration offered security of funds, confidence, freedom from forfeiture, and elasticity in making payments. As a long-term investment the inducements offered were superior to those offered by private companies. But could it become an effective instrument for achieving security in old age on the part of the average workman? Could any voluntary scheme actually meet the income maintenance problems involved? For skilled workers regularly employed, and for middle-class people, an additional outlet for savings devoted solely to the building up of an old age annuity might become an attractive prospect. But for the average factory worker it was expecting too much in terms of discipline and sacrifice. His surplus, if any, was small, and there were too many current risks demanding accessible savings to make it possible for him to tie up regular sums for a distant prospect. The whole Act insofar as it was intended to serve the needs of workingmen was based on misconception of their way of life.[75]

A random sample of annuity contracts examined in 1915 indicated that "purchasers were mainly people in the lower-paid professions (notably teachers and clergy), clerks, skilled tradesmen, farmers and small businessmen. Labourers accounted for only 4 percent of sales."[76] Between 1908 and the beginning of the Old Age Pensions Act in 1927, only 7,713 annuities were issued, leaving the vast bulk of ageing, needy Canadians dependent upon families, friends, or organized charity, often in the form of indoor relief.

Public Assistance at the Turn of the Century

One aspect of the social minimum concept in Canada prior to the First World War was the form of public aid to people in financial need. Up until the war, the only type of public assistance available was that provided on an emergency basis by municipalities or by private charities acting as their agents, and generally referred to as "outdoor relief." Most of the help given was assistance in kind—that is, in the form of grocery hampers, second-hand clothing, and orders for fuel. Very little cash was provided, in keeping with the prevailing view that poverty was intimately related to, among other human frailties, a chronic inability to budget properly. Such help that was provided, whether in cash or in kind, was given as emergency aid with little in the way of assistance on a regular, continuing basis.

The amount and form of help given to the dependent poor were conditioned by the famous (or infamous) English poor law principle of *less eligibility*. This principle, first enunciated by the Poor Law Reform Commission of 1834, decreed that in Britain the standard of living provided by the municipality for its dependent poor must be at a less favourable standard than that which the lowest-paid labourer could earn for himself and his family. While not given formal recognition in Canada, the principle of less eligibility pervaded the administration of public assistance to the poor from the outset, resulting in meagre subsistence-level handouts, which for long-term dependencies (as in the case of a mother left to care for a family of small children) became a threat to the health of the individuals and families assisted.

An extension of the less eligibility belief that also infiltrated into Canada from England was the workhouse test. This had the dual aim of detecting fraudulent claims for assistance as well as implementing less eligibility as a principle. As it was not always thought possible to provide assistance in amounts less than that of the lowest-paid independent wage earner, as that class of labourer might well be at a bare subsistence level, the condition of the recipient of welfare was made less favourable by providing assistance in an unpalatable form—indoor relief. The offer of help conditional upon entry into one of the poor law institutions was called the "workhouse test." People who refused to accept this form of help were considered to have fraudulently asked for assistance. Those who accepted it were clearly those in most desperate need and therefore the proper subjects for charity.

As Canada approached the end of the nineteenth century, there was increasing "uneasiness at the idea of building large institutions, named after the most lavish contributor to house people who needed care,"[77] and outdoor relief became more common. The workhouse test now became the work test, which meant that an applicant for public assistance, unless he had a medical certificate excusing him from work, could be required to saw cordwood or break rock as a condition for receiving help. In 1915, for example, the House of Industry in Toronto required an applicant for relief to break up a crate of rocks weighing 650 pounds.[78] Once again it was held by welfare administrators and those responsible for policy that such a requirement separated the genuine case of hardship from the fraudulent, as well as making the conditions of life for the assisted poor "less favourable" than for the unassisted. The amount of help provided as outdoor relief, following the less eligibility concept, was so minimal that the recipient was often forced to supplement this aid by applying to private individuals and charitable organizations for additional help. In effect, public aid had to be supplemented in many cases by begging. In the larger cities, particularly during the winter months or during periods of economic recession, an array of charitable agencies would spring up as a result of public concern for the poor. This in turn resulted in a movement, at about the turn of the century, to organize the various charities and introduce a more systematic approach to relief-giving as a means of avoiding duplication of effort and cutting down on fraudulent application—the latter subject generating, then as now, more interest than it deserved.

Attitudes toward the poor and explanations of the causes of poverty in the decade prior to the First World War appear to have changed very little from what they were in the nineteenth century, the research of H.B. Ames notwithstanding. The Associated Charities of Winnipeg, formed in 1908, stated in their first annual report that, although they had "no exact record," they were satisfied that intemperance was an important contributing factor in 80 per cent of cases of destitution.[79] In a 1912 report this same organization, in explaining its function to the public, revealed a characteristic view of poverty held by charitable agencies: "if material assistance was all that was needed, if the families seeking it could in all cases be relied upon to use it in such a way that they would quickly become self-supporting the work of this department would be easy. Unfortunately, the large majority of applications for relief are caused by thriftlessness, mismanagement, unemployment due to incompetence, intemperance, immorality, desertion of the family and domestic quarrels. In such cases the mere giving of relief tends rather to induce pauperism than to reduce poverty."[80]

As long as this definition of poverty prevailed, a limited, residual approach to social welfare seemed to many to be justified. It was only when the causes of poverty began to be decisively redefined that a foundation for changes in the social security system was laid. These changes came about as a result of a host of socioeconomic forces unleashed by industrialization. The first of these developments was the workers' compensation movement.

Notes

1. Donald Creighton, *Canada's First Century* (Toronto: Macmillan 1970), 24.
2. In 1871 there were only nineteen urban centres in Canada with a population of over 5,000. By 1891 the number was forty-four, by 1911 seventy-six. Leroy O. Stone, *Urban Development in Canada* (Ottawa: DBS 1967), 69, Table 4.1.
3. Canada, *Report of the Royal Commission on the Relations of Labor and Capital in Canada* (Ottawa 1889), 87 (hereafter cited as the Labor Commission).
4. J.S. Woodsworth, *My Neighbor* (1911; reprint, Toronto: University of Toronto Press 1972), 18.
5. For a brief extract of the 1882 report, see Michael Cross, ed., *The Workingman in the Nineteenth Century* (Toronto: Oxford University Press 1974), 74. Note that in a survey of 465 mills and factories, 173 children under ten were recorded as employees and over 2,000 between the ages of ten and fourteen.

6. Unions were legalized in 1872 by the Canadian Trade Unions Act. It applied only to those trade unions and their members properly registered with the Registrar General of Canada. Unregistered trade unions might still be prosecuted as conspiracies. Accompanying this act was another that weakened its effect—the Criminal Law Amendment Act, 1872, modelled on a British law that made picketing illegal, thus seriously limiting union action. In 1876 this Act was repealed, and peaceful picketing became legal. J.E. Cameron and F.J. Young, *The Status of Trade Unions in Canada* (Kingston: Jackson Press 1960), 29.

7. Greg Kealey ed., *Canada Investigates Industrialism* (Toronto: University of Toronto Press 1973), ix. I am indebted to Kealey's introduction to his abridged version of the royal commission reports and evidence for the following discussion.

8. Ibid., xviii.

9. Labor Commission, *Second Report*, 89. See as well Kealey, *Canada Investigates Industrialism*, 110–11.

10. Labor Commission, *Second Report*, 91.

11. Kealey, *Canada Investigates Industrialism*, 408.

12. Ibid., 105.

13. Labor Commission, *First Report*, 8, and Appendix A, 17.

14. Labor Commission, *Second Report*, 78–79.

15. Ibid., 117.

16. Labor Commission, *First Report*, 8.

17. Labor Commission, *Second Report*, 116.

18. Labor Commission, *First Report*, 8.

19. Ibid., 29.

20. Labor Commission, *Second Report*, 84.

21. For a more complete discussion on workers' compensation legislation, see the next chapter.

22. Kealey, *Canada Investigates Industrialism*, 181.

23. Ibid., 198.

24. Ibid., 204.

25. Ibid., 429.

26. Labor Commission, *Second Report*, 82. For references to union benefit schemes in evidence presented to the commission, see Kealey, *Canada Investigates Industrialism*, 140, 150, 191, 278–79.

27. Kealey, *Canada Investigates Industrialism*, 414, and the Labor Commission, *First Report*, Table of Wages, 187.

28. Labor Commission, *First Report*, Appendix C. The employees had no voice in the operation of the benefit society.

29. Labor Commission, *First Report*, 13.

30. See Kealey, *Canada Investigates Industrialism*, xx. In addition to the recommendations already noted with regard to annuities and the sanitary inspection of houses, the *First Report* also recommended that a government-operated scheme of insurance be instituted to protect the heirs of persons killed in industrial accidents and that the government also invite tenders from private insurance companies to provide insurance for work-related injuries. The commissioners called for improved safety measures for the workforce, particularly on the railroads and Great Lakes shipping. They recommended that factories be inspected more thoroughly and regularly and that only certified engineers be permitted to operate steam boilers. The commissioners recommended that the punishment of child employees by foremen be made a criminal offence; that the system of fining employees be prohibited; and that hours of labour be restricted to ten hours per day, fifty-four hours per week. The commissioners urged that boards of arbitration should be established; that opportunities for technical education be expanded; and that certain laws that weighed heavily on workers be modified or eliminated, such as the *Master and Servants Act*, the seizure of household property for non-payment of debts, and the practice of charging the debtor with the costs of debt collection (frequently reported as greater than the debt owed). A Bureau of Labour was proposed to compile and publish statistical information on wages, working conditions, and other relevant information.

31. In the following discussion, free use has been made of the insights provided by Elisabeth Wallace, "The Origin of the Social Welfare State in Canada 1867–1900," *Canadian Journal of Economics and Political Science* 16 (1950):383–93.

32. The advent of the public school was particularly significant for the education of girls. When families had to bear the costs of educating their children privately, the education of sons tended to be given priority if money for educational purposes was scarce. See Ian E. Davey, "Trends in Female School Attendance in Mid-Nineteenth-Century Ontario," *Histoire sociale/Social History* 8 (May 1975):253.

33. Judith Fingard, "Attitudes toward the Education of the Poor in Colonial Halifax," *Acadiensis* 2 (spring 1973):26. See as well Susan E. Houston, "Policies, Schools and Social Change in Upper Canada," *Canadian Historical Review* 53 (1972):249–71.

34. Anthony Platt, "The Triumph of Benevolence: The Origins of the Juvenile Justice System in the US," in *Criminal Justice in America*, ed. Richard Quinney (Boston: Little Brown 1975), 370.

35. Ibid., 389. Provincial governments began to enact their own factory acts beginning with Ontario in 1884.

36. This included 80 per cent of labourers, 56 per cent of the artisans, and 59 per cent of the business employees (primarily clerks). Qualifications for municipal elections were less onerous. See Michael B. Katz, *The People of Hamilton, Canada West* (Cambridge: Harvard University Press 1975), 27.

37. The exception to this was in Lower Canada, where from 1809 to 1834 women with the necessary property qualifications could vote.

38. Prince Edward Island granted women the vote in 1922; Quebec women had to wait until 1940. The Dominion of Newfoundland permitted women at the age of twenty-five to vote in 1925. The age qualification was reduced to twenty-one in 1946 (*Report of the Royal Commission on the Status of Women in Canada* [Ottawa 1970], 337).

39. H.W. Arthur, "Developing Industrial Citizenship: A Challenge for Canada's Second Century," *Canadian Bar Review* 45 (1967):792.

40. Martin Robin, "Registration, Conscription and Independent Labour Politics, 1916–1917," *Canadian Historical Review* 47 (1966):117.

41. Herbert Brown Ames, *The City below the Hill* (Toronto: University of Toronto Press 1972). This work was first published in book form in 1897 following its initial appearance as a series of newspaper articles.

42. Ibid., 7.

43. Charles Booth, *Life and Labour of the People of London* (London: Macmillan 1904). The results of Booth's work, which took ten years to complete, began to appear as early as 1889.

44. Ames, *City below the Hill*, 72.

45. Ibid., 73.

46. Kealey, *Canada Investigates Industrialism*, 234.

47. Ames, *City below the Hill*, 75.

48. Ibid., 76.

49. "If private enterprise does not furnish sufficient opportunity for willing men to provide for their families the absolute necessities of life, during the four cold winter months, then the municipality, by carefully considered relief works conducted at a minimum wage, should come to their assistance" (Ames, *City below the Hill*, 76–77).

50. Ames called for "legislation that will abolish the rear tenement and the out-of-door closet and will create breathing places for the people" (ibid., 115).

51. Ibid., 107–10.

52. "We may safely fix the limit of decent subsistence at $5.00 per week" (ibid., 68).

53. Ibid., 33.

54. Ibid., 36. This assumes more than one wage earner per family.

55. Terry Copp, *The Anatomy of Poverty* (Toronto: McClelland and Stewart 1974), 32. Ames's poverty line of $5 a week for a family was dangerously low, and the evidence he compiled on death rates supports this contention.

56. For an excellent overview and sampling of issues, see Paul Rutherford, ed., *Saving the Canadian City: The First Phase 1880–1920* (Toronto: University of Toronto Press 1974).

57. Splane, *Social Welfare in Ontario*, 265 ff. In Ontario, prior to 1900, charity was seen as a religious function. This, too, militated against public responsibility for social welfare and accounted for the proliferation of charitable agencies as each denomination attempted to deal with the social welfare problems of its adherents (see Stephen A. Speisman, "Munificent Parsons and Municipal Parsimony," *Ontario History* 65 [March 1973]:34–49).

58. Rutherford, *Saving the Canadian City*, 195–208. Urban reform is also the subject of J.S. Woodsworth's *My Neighbor*.

59. For a full account of the social gospel movement in Canada, see Richard Allen, *The Social Passion, Religion and Social Reform in Canada, 1914–28* (Toronto: University of Toronto Press 1971). I am indebted to this work for the following discussion.

60. Stewart Crysdale, *The Industrial Struggle and Protestant Ethics in Canada* (Toronto: Ryerson Press 1961), 19–20.

61. For some idea of the range of social welfare activities conducted by churches at this time, see Woodsworth, *My Neighbor*, Chapter 10.

62. A.E. Smith, "Cutting Down an Evil Tree," *Social Service Congress, Report of Addresses and Proceedings* (Toronto: The Social Service Council of Canada 1914), 204–06.

63. G.C. Pidgeon, "The Church and Labour in British Columbia," ibid., 46–53.

64. James Simpson, "The Extension of Social Justice," ibid., 39–41.

65. W.M. Rochester, "The Weekly Rest Day and National Well-Being," ibid., 17–24; Marie Christine Ratte, "Rescue Work for Girls," ibid., 222–25; Ven. Archdeacon Cody, "Why Is It Wrong to Gamble," ibid., 340–51; and Sara Rowell Wright, "The W.C.T.U. Programme," ibid., 322–26.

66. As just one of several examples, J.J. Kelso, "The Importance of Child Welfare," ibid., 91–93.

67. Rose Henderson, "Mothers' Pensions," ibid., 109–15.

68. For a complete account of the development of old age pensions in Canada (including the development of the Government Annuities Act of 1908), see Kenneth Bryden, *Old Age Pensions and Policy-Making in Canada* (Montreal: McGill-Queen's University Press 1974).

69. Labor Commission, *First Report*, 13.

70. Splane, *Social Welfare in Ontario*, 103. This royal commission report, which Splane describes as "one of the outstanding documents in the literature of social welfare in Canada" (56), identified poverty and the failure to develop policies and programs in the social welfare area as contributing in a major way to crime and vice in society.

71. Canada, Department of Labour, *Labour Gazette* 1 (October 1900):51–52 (hereafter referred to as *Labour Gazette*).

72. *Labour Gazette* 6 (August 1905):177.

73. Bryden, *Old Age Pensions*, 49.

74. *Canadian Annual Review* (1906), 234, quoting an editorial from the Toronto *Globe* of 23 May 1906. See also 215 ff.

75. Joseph E. Laycock, *The Canadian System of Old Age Pensions*, vol. 1 (PhD diss., University of Chicago School of Social Service Administration 1952), 31.

76. Bryden, *Old Age Pensions*, 52.

77. Wallace, "Origin of the Social Welfare State," 387.

78. See evidence of Arthur Laughlen, superintendent, presented to the Ontario Commission on Unemployment, *Report of the Ontario Commission on Unemployment* (Toronto 1916), 234. In the 1880s the Toronto House of Industry's work test involved cutting wood. In their annual report of 1886, the directors noted that because they had experienced difficulty in disposing of the wood, they were forced to discontinue the work test. Apparently they found a market for crushed rock! See "Charity in Toronto," *The Workingman in the Nineteenth Century*, ed. Michael S. Cross (Toronto: Oxford University Press 1974), 205–06.

79. Cited in Woodsworth, *My Neighbor*, 63.

80. Alan F.J. Artibise, *Winnipeg: A Social History of Urban Growth, 1874–1914* (Montreal: McGill-Queen's University Press 1975), 188.

2

Blood on the Factory Floor

The Workers' Compensation Movement in Canada and the United States*

ROBERT H. BABCOCK

Introduction

DURING THE LATE NINETEENTH and early twentieth centuries, a movement to reduce the socio-economic impact of workplace injuries through a non-litigious method of compensating victims or their dependents gained momentum. Originating in Europe and New Zealand during the late nineteenth century, the movement quickly swept across the United States and Canada between 1890 and 1920 in campaigns waged at both the state, or provincial, and federal levels. While organized labour and powerful business interests exerted a preponderant influence on the content of the statutes in each of the nearly sixty state or provincial jurisdictions, myriad intervening variables provoked somewhat different outcomes. To a significant extent, those states or provinces that had pioneered in workers' compensation legislation provided models that shaped later debates in the remaining political arenas. Robert Asher concludes that "workmen's compensation was the most widespread and palpable legislation bringing tangible benefits to workers to be enacted by the American states before World War I."[1]

After examining the problem of industrial accidents in North America at the turn of the century, this paper summarizes the existing literature explaining the origins of workers' compensation legislation in several American states and Canadian provinces. To this survey the author adds findings from his own investigation of the reform movement in the state of Maine and the province of New Brunswick. There is a widely held assumption among social scientists that Canadians rely more heavily than Americans upon collectivist solutions to social problems.[2] But the history of the origins of workers' compensation laws belies that assertion, because in this case statist mechanisms surfaced on *both* sides of the 49th parallel. Indeed, the evidence presented here suggests that pioneering laws, rather than values derived from a more collectivist political culture, exerted greater influence on Canadian legislation in this field.

---

* This chapter was first published as "Blood on the Factory Floor: The Workers' Compensation Movement in Canada and the United States," in Raymond B. Blake and Jeff Keshen, *Social Welfare Policy in Canada. Historical Readings* (Toronto: Copp Clark Ltd., 1995): 107–21.

The Scope of the Industrial Accidents Problem

During the age of iron and steam, the factory became an increasingly dangerous work-place. Exploding boilers, rapidly spinning shafts, exposed gears and cogs, unprotected saw blades and planing knives, clouds of dust, overcrowding, poor sanitation, and the absence of fire escapes all magnified the dangers. Piece work intensified the labour process and thereby increased the risk of injury. On the American side, defining the scope of this prob-lem remains complicated by the absence of a central source of national data on industrial accidents. Much of the information on the frequency of mishaps is buried in the reports of state bureaus of industrial statistics; only a small portion has been correlated. One turn-of-the-century student who examined the problem reported that, between 1899 and 1908, 19,469 coal miners were killed and 5,316 injured in mines located in twenty-two states that produced 98 percent of American coal.[3] In nearly the same period (1900–1907), 23,895 employees of American railways lost their lives, and 335,946 were injured.[4] He also estimated that one-half of 126,567 deaths reported in the U.S. Census between 1900 and 1906 resulted from accidents to males in American factories.[5] Not only the workers them-selves suffered: between 1899 and 1908 the 11,328 coal miners killed at work in Illinois and Pennsylvania left 6,183 widows and 14,444 children.[6] Nationwide, it was estimated that more than 10,000 widows and 25,000 children could be "charged to the account of American coal production" during this decade.[7] A recent student of the compensation reform movement concludes that the United States suffered the highest accident rates of any leading industrial power before World War I.[8]

   In Canada, the task of finding national industrial accident data is somewhat easier. Ottawa set up a Department of Labour in 1900, which, among other tasks, accumulated information on workplace mishaps. Each month the department's *Labour Gazette* report-ed accident data; each year it summarized fatal and non-fatal accidents according to a variety of industries or trades. Table 1 presents the data for 1904. Assuming the popula-tion of Canada to be about one-tenth that of the United States in 1904, the chart suggests

Table 2.1. Industrial accidents in Canada during 1904

	Non-Fatal Accidents	Fatal Accidents
Lumbering	59	119
Mining	106	117
Building trades	43	139
Metal trades	73	492
Woodworking trades	12	154
Printing trades	–	10
Clothing trades	3	20
Textile trades	4	25
Food, tobacco preparation	6	55
Leather trades	2	4
Railway service	273	360
General transport	104	169
Miscellaneous trades	43	191
Unskilled labour	30	121

Source: *Labour Gazette* 5 (Jan. 1905), 742–73 (totals include agriculture and fishing).

that, proportionately, death and injury rates may not have been as great north of the border as those in the United States reported by Campbell. Then again, the pace of industrial capitalist development in Canada lagged behind that of its neighbour. No doubt many accidents that had taken place in remote locations on the staples-driven frontier were never reported. In any case, the fact that Ottawa took pains to collect this data suggests that many Canadians considered the industrial carnage to be a significant socio-economic problem.

Until the turn of the century, victims of industrial accidents and their families could only seek legal remedies if they believed they were not at fault and if they possessed sufficient resources (most did not) to employ counsel and pay court fees. Even if they could afford a lawyer, common law precedents in both Canada and the United States stacked the deck in favour of the rights of employers. First of all, the assumption-of-risk doctrine held that victims of industrial accidents had already accepted "the natural and ordinary risks and perils" of a job when they had begun work, and normally they could not hold the employer responsible. In theory, judges expected workers to reject conditions they considered to be dangerous by quitting and seeking "safer" work; in reality, too many workers chased too few jobs for anyone to be that choosy. Secondly, in order for judges to find employers liable for unsafe conditions, the injured worker was required to prove that the employer himself, and not just his foreman or manager, had contributed to the "extraordinary" danger. A bold worker might make this charge, but it was easy for the boss to deny responsibility and difficult for the worker to prove it. Thirdly, according to the courts' fellow-servant rule, employers could not be held accountable if the injured worker or another employee had been partially responsible for the mishap.[9] Judges implied that the victim could sue his shopmate, but from the injured's viewpoint it made no sense to bring costly legal action against an impoverished co-worker. As a result of these well-entrenched common law doctrines, then, the vast majority of injured workers and their families found themselves dependent upon an employer's sympathy, their family resources, or public charity rather than on courts of law. Only an estimated 15 percent of injured workers actually obtained damages through lawsuits, and lawyers often claimed a big chunk in fees. To protect themselves, workers in a few larger shops organized into mutual benefit societies for insurance purposes, and some skilled craftsmen ultimately earned enough to afford insurance policies purchased from trade unions or fraternal orders. But for the vast majority of turn-of-the-century Canadian and American workers, blood-stained factory floors seemed tilted in favour of employers. Over the next two decades, the balance between labour, capital, and the state gradually shifted in both Canada and the United States and, as a result, the tilt and the colour of North American factory floors began to change.

Three nations initially addressed the problem of industrial accidents. In 1871 Germany placed more liability for accidents upon employers, and fourteen years later required them to provide accident insurance.[10] An English employers' liability statute of 1880 put some limits on common law judgments by abolishing the fellow-servant rule; then a compensation law enacted in 1897 allowed workers to choose between seeking a legal remedy or accepting a fixed schedule of payments based upon the severity of the injury. Finally, in 1906, England adopted a comprehensive no-fault compensation system paying benefits to injured workers or their kin.[11] New Zealand, the third pioneering society, adopted a wide range of industrial reforms, including no-fault accident compensation, during the last decade of the nineteenth century. An influential group of North American reformers, including Henry Demarest Lloyd and Richard T. Ely in the United States and W. Frank Hatheway in Canada, closely followed events in these countries. Lloyd returned from a visit determined to "New Zealandize" America, concluding that "the state could and should create a just social and economic order."[12] Soon workers' compensation became a continental movement in which German, English, and New Zealand laws were heralded as models.

The Movement for Workers' Compensation Legislation in the United States

Only a few scholars have investigated the origins of workers' compensation legislation in a handful of states or provinces, and consequently much of what is known in others comes from barebones surveys by contemporary Washington and Ottawa bureaucrats. In the United States, the earliest legislation appeared at the turn of the century. First, employers' liability laws redefined portions of the common law precedents and often placed limits on juried awards, but they did not abandon the legal principle of fault-finding. As a result, lawsuits remained the only compensatory remedy. Later, workers' compensation bills adopted a no-fault stance, considering accidents to be an unavoidable cost of doing business, and established a benefit schedule for workplace victims. Now businessmen could estimate the costs of accidents by covering their liability through insurance policies whose annual premiums were passed on to the consumer.

By 1907, twenty-seven states or provinces had adopted employers' liability laws; most of them modified the fellow-servant doctrine while a few limited the other two court tests (assumption of risk and contributory negligence) as well.[13] In 1902, Maryland enacted the first North American law to provide benefits without suit or proof of negligence, but only two years later a court ruled it unconstitutional.[14] In 1908 Congress drew attention to the problem when it granted certain government employees the right to compensation for injuries sustained at work. A year later, Montana became the first state to enact a compulsory law requiring contributions from both employers and workers, but once again a court threw it out. The Massachusetts bill of 1907 escaped this fate only by allowing employers to elect to participate.[15] Canadian legislatures enacted compensation laws during the same era. British Columbia set up a compensation plan in 1902; Alberta followed in 1908, Quebec in 1909, and Manitoba in 1910. Most were initially employers' liability statutes that mirrored British legislation. Soon on both sides of the border the movement for no-fault compensation accelerated, governments acted, judges yielded, and by 1920 forty-three states and seven provinces (plus the Yukon) had joined the reform bandwagon.[16]

Because outcomes of the various provincial and state battles for workers' compensation laws differed, it is necessary to examine these movements separately (and to some extent chronologically) before hazarding any generalizations. Nearly thirty years ago, Roy Lubove and James Weinstein presented two distinct but overlapping interpretations of the origins of workers' compensation in the United States. Lubove traced the movement to popular indignation over high industrial accidents and to studies challenging the conventional wisdom that 95 percent of accidents were a result of worker carelessness. For instance, evidence from the Pittsburgh Survey, a social science study completed in the early twentieth century, revealed that only 21 percent of factory mishaps could be attributed to this factor. Employers welcomed the no-fault principle, Lubove argued, for two reasons: first, they found existing employers' liability laws to be too slow, wasteful, and unfair, and secondly, they believed that compensation "would substitute a fixed, but limited charge for a variable, potentially ruinous one."[17] In short, compensation became a form of cost control. Lubove concludes that business imperatives rather than a desire for equity "proved more influential in shaping the workmen's compensation System."[18]

Starting from a somewhat different perspective on the Progressive Era, James Weinstein shares many of Lubove's conclusions about the importance of business interests in establishing no-fault workers' compensation. Big businessmen wanted to stabilize their position and undercut efforts by workers to engage in independent political action. Organized labour, fearing state intervention, initially opposed workers' compensation but reversed its position after 1908 when the National Civic Federation (NCF), an alliance of big businessmen and labour leaders, "threw its whole weight into the fight for compensation legislation."[19] The NCF circulated a model bill, based on German and English laws, to state legislatures. By early 1909, several states had appointed commissions to look into workers' compensation acts; the big battle took place in New York State, Weinstein says, where businessmen conceded a higher benefits package in return for funding payments through private rather than state insurance.[20]

To date Robert Asher offers the most extensive, systematic study of the workers' compensation movement in the United States through a comparison of the origins of these laws in New York, Wisconsin, Minnesota, Massachusetts, and Ohio. He concludes that the business community reflected a diversity of views on the no-fault approach and failed to dominate the legislative process as much as Lubove and Weinstein had argued. The middle class supported the movement in order to relieve class tensions; labour ultimately endorsed it because more workers gained than those who might hope to win juried cash awards.[21] But the interaction of these interest groups, as we will see below, differed in the six states examined here: Massachusetts, Wisconsin, Minnesota, Washington, New York, and Maine.

In Massachusetts, Asher finds, workers' compensation came about as a result of a business-labour consensus. A "moderate" employers' liability law adopted in 1887 proved ineffectual because of congested court dockets and high lawyers' fees. Employers worried about rising insurance costs. Organized labour, initially opposed to no-fault compensation, finally endorsed it. A voluntary law was adopted in 1908 but covered only 20 percent of the industrial force in the state. Soon large employers demanded a more stringent act. The legislature debated three different bills initially barring casualty companies from writing compensation insurance, but the insurance industry's lobbyists won amendments scuttling this provision. Finally a bill covering 80 percent of the state's industrial workforce became law in 1910. Asher concludes that Weinstein overstated the role of the big business and failed to note the "negative effects [of] cost-conscious conservative employers" on the reform movement. The Massachusetts law, he says, was "truly a compromise measure, ... supported by labor and either endorsed or tolerated by employers" because of their dissatisfaction with earlier liability laws.[22]

In Wisconsin, Asher finds, Progressive Republicans endorsed workers' compensation legislation for a quite different reason: they wanted to detach the working-class vote from that state's prominent, ethnically rooted social democratic movement. Organized labour worked with businessmen on bills to replace the antiquated liability system with a no-fault law. While they fought over the details, Wisconsin's 1911 compensation act also reflected compromises between these two interests. Workers could elect common law defences rather than scheduled compensation benefits; private casualty companies rather than a state insurance fund would continue to underwrite employer's liability.[23]

In Minnesota, a radical political movement, the Non-Partisan League, provoked an ideological conflict over state insurance of workers' compensation. Some private insurance companies backed such laws because they were believed to promise the industry higher premiums and more predictable losses, while others opposed them because they feared the competition from monopoly state insurance. Organized labour sided with the League but was unable to overcome opposition in the upper house of the Minnesota legislature. Ultimately, postwar hostility toward government intervention and fear of radicalism eroded the League's support and killed state insurance. Among other factors, Asher concludes, "an extensive network of private [insurance] organizations was already functioning in the compensation field" in Minnesota, and legislators decided these could be regulated rather than replaced.[24]

The workers' compensation movement in the state of Washington was the product of a consensus among labour leaders and businessmen in one industry—lumber. In fact, Washington State lawmakers, not Canadian provincial legislators, set up the first North American government-run insurance fund. By 1910, 65 percent of the state's wage earners worked in the lumber industry, and west coast lumbermen were "anxious to rid themselves of personal injury litigation." Higher accident rates, falling prices, a growing number of lawsuits, and escalating insurance rates forced lumber entrepreneurs to stabilize costs. "There was no denying the mutual desire of labor and lumbermen," Joseph Tripp concludes, "to escape the morass of litigation." Despite opposition from many lawyers, urban businessmen, and other so-called "progressives," the Washington legislature enacted a workers' compensation law in 1911 that established a state accident fund administered by an independent commission. Ultimately, seven more states and most, if not all, Canadian provinces followed Washington's example.[25]

While acknowledging the contributions of social progressives to the movement for workers' compensation laws, Weinstein, Asher, and Tripp maintain that big business played a major role in several American states in order to establish control over labour costs. Later, organized labour, initially sceptical of government intervention into labour–capital relations, joined the campaign. Robert Wesser identifies all three groups in the New York State reform effort, but he argues that labour played a more important role in this state than business did. A state commission established in 1909 systematically collected information on German and English laws before conducting public hearings. Its report incorporated many suggestions from organized labour, lauded the British plan, and urged elimination of the assumption-of-risk rule and relaxation of the other two common law doctrines. Nevertheless, two-thirds of the state's businessmen remained opposed to the commission-sponsored legislation, mostly because workers could still choose between fixed compensation and a lawsuit. State courts declared the law unconstitutional in 1911. Over the next two years, organized labour in New York State, capitalizing on rivalry between Democrats and Republicans, as well as on the latter's split between factions favouring either William Howard Taft or Theodore Roosevelt, took control of the movement for workers' compensation. In 1913, the New York State legislature enacted a law providing for compulsory compensation with benefits administered by a state commission. Employers could choose a variety of ways to insure themselves. Wesser concludes that the New York workers' compensation law was a "significant triumph" for organized labour rather than for big business.[26]

At the turn of the century, the relatively small labour movement in rural Maine, as in many other states, actively promoted an employers' liability bill. But the dominant Republican Party, a stalwart defender of property rights, steadfastly ignored these requests until their grip on the political situation began to weaken. When the state's biggest business, the pulp and paper industry, demonstrated an interest in stabilizing the costs of industrial accidents, Republicans enacted an employers' liability law in 1909. The measure modified common law assumptions, put limits on the size of awards, but excluded farm workers, domestic servants, and those engaged in the lumber industry. If workers accepted benefits under the law, they were barred from filing lawsuits.[27]

In 1910, the national Progressive political whirlwind swept through Maine, and a year later the Democrats, aided by a strong labour vote, won control of both houses and the governorship for the first time in decades. Three laws were promptly enacted on behalf of the state's workers. The first upgraded a bureau of labour statistics into a full department in the governor's cabinet whose head was given power to collect accident data and to order employers to promote workplace safety. The second law required factory supervisors to report all deaths or serious injuries within ten days. Under the provisions of this law, 814 accidents were tallied from mid-1911 to mid-1912, thirty-one of them fatal. The third measure required Maine's employers to pay weekly wages. At the same time, the legislature rejected a bill to require safeguards on machinery or to exempt injured workers from proving that they had been exercising "due care" at the time of their accident. As a result, courts still found workers liable for seven-eighths of all accidents, and the injured received less than 40 percent of juried awards.[28]

During the next four years (1910–1914) the reform tide ebbed and flowed within the ranks of Democrats, Republicans, and Progressives. Gradually, elements of all three parties—big business among traditional Republicans, organized labour in the Democratic Party, and social reformers in the Progressive fold—converged behind a call for no-fault workers' compensation legislation. By 1914, all three parties had nailed this plank to their party platforms, and a bill was introduced in the legislature. Yet powerful Maine lumbermen, unlike their counterparts in Washington State, remained strongly opposed to compensation legislation, probably because the industry in the Pine Tree State still consisted of small units that subcontracted much of their work and engaged mostly seasonal, part-time employees. Since woods workers laboured by themselves, employers said, businessmen should not be held responsible for their injuries. Ultimately the bill was scuttled through a complicated parliamentary manoeuvre.[29]

When the Democratic Party captured both the governorship and the lower house of the state legislature in 1914–15, prospects for a workers' compensation bill measurably improved, and a no-fault law went into effect on 1 January 1916. It covered just 73 percent of the state's labour force, excluding farm labour, domestic service, loggers, part-time workers, and small shops with less than six employees. Covered workers gave up their right to sue, and employers lost common law protections if they refused to participate. Court appeals were limited only to questions of law. No state-administered fund was specified; businessmen could insure themselves or buy liability insurance from private companies. The Maine compensation statute fixed dollar limits for both partial and full disabilities. A three-person board administered benefits, originally fixed at 50 percent of wages and later raised to 60 percent.[30]

Despite the law's obvious shortcomings, some Maine labour leaders justifiably called it "without doubt the most important piece of legislation ever passed in Maine in favor of industrial employees." Others lamented the compromises and pressed for amendments at the next session. In 1919, the law was rewritten to reduce the waiting period, raise benefits, expand the state governing board to four members, and allow its chair to take legal dispositions. Having received endorsements from both parties and the governor, the revised statute sailed into law. One Maine labour leader concluded that the 1919 version of workers' compensation was "one of the best there is in the United States."[31]

In Maine as in the other states, large and small businessmen, organized labour, and a shifting political context affected the drive for workers' compensation legislation. Gains by the state Democratic Party and a split in Republican ranks after 1910 created a political opening for the reform movement. Divisions in the business community between small woods contractors and giant pulp and paper companies initially blocked legislation in 1913, but two years later organized labour tilted the balance in favour of a compensation law that was subsequently refined and adjusted for wartime inflationary conditions. Thanks to the influence of big business and its servants, the casualty companies, a state insurance fund was never considered.

The Movement for Workers' Compensation in Canada

The origins of workers' compensation laws in Canada are less well-known, and thus far scholars have examined the movements only in Quebec, Ontario, and New Brunswick. In the course of surveying the condition of Montreal workers at the turn of the century, Terry Copp briefly reviewed the industrial accidents problem. He noted that Quebec's inspectors described the factory floor as "a real battlefield with its dead and wounded." Between 1890 and 1907, inspectors looked into 4,608 accidents in which 263 workers were killed, yet only one in three mishaps had been reported as required by law. The casualties left the province's charitable institutions "hard-pressed." Aware of growing concern in Europe and North America about this problem, in 1907 a Quebec government-appointed commission recommended enactment of a provincial compensation law. While both the province's employers and organized labour supported the measure, most of the initiative for the Quebec workers' compensation law of 1909 came from neither business nor labour but from a successful lobbying campaign by Louis Guyon, Quebec's factory inspector. Although not, as Copp claims, the first such act in North America, the Quebec law did establish a schedule of payments and death benefits. Courts administered it until an independent board was set up in the early 1930s.[32]

The workers' compensation movement in Ontario was particularly influential because the outcome regulated Canada's largest and most industrialized province and served as a model for less industrialized provinces. In 1886, Ontario adopted an employers' liability law based on the 1880 British statute; at first "justice was irregular and sporadic,"[33] although workers won more verdicts after 1900.[34] Labour, not big business, initiated the movement for reform, and workers' compensation became their "central issue." Responding to a rising tide of working-class political consciousness, in 1910 a Conservative government appointed the province's chief justice, William Meredith, to head a commission of inquiry. At the hearings, the Canadian Manufacturers Association (CMA) endorsed the principle of no-fault compensation; like so many of their American counterparts, Ontario businessmen complained about expensive liability insurance, ambulance-chasing lawyers, and the need to regularize and reduce costs. Yet when the commission finally presented a bill, the CMA condemned it because they thought the benefits were too high and they wanted employees to contribute to insurance costs.[35]

Ultimately the Ontario compensation law of 1914 represented a compromise between business and labour. Businessmen obtained a simpler measure covering all workers. The law divided employers into groups according to relative risks and assessed their payrolls proportionately. They also called for state insurance like their counterparts in some American jurisdictions such as Washington State because they believed it would be less expensive. A provincial workers' compensation board levied payroll assessments and administered the benefits. Rather than abolishing all common law rights of recovery, the Ontario law suspended them if the worker accepted compensation under the new law. Like most North American acts, the Ontario law excluded those working in agriculture and domestic service; unlike American legislation, it covered the victims of many industrial diseases. Organized labour subsequently agitated for additional benefits such as the cost of medical treatment.[36]

Why did Ontario set up a provincial compensation board and a state-controlled insurance fund? Not primarily as a result of an inherent bias in favour of state action, it would appear. First of all, the insurance industry "made surprisingly little effort" during and after the hearings to avoid this result. Their lawyers appeared late in the sessions and "neither their participation nor their briefs were impressive or forceful defences of insurance."[37] Secondly, the head of the inquiry, Chief Justice Meredith, was determined to block judicial administration of benefits. Thus Ontario's compensation legislation came about because the CMA had openly endorsed the principle, labour had shown "strong and widespread support," and "most important[ly]," because of Meredith's influence.[38]

The reform movement in New Brunswick, as in Maine, reflected motley internal and external influences. Initially a small group of middle-class Saint John progressives led by W. Frank Hatheway, a tea merchant, joined with leaders of the powerful local longshoremen's union in the spring of 1901 to study the "labour question." Discussion soon turned to the need for employers' liability laws. After the group had examined the English statute, it asked the provincial government to enact a similar measure.[39] Rather than run an unnecessary political risk, the reigning Liberals postponed action until they had won an election. Then they enacted a modest bill that somewhat modified common law doctrine but required workers to continue to press claims through lawsuits. Subsequently, the Grits also approved a factory law in 1905, which provided for the inspection of workplace conditions. Neither went far enough to satisfy the province's workers, particularly the most politically conscious segment in Saint John, and the Tories, Hatheway among them, swept into provincial office in 1908.[40]

From his position in the assembly, Hatheway promptly orchestrated a movement to enact a tighter liability law. The new measure, endorsed by Saint John longshoremen and millmen, set aside the fellow-servant rule, made employers liable for accidents caused by unsafe machines, and established a benefit schedule. Nevertheless, workers still faced the costs, delays, and dilemmas of proving their injuries in a court of law. Businessmen still lacked a financial incentive to introduce safety measure.[41] "When I suggest that some dangerous parts of machinery should be covered," the factory inspector complained, "I am told it is not necessary, because it has been in that condition some five, ten or fifteen years, and no one has been injured."[42] With the gradual dissipation of the provincial labour movement after 1907, the movement to enact a comprehensive, no-fault compensation law ground to a halt.

By 1916, three factors had impelled the government of New Brunswick to change its stance. As an election approached, the Tories found themselves in political trouble and prepared to shore up their position. Secondly, the rate of industrial accidents showed no signs of diminishing; there were seventy-four in 1916, eight of them fatal. Thirdly and perhaps most importantly, in 1915 Nova Scotia had enacted an up-to-date, no-fault law. Assured of support from the Tory premier, a revitalized New Brunswick Federation of Labour immediately launched an all-out effort to get a law modelled on both the Nova Scotia and Ontario statutes. When the Tories subsequently dragged their feet, going only so far as to appoint a commission to conduct another study, they lost labour's confidence as well as the ensuing election.[43]

Although the Liberals were returned to power, the report commissioned by their Tory predecessors set the stage for New Brunswick's abandonment of the old common law doctrines regarding fault. The report identified three types of laws: (1) employers' liability acts similar to those that had been adopted in 1903 and 1908; (2) a system whereby employers' submitted payrolls to a government agency that grouped the industries according to risk and levied varying assessments in order to carry the liability; and (3) a state insurance fund.[44] Ontario had been the first province to implement the second type, in 1915, followed by British Columbia and Nova Scotia. In 1918, the new Liberal government of W.E. Foster in New Brunswick followed their example. Citing Ontario's experience as well as provisions of the Nova Scotia act, it abolished the fellow-servant rule. Then contributory negligence was taken out of the hands of judges and juries and given to an impartial board that would take this factor into account when assessing damages. A government-appointed workers' compensation board (whose labour member had been active in the fight for the law), rather than the provincial treasurer, received funds collected from employers. The board also took over the courts' power to make awards. The new act covered millmen but excluded farm labour, domestic servants, miners, fishermen, city employees, clerks, part-time workers, and—notably—loggers, a particularly contentious omission in this heavily forested province. In 1920, the Liberals, perhaps worried about the impact of a local United Farmers' movement on their political standing, upgraded the workers' compensation statute, adopting a schedule for industrial diseases, increasing benefits, and extending coverage to workers in the lumber industry.[45]

In retrospect, several factors shaped both the timing and content of New Brunswick's response to the problem of industrial accidents. Most importantly, a rising political consciousness among workers, particularly in Saint John, goaded politicians into responding to an accelerating social problem. Secondly, at different periods both middle-class progressives and working-class leaders played key roles in articulating solutions borrowed from path-breaking laws already enacted in the British Empire rather than from American models. Thirdly, because neither the Grits nor the Tories securely controlled the levers of power during this period, both parties vied for the attention of working-class voters more than they had been accustomed to doing. Fourthly, unlike the situation in Ontario, representatives of the insurance industry testified in Fredericton on behalf of their interests, and the final bill contained a provision authorizing the provincial cabinet to sanction private insurance for any employer who petitioned for it.[46] Hence New Brunswick actually established a competitive (state-controlled or private) fund like those in nine American states.

Conclusion

While business, organized labour, and reform-minded individuals or groups played significant parts in all these jurisdictions, outcomes differed from place to place depending upon such variables as the specific political contexts, the relative influence exerted by the contending interest groups on the political process, and the model laws most appealing to the interested parties. The trend in both countries was toward the establishment of no-fault, government-run workers' compensation commissions rather than the perpetuation of fault-finding by the courts. Several states and provinces appointed commissions to conduct investigations, hold hearings, and draft model bills for legislators to consider. In all of these jurisdictions, either the advocacy or at least the acquiescence of some important sectors of the business community was vital to the ultimate success of the movement. Similarly, organized labour played a crucial role in both nations, although it appears to have been a more important factor in Ontario, New Brunswick, New York, and Maine than in some other jurisdictions. The significant role of progressive-minded leaders crops up time and time again in the origins of workers' compensation, whether it was Louis Guyon in Quebec, Chief Justice Meredith in Ontario, Frank Hatheway in New Brunswick, Judge Wainwright in New York, or Carroll Wright in Massachusetts.

A comparison of provisions in American and Canadian accident compensation laws in 1920 suggests the controlling influence of historical contingencies rather than underlying national values in explaining the differences.[47] For instance, the "remarkably uniformity" in Canadian laws noted by Hookstadt resulted from the overriding influence of two models—the British statutes and Ontario's pioneering compensation law—rather than from an underlying "statist" disposition. In 1920 all the Canadian compensation statutes were compulsory for employers while a majority (thirty-one) of American laws remained elective. But this difference most likely reflected the impact of court decisions in states like Massachusetts, which had forced lawmakers to insert elective provisions that usually denied common law protections to those employers who opted out. Canadian jurists, traditionally less interventionist in the political process and probably more closely attuned to legal developments in the United Kingdom, simply did not throw out compulsory accident compensation legislation after 1900 like their American counterparts. Finally, we should note that the workers' compensation laws in fourteen American states were no less compulsory in 1920 than the statutes in Canadian provinces.

As for the issue of state vs. private casualty insurance, it would appear once again that statist values did not divide at the 49th parallel. By 1920 in Canada, five of the seven jurisdictions with accident compensation laws had erected state insurance funds, whereas in the United States seventeen of the forty-five states had either exclusive or competitive state funds, and twenty-eight states relied solely upon private casualty or mutual insurance firms. These facts hardly support the notion of a rigidly statist or anti-statist bias in either Canada or the United States.

But there was one underlying difference between the approaches of the two nations in dealing with this problem between 1890 and 1920 that deserves mention. Canadian laws assumed liability on the part of the province; that is, injured workers received payments regardless of whether or not employers had contributed their premiums to a province-run compensation fund. Defaulting employers could be sued by the provincial workers' compensation board. No American states assumed such liability, and as a result injured workers lost compensation benefits when the employer or insurance carrier fell into insolvency. In short, whereas Canadian provinces assumed ultimate responsibility for the welfare of the injured, American states did not.

Notes

1. Robert Asher, *Dissertation Abstracts International* 1971, 2587-A.
2. For a recent statement of this view see S.M. Lipset, *Continental Divide: The Values and Interpretations of the United States and Canada* (Toronto: C.D. Howe Institute, 1989).
3. Gilbert Lewis Campbell, *Industrial Accidents and Their Compensation* (Boston, 1911), 10.
4. Ibid., 15.
5. Ibid., 5.
6. Ibid., 22.
7. Ibid.
8. Robert Asher, "Industrial Safety and Labor Relations in the United States, 1865–1917," in *Life and Labor: Dimensions of American Working-Class History*, ed. C. Stephenson and R. Asher (Albany, 1986), 116.
9. For common law precedents see J.R. Commons and J.B. Andrews, *Principles of Labor Legislation* (New York, 1967 reprint), 227–31.
10. Ibid., 232.
11. Durand Halsey Van Doren, *Workmen's Compensation and Insurance* (New York, 1918), 33–34, 45.
12. Peter J. Coleman, "New Zealand Liberalism and the Origins of the American Welfare State," *Journal of American History* 69 (Sept. 1982): 372–91.
13. James Weinstein, "Big Business and the Origins of Workmen's Compensation," *Labor History* 8 (1967): 159.
14. Commons and Andrews, *Principles of Labor Legislation*, 236.
15. Ibid., 236–37.
16. Ibid., 256; Roy Lubove, "Workmen's Compensation and the Prerogatives of Voluntarism," *Labor History* 8 (1967): 262–63.
17. Lubove, "Workmen's Compensation," 259–62.
18. Ibid., 268.
19. Weinstein, "Big Business and Origins of Workmen's Compensation," 162.
20. Ibid., 167–70, 174.

21. Asher, "Workmen's Compensation in the US, 1880–1935," *Dissertation Abstracts International*, 1971, 2587-A.

22. Robert Asher, "Business and Workers' Welfare in the Progressive Era: Workmen's Compensation Reform in Massachusetts, 1880–1911," *Business History Review* 43 (1969): 452–75.

23. Robert Asher, "The 1911 Wisconsin Workmen's Compensation Law: A Study in Conservative Labor Reform," *Wisconsin Magazine of History* 57 (1973): 123–40.

24. Robert Asher, "Radicalism and Reform: State Insurance of Workmen's Compensation in Minnesota, 1910–1933," *Labor History* 14, 1 (Winter 1973): 19–41.

25. Joseph F. Tripp, "An Instance of Labor and Business Cooperation: Workmen's Compensation in Washington State (1911)," *Labor History* 17 (Fall 1976): 530–50.

26. Robert Wesser, "Conflict and Compromise: The Workmen's Compensation Movement in New York, 1890s–1913," *Labor History* 12, 3 (Summer 1971): 345–72.

27. *Maine Register*, 1900, 162; 1902–03, 158; 1905–06, 160; 1907–08, 160; *Maine Legislative Graveyard*, 1907, RG1, box 928, folder 5; box 956; *Maine Legislative Record*, 1909, 65, 67, 186, 268, 300, 750, 814, 838, 974; *Acts and Resolves*, 1909, 30; Maine Department of Labor and Industry, *Report*, 1911–12, 248–51; 1913, 151–52; *10th Annual Report of Maine State AFL*, 1913, 25.

28. *Maine Register*, 1911–12, 160; 1920, 221–22; *Original Papers of the Maine Legislature*, 1911; *10th Annual Convention of the Maine AFL*, 1913, 27.

29. *Maine Register*, 1913–14, 160; 1915–16, 160; 1920, 221–22; Legislative Committee, *10th Annual Convention of Maine AFL*, 1913, 2 ff., 37–41; *Maine Legislative Graveyard*, 1913, box 1000, folders 2, 3, 4; *Maine Legislative Record*, 1913, 8, 256, 258, 278, 321, 1142; Maine Department of Labor and Industry, *Report*, 1913–14, 252.

30. *Maine Legislative Record*, 1915, 1103–06; *Workmen's Compensation Act of the State of Maine, Effective January 1, 1916* (Waterville, 1917); *Third Biennial Report of the Department of Labor and Industry*, 1915–16, 9.

31. Maine State AFL, *Proceedings*, 1917, 19–20; 1918, 33; 1919, 37, 71; *Maine Legislative Record*, 1917, 624–25, 636, 819–20, 1036–40; 1919, 1085, 1087–88, 1203; Maine Department of Labor and Industry *Report*, 1917–18, 9-18.

32. Terry Copp, *The Anatomy of Poverty: The Condition of the Working Class in Montreal, 1897–1929* (Toronto, 1974), 106–25.

33. Michael J. Piva, "The Workmen's Compensation Movement in Ontario," *Ontario History* 67 (1975): 43.

34. R.C.B. Risk, "'This Nuisance of Litigation': The Origins of Workers' Compensation in Ontario," in *Essays in the History of Canadian Law*, vol. 2, ed. David H. Flaherty (Toronto, 1983), 432.

35. Piva, "The Workmen's Compensation Movement," 39–56.

36. Ibid.

37. Risk, "'This Nuisance of Litigation,'" 465.

38. Ibid., 472.

39. Saint John *Daily Sun*, 24 April, 11 Sept., 9 Oct. 1901; Saint John *Daily News*, 13 Nov. 1901; card, *The Fabian League* in H.H. Stuart Collection, box 1, no. 14 "Labor," Harriet Irving Library, University of New Brunswick (hereafter UNB), Fredericton; letters W.F. Hatheway to Premier L.J. Tweedie, 15, 23 Jan., 14 Feb. 1902, in Legislative Council Records, Provincial Archives of New Brunswick (henceforth PANB), Fredericton.

40. "Our New Brunswick Policy Is ..." campaign flyer used in 1903 election, W.F. Hatheway Papers, Harriet Irving Library, UNB; *Canadian Annual Review*, 1903, 169–71, 1904, 330, 1905, 332, 338; 1906, 395–406; 1907, 623–28; 1908, 388, 390, 397; New Brunswick *Synoptic Report*, 30 April 1903, 135; 6 May 1903, 182–84. Trades and Labor Congress *Proceedings*, 1903, 22; *Labour Gazette* 5 (June 1905): 1364–66; Saint John *Sun*, 31 Jan., 1 Feb. 1908.

41. New Brunswick, *Journals of the House of Assembly, 1909*, Supplementary Appendix, Factory Inspector's Report 1908–09, 142–49; *Eastern Labor News*, 24 Dec. 1910.

42. New Brunswick, *Journals of the House of Assembly, 1912*, Supplementary Appendix, Report of the Factory Inspector, 28.

43. *Canadian Annual Review*, 1916, 631, 638; 1917, 695, 697; Trades and Labor Congress, *Proceedings*, 1915, 32–33; 1916, Report of the NBFL, 76–77; NB *Synoptic Report*, 1916, 172.

44. NB Journals, 1917, Supplementary Appendix, *Report of the Commission Appointed into the Working of the Ontario and Nova Scotia Workmen's Compensation Act*; 8 George V (1917), c. 30.

45. *Canadian Annual Review*, 1918, 661; 1919, 707; 1920, 696, 704, 714; NB *Synoptic Report*, 1918, 33–34, 250, 260, 277–79; 1919, 234, 245–52; 8 George V (1918), c. 37; 9 George V (1919), c. 7; 10 George V (1920), c. 12.

46. NB *Synoptic Report*, 1917, 71; 8 George V (1918), c. 37, s. 53.

47. Carl Hookstadt, *Comparison of Workmen's Compensation Laws of the United States and Canada up to January 1, 1920*, U.S. Dept. of Labor, Bureau of Labor Statistics No. 275 (Washington: GPO, 1920), 131–40.

3

"In the Interests of the Children"

Mothers' Allowances and the Origins of Income Security in Ontario, 1917–1930*

JAMES STRUTHERS

THE ORIGINS OF INCOME SECURITY in Ontario begin with motherhood. With the creation of mothers' allowances in 1920, women became the first clients of provincial social assistance. In singling out impoverished widows with children as a category deserving special public recognition and entitlement, Ontario was by no means breaking new ground. Between 1911, when the state of Illinois enacted North America's first mothers' pension scheme, and 1920, thirty-nine American states and all four western Canadian provinces set up similar schemes providing pensions or allowances to dependent widows and their children.[1]

Why did the needs of widows with children, rather than those of the unemployed, the disabled, or the elderly, break the mould of local poor relief and private charity that had dominated the response to poverty and dependency in Ontario, as elsewhere in North America, throughout the nineteenth and early twentieth centuries? On what terms did mothers receive assistance from the state, and how did their claims differ from those of men? In what ways did mothers' allowances, as Ontario's first income security program, establish a welfare framework that would shape the provincial response to other forms of poverty in this century? To what extent did the provision of "pensions" for mothers represent a new departure in thinking about the minimum needs of Ontario families for an adequate and decent social life?

These questions reflect the extent to which mothers' allowances are central to any understanding of the gendered basis of the welfare state both within Ontario and elsewhere in this century. As feminist historian Linda Gordon has argued, "if the state were a family, it would be assumed that welfare is a woman's affair.... [W]omen constitute most of the recipients and providers of 'welfare.'"[2] Within Ontario, women were critical in the campaign to bring about mothers' allowances between 1912 and 1920, and they formed the core staff, although not the key administrators, within the program's early bureaucracy. As Theda Skocpol argues within an American context, mothers' allowances represented the most fully realized vision of a maternalist welfare state, built by and for women.[3]

---

* This chapter was first published as "In the Interests of the Children': Mothers' Allowances and the Origins of Income Security in Ontario," in James Struthers, *The Limits of Affluence: Welfare in Ontario, 1920–1970* (Toronto: University of Toronto Press, 1994): 19–49.

Moreover, policies and regulations aimed at the female clients of mothers' allowances serve to illustrate another key element of the welfare state within Ontario. It operated as a powerful reinforcement for existing assumptions about the essential differences in the needs, roles, and responsibilities of women and men within society. If social policies aimed at men were designed principally to foster the ideal of wage-earning independence, "women's policies turned on motherhood."[4] Quite simply, women's right to state aid presupposed their reproductive role within the family and their economic dependency upon men. Only women still fulfilling the first role and deprived of the second were considered eligible for state support.

As a consequence, within mothers' allowances, women in Ontario entered into a unique moral relationship with government. On the one hand, state allowances paid on a regular monthly basis to those women who met the eligibility criteria provided a minimal guarantee of income sufficient to allow them to stave off absolute destitution and, most importantly, to keep their families intact and their children free from the orphanage or foster care. On the other hand, the state, through Ontario's Mothers' Allowance Commission and its cadre of investigators and local boards, explicitly took the place of the absent husband. Financial support and the right to retain care of one's children were given only in exchange for strict fidelity to specific moral norms and expectations concerning the proper external behaviour and innate qualities of a "good mother" and housekeeper. Women received help not as independent citizens in their own right, but as paid caregivers for the state. Mothers' allowances, Ontario officials argued at the scheme's inception, were justified "primarily in the interests of the child—the future citizen of the country; the mother being only a secondary from the standpoint of the State."[5] In this respect, provincial social policy alleviated women's need while at the same time it reinforced their social subordination. Within the early years of mothers' allowances, then, can be found many of the essential contours and contradictions of the gendered response to poverty in twentieth-century Ontario.

The campaign for mothers' allowances in Ontario began, as elsewhere in North America, in the decade before the First World War. The centre of activity was Toronto, the city whose social reform, philanthropic network, and large population would be instrumental in provoking much of the province's response to welfare throughout the remainder of the century. As with most concerns affecting Ontario children in this era, the earliest exponent of mothers' allowances was John Joseph Kelso, a former Toronto newspaper reporter who was the driving force behind the creation of Children's Aid Societies across the province in the early 1890s.[6] In 1893 Kelso was appointed Ontario's first superintendent of neglected and dependent children, responsible for overseeing the regulation of child welfare and protection work across the province. Brought into constant contact with needy widows driven to surrender their children to foster care because of poverty alone, Kelso soon became a forceful advocate of some form of regular financial aid for such women, through a partnership between local government and private charity, to prevent the unnecessary breakup of otherwise worthy families. "It is no real charity or help to a poor mother to close up her home and send her children, one to this institution and one to that, thus robbing both of the ties and influence that are, after all, the only thing worth living for," Kelso argued on behalf of widows' pensions in his annual reports to the Ontario legislature from 1895 onwards.[7]

Although Kelso and the Children's Aid Society movement were the earliest advocates of the idea, it gained momentum in the years immediately before the First World War when the campaign was taken up by a wider coalition of women's groups, social service professionals, juvenile court magistrates, labour leaders, and child welfare advocates. They came together through an umbrella Committee on Mothers' Allowances led by the Reverend Peter Bryce, a reform-oriented Methodist minister who was instrumental in settlement work among British immigrant families in the Earlscourt or "shacktown" district of Toronto.[8]

Bryce was one of the leaders in Toronto's social reform movement. A British immigrant and theology graduate who had studied sociology and political economy with Professor James Mavor at the University of Toronto, Bryce was at the centre of a wide network of child welfare activities within the city. Through his Earlscourt church he administered Canada's biggest Sunday school, with more than 2000 children. Along with publisher and fellow Methodist Joseph Atkinson, he was the originator of the *Toronto Star*'s Santa Claus Fund, and his Earlscourt Children's Home was one of the largest and most energetic Protestant orphanages and day-care facilities within the city. He was also the first president of Toronto's Federation of Community Services, its Child Welfare Council, and the Neighborhood Workers' Association, the city's largest organized charity. He would also become the first director of Ontario's Mothers' Allowance Commission. Bryce's career in social reform in the first two decades of the new century ably captures the transition from evangelism and moral uplift to a growing faith in the redemptive powers of government. "At one time Child Welfare had its source in the ministering spirit inculcated by religion, then in the natural impulses of human sympathy," he argued in 1920. "Now it is part of the defensive foresight of citizens who would protect the future of the state."[9]

Although Bryce, like Kelso, provided important leadership in the campaign for mothers' allowances, the core constituency of this reform movement, in Toronto as elsewhere throughout North America, came from the growing ranks of middle-class women involved in voluntary, philanthropic activity. As Gwendolyn Mink argues, "women's policies were the achievement of middle-class women's politics." Even before they had the vote, women across the continent used the politics of motherhood as a "wedge into the political community, attempting to feminize political life through asserting the centrality of motherhood, home, and family life to national efficiency, moral character, and the productivity of the state."[10] Within Toronto, organizations such as the Wimodausis Club (wives, mothers, daughters, sisters) provided the core financing and administrative support for the work of Bryce's Earlscourt Children's Home. Through this volunteer work, middle- and upper-class Toronto women were exposed to the problems that drove widowed, abused, deserted, and unwed women to place their children in residential care; at the same time, they gained an institutional vehicle for the assertion of their own social and political power within the community.[11] As a consequence, improving the conditions of maternal and child welfare became the crucible within which women forged their own political identity in the pre-suffrage years. Pensions for mothers became one of their most important strategic victories.

Within Toronto, the Local Council of Women took the first step in the mothers' allowance campaign. In 1914, three years after the enactment of the first mothers' pension act in Illinois, the council sponsored an "experiment" by providing a monthly subsidy for one year to six needy widows and their families in order to demonstrate to government the feasibility and necessity of mothers' pensions. The experiment was "an unqualified success ... [with] absolutely no pauperizing tendency observed," the council argued, and the unmet need it revealed was immense. When the project received publicity, "applications for help poured in from all sides, even from men who were out of work and wanted assistance for their families."[12] The design of the experiment closely prefigured the final shape of Ontario's 1920 mothers' allowance scheme. The women received help only "after the most thorough investigation as to their worthiness and their necessity," and only in return for "direct supervision of the conditions in each home" by a public health nurse who visited each family regularly, "advising as to the best means of maintaining the health of the children ... and emphasizing at all times the fact that the mother's duty was to remain at home and to care for the children." The visitor also advised the mothers "in a friendly manner as to the best outlay of the pension money" and required written monthly statements from each one showing what she had spent for food, clothing, shelter, and fuel.[13] As Mariana Valverde has argued, the creation of the welfare state was as much a project of private philanthropy as it was the result of efforts by politicians and civil servants. This is certainly evident in the campaign for and design of mothers' allowances. As Ontario officials themselves concluded in appraising the Local Council of Women's experiment, "private philanthropy must always point the way for state legislation in matters pertaining to charities or pensions."[14]

Lobbying for mothers' pensions received help from other quarters as well. By the second decade of the new century, overcrowding and high death rates within children's institutions created a growing critique of their role as the primary response to the plight of dependent children. Few of the residents of Toronto's so-called orphanages, as elsewhere in North America, were in fact orphans at all. At the Earlscourt Children's Home, for example, 79 percent of the children receiving residential care were discharged to their own families, and more than one-third came from mother-led households. A 1918 survey of all 1741 children in institutional care within Toronto uncovered only twenty who had lost both parents. Two-thirds of the remainder were there because of the death, illness, or desertion of one parent, a statistic underscoring the financial fragility of most working-class households. These homes functioned most frequently as the last resort for families in financial crisis rather than as refuges for the parentless, and mothers deprived of the earnings of a male breadwinner constituted their most regular clientele.[15]

Within Toronto's public health, child welfare, and social service community the anomaly of orphanages providing care principally to children with living parents who, but for financial necessity, wished to keep their families intact was a growing mockery of the sanctity of motherhood, home, and family life. Concern reached a climax during the final years of the First World War. Public health officials pointed to high death rates due to contagious disease among infants surrendered to institutions by working mothers. "One of the most essential things if the babies are to survive is that they should have mother's care; that they should be nursed through the period of infancy," Toronto's medical health officer told Ontario officials in making the case for a mothers' pension scheme. "Now, hundreds, probably thousands of children are weaned because the mother has to go to work to earn a living." Pensions for mothers would also provide an inducement to persuade tubercular fathers to seek sanatorium care, thus reducing the risk of infection to their families.

Toronto school officials pointed to the high dropout among fatherless children and noted that sixty-two exemptions from school had been granted in one year to children under fourteen "because their mothers were wage-earners requiring [their] help."[16]

As in other North American cities, juvenile court magistrates also played a key role in making the case for mothers' pensions as an antidote to delinquency. Three of the twenty-six members of Bryce's Committee on Mothers' Allowances were from the city's juvenile court system and all made direct linkages between working mothers and youth in trouble with the law. "Children who carry the key while their mothers work all day are not long in getting beyond their mothers' control," the commissioner of Toronto's juvenile court argued in support of keeping women at home through a mothers' pension scheme. Others pointed out that public money spent on mothers' allowances would be returned "in saving our boys from penitentiaries and our girls from houses of ill fame."

Even those in charge of children's institutions confessed to increasing disillusionment with the results of this form of care. "The insufficiency of institutional life, the stigma later attached to the institutional child, the over-crowding of our institutions, and the increasing cost of their upkeep" were all arguments in favour of launching a publicly funded program of mothers' pensions, child welfare workers maintained. As one of Toronto's leading Catholic refuge directors put it, "one of the biggest mistakes that can possibly be [made is] to place any child in any institution, if it is possible to keep it out.... [T]he best institution under the best management is not equal to the poorest home, provided that home be morally correct.... Under present conditions we are obliged to put children into institutions who really should not be there." Mothers' pensions and the "proper home training" they would provide would produce "much better citizens of the country." Other infant home directors complained that overcrowding in their institutions was a "terrible problem.... Our cities are growing, and war conditions are making things worse." Mothers' pensions were "absolutely necessary" and could reduce the number of children in infant homes by 40 percent, at great savings to the wider community. Institutionalization was a "most extravagant way of dealing with the children," Ontario's superintendent of prisons and charities argued in making the case for mothers' pensions. "The total cost of keeping the individual homes together would be but a small fraction of the sum" spent on maintaining them within orphanages.[17]

Union leaders, anxious to keep working-class families intact and to reduce the threat of low-wage competition from poverty-stricken working women and children, were a final important constituency behind the drive for a provincial mothers' pension scheme. Fresh from their successful campaign to achieve state-administered workers' compensation in 1914, Ontario labour leaders saw pensions for mothers as a logical next step on the road to protecting the incomes of working-class families. Why should the widow of a man killed through an industrial accident receive 55 percent of his former earnings, while the widow of a man dying from tuberculosis receive nothing, the *Toronto Star* asked, in making the connection between workers' compensation and mothers pensions. "In both cases there is the personal loss, but the one family has security of social status, while the other falls into the abyss of poverty." Labour leaders agreed. Three union officials were represented on the Committee on Mothers' Allowances, and resolutions endorsing the concept poured into Queen's Park from local labour councils across the province in the years between 1914 and 1919. Of all advocates of mothers' pensions, unionists were most in favour of an all-inclusive scheme incorporating not just widows, but deserted, divorced, and unwed mothers as well. "It is up to the Country to see that [these] children get a fair chance for their bringing up and for their education," Hamilton labour leader Walter Rollo argued before a government inquiry into the subject. "It is through no fault of the child that such conditions exist. We believe that the *Act* should be made as wide as possible and should cover every case.... It keeps the family together." Ironically, as the minister of labour in charge of implementing Ontario's first *Mothers' Allowance Act* in 1920, Rollo would find himself presiding over a measure far more restrictive than this generous vision.[18]

The First World War provided the political context for mobilizing these diverse arguments and constituencies above the critical threshold for government action. On the one hand the enormity of the slaughter produced by the war itself heightened the already growing prewar concern that the conservation of children was essential to the productivity and social efficiency of the nation. "Losses on the battlefield," Veronica Strong-Boag writes, "could most logically be made up by renewed efforts to reduce infant mortality. Improved care for mothers and their children would also ensure a generation physically and morally fit to inherit the 'brave new world' for which Canada's soldiers had fought." Mothers' pensions thus formed a core component of this war-heightened campaign to shore up family life and redeem the colossal sacrifice of the battlefield.[19]

At the same time, the mobilization of voluntary effort through the Canadian Patriotic Fund to care for the needy families of men overseas provided a practical illustration of the benefits and the methods of administering regular allowances for women raising children. The Patriotic Fund in many ways was nothing but a national illustration, enormously expanded in scale, of earlier experiments, such as Toronto's, in the provision of aid to deserving mothers. "The experience gained from the administration of pensions to soldiers' dependents by the Patriotic Fund," Ontario officials argued during war, served as "a guide" to their efforts in designing mothers' allowances for a postwar world.[20]

Three features of the fund's experience with women were particularly important in this regard. The first was the necessity for "strict supervision through regular home visiting of the mothers receiving support, given the lack of foresight shown by some of the women who receive[d] Patriotic Fund money." Women getting help needed "the supervising and personal touch" to enable them to "do the best with the sum allowed," while the community needed a "safeguard [to] prevent an unintelligent distribution of public moneys." As a result of such close moral supervision, "in a great many cases [the mother] ... has become a very much better woman."[21]

Second, the work of the Patriotic Fund demonstrated that "in every locality there are public spirited and socially minded men and women ready and anxious to give their services in the cause of public welfare." The fund had worked through the close cooperation of central administrators with local committees of volunteers and visitors operating at the municipal and county level. Ontario advocates of mothers' pensions argued that this model could be transferred successfully to the administration of mothers' pensions.[22]

Paradoxically, the third lesson drawn from the Patriotic Fund experience was that there was "no suggestion of charity" in receiving money from the fund. Given the close moral supervision and the regular involvement of volunteer women visitors in the intimate details of a client's family life, all of which was borrowed directly from the charity organization model, this insistence that the stigma of charity was entirely absent from the Patriotic Fund's operation was somewhat surprising. However, fund officials gave two critical reasons why this should be so. The first was that the money was "given in recognition of the service of the husband." Although mothers' pensions would be justified on the basis of a mother's "service to the state," this was not the case with the Patriotic Fund. At bottom, it was the man's sacrifice, not his wife's, which dictated the basis of entitlement. By implication, the moral policing of her household was simply the fund's attempt to look after his interests while he was absent overseas.[23] Second, fund officials argued that the taint of charity was eliminated because they "provided what we thought was sufficient to give a decent living and a decent living was dependent altogether on the cost of living in the locality. We didn't follow out the principle of the English Poor Law, which gives them just enough to keep up an existence. That would have been a very easy matter to do, but we tried to place them on the basis of a decent living in the community in which they did live.... We tried to give them sufficient to keep on their house."[24]

When asked by Ontario government officials investigating mothers' pensions what such a standard of "decent living" might be, fund officials did not hesitate to provide explicit answers. "Based on the [Patriotic Fund] allowance a widow and two children would now get a minimum of ... $65 a month," a Hamilton representative pointed out. For a mother with seven children the allowance might range up to "$100 a month."[25] Simply put, the stigma of charity was dispelled by paying women and their children an adequate and decent allowance geared to actual living costs in the community. Although mothers' allowances in Ontario would borrow much from the Patriotic Fund experience in its design and operation, this commitment to basic adequacy as the cost of avoiding stigma and humiliation for its clients was deliberately forgotten.

The war also provided one last tangible benefit to those interested in the design and implementation of a mothers' pension scheme in Ontario. Through National Registration, government officials knew with a fair degree of accuracy both the number and the location of widows with children in the province and could make a reasonable estimate of how much different versions of a mothers' allowance act were likely to cost. When Department of Labour officials were given the go-ahead by Conservative premier William Hearst at the beginning of 1919 to begin work on the design of "as sound and perfect a scheme as possible," they had the models of forty-three American and western Canadian schemes to drawn upon as well as a solid database on the target population within Ontario.[26] A sample of more than four hundred widowed women, selected from the National Registration files, were visited by special investigators sent out by the Department of Labour to determine "in what percentage of cases the Government would be justified in providing funds."[27] The questions they asked, borrowed from the operation of mothers' pension schemes elsewhere, ultimately shaped the structure of entitlement under Ontario's mothers' allowance program. Government investigators wanted to know:

> the number and ages of the children; their nationality; the number of children at home; at school; and working; whether the family occupied the whole house or part; kept lodgers or boarders; whether the mother worked or stayed at home with the children; if she worked, for whom and at what wage; what other income the family received, whether from children or otherwise; what other assets were available, whether in property or insurance;

how long the family had lived in Canada and in Ontario; and in addition ...
some estimate of the general circumstances of the home, and of the ability of
the mother as a homemaker.[28]

Behind all these questions lay the core assumptions concerning who was or was not
entitled to state support and under what circumstances. On this basis, department officials determined that 80 out of the 400 families visited, or one-fifth of the total, would
be eligible for mothers' allowances should such a scheme be implemented within Ontario.
Extrapolated to the more than 16,000 widows in the province, this yielded the estimate
of a probable caseload of 3,200 families at a cost of almost $1 million annually—figures
that would be reached within the first two years of the scheme's operation. Unlike old age
pensions, which would be launched a decade later with wildly inaccurate estimates of the
population initially eligible, mothers' allowances would be based on remarkably accurate
forecasts of costs and caseload size.[29]

Of all the key decisions surrounding the inauguration of mothers' allowances in
Ontario, none was more critical than which mothers should be entitled to receive the
state's support. Once the decision was made by the Hearst administration early in 1919 to
launch such a scheme, public hearings were scheduled in Ontario's four largest cities to
test public opinion on the issue. In all, ninety-three witnesses testified at these hearings
and none of them spoke against the concept. "It was distinctly evident ... that this idea of
the State employing the mother of its future citizens to rear her children according to approved standards, and subsidizing the home for this purpose where need exists, has taken
hold of a very large element in the community," labour department officials observed.[30]

But which mothers? Evidence given at the public hearings gave conflicting points of
view. On the one hand, much of the rationale for mothers' pensions came out of their
supposed efficacy in a postwar attack on poverty. "The day is past when thinking men
and women could take poverty for granted," Ontario officials argued in making the case
for such a scheme. "The causes of poverty ... may be to a large extent eradicated," and,
among them all, the absence of a parent through sickness, death, or desertion was the
leading source of hardship for most families in need. Of almost 2,000 Toronto children
removed from their families to institutions in 1918, one-half were there because of the
illness or desertion of a parent, one-quarter because of the death of a parent, and less than
10 percent because of emotional or physical neglect. Only 1 percent were true orphans.[31]
If rescuing innocent children from poverty was the principal rationale for mothers' pensions, statistics such as these made a strong case for making the scheme as comprehensive
and all-inclusive as possible.

Much of the evidence presented at the public hearings in 1919 lent weight to this point
of view. If mothers' allowances were restricted only to widows, as was the case in most
other jurisdictions, "the majority of the children will remain where they are," since only 12
percent of the population of Toronto's orphanages were there because of the death of their
fathers. Insofar as infant mortality was an argument for mothers' pensions, this too miti-
gated in favour of extending the scheme to "all dependent mothers, whether widowed, or
deserted, or unmarried, as only if the mother can nurse her own child, has the child a fair
chance to survive," public health and children's aid workers in London, Ontario, argued.
Finally, "no need was presented more frequently at the Public Hearings" than the plight of

deserted wives with children. Many of these were "worthy women ... deserted by worthless husbands," and their children would be "an asset to the State, just the same as children who have lost their fathers by death," witnesses argued.[32]

While recognizing the legitimacy of these concerns, both government officials and the leaders of most social work and women's organizations lobbying for mothers' pensions came out strongly against including deserted and unmarried women in the scheme. Toronto's powerful Committee on Mothers' Allowances did not even mention the possibility of including any group other than widows in the legislation. Women leaders were the most forceful advocates of a plan restricted to widows only, largely because of moral concerns. Despite paying lip service to the idea of deserving women deserted by "worthless" men, a strong aura of suspicion and moral disapprobation hung over the heads of women abandoned by their husbands. Only 16 percent of their number living in poverty, social workers estimated, would qualify for mothers' allowances "under an Act strictly administered according to approved home standards," and even in these cases the "worthiness of the wife would require special investigation." Other witnesses, such as Elizabeth Shortt, one of the province's leading advocates of mothers' pensions, argued that "the present unsettled domestic relations due to the war" militated against any financial inducement being provided by the government for men to abandon their families. In cases of desertion, most women witnesses agreed, the state's core obligation was to "provide some way for getting after the man and making him provide for his family," not to take his place as the family's chief source of financial support.[33]

If relieving the plight of deserted wives through mothers' pensions was morally dubious, doing so for unwed mothers was downright dangerous. "When we open these doors the flood that will appear makes a man sit back and say 'Who will foot the bill?'" clerics testified before the inquiry. Most of these mothers were "not women who could safely be trusted with the upbringing of children," infant home directors observed. "In so many instances [they] are feeble-minded or irresponsible" and only "a small percentage ... have been very worthy." Although many wanted to keep their children, in most cases it was "in the better interest of the child if it were adopted into some other family." Nor were government officials willing to give any estimate of the anticipated cost of including unwed mothers within the legislation. "What would be the effect in relation to the present Anglo-Saxon regard for marriage as a national institution if the State undertook to support ... the children of unmarried parents?" labour department officials asked. Although some doctors and nurses argued that unwed mothers should be supported for at least nine months while they nursed their children, only union leaders expressed unreserved support for their equal right to mothers' allowances. "It is not so much a pension for the mother ... as it is looking after the child. The child has no choice as to whether it is born in the home of the unmarried or the married mother," and many illegitimate children grew up to "become some of the brightest citizens of this and other countries ... I don't think we should allow sentiment to enter into it," Trades and Labour Congress president Tom Moore argued. This view remained exceptional, however.[34]

A final but decisive factor governing entitlement to mothers' pensions was the scheme's initial cost. Dr Walter Riddell, superintendent of labour within the Ontario government and architect of the province's first *Mothers' Allowance Act*, had been warned by Hearst in drafting the legislation to develop "carefully thought out provisions ... to prevent abuse."

Considerations of cost as well as moral regulation weighed heavily on his mind in design-ing Ontario's scheme. "One thing I am trying to get at is some of the limits we would fix ... to get it in such a way that it will not be abused," Riddell told witnesses at the public hearings. The inability even to estimate the cost of including unwed mothers rendered them ineligible for support for fiscal as much as for moral reasons. Moreover, compared with the certainty of counting widows, the number of deserted wives who might seek aid could only be roughly guessed. In order to limit costs, Riddell went so far as to maintain that widows with only one child should be excluded from coverage. Although nearly 8000 women in Ontario fell into this category, their need was not desperate, the superintendent of labour argued. "There are ... numerous good homes open to a mother with one child, where she might go in as more or less of a working housekeeper and take her child with her. The influence of that home would probably be excellent.... [I]t might be the best thing in the world not to pension the mother, so that the child would have the added advantage of being in a good home." More to the point, cutting out this group, comprising half the widows in the province, from coverage "would make a great difference [to] the cost of the scheme." In launching mothers' allowances, Riddell wished to keep "our position ... com-paratively conservative.... [A] solid foundation, well-laid, is the best assurance of a really adequate administration and to secure this at the beginning of so new an undertaking, the doors should not be thrown open wide to all classes of applicants." Similar arguments prevailed in the decision to limit eligibility to women owning less than $2000 in property and with liquid assets of less than $500. Only "British subjects" who had lived at least three years in Canada and two years in Ontario prior to their application were eligible for support.[35]

Apart from narrowly restricting the scope of entitlement, the other main determi-nant of the scheme's cost was the amount to be paid to each mother. Without knowing the extent of need within individual families, Riddell's department used only two rough guidelines to calculate cost estimates. The first was the expense of caring for children within institutions in Ontario, which worked out to $10 per child per month. The second was the average monthly payment of $35 made by Manitoba's mothers' allowance scheme, which had been launched in 1916. Both figures yielded initial estimates in the range of $800,000 to $1 million annually for a mothers' allowance scheme in Ontario restricted to widows with two or more children. Although in many other respects the Patriotic Fund provided the most immediate point of comparison for mothers' pensions, this did not prove to be the case in deciding how much was enough for Ontario widows and their children. In designing the *Mothers' Allowance Act*, government officials, despite arguing that the legislation should "provide an amount adequate to secure for the child proper home care," took as their point of departure a monthly level of support roughly half that used by Patriotic Fund administrators as the standard for a "decent living." Moreover, in another precedent that would echo throughout the building of Ontario's welfare bu-reaucracy, Riddell's report, although refusing to specify a minimum level of entitlement, argued that it was "necessary that a *maximum per family* should be determined, based on a cost of living budget." Like much else within the province's emerging welfare structure, mothers' allowances would have a ceiling but not a floor.[36]

Given the critical importance placed on ongoing supervision to ensure the "moral worthiness" of mothers to receive support, women witnesses at the public hearings also argued strongly against the payment of any routine, fixed amounts to families as was done for injured men through workers' compensation. Within the mothers' allowance program, women's judgment, not any pre-fixed formula, was the best means of determining a mother's level of entitlement. "Women ... have been dealing with these problems all these years without assistance from the Government," female charity workers testified at the public hearings, "and would be thoroughly trained to take each case on its merits.... [I]t would be ill-advised to have hard and fast cast iron rules laid down on this question.... [I]t should be left to the Committee in charge to judge each case." Local mothers' allowance boards should be composed equally of men and women, and the latter should be left in charge of the details of family investigation and supervision, these women told Riddell.[37]

As a consequence, within Ontario, as in the United States, mothers' allowances emerged as part of what Nelson has called the two-channel welfare state. "Industrialists set the terms for the male, work-based parts of the welfare state while their wives, through charity organization work, set the terms for the female, motherhood-based segments." Unlike workers' compensation, which was "male, judicial, public and routinized in origin," mothers' allowances from their inception were "female, administrative, private, and nonroutinized in origin," with levels of discretion and moral judgment borrowed directly from the realm of charity organization rather than the insurance industry, the other main administrative model for social reform.[38]

Although Ontario's *Mothers' Allowance Act* was developed by Hearst's Conservative administration in time for the 1919 provincial election, the first ever in which Ontario women would cast a vote, Hearst did not benefit from its preparation. Instead, victory fell to the insurgent United Farmers of Ontario in tandem with the Independent Labour Party of Ontario. Together these two groups would enter into a coalition government, led by Simcoe County farmer Ernest Drury, which in 1920 would introduce mothers' allowances within the province. However, the details of the legislation were identical to those already worked out by Riddell during his 1919 investigations. Like the Patriotic Fund, mothers' allowances in Ontario would be administered through a central commission, not a department of government, working with ninety-six municipal and county boards to be established throughout the province. A locally administered scheme without "centralized control," government officials concluded, would be too "irresponsible."[39]

The province would finance half the cost of the scheme and would retain final decision-making authority over who was entitled to receive support. Local governments would finance the other half and, through their mothers' allowance boards, would receive initial applications for support and advise the central commission in Toronto concerning their worthiness. A staff of seventeen paid investigators, employed by the commission, would undertake the initial home investigation and maintain ongoing supervision of the women who qualified for help. Although Riddell's report had recommended that these investigators should be chosen from among the ranks of experienced social workers and should be free from the taint of patronage, such was not the case. More than three hundred people applied for these positions, and those chosen were often women with public health or educational, but not social work training, who owed their appointments to good political connections.[40] They also endured considerable hardship in physically getting to their clients, particularly in remote rural areas. Investigators commented in their reports on enduring "a drive or horse-back ride of thirty miles ... long walks of twelve to fifteen

miles" or occasionally the necessity "to travel by hand-car back into the mining districts."
Some told of "travelling ... by stone-boat" or surviving "drives in the North through snow
so deep that it has to be left to the horses to stick to the trail."[41]

Peter Bryce was chosen first chairman of the five-member Mothers' Allowance
Commission. Other representatives included Elizabeth Shortt; Minnie Singer, a nominee
of the labour movement; Arthur Reynolds, a dairy farmer; and Major Thomas Murphy, a
lawyer. Three years later, however, Bryce would be gone. When the Conservatives returned
to power in 1923, Bryce was replaced by veteran Tory backbencher David Jamieson, an elderly doctor from Durham, Ontario. In 1927 Shortt resigned in protest against Jamieson's
blatant use of patronage in hiring commission investigators. Local mothers' allowance
boards were also required to duplicate the central commission's pattern of reserving two
out of five positions for women, although out of ninety-six boards across the province,
only twelve were chaired by women. In terms of eligibility, the Mothers' Allowances Act
of 1920 was only slightly different from the criteria recommended in Riddell's report.
Allowances would be restricted to needy widows with two or more children who were
British subjects, owned less than $2500 in property and $350 in liquid assets, and had
lived at least three years in Canada and two years in Ontario before applying for support.
Women with husbands whose whereabouts had been unknown for seven or more years
were also deemed eligible for support, as were wives of men with total and permanent
physical incapacitation. This latter group would prove to be a steadily rising percentage of
mothers' allowance families, reaching almost one-quarter of the total caseload by the late
1920s, with tuberculosis the leading cause of dependency.[42]

Most importantly, even if these criteria were met, entitlement to state support was by
no means automatic. Widowed mothers still had to meet one more key moral requirement. They must be deemed "fit and proper persons" to rear their own children, a test of
character and worthiness familiar to most other mothers' pension schemes throughout
North America. "The Act was framed in the interests of the children," its administrators
pointed out in their first annual report. "The mother is regarded as an applicant for employment as a guardian of future citizens of the State, and if she does not measure up to
the state's standards for such guardians, other arrangements must be sought in the best
interests of the children." The allowance was "a reward for service, not a form of public
relief," a distinction deemed critical by the scheme's administrators in order to forestall
"any humiliating feeling of 'charity.'" "Family pride is ... a valuable asset to the state and
one which we cannot afford to break down." More to the point, this strict insistence on the
moral probity and deservedness of mothers receiving help was a necessary corollary to the
sanctification of motherhood itself upon which the campaign for mothers' pensions had
been constructed. As Mink puts it, "these policy victories socialized motherhood rather
than citizenship," and women entitled to help had to live up to prevailing Anglo-Saxon
standards of the maternal ideal.[43]

Within Ontario's *Mothers' Allowance Act*, the regulation and enforcement of these
standards were left up to the discretion of local mothers' allowance boards and the commission's own corps of investigators, all but one of them women. For the most part their
reports on the lives of the women they visited read like a discourse on their own ideals of
middle-class, British, Protestant family life. In the homes of deserving mothers, "cleanliness and neatness await the visitor instead of untidiness," their rooms had "clean curtains

... flowering plants ... [and] good bedding" and their tables were set "with a clean white cloth, a warm bright fire, and the children sitting around a simple, but wholesome meal." These women kept "a close track of every penny that comes into the house," made their purchases "economically ... sew [instead of] buy ready to wear articles ... cook wholesome dishes ... [and] pay ... a little monthly on their old debts." They took care to "watch closely [over] the physical development of [their] children," ensured their regular church and school attendance, and were not "overworked ... anxious ... or irritable." They took "pride in their homes and gardens and [made] ... great efforts to beautify and make them comfortable." They also paid attention to their own personal grooming, appearing in "a clean, neatly worn dress, [with] hair nicely arranged," and where possible wore "a look of hope and contentment on [their] face[s]" when the investigator came to call. They did not look for full-time work, but in consultation with their investigator, undertook a selected range of approved part-time labour in order to "adequately supplement the allowance and yet maintain the position of homemaker." Women living in the countryside grew "much of their food stuffs," or sold "ice cream and home made baking" at the road side. Others made "plasticine work, women's wool hats, christmas tree decorations, carding buttons, artificial flowers, reedwork ... brushes ... slippers ... canvas shoes, dresses, millinery ... shirts ... [and] flower buttonholes." They took in boarders, did laundry, or most frequently laboured as part-time domestics or charwomen in other people's homes. Above all, they managed, without complaining, on whatever allowance they were granted by the commission, demonstrating their "ability ... to maintain a good standard home on a very small income" through a process of "wonderful thrift" and "pride in their efforts" that was often "nothing short of amazing." In this they provided a "training ... [for] the children [which] is greatly to the advantage of their future citizenship." Needless to say, "fit and proper" mothers did not drink, use bad language, or consort with men.[44]

Unfit mothers failed to meet these standards. They had a "record of immorality, neglect of [their] children, or of feeblemindedness with its consequent shiftlessness, inefficiency, and dirt." They would not provide "necessary information [such as] the names and addresses of relatives" to investigators, claimed they were "too sick to work but will not go to the doctor," or "refuse[d] to move from an unsanitary home or a demoralizing neighborhood." They could not control their children, failed to keep them regularly attending school or off the streets, were not seen in church, and could not manage on the money they were given. They took single men into their homes. They drank or used bad language. Above all, they were dirty. Untidiness and lack of cleanliness, in fact, is the most common complaint in the early reports of mothers' allowance investigators, testifying to a connection between dirt, vice, and immorality which, as Valverde has argued, was a central metaphor for the moral reform and social purity movements of this era. Within the maternal feminism of the 1920s, she observes, lay a "parallel between what was known as 'political purity' and personal hygiene. Physical and sexual hygiene—which were to a large extent in women's sphere—were the microcosmic foundation of the larger project of building a 'clean' nation."[45]

In this sense, the connection routinely made by mothers' allowance investigators between mothers' "service to the state" and the physical conditions of their homes is hardly surprising. As one visitor put it, "marked improvement in cleanliness of both home and children show the awakening of ambition in the mother," with results that augured well for the future of her offspring. Throughout commission reports of the 1920s, the moral transformation of women's households through cleanliness imposed by mothers' allowance investigators was a dominant and recurring theme. One recounted her initial visit to a home "dirty beyond description" in which the language of the children and the mother was "frightful" and "appalling." "This woman was given instructions as to cleanliness, language, and the home education of her children. The change was far more rapid than one could hope for.... On my last visit both she and the home were the acme of neatness and cleanliness, nice curtains covered the windows and the house was nicely arranged and the children were neat and clean." It was "one of the most remarkable cases of social regeneration that I have ever met with." Another described a family "living in a one room shack and the floor, walls, and tables were very dirty, the room was filled with flies. The mother was far from clean and was of slovenly appearance. [I] gave careful instruction in detail as to scrubbing and cleaning and advised the mother as to looking for more suitable quarters. Six months later the family had moved to a semi-detached frame house.... The home was clean and neatly arranged and the mother and children showed better personal care."[46] A third investigator recalled a:

> family ... found housed in an old shack, surrounded by factories and warehouses, and almost destitute of sunshine and fresh air. Dirt and unsanitary conditions abounded. The children were in rags and had no change of clothing, and the furniture was of the scantiest description. The mother ... had no training in caring for a house or children. The visitor made almost daily visits to this home in the early days after the pension was granted, keeping the mother constantly mindful of what was expected of her ... Little by little changes were made, bedding and clothing procured, and the mother has gradually become a better housekeeper. After 15 months of careful watching and regular income, the family is now in a little five room cottage in a much better district. This new home shows many signs, outside of its improved cleanliness and better furnishing, of the family's new spirit.[47]

Other investigators reported similar transformations of their clients "from a despondent downcast drudge ... [to] a cheerful mother who can take an interest in her home and family, and the home and family show the result of her interest in their greater cleanliness and neatness." Such clean and tidy homes created within children "an appreciation of their home and a willingness to work in and for it that indicates they value such home life and their right to it in the interest of future citizenship." These "manly boys and tidy girls" soon developed a "spirit of independence and are ready to insist that they be given equality of opportunity with other children."[48]

Alone among welfare programs, mothers' allowance during its first decade developed a discourse which, in a complete reversal of the assumptions of organized charity, linked the provision of regular and certain state relief to the building of character and independence in its clients, through the central metaphors of motherhood and better housekeeping. Within the early years of mothers' allowances, welfare was, in theory, uplifting, not degrading. "We have seen the beneficial results of state aid in improved home conditions, where before was nothing but poverty and distress, the mother untidy and discouraged," the commission argued. "All of this has been changed as if by magic. The whole atmosphere of the home breathes happiness and comfort under the wise and always beneficent influence of the *Mothers' Allowance Act*, replacing private charity, with the limitations of amounts, its demoralizing effects, and its destruction of self-respect among our people."[49] In this new framework, private charity, not the state, was the agency of demoralization.

Why this should be so pertained exclusively to the scheme's exaltation of motherhood. Unlike other clients of the emerging welfare state, women staying at home to raise their children were at work performing an essential service. It was for this reason, the commission argued, that mothers' allowance was "regular in its payments, giving a sense of stability. The recipient looks upon it as in some sense a wage for public service rather than as a dole to a pauper. This makes for self-respect.... The whole tone of the home has been raised by the receipt of an allowance. Mothers who have been indifferent housekeepers and home makers, through the efforts of the Investigator and the local Board, become thrifty, cleanly, and painstaking. The children are better clothed, better fed, and even better mannered, and a chance for education and advancement is given them."[50]

Although the logic was impeccable, during the 1920s it was not expanded beyond the boundaries of a select group of needy widows with more than one child. Other widows, deserted wives, and divorced or unwed mothers attempting to raise children on their own were kept outside the "magic" of mothers' allowances and remained dependent on irregular earnings and the uncertain support of absent men, families, friends, and private charity.

As the widowed mother's new employer, the state drove a hard bargain. Mothers' allowance, although ostensibly geared to a "cost of living schedule," did not pay anything close to the real monthly costs of raising a family, nor did it draw upon already existing levels of entitlement developed through the wartime Patriotic Fund. Initially, the Mothers' Allowance Commission asked each local board to draw up cost-of-living schedules for mothers with two or more children in their own communities. Although some did, their findings were not reflected in the benefit structure developed by the commission in 1920. Lanark County's board, for example, developed a detailed budget schedule in 1921 showing that $65 was the minimum needed for a mother with four children "to live in Lanark one month," but the average monthly mothers' allowance payment in that county was only $30, and the commission itself set a maximum payment ceiling of $40 a month for women in this category living in rural areas.[51]

During its first year of operation, the Mothers' Allowance Commission developed a sliding scale for maximum ceilings of monthly aid based on the number of children in a family and its rural or urban location. Within cities, mothers with two children and no other means of support could get up to $40 monthly, while those with five or more children in the same situation received $55. In rural areas the corresponding payments were $10 less. However, these were maximum levels of support. Deductions were routinely made for income from any assets, or the earnings of the widow, her children, or any support from other relatives. Widows with assets such as the insurance policies of their dead husbands were told to invest the amount in the purchase of homes. Unemployment was not considered a legitimate reason for the deferral of such support and, "where the family could be self-sustaining without an allowance, were all the members employed, it is not considered eligible" unless the reason was incapacitation due to sickness.[52]

During the scheme's early months of operation, monthly payments averaged more than $43, but thereafter dropped steadily so that by the year's end $35 was the normal allowance, a level that remained constant throughout the decade. The processing of neediest families first, and, more importantly, the commission's increasing experience in the investigation of income and assets, accounted for this 18 percent drop in the average size of monthly allowances. In its first year of operation, 2,660 women qualified for aid. By the end of the decade, steady but modest caseload growth would push the number of families dependent on the program to more than 5,600, including almost 17,000 children, at an annual cost of almost $2,400,000 Although the criteria for eligibility or the incidence of widowhood did not change markedly, Ontario's growing population and a rapid rise in the applications of physically incapacitated fathers accounted for the largest elements of program expansion.[53]

The commission acknowledged from the start that the allowances it paid were "insufficient to maintain the family and can only be regarded as supplementary to the mother's own earnings or other source of income." Mothers were expected to work on a part-time basis to bridge the gap between their allowance and a basic level of adequacy for their families, and about 60 percent of them derived income from a wide variety of tasks. Charwork, sewing and knitting, and keeping boarders provided the overwhelming source of extra funds for most mothers. Factory work, because it removed the mother from the home and supervision of her children, was explicitly discouraged. Forty percent of those receiving allowances reported no employment at all.[54]

If these deserving mothers were truly "servants of the state," why were they not paid a living wage to support their children, particularly in light of the uplifted conception of motherhood and full-time care of children which underpinned the scheme? Throughout the first decade of its operation, the rationale for this contradiction shifted in revealing ways. In its inaugural year the commission chairman, Peter Bryce, argued that the "very large number of applications, many more than at first anticipated," was the primary reason behind the decision to keep maximum payments within the range of $30 to $55 a month.[55] However, since $35 was the average monthly payment on which Riddell's 1919 investigation had based its initial cost estimates of the scheme, it is hardly surprising that this figure soon became the actual average payment made by the commission. Before long the necessity of mothers working part-time in order to make ends meet was heralded as a positive virtue of the legislation. As Bryce put it in his 1924 annual report: "While the allowance does not cover the full maintenance of the family yet it is just enough to give encouragement to the mother so that, with careful management on her part and by doing a little work to supplement the allowance, she is able to keep herself and family comfortable in every respect. Were the allowance made to cover full maintenance it would create wastefulness and probably laziness.... The encouragement thus given to the mother to be industrious ... has a good deal to do in making her family likewise."[56]

Apart from this moral reinforcement of thrift and the work ethic, the labour and earnings of mothers were also deemed useful "so that the children may benefit to the fullest extent from the Mothers' Allowances." In other words, the monthly payments were principally for the upkeep of the children, not the mother, who was expected to earn the cost of her own maintenance. Most women were allowed a total income of about $55 a month, inclusive of the average $35 mothers' allowance payment, without suffering any financial penalty. In this respect the program was unique in being the first to provide a financial incentive for supplemental earnings without dollar for dollar deductions from the allowance paid.[57]

The commission soon argued that even $35 a month, without any additional income, was sufficient for those women, particularly in rural areas, who were wise and efficient money managers. One mother with three children living on only $36.50 a month who kept "close track of every penny that comes into the house" was lauded for her "amazing ability to maintain a good standard home on a very small income." Her family was "well and receiving excellent care." Another woman living in a small village, also with three children, received "an allowance of $33 per month and is keeping up a ... comfortable home without debt," with additional monthly earnings of only $2. A third, with two children, received $30, earned another $3.75 a week, and "on this income maintains a good home where her children have excellent care.... She has no debt and about $50 in savings."[58] And so on. The subtext of these tales, which appeared constantly in commission reports in the middle and later years of the decade, was clear. Thrifty mothers could manage well on the income paid through mothers' allowances, particularly if they moved out of the city, and local boards constantly exhorted their mothers "to try to get along more economically."[59]

Those who could not were judged the authors of their own misfortune. If they ended up in debt, ran out of food near the end of the month, could not pay the rent, or failed to clothe their children properly, the fault lay within themselves, not in any basic inadequacy of mothers' allowances, and such women faced interviews by their local boards "regarding unpaid accounts." The penalties for such failure could be severe. Investigators were constantly reminded that one of their chief tasks was to monitor "the mother's ability to wisely expend the allowance," and the commission's annual reports noted that "often the allowance has actually to be administered to insure the family deriving the proper benefit from it, particularly where the mother is of low mentality," usually through the offices of the local clergyman's wife, the storekeeper, a member of the local mothers' allowance board, or as in one case, "the wife of the [township] relief officer [who] ... arranged with Mrs. H. to help her manage her money affairs for a period of 2 months." In these cases, control over the expenditure of her allowance would only be restored when the mother demonstrated her ability to "pay the rent regularly, keep out of debt, and buy food of good nutritive value without extravagance." One widow with five children, deemed "a good mother but inclined to be easy with her family" by her local board, lost control of her allowance simply because of her inability to compel her two eldest children to earn enough to keep the family out of debt. "For this reason it was thought advisable that she should have some supervision or guidance in the handling of an allowance. Her older children would in this way be taught that it is necessary for them to be responsible for themselves." Her cheque was initially turned over to the wife of the local clergyman and eventually was administered through the local storekeeper and postmistress. Some local board members reported visiting mothers "twice a week, helping the mother in the spending of her allowance and in the care of her home," leading one exasperated former board member to complain, "why any fur-coated investigator should be allowed to go into a widow's home and demand that she give an account to her of every cent of her allowance is more than I could ever swallow for justice or sympathy." As a final threat, in homes where "poor conditions" continued to prevail, the local Children's Aid Society would be called in to remove the offspring. Faced with the prospect of losing control, first of their allowances and then of their children, through failure to make do on the money paid, few mothers were apt to complain to their local boards or the commission about the adequacy of their entitlement.[60]

Local mothers' allowance boards, during the scheme's early years, played a critical, albeit idiosyncratic role in regulating the lives of the women under their jurisdiction. Decisions of the central Mothers' Allowance Commission were final, but local boards had influence because municipalities and counties were responsible for half the cost of all allowances paid. In addition, they were able to keep a closer scrutiny over women collecting mothers' allowance than the commission's staff of seventeen investigators, spread across the entire province, with caseloads averaging more than 300 clients each.

In making their initial recommendations about mothers who were "fit and proper persons" under the meaning of the legislation, local boards were apt to be swayed by rumour, gossip, ethnic and racial prejudice, or their own personal judgment of the reputation and often shifting circumstances of the families under their purview. In contrast, the Mothers' Allowance Commission in Toronto placed more emphasis on strict interpretation of the language of the act itself. Whether women benefited from the gaze of their local boards depended on where they fit within a hierarchy of moral deservedness. During the scheme's early years, when the extent of discretionary judgment permitted by the Act was not always clear, this idiosyncrasy of local board decisions was particularly pronounced. In some cases recently deserted, rather than widowed wives, or mothers with only one child, would be recommended for an allowance by local boards when their plight seemed particularly deserving. "[She] has only one child but the mother is an invalid," Lanark County's board pleaded on behalf of one applicant. "[She] is in very poor health. Her husband having been heard of in recent months would make her ineligible, but [it] was decided ... that this application be sent to [the] Commission," they agreed in another case. Brant County's board, in its early years, also proved willing to recommend applications for clients who "did not come under the Act" when moved by their plight, as did Lincoln County. "While the resident clause would apparently bar a pension," this board argued on behalf of one recently arrived family, "we are of the opinion there is a moral claim that should not be set aside. The children are not too rugged and unless nourishment is furnished them, there is just a chance of trouble ahead." Another mother of eight, recently deserted and abused by her husband and who "lived in terror of him ever since," was also recommended for an allowance. "She experienced nothing but hardship all her married life and our Board, several of whom have known the case for sometime, feel that Mrs. J. is MOST DESERVING of help and ... they strongly recommend that allowance be granted."[61]

Almost always such claims were rejected by the central commission, no matter how tragic the circumstances, on the grounds that only the strict language of the act itself, not hardship or suffering, conferred entitlement. "We cannot understand anybody ... telling Mrs. J. that her case would be made a 'special' one," commission administrators told Lincoln County board members in a stiff rebuke regarding the case cited above. "May I point out that the Act does not provide for an allowance unless that applicant is a widow, or the wife of the father of her dependent children if the husband is incapacitated or has disappeared for ... years ... We are sorry for the difficult circumstances in which this woman finds herself ... especially in view of the fact that the Commission is unable to render any assistance."[62]

More often, however, the closer scrutiny of the local boards was employed as a check upon mothers who, either for reasons of behaviour or additional income, were deemed no longer worthy or in need of government support. In these cases the role of gossip, rumour, and local reputation often proved critical. Even during a time when entitlement was restricted only to the most "deserving" of mothers—widows with two or more children—a climate of suspicion always coexisted alongside the lofty rhetoric portraying mothers as "servants to the state." Lanark County's board, in only its second year of operation, noted "there is considerable criticism of the many recipients" and argued that "many ... were now receiving the allowance but ... not living up to their obligations."[63] As eligibility under the act expanded in the years to come, the scope for doubt within the community concerning the moral deservedness of its clients would widen even further.

Four areas of women's lives were particular subjects of attention by local boards. The first was sex. On the one hand, widowed mothers were expected to remarry. "[T]his return to the normal home where the man is the wage earner and the mother is the home-maker constitut[es] the best solution of the problem of the support and care of these dependent children," the commission argued.[64] On the other hand, women seen fraternizing too closely with men risked being viewed as unfit mothers under the meaning of the act. In the case of one Brant County mother, the local board, while "recogniz[ing] the great financial need of [the] family," refused to recommend an allowance "on account of the reputation of the mother which does not seem to be all that could be desired." A Lanark County mother was terminated because her "conduct was the occasion of a great deal of talk." In Lincoln County "rumours of the conduct" of another mother led to an "investigation" and suspension of her allowance. A neighbour's letter sent to this same board in another case triggered the suspension of a woman's allowance and the recommendation that her "home [be] kept under observation for two months." Her crime was to have been seen going with a man "to a doctor's office and later to a beverage room and from a reliable source [we were] told this was a common occurrence in Grimsby on Saturday night." She, too, lost her allowance. In her wide-ranging research into mothers' allowances in this era, Margaret Little has also uncovered numerous instances of women cut off from support on the grounds of alleged sexual impropriety. "These women were supposed to donate all their time and attention to their children and to never show another interest in a man as long as they received the MA cheque," she argues. "Just as their husband had financially supported them in return for sexual monogamy, the state struck the same bargain."[65]

Mothers also had to live up to strict standards of housekeeping in the eyes of their local boards, but even here there was a fine line to be drawn between keeping their physical surroundings "neat and tidy" and spending too much on their homes. Reports to London's board that a mother was living in "quarters unsuitable for the bringing up of children" was sufficient reason for denying her a pension. Lincoln County's board accused a St Catharines mother of "living ... in such a condition of filth and degradation as to remove her entirely from our Branch of the work." Her allowance was suspended. "Untidy conditions" in another home were taken as evidence that the mother "was not a good housekeeper." A third mother was told bluntly that her "living conditions ... were brought to the attention of our Board at their last meeting and at that time I was instructed to warn you that unless these conditions are improved immediately, your allowance will be cut off." Yet when another woman "bought ... new furniture, had a new bathroom put in, new linoleum on floors, new curtains etc, since her husband died," these actions were considered sufficient grounds for why "our Board could NOT recommend this case." Only recognition by the central commission that the mother was using her husband's estate correctly to improve living conditions for her children succeeded in winning a pension for this widow, against the wishes of her local community.[66]

The capacity of other family members to come to the aid of widows in need was the third area in which local boards were given free rein to exercise discretionary moral judgments. Since local taxpayers were responsible for 50 percent of the cost of mothers' allowances, this was a particularly sensitive issue within counties and municipalities across Ontario, and local gossip and monitoring by neighbours provided local boards with a critical conduit of information on the shifting financial circumstances and earnings of family members. "A lady called me up over the 'phone this morning respecting [a] mother's pension beneficiary—Mrs. H.," London's city clerk told the local board. "She claims that the man is going around dressed in white flannels like a well-to-do merchant prince. A daughter is working in the Bell Telephone Co., and the brother is an insurance agent making big money. The woman is working regularly, and generally they are living in opulence and wealth. She claims that they are not deserving a mother's pension and that it is a crime against the general taxpayer."[67] In Brant County, grandparents were considered, in another case, to have "some responsibility in the care of [a widow's] children and ... are financially able to look after them without public assistance." A similar view prevailed with respect to a Lincoln County mother. "While the applicant appears to have no assets," the local board argued, "we feel that the ability of the parent to assist should be considered in deciding the amount of allowance to be granted." More commonly, other widows had their pensions reduced or suspended altogether because of the expectation, as Lanark County's board put it, that "so many adult children should maintain the mother and child," or because "wage earners should contribute more to the house." "The applicant should have some help," Brant County's board argued in a typical case, "but [we] took into consideration that there were children 16 & 17 yrs who should be helping the [mother]." As would become the rule with Old Age Pensions in the 1930s, this anticipated income from siblings, children, and parents was counted against a woman's monthly entitlement whether or not it was actually received.[68]

Finally, regular school attendance and the appearance, language, and behaviour of their children within the community were a constant measurement of how well mothers were living up to their role as "servants to the state." As the commission gained experience in administering the program, new methods were sought to "get better results ... for the allowance granted."[69] One of the most effective was demanding the monthly return of school attendance cards by mothers to the central commission offices in Toronto, and "if the card is not in by the 20th of the month, the beneficiary knows that her cheque will be withheld," officials pointed out. In cases where attendance was deemed unsatisfactory, a financial penalty would be deducted from the family's monthly allowance. Here, for example, are typical entries appearing in the Lanark County board minutes between July and November 1929. "Mrs. L, Perth, decreased from $35 to $30. Arnold not at school. Mrs. S. decreased $35 to $30. Bonnie not at school. J.D., Maberly, cancelled, only 1 at school ... M.L., decreased $30 to $25. Laura not at school. A.D, decreased $45 to $40. Jonathan not at school."[70] And so on. Through these bureaucratic devices not only mothers but children themselves were made directly aware of the strict relationship between behaviour and entitlement. As the commission put it: "The mother knows at once that her children must have her first care ... she is told her children must not keep bad company, must not be out late at night, in addition the children as they grow older know the income into their home depends largely on how they conduct themselves, they know that periodical school reports are sent to Head Office, and so the boys and girls are under this steadying influence all the time, and especially at that critical age of fourteen to sixteen when so many ... make a wrong turn."[71]

Local police appreciated this extra control mechanism on children's behaviour. "A chief of police of one city ... says he has little or no trouble with children of beneficiaries," the commission reported. "If he meets one with a tendency to misbehaviour he has only to threaten to report to the Investigator, it has the desired effect." Cooperation of mothers with doctors and local public health officials in seeking treatment for themselves or their children was also essential in their retention of a monthly allowance; investigators armed with the threat of withholding monthly income "succeeded where others have failed in persuading a mother to have her child admitted to a hospital, or taken to a doctor." In short, through developing new channels of information with other agencies of the state such as school officials, public health nurses, and the police, the Mothers' Allowance Commission and its local boards by the later 1920s were able not only to "merely collect information in order [to] ... decide on the eligibility of an applicant, [but] rather [to become] vitally interested in every phase of the family life." In this way its moral gaze into the lives of its clients became ever more penetrating.[72]

The race and ethnicity of clients also influenced the way local boards judged their deservedness in the program's formative years. The requirement that applicants be British subjects, along with the scheme's strict residence requirements, acted as an arbitrary bureaucratic filter for excluding many immigrant widows and their children from coverage. Throughout the 1920s the ethnic origins of over 90 percent of mothers getting aid through the program were either Canadian, British, English, Scottish, or Irish, compared with only 9 percent born elsewhere, at a time when almost 15 percent of Ontario's population was of non-British or French ancestry.[73] Apart from this formal stipulation, other barriers of ethnocentrism and racism excluded mothers of non-Anglo-Celtic origin from equal treatment. Some local boards, Little discovered, disqualified ethnic minority women "because they could not read or write English." Inability to produce the necessary legal documentation proving marriage, widowhood, or the birth of their children operated as a further bureaucratic obstacle excluding many immigrant women of non-English ancestry from eligibility. It is also clear, as Little argues, that "families from ethnic minority backgrounds underwent more intense investigation than their WASP counterparts" and that "neighbours were more likely to spy and complain about minority families." In Lincoln County's surviving case files, the claims of some mothers with non-British names, no assets, and debts sometimes totalling over $750 were dismissed simply on the grounds that "we think she can manage" or because "she lives in a fruit section where both she and her family can obtain almost steady employment." In other cases a mother was "cut off ... because of her anti-British sympathies" or because of "evidence of disloyalty." In contrast, other applicants, as Little notes, could be congratulated for coming from "a beautiful Scotch family" or being "very worthy, reticent, Scotch people." In this way local boards, by reflecting existing community patterns of ethnocentrism, prejudice, and discrimination in their recommendations, cut off many otherwise eligible and deserving mothers and children from the support available through the program.[74]

Despite the powerful role of moral judgment, community scrutiny, rumour, and prejudice in the administration of mothers' allowances, which undercut the program's continual claim that it was free from any "stigma or taint of charity," and regardless of the inadequate benefits it paid, there is no doubt that the program's arrival in Ontario during the 1920s was a blessing to the thousands of women who qualified for its support. That this was the case can be seen from the letters they sent to the commission itself, from the conditions they faced prior to applying for help, and from the desperate pleas of thousands more deserted, divorced, or unwed mothers who could not qualify for support under its terms. "I wish I could tell you the joy it is for me to be able to stay at home and make our home bright and comfortable for my children," one mother wrote on receipt of her allowance. "My own health was failing and I do not like to think of how we would have lived this winter without help." "What a blessing your pension is," wrote another in a letter typical of many others sent to the commission. "Now we poor widows and orphans can live like other people and have some pleasure. Before we had this pension our poor kids were certainly to be pitied, but now they can pass with the others and be safe from hardships." "Without your help I don't know what would have become of my children and myself," a third simply stated.[75]

For the mother who had "lost her home and her furniture was set out on the road"; for the woman who occupied "the most needy home I was ever in, positively bare, some boxes for table and boxes to sit on"; for the family "depending on whatever their brothers give them"; for the mother with three children living entirely on "two dollars per week for the last two years from North Grimsby Township Council"; or the mother of three getting "$10 per month as a domestic"—the regularity of a $35 or $40 monthly mothers' allowance cheque made an extraordinary difference in their lives and those of their children.[76] If it was not, to be sure, an adequate and decent standard of living, it was nonetheless the difference in many cases between keeping a family intact on the death of the husband and surrendering children to the uncertain fate of institutional or foster care. In many cases it represented the first regular income such women had ever seen. However, it was also an allowance paid for the care of the children, not the mother. When they turned sixteen, she was left to the care of her own children or, failing that, to relief or to private charity. Yet as a woman too young for the means-tested old age pension, she was often too old or too ill for paid employment. "I have been a widow for the past three years and have two children, a girl sixteen in December and a boy twelve years," one mother wrote Premier Howard Ferguson in despair on learning that her allowance was to be cancelled. "By the help of the Mothers' Allowance so far I have been able to manage ... Mrs. Preston ... who visits me on official business concerning the Mothers' Allowance on her last visit spoke as though I would be without this support as soon as my girl was sixteen. I am at a loss to know what to do to meet expenses from now until such times as my boy is able to take a man's place on the farm." Ferguson's reply was short and to the point. "There frequently arises cases similar to yours ... but there are no monies available.... I am very sorry that this should be the case." Mothers' allowance, Ferguson responded to all such queries, "was not a pension scheme. It is merely intended as an aid to mothers to enable them to provide a home and properly rear their children." When their reproductive work was finished, so too was their claim upon the state for support.[77]

Mothering was a central metaphor for the development of Ontario's welfare state. The claims of motherhood as a service to the state provided the first compelling arguments for breaking down the tradition of exclusive local responsibility for the care of the poor. Within Ontario's mothers' allowance program, moreover, lay the seeds of a new basis for thinking about welfare as entitlement rather than as charity. The rationale employed by women's groups and other social reform constituencies for legitimizing mothers' allowances, and in the reports of the commission itself during the first formative decade of its operation, was always that state support to mothers was a reward for service, that it did not stigmatize, that it fostered independence, and that it uplifted the character of both the women and the children who received it. Simply put, mothers' allowance during the 1920s was the first means-tested social program based on the premise that steady and certain state assistance was not demoralizing, and that the reproductive work of women merited some degree of social entitlement.

However, both the level and the scope of this entitlement remained highly ambiguous. Although better than the uncertain support of relatives, neighbours, local relief, or private charity, mothers' allowances never came close to providing a sufficient income in itself for a decent standard of living even as defined within the context of the 1920s.[78] Nor was it meant to. Even the most deserving of the poor—worthy widows of British stock with two or more children—were still expected to need an "incentive to effort" in the form of part-time work, in order to underwrite the cost of their own care, to motivate their children towards self-reliance, and to bridge the gap to a minimally adequate living standard. By failing to come close to adequacy despite recognizing entitlement and need, mothers' allowances thus became an ominous indicator of contradictions that would soon bedevil other welfare programs to emerge within Ontario.

Despite its claim of fostering independence, moreover, the program did not leave mothers on their own. Commission investigators, local boards, other agents of the state such as school officials or public health nurses, and neighbours subjected the lives of mothers in the program to an unrelenting moral scrutiny and supervision. Widows on mothers' allowance may not have been stigmatized, but as women living on their own at the expense of taxpayers they were always morally suspect and the conditions of their entitlement required unremitting attention to their standards of character, homemaking, sexual behaviour, thrift, and industry. Deviations from these standards, or simply inability to cope, could and did result in loss of control over their allowance or, in extreme cases, in loss of their own children. As the program was expanded to include deserted wives and, ultimately, unwed mothers in the decades to come, the grounds for suspicion of moral worthiness would expand even further.

Finally, mothers' allowances were justified "in the interests, of the children." Although paid to mothers, the allowances were intended for their children. Thus an unresolved contradiction between the needs of women and children was embedded in the program from its inception. Were mothers' allowances truly a payment to women in reward for service to the state, or were they instead a sum entrusted to mothers for the care of their children? In the former concept there was a sense of earned entitlement; in the latter, only stewardship. As the plight of mothers whose children turned sixteen clearly revealed, it was stewardship, not entitlement or a reward for effort, which underpinned mothers' allowances in Ontario. When their nurturing task was done, women were cut off from the program's support at an age and often in a state of health which made paid employment uncertain at best. From their ranks, as well as others, would emerge a new category of aged women living in poverty.

Notes

1. On the mothers' pension movement in the United States see Gwendolyn Mink, "The Lady and the Tramp: Gender, Race, and the Origins of the American Welfare State," and Barbara J. Nelson, "The Origins of the Two-Channel Welfare State: Workmen's Compensation and Mothers' Aid," in Linda Gordon, ed., *Women, the State, and Welfare* (Madison 1990), 93–151; Joanne Goodwin, "An American Experiment in Paid Motherhood: The Implementation of Mothers' Pensions in Early Twentieth-Century Chicago," *Gender and History* 4, 3 (autumn 1992), 323–42; and most recently, Theda Skocpol, *Protecting Soldiers and Mothers: The Political Origins of Social Policy in the United States* (Cambridge 1992), 424–79. For an analysis of the same movement in Canada see Veronica Strong-Boag, "'Wages for Housework': Mothers' Allowances and the Beginnings of Social Security in Canada," *Journal of Canadian Studies* 14, 1, (spring 1979), 24–34, and more recently, Margaret Hillyard Little, "'A Fit and Proper Person': The Moral Regulation of Single Mothers in Ontario, 1920–1940," paper presented to the Canadian Women's Studies Association, Kingston, 30 May 1991, and Suzanne Morton, "Women on Their Own: Single Mothers in Working-Class Halifax in the 1920s," *Acadiensis* 21, 2 (spring 1992), 90–107.
2. Linda Gordon, "The New Feminist Scholarship on the Welfare State," in her *Women, the State, and Welfare*, 9.
3. Skocpol, *Protecting Soldiers and Mothers*, 424–79.
4. Mink, "The Lady and the Tramp," 101.
5. Archives of Ontario (AO), RG 7, series II-1, box 2, "Memo on Mothers Pensions Prepared by the Superintendent of Trades and Labour," 1917, 2.
6. On Kelso and the origins of the Children's Aid Societies of Ontario see Andrew Jones and Leonard Rutman, *In the Children's Aid: J.J. Kelso and Child Welfare in Ontario* (Toronto 1981), and John Bullen, "J.J. Kelso and the "New" Child-Savers: The Genesis of the Children's Aid Movement in Ontario," *Ontario History* 82, 2 (June 1990), 107–28.
7. As cited in Margaret Hillyard Little, "'No Car, No Radio, No Liquor Permit': The Moral Regulation of Single Mothers in Ontario, 1920–1993" (PhD dissertation, York University 1994), 53. I am indebted to Little for drawing the centrality of Kelso's early role in Ontario's mothers' allowance movement to my attention.
8. The list of organizations involved in Toronto's Committee on Mothers' Allowances included, besides Peter Bryce as convener, representatives from the Juvenile Court, the Social Service Council of Ontario, the Trades and Labour Council, the Social Service Commission of Toronto, the Superintendent of Catholic Charities, the Bureau of Municipal Research, the Local Council of Women, the Department of Public Health, the Superintendent of Neglected and Dependent Children, the Neighborhood Workers' Association, the Women's Institutes, the Machinists' Union, the Inspector of the Feeble-Minded, and the Head of Separate Schools. Ontario, Department of Labour, *Mothers' Allowances: An Investigation* (Toronto 1920), 15.
9. Biographical material on the Reverend Peter Bryce is taken from Carol Thora Baines, "From Women's Benevolence to Professional Social Work: The Case of the Wimodausis Club and the Earlscourt Children's Home, 1902–1971" (PhD dissertation, University of Toronto 1990), 48–50; the quotation is originally cited in Doug Owram, *The Government Generation: Canadian Intellectuals and the State, 1900–1945* (Toronto 1986), 124.

10. Mink, "The Lady and the Tramp," 93, 97–98, 107. See also Mimi Abramovitz, *Regulating the Lives of Women: Social Welfare Policy from Colonial Times to the Present* (Boston 1988), and Jane Lewis, *The Politics of Motherhood: Child and Maternal Welfare in England, 1900–1939* (London 1980). Skocpol, in *Protecting Soldiers and Mothers*, 442–48, provides the most important new interpretation of the mothers' pension movement in the United States, arguing that its origins can be traced to the power of a middle- and upper-class women's reform movement, led by organizations such as the National Congress of Mothers and the General Federation of Women's Clubs, which had branches in cities and towns across the nation. "These upper and middle-class women were trying to embrace as sisters, as fellow mothers, the impoverished widows who would be helped by mothers' pensions" (479).

11. On the symbiotic relationship between exposure to the needs of working-class women and the achievement of social power by women charity workers see Baines, "From Women's Benevolence to Professional Social Work," 60–93.

12. AO, RG 7, "Memo on Mothers' Pensions," 1917.

13. Ibid.

14. Mariana Valverde, *The Age of Light, Soap, and Water: Moral Reform in English Canada, 1885–1925* (Toronto 1991), 160; AO, RG 7, "Memo on Mothers' Pensions," 1917.

15. On the primary role of orphanages in providing care for the children of indigent parents see Bettina Bradbury, "The Fragmented Family: Family Strategies in the Face of Death, Illness, and Poverty, Montreal, 1860–1885," in Joy Parr, ed., *Childhood and Family in Canadian History* (Toronto 1982), 199–28. As Ann Vandepol writes, "These asylums quickly developed into the major social mechanism for sustaining children of low-income parents faced with unemployment, financial collapse, or death of a male breadwinner. At many asylums, half-orphans (children with one parent alive) outnumbered full orphans by a wide margin. In California by 1900 there were 5399 half-orphans and only 959 full orphans housed in institutions throughout the state," cited in Nelson, "The Origins of the Two-Channel Welfare State," 137–38; Baines, "From Women's Benevolence to Professional Social Work," 104–06; Ontario, *Mothers' Allowances*, 22–23.

16. Ontario, *Mothers' Allowances*, 24–26, 28–29. The risk to children in institutional care of death from infection was quite real in this era. Within the Earlscourt Home, fourteen children died between 1913 and 1929 owing to contagious disease. Baines, "From Women's Benevolence to Professional Social Work," 110. Even official institutional death rates among children were often understated. As one doctor testifying before Ontario's 1919 Inquiry into Mothers' Allowances pointed out, "the main advantage of this Pension scheme is that it will take these children out of Infant Homes, no matter how well they may be managed. In some of these places, in order to keep their mortality down, they ship the sick child into hospitals, and then the death does not appear in the books." AO, RG 7, series II, box 2, file "Mothers' Allowance, 1919," verbatim testimony, "Mothers' Pension Allowance: Hamilton Enquiry, 20 February 1919," testimony of Dr Mullin.

17. Ontario, *Mothers' Allowances, an Investigation*, 1920, 26–27; AO, RG 7, series II-1, box 2, "Mother's Pension Allowance: Hamilton Enquiry, 20 February 1919," testimony of Mrs Evans; RG 7, "Memo on Mothers' Pensions, 1917," citation from Report by Dr Bruce Smith, April 1913. Chronic overcrowding and high death rates among institutionalized children were also critical factors in the success of campaigns for mothers' pensions in American states. As Mimi Abramovitz notes, "In 1910, one year before the enactment of the first Mothers' Pension program, the number of children housed in institutions peaked at more than 126,000, representing more than three per 1000 of the child population ... High infant mortality rates, outbreaks of contagious diseases, the exploitation of child labor, and the overall poor care provided to the children who survived discredited the original child-saving methods as a way to socialize children and conserve them as an important national resource." *Regulating the Lives of Women*, 196.

18. *Toronto Star*, 15 January 1920, cited in Ontario, *Mothers' Allowances*, 19; ibid., 12, 15; AO, RG 7, series II-1, box 2, "Mother's Pension Allowance: Hamilton Enquiry, 20 February 1919," testimony of Walter Rob. On similar arguments for mothers' pensions by organized labour

in American states see Nelson, "The Origins of the Two-Channel Welfare State," 139, and Goodwin, "An American Experiment in Paid Motherhood" (327). Nelson observes that although union leaders lent their support to the mothers' pensions movement, unlike workers' compensation legislation it was "never a priority for organized labor." This was probably the case in Ontario as well. It is also important to note the critical distinction Nelson makes between the conceptualization and operation of these two early state initiatives into income security. "Workmen's Compensation was a program developed for the white northern men employed in heavy industry ... [and] it set the tone for the first channel of the welfare state, which was male, judicial, public, and routinized in origin. In comparison, Mothers' Aid was originally designed for white impoverished widows of men like those eligible for Workmen's Compensation. It set the tone for the second channel of the welfare state, which was female, administrative, private, and nonroutinized in origin" (133).

19. Strong-Boag, "Wages for Housework," 25.
20. Ontario, *Mothers' Allowances*, 17.
21. AO, RG 7, "Memo on Mothers' Pensions, 1917"; Ontario, *Mothers' Allowances*, 84; RG 7, series II-1, box 2, "Mothers' Pension Allowance: Hamilton Enquiry, 20 February 1919," testimony of W.H. Lovering.
22. Ontario, *Mothers' Allowances*, 75.
23. Ibid., 17; RG 7, series II-1, box 2, "Mothers' Pension Allowance: Hamilton Enquiry, 20 February 1919," testimony of W.H. Lovering.
24. "Mothers' Pension Allowance: Hamilton Enquiry, 20 February 1919," testimony of W.H. Lovering.
25. Ibid. This was an amount adjusted for postwar price increases. During the war itself, the Patriotic Fund paid up to a ceiling of $45 per month for the mother and a progressively smaller amount for each child, depending upon the circumstances of each family. Local committees in each community were given discretionary authority to set their own scales up to the level of this maximum. See Philip Morris, ed., *The Canadian Patriotic Fund: A Record of Its Activities from 1914 to 1919* (np, nd), 30. See also Margaret McCallum, "Assistance to Veterans and Their Dependants: Steps on the Way to the Administrative State, 1914–1929," in W. Wesley Pue and Barry Wright, eds., *Canadian Perspectives on Law and Society: Issues in Legal History* (Ottawa 1988), 157–77.
26. Ontario, *Mothers' Allowances*, 9–10; AO, RG 7, series II-1, box 2, "Mothers' Allowance, 1919," W.H. Hearst to W.A. Riddell, 16 January 1919.
27. Ontario, *Mothers' Allowances*, 10.
28. Ibid., 30.
29. Ibid., 30–31. By the end of 1921–22 mothers' allowances in Ontario would have a caseload of 3,559 widows and 10,922 children at a total cost of $1,382,138, compared with $774,667 spent on 2,660 mothers in its first year. Ontario, *First Annual Report of the Mothers' Allowance Commission of Ontario 1920–21* (hereafter *First Annual Report, 1920–21*), 15; *Second Annual Report, 1921–22*, 9. On the gross inaccuracy and lack of administrative preparation surrounding Ontario's first foray into old age pensions see James Struthers, "Regulating the Elderly: Old Age Pensions and the Formation of a Pension Bureaucracy in Ontario, 1920–1945," *Journal of the Canadian Historical Association*, new series, 3 (1992), 235–55.
30. Ontario, *Mothers' Allowances*, 16.
31. Ibid., 21–22.
32. Ibid., 23–25, 49–50.
33. Ibid., 35, 50–53, 68.
34. Ibid., 54–58; RG 7, series II-1, "Mothers' Pension Allowance: Hamilton Enquiry, 20 February 1919," testimony of Mrs Hawkings, Walter Riddell, and Mr Axford. For further support by labour for the rights of unwed mothers, see the testimony of Walter Rob.
35. AO, RG 7, series II-1, box 2, "Mothers' Pension Allowance: Hamilton Enquiry, 20 February 1919"; Mothers' Allowances, 31, 53, 68, 86, 88.
36. *Mothers' Allowances*, 59–65, 88 (original emphasis); AO, RG 7, "Mothers' Pension Allowance: Hamilton Enquiry, 20 February 1919," testimony of W.H. Lovering.

37. AO, RG 7, series II-1, box 2, "Mothers' Pension Allowance: Hamilton Enquiry, 20 February 1919," testimony of Mrs P.D. Crerar, *Mothers' Allowances*, 82–84.

38. Nelson, "The Origins of the Two-Channel Welfare State," 124, 133, 136, 140–41. As Nelson points out, "a key difference in the administration of the two programs is that Mothers' Aid was given in return for an ongoing service rather than in response to a realized risk.... [T]he administrators of Workmen's Compensation cared if alcohol contributed to accidents ... but they did not care, or, more important, they could not control the beneficiary who spent all of his or her benefits on drink. The behaviour of Mothers' Aid beneficiaries, on the other hand, was closely monitored. Thus, it was the *capacity to care* that was supported in Mothers' Aid" (original emphasis).

39. *Mothers' Allowances*, 60.

40. Ibid., 80; *First Annual Report, 1920–21*, 10. Patronage in the appointment of Mothers' Allowance investigators was a frequent complaint from the ranks of Canadian social work in the 1920s. See James Struthers, "A Profession in Crisis: Charlotte Whitton and Canadian Social Work in the 1930s," *The Canadian Historical Review* 62, 2 (1981), 169–85, and Margaret Kirkpatrick Strong, *Public Welfare Administration in Canada* (Chicago 1930), 135.

41. *First Annual Report, 1920–21*, 16–17.

42. Ibid., 10–11; *Tenth Annual Report, 1929–30*, 13. On Elizabeth Shorn's resignation see Clifford J. Williams, *Decades of Service: A History of the Ontario Ministry of Community and Social Services, 1930–1980* (Toronto 1984), 38.

43. *First Annual Report, 1920–21*, 12, 23, 27. On the prevalence of "fit and proper person" clauses in most mothers' pensions schemes see Abramovitz, *Regulating the Lives of Women*, 200–3; Mink, "The Lady and the Tramp," 93, 110.

44. *First Annual Report, 1920–21*, 20, 23–24 *Second Annual Report, 1921–22*, 24, 26–29.

45. *First Annual Report, 1920–21*, 27–28; Valverde, *The Age of Light, Soap, and Water*, 28.

46. *Fifth Annual Report, 1924–25*, 12–13; *Second Annual Report, 1921–22*, 27.

47. *Second Annual Report, 1921–22*, 30.

48. *Third Annual Report, 1922–23*, 18–19; *Fourth Annual Report, 1923–24*, 15.

49. *Fourth Annual Report, 1923–24*, 16.

50. Ibid., 16.

51. AO, MG 26 1739/31, vol. 1, Lanark County Mothers' Allowance Board, Minutes, 8 January 1921; *First Annual Report, 1920–21*, 65.

52. *First Annual Report, 1920–21*, 28, 65.

53. Ibid., *Tenth Annual Report, 1929–30*, 5. The length of time required for the desertion of husbands whose whereabouts were unknown, as a requirement for eligibility, was dropped from seven years to five in 1921. Physical incapacitation of husbands, as a criterion for eligibility, jumped from 7.6 percent to 22 percent of the total caseload between 1921 and 1930.

54. *First Annual Report, 1920–21*, 21; *Second Annual Report, 1921–22*, 21.

55. *First Annual Report, 1920–21*, 10–11.

56. *Third Annual Report, 1922–23*, 17.

57. *Fourth Annual Report, 1923–24*, 16; *Third Annual Report, 1922–23*, 20, 22.

58. *Second Annual Report, 1921–22*, 27–28; *Third Annual Report, 1922–23*, 18, 22.

59. AO, Lincoln County Records F 1741, "Minutes of the Lincoln County Mothers' Allowance Board," meeting of 18 May 1927.

60. Ibid., meeting of 20 October 1927; *First Annual Report, 1920–21*, 18, 27; *Second Annual Report, 1921–22*, 30–31; *Third Annual Report, 1922–23*, 18; AO, F 1741, Lincoln County Mothers' Allowance/Pension Commission, Case Records for Mothers' Allowances, 1920–1949, box 3, Jean Davidson to H. Bentley, 31 1938; case of E.H., 10 May 1939; letter from Mrs E. Nolan to the *Toronto Star*, 3 February 1926, originally cited in Margaret Hillyard Little, "'A Fit and Proper Person': The Moral Regulation of Single Mothers in Ontario, 1920–1940," paper presented to the Canadian Women's Studies Association. Kingston, 30 May 1991, 10.

61. AO, MG 26 1739/31, vol. 1, Lanark County, Minutes, Mothers' Allowance Board, 1920–38, meeting, 12 March 1921, 19 December 1925; AO, F 1551/14/1, Brant, County of: Mothers' Allowance Board Minutes, 1920–1937, 15 December 1920, 22 January 1921; F 1741, box

3, Lincoln County Mothers' Allowance/Pension Commission, Case Records for Mothers' Allowances, 1920–49, case of E.J., 16 February 1928; case of M.J., 4 December 1938 (original emphasis).

62. AO, F 1741, box 3, H. Bentley to Jean Davidson, 15 December 1938.

63. AO, MG 26 1739/31, vol. 1, Lanark County, Minutes, Mothers' Allowance Board, 1920–38, 16 March 1922.

64. *First Annual Report, 1920–21*, 28.

65. AO, F 1551/14/1, Brant, County of: Mothers' Allowance Board Minutes, 1920–37, 16 May 1925; AO, MG 26 1739/31, vol. I, Lanark County, Minutes, Mothers' Allowance Board, 1920–38, 18 March 1927; AO, F 1741, Lincoln County Pension/Mothers' Allowance Commission, 1937–49, Minutes, 25 May 1934, 5 January 1937, 27 July 1937; Little, "No Car, No Radio, No Liquor Permit," 14–15. As Little points out, Mothers' Allowance Commission investigators also took the same strict approach to enforcing sexual propriety. "They interrogated the mother, her parents, her friends and neighbours, public officials—asking them to comment on the number and type of visitors to the home, the number of times the mother socialized outside the home and with whom, and the type of clothing the mother bought and wore" (15). See also her "The Policing of Ontario's Single Mothers during the Dirty Thirties," paper presented to the Canadian Historical Association Annual Meeting, Charlottetown, May 1992.

66. University of Western Ontario (UWO), Regional History Collection, London, Minutes of Seventh Meeting of Mothers' Allowance Board, 27 September 1929, case no. 609; AO, F 1741, Lincoln County Mothers' Allowance/Pension Commission, Case Records, box 3, Jean Davidson to Central Board, 19 November 1938; case of I.H., 22 April 1940; case of L.C., 21 October 1936; case of J.B., 3 January 1939. In this instance the central commission overruled the recommendation of the local board on the grounds that the mother was using up the balance of her husband's estate correctly to improve the home conditions of her children. H. Bentley to Jean Davidson, 3 January 1939.

67. UWO, Regional History Collection, Minutes of Seventh Meeting, Mothers' Allowance Board, 27 September 1929, case no. 613.

68. AO, F 1551/14/1, Brunt, County of, Mothers' Allowance Board Minutes, 1920–37, 16 July 1932; F 1741, box 3, Lincoln County Mothers' Allowance/Pension Case Files, 1920–49, case of M.D., 10 June 1935; AO, MG 26 1739/31, vol. 1, Lanark County, Minutes, Mothers' Allowance Board, 1920–38, 18 February 1935, 14 September 1936; Brunt, County of, Mothers' Allowance Board Minutes, 1920–37, 28 December 1925. On old age pensions see Struthers, "Regulating the Elderly."

69. AO, F 1741, Lincoln County Pensions/Mothers' Allowance Commission 1937–49, box 1, Minutes of the Lincoln County Mothers' Allowance Board meeting of 18 May 1927.

70. *Eighth Annual Report, 1927–28*, 14; AO, MG 26 1739/31, vol. 1, Lanark County, Minutes, Mothers' Allowance Board, 1920–38, meetings of 31 July and 14 November 1929 (names changed from original).

71. *Seventh Annual Report, 1926–27*, 21.

72. *Eighth Annual Report, 1927–28*, 14–15. For a stimulating application of the ideas of Michel Foucault to the state's "moral gaze" over family life, through a web of interconnected social agencies, see Jacques Donzelot, *The Policing of Families* (New York 1979), especially chapter 4.

73. *Tenth Annual Report, 1929–30*, 14; Warren E. Kalbach, "Growth and Distribution of Canada's Ethnic Populations, 1871–1981," in Leo Driedger, ed., *Ethnic Canada* (Toronto 1985), table 8.

74. Little, "'A Fit and Proper Person,'" 26–28; AO, F 1741, Lincoln County Mothers' Allowance/Pension Commission, Case Records, 1920–49, box 3, case of M.S., 21 September 1938; case of K.O., 12 June 1940; case of H.P., 12 March 1941; case of C.M., 17 December 1940. Little also notes, from her research, that black and aboriginal women "suffered most. Almost every Black mother who applied had experienced neighbours attempting to besmudge her reputation." Aboriginal mothers often had their claims dismissed because of inadequate documentation by Ottawa of Indian births.

75. *Second Annual Report, 1921–22*, 31–33.

76. AO, F 1741, Lincoln County Mothers' Allowance/Pension Commission, Case Records, 1920–49, box 3, case of R.H., 20 December 1934; case of M.D., 16 January 1929; case of S.C., 26 September 1935; case of M.D., 17 November 1927.

77. AO, RG 3, Ferguson Papers, box 100, file "Mothers' Allowance Commission," Mrs Ethel Bagley to Howard Ferguson, 30 October 1928; Howard Ferguson to Mrs Ethel Bagley, 5 November 1928; Howard Ferguson to F.W. Stapleford, 14 January 1927. See also the quite typical case of B.F. with five children under the age of sixteen whose husband died of a brain tumour in 1928. She applied for and received a mothers' allowance at the age of thirty-four in February 1928. After sixteen years of support, her allowance of $30 a month was cut off automatically in June 1944 "as the last child turned 16." She thus faced the labour market at the age of fifty, without any income or savings, and with a twenty-year wait for eligibility for a means-tested Old Age Pension. AO, F 1741, Lincoln County Mothers' Allowance/Pension Commission, Case Records, 1920–49, box 3, case of B.F., 21 February 1928.

78. In her recent study of mothers' pensions in the United States, Theda Skocpol argues that inadequate benefits, averaging $21 monthly across the United States, reflected the inability of women's reform organizations, which pioneered the legislation, to exercise continuing influence over its administration once such programs passed into the hands of "bureaucrats and social workers." Within Ontario, however, there is no evidence that women's organizations campaigned vociferously for higher benefits levels than the ones provided. See Skocpol, *Protecting Soldiers and Mothers*, 476–9. Suzanne Morton notes that in Nova Scotia, mothers' allowances initially paid $35 a month, while workers' compensation paid benefits to a maximum of $60 a month. Morton, "Single Mothers in Halifax," 100, n55.

4

Scandal and Social Policy

The Ideal Maternity Home and the Evolution of Social Policy in Nova Scotia, 1940–1951*

KAREN BALCOM

A SCANDAL WAS BREWING in the small seaside village of East Chester, Nova Scotia in the mid-1940s. At the heart of the controversy were William and Lila Young, proprietors of the recently expanded Ideal Maternity Home (IMH). Since 1928, William (a chiropractor) and Lila (an "obstetrical specialist") had provided maternity care and adoption services to unwed mothers looking for a haven where they could give birth to their children and hide from the harsh condemnation society directed toward unmarried pregnant women.[1] The IMH prospered in the 1930s, and grew still more as the dislocations of war-time Nova Scotia brought increasing numbers of women "in trouble" to the Youngs' doorstep.[2] By the mid-1940s, the IMH was the largest maternity home in Eastern Canada, with between 80 and 125 babies in the nursery. Estimates of the total number of children born at the Home between 1928 and 1946 range from 800 to 1,500.[3]

As the Home expanded, the Youngs and their business attracted attention from both admirers and bitter critics. Admirers, who included politicians, local businessmen, and prominent Nova Scotian families, praised the Youngs for their contributions to the local economy, for their dedicated work in the "mission field" of service to unwed mothers and for their success in creating happy families by arranging adoptions. Less charitably, the Home's supporters noted the Youngs also saved local rate-payers the expense of support-ing destitute unwed mothers and their children.[4] The Home's detractors, centred in the province's Department of Public Welfare, held a darker view, arguing that the Youngs' fee structure exploited birth mothers and adoptive parents and that standards of nutrition, medical care, and cleanliness at the Home were abysmal. They accused the Youngs of disregarding the health and happiness of the children, resorting to fraud and blackmail to collect fees, deliberately trying to evade provincial laws and effectively "selling" babies on an international black market in children.[5]

Between 1934 and 1946, Nova Scotia's minister of public welfare, Dr. Frank Davis, and his senior departmental staff engaged in a "twelve year running battle" with the Youngs and their supporters as provincial officials tried to control and then to shut down the IMH.[6] The other key combatants in this "battle" were Deputy Minister of Public Welfare

---

* This material chapter was first published "Scandal and Social Policy: The Ideal Maternity Home and the Evolution of Social Policy in Nova Scotia, 1940–51," *Acadensis* 31 2 (2002): 3–37.

Ernest Blois and provincial Director of Child Welfare Fred MacKinnon, arguably the two most important figures in the development of social policy in Nova Scotia in the 20th century.[7] As the fight to close the IMH intensified, these provincial officials collected more and more evidence of the Youngs' misdeeds and questionable practices. When some of this evidence became public between 1945 and 1947, the Youngs lost favour among many of their former supporters and their public reputation disintegrated. Behind the scenes, a more complete and horrific accounting of events at the Home became ammunition for Davis, Blois, and especially MacKinnon, as they pushed for changes in provincial child welfare and adoption laws which would give them the power they needed to shut down the Home. By 1946, this strategy was successful and the IMH was—at least officially—out of business.[8]

On one level, the story of the IMH can be read as a cautionary tale of shame and tragedy. The Home was an increasing embarrassment to the provincial government and to the small group of professionally trained child welfare workers in the province. It demonstrated key weaknesses in the province's child welfare system and marked the province as backward in some aspects of its social policy. The legislative and policy changes Nova Scotia enacted to fill the regulatory void and clamp down on the IMH, or justified because of the Home, also had an important long term effect on the evolution of the social welfare system. Thus, the tragedy of the IMH was an opening for the reform of social policy in the province. In the short term, there were direct links between the IMH and changes in the Nova Scotia adoption and maternity boarding houses legislation. In the longer term, the IMH experience is linked, though less directly, to the repeal of the *Nova Scotia Illegitimate Children's Act* in 1951 and to the growing push for professional standards in child welfare services in the province beginning in the 1940s.

The first question to ask is why the IMH scandal was so influential, given that there were other potentially "scandalous" problems in the administration of social policy in Nova Scotia in this period. In 1944, George Davidson (executive director of the Canadian Welfare Council) produced a *Report on Public Welfare Services in Nova Scotia* for the Dawson Royal Commission on Provincial Development and Rehabilitation. In Davidson's report, the IMH featured as a core problem in the province's welfare system. According to the report, it demonstrated the need for widespread reform touching many areas of the social welfare structure from amendments to the adoption law and repeal of the province's *Illegitimate Children's Act*, to a desperately needed re-vamping of the province's outmoded poor law. As Janet Guildford has argued however, Davidson's most trenchant critiques and most extensive recommendations for reform were directed toward the poor law system. Davidson was appalled by conditions in the county poor houses where the aged, the indigent, and the insane were often housed together in unsanitary and depressing conditions. He described the homes as a "convenient dumping ground for any problem cases arising within the local area," and was horrified to discover that "in some instances unmarried mothers are taken into the local county home for confinement and are kept there, after the child is born, for indefinite and sometimes prolonged periods."[9]

Clearly, there were other places to locate "scandal" in the treatment of unwed mothers and their children in Nova Scotia in the 1940s, as well as in other areas of social policy. But neither the condition of the poor in the county homes, nor the generally bleak options facing unmarried pregnant women attracted the attention and sympathy of Nova Scotians and their politicians during this decade. In contrast, the IMH—or, rather, a very specific construction of the scandalous IMH—attracted much attention and became the impetus for important changes in social policy. Although the story of the rise and fall of the Youngs and their maternity-adoption business was complex, the tale could be, and often was, sold to the public and to politicians simply and directly through the faces and the fates of the children born at the Home. Were these children cared for properly? Were they neglected? Were they placed with (sold to?) good parents? With bad or unworthy parents? What authority did the government need—must the government have—to protect these children? What further tragedies would develop in the absence of government control? In this version of the IMH story, the unwed mother, after giving birth, did not disappear completely. She was, however, pushed to the background while her child was, quite consciously, pulled to the foreground. The "innocent" babe could excite public opinion and become a vehicle for social change in a way that the possibly "destitute" and probably "sinful" unwed mother could not.

Beyond the "public relations" value of the IMH babies, the developing scandal turned on the clash of strong personalities and on conflicting visions of the proper role of government in the administration of social welfare.[10] The Youngs were quarrelsome, aggressive, and outspoken, and they championed the right of the entrepreneur to conduct business without undue interference and harassment from government officials. In contrast, Minister Davis, Deputy Minister Blois, and Director of Child Welfare MacKinnon presented themselves as the voice(s) of reason, logic, experience and, above all, professional authority. Within this group, MacKinnon's personality, which mixed a careful sense of bureaucratic propriety with a strident commitment to "progress" in social welfare, was the most interesting and the most significant in terms of the subsequent development of social policy in Nova Scotia. While Blois retired in 1947 and Davis died in office in 1948, MacKinnon remained as the senior bureaucrat in the provincial Department of Public Welfare until 1980.

MacKinnon was in many ways the archetypal bureaucrat, loyal to his superiors and always aware that his ability to shape policy depended on finding allies. He was conscious of the need to prepare the public (and the politicians) before presenting new ideas. When he felt he had strong support, he was willing to exercise the authority of his office but otherwise he was cautious. At the same time, MacKinnon had a clear vision of how to improve social welfare services in Nova Scotia and he saw himself as a key advocate for progress. For MacKinnon, such progress required an increasingly activist government over-seeing an expanded array of public and private social welfare agencies staffed and administered by professionally trained social workers.[11] Not surprisingly, MacKinnon's views reflected dominant themes in professional social work thought and practice across North America in this period. As James Struthers has argued, "Building welfare state programs ... meant creating employment for social work and expanding the profession's potential power through enhancing the claims of its specialised knowledge and expertise."[12] When he took up his first position with the Nova Scotia government in 1939, MacKinnon was fresh from a year of study at the University of Chicago's prestigious graduate School of Social Work. As a well-educated young man dedicated to a career in social welfare, MacKinnon was in many ways the literal embodiment of new directions in the development and administration of the welfare state.[13]

To a large extent, this study considers the IMH scandal from MacKinnon's professionalizing/state-building perspective, from inside a logic which establishes the major "problem" surrounding the IMH as the absence of government regulation and then defines the "solution" as the expansion of state authority backed by professional expertise. This understanding of problem and solution explains the path taken from scandal to social policy.[14] It does not follow, however, that MacKinnon and his supporters were always consistent in their actions, or that the Nova Scotia reformers followed up on all of the implications of their own ideas and supposed priorities. Nor did their professionalizing/state-building perspective go unchallenged. There was considerable opposition—inside and outside of Nova Scotia—both to the depiction of the Youngs and their business in the IMH scandal, and to the vision of a more authoritative welfare state which informed the policy response.

The basic story of the IMH will be familiar to many readers. Nearly forgotten for 40 years, the story of the Home was revived in the late 1980s through the work of journalist Bette Cahill. In *Butterbox Babies: Baby Sales, Baby Deaths and the Scandalous Story of the Ideal Maternity Home*, Cahill traced the contours of the Youngs' lucrative business. Unwed mothers paid the Youngs $500 or $600 for secrecy, shelter, medical care, and an "adoption" transfer plan.[15] Women who could not afford the IMH prices worked off their debt before and after the birth of their children by doing the laundry, cooking, and childminding. Because the Home employed very few professionally trained nurses, the young mothers did most of the nursing work as well.[16]

Adoptive families from across eastern Canada and the Northeast United States, desperate to find healthy, white, adoptable infants in a very tight adoption market, paid "fees" or gave "donations" to the Home that ranged from a few hundred dollars to, perhaps, as much as $10,000. It is unlikely that many parents adopting children from the Home paid anything near this higher figure, and child welfare leaders from Canada and the United States who investigated the IMH could not confirm payments higher than several hundred dollars.[17] They nonetheless felt that fees at the IMH were "exorbitant," and regarded the Youngs' operation as a clear example of "black market practices." Without question, the Youngs were prospering. By 1944, the family had a new private residence and the IMH had moved into a 54-room building with extensive grounds.[18]

The Youngs advertised extensively in American and Canadian newspapers, offering "lovely babies for adoption; excellent health background and healthy bodies."[19] Word of mouth also helped the business and by the early 1940s the Youngs had an extensive clientele in both countries. They developed a close connection with Jewish families in the New Jersey and New York City area, who found it almost impossible to adopt children through licensed social agencies. Adoption and child welfare laws in most states and provinces in the 1930s and 1940s forbade adoption placements across religious lines and as a result there was a particularly acute shortage of Jewish children available through reputable child welfare organizations.[20] The adoption law in Nova Scotia did not require that children be placed within the same religious group, and the Youngs consciously rejected the principle of same-religion placement. When adopting parents were concerned about religious matching, the Youngs would often claim a specific child was born to a Jewish mother. It is unlikely, however, that large numbers of Jewish women sought out the rural Nova Scotia Home for their confinements.[21]

Although adoptive parents approaching the IMH for children were required to provide letters of reference and proof of financial standing, these materials were not checked in any way. Parents chose their new child out of the nursery, or in some cases selected the child before birth, after observing the expectant mothers at the Home. Before 1943, the adoptions were processed quickly (sometimes within 24 hours) in the local county court when the children were as young as two to three days old. If the family was returning to the United States, obtaining a Canadian passport and an American entry visa for the child took an additional two weeks. Often, parents were back at home with their new charge within three weeks. There was no provision in the IMH procedure for any follow-up or investigation of the new family before or after the adoption.[22]

All of this flew in the face of the adoption procedures recommended by child welfare leaders in Canada and the United States. By the 1940s, child welfare leaders in both countries had developed recommended procedures in adoption referred to collectively as "sound adoption practice." The key concepts in sound adoption practice were investigation, matching, supervision, and regulation. Child welfare leaders regarded adoption as a complicated social and legal procedure which could go wrong at many stages and which, therefore, needed to be approached with the greatest care. The first step was the proper counselling of the birth mother to make certain that she understood her options and had made a realistic choice about relinquishing her child for adoption.[23] The next step was a thorough "social" investigation of both the mother and the putative father that delved into the "moral" and genetic background of the birth parents. The investigation looked at physical characteristics from race to eye colour and skin tone of the mother and father, and for any evidence of either physical or mental illness in the family. Also important were the religion, socio-economic class, occupation, and education of the birth parents. After birth, the infant had to be observed and tested for at least several months to make certain there were no obvious physical or neurological defects.

Prospective parents had to undergo a similar series of investigations delving into their physical and psychological health, their moral and financial standing, and their reasons for wanting to adopt a child. All of this information was considered critical in the next step: finding a "match" between adoptive parents and adoptable children in which racial background, religious faith and the more vaguely defined "developmental potential" of the child were the most important factors. Once the match was made, adoption reformers recommended the child be placed in the adoptive home for a probationary period so the new family could be observed and evaluated by a professionally-trained social worker. The final adoption order would be processed six months to two years later, after a satisfactory report from the social worker.[24]

The Youngs' rapid-fire approach to adoption completely bypassed these procedures. As Nora Lea of the Canadian Welfare Council explained to a worried New Jersey child welfare official, "the real source of trouble with the Ideal Maternity Home is their complete violation of ordinary accepted standards in adoption placement."[25] But there were other problems as well. Adoption reformers argued that placements worked best when the entire process was overseen by a single social agency (ideally, by one worker) familiar with the birth mother, the child, and the adoptive parents. This meant a strong preference for working within a limited geographic area and placing children locally. "Distance placements" were possible, but required careful co-ordination and communication between social agencies which was difficult to arrange, especially when children were moved across the physical boundaries separating one unit of government (and therefore one unit of legal jurisdiction) from another. When children crossed borders between one state and another, between one province and another, and between one country and another, child welfare leaders feared it was possible (even probable) that children and parents would "fall through the cracks" and that adoption placements would occur without adequate input, guidance, or protection from social workers and state officials.[26] From the perspective of government officials and professional social workers inside and outside of Nova Scotia, the Youngs moved babies across borders in a deliberate effort to avoid government regulations and professional oversight. The result, they argued, was the dangerous exploitation of birth mothers, adoptive parents, and, above all, innocent children.[27]

In *Butterbox Babies*, Cahill explored disturbing rumours that the Youngs deliberately starved and neglected babies with some physical or mental defect who could not easily be placed for adoption. She records the long-standing suspicion that at least 100 babies are buried in unmarked graves near a local cemetery in Fox Point, Nova Scotia, and that other bodies were either dumped at sea or thrown into the Home's incinerator. The Youngs were never convicted of the murder of an infant, and there does not appear to be documentary evidence in support of Cahill's most disturbing allegations. But there is solid proof that there were serious deficiencies in sanitary conditions and medical standards at the Home and that many of the children in the nursery were neglected and malnourished.[28] In 1945, one potential adoptive mother, appalled by what she had seen, reported her experiences to an adoption worker in New York. Describing the nursery at the Home, she reported that:

> The smell and stench of stale urine overcame her to such an extent that she was ready to fly from the place. The cribs had three children in each one. The floors were bare, and she noticed that the children who should be getting solid foods were getting pabulum in their milk bottles. No child was getting personal care and all looked undernourished, pale and soiled.[29]

In an early draft of the *Report on Public Welfare Services in Nova Scotia*, George Davidson of the Canadian Welfare Council reported that:

> Although the Home confines upwards of a hundred mothers or more a year, and cares for as many as seventy babies at a time, there is a total lack of qualified medical supervision, and a serious inadequacy of properly qualified, fully trained nursing care. The room in which the babies were kept was, on the occasion of the survey visit, distressingly overcrowded, with the obvious result that it was impossible to prevent the spread of colds (and this would apply to similar infectious diseases).... On at least one previous occasion, infant deaths at this institution have reached epidemic proportions, and it is the opinion of this survey that nothing except great good fortune has prevented similar tragedies from recurring on more frequent occasions.[30]

These passages are disturbing, even heart-rending, and could be supplemented by many similar examples. From at least 1935, when the Youngs were unsuccessfully prosecuted for manslaughter in connection with the death of a mother and her infant, provincial officials were aware of some of the Home's problems and shortcomings.[31] Why, then, did it take so long for provincial officials to take effective action? Why was it so difficult to close the Home? From MacKinnon's professionalizing/state-building perspective, the first answer to these questions is that through the 1930s, and well into the 1940s, the provincial government had no authority to inspect or regulate either the IMH or other similar institutions. There was no provincial mechanism for the inspection of maternity homes or private hospitals. The adoption law, as measured against the standard of "sound adoption practice," was also seriously deficient. There was no requirement in the law that parents or children be investigated before an adoption; there was no opportunity for provincial authorities to give or withhold approval for a particular placement; there was no provision for a probationary period before a final adoption decree.[32] In this situation, it was difficult for provincial authorities to find proof to support their growing suspicions about the Home, and, therefore difficult to build a convincing case for the expansion of state authority necessary for them to take action.

The carefully guarded secrecy surrounding the IMH made things still more difficult for provincial authorities. At the same time, this secrecy was a critical part of the Home's appeal to its clients. Despite the rising popularity of infant adoption, many adopting parents tried to hide the new child's origins from friends and neighbours. The Youngs promised never to reveal information about the adopted babies, and sometimes offered cover stories for anxious parents.[33] In newspaper advertisements and brochures directed toward women pregnant out of wedlock, the Youngs promised a "Complete Service Free From Publicity." To underscore the importance of the (private, publicity-free) "Mothers' Refuge" offered at the IMH, the Youngs pointed out that "Dame Gossip has sent many young lives to perdition after ruining them socially, that might have been BRIGHT STARS in society and a POWER in the world of usefulness HAD THEY BEEN SHIELDED from gossip when they made a mistake."[34]

It is not difficult to understand why this rhetoric appealed to unwed mothers. Their best hope for resuming "normal" lives after the birth of their children lay in hiding their pregnancies from their communities and perhaps even from their families. The women also needed shelter, medical care, and reassurance they were making good choices for their babies. The Youngs promised all of this, and many women got exactly what they needed and wanted from the Home. Another explanation, then, for why the IMH continued the thrive in the 1940s was that the institution provided a service which was valued by adoptive parents, and desperately needed by women pregnant out of wedlock.[35] Because of the (highly valued) secrecy surrounding the Home, there was little chance that a woman entering the IMH would know anything about the rumoured problems with medical standards and child care which worried provincial officials. Some women detected no significant problems during their stay at the IMH. Those who did spot problems, were worried about the standard of child care, or felt they had been mistreated, could not report what they had experienced without forfeiting the anonymity which drew them to the Home in the first place.[36]

Although Davidson also emphasized the lack of "social care" and "sympathetic helpful understanding" for the unwed mother that made the commercial maternity home look like an attractive option for Nova Scotian women, he concluded that the "problem" of the IMH was created and sustained by gaps in the province's regulatory structure.[37] In early drafts of his report, Davidson wrote explicitly and at length about the Home and its deficiencies. He also described the rampant animosity between the Youngs and senior officials at the Department of Public Welfare and detailed attempts by the Youngs to deliberately evade provincial regulations.[38] In later versions of his report, Davidson removed most specific references to the Home and toned down his comments, but he kept more than a dozen unmistakable, and highly critical, references to a "certain commercial maternity home" engaged in an "export baby business."[39] Starting with the IMH as evidence of shortcomings in the province, Davidson went on to recommend a series of reforms designed to control the home while at the same time strengthening the overall provincial welfare structure.

Davidson was not an employee of the province, nor was his report binding on the provincial government. Nonetheless, the report—along with Davidson's letters and notes on the project—laid out the connections between the IMH, the need for immediate changes in provincial laws and longer-term directions for reform in the province.[40] Of necessity, Davidson worked closely (though not always without tension) with key staff members at the Department of Public Welfare, including MacKinnon.[41] The two men had much in common in their professional outlook and MacKinnon identified closely with the themes of professional development and expanded state authority which ran through Davidson's report. MacKinnon, quite characteristically, felt that many of Davidson's recommendations for reform were unrealistic and ignored the fiscal, social and political realities of mid-twentieth-century Nova Scotia but the two clearly shared a commitment to change that went well beyond closing the IMH.[42]

When Davidson arrived in the province, some changes were already in place. In 1940, Dr. Frank Davis and his staff at the Nova Scotia Ministry of Public Welfare successfully sponsored a new piece of legislation, the *Maternity Boarding Houses Act*, which extended provincial control over institutions like the IMH. Under the legislation, most institutions receiving payment for keeping children under three years of age were required to obtain a licence from the province. One condition of the licence was that the facility and its records had to be open at all times for inspection by the director of child welfare and certain of his representatives. Other provisions effectively prohibited institutions from advertising that they had children available for adoption or were willing to arrange adoptions. The law established penalties for institutions operating without a licence or violating other provisions of the legislation. The director of child welfare, "at his absolute discretion," was given the authority to evaluate any application for a licence and to cancel any licence already granted. The legislation also had weak provisions for establishing provincial authority over adoption, specifying that any adoption placement originating from a licensed maternity boarding house had to be approved by the local Children's Aid Society, the director of child welfare or a court.[43]

In the short term, provincial officials moved slowly and chose not to exploit the full potential of the new legislation. In 1940, 1941, and again in 1942, Nova Scotia granted the Youngs a licence under the *Maternity Boarding Houses Act*, and provincial officials contented themselves with a rudimentary reporting from the Youngs on the Home's activities. The most obvious explanation for why the province issued these licences is that MacKinnon, Blois and Davis felt they were not in a strong enough position to take action against the still-popular and politically connected Youngs.[44] The Youngs, meanwhile, were quick to put their new status to good advantage, producing publicity pamphlets touting the IMH as a "licenced facility approved by the Nova Scotia government."[45]

In 1943, as provincial officials were building greater support for a tougher application of the law, the Youngs took advantage of a loophole in the 1940 legislation which exempted incorporated institutions from the provisions of the *Maternity Boarding Houses Act*. The exemption was originally intended to exclude the large denominational maternity homes in Halifax and Sydney from the requirements of the legislation. The explanation for this provision was that the denominational maternity homes—created by individual acts of the provincial government and regulated under these acts—were already reporting to the province of their own accord. For the IMH, the incorporation loophole was a way to slip out from under the control of provincial officials.[46] The "Ideal Maternity Home" became the "Ideal Maternity Home and Sanatorium, Inc.," with Senator William Duff, a powerful Nova Scotia political figure, serving as president.[47] Davidson, surveying these developments, was appalled. He argued that the fact "the largest institution of its kind in the province ... resorted to incorporation for the obvious purpose of escaping supervision," demonstrated that the *Maternity Boarding Houses Act* must be strengthened.[48]

Davidson saw greater potential in the province's "excellent amendments" to the Adoption Act in 1943. The key reform was a provision requiring a probationary period of one year before an adoption could be finalized. During that year, the director of child welfare, or his representatives, would have the chance to supervise and investigate the adoptive placement. Later, these officials had the option to give evidence and recommend approval or disapproval at the final adoption hearing, although the decision still rested in the hands of a county court judge.[49] The legislation effectively increased the regulatory authority of provincial officials and, in accord with the tenets of sound adoption practice, established the provincial interest in overseeing "social" as well as "legal" aspects of adoption transactions. In an early draft of his report, Davidson noted that one effect of this amendment was to "increase congestion" at the IMH, "since children can no longer be disposed of so readily." In the published version, he argued that the new provisions had "put an effective stop to an 'export' business in babies for adoption on an 'over-the-counter' basis."[50]

This prediction was premature. The Youngs and their lawyers soon found a way around the new legislation by instructing the adoptive parents to take children to New Brunswick for the court appearance and adoption.[51] Under New Brunswick regulations there was no requirement that either the child or the parent be a resident of the province, and there was no probationary period before the a final adoption decree was issued.[52] In letters to Americans seeking children to adopt, William Young explained in detail how couples could evade the laws of Nova Scotia and obtain quick adoption decrees in New Brunswick.[53]

Considerable opposition to the new adoption legislation emerged within the province as well, and in early 1944 provincial officials were preparing for a challenge to the new *Adoption Act* at the spring sitting of the legislature. Davidson hinted broadly that the Youngs were behind the challenge. There were, though, other potential sources of opposition to the new regulatory regime.[54] Across North America during the 1940s and 1950s, child welfare leaders advocating adoption reform and calling for increased professional supervision and more state regulation of the adoption process often met with resistance from the public, from politicians and even from some members of their own profession.[55] In some areas, the principles of sound adoption practice were well-entrenched in law and professional practice, but elsewhere standards (as measured by adoption reformers) were low. While reformers argued that stringent professional oversight was necessary to protect children and parents, critics noted the threat of unnecessary delays, increasing expenses, and an unwarranted intrusion into the private lives of adoptive families. Complaints that social workers deliberately surrounded adoption procedures with "red tape" and "bureaucracy" in order to protect their jobs were frequent, as were charges that the so-called "protections" of "sound adoption practice" were responsible for preventing thousands of lonely families and abandoned children from finding happiness together. In 1945, the grandmother of an IMH-adopted baby lectured a New Jersey child welfare worker on what a "shame" it was "that New Jersey agencies work so hard to prevent families from adopting children." She went on to "point how very gracious the people in Canada [at the IMH] were to her daughter, as a decided contrast."[56]

The Youngs proved adept at exploiting latent opposition to the intrusion and delay associated with increased state control of adoption. Often, couples came to the IMH in search of babies specifically because they were tired of waiting for heavily regulated adoptions conducted under the laws of their home provinces or states. Others came because they had been rejected as adoptive parents under the strict guidelines (including religious matching) of adoption agencies employing the new professional standards. For many Nova Scotians, it seemed unnecessary to spend time and tax dollars to launch invasive studies of adoptive placements and add complications to the simple process of bringing home a child to love, particularly if that child might otherwise become a financial burden on the community. The Youngs had, after all, successfully crafted a public image as dedicated and skilled practitioners in service of children and families. In a 1944 booklet aimed at adoptive parents and the public at large, for example, Senator Duff praised the Youngs for keeping true to their "strong faith in God and determination for the betterment of humanity," as they overcame obstacles and "nobly pioneered the work of child welfare by developing strong healthy babies within delightful surroundings for both mother and child." The same booklet featured a smiling photo and glowing endorsement of the IMH from Mr. and Mrs. John Stewart Kendall (the son and daughter-in-law of the province's lieutenant governor) who had recently adopted a child from the Home.[57] Reformers at the Nova Scotia Department of Public Welfare might talk about the need to protect children in adoption, but it simply would not have been evident to most of those outside of their circle what dangers lurked behind unregulated adoptions from the IMH or any other maternity home which would justify state intervention and oversight.

The circle of reformers who were aware of problems at the IMH and committed to changes in the province's child welfare structure included a small but growing group of professionally trained social workers and supporters of reform concentrated in the Halifax area. Since 1941, a committee of the Halifax Council of Social Agencies had been studying the province's adoption act.[58] In 1943, the Council lobbied the legislature in support of amendments to the Act which increased provincial oversight and professional intervention.[59] In 1944, when these amendments seemed threatened, MacKinnon told the Council that "he did not think sufficient preliminary education had been given to amendments before they were passed," and he asked that the Council send out information on adoption reform to "all interested organisations in the province." The Council also organized a committee to watch the proceedings of the legislature closely and "be ready with material, etc. to meet any opposition." The Halifax Children's Aid Society, a member group of the Council, sent briefs to local Children's Aid Societies around the province asking their board members, who generally were prominent local citizens, "to invoke the interest of their local representatives in the matter."[60]

Acting in his official capacity as director of child welfare, MacKinnon responded to the challenge by preparing and distributing a booklet, *Adoption of Children: Selection of Opinions from British, American and Canadian Sources*. While this publication made no specific mention of the recent Nova Scotia amendments, the booklet presented examples of legislation and professional opinion on adoption reform, made an implicit argument in support of the reforms undertaken in the province and pointed toward further advances.[61] The publication illustrates the self-referential logic which lay behind MacKinnon's quest to expand state authority and professionalize adoption practice in the province; to prove the need for more professional authority and state power, MacKinnon quoted other professionals and law makers who shared his perspective. The collective lobbying and educational efforts of provincial officials and their supporters outside of government seems to have been successful. The *Adoption Act* was neither repealed nor weakened during the 1944 legislative session.[62]

By 1945, Davis, backed by Blois and MacKinnon, felt he was in a strong enough position to push for further reform and greater authority. In that year, the RCMP, at the request of the province, began to investigate the Home's adoptive placements and to interview birth mothers on their experiences with the Youngs.[63] In the spring, the legislature amended the *Maternity Boarding Houses Act* to remove the "incorporation loophole" which had allowed the Youngs to avoid provincial control. This change left the Youngs in a precarious position. From this point forward, they would be required to obtain an operating licence from the province, granted or refused at MacKinnon's discretion.[64] In July 1945, the Youngs applied for a licence. MacKinnon inspected the Home in August and then turned down the application. In his report on the inspection, MacKinnon noted that he had found babies lying in their own vomit and fecal matter.[65]

The Youngs responded to this new situation with an enhanced, and more public, attack on Davis, Blois and MacKinnon and on the policies of the Department of Public Welfare. This animosity was not new. In 1944, Davidson had been struck by their "open and strenuous hostility towards the Director of Child Welfare and towards the entire Department of Health."[66] Davidson removed direct references to this conflict from his report at the request of MacKinnon, but added a plea for support for the Department's beleaguered officials in his final version: "There should therefore be the strongest possible measure of support for any steps which the Department of Public Health may take to insure that institutions of this kind measure up to tolerable standards."[67]

MacKinnon was not the only target of these attacks. Davis and Blois had been in conflict with the Youngs since the mid-1930s. By 1945, Blois was nearing the end of a 32-year career in social welfare during which he pioneered key areas of social policy in the province and helped to establish the provincial Department of Public Health and later the Department of Public Welfare. Frequently prickly and apt to take criticism of the provincial social welfare structure as an attack on his personal integrity, Blois was clearly feeling frustrated and pressured by the IMH struggle.[68] That summer, Lea, George Davidson's successor at the head of the CWC, reported on a meeting with Blois in which the Nova Scotian noted that "they [the Youngs] are organising a very active campaign in the province against the Minister of Health and Welfare (sic) and tending to discredit them in the eyes of the public." Blois expressed to Lea his belief that, "a public official can stand only so much of this and then it becomes harmful to the Department and its projects."[69]

For Davis, the new assault from the Youngs meant an attack on his personal reputation and a challenge to his Department of Public Welfare; it also was a direct threat to his political future. Davis, in addition to serving as minister of public welfare, was the member of the legislative assembly for Lunenburg County—the electoral riding in which the IMH was located. The IMH generated a lot of business in the local area, and the Youngs had the support of most of the business community in the town of Chester. Many of these businessmen were supporters of Davis's party—the Liberal party—and 1945 was an election year.[70] Through the fall of 1945, the Youngs spearheaded a direct effort to defeat Davis in the election, organizing and speaking at anti-Davis lectures and placing posters around the county urging the voters to "RESTORE DEMOCRACY" by making election day "V-DAY" for "VICTORY OVER DAVIS AND DICTATORSHIP."[71]

The hyperbole the Youngs employed in this effort was astounding. They compared Davis to the fascist dictators of Europe, basing their claims on the "dictatorial powers" the legislature had recently granted the director of child welfare: "Since a war has just been fought to end dictatorship in Europe.... We can't afford to let it continue here, so away with Davis and Dictatorship!"[72] The Youngs, in turn, portrayed themselves as the innocent victims of persecution, the objects of an unreasonable personal vendetta on the part of Davis and his staff. They wrote confidently to their American supporters that, "our campaign against Dr. Davis is going over in a big way. In the six lectures already held, we have spoken to about three thousand people. It is costing us considerable, but we feel that any sacrifice is necessary for these helpless babies."[73]

This "sacrifice" was to be in vain. Davis fought back steadily, challenging his opponents to "step out from behind women's petticoats," a reference to Lila Young's leadership in the anti-Davis campaign. He gathered support from social welfare professionals and major social organizations from across the province and won the election easily as part of the Liberal sweep of the province. He also filed (although later withdrew) a libel action against the Youngs. Davis thus emerged from the election with his political base largely intact and with solid support from the newly elected and popular premier, his old friend Angus L. Macdonald.[74]

Earlier in 1945, Lea confessed her "shrewd suspicion that the Nova Scotia authorities are a little bit afraid of this institution [the IMH] and, hence, are walking warily." In 1944, Davidson expressed the same sentiment, writing to R. MacGregor Dawson that the Nova Scotian authorities were pressuring him to tone down his report because they feared they might be sued by the Youngs.[75] Although Blois, MacKinnon, and Davis may have had some personal, professional, and political inclinations to be cautious—even fearful—in their dealings with the Youngs in earlier years, there was little reason to maintain that reserve beyond the summer and fall of 1945. After the Youngs stepped up their very public criticism of Davis and his staff, there was no motivation for the provincial officials to act cautiously in an effort to avoid scandal. The Home thrived on the secrecy surrounding the specifics of its operation and had been protected by it. But as the Youngs complained of "persecution" at the hands of Davis, Blois and MacKinnon, they drew more and more attention to themselves and presented a new public face that was far less scripted—and far less appealing—than the image which appeared in their promotional brochures. Nova Scotians were left to judge whether they felt that new provincial regulations for maternity homes and new oversight in adoption really constituted the advance of tyranny in the province. Some, undoubtedly, believed that it did. Others, whether or not they were convinced by the logic of professionalizing child welfare, saw exaggeration and hyperbole in the Youngs' attacks on the well-respected Davis and his staff.[76]

The reformers emerged from the nastiness of the election campaign in a stronger position and quickly pressed their advantage. In early November, MacKinnon sent the Youngs a long letter detailing changes in record keeping, medical care, nutrition, child care and physical plant that would have to be made at the IMH before he would consider a new application for a maternity boarding home licence.[77] The Youngs' vocal supporters in the Chester business community complained that it was impossible for the IMH, or any other institution in the province, to meet the criteria MacKinnon set out in his letter, and in this they were probably correct.[78] They argued that the length of time between MacKinnon's initial inspection in July (there was a second inspection in October) and his formal report back to the institution in November indicated that the province had no interest in change at the IMH but only wished to close it down. Here, the Chester businessmen were probably also correct. A petition to the premier and the Nova Scotia legislature filed by the Chester Board of Trade described the "bitter persecution" of the IMH, which culminated in "discriminating dictatorial legislation," as an attack on the right of the Youngs (and of local businessmen) to a fair return on their invested capital.[79] In a long "Report on Ideal Maternity Home" directed "without prejudice" to the premier, the president of the Chester Board of Trade, Phil Moore, argued that "the continual hounding of the Ideal Maternity Home ... is in the opinion of this Board the most astounding project of studied injustice that has ever been perpetrated by Government officials anywhere in the Dominion." Later in the same report, Moore accused Davis and his staff of using "Gestapo methods" and argued that the minister was "using the powers of his high office to promote his own chances in a *private* quarrel with Dr. and Mrs. Young."[80]

None of these complaints got a sympathetic hearing. The premier responded strongly to Moore's attack on Davis, writing that "I cannot remain silent when a colleague of the calibre of Dr. Davis is attacked in this way, unfairly."[81] The Youngs were worried. They told supporters in the United States to encourage friends to hurry to Nova Scotia to collect babies because the Home might not be able to stay in business after the spring 1946 sitting of the legislature.[82] During the spring session, the legislature replaced the *Maternity Boarding Houses Act* with a new act which continued the provisions of the former legislation while adding some important new items. For example, the new Act specified that "no child who is kept or maintained in a maternity home shall be given out for adoption ... except with the consent of the Director [of Child Welfare]." As well, it provided an expanded, clarified definition of a maternity home, established the authority of the director of Child Welfare to make further regulations respecting maternity homes and specified that every day an institution operated in contravention of the terms of the Act was a separate, punishable offence.[83] The Youngs, in other words, could no longer place children for adoption, whether the actual adoption was finalized inside or outside of the province, without the consent of the director of child welfare. Every instance in which the IMH made an unauthorized placement, as well as every day it remained open without a licence, could be the basis for a separate legal complaint.

Even before the legislation was passed, the Youngs faced serious trouble from legal prosecutions for violations of the original *Maternity Boarding Houses Act* and the provincial *Medical Act*. The subsequent trials, which kept the Youngs in court for much of the spring of 1946, were not a new experience for the couple. In 1936, the Youngs were acquitted on two charges of manslaughter stemming from the death of a mother and her baby at the home. In 1935, they were convicted of fraud for their attempt to collect expenses for the care of a child after the child died.[84] In 1942, they were forced to appear before a board of inquest studying the death of a child recently adopted from the Home.[85] The Youngs emerged from these encounters relatively unscathed, but the court actions in the spring of 1946 brought a series of convictions and negative publicity.

William and Lila Young successfully defended themselves against charges under the *Medical Act*, which concerned whether William, a chiropractor, was posing and/or acting as a medical doctor and whether Lila, who described herself as an "obstetrical specialist," was reaching beyond her (questionable) qualification as a midwife and performing procedures for which she was neither qualified nor licensed.[86] It was more difficult to defend themselves from charges that they had violated the *Maternity Boarding Houses Act*. The evidence against them, drawn from the RCMP investigations, was strong and the Youngs were convicted on seven of nine charges.[87] The court fined them $50 or $100 for each conviction plus costs. The negative publicity was the most damaging aspect of the trials, as the proceedings were covered extensively in the province's newspapers.[88] As the public looked on, MacKinnon explained in detail how the Youngs were flaunting provincial laws while Lila Young ranted about persecution and William Young persisted in untenable denials of his role in arranging adoptions. The Youngs' behaviour drew the ire of judges and lawyers, and the couple came across poorly in newspaper accounts of the proceedings.[89]

Outside the province, social welfare reformers in both Canada and the United States watched the events of spring 1946 with hope and expectation. Lea, writing to a colleague in the United States, noted that the new Nova Scotia legislation "will certainly put a spoke in the wheel of the Home."[90] By June, with convictions mounting and the new legislation about to come into effect, the Youngs appeared to have had enough and their lawyer announced that the IMH was closing. MacKinnon reacted with relief as the increasingly public scandal surrounding the Home was embarrassing as well as useful. He wrote Lea expressing his satisfaction that political barriers to strong action against the Home had been overcome. He argued, perhaps too optimistically, that, "I think you will agree that none of these things in the administrative field can be cleared entirely from political colour, but I also think that it can be said that in this case a fundamental issue was involved which was finally and definitely settled devoid of any prejudice or political considerations. Some of us could not stand such indignities any longer."[91] The timing of the Youngs' announcement was fortuitous as the Canadian Conference on Social Work was set to have its annual meeting in Halifax in late June. Blois was president of the conference, an important honour as he neared the end of a career spent shaping the welfare structure of Nova Scotia. "I can't tell you," wrote MacKinnon, "how pleased I am to know that the whole sordid mess is settled before the Conference comes to Nova Scotia."[92]

This was not, however, the end of either the Youngs or their home; the "sordid mess" could be neither cleaned up nor forgotten easily. While in Nova Scotia for the Canadian Conference on Social Work meeting, the American Children's Bureau adoption expert Maud Morlock noted that there were still many children at the Home "for whom some plan must be made."[93] The Youngs "officially" turned the IMH into a tourist hotel and old age care centre called the "Battle Creek of Nova Scotia Rest Haven Park." Lila, however, still operated a "private" obstetrical care and adoption business under her own name for several years. The court battles also continued. During the fall of 1946, the Youngs appealed their convictions under the *Maternity Boarding Houses Act*, but were successful in only one case. In early 1947, William was in court successfully defending himself against a perjury charge stemming from the previous spring's court appearances. Lila plead guilty to two additional charges under the *Maternity Boarding Houses Act* based on her most recent activities.[94]

The Youngs' courtroom career reached a dramatic climax in May 1947 when a libel suit they instigated against the *Montreal Standard* came to trial. In August of 1946, the *Standard* published an exposé by staff reporter Mavis Gallant: "Traders in Fear: Baby Farm Rackets Still Lure Girls Who are Afraid of Social Agencies." The article painted the IMH in a damming light, charging that the Youngs exploited young girls in desperate circumstances, bullied them into giving their children up for adoption, ignored accepted standards for choosing and supervising adoptive placements and provided a questionable standard of medical care. Gallant described William and Lila Young as "blatant" participants in an international traffic in babies.[95] Although the Home was closed when the article appeared, the Youngs insisted they had been "greatly injured in their character, credit and reputation and had suffered general damages." They sued for $25,000. It was the trial itself, however, which proved most damaging to the couple's character and reputation. As the *Standard*'s lawyer set out to prove the charges in the article, the proceedings turned into a parade of the Young's misdeeds and Lila's stormy defiance. The entire drama was played out in excruciating detail on the front pages of the Halifax newspapers.[96] One particularly effective exchange for the defence concerned the accusation that the Youngs buried dead infants in "butter boxes" obtained from the local grocer. Lila Young insisted that these wooden boxes were turned into respectable coffins lined with "beautiful sateen," but the image of babies tossed aside in leftover packaging remained and became a symbol of the Youngs' questionable practices.[97]

After four days of testimony, the presiding judge dismissed the complaint. The Youngs' reputation was in shreds and by this time most of their former supporters had grown silent or turned against the couple. In the aftermath of the libel trial, there were no more letters to the premier decrying the "persecution" of the Youngs. By 1948, Lieutenant Governor Kendall, the adoptive grandfather of an IMH baby, was acknowledging problems with the IMH in correspondence with federal officials.[98] MacKinnon described the day the libel case was dismissed as "the best day of my life." He had reason to be pleased. He testified at the trial concerning the poor conditions he found at the Home and the failure of the Youngs to meet the province's licensing standards or to acknowledge the widely accepted professional standards for investigation and "matching" in adoptive placements. His testimony, with its references to new laws, newly enforced standards and new principles in adoption practice, was itself an indication of how the IMH contributed to what MacKinnon would call "progress" in the province's child welfare system.[99]

As the immediate scandal wound down, the province was left with the negative publicity as well as with a strengthened regulatory framework in the form of the *Maternity Boarding Houses Act* and the amended *Adoption Act*. In subsequent years, MacKinnon devoted more attention to these two pieces of legislation, filling in potential loopholes and strengthening the position of the department and its agents. In 1949, the legislature amended the *Maternity Boarding Houses Act* to require that any person taking a child out of the province for adoption first obtain a special certificate from the director of child welfare, issued only after an investigation of the proposed adoptive home.[100] MacKinnon continued to work steadily on adoption reform, looking for ways to control out-of-province adoptions and trying to surround legal consents to adoption with protections that would safeguard the interests of adoptive parents and birth mothers.[101] At the national level, he emerged as a leader in the biannual gatherings of the provincial directors of child welfare. Throughout the 1950s, this group devoted much of its attention to refinements in adoption law, and paid particular attention to the challenge of regulating interprovincial and international adoption placements. By the mid-1950s, the Nova Scotia Department of Public Welfare became a Canadian pioneer in a new movement to search nationally and internationally to locate adoptive homes for so-called "hard-to-place" children—mixed-race, Native, and handicapped children. MacKinnon had come full circle; he began as the steadfast opponent of cross-border placements, and ended as an advocate for professionally sanctioned and carefully controlled cross-border adoptions, at least for some children. In both poses, he remained an advocate of professional supervision and state authority in adoption.[102]

This new regulatory regime for adoption and maternity boarding houses did not, however, solve all of the "problems" revealed by the IMH, nor did it mark the extent of the scandal's influence on provincial welfare structures. The province gained a mechanism to control the IMH and other smaller, less controversial charitable and commercial maternity homes operating in the province, but none of this did anything to address the very pressing needs of single, unwed women for material aid. The IMH appealed to women pregnant out of wedlock because it offered shelter and protection and made it possible for the women to resume "normal" lives after the births of their babies. Before and after the IMH scandal, the province offered no comparable service. From this perspective, the demise of the IMH was a loss for some single pregnant women.[103]

MacKinnon and his colleagues were by no means insensitive to this issue, but worried they could not break through the bitter prejudice against the unmarried mother and build support for expanded services for these women. MacKinnon chose to direct the initial battle against the IMH through the issue of adoption, feeling that the mistreatment of babies was far more likely to draw public support than the exploitation of unwed mothers. This was a political decision with material consequences for unmarried mothers.[104] In 1944, George Davidson argued, quite reasonably, that it was not possible get rid of the commercialized baby business without addressing the needs of the mother as well as the danger to the child:

It should be constantly kept in mind that the reason why commercialised maternity homes come into existence and flourish is because no adequate social facilities are available to provide the necessary care and help to the unmarried mother and her child. It is not, therefore, sufficient to put out of business, or to establish minimum control over, commercialised maternity houses operating in this field.... It is even more important that the province should assume the responsibility of developing, through its Child Welfare Branch and through the Children's Aid Societies of the province, a case work service that will adequately meet the needs of the unmarried mother in her period of difficulty.[105]

Davidson had an expansive view of what those needs were and what services would be required to fill them. He argued that the province required a much larger staff of trained social welfare professionals who would be available to provide sympathetic support for every unwed mother. The social workers would assist the woman during her pregnancy and delivery and help her to make a plan for her baby after the birth. He argued that the mother had the "first rights to her own child" and that she should be provided, if necessary, with the financial support to enable her to keep her baby if that is what she chose to do after consultation with a social worker. Davidson believed that if such a plan were implemented, the commercialized maternity homes would have no more clients. "Unmarried mothers will come to the Children's Aid Societies or the Provincial Welfare Representatives for advice in planning as to how they shall be confined and what plan they should make for themselves and their baby after it is born."[106]

Davidson's vision was generous in some ways. His plan for financial support for unwed mothers, and his assertion of an unwed mother's right to keep her child, put him out of step with social welfare practice and even with professional opinion on adoption and un-wed motherhood in this period.[107] But this vision was also naive. It ignored the very good reasons unwed mothers had for placing a high value on secrecy and distrusting intrusive social workers. Approaching public officials for help, even if those officials were sympathetic, meant braving public knowledge of the pregnancy. It was difficult, for instance, for social workers to investigate the mother and her background without alerting family and friends of her pregnancy. Turning to social workers for help could only be as attractive as Davidson assumed if there was a radical change in public attitudes toward the single pregnant woman, an unlikely revolution in thought and practice. The plan also assumed financial and professional resources which were simply not available in the province, nor likely to be available.

MacKinnon recognized that the province was letting down unwed mothers, but disagreed strongly with many of Davidson's recommendations. The cautious and pragmatic bureaucrat in MacKinnon felt Davidson's measures would never be approved by the provincial legislature. MacKinnon also believed that providing minimal, inadequate, financial support to unwed mothers would only doom the mothers and their children to poverty. And it did not seem creditable that there would be a sudden change of opinion and practice among the mostly untrained Children's Aid workers around the province.[108] During the 1930s, these same workers proved some of the harshest critics of the unwed mothers; their annual reports often portrayed women pregnant out of wedlock as moral and financial threats to the community.[109] In the late 1940s, the executive secretary of the Halifax Children's Aid Society, Gwen Lantz (a professionally trained social worker) was criticized by fellow social workers in the city for her harsh treatment of the unwed mothers who came to the Children's Aid Society for help.[110]

There was one area where MacKinnon agreed with Davidson's recommendations on "illegitimacy and work with unwed mothers": the province's *Illegitimate Children's Act* had to repealed and replaced. Davidson called the Act, which set the terms under which an unwed mother could use the court system to seek financial support from the father of her child, "the greatest weakness in the entire chain of child protective services in the province." Neither this Act, nor any other piece of legislation on the provincial books, made any provision for the kind of support and guidance which Davidson referred to as constituting proper "social care" of the unwed mother. Davidson also pointed out that the legislation was directly tied to the province's antiquated poor law system and was set up to protect the financial interests of the local poor district, often to the detriment of the mother and her child.[111]

Until the late 1950s, general relief in Nova Scotia was administered under a poor law inherited from Great Britain and largely unchanged in administration and spirit from the 18th century to the mid-1900s. Under this system, the province was divided into more than 300 tiny poor districts, each responsible for raising funds to support the poor having settlement in that district.[112] But how did the connection between the poor law and the *Illegitimate Children's Act* affect the unwed mother? The answer to this question depended on the financial and familial resources available to a woman. The most fortunate had families or lovers who gave them care and shelter or provided financial support, perhaps enough to pay for a commercial maternity home.[113] Other women managed, as at the IMH, to work off their bills at commercial homes, or chose the charitable maternity homes run by the Catholic and Protestant churches in Halifax and Sydney.[114] Unless these options were unavailable or unacceptable, a Nova Scotian pregnant out of wedlock was unlikely to turn to the poor law and/or the *Illegitimate Children's Act* for help.

The Act was divided into two parts: the first treated "Proceedings on Behalf of the Poor District"; the second treated "Proceedings on Behalf of an Illegitimate Child and Its Mother."[115] Under Part II of the Act, the mother of an illegitimate child (or her parents, or "any person or corporation having maintained such child") could bring an action against the putative father of the child to force the father to contribute to her medical expenses and to the ongoing maintenance of the child. In order to secure payment, the mother was forced to appear in open court for a humiliating inquiry into the circumstances of her pregnancy where the putative father could defend himself by questioning the mother's character and sexual history.[116]

If the judge believed the mother had accurately named the father of the child in question, the father could be ordered to pay the woman a maximum of five dollars per week, depending on his financial resources. The mother was, however, prohibited from pursuing the father under Part II of the Act if there had been a previous action against him under Part I of the Act. This protected the interests of the poor district. If, at any point before or after the birth of her child, the mother turned to the local overseers of the poor for relief (for medical care during her delivery, housing in the Poor House, boarding care for the child) then she could be forced by the overseers of the poor, or by any ratepayer in the poor district, to name the father of her child before a judge and thus commence legal proceedings under Part I of the Act. In this proceeding (that is, one initiated on behalf of the local poor district), the mother still had to face the open court inquiry, but any funds recovered would go to pay the expenses incurred by the overseers of the poor. The total liability of the father in an action under Part I was limited to $500. In other words, the claim of the poor district for the repayment of short-term expenses outweighed the claim of the mother for either short-term costs or long-term support for her child. Overall, the process was traumatic for women, and the chances of a successful prosecution of the father low. If either a mother or a poor district succeeded in securing an order under the act, the amount of money was likely to be small and difficult to collect from uncooperative fathers. In most of the province, there were few prosecutions under the act by the 1940s.[117]

As early as 1930, the *Nova Scotia Illegitimate Children's Act* was recognized as the most backward legislation of its kind in the country.[118] Blois, prodded by Canadian Welfare Council leaders, made several attempts to draft new legislation but there was no concentrated push from within the province to get a new law until 1945–46—at the height of the IMH scandal. In late 1945 and early 1946, MacKinnon was corresponding with Lea at the Canadian Welfare Council, seeking her advice on the drafting of a new *Unmarried Parents Act* which would, among other things, treat the unmarried mother more gently in filiation proceedings and place her interests above those of the poor district.[119] MacKinnon hoped, in vain, to get the new legislation through the legislature in 1946. In the fall of 1946, the cause of reform was strengthened when the Child Welfare Division of the Halifax Council of Social Agencies, a group in which MacKinnon was quite influential, began work on its own draft bill. The Council hoped that through study and publicity it would be able to "create interest locally in the passing of a new act" much as it had been able, earlier in the decade, to consolidate support for the *Adoption Act*.[120] At the same time, the newly formed Nova Scotia Association of Children's Aid Societies began a similar study.[121]

The fight to get a new act through the legislature was long and bitter and the new *Children of Unmarried Parents Act* was not passed until 1951. As MacKinnon predicted, it was difficult to build public support for a better deal for unwed mothers—support which was needed to prod legislators. There were even serious divisions within the professional reform community. Reformers at the Halifax Council of Social Agencies felt that the bill supported by the Nova Scotia Association of Children's Aid Societies was still marked by an attitude of condemnation toward the unmarried mother. They were pleased when legislation passed in 1951 "more nearly resembled" the Council of Social Agencies' vision.[122] The most important features of the new bill placed the mother's claim first in the collection of payments from the father; there was no provision for the overseers of the poor (or anyone else) to initiate action on behalf of the poor district. Other changes increased the amount of money a court could order the father to pay in a lump sum (from $500 to $1,500) and made provisions for the court to order regular payments for maintenance until the child turned 16. Court proceedings under the Act were closed to the public, but the director of Child Welfare was given the option to attend, give evidence and call witnesses in these proceedings.[123]

These were significant advances, but any advance toward "social care" of the unwed mother was implied rather than required, and the potential awards to mothers were still relatively small and often difficult to collect.[124] In many cases, the mothers did not have direct control over the funds these proceedings secured. The court designated "a person who in the opinion of the magistrate is capable of applying the money properly and can be relied upon to do so." This "responsible person" could be the mother, but the wording of the act (along with discussions leading up to the legislation) permitted alternatives.[125] With the poor law still in place, women who needed additional help still faced local condemnation and restrictions on their choices. In the mid-1950s, overseers of the poor in Lunenburg County were still known to use the threat of incarceration in the poor house to force single mothers to surrender their children for adoption or to support them in specific boarding placements. MacKinnon and other supporters of the new legislation felt, however, that the new legislation represented a recognition of problems with the poor law system and a step toward its demise. MacKinnon, celebrating the new *Unmarried Parents Act* described the old act as "a companion piece" of the *Poor Relief Act*. Halifax City Solicitor Carl Bethune called the new act a "tremendous improvement from the point of view of municipalities," and added "I hope it might be a forerunner to an attempt to do a job on the Poor Relief Act."[126]

MacKinnon, like most leaders in his profession, believed that enacting laws and regulations was only the first step to improving social welfare services; new regulatory regimes would have limited effect unless they were implemented by trained social work professionals. During the same period that MacKinnon was fighting the IMH, he was working with the small group of professionally trained or oriented social workers and administrators in the province to found the Maritime School of Social Work. The school opened its doors in 1941, and expanded through the decade. In the early 1940s, MacKinnon also instituted regular training seminars for the (mostly untrained) Children's Aid workers around the province.[127]

The IMH, at the very least, gave MacKinnon an extra argument in favour of complementing the new legislation with increased training and a platform from which to promote new, higher professional standards in child welfare. He received support in this effort from national child welfare leaders at the Canadian Welfare Council. In late 1945, MacKinnon invited Lea to Halifax to conduct a training institute with rural child welfare workers on the topic of adoption, noting that "As far as adoption is concerned—we have had three years of experience here with the amended Act and the whole field is an interesting one, especially in view of the activities of the Institution at Chester." A few months later (in the midst of the IMH court cases) MacKinnon told another Canadian Welfare Council worker that "current interest in the prosecution of the Ideal Maternity Home" was leading to increased interest in the province in the "socially acceptable types of care for the unmarried mother."[128] At this point, MacKinnon's boss, Blois, had already invited Maud Morlock, the United States' Children's Bureau expert on adoption and work with unmarried mothers, to headline the June 1946 Canadian Conference on Social Work meeting in Halifax. Morlock came to Halifax with Lea. Together, the two led a series of well-attended seminars on adoption, maternity boarding houses, and work with unwed mothers in which they emphasized the importance of professional training for social workers. The IMH was the (almost literal) backdrop for these discussions.[129]

Not everyone appreciated the effort MacKinnon and like-minded colleagues devoted to the effort to professionalize child welfare in Nova Scotia. The push for professionalization was closely tied to the increased assertion of provincial authority in child welfare and for some this was a threatening, or at least unwelcome, development. Traditionally, provincial authorities had little authority over the Children's Aid Societies which did most of the day-to-day child welfare work in communities around the province. MacKinnon's reform agenda was interpreted as an effort to assert central control over the children's aid system and replace or upgrade the "amateur" workers who had staffed the Children's Aid Societies for years or even decades.[130] Background grumblings spilled into open revolt at the 1946 conference of the Nova Scotia Association of Children's Aid Societies when Cape Breton social worker Elizabeth Torrey attacked Blois and MacKinnon, complaining of "undue interference" by the provincial government in the work of the local Children's Aid Societies. Torrey pointed to the recent amendments of the adoption act (a direct outcome of the IMH scandal) as a prime example of provincial encroachment on local territory.[131] The dispute was ugly and well publicized, but Torrey and her supporters were not in the majority. The same conference passed one resolution "to the effect that the conference wished to cooperate with the Department of Public Welfare" and another commending "the Attorney-General's Department in prosecuting a maternity home for infractions against the Maternity Boarding Houses Act of 1940." These prosecutions, of course, depended on the work that MacKinnon, Blois, and Davis had done to strengthen the authority of the province with respect to adoption and maternity boarding houses. Torrey was correct, however, in her intimation that ever greater levels of provincial control over the Children's Aid Societies were in the offing. In 1950, the *Children's Protection Act* was amended to institute a "grading system" where provincial grants to the Children's Aid Societies were tied to a provincial assessment of the standards and practices of each society.[132]

The connections between the IMH, the Unmarried Parents Act, and the push to professionalize and centralize child welfare work in Nova Scotia are not as obvious as the ties between the IMH scandal and earlier regulatory reform. The IMH debate, though, drew attention to deficiencies in the social services and legal protection provided to unmarried mothers in Nova Scotia, and helped create momentum for new legislation. Similarly, the IMH scandal created obvious centres of interest for professional training, thus reinforcing MacKinnon's pre-existing commitment to "professionalize" child welfare in Nova Scotia. Directly and indirectly, the IMH scandal served as a vehicle to expand state and professional authority in Nova Scotia.

The IMH scandal had implications that extended beyond the development of social policy in Nova Scotia. The adopted children went to families across eastern Canada and, especially, the northeastern United States, and child welfare authorities in these jurisdictions also had an interest in the standards and practices of the Home. The IMH, and the larger cross-border "traffic in babies" of which it was a part, presented a social problem that crossed borders and ignored the neat divisions between units of governmental jurisdiction. Bureaucrats and social welfare reformers both inside and outside of Nova Scotia knew that controlling the baby trade from Canada to the United States required reforming adoption practices in Canadian provinces and American states, as well as developing new co-operative mechanisms that could link provincial, state and national governments in a common effort.[133]

At this international level the IMH worked as a catalyst for reform in much the same way as it did within Nova Scotia. The IMH, as an example of tragedy and exploitation, was a powerful weapon in the hands of reformers seeking to modernize adoption in both countries and to prompt reluctant legislators to tighten adoption regulations. In the United States, the IMH case, along with other instances of cross-border adoption, led the Children's Bureau to convene interstate conferences on the problem of the state-to-state transfer of children, as well as the transfer of children from Canada and the United States. In Canada, the IMH helped put interprovincial and international protocols for adoption placement on the agenda of the provincial directors of child welfare and of the Canadian Welfare Council's Committee on Adoption in the 1950s.[134]

Canadian Welfare Council and United States Children's Bureau officials used their national networks to collect information on the IMH operation and then passed this "evidence" of wrongdoing and/or dangerous practices to Blois and MacKinnon in Nova Scotia.[135] Throughout the 1940s, Canadian Welfare Council officials offered advice and consultation on the reform of Nova Scotia's laws and also tried (always discreetly) to push the Nova Scotians to take quicker and more decisive action against the IMH.[136] The Canadian Welfare Council applied similar pressure to politicians and social welfare bureaucrats in the neighbouring provinces of New Brunswick and Prince Edward Island in 1945 and 1946. Lea successfully used the IMH scandal to leverage long-desired adoption reform in New Brunswick. New adoption regulations enacted in late 1945 made it more difficult for adoption operators from other provinces (including the IMH) to process quick adoptions through the New Brunswick courts. In 1946, the province passed its first formal adoption law, which took effect in 1947. In 1945, Prince Edward Island officials heeded a warning from Lea that they must tighten adoption regulations to avoid becoming the next "funnel" for IMH adoptions once New Brunswick enacted reforms.[137]

The tragedy of the IMH is most often thought of as a black mark on the history of social welfare in Nova Scotia and there is great justification for this view. But the tale of exploitation and of cruelly limited options that lie at the heart of the IMH saga, and the experience of "closing the IMH," helped to jump-start important short-term and long-term reforms of social policy in the province. The shape of these reforms had much to do with the professionalizing and state-building priorities of MacKinnon, who was early in his career when these events took place. When Blois retired in 1948, MacKinnon became the acting deputy minister of welfare, with responsibilities which stretched beyond child welfare to the entire scope of social welfare services in the province. He remained as acting or permanent deputy minister for the next 32 years. How the case of the IMH affected MacKinnon's professional outlook and subsequent developments in social policy in the province requires further research. In the aftermath of the IMH tragedy, important changes in the organization and supervision of child welfare in the province helped to remove some of the worst abuses of the older system. It is not clear, however, whether the closing of the IMH and the related regulatory reforms really improved the situation of unwed mothers, their children, or adoptive parents.

Notes

1. *Ideal Maternity Home: No Publicity—Mothers Refuge*, 1944, MG 100. vol. 100. file 59, Public Archives of Nova Scotia [PANS]. Research for this paper was supported generously by the Social Science and Humanities Research Council of Canada through the Doctoral Fellowship Program, and by grants from the American Historical Association, the New York State Archives

and Records Administration, and the Graduate School at Rutgers University. I am grateful to Alice Kessler-Harris, Kathleen Brown, Danny Samson. Gail Campbell and the anonymous reviewers of *Acadiensis* for comments on earlier versions of this paper. Suzanne Morton and Shirley Tillotson gave me permission to cite their work-in-progress, and discussions with both helped me refine this paper. Various members of the support group the Friends and Survivors of the Ideal Maternity Home in Canada and in the United States agreed to share their personal stories and their private documents with me.

2. Through 1936–44, the ratio of births out of wedlock to live births in Nova Scotia never dropped below 6 per cent, while no other Canadian province recorded a rate above 5 per cent. In 1945, the out-of-wedlock birth rate in Nova Scotia rose to a peak of 7.9 per cent—or 1,228 births—against a national average still well below 5 per cent. See George Davidson, *Report on Public Welfare Services in Nova Scotia*, Royal Commission on Provincial Development and Rehabilitation. Volume 4 (Halifax, 1944), p. 153; Number of Illegitimate Live Births and Percentage of all Births in Canada by Province, 1926–48. MG 28 I10, vol. 60, file 491, National Archives of Canada [NAC]. On contemporary attempts to explain the province's comparatively high rate of out-of-wedlock births, see Suzanne Morton, "Nova Scotia and Its Unmarried Mothers, 1945–75," in Michael Gauvreau and Nancy Christie, eds., *On the Margins of the Family* (Montreal and Kingston, 2004).

3. "Evidence Heard in Maternity Home Case," *Halifax Herald,* 2 May 1946; Bette Cahill, *Butterbox Babies: Baby Sales, Baby Deaths and the Scandalous Story of the Ideal Maternity Home* (Toronto, 1992), p. 116: William Young to Mr. Morris, 19 July 1945, MG 28 I10, vol. 45, file 405 (1941–45), NAC: Young to Mr. and Mrs. Barnes, 18 September 1945, Archival Collection of Author [ACA]; Fred MacKinnon, interview with author, 3 December 1993.

4. See testimonials, especially from Senator William Duff, in *The Child of Today is to Become the Man or Woman of Tomorrow,* 1944, RG 25, series C, vol. 9, file 7, Petition, 22 November 1945, MG 2, vol. 897, file 17-1/3, PANS.

5. See, for example, MacKinnon to Young, 7 November 1945, RG 39, series C, vol. 934, SC13226, PANS.

6. Mavis Gallant, "Traders in Fear: Baby Farm Rackets Still Lure Girls Who Are Afraid of Social Agencies," *Montreal Standard,* 31 August 1946, copy in MG 100, vol. 87, file 18, PANS.

7. On the impact of Blois, see Fred MacKinnon, *The Life and Times of Ernest Blois* (Halifax, 1992); *Annual Report of the Director of Child Welfare for 1943* (Halifax, 1944). On MacKinnon, see "Three Nova Scotians among Order of Canada Inductees," *Halifax Mail-Star,* 25 June 1992.

8. The institutional affiliations of the key players changed over the course of this study. Frank Davis was first appointed Nova Scotia's minister of public health in 1933, while Ernest Blois served, at this time, as the director of child welfare. From 1939–44, MacKinnon was the assistant director of child welfare. In 1944, the Department of Public Health was re-organized as the Department of Public Welfare, and Davis became minister of public welfare, Blois became deputy minister of public welfare and MacKinnon was appointed director of child welfare. For clarity, I have used the titles in place from 1944 throughout this paper.

9. Janet Guildford, "Closing the Mansions of Woe: The End of the Poor Law in Nova Scotia, 1944–65," (paper presented at the Canadian Historical Association Conference, St. John's, Newfoundland, June 1997); Davidson, *Report on Public Welfare Services*, pp. 104–09, 122–26.

10. As Shirley Tillotson has recently argued, "large transformations in political culture are lived out in a myriad of apparently petty struggles, and engage their participants in power relations at multiple levels, from the interpersonal to the institutional to the ideological." See Tillotson, "'Too Much Planning in Secret': Publicity and Democracy in Child Welfare, 1925–1952," in Judith Fingard and Janet Guildford, eds., Mothers of the Municipality: Women in Halifax, 1945–2000 (2004).

11. The docudrama *Butterbox Babies* (Sullivan Entertainment, 1994) portrays MacKinnon as crusader who ignored bureaucratic protocol, pressured his superiors and risked his job in the effort to shut down the IMH. This is a highly inaccurate picture. My portrait of MacKinnon's personality is drawn from Bette Cahill's discussion of MacKinnon in the book *Butterbox Babies*, my interview with MacKinnon in 1993 and my reading hundreds of pages of MacKinnon's

correspondence, speeches, and articles found in the archival collections of the Department of Community Services and the Angus L. Macdonald papers at PANS, the Canadian Council on Social Development papers at NAC and the library of the Nova Scotia Department of Community Services in Halifax. See also Tillotson, "'Too much planning in secret.'"

12. James Struthers, *The Limits of Affluence: Welfare in Ontario, 1920–1970* (Toronto, 1994), p. 274.

13. MacKinnon was a case worker for the Children's Aid Society in Colchester County in the late 1930s. Blois recruited MacKinnon to provincial service and arranged for the younger man to receive a Rockefeller Foundation Scholarship to finance his studies in Chicago. MacKinnon then committed to a profession (social work) and a subfield (child welfare) that was numerically dominated by women. Historians of social welfare in the United States and Canada have noted that larger numbers of men moved into the social work field as the expanding welfare state created new, relatively well-paid positions in the administration of large social welfare agencies and government programs. See MacKinnon interview; James Struthers, "'Lord Give Us Men': Women and Social Work in English Canada. 1918–1953," in Allan Muscovitch and Jim Albert, eds., *The Benevolent State: The Growth of Welfare in Canada* (Toronto, 1987), pp. 126–43; R.L. Schnell, "Female Separatism and Institution Building: Continuities and Discontinuities in Canadian Child Welfare, 1913–1935," *International Journal of History and Political Science* 25, 2 (1988), pp. 14–40; Cynthia Commachio, *Nations Are Built of Babies: Saving Ontario's Mothers and Children, 1900–1940* (Montreal and Kingston, 1993), pp. 4, 238. Tillotson describes "gendered shifts in authority" in the developing welfare state with specific reference to MacKinnon and developments in Halifax in "'Too much planning in secret.'" For an introduction to the voluminous American literature on gender, professional authority and the welfare state, see Robyn Muncy, *Creating a Female Dominion in American Reform* (New York, 1991); Linda Gordon, *Pitied but not Entitled: Single Mothers and the History of Welfare, 1890–1935* (New York, 1994). Regina Kunzel describes these issues with specific reference the history of unmarried mothers and adoption in *Fallen Women, Problem Girls: Unmarried Mothers and the Professionalization of Social Work, 1890–1940* (New Haven, 1993).

14. From a broader perspective, this problem-solution dyad, which promised to "fix" social problems through the application of bureaucratic control and professional expertise was an important dynamic in the development of welfare state programs at the provincial and federal level across Canada. This dynamic appears to have been more influential in the field of child welfare than in the field of income support (i.e., unemployment insurance and old age pensions) where the expansion of the welfare state was so closely linked to fiscal and constitutional negotiations between the provinces and the federal government. For a thorough and well-balanced analysis of the myriad factors (including the professionalizing/state building impulse) feeding the development of the Canadian welfare state, see Struthers, *The Limits of Affluence*, pp. 3–17, 126–35, 261–75. See also James Struthers, *No Fault of Their Own: Unemployment and the Canadian Welfare State, 1914–1941* (Toronto, 1983); Dennis Guest, *The Emergence of Social Security in Canada* (Vancouver, 1985): Margaret Jane Hillyard Little, *"No Car, No Radio, No Liquor Permit": The Moral Regulation of Single Mothers in Ontario* (Toronto, 1999); Muscovitch and Albert, *The Benevolent State*; Nancy Christie, *Engendering the State: Family, Work and Welfare in Canada* (Toronto, 2000). For works which focus on child welfare systems, see Commachio, *Nations Are Built of Babies*; Patricia Rooke and R.L. Schnell, *Discarding the Asylum: From Child Welfare to the Welfare State in English Canada 1800–1950* (Lanham, Maryland, 1983); Neil Sutherland, *Children in English Canadian Society* (Toronto, 1976).

15. Cahill, *Butterbox Babies*. Under the adoption transfer plan, expectant mothers paid the Youngs $300 ($350 if they did not sign the transfer document until after the birth) to place their children for adoption and care for them until the adoption placement. The mothers often understood the adoption transfer agreement as a legally binding, formal consent to adoption, but the document was not a legal instrument for this purpose. See Ideal Maternity Home and Sanatorium Limited Price List, undated (1944), RG 39, series C, vol. 934, SC13226, PANS; Cahill, *Butterbox Babies*, p. 82.

16. The adoption placement fee seems to have been a unique IMH innovation. The issue of fees charged to the women is complicated. Undoubtedly, there were homes which charged more

than the IMH for board and medical care and most homes charged boarding fees for children until they were adopted or removed from the home by the birth mother. But as Rickie Solinger points out, commercial maternity homes which charged parents fees for arranging adoption (or engaged in the outright selling of babies) usually attracted pregnant women by offering them free care in exchange for their children. See Solinger, *Wake Up Little Suzy: Single Pregnancy and Race Before Roe v. Wade* (New York, 1992), pp. 177–86.

17. Historians of adoption date a rapidly rising demand for infant children to adopt, and hence the appearance of an adoption marketplace where there was a distinct "shortage" of some kinds of children, from the late 1930s. The adoption marketplace was segregated by race; the demand was very specifically for white children. The IMH took in only white mothers, and children born "not white" were excluded from the adoption transfer plan. See Transfer Agreement, 1944, RG 39, series C, vol. 934, SC13226, PANS; Rickie Solinger, "Race and Value: Black and White Illegitimate Babies, in the USA, 1945–1965," *Gender and History* 4, 3 (Autumn 1992), pp. 343–63; Kunzel, *Fallen Women, Problem Girls*, pp. 144–70: Julie Berebitsky, *Like Our Very Own: Adoption and the Changing Culture of Motherhood, 1851–1950* (Lawrence, Kansas, 2000), pp. 9–11, 128–29, 168–69.

18. A wealthy New Jersey couple told Cahill they paid nearly $10,000 to an IMH lawyer in connection with the adoption of their son and Cahill cites other examples of families who paid between $1,000 and $3,000. MacKinnon suspected the standard fee was between $800 and $1,000. See Cahill, *Butterbox Babies*, pp. 111–13, 122; IMH, 3 April 1946, MG 28 I10, vol. 45, file 405 (1946), NAC; Sarah Scott to Maud Morlock, 1 November 1945, RG 102, series 3B, 1949–52, box 445, file 7-3-1-3, (January-May 1949), United States National Archives [USNA], Washington. Pictures of the Youngs' new buildings and grounds dominated a glossy brochure on the IMH first distributed in 1944. See *The Child of Today is to Become the Man or Woman of Tomorrow*, 1944, RG 25, series C, vol. 9, file 7; Petition. 22 November 1945, MG 2, vol. 897, file 17-1/3, PANS.

19. Advertisement copy attached to William P. Young to Manager, Classified Advertising the *Elizabeth Daily Journal* (New Jersey), 6 November 1944, MG 28 I10, vol. 45, file 405 (1941–45), NAC. Such advertisements were illegal under New Jersey law. See Ellen Potter to Morlock, 17 May 1945, RG 102, series 3B, box 445, file 7-3-1-3, USNA.

20. Often religious matching regulations appeared in the *Children's Protection Act* as well as, or instead of, the *Adoption Act*. In both Canada and the United States, religious placement laws had their origin in the legal standard of ensuring the "best interests of the child," but also in earlier debates about the existence and funding of Protestant and Catholic public schools and social welfare institutions. In both countries, these laws were challenged in the 1950s and in most jurisdictions religious matching became discretionary (though still influential) instead of mandatory. See "Survey of New Jersey Adoption Law," *Rutgers Law Review*, XVII, 2 (Winter 1962), pp. 410–15; Laura Schwartz, "Religious Matching for Adoption: Unravelling the Interests Behind the 'Best Interests' Standard," *Family Law Quarterly* XXV, 2 (Summer 1991), pp. 171–92; David Dehler, "Church and State: The Problem of Interfaith Adoption in Ontario," *Revue de l'univeristé d'Ottawa* 36, 1 (1966), pp. 66–85. On the appeal of the IMH to Jewish families in the United States, see Rose Weinheimer to Nora Lea, 21 August 1946, MG 28 I10, vol. 45, file 405 (1946), NAC. For the role of religious matching laws and traditions in creating a "surplus" of Catholic children in Quebec and its impact on cross-border adoptions from Quebec into the Northeastern United States, see Karen Balcom, "'The Traffic in Babies': Cross-Border Adoption, Baby-Selling and the Development of Child Welfare Systems in the United States and Canada, 1930–1960," Ph.D. dissertation, Rutgers University, 2002.

21. The *Nova Scotia Children's Protection Act* specified that Protestant children could not be placed in Roman Catholic institutions or "in any family the head of which is a Roman Catholic," and also made the reverse stipulation. But the Act referred only to neglected and dependent children taken into care, and this did not apply to the children born at the IMH. In addition, this law made no mention of religious identities other than Protestantism and Roman Catholicism. See *Statutes of Nova Scotia*, c. 166, s. 30, 1923. On the IMH argument against religious matching, see Charles Longley to Potter, 31 August 1945, RG 102, series 3B, box 445, file 7-3-1-3,

USNA. On lies to parents, see Scott to Blois, 13 August 1945, RG 102, series 3B, 1949-52, box 445, file 7-3-1-3 (January-May 1949), USNA.

22. Couples were required to produce 12 notarized documents (11 of which pertained to the family's financial standing) along with the names of two people who *could be* contacted as character references. The financial documents were required to obtain the American entry visa. See Longley to Mrs. Pippos, 26 February 1945, MG 28 I10, vol. 45, file 405 (1941–45), NAC: Robert Hartlen, *Butterbox Survivors: Life After the Ideal Maternity Home* (Halifax, 1999), p. 21.

23. As Solinger and Kunzel point out, the *realistic* options presented to women by social workers varied over time. Early in the century, women pregnant out of wedlock were pressured to keep their children. By the 1940s, there was tremendous pressure on white women (and white women only) to relinquish their children for adoption. See Solinger, *Wake Up Little Suzy*, pp. 148–204; Kunzel, *Fallen Women, Problem Girls*, pp. 144–70. On options for women pregnant out of wedlock in Nova Scotia, see Morton, "Nova Scotia and its Unmarried Mothers."

24. These principles were laid out for Canadian social workers in Canadian Welfare Council, *Essentials in Adoption Service* (Ottawa, 1944). The equivalent American publication, produced by the United States Children's Bureau, was widely available in Canada both in its early draft form (1944) and later (1949) as a formal Bureau publication. Over time, adoption reformers shortened the recommended period for observing and testing the newborn infant before placement, but the standard in the 1940s was three to four months. See United States Children's Bureau. *Essentials in Adoption Practice* (Washington, 1949); *Preliminary Draft of Essentials of Adoption Law and Procedures*, December 1945, RG 102, series 3B, 1945–48, box 191, file 10-12-5 (January-June 1945), USNA. See also, Berebitsky, *Like Our Very Own*, pp. 128–65; E. Wayne Carp, *Family Matters: Secrecy and Disclosure in the History of Adoption* (Cambridge, 1998), pp. 15–35.

25. Lea to Potter, 10 August 1945, RG 102, series 3B, 1945–48, box 154, file 7-3-1-3 (August-December 1947), USNA.

26. In 1945, Morlock of the United States Children's Bureau explained the professional objection to distance placement and international adoptions in an article prompted by the developing IMH scandal. See Maud Morlock, "Chosen Children," *Canadian Welfare*, 15 April 1945, pp. 3–8.

27. Significantly, nationalist objections to the "export" of Canadian babies did not feature prominently in complaints against the Youngs, although child welfare leaders did worry that adopting parents might not take the necessary steps to secure American citizenship for their new children. In other cases, notably the Alberta "Babies-for-Export" scandal uncovered by Charlotte Whitton in 1947, Canadian social welfare leaders and politicians made much more of Canada's "loss" of future citizens and the children's "right" to their Canadian heritage. See Patricia Rooke and R.L. Schnell, "Charlotte Whitton Meets 'The Last Best West': The Politics of Child Welfare in Alberta, 1929–49," *Prairie Forum* 6, 2 (Fall 1981), pp. 143–63; Charlotte Whitton, "Better Controls for Baby Adoption Needed When Babies Cross Borders," *Saturday Night* 63, 36 (June 12, 1948), pp. 6–7.

28. Cahill relied largely on interviews with local residents in Chester and former employees of the Home. Her strongest testimony comes from a handyman who worked at the Home and who recalled burying large numbers of children. I did not talk to any of Cahill's interviewees (with the exception of MacKinnon) and relied instead on correspondence and records about the IMH case located in Canadian and American archives. I found no references to the Youngs as deliberate mass murderers of children, even in records produced by the Youngs' harshest critics. See Cahill, *Butterbox Babies*, pp. 225–27.

29. Ruth Bremmer to State Department of Social Welfare, 29 November 1945. RG 102, series 3B, box 445, file 7-3-1-3, USNA.

30. Davidson's reference to poor sanitary conditions and infant deaths at "epidemic proportions" may help to explain rumours about the murder of children at the Home. See Davidson quoted in Lea to Jane Rinck, 31 May 1945, RG 102, series 3B. 1945–48, box 154, file 7-3-1-3 (August-December 1947), USNA. This passage was edited out of Davidson's published report.

31. On the 1935 manslaughter trial, see Cahill, *Butterbox Babies*, pp. 35–41.

32. By 1941, five Canadian provinces (British Columbia, Alberta, Saskatchewan, Manitoba and Ontario) had adoption laws which gave provincial authorities some authority to compel and

oversee adoption investigations. By 1939, state departments of social welfare in the United States held similar authority in 11 states. The 1940s were a critical decade in the reform of adoption laws in both countries. See Agnes Hanna to Charlotte Whitton, 24 March 1941, MG 28 I10, vol. 45, 405 (1941–45), NAC; Mary Ruth Colby, *Problems and Procedures in Adoption* (Washington, 1941). On the need for legislation to control private hospitals in Nova Scotia, see Davidson, *Report on Public Welfare in Nova Scotia*, pp. 19–20, 157–58.

33. In the case of one New Jersey family which adopted two children from the IMH, the official story was that the (supposedly pregnant) adoptive mother deliberately traveled from urban New Jersey to rural Nova Scotia for the quality obstetrical care available at the IMH, twice. Another story which recurs within IMH families is that of the (supposedly) heavily pregnant (adoptive) mother who accompanied her husband on a fishing trip to Nova Scotia and was then forced to give birth at the IMH. The best source on changing attitudes toward secrecy and openness in adoption over the course of the 20th century is Carp, *Family Matters*. On IMH cover stories, see David William Vosburgh (born Rex McBride, named unchanged at informant's request), interview with author, April 1997; Hartlen, *Butterbox Survivors*, p. 208.

34. *Ideal Maternity Home—No Publicity—Mothers' Refuge*, undated, MG 100, vol. 54, file 59, PANS.

35. In Nova Scotia and elsewhere, commercial maternity homes offered unwed mothers-to-be the protection of secrecy without the moral condemnation or rehabilitative programs which came with maternity home care under the control of churches or professional social workers. On the appeal of the commercial maternity homes, see Solinger, *Wake Up Little Suzy*, pp. 177–86; Kunzel, *Fallen Women, Problem Girls*, p. 70. On the priorities of Canadian women seeking maternity home care, see Anne Petrie, *Gone to An Aunt's: Remembering Canada's Homes for Unwed Mothers* (Toronto, 1998); Andrée Lévesque, "Deviants Anonymous: Single Mothers at the Hôpital de la Misericorde in Montreal, 1929–1939," in Katherine Arnup, ed., *Delivering Motherhood* (London, 1990), pp. 108–25.

36. For positive and negative personal recollections from several women who gave birth at the IMH, see Hartlen, *Butterbox Survivors*, pp. 2–28. One of the women in Hartlen's sample noted that when she decided to keep her baby she was told by the Youngs that the child was dead. She also reported, however, that "other than lying to us about our babies, the Youngs could have treated us a lot worse," p. 14. A negative account from a woman who gave birth at the Home can be found in "'Never Heard So Many Lies, Lila': Mothers, Character Witnesses Take Up Third Day of $25,000 Libel Suit," *Halifax Chronicle*, 14 May 1947.

37. Quotation from Davidson, *Public Welfare in Nova Scotia*, pp. 156, 160.

38. Excerpts From Dr. Davidson's Memo Re: Nova Scotia, no date, MG 28 I10, vol. 216, file 13, NAC; Davidson to R. MacGregor Dawson. 22 March 1944, MS 2, vol. 256, file F.I.C.39, Dalhousie University Archives [DUA]; Lea to Rinck, 31 May 1945, RG 102, series 3B, 1945–48, box 154, file 7-3-1-3 (August–December 1947), USNA.

39. Davidson, *Report on Public Welfare Services*, p. 19.

40. My argument is not that Davidson provided a blueprint for changes in the province which was then followed by provincial officials, but rather that his report laid out an argument and a logic around the IMH which mirrored and supported developments already under way in the province. See MacKinnon. *Life and Times of Ernest Blois*, pp. 23–24.

41. Deputy Minister Blois disagreed with Davidson's criticisms of provincial practice with respect to the administration of pensions, hospitals and care for mentally handicapped children, though he felt "bound to say that with many of [Davidson's] recommendations, but by no means all," he was "heartily in agreement." MacKinnon recalls that Blois was reluctant to enact many of Davidson's suggestions and that the main recommendations concerning the poor law system could not be implemented until federal-provincial fiscal relationships were renegotiated. The closest ties between Davidson's recommendations and provincial action came in the child welfare practices touched by the IMH scandal. See Blois to Davidson, 29 March 1944, 5 April 1944, MS 2, vol. 256, F.I.C.39, DUA; MacKinnon, *Life and Times of Ernest Blois*, pp. 23–24. On Davidson's overall assessment of the province's public welfare services, see Guildford, "Closing the Mansions of Woe." On the generally disappointed reaction to the Dawson Royal

Commission report as a whole, see J. Murray Beck, *The Politics of Nova Scotia, Vol. 2, Murray-Buchanan, 1896-1988* (Tantallon, Nova Scotia, 1988), pp. 199-200.

42. MacKinnon interview. See also MacKinnon, *Life and Times of Ernest Blois*, pp. 23-24.

43. Since IMH adoptions were already approved by local courts, this provision had little impact. See *Statutes of Nova Scotia*, c. 9, 1940.

44. This explanation is supported by Cahill's interviews with MacKinnon, in which MacKinnon expressed some discomfort with the decision to grant the Youngs a licence. See Cahill, *Butterbox Babies*, pp. 80-1. In 1946, the Youngs' supporters at the Chester Board of Trade would argue that since the Youngs were first granted and then denied a licence there was proof of a capricious persecution of the couple by provincial officials. See Report of the Chester Board of Trade, 5 July 1946, MG 2, vol. 897, file 17-1/14, PANS. Local businessmen had obvious financial reasons for supporting the home. What other motivations may have influenced their position are not clear, but ongoing research by Danny Samson and Erik Kristianson suggests possible connections between the Home, the wide-spread popularity of eugenic ideas in the province and the development of provincial welfare policy.

45. *Ideal Maternity Home*, 1942, MG 100, vol. 100, file 59, PANS.

46. Section 13 of the *Maternity Boarding Houses Act*, mentions specific institutions operating in the province (Halifax Infants Home, Home of the Guardian Angel, Mercy Hospital) and grants a blanket exemption to "incorporated institutions." See Notes for Reply to Robin Hennigar, 25 February 1946, MG 2, vol. 897, file 17-1/1, PANS.

47. The Youngs retained control of the new corporation, holding all but the three shares which were distributed Senator Duff and Chester businessmen Philip Moore and Robin Hennigar. See Hennigar to Angus L. Macdonald, 16 February 1946, MG 2, vol. 897, file 17-1/2. PANS.

48. Davidson recommended that the incorporation provision be repealed and also argued that the province needed to pass new legislation giving it authority over private hospitals. See Davidson, *Report on Public Welfare in Nova Scotia*, pp. 66, 157, 377.

49. Davidson, *Report on Public Welfare in Nova Scotia*, p. 150; *Statutes of Nova Scotia*, c. 18, 1939.

50. Lea to Rinck, 31 May 1945, RG 102, series 3B, 1945-48, box 154, file 7-3-1-3 (August-December 1947), USNA; Davidson, *Report on Public Welfare Services*, p. 151.

51. Toward this end, the Youngs acquired a new partner, Saint John attorney Benjamin Guss. As pressure mounted in Nova Scotia, Guss became more and more important. In 1946, he urged the Youngs, to no avail, to move the IMH to New Brunswick. After the IMH closed, Guss became an independent operator, building up his own black market baby business out of Saint John, New Brunswick. See Longley to Mr. and Mrs. Barnes, 26 February 1945; Sarah Jones [IMH nurse] to Mrs. Barnes, 26 March 1947, ACA: John B. McNair to Louis St. Laurent, 16 March 1948. RG 25, vol. 3937, file 9463-40 (1947-49), NAC.

52. Until the late 1940s, New Brunswick did not have an *Adoption Act* and adoptions were processed under regulations contained in the *Judicature Act*. See *Statutes of New Brunswick*, c. 113, 1927, order 56, rules 56-62; amend. 1943, order 56, rule 58, 1944, order 56, rule 57. See also Canadian Welfare Council, *The Adoption Laws of the Canadian Provinces* (Ottawa, 1946), pp. 18-20.

53. Young to "Dear Friend," January 1945 and Young to Morris, 19 July 1945, MG 28 I10, vol. 45, file 405 (1941-45), NAC.

54. "Other pressures and protests have, of course, arisen in Nova Scotia, inspired by sources which, to say the least, have an interest in the problem which is not always identical with the interests of the children involved." See Davidson, *Report on Public Welfare Services*, p. 151.

55. Kunzel documents conflicts between professionally trained social workers and "amateur" charity workers, as well as conflicts between social workers, over the proper professional approach to the treatment of unwed mothers and their children. See Kunzel, *Fallen Women, Problem Girls*, pp. 36-64, 115-43.

56. For an example of popular criticism of sound adoption practice, see Edith Liggett, "Red Tape and Runaround in Adoption," *The Woman*, June 1946, pp. 29-32. Resistance to adoption reform is also discussed in Morlock, "Chosen Children." On the New Jersey grandmother, see Scott to Lea, 23 October 1945, MG 28 I10, vol. 45, file 405 (1941-45), NAC.

57. *The Child of Today is to Become the Man or Woman of Tomorrow*, 1944, RG25, series C, vol. 9, file 7, PANS. See also *Make Yours a Happy Home by Adopting a Baby*, no date, MG 100, vol. 54, file 59, PANS.

58. From 1930 to 1950 this organization was known as the Halifax Council of Social Agencies: afterwards it became the Halifax Welfare Council. Since most of my references to this group precede the change, I have used Halifax Council of Social Agencies throughout.

59. The Council recommended a stronger law than was eventually passed. In the Halifax Council of Social Agencies version, the director of child welfare had to give his consent before any adoption was finalized. Before giving this consent, the director had to prove that "the conduct of the applicant and the conditions under which the infant has lived have been such as to justify the making of the order." See Memorandum of the Council of Social Agencies Concerning the *Adoption Act*, undated (1943), MG 20, vol. 408, file 2.13; Division A, Child Welfare, Minutes, 18 November 1941, MG 20, vol. 408, file 2.5, PANS.

60. Division A, Child Welfare, Minutes, 31 January 1944, MG 20, vol. 408, file 2.20, PANS.

61. Director of Child Welfare, *Adoption of Children: Selections of Opinion from British. American and Canadian Sources* (Halifax, 1944). Davidson used a similar tactic throughout his report—building support for reform in Nova Scotia by comparing changes (or proposed changes) in the province to reforms already undertaken elsewhere in the Dominion. See Davidson, *Report on Public Welfare Services*, pp. 150, 155.

62. It is not clear how far this challenge went, or exactly where it was directed, but it certainly was taken seriously by the provincial reform community. There is no Hansard for the Nova Scotia legislature for this period, and published accounts of legislative debate during the spring 1944 session make no mention of the 1943 adoption reforms or possible opposition. See Minutes of the Child Welfare Division of the Halifax Council of Social Agencies, 21 February 1944, MG 20, vol. 408, file 3.1; *Annual Report of the Halifax Council of Social Agencies for 1945*, MG 20, vol. 47, file 1.41, PANS.

63. The Home's supporters among Chester businessmen charged that the RCMP investigations constituted a cruel and unwarranted invasion of the privacy of the IMH mothers. See Moore to Macdonald, undated (March 1946), MG 2, vol. 897, file 17-1/6, PANS. New Brunswick officials requested a similar investigation very soon thereafter. See Memorandum for the Secretary of State for External Affairs, 26 May 1948, RG 25, vol. 3937, file 9463-40, 1947–49, NAC. RCMP files on the New Brunswick and Nova Scotia investigations are no longer extant.

64. *Statutes of Nova Scotia*, c. 68, 1945.

65. MacKinnon to Young, 7 November 1945, RG 39, series C, vol. 934, file SC13226, PANS.

66. Davidson quoted in Lea to Rinck, 31 May 1945, RG 102, series 3B, 1945–48, box 154, file 7-3-1-3 (August-December 1947), USNA.

67. Davidson, *Report on Public Welfare Services*, p. 157; Comments Regarding Davidson Report, 5 April 1944, MS 2, vol. 256, file F.I.C.39, DUA; Davidson to Dawson, 14 April 1944, MS 2, vol. 256, file F.I.C.39, DUA.

68. Blois's contributions to social welfare in the province are outlined in MacKinnon. *The Life and Times of Ernest Blois*. For evidence of Blois's defensiveness see Blois to Whitton, 27 February 1930, Whitton to Blois, 20 January 1934, MG 28 I10, vol. 1, file 4, NAC.

69. Lea to Morlock, 14 August 1945, RG 102, series 3B, 1945–48, box 154, file 7-3-1-3 (August-December 1947), NAC.

70. The Liberal political affiliation of most of the Chester Board of Trade leadership was pointed out very clearly in a letter from the president of the board to Davis protesting the government's persecution of the IMH (and by extension the Chester business community). See Moore to Frank Davis, 26 November 1945, MG 2, vol. 897, file 17-1/7, PANS.

71. "Restore Democracy," 1945, MG 2, vol. 897, file 17-1/1A, PANS.

72. Ibid. The Youngs' campaign against Davis appears to have been their own project, but there were tantalizing ties to the larger Progressive Conservative campaign in the province. First, one of the Conservative candidates opposing Davis was Clifford E. Levy, a Chester lawyer who frequently worked for the Youngs and who served as clerk for the Chester Municipal Council. a body that stood staunchly in support of the Youngs. Second, the Youngs' attack on Davis

as a "dictator" granting unreasonable amounts of power to the bureaucrats who worked for him resonated well with the Progressive Conservative campaign plank criticizing the expanded authority and size of the provincial bureaucracy. See "A Message to the Voters of Lunenburg County," *Bridgewater Bulletin*, 17 October 1945; "The Dictators," *Halifax Herald*, 12 October 1945; "Preserving Liberty," *Halifax Mail*, 16 October 1945.

73. Young to Mr. and Mrs. Bendett, 18 September 1945, ACA.

74. "Minister of Health Answers Criticism Regarding Maternity Home," *Bridgewater Progress-Enterprise*, 17 October 1945; Macdonald to Moore, 22 March 1946, MG 2, vol. 897, file 17-1/5, PANS; MacKinnon interview.

75. In the end, many of Davidson's cuts were motivated by *his* fear that he might be sued by the Youngs. See Lea to Morlock, 14 August 1945, RG 102, series 3B (1945–48), box 154, file 7-3-1-3 (August–December 1947), USNA; Davidson to Dawson, 14 April 1944, 22 March 1944. MS 2, vol. 256, file F.I.C.39, DUA.

76. "Consider Carefully Before Voting," *Bridgewater Progress-Enterprise*, 17 October 1945: Cahill, *Butterbox Babies*, pp. 130, 134.

77. MacKinnon to Young, 7 November 1945, RG 39, series C, vol. 934, file SC13226, PANS.

78. Moore to Macdonald, [March 1946], MG 2, vol. 897, file 17-1/6, PANS. Moore, president of the Chester Board of Trade and a persistent champion of the Youngs, argued that the denominational maternity homes in Halifax and Sydney were specifically exempted from the 1945 Maternity Boarding Houses Act because they could never meet the standards the province required as a condition for licensing the IMH. See Moore to Macdonald, [March 1946], MG 2, vol. 897, file 17-1/6, PANS; MacKinnon interview.

79. Hennigar to Macdonald, 16 February 1946, MG 2, vol. 897, file 17-1/2; Petition, 22 November 1945, Resolution, 19 January 1946, MG 2, vol. 897, file 17-1/3; Report of the Chester Board of Trade, 5 July 1946, MG 2, vol. 897, file 17-1/14, PANS.

80. Moore to Macdonald, [March 1946], MG 2, vol. 897, file 17-1/6, PANS. Although Moore signed this document, there is evidence that it was written by Dr. Young.

81. Macdonald to Moore, 22 March 1946, MG 2, vol. 897, file 17-1/5; Notes for reply to Robin Hennigar, 25 February 1946, MG 2, vol. 897, file 17-1/1, PANS.

82. Young to Rachel Salman, 5 December 1945, ACA.

83. *Statutes of Nova Scotia*, c. 8, 1946.

84. Cahill, *Butterbox Babies*, pp. 35–41, 43–48; "Dr. and Mrs. Young Acquitted of Manslaughter Charges: Freed on All Counts," *Halifax Herald*, 29 May 1936.

85. The child died of a middle ear infection and blood poisoning. The jury decided that "the death of the child was due to natural causes." but also recommended "that conditions at the Ideal Maternity Home be investigated." See "Decide Death due to Natural Causes," *Halifax Herald*, 9 January 1942. Through the same period, the litigious Youngs launched several civil suits of their own seeking payment from their maternity home clients and contesting a land transaction. See vol. 841, series C, SC 5589, file 5590; vol. 62, file CC7285; vol. 84, file CC7793; vol. 889, file SC8455, PANS; Cahill, *Butterbox Babies*, pp. 47–48.

86. "Maternity Home Case Continues," *Halifax Herald*, 16 May 1946; "Counsel States Home to Close," *Halifax Chronicle*, 5 June 1946; Cahill, *Butterbox Babies*, pp. 150–1.

87. One conviction was for operating without a licence, one for unlawfully keeping mothers for gain and five for contracting illegal adoptions without complying with the terms of the Act. One additional charge under the *Maternity Boarding Houses Act*, which dealt with illegal advertising of children available for adoption, was dismissed and a final charge dealing with the unlawful boarding of children was dropped. See "Maternity Home is Convicted on Two Charges," *Halifax Herald*, 28 March 1946; "Ideal Will Appeal Two Decisions," *Halifax Herald*, 20 June 1946.

88. See, for example. "Maternity Home Faces 7 Charges," *Halifax Herald*, 21 March 1946; "Maternity Home Fined," *Halifax Herald*, 17 April 1946; "Evidence Heard in Maternity Case," *Halifax Herald*, 2 May 1946; "Ideal Will Appeal Two Decisions," *Halifax Chronicle*, 20 June 1946.

89. "Verbal Battle in Home Case: Magistrate Asks Mrs. Young 'Not to be so flip', Orders Lawyers to 'Sit Down'," *Halifax Chronicle*, 2 May 1946; "Ideal Home Perjury Case: Stenographer 'Only Vaguely' Remembers," *Halifax Chronicle*, 21 March 1947.

90. Lea to Scott, 25 April 1946 and Scott to Lea, 23 April 1946, telegram, 17 May 1946, Ideal Maternity Home, 3 April 1946, Memo of Discussion with Mr. MacKinnon, 2 April 1946, MG 28 I10, vol. 45, file 405 (1946), NAC.

91. "Counsel States Home to Close," Halifax Chronicle, 5 June 1946; MacKinnon to Lea, 12 June 1946, MG 28 I10, vol. 45, file 405 (1946), NAC.

92. MacKinnon to Lea, 12 June 1946, MG 28 I10, vol. 45, file 405 (1946), NAC; MacKinnon, The Life and Times of Ernest Blois, pp. 23–5.

93. Morlock to Lawrence Cole, 22 August 1946, MG 28 I10, vol. 45, file 405 (1946), NAC.

94. "Ideal Wins One, Loses 5 Appeals," Halifax Chronicle, 24 October 1946; "Guilty Plea to Two Charges," Halifax Chronicle, 22 March 1947; "Dr. Young Cleared of Perjury Charge: Judge is Critical of Decision of Petit Jurors in Case," Halifax Chronicle, 22 March 1947.

95. Gallant, "Traders in Fear."

96. "Open $25,000 Libel Suit," Halifax Chronicle, 9 May 1947; "Bury Babes in Butter Boxes: Interesting Testimony at Trial of Young $25,000 Libel Suit," Halifax Chronicle, 10 May 1947; "Says 'Took Rap for Wily Girl': Libel Suit Evidence Mentions Bad Smell at Chester," Halifax Chronicle, 13 May 1947; "'Never Heard So Many Lies, Lila': Mothers, Character Witnesses Take up Third Day of $25,000 Libel Suit," Halifax Chronicle, 14 May 1947; "$25.000 Libel Suit Dismissed by Court: Judge Compliments On Decision In Action Against Montreal Newspaper," 15 May 1947. The Halifax Herald used less sensational headlines, but presented even closer coverage of the trial. See "Libel Case Evidence Heard," 10 May 1947; "Further Evidence To be Taken in Libel Action," 12 May 1947; "Libel Action May Go To Jury This Afternoon," 13 May 1947; "Defense Closes Case in Libel Action at Halifax," 14 May 1947; "Decision in Libel Action Favours Publishing Company," 15 May 1947. See also Cahill, Butterbox Babies, pp. 159–89.

97. "Bury Babes in Butter Boxes: Interesting Testimony at Trial of Young $25,000 Libel Suit," Halifax Chronicle, 10 May 1947.

98. H.E. Kendall to W.R.J. O'Meara, 5 March 1947, RG 25, vol. 3937, file 9463-40 (1947–49), NAC.

99. Cahill, Butterbox Babies, p. 187; "'Never Heard So Many Lies, Lila': Mothers, Character Witnesses Take up Third day of $25,000 Libel Suit," Halifax Chronicle, 14 May 1947; MacKinnon interview.

100. Statutes of Nova Scotia, c. 63, 1949. In 1950, the Maternity Boarding Houses Act was folded into the province's new Children's Protection Act.

101. MacKinnon to Scott, 16 June 1947, RG 72, vol. 9, file 2, PANS; Statutes of Nova Scotia, c. 2, 1952.

102. On MacKinnon's national role, see, for example, Minutes of Directors of Child Welfare Meeting, 14 October 1955, MG 28 I10, vol. 183, file 10, PANS; Across-Border Placement Meeting, 10 August 1954, SW 109, box 12, file Children in Migration, Social Welfare History Archives [SWHA], University of Minnesota. On the Nova Scotian effort with respect to hard-to-place children, see Minutes of Meeting of the Directors of Child Welfare, 16–17 June 1956, MG 28 I10, vol. 183, file 11, NAC; Minister of Public Welfare for Nova Scotia, Social Welfare Pioneers in Nova Scotia (Halifax, 1964), entry for "Lillian Romkey," pp. 25–31. On the larger movement to arrange border-crossing adoptions for hard-to-place children, see Roberta Hunt, Obstacles to Interstate Adoption (New York, 1972).

103. The IMH was an exploitative institution which, on the whole, treated both mothers and children poorly. But most choices for women pregnant out of wedlock were not attractive.

104. MacKinnon interview. Measuring societal prejudice against unmarried mothers is a difficult task. Most of the literature on unwed pregnancy in this period describes, on the basis of considerable evidence, a general tone of harsh condemnation directed against women giving birth out of wedlock. Recent work by Mary Louise Hough on unmarried mothers in rural Maine—a region that is in many ways comparable to Nova Scotia—suggests that in local pockets these women received a more sympathetic reception. I am grateful to Suzanne Morton for drawing my attention to this work. See Mary Louise Hough, "'I'm a Poor Girl ... in Family and I'd Like to Know if You Be Kind': The Community's Response to Unwed Mothers in Maine and Tennessee, 1876–1956," Ph.D. Dissertation, University of Maine, 1997. See also Suzanne Morton, "Nova Scotia and its Unmarried Mothers."

105. Davidson, Report on Public Welfare Services, p. 159.

106. Davidson, Report on Public Welfare Services, pp. 156–60.

107. Solinger and Kunzel argue that from the 1940s a rhetoric of "choice" for unwed mothers was undercut by continual pressure on white women with "normal," "adoptable" children to recognize adoption as the responsible choice. For non-white women, the pressure was reversed. See Solinger, *Wake Up Little Suzy*; Kunzel, *Fallen Women, Problem Girls*.

108. MacKinnon interview. As Suzanne Morton has noted, MacKinnon's position was quite paternalistic. He assumed that he, as representative of the state and professional social welfare, "knew better" than the mothers what was best for their children and for themselves. Personal communication with Suzanne Morton, April 2001.

109. See, for example, annual reports of the Children's Aid Societies of Colchester and Cumberland counties, published in *Annual Report of the Director of Child Welfare for 1938* (Halifax, 1939), pp. 30, 45.

110. This was only one of many complaints against Lantz. See Tillotson, "'Too much planning in secret'"; Memo to File, 18 February 1950, MG 28 I10, vol. 227, file 26, NAC; Minister of Public Welfare of Nova Scotia, *The Nova Scotia Association of Children's Aid Societies: 1926–1956* (Halifax, 1972), p. 47.

111. Davidson, *Report on Public Welfare Services*, pp. 153–54.

112. For an examination of the poor law, see Guildford, "Closing the Mansions of Woe": L.T. Hancock, "The Function and Status of Poor Boards in Nova Scotia," 10 September 1954, MS 1-22, file Canadian Public Health Association Atlantic Branch, DUA.

113. Morton, "Nova Scotia and Its Unmarried Mothers"; Hough, "I'm a Poor Girl ... in Family."

114. The religious homes did not charge fees, but the help they provided came tied up with a strong message about the woman's "sin" and her need for redemption. MacKinnon described the Catholic Home of the Guardian Angel and Protestant Halifax Infants' Home during the 1940s as "operating out of the nineteenth century" in the punitive application of religious doctrine. See MacKinnon interview. On women's experiences in religious maternity homes, see Lévesque, "Deviants Anonymous"; Petrie, *Gone to an Aunt's*; Maire-Aimée Cliché, "Morale chrétienne et 'double standard sexuel': les filles-mères à l'hôpital Miséricorde à Québec 1874–1972," *Histoire sociale/Social History* 24, 47 (mai/May 1991), pp. 85–125. Canadian and American historians argue that many women were able to take what they needed from charitable or religious maternity homes while resisting efforts to "reform" their behaviour or "save" their souls. See Lévesque, "Deviants Anonymous"; Petrie, *Gone to an Aunt's*; Solinger, *Wake Up Little Suzy*; Kunzel, *Fallen Women, Problem Girls*.

115. *Revised Statutes of Nova Scotia*, c. 49, 1923 and amendments as specified in *Statutes of Nova Scotia*, c. 24. 1920, c. 22, 1934, c. 20, 1938, c. 31, 1941.

116. Judge R.H. Murray, "Nobody's Child," *Public Affairs* 1, 1 (August 1937). In 1938, the *Illegitimate Children's Act* was amended to specify that if a putative father tried to defend himself by producing a witness who claimed that he also had sexual intercourse with the mother, both men could be held liable under the terms of the Act. This seems a strong indication that this kind of defence was a regular occurrence. See *Statutes of Nova Scotia*, c. 20, 1938.

117. Morton, "Nova Scotia and Its Unmarried Mothers." Morton notes that one possible exception to this trend was Lunenburg County, where there were more frequent legal cases.

118. Memorandum re: Discussion of Possible Changes Unmarried Parenthood Legislation in Nova Scotia, August 1931: Whitton to Blois, 20 January 1934, MG 28 I10, vol. 1, file 4, NAC.

119. MacKinnon to Lea. 12 February 1946, MG 28 I10, vol. 216, file 13, NAC.

120. MacKinnon urged consideration of the *Illegitimate Children's Act* on the Child Welfare Division as early as November 1944. In 1947, he was on the subcommittee which worked on the a new Unmarried Parents Act, though he did not agree with all of the provisions suggested by this body. See Minutes of the Child Welfare Division of the Halifax Council of Social Agencies, 6 November 1944, 6 March 1947, 17 November 1947, MG 20. vol. 408, file 3.1, PANS; Gwen Shand, *A History of the Welfare council of Halifax Nova Scotia* (Halifax, 1960), p. 14. On MacKinnon's influence inside the Council, see Tillotson, "'Too much planning in secret.'"

121. Minister of Public Welfare of Nova Scotia, *Nova Scotia Association of Children's Aid Societies*, pp. 22, 33; Walter Wood to MacDonald, 24 January 1948, MG 2, vol. 933, file 26.5, PANS. MacKinnon was also a significant presence in the Nova Scotia Association of Children's Aid Societies, serving as honorary president through the second half of the 1940s.

122. The Nova Scotia Association of Children's Aid Societies bill was largely influenced by Gwen Lantz, of the Halifax Children's Aid Society. Many at the Halifax Council of Social Agencies, and some at the Nova Scotia Association of Children's Aid Societies, felt that Lantz sabotaged efforts to merge the Halifax Council of Social Agencies and Nova Scotia Association of Children's Aid Societies draft bills and perhaps tried to derail the new legislation altogether in her 1951 testimony before the Committee on Bills of the Nova Scotia legislature. One point of conflict was Lantz's supposed unwillingness to see unmarried mothers treated more gently. Another was her insistence (this time shared with her Nova Scotia Association of Children's Aid Societies colleagues) that the director of child welfare receive and re-distribute all monies paid out under court orders. The Children's Aid Societies want to avoid responsibility for collecting the money because of the workload involved. When a similar suggestion was made in any early stage of the Halifax Council of Social Agencies debates, MacKinnon argued that having all money paid to the director's office made for too great a concentration of authority. The eventual legislation specified a number of responsible bodies or individuals who could collect the money. See Bessie Touzel, *Halifax (NS) Study of the Children's Aid Society and Its Relation to Other Agencies*, 1952, MG 28 I10, vol. 228, file 1, pp. 6–8, NAC; Minutes of the Child Welfare Division of the Halifax Council of Social Agencies, 6 March 1947, 9 January 1948, 6 February 1948, 13 February 1948, 28 November 1950, MG 20, vol. 408, file 3.1, 4, PANS; Minister of Public Welfare, *Nova Scotia Association of Children's Aid Societies*, pp. 45–47; "Bill Widening Scope of Act Favoured in Principle," *Mail-Star*, 31 March 1951.

123. *Statutes of Nova Scotia*, c. 3, 1951.

124. Suzanne Morton argues that the 1951 legislation did not significantly improve the situation of unwed mothers. She notes that women often did not have control of the money paid on their behalf and argues that enforcing court orders remained difficult. She also points out that since the previous legislation was not widely used, there is reason to question how often the new legislation resulted in court orders. Both the new legislation and the old had provisions for the collection of money owed under court orders. In the new legislation these provisions were extended to provide for the seizure and sale of the father's goods. But the text of the Act suggests little about actual enforcement. More research is needed on the use of the new legislation and on the issue of enforcement. See *Statutes of Nova Scotia*, c. 3, 1951, s. 8–10, 34; Morton, "Nova Scotia and Its Unmarried Mothers."

125. The Act was divided into two sections. Part I laid out the process for a formal filiation proceeding, in which the judge ruled on the paternity of the child and named the recipient of funds. Part II lays out less formal procedure for determining the civil liability of a father, where paternity is not contested and is not determined by the court. Part II provides for the payment of funds from the father of the child to the mother or to her parents. See *Statutes of Nova Scotia*, c. 3, 1951, s. 3.3, 7.1, 11.1, 33.

126. Conway Ellsworth to L.T. Hancock, 18 August 1954, MS 1, vol. 22, file Canadian Public Health Association. Atlantic Branch, DUA; "Bill Widening Scope of Act Favoured in Principle," *Mail-Star*, 31 March 1951.

127. Memo for the Nova Scotia Provincial Child Welfare Department File, February 1944, MG 28 I10, vol. 216, file 13, NAC.

128. MacKinnon to Lea, 18 December 1945, Memo of Discussion with Mr. MacKinnon, 2 April 1946, MG 28 I10, vol. 216, file 13, NAC.

129. Blois to Morlock, 19 December 1946, RG 102, series 3B, 1945–48, box 171, file 8-4-2 (August–September 1946), USNA; Canadian Conference on Social Work, *Proceedings of the 10th Biennial Meeting of the Canadian Conference on Social Work* (Halifax, 1946). Blois was the president of the conference, Lea was on the program committee and MacKinnon was deeply involved in the planning process. Morlock and Lea were intimate friends who worked together closely in the effort to regulate the movement of Canadian children to the United States for adoption. I discuss their collaboration in connection with the IMH in Balcom, "The Traffic in Babies."

130. Complaints were directed against both Blois and MacKinnon. See, for example, Elizabeth Torrey to Lea, 8 June 1945, MG 28 I10, vol. 223, file 19; E.S.L. Govan, Notes from Field Trip to Nova Scotia, 16–18 February 1950, MG 28 I10, vol. 241, file 11, NAC.

131. Minister of Public Welfare of Nova Scotia, *Nova Scotia Association of Children's Aid Societies*, pp. 28–33; "Children's Aid Delegates in Session: Critical of Relations with Welfare Branch," *Halifax Herald*, 25 April 1946. Torrey was backed by Lantz and by Whitton, who was visiting Nova Scotia at the time of the conference. Whitton's resistance to what she viewed as the over-extension of government authority in social welfare is explored in Struthers, "Lord, Give Us Men," pp. 126–43; Patricia Rooke and R.L. Schnell, "Making the Way More Comfortable: Charlotte Whitton's Child Welfare Career, 1920–1948," *Journal of Canadian Studies* 17, 4 (Winter 1982–3), pp. 33–45. The personal animosity between MacKinnon and Lantz is explored in Tillotson, "'Too much planning in secret."

132. *Statute of Nova Scotia*, c. 2, 1950, s. 9.C, 15. In 1952, the legislation was further amended to allow the minister to "suspend or stop payment" to a society if that body "has not adopted or is not maintaining the standards and methods of work prescribed" by provincial regulations. See *Statutes of Nova Scotia*, c. 78, 1952, s. 2.3. Nova Scotia adapted the grading system for Children's Aid Societies from one already in place in Ontario. See Struthers, *The Limits of Affluence*, p. 130.

133. For a more complete treatment of how the IMH fits with the formal and informal international networks connecting leading child welfare reformers at the Canadian Welfare Council and the United States Children's Bureau, the Alberta Babies-for-Export Scandal, and the role of *La Société d'Adoption et de Protection de l'enfance* in the placement of Catholic children from Quebec in Catholic homes in the northeastern United States, see Balcom, "'The Traffic in Babies." Unlike the IMH case, the Alberta and Quebec placements do not seem to have involved the transfer of dollars and a literal selling of babies. On the Alberta case, see Rooke and Schnell, "Charlotte Whitton Meets 'The Last Best West," pp. 143–63. For an institutional history of *La Société d'Adoption et de Protection de l'enfance*, see Marie-Paule Malouin, dir., *L'univers des enfants en difficulé au Québec entre 1940 et 1960* (Montreal, 1996).

134. For American discussions see Smith to Lea, 4 November 1946, RG 102, series 3B (1945–48), box 154, file 7-3-1-3 (August-December 1947); Summary Report of Midwest Conference on Interstate and International Placement of Children, Grafton, Illinois, October 1947, RG 102, series 3B (1945–48), box 154, file 7-3-1-3 (January-March 1948); Problems in the International Placement of Children, July 1948, RG 102, series 3B (1945–48), box 154, file 7-3-1-3 (April-December 1948), USNA. For Canadian discussions see Canadian Welfare Council, Committee on Adoption, *Report of the Committee on Adoption* (Ottawa, 1948), Canadian Welfare Council, Committee on Adoption, *Report of the Adoption Committee* (Ottawa, 1953), Canadian Welfare Council, *A Policy Statement on Adoption Across Borders* (Ottawa, 1956), Minutes of Directors of Child Welfare Meeting, 14 October 1955, MG 28 I10, vol. 183, file 10, NAC.

135. For example, New Jersey and Rhode Island officials collected letters the Youngs and their lawyers wrote to prospective clients in these two states. The letters laid out the IMH plan to circumvent Nova Scotia's adoption laws by taking the babies to New Brunswick for adoption. Such letters, passed from the states to the United States Children's Bureau to the Canadian Welfare Council and back the governments of Nova Scotia and New Brunswick, bolstered the argument for further adoption reform in both provinces. In 1945 New Jersey, responding to a request from Nova Scotia, funnelled through the Canadian Welfare Council and the United States Children's Bureau, agreed to do follow-up studies on adoptive families in New Jersey who had taken children from the IMH. Scott of the New Jersey Department of Institutions and agencies then forwarded a detailed (and damning) report to Blois. See Scott to Blois, 13 August 1945, RG 102, series 3B, box 445, file 7-3-1-3, USNA.

136. Morlock to Blois. 19 May 1945, RG 102, series 3B, 1945–48, box 191, file 10-12-5 (January-April 1947), USNA; Lea to Morlock, 21 November 1945, RG 102, series 3B, 1945–48, box 154, file 7-3-1-3 (August-December 1947), USNA.

137. Lea to McNair, 29 April 1946, MG 28 I10, vol. 216, file New Brunswick Department of Health and Social Services, (1935–50); Lea to E.B. McLatchy, 19 April 1946, MG 28 I10, vol. 216, file New Brunswick Department of Health and Social Services, (1935–50); Lea to W.J. Brawders, 27 December 1945 and 19 December 1945, MG 28 I10, vol. 45, file 405 (1946), NAC.

5

"Forward to a Farm"

Land Settlement as Unemployment Relief in the 1930s*

DAWN S. BOWEN

DURING THE 1930S, severe drought and economic depression irrevocably altered the nature of Canadian society. Governments tried to alleviate some of the most acute suffering, but the measures undertaken were insufficient to provide for all of those in need. The most contentious issue during the period was relief: seed relief for farmers, relief camps for the single unemployed, and direct relief for families in the cities. Unemployment reached cataclysmic proportions and relief became a way of existence for many. Faced with escalating costs, however, government officials sought new alternatives to direct relief. The land offered one solution. Land had served as a safety net in Canadian society, and popular opinion held that if a man could not find work in the city, he could always support his family on a farm. Individual families who returned to the land of their own accord made up the bulk of the settlers in the 1930s, but the back-to-the-land movement also reflected new government policies designed to encourage urban relief recipients to take up homesteads.[1] This practice was carried out at all levels of government from the local to the federal. In several provinces interest in the back-to-the-land movement was initiated at the local level, where cities sought to provide alternatives to direct relief and thus limit their expenditures. An important factor distinguishing the 1930s migration from its predecessors is that government actively encouraged and provided financial assistance for indigent urban dwellers to obtain new homes in the country. While individual decisions certainly played a role in determining who joined the movement, it was often government that set the process in motion. The idea was not a novel one for government had long taken a leading role in promoting settlement in the prairie region, and had directed the placement of returned soldiers on the land following World War I.[2] This article demonstrates how state-assisted policy developed, and examines the early stages of the process in Saskatchewan, where a number of cities promoted settlements for unemployed workers in the northern part of the province. It argues that because the federal government was reluctant to practice deficit spending, the adoption of a back-to-the-land strategy offered a reasonable alternative to direct relief. Finally, it challenges the recent assertions of scholars who interpret this movement as an attempt on the part of the state and big business to create a rural peasantry.

* This chapter was first published as "'Forward to a Farm': Land Settlement as Unemployment Relief in the 1930s," *Prairie Forum*, 20, 2 (1995): 207–229. An earlier version of this article was written for a graduate seminar at Queen's University. The author wishes to thank Dr. Ian McKay and seminar members for their helpful criticisms.

In *Canada 1922–1939: Decades of Discord*, John Herd Thompson traces the political, economic and social roots of the Depression through the 1920s and analyzes conditions in Canada during the very depths of the Depression. He suggests that during the political reign of R.B. Bennett, the principal issue was unemployment and how this problem might be most effectively handled. During his campaign, Bennett had promised work to every man who wanted it, and by implementing a restrictive tariff, he expected that Canada would "blast her way" into world markets. A short-lived series of public works projects and the protective tariff were the only solutions Bennett had to offer the unemployed. Yet there was another option which the government implemented to deal with the crisis. Thompson acknowledges that a back-to-the-land movement occurred during the 1930s, but the few words devoted to the topic lead one to conclude that it was an insignificant part of the Depression experience. To be fair, *Canada 1922–1939* is simply a survey of this tumultuous period in Canadian history, and it would not have been possible for Thompson to consider every social or economic development that was taking place. The author, however, relies on only a few secondary sources to assess the back-to-the-land movement and concludes that the relief settlement scheme was "an attempt to turn back the clock to a peaceful, pre-industrial Canada, when the peasantry starved quietly on the farms during lean years."[3]

Another critic of the back-to-the-land movement, James Struthers, devotes more attention to the subject, but suggests simply that it was a popular panacea for unemployment because it served the class interests of farmers and big business.[4] A central thesis of his work is that the "indifference to the plight of the unemployed reflected Canada's preoccupation with the land." Unemployment insurance was deemed inappropriate for Canada because of its "agrarian nature." To support this view, Struthers quotes farm and industry spokesmen who questioned the necessity of providing relief to idle men in the city when there was work to be done on the frontier. These same class interests also believed that a back-to-the-land movement would create a "reserve army" of labour that could be maintained cheaply on the land and recalled to industry when economic conditions improved. Taking these ideas to their logical conclusion, Struthers argues that employing a back-to-the-land strategy to combat unemployment "ensured that this 'reserve army' would be willing to work under conditions and for rates of pay that were unattractive by any standards."[5] The evidence provided to support these claims is, however, one-sided, and reflects the ideas of a vocal group of economic leaders who were eager to protect and advance their interests. Such opinions were widely voiced throughout the era, and thus one must not assume that they simply represent conjecture on the part of the author. But until further research is conducted into the ways in which both the labouring classes and the industrial elite reacted to back-to-the-land as an unemployment relief strategy, the matter will remain unresolved.

Two other works, written while the back-to-the-land movement was underway, provide important yardsticks against which the settlement plan might also be measured. In both instances, the authors supported in principle the idea of relief land settlement. In his study of labour and agriculture, George Haythorne demonstrated the need for scholars to examine the counterflow of migrants from the cities, described the social consequences of the back-to-the-land movement, and suggested a number of ways to judge the relative merits of newly established settlements. One recurrent theme in Haythorne's work was that farming and rural life were Canadian traditions: "agriculture," he maintained, "is still fundamental in the Canadian economy and in Canadian life." Of greater relevance was his contention that agriculture "is looked to hopefully as the medium through which the unemployed may be reestablished in depression."[6] In measuring the human and financial costs of the 1930s settlement experience, Haythorne believed that for those who "made the grade," the benefits in "physical, psychological, and social gains" could not be calculated in financial terms. Echoing the words of many of his contemporaries, Haythorne offered this support for the movement: "Against the alternative of life in a city slum area perpetuated by a cash dole affording only meagre subsistence, settlement offers the boon of self-respect, the chance of a self-supporting occupation, hard but varied and satisfying work, in a healthy environment."[7]

In 1936, Robert England, an expert on immigration and settlement employed by the Canadian National Railway, provided another perspective on the back-to-the-land phenomenon then taking place in western Canada. Demand for farms in the northern parts of the provinces, he suggested, reflected settlers' interest in land where "building logs, fuel and even game" were available, and indicated a lack of capital and a "desire to engage in a more self-sufficing type of agriculture."[8] England asserted that although the back-to-the-land movement had its critics, the movement did "emphasize the fundamentals of life." Life in the country was a tonic which could cure those urban dwellers who had some previous relationship with the land. Despite the fact that the land settlement scheme was simply a relief project, officials truly hoped that those who participated in the plan would be able to improve the quality of their lives. England reported that the "de-urbanized settler [had] acquired a distrust of urban life, ... has as his primary objective the provision of food and shelter, [and] is located where the securing of these needs is possible." The belief in farming as a way of life, in England's words "a family affair with an atmosphere of frugality, industry and thrift," was still very much alive and, he believed, should be encouraged.[9]

Clearly, the assessments of the back-to-the-land movement made by these writers are problematic. A principal concern is that the conclusions drawn by some modern scholars are not based on any original research. To be sure, scholarly investigations into the process are few, but care must be taken not to make generalizations based only on secondary sources. Similarly, the writers who witnessed the movement firsthand, one of whom had a vested interest in promoting the plan, do not take into consideration the long-term outcome of the back-to-the-land policy, nor do they adequately consider the interests of government in promoting settlement as a relief measure. It is also clear that these men were very much influenced by the economic conditions of the time, and by prevailing attitudes about rural life and agriculture. It is not fair to evaluate the back-to-the-land policy without placing it squarely within its full context. If the evidence at the local, provincial, and federal level is examined closely, it is likely that a more balanced interpretation of the back-to-the-land movement will emerge.

Canada in the Depression

Blair Neatby has written that Canada was at a turning point during the Depression of the 1930s. Many Canadians had lost faith in institutions which had permitted economic collapse and began to analyze seriously the structure of society and the role of social institutions; they concluded that both would have to change. Because government exercised power, Canadians demanded political action. While they admitted that relief was a first step, they expected government to take control of the economic system, to provide some direction for the economy, and to end the Depression. In contrast to the ruling party in the United States, which pumped tremendous amounts of cash into the American economy, the government of R.B. Bennett was not one to provide creative leadership or to take chances. Bennett staunchly believed in balanced budgets. No matter how bad the economic calamity may have been for working-class Canadians, relief would have to be limited to that which could be provided within the constraints of fiscal responsibility.[10] Michiel Horn provides a critical view of the approach of Canadian governments during the Depression. Despite calls for fiscal belt tightening, the total national debt increased by 27 percent between 1930 and 1937, but none of these expenditures was used for any "boldly innovative" projects. "Boldness, indeed," Horn declares, "is the last word to describe the policies of the federal government, whether directed by R.B. Bennett's Conservatives or William Lyon Mackenzie King's Liberals."[11] Of paramount concern for both governments was the avoidance of new government responsibilities, particularly for the unemployed, that "might prove costly or politically unrewarding." In short, this meant that neither government was willing to expend the money that was necessary to see Canada and Canadians through the worst of the Depression.

It is true that no one could have predicted the intensity of the economic collapse, but there were warning signs. The nation had industrialized, but little thought was given to the implications for both workers and farmers. Neatby states that Canadians were so mesmerized by economic expansion that increasing economic insecurity was ignored. After World War I, Canada shifted from a rural society to an urban one, and its economy expanded from one based in agriculture to one rooted in industry. Rapid urbanization accompanied this industrialization and seriously disrupted the balance of urban and rural populations. Writing about this process, John Herd Thompson quotes a popular tune, "How're you gonna keep 'em down on the farm after they've seen Paree?" but maintains that Groucho Marx was closer to the mark when he quipped, "How're you gonna keep 'em down on the farm after they've seen the *farm*?"[12] The social and economic gains made in the cities far outpaced similar improvements in rural life and contributed to the exodus from the farm. Analyzing a similar movement in the United States, Leon Truesdell claimed that superficial reasons such as the glitter and excitement of the city were often discussed, but, in fact, there were three fundamental and far-reaching economic changes which made the migration from the farm to the city almost inevitable. These were: 1) the development of factory production which meant that the farmer and his farm were no longer self-sufficient enterprises; 2) the improvement of farming techniques through mechanization and specialization; and 3) a rising standard of living.[13] T. Lynn Smith, a prominent American rural sociologist, agreed. The small farmer and farm labourer had become marginalized in the American economy. When people were crowded out of all other industry or more rewarding agriculture, Smith believed, the subsistence farm became the "employer of last resort."[14] This condition was exacerbated by the Depression.

In Canada, the federal government attempted to ease the situation by providing work relief, but in 1932, with costs escalating, Prime Minister Bennett declared that all public works projects would be terminated. Direct relief became the only option available to most destitute families. By the early summer of 1932, however, another plan, known as relief land settlement, was being promoted. Although only a small number of families could ultimately benefit from this plan, it was widely heralded as a positive step. Canada's identity as an agrarian nation is key to understanding the back-to-the-land scheme as a solution to the unemployment crisis. The ability of an unemployed man to help himself and his family by returning to the land served to confirm the belief that agriculture was the foundation of society. The Conservative government's encouragement of the dispossessed to return to the land as a means of self-help also demonstrates its reluctance to rely on industry to provide the country's unemployed with a promising future. If recovery was to be achieved, it would result largely from the actions taken by those without work to help themselves. Although the government provided assistance to the jobless who wanted to go to the land, distributing funds in this manner was viewed as a logical alternative to the provision of direct relief. Underwriting settlement was a worthy expenditure if people could subsequently help themselves and emerge from the morass of relief.

Back-to-the-Land as a Federal Response to Unemployment

In the spring of 1931, with unemployment levels increasing dramatically, the federal Department of Immigration and Colonization decided to restrict immigration into the country. In summing up department policy, Wesley A. Gordon, minister of Immigration and Colonization wrote, "It is obviously unfair to the newcomer and immeasurably more unfair to our own people to encourage immigration of a type that will in any way aggravate our own internal difficulties." In addition to curtailing immigration, Gordon suggested that the two national railways, the Land Settlement Branch of the Department of Immigration and Colonization, and the provincial colonization departments undertake a coordinated effort to place Canadians on available farmland. Further, the minister suggested that "it is entirely logical that a substantial number of families ... now in our cities should, under existing conditions, be seriously turning their thoughts to the security to be found on the farm.... Assured shelter and food are strong incentives to families and individuals who are either out of employment or whose probable tenure of employment is precarious."[15]

Commentators such as J.B. MacLean, President of the MacLean Publishing Company, agreed that the cooperative plan was "the first constructive step in the solution of our present problems." He continued:

> Rural populations have not required doles of any kind, and have been living comparatively well; have plenty of money, particularly in Ontario and good parts of the West. In short, there has been no unemployment or lack of food on the farms.[16]

Others, including the committee charged with overseeing the coordination of the settlement activities, echoed this viewpoint. In a report to Minister Gordon in August 1931, committee members argued that the "agricultural industry ... constitutes a stabilizing influence in our national structure [and] offers ... a productive field for the absorption of a large number of our Canadian unemployed."[17] Observations such as these provided a good indication that a policy of agricultural settlement for the jobless might be a reasonable response to the unemployment crisis, and might alleviate some of the burden that was being placed on governments to care for ever-increasing numbers of indigent citizens. They also suggest that long-held assumptions about land and rural life would influence the course of federal relief policy.

The policy initially met with a good deal of success. In a two-year period ending in September 1932, over 9,000 families had been settled on farms and nearly 21,000 single men had been placed in farm work throughout the Dominion. The government believed that the placement of unemployed single men in useful work on farms had served two objectives. Not only did this action remove a large number of potential agitators from the cities, but it was taken without additional cost to the government. The same staff that had previously been engaged in attracting immigrants into the country were now charged with placing Canadians on the land, and no funds were expended from the public purse to assist this migration.[18] Officials, however, quickly came to the realization that simply helping families to locate land was not enough. Families with the financial resources to return to the land on their own accord were in short supply and those who had wanted to take up land had already done so. Yet, there were still other families who were willing to leave the city and try their luck on a pioneer farm. It soon became apparent to those in charge of settlement that families without adequate means would also benefit from returning to the land and deserved a chance to become self-supporting on a farm of their own. The urban experience had been very disappointing for many of these families, and officials believed that they would welcome an opportunity to return to a rural life.[19]

Many members of Parliament appeared to agree that a number of deserving families with agricultural backgrounds should be assisted to return to the land. In March 1932, F.W. Gershaw, the Honourable Member from Medicine Hat, Alberta, suggested that the federal government finance a plan similar to the joint venture of the federal and railway colonization departments. The people he had in mind were those who were out of work, but "who might if suitably placed on the land be able to produce food and supplies for themselves." It was a scheme, he believed, which would provide genuine assistance to those with farming experience. It was also his opinion that these people could be "supported on the farms at a smaller cost to the state than [it] must meet [at present]." Gershaw added that some people might charge that the government could not afford to undertake such a scheme, but the people he would encourage to settle were already being supported by some government, and that "three, four or five hundred dollars a year must be advanced to keep them from starvation." If some small amount of these funds were advanced as a credit, the people carefully chosen, and the lands properly selected, then "many of the unemployed who now have no hope for the future would be given fresh courage, and their conditions vastly improved." Gershaw also claimed that if, in the end, such a scheme added to the overproduction of farm products as some critics had charged, then the scheme would have "succeeded far beyond our hopes." In short, he did not see the plan as being more than a way to promote self-sufficiency.[20]

A month later, the MP from Saskatoon, F.R. Macmillan, also expressed his support for a back-to-the-land policy. In 1931, he reported that his city had sent "some forty-two families who were on the unemployed list [to lands in northern Saskatchewan]. We financed them to some extent, and I am glad to say that forty of the forty-two families will remain in the area, and that they are doing exceptionally well." In the spring of 1932, the cities of Saskatoon, Regina and Moose Jaw, in conjunction with the provincial government, came up with a plan to relocate 2,000 unemployed families to farms in the north with the assistance of the federal government. The cities had already agreed to contribute $100, as had the province, and provincial officials had asked the Dominion to make the same contribution. With a total of $300, Macmillan believed, these families could be put into "productive work whereby they can earn their living."[21] With the city scheme having already produced tangible results, Macmillan recommended that the federal government support a similar plan, and offer financial assistance to the provinces that had citizens willing and able to earn their living from the land.

Not all members were so enthusiastic about the back-to-the-land movement, nor about the federal government's statements on the success of its current policy. Angus MacInnis, a western Labour MP, declared that the back-to-the-land movement "tends towards the creation of a peasantry in Canada, a peasantry which will eke out a precarious living from the land when there is nothing to be done in the city. That peasantry will form a labour reserve to be called upon at a time when working conditions in the cities improve."[22] Although this view may have reflected the opinion of one section of the labour movement, another organization, the Trades and Labour Congress (TLC), expressed a very different view. In the fall of 1933, the TLC went on record as being "heartily in accord" with the settlement policy. Tom Moore, president of the TLC, was satisfied with the efforts to locate unemployed workers on the land, and expressed hope that the policy be "continued and developed [so that] ... all those capable and willing to provide for themselves and their dependents by farming may be placed in a position to do so."[23] Smaller labour groups also promoted various back-to-the-land schemes as a way to relieve unemployment. In Saskatoon, the British Workers' Association forwarded a plan to the city council in which a dozen families would be placed on homesteads in the northern part of the province, and machinery and equipment would be held on a community basis.[24] In Moose Jaw, a delegation from the Federal Workers' Union asked city council to advance a loan to permit forty-two unemployed married men to file on land under the provincial land settlement scheme.[25] Both plans were eventually turned down by the councils because they implemented other schemes instead, but they do suggest that these labour groups recognized that land settlement offered immediate benefits and hope for the future. Although the only evidence that the Trades and Labour Congress supported the idea of a back-to-the-land scheme for unemployed workers is provided above, newspapers contain frequent references to local labour organizations which lobbied city councils and provincial governments to approve various plans. Not all labour groups were of one mind on this issue as the statement of Angus MacInnis aptly demonstrates, and perhaps it is significant that this was so. Nonetheless, the evidence marshalled here suggests that many of these organizations, particularly at the local level, were supportive of the settlement idea, even if only as a temporary palliative.

In the spring of 1932, the federal government began to consider seriously a policy of state-aided land settlement as a measure to relieve unemployment. At the request of Minister Gordon, W.M. Jones, commissioner of Colonization in the federal Department of Immigration, formed a committee which met to weigh the relative merits and potential problems associated with such a program. Prior to its first meeting, Jones circulated a memorandum to W.J. Black, the director of Colonization for the Canadian National Railways and J.N.K. Macalister, chief commissioner of Colonization for the Canadian Pacific Railway, the two other committee members. The memo raised a number of issues for discussion, including whether land settlement should be undertaken as a practical means of relieving the national problem of unemployment, whether it was feasible for the federal government to participate financially in such an undertaking, and how a project might take shape.[26] At its meeting, the committee concluded:

> Unemployment relief applied in the placement of families on the land— embodying as it does the essential element of helping people to help themselves—would be in the public interest, both from the stand-point of the families assisted and the Canadian tax payers who are called upon to shoulder the burden of relief costs.[27]

The real issue concerned the cost of maintaining families in idleness on direct relief, as opposed to the "cost of placing these same families, whose practical experience and present condition indicate the possibility of reasonable success, on farms where they will contribute to their own maintenance and in due course become self-sustaining."[28] Examined in this manner, there was no doubt that money spent on direct relief would be better channelled into a program of land settlement, where families could provide for their own support and place less of a burden on the relief system. The committee recommended that the federal government incorporate a policy of land settlement into the present relief policy. Settlement was a "constructive method of actually reducing unemployment," and would permit families to help themselves. Further, it was "in the interest of the Provinces and the Dominion to have these families return to a rural life."[29] Clearly, rural life was viewed as preferable to life in the city, and any attempt to return urban residents with rural roots to the land was a positive step.

The plan advocated by these men was not a hastily conceived measure. Each had considerable experience in colonization work, and their years of experience enabled them to formulate a solid plan of relief settlement. The selection of suitable families was crucial to its success, for, as committee members maintained, "it would be a waste of money to endeavour to settle any family that was totally unsuitable for rural life." They recommended that only families with actual farming experience be allowed to participate in the scheme; in addition, those families selected "must be keenly anxious to return to rural life." Limiting expenditures was also an important prerequisite for the plan, and the committee reported that "many of these families could live much more cheaply in the country than in the city provided that they had suitable housing accommodation, a supply of milk and vegetables and their own fuel." In conclusion, they declared:

> a policy of settlement ... might not absorb any large number of unemployed families for the present winter; nevertheless the plan is a constructive one and decidedly in the interests of our national development. It will relieve the problem at points where there is considerable congestion, and above all it will enable a number of good families to be self-sustaining and to re-estab- lish themselves in rural life where they desire to be.[30]

In late April 1932, the federal government, bowing to pressure from the provinces and a number of its own ministers, announced plans to include a land settlement scheme as part of its unemployment relief policy. The Dominion government would contribute one-third of the cost, while each province would share the remaining two-thirds with the municipality from which the family originated. Land settlement was stressed as an unemployment relief measure, and its purpose was to promote subsistence farming only. "This is in no sense a Government-aided land settlement scheme," Gordon stated, "but an application of relief expenditure to enable families receiving relief to contribute to their own maintenance by labour on the land, where they may eventually establish themselves on a self-supporting basis."[31] All provinces except Prince Edward Island elected to participate in the scheme, and accepted responsibility for the settlement arrangements and selection of families. Each province would be assisted in this endeavour by an advisory committee consisting of representatives from the municipalities, the federal Department of Colonization, and the Canadian Pacific and the Canadian National Railways. The agreements made with the provinces stated that all families selected must be residents of Canada and be on direct relief. It was further provided that selections be made without regard for race, religious views, or political affiliation.[32]

The back-to-the-land movement was not a panacea for the myriad problems associated with the Depression. It did, however, offer an alternative to bare subsistence in the city, where opportunities for gainful employment were few. A back-to-the-land policy would also not cure the unemployment problem, nor would it actually help more than a few thousand families to become self-supporting, but relief land settlement did provide the government with an opportunity to demonstrate that it was attempting to redress some of the problems associated with urbanization and industrialization. Minister Gordon argued that a fundamental cause of the Depression was the imbalance between rural and urban populations. A necessary component of economic recovery, therefore, was the return of surplus urban populations to the land. Gordon had long supported the idea of land settlement, in large part because he adhered to those age-old beliefs that the land could sustain and nurture a morally responsible and law-abiding populace. When he announced the federal plan in Parliament, Gordon explained that, in his opinion, the phrase "back to the farm" was a misnomer. A more correct expression, he suggested, would be "go forward to a farm" because in the final analysis, "if Canada is to survive ... it will be by reason ... of the products of the first six inches of her soil."[33] The land, then, offered not only a temporary respite for the unemployed, but reestablishing people in agriculture would fundamentally alter the nature of Canadian society. Other proponents asserted that a back-to-the-land movement was a "remedy suited to [the] national economy," which would permit the "re-establishment of an equilibrium destroyed by a too rapid industrial expansion." Thus, in the minds of those promoting the plan, relief settlement would direct people toward agriculture which, unlike industry, did not refuse work to those who were willing, and offered them shelter and sustenance.[34]

After a brief period of public works projects, back-to-the-land became Canada's only immediate response to the unemployment crisis. Land settlement did not pretend to end the problem of unemployment, but it was one strategy which would permit people without adequate means to help themselves. It was also viewed as a means of establishing a more equitable balance between urban and rural populations which many observers believed would ultimately ease the problem of unemployment. In Saskatchewan, the city of Saskatoon took an active interest in promoting back-to-the-land as a relief strategy. Soon, a number of other Saskatchewan cities, recognizing the advantages for themselves and their indigent citizens, expressed their support for a land settlement program. The back-to-the-land movement in Saskatchewan is used as a case study to demonstrate how the scheme was implemented at the provincial level, to document the early months of one relief settlement community, and, where appropriate, to give voice to the settlers who abandoned the urban world and became pioneers on the province's northern frontier.

Saskatchewan, 1931–1934

In August 1931, the provincial premiers received a telegram from the Department of Labour asking for an estimate of the number of unemployed and the localities where the greatest problems existed. In reply, the premier of Saskatchewan declared that over 21,000 people, fully 10 percent of the urban population, were without work.[35] Unemployment was largely a result of "general causes," but crop failures had induced a large number of farm labourers to drift into urban centers. In many cases, these workers "arrived penniless as farmers were without funds to pay wages."[36] Relief numbers were generally at their lowest in the summer, but by mid-1932 over 1,600 families were still receiving relief. This figure represented an increase of 150 percent over the previous summer. In the first six months of 1932, the province had expended more on relief that it had in all of 1931, and there was no sign that the situation would soon improve.[37]

The provincial government, faced with greater numbers of destitute citizens and a nearly depleted treasury, sought ways to alleviate the economic crisis.[38] Its solution was to encourage people to return to the farm. In March of 1931, Saskatoon's mayor, John W. Hair, presented a plan to city council which called for the placement of 500 unemployed city men and their families on farms, where they could grow sufficient produce to meet their own needs. Hair suggested that the farms be forty to eighty acres in size and be grouped in small clusters so that buildings and equipment might be shared by four families. The objective of the plan was not to expend vast amounts of money to establish families, but rather to provide sufficient assistance so that they could help themselves. The mayor concluded that "by raising poultry, dairying in a small way, and growing potatoes and garden crops, families should have no difficulty in making a living."[39]

Provincial officials recognized that plans such as the one noted above might well have some effect on the unemployment crisis, and at the very least might encourage a number of families to leave the city, thereby reducing relief expenditures. Government officials and the public both favoured back-to-the-land schemes as a means of providing relief. Unemployed workers' associations were also interested in the idea and lobbied local authorities to adopt a back-to-the-land program for the urban poor.[40] City officials in Saskatoon recognized that a back-to-the-land movement had some genuine advantages: not only would a number of families be removed from the city and its relief rolls, but those same families would be working toward a goal of self-sufficiency. Politicians recognized that the movement would have to be limited to a small number of the unemployed, but some form of relief settlement held out the possibility of "independence, health and happiness," whereas direct relief could only lead to "discontent, bitterness and despair."[41]

When the mayor announced his settlement plan in March, the response was over-whelming. Within little more than a week, 156 families had applied to the city relief officer, who reported being "literally besieged" by prospective settlers.[42] A number of these family heads also went to the CNR Colonization office in Saskatoon to solicit an opinion about the mayor's farm plan. The CNR agent advised the group to take up homestead land rather than waiting to see if the forty-acre scheme would be approved. Twenty-five of these families got together and interviewed Mayor Hair, who then suggested that they meet with Major Barnett, the Deputy Minister of Natural Resources. Barnett informed them that if they were able to secure stock and equipment and file on homestead lands, they would become eligible for a $500 provincial land settlement loan. With this information in hand, the group decided to explore settlement possibilities. The families selected four represen-tatives who, in the company of two railway officials, travelled to the northern part of the province to select a block of homestead land. They found a tract of land near Loon Lake, a small settlement in northwestern Saskatchewan, 175 miles northwest of Saskatoon (see Figure 1). The land was described as level or gently rolling, with good soil. It was also well located as none of the homesteads were more than ten miles from a proposed railway that

Figure 5.1. Map of study area showing location of the Loon Lake settlement ("Little Saskatoon")

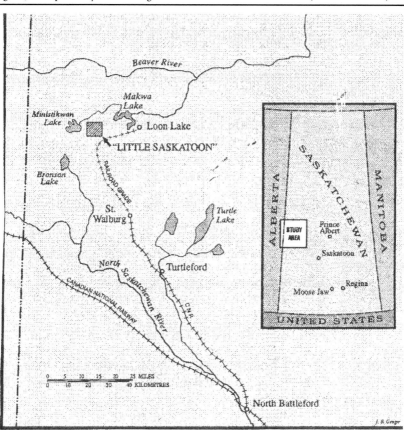

would open up the country in the near future. The group returned "well satisfied" with their selection.[43]

As a result of this action, city leaders became aware of the possibility of settling families in northwestern Saskatchewan. According to CNR officials, it was only after this opportunity came to light that city officials contacted the provincial government about the possibility of funding families to return to the land.[44] In March, the Saskatchewan Legislature had passed a land settlement act, which included a loan of up to $500 to assist in settling qualified people on unoccupied provincial lands. Like the plans developed later by the federal authorities, this act was not designed to be a land colonization measure; rather it was intended as a means to enable families living on relief in the city to become self-supporting through the establishment of homesteads.[45] Applications were reviewed by a special committee in each city, and those selected were sent to a provincial committee for final approval. If an application was passed, the province asked for an inspection of the designated quarter section, and made arrangements to transport the family to the land.[46] Mayor Hair declared that large numbers of the city's residents "realize that they would be better off on a farm of their own than trying to make their way in the city under present conditions."[47] There was no illusion that they would become commercial grain farmers, but it was thought that through hard work they could feed their families and perhaps have a small surplus to barter for the items that they could not produce.

The delegation of men who had travelled to northwestern Saskatchewan conferred with the other family heads and decided to file on the land they had seen in the Loon Lake area.[48] Once they applied for homesteads, most of the families in this group submitted requests to the province for settlement loans. Applicants were required to be British subjects and to have resided in the province for at least five years.[49] The application form inquired extensively into the men's personal backgrounds, their occupations and training, and, most importantly, their farming experience. Questions included where this experience had been obtained (that is, prairies or bush country), and what type of farming had been practiced (that is, grain, livestock, or mixed farming). Farming skills were seen as necessary to ensure success, but the province also wanted to know what other skills family members had which could help secure additional funds when necessary. All men selected to participate in the scheme had farming experience; most had been raised on farms, and had been farmers themselves, or, at the very least, had worked as farm labourers. After their arrival in the city, the men had taken up new occupations. Counted among the settlers in this back-to-the-land movement were carpenters, railroad workers, machinists, teamsters, and even a few salesmen.[50]

Selection of men with the potential to succeed was of paramount concern, but equally important in the minds of relief officials was the willingness of their wives to offer their full-fledged cooperation. "Fully 50 percent of the success of such a venture," a newspaper reporter commented, "depended upon the women."[51] Women were also active participants in the application process. They, too, were questioned about their farming experience and whether they were "fully conversant with the conditions of life on a pioneer farm." Finally, wives were asked if they approved of their husbands' applications, and if they "willingly joined" them in taking up land.[52] A report of the interview with the William Taylor family demonstrates how important women were in this equation: Mrs. Taylor is "a real Scotch homemaker," wrote the inspector. "She is fully experienced, able and willing to do her bit to make a success of farming with her husband."[53]

The first group of Saskatoon residents left the city with high hopes as they prepared to establish new lives in the north. The city had little to offer them except a chance to own a piece of land so they could become self-supporting once again. They would still be dependent on the government for assistance, but at least they could avoid the stigma of direct relief. These men would be working again, not on a make-work project, but on developing their own homesteads. Although funds were in short supply, the city did its best to aid the settlers. Noting that some of the settlers were "not overly blessed with worldly goods," the mayor appealed to local citizens to donate any equipment they could spare: "An old wagon, plow, harrow, garden tools, an old horse, and even clothing would be greatly appreciated." The Hudson's Bay Company also supported the effort and supplied each family with an ax.[54] The families departed in the late spring of 1931, and were transported by rail to the end of the line at St. Walburg, a farming town forty miles short of their destination. With their meagre possessions and some livestock loaded in trucks and wagons, they followed the railroad grade north to their homesteads at Loon Lake.

The settlers at "Little Saskatoon," as the community was commonly known, appeared eager to make the best of their situation. They were well aware that the first two or three years would not be any "picnic," but they were prepared to work hard. When they arrived on their homesteads, they built shacks and cleared a small amount of land for a garden. One enthusiastic resident, Stanley Sly, described the area as a "regular little heaven," and suggested to a Saskatoon reporter that "it would be impossible to induce any of [the settlers] to return to the city." Fish and game were plentiful and wild fruit grew in abundance. Sly optimistically concluded, "While we have been there only a few weeks we are now practically self-supporting."[55] The newspaper's editor responded that although the claims of self-sufficiency may have been a "little exaggerated," it nonetheless appeared that the settlers were content and that the scheme was off to a good start.[56] In the fall, another homesteader, Ray Gearhart, offered to ship two tons of fish to the city relief office in repayment for the assistance that the city had given to him and his friends. Gearhart, who was no doubt a better promoter than a settler, also reported that plenty of timber was available, and was visiting Saskatoon in an effort to secure a market for the wagons, sleighs and other agricultural equipment that he expected to produce in his wood-working plant.[57]

Other positive reports on activities in the north arrived the following spring. In March 1932, George Hoffman, another former Saskatoon resident, told the *Saskatoon Star-Phoenix* that the greatest problem facing the Loon Lake settlers was a shortage of livestock feed, but that community members were "otherwise happy and contented with their lot."[58] In April, when the House of Commons was debating the possibility of federal support for the back-to-the-land movement, MP Macmillan read a letter from a former city resident that confirmed this view. The settler wrote:

> Sure, it is great! When working for oneself it is a pleasure. We have got things comfortable. The cabin, or mansion, is a kitchen, dining-room, sitting-room, combined, with a nice big pantry, also good sized bedroom and clothes closet.
>
> Last week I built an addition to it, 8x15, joining the kitchen which I have piled up with wood so the wife don't have to keep running outside every

time she needs some. Have also built a chicken house, ... and cleared about 12 acres of land ready for breaking.... I am starting to get logs out for a pig pen and a barn.... As far as the wife and I are concerned, we say the government will never have this homestead again, as I have no fear it will all turn out all right.[59]

Still another letter arrived at the city relief office from a Loon Lake settler who encouraged the city to send more unemployed families north. Conditions were not ideal, but at least the settlers appeared to be satisfied with their prospects:

Thought I would drop you a few lines, just to let you know that we are still alive. I have not been able to call at your office this winter for a work card or relief, thank God.... With us the future looks good. We have something to work for.

We have a very nice log cabin.... There's one real good feature about it, there's no one coming along every month demanding rent or telling us to get out.... I am the landlord....

Last year at this time we owned nothing, now we feel as if we have the world on a downhill pull. It may be slow, but it is success none the less.... My advice is if you have more men down there that ... can get away from mother's apron strings, also their wives have real backbone and if you can find your way clear for them to homestead let them go. It's hard grinding, but when it's time for one's self, who cares.[60]

Encouraged by these and other reports, and facing near daily requests from the unemployed to participate in the settlement scheme, the province continued to discuss various schemes to place unemployed workers on the land.

Table 5.1. 1932 Land Settlement Plan, Province of Saskatchewan

	1932	1933
Number of Settlers	394	114
Number of Dependents	1445	435
Located on Crown Land	235	49
Located on Purchased Land	159	65
On Land	353	113
Abandoned	41	1
Total Expenditure	$164,873	$30,285
Average per Settler	$411	$288
Number of Settlers Contributed from Saskatchewan Cities		
Saskatoon	193	48
Regina	77	30
Moose Jaw	59	0
Prince Albert	12	6
Weyburn	4	3
Swift Current	2	1
Yorkton	1	1
Towns & villages	46	25

Source: NA, RG 30, vol. 8395, file 3840-4, "Saskatchewan Relief Settlement Plan."

The province expected to continue with its program of relief settlement in 1932, but hoped to get more support from the federal government.[61] Later that year, when the federal government finally agreed to fund the back-to-the-land movement, the province of Saskatchewan eagerly participated (see Table 1). It viewed its own settlement plan of the previous year as a success, and believed that with the assistance of the federal government more unemployed relief recipients could be encouraged to return to the land. Although it is uncertain precisely how provincial officials judged the success of the plan, one tangible measure was cost. Even after supporting the families through the winter, the province had only spent an average of $150 per family, a figure considerably less than the cost of maintaining a similar family on city relief.[62] Faced with no other viable alternative, the provincial government agreed that relief funds would be better spent on reestablishment than for the dole.

In the spring of 1932, a United Church missionary toured the new settlements, but the portrait that he painted was not quite so inspiring. In a report to *The Western Producer*, Reverend A.R. Taylor described the conditions he had encountered. In many of the homes visited, "women were in a highly nervous state due to loneliness," and both scabies and impetigo were in evidence as "clothing [was] not sufficiently plentiful to be changed frequently." Few of the city men, Taylor warned, had accomplished much in the way of farm work, and he believed that the placement of these men on the land was not an unqualified success. Commenting on this report, the United Farmers expressed sympathy with the desire of authorities to solve the unemployment problem, but demanded that before any further settlement of the unemployed be made, the province undertake a thorough and disinterested investigation to discover the truth about the settlement scheme.[63]

There can be no doubt that conditions in the north were difficult, but were they, in fact, significantly worse than those experienced by relief recipients in the city? Access to medical services, schools, churches, and stores was certainly more limited, but those amenities were still available to the settlers. A Red Cross hospital was opened at Loon Lake in the fall of 1931, the settlers erected two schools to educate their children, and visiting missionaries attended to the spiritual needs of the homesteaders.[64] It is true that the men had in fact made little progress in their agricultural endeavours, but they had been on the land less than a year when the minister made his visit. All participants were aware that they would be pioneers on a new frontier, and due to their late departure in the 1931 season, no one expected that they would achieve more than the planting of a small garden and the clearing of a couple of acres.[65] It is also true that their isolation far from the city meant their that concerns could be easily ignored, but for the first year or two, the city tried to keep in touch with its former residents and to provide them with as much assistance as possible.[66] And the settlers' correspondence does suggest that, initially at least, they were optimistic about their prospects for reestablishment.

Attempts to ease the transition from urban life to life on a pioneer farm were made by both relief officers and CNR colonization agents, but the back-to-the-land settlers still confronted many harsh realities. At first, it may have seemed adventurous to move to the north and try one's hand at farming, but the initial attraction soon gave way to stark reality. In September 1934, F.B. Kirkwood, superintendent of land settlement for the CNR, made an inspection of the Loon Lake region. His report provided a sad commentary on the status of the back-to-the-land movement:

money is very scarce and in many cases non-existent. It is extremely difficult for homesteaders to obtain ready cash as they have nothing to sell. Where formerly homesteaders were able to secure work for wages, ... today the homesteader has no opportunity along this line. He is too far from market to hope to sell cordwood; his equipment is generally inadequate, and thus he has been unable to bring much land under cultivation, which means that he has no crops to sell.[67]

Citing the "indifference of the administration" and "lack of funds," Kirkwood stated that he did not expect the province to continue with the plan in 1935. There was clearly a need, he believed, for the province to spend more money on these settlers, particularly in the form of development work on the farms. Yet, given the high cost of relief and the numerous other demands being placed on the system, it was not likely that anyone could convince provincial officials to spend even more money on the settlers.[68] For the back-to-the-land scheme to be truly successful, governments would have to provide infrastructure, supervision, and off-homestead employment. None demonstrated a willingness to make the financial commitment that was necessary to permit these settlers to become permanently reestablished on the land.

Although a thorough analysis has yet to be made, it does appear that the back-to-the-land schemes in Saskatchewan, at least, experienced some success. Of the twenty-five Saskatoon families who moved to Loon Lake, for example, more than half eventually gained title to their homesteads. It appears, also, that the first two years of settlement were critical. Of the settlers approved under the 1932 relief settlement plan, 23 percent had abandoned their properties within the first two years. Four years later, that figure had only reached 27 percent.[69] These numbers compare favorably with those for Manitoba, where 24 percent left within two years and 38 percent within four. More than nine out of ten settlers eventually abandoned their holdings in Manitoba, although half remained on the land for at least five years and 20 percent lasted for over a decade.[70] A considerable number of people who were accepted into the program never actually settled on the land, and this fact may falsely inflate the failure rates, but many of those who did settle were simply unsuited for the task. Illness, domestic trouble, and general unsuitability were frequently cited as reasons for abandonment, but in some cases the recorder was more specific. For two settlers who abandoned their homesteads in Manitoba, the clerk provided as reasons: "absolutely useless as a settler," and "salvaged at his own request."[71]

Upon initial inspection, these figures are appalling, and suggest that the policy was a miserable failure. In reality, however, settlement in the prairie provinces was not an easy undertaking. A harsh climate, poor land, pests, and uncertain market conditions each raised the odds against eventual success. In *The Canadian Prairies*, Gerald Friesen discusses the work done by Chester Martin to calculate failure rates among homestead applicants. Friesen describes the rate of attrition as "extraordinary." In Alberta, 45 percent of entries made between 1905 and 1930 were abandoned, while in Saskatchewan for a similar period, the figure was 57 percent.[72] It must be remembered, too, that these settlers were usually farmers, who intended to acquire a homestead in western Canada. In addition, many of them were European settlers who Martin claimed were better homesteaders than settlers of Anglo-Saxon origin.[73] The back-to-the-land settlers of the 1930s had farming experience, but they had also become urbanized. That their rates of failure compared favorably with those of settlers of an earlier era is testimony to their diligence and perseverance.

Reflections on the Back-to-the-Land Scheme

Back-to-the-land was not born of the Depression, yet it was very much affected by both the disastrous economic conditions of the 1930s, and the more prosperous decade of the 1920s. The historians who have characterized the movement as an attempt to create a rural peasantry have done so unfairly. They have not given due consideration to the social and economic conditions of the time, to the ideological roots of the back-to-the-land philosophy, or to the actual people who participated in the process. This article does not pretend to have completely addressed each of these points, but it does take a step in the right direction. Until such time as a thorough investigation of the back-to-the-land movement is made, scholars must not be quick to judge the scheme too harshly. There were serious inadequacies in the schemes adopted and promoted by provincial and federal governments, and these problems were compounded by insufficient financial resources. Nevertheless, the back-to-the-land movement did hold out opportunity for many Canadians who had no other hope.

One critic has charged that Canada's preoccupation with the land kept it from confronting the unemployment problem and finding innovative solutions to the crisis that was enveloping the country. But land was fundamental to Canadian identity. Canada was a nation of farmers, and while many of those farmers were no longer on the farm, the sentiment remained. In prosperous times, people left the land for the city; in times of economic distress, people were willing to give the land another chance. This ebb and flow of humanity reflected the fortunes of an uncertain and sometimes unsound economy. Although the land could provide sustenance, cities and their industries, reformers charged, could not support densely concentrated populations. In urban environments, people had nothing to fall back on. On the farm, at least, they would not starve. The ideological roots of this belief in the land lent both credence and support to the back-to-the-land schemes adopted by the government. Canada's long agrarian tradition, and the fact that agriculture provided the underlying support for much of the Canadian economy, also helped to convince people and their government that a return to a simpler rural life would benefit society.

Financial considerations are central to understanding the Depression-era back-to-the-land movement. Time and again, politicians and civil servants advised that land settlement would be a cost-saving measure. Families could be supported on the land more cheaply than similar families in the city. And given Bennett's fiscal conservatism, reduction of costs became an overriding concern in any relief measure. In the spring of 1932, when public works programs were suspended in favour of direct relief, the principal motivation had been cost. Public works were ten times more expensive than direct relief, and despite the fact that many useful projects had been undertaken, Bennett refused to engage in any form of deficit spending if it meant jeopardizing Canada's credit rating. Returning people to the land had the advantage of reducing local relief burdens, and offered, potentially at least, the chance to permanently reestablish people who could become self-supporting. It no doubt seemed reasonable to politicians that if men could not find work in the cities, they could always support their families on the farm. The Depression did not alter this attitude. It only added impetus.

Finally, the back-to-the-land plan was packaged as an opportunity for men on relief to save face. On the land, men and their families could work to feed themselves and did not have to experience the near daily humiliation of city doles. Effort put into their homesteads would provide satisfaction because settlers knew that it was home. These were the potential benefits and the tangible results that might be realized. The reality was often very different. Land settlement schemes were, in fact, emergency responses to adverse conditions, rather than carefully planned colonization initiatives which were necessary to ensure success. The federal government repeatedly declared that its plan was simply designed to provide relief, not to create new communities. Land settlement may have provided an alternative to direct relief, but without sufficient financial resources, adequate guidance in agricultural matters, or the provision of any infrastructure, the land settlement scheme could not begin to address the problems of the urban poor. In the final analysis, neither the cities, the province nor the federal government were prepared to expend the funds necessary to support a full-fledged back-to-the-land movement. It was in reality a stop-gap measure for a government bankrupted by relief payments and, with no end to the Depression in sight, it was the only tangible program it could offer a populace clamouring for action.

Notes

1. T.J.D. Powell, "Northern Settlement, 1929–1935," *Saskatchewan History* 30, no. 3 (Autumn 1977): 81–98.
2. See, for example, Gerald Friesen, *The Canadian Prairies: A History* (Toronto: University of Toronto Press, 1984); John McDonald, "Soldier Settlement and Depression Settlement in the Forest Fringe of Saskatchewan," *Prairie Forum* 6, no. 1 (Spring 1981): 35–55; E.C. Morgan, "Soldier Settlement in the Prairie Provinces," *Saskatchewan History* 21, no. 2 (Spring 1968): 41–55.
3. John Herd Thompson with Allen Seager, *Canada 1922–1939: Decades of Discord* (Toronto: McClelland and Stewart, 1985), 218.
4. James Struthers, *No Fault of Their Own: Unemployment and the Canadian Welfare State, 1914–1941* (Toronto: University of Toronto Press, 1983), 8.
5. Ibid., 9.
6. George V. Haythorne, *Land and Labour: A Social Survey of Agriculture and the Farm Labour Market in Central Canada* (Toronto: Oxford University Press, 1941), ix.
7. Ibid., 437.
8. Robert England, *The Colonization of Western Canada: A Study of Contemporary Land Settlement (1896–1934)* (London: P.S. King and Son, Ltd., 1936), 122.
9. Ibid., 134–35.
10. H. Blair Neatby, *The Politics of Chaos: Canada in the Thirties* (Toronto: Macmillan, 1972).
11. Michiel Horn, *The Great Depression of the 1930s in Canada* (Ottawa: Canadian Historical Association, 1984), 8.
12. Thompson, *Canada 1922–1939*, 96.
13. Leon Edgar Truesdell, "The Extent and Significance of Farm Migration," in Wilson Gee, ed., *The Country Life of the Nation* (Chapel Hill: University of North Carolina Press, 1930), 39–53.
14. T. Lynn Smith, *Studies of the Great Rural Tap Roots of Urban Poverty in the U.S.* (New York: Canton Press, 1974).
15. National Archives of Canada (NA), RG 30, Canadian National Railways Files, vol. 8394, file 3860-4, sec. 1, letter from W.A. Gordon to Colonel J.B. MacLean, 22 June 1931.

16. NA, RG 30, vol. 8394, file 3860-4, sec. 1, letter from J.B. MacLean to W.A. Gordon, 15 June 1931.

17. Ibid., sec. 2, memorandum from the Central Committee to W.A. Gordon, 28 August 1931.

18. House of Commons, *Debates*, 20 July 1931, p. 3973.

19. NA, RG 30, vol. 8394, file 3860-4, sec. 2, memorandum from the Central Committee to W.A. Gordon, 28 August 1931, and memorandum to W.A. Gordon, n.d. [Fall 1931].

20. House of Commons, *Debates*, 11 March 1932, pp. 1055–56.

21. Ibid., 4 April 1932, p. 1663.

22. Ibid., 2 March 1933, p. 2657.

23. J.A.P. Haydon, "Filling up Canada's Vacant Spaces," *Canadian Congress Journal* 12, no. 9 (September 1933): 15–16.

24. "Unemployment Scheme Liked," *Regina Leader-Post*, 14 May 1931, p. 2.

25. "City May Finance Unemployed to Get on Northern Land," *Moose Jaw Evening Times*, 16 May 1931, p. 7; "Details of Land Settlement Plan Will be Sought," *Moose Jaw Evening Times*, 19 May 1931, p. 5.

26. NA, RG 30, vol. 8394, file 3860-4, sec. 3, "State Aided Land Settlement as a Measure to Relieve Unemployment," 21 March 1932.

27. Ibid., "Unemployment Relief Land Settlement," 29 March 1932.

28. Ibid.

29. Ibid., sec. 2, memorandum to W.A. Gordon, n.d. [Fall 1931].

30. Ibid.

31. *The Labour Gazette* 32, no. 5 (May 1932): 478.

32. Ibid., 32, no. 7 (July 1932): 789.

33. House of Commons, *Debates*, 28 April 1932, p. 2453.

34. NA, MG 26, R.B. Bennett Papers, reel 1279, pp. 346995–996, "Some Remedies for Unemployment."

35. Ibid., reel 1433, p. 477260, Premier J.T.M. Anderson quoted in letter from federal Labour Minister, G.D. Robertson, to R.B. Bennett, 11 August 1931.

36. Ibid., p. 477886, "Unemployment Relief Report," 1932.

37. Ibid., reel 1434, p. 478722, "City of Saskatoon: Unemployment Relief Statistics," 1932.

38. John H. Archer, *Saskatchewan: A History* (Saskatoon: Western Prairie Producer Books, 1980), chapter 12.

39. "Suggests Establishing 500 Jobless on Stocked Farms," *Saskatoon Star-Phoenix*, 4 March 1931, p. 4; "Hair Would Put Jobless on Farm Land," *Saskatoon Star-Phoenix*, 7 March 1931, p. 3.

40. "Men Ask Cash to Settle on Farms," *Saskatoon Star-Phoenix*, 16 May 1931, p. 7; "Dr. Anderson Answers Macauley's Criticisms," *Saskatoon Star-Phoenix*, 29 March 1932, p. 12; "Unemployed Ask $400 for Each Family," *Saskatoon Star-Phoenix*, 3 May 1932, p. 3.

41. "Going to the Land," *Saskatoon Star-Phoenix*, 18 May 1932, p. 11.

42. "Interest Keen in Settlement Plan," *Saskatoon Star-Phoenix*, 14 March 1931, p. 3.

43. NA, RG 30, vol. 5614, file 2231 -D, letter from J.P. Martin to A.G. Sinclair, 31 April 1931.

44. Ibid., "Land Settlement Activities."

45. "An Act to provide for the Settlement of Provincial Lands," *Statutes of the Province of Saskatchewan, 1931*, c. 22; "Scores Now Planning to Obtain Land," *Saskatoon Star-Phoenix*, 20 April 1931, p. 3; "25 Families Seek Farms," *Saskatoon Star-Phoenix*, 14 April 1931, p. 5.

46. The 1931 plan was quite similar to the 1932 federal-provincial scheme. See "Settlement Plan Ready for Action," *Saskatoon Star-Phoenix*, 10 May 1932, p. 3; "Provincial and City Committees Formed to Pilot Land Plan," *Saskatoon Star-Phoenix*, 13 May 1932, p. 7.

47. "Scores Now Planning to Obtain Land," *Saskatoon Star-Phoenix*, 20 April 1931, p. 3.

48. "Choose Land in Loon Lake Area," *Saskatoon Star-Phoenix*, 21 April 1931, p. 3.

49. R.W. Murchie, *Land Settlement as a Relief Measure* (Minneapolis: University of Minnesota Press, 1933), 16.

50. Saskatchewan Archives Board (SAB) (Saskatoon Office), homestead files of selected Saskatoon settlers who located on land near Loon Lake.

51. "25 Families Seek Farms," *Saskatoon Star-Phoenix*, 14 April 1931, p. 5.

52. SAB (Saskatoon Office), "Application for an Eligibility Certification, Department of Natural Resources, Province of Saskatchewan," located in the homestead file of William Thomas Taylor, SW 33, Township 58, Range 23, West of the 3rd Meridian.

53. Ibid.

54. "Thirty Families Prepare for Trek to Farm Location," *Saskatoon Star-Phoenix*, 6 May 1931, p. 3.

55. "New Settlers Are Sold on 'Little Saskatoon,'" *Saskatoon Star-Phoenix*, 20 June 1931, p. 3.

56. "Little Saskatoon," *Saskatoon Star-Phoenix*, 23 June 1931, p. 9.

57. "Offers Fish to Repay This City," *Saskatoon Star-Phoenix*, 14 September 1931, p. 3.

58. "Feed For Cattle Chief Problem at Loon Lake," *Saskatoon Star-Phoenix*, 9 March 1932, p. 3.

59. House of Commons, *Debates*, 4 April 1932, p. 1664.

60. "Saskatoon People Making Good on Loon Lake Farms," *Saskatoon Star-Phoenix*, 28 March 1932, p. 3.

61. See, for example, "Settlement of Jobless is Proposed," *Saskatoon Star-Phoenix*, 27 February 1932, p. 3; "Settlement Proposal to be Discussed," *Saskatoon Star-Phoenix*, 5 March 1932, p. 3; "May Act on Settlement This Evening," *Saskatoon Star-Phoenix*, 1 April 1932, p. 3; and "Claims Return to Land is Solution of Unemployment," *Saskatoon Star-Phoenix*, 22 April 1932, p. 3.

62. NA, RG 30, vol. 8394, file 3860-4, sec. 3, letter from E.M. Johnson to T. Magladery, 11 May 1932.

63. "Conditions Bad in Loon Lake District," *The Western Producer*, 31 March 1932, p. 5.

64. "Face Winter Confidently," *Saskatoon Star-Phoenix*, 31 October 1931, p. 3; "Loon Lake," *Saskatoon Star-Phoenix*, 4 January 1932, p. 6; "Loon Lake," *Saskatoon Star-Phoenix*, 5 March 1932, p. 13.

65. "Thirty Families ..." *Saskatoon Star-Phoenix*, 6 May 1931, p. 3.

66. "Harness Needed by Loon Lake Man," *Saskatoon Star-Phoenix*, 27 April 1932, p. 9; "Saskatoon Leads Settlement Work," *Saskatoon Star-Phoenix*, 27 June 1932, p. 3; "New Settlers in Need of Clothes," *Saskatoon Star-Phoenix*, 23 September 1932, p. 10; "Loon Lake People in Call for Toys," *Saskatoon Star-Phoenix*, 16 November 1932, p. 3.

67. NA, RG 30, vol. 5639, file 5540-5, memorandum from F.B. Kirkwood, 26 September 1934.

68. Ibid., letter from F.B. Kirkwood to A.G. Sinclair, 25 September 1934.

69. NA, RG 27, Department of Labour Records, vol. 2260, "Province of Saskatchewan, Relief Land Settlement (1932), Settlers Who Have Abandoned the Land."

70. Ibid., vol. 2260, "Province of Manitoba, Relief Land Settlement (1932), Settlers Who Have Abandoned the Land." Abandonment data beyond 1935 for the province of Saskatchewan has not been recovered, so it is not possible to compare later developments in Saskatchewan with those in Manitoba.

71. Ibid.

72. Friesen, *The Canadian Prairies*, 309.

73. In Saskatchewan, two-thirds of the settlers selected under the 1932 settlement plan were of British origin. See NA, RG 27, vol. 2266, file C, "The Relief Act 1932, Approved Settlers under Relief Settlement Plan, Province of Saskatchewan, 31 December 1933."

6

History According to the Boucher Report

*Some Reflections on the State and Social Welfare
in Quebec before the Quiet Revolution**

B.L. VIGOD

IN DECEMBER 1961, the Quebec Government appointed a Committee to study the prevailing system of social assistance, or as it was still quaintly but revealingly called, "assistance at home." The members of the committee were J. Emile Boucher, Chairman of the Board of Directors of the Société nationale de fiducie, Marcel Bélanger, an accountant teaching in the Laval University Faculty of Commerce, and Claude Morin, teaching in the Social Sciences faculty at Laval. The two secretaries, Jean-Paul Labelle and Marcel Lemieux, were provincial welfare administrators. The committee therefore included no historians, it lacked the status of a Royal Commission (unlike the Parent Inquiry into education), and its mandate was very precise and limited. It was to examine the size and criteria of benefits, means of cooperation between government and private agencies, and "the overall problem of financial assistance at home, its financial and social implications, prevention and rehabilitation." So one would hardly have expected the Report of such a committee to contain a historical treatise. But the Boucher Report of June 1963 attached a great deal of importance to the history of its subject. It argued that the unsatisfactory nature of existing arrangements for social assistance was the product of a unique historical development stretching back to the very birth of Quebec society. And it very strongly implied that to reform its social welfare system in the 1960s, Quebec had to escape from its institutional and ideological past.[1] This is a fine, indeed classic example of the historical mythology created by the authors and partisans of the Quiet Revolution: "avant nous, rien." The history of modern Quebec is divided into "the uniform bleakness of the pre-Quiet Revolution years (la grande noirceur) and the long-delayed liberation of the post-Quiet Revolution period."[2] As is the case in other spheres of public activity, this generalization about the evolution of social assistance in Quebec distorts the historical record. On the other hand, it sheds considerable light on the outlook and interests of these particular reformers at the time they mapped out the future of social service in Quebec.[3] Historians of the Quiet Revolution are in that sense indebted to documents such as the Boucher Report.

---

* This chapter was first published as "History According to the Boucher Report: Some Reflections on the State and Social Welfare in Quebec Before the Quiet Revolution," in Allan Moscovitch and Jim Albert, eds., *The Benevolent State: The Growth of Welfare in Canada* (Toronto: Garamond Press, 1987): 175–86.

The Boucher Commission and the History of Social Welfare

According to the Boucher Report, the history of social assistance in Quebec was one of remarkable continuity. Institutional developments from the early seventeenth to the late nineteenth century conformed closely to the teaching of the Roman Catholic Church. The system which evolved, was, in the words of Esdras Minville's earlier study for the Rowell-Sirois Commission, which are quoted approvingly, "the concrete expression of a doctrine [of social justice and charity]." Under the French regime, the state was "too busy with quarrels ... to pay attention" to social needs; and in any case most people considered their problems too intimate or personal to confide to royal officials. Thus, even the forerunner of "assistance at home," the so-called Committees for the Poor established in the mid-17th century, were an exercise in community responsibility organized by the Church, albeit under Royal authority.[4]

Although French Canada was briefly subject to the Elizabethan Poor Law, and although the Committees for the Poor tended to wither away, the effect of the British Conquest was essentially to strengthen community bonds and private and personal notions of charity. This, the Boucher Report attributed on one hand to French Canadians' fear of the new alien authorities, and on the other hand to the re-establishment of French Civil Law under the Quebec Act. In the first half of the 19th century, St. Vincent-de-Paul societies arose to assume responsibilities for local relief, and there was a gradual expansion of institutions caring for indigents: hospitals, asylums, and orphanages. There was some state support for these, but they were largely the work of religious orders recently imported from France.

Because the state's role was so limited, Confederation had no special impact on social assistance: it merely established the theoretical jurisdiction of the provincial government. What did alter the system were the economic changes of the late nineteenth century, which found private [i.e., religious] charitable agencies unable to cope with urban, indus-trial society. Herein lies the great tragedy, according to the Boucher Report. Responding to a "historical necessity," the Provincial Legislature passed the *Public Charities Act of 1921* to increase and regularize state support for institutions which cared for indigents. But despite this promising initiative, neither the concept of indigence nor the range of state activity was brought into line with social reality thereafter. The system failed to acknowledge that economic weakness, not utter destitution, was the prevalent social problem; and it there-fore failed to shift the emphasis from institutional support to "social assistance at home." Although some modest allowances were introduced during the late 1930's, this basic fail-ure created a vacuum soon filled by federal legislation of "Anglo-Saxon inspiration" which was ill-suited to Quebec needs, and which itself contributed to the postwar malaise.[5]

How did the Boucher Committee explain the failure to modernize social assistance? Basically, with the categorical statement that "there had long existed in Quebec a pro-found misconception of the true role of the state in welfare matters ...." The misconception was that the state should play an inferior, supplementary role vis-à-vis private initiative, limited in effect to channelling funds through private agencies. When social realities be-gan to threaten this doctrine, the private sector "froze in a rigid and suspicious attitude." For its part, the public sector (i.e., the provincial government) had its own motives for respecting the doctrine and maintaining the fiction—even while assuming the lion's share of costs. The result was a "composite administrative organization over which neither [sector] has full authority." Social needs weren't being met, but the private institutions were too satisfied with their power and status to notice.[6]

The state's acceptance of a subordinate role had dire consequences. Its administrative personnel thought only in terms of controlling public funds; in times of restraint they could be a positive hindrance through false economies. They did not evaluate the quality or adequacy of social services. Indeed, when the Department of Social Welfare finally did hire some professionals in social welfare, their presence was deeply feared by the lawyers and accountants in place. In the same way, legislation never reflected any fundamental changes in thinking about social assistance. Amendments to the *Public Charities Act* were mere housekeeping: changes in categories of assistance, absorption of new federal-provincial programs, and so on. Even the Great Depression produced only emergency relief and a grudging addition of "institutions without walls" to the list of agencies which could be subsidized. The essentially rural notions of indigence, community responsibility and the role of extended families were never formally abandoned. The Committee conceded that there is always a time lag between changing realities and appropriate legislation. But Quebec's failings could not be considered normal in this sense: the resistance to change was determined, even obsessive.[7]

Thus, the Boucher Report not surprisingly recommended an explicit rejection of these anachronistic ideas. "The Quebec Government should acknowledge in theory and practice an increasingly dynamic and creative role in social security matters ... [and] accept in a positive and realistic manner all consequences resulting from this necessary role."[8]

Quebec Social Welfare, 1920–1950: An Alternative View

How should a professional historian react to this version of the past? For the pre-1921 period, he can point to a few contradictions and misconceptions, but nothing terribly serious. Most of them derive from an overemphasis on continuity—the assumption that since religious doctrines were always involved, there were no significant alternations in the relative importance of Church and State in the realm of social assistance. Thus we have a significant downplaying of the powers and initiatives of the civil authority in New France after 1663, and little sense of the impact of the ultramontane triumphs of the mid-19th century, both institutional and ideological. The Report even contradicts itself on this subject, claiming at the outset that Church teaching brought about the acceptance of family and community responsibility without civil compulsion, but later suggesting that the re-introduction of French Civil Law in 1774 created "legal norms [which were] a powerful instrument assuring cohesion and continuity of the family's responsibilities in welfare matters."[9]

But these are minor quibbles. More surprising is the failure to acknowledge the complexities of the period after 1921. A study of the period between 1921 and 1945 reveals something other than "uniform bleakness." There were discernible advances in thinking about social assistance and the role of the state, and if the system in 1960 was unbelievably antiquated and chaotic, the explanation lay in the immediate rather than the distant past. Perhaps the Committee did not want to sound politically partisan, or perhaps it was using history to undermine the legitimacy of the clerically-dominated structure whose displacement it was about to propose. Whatever the reason, it ignored the possibility that the villain was no older than the postwar Duplessis regime itself, which conducted a self-serving but shortsighted and unconscionable resistance to many forms of political modernization. True, a threatened clerical and lay elite in the private sector acquiesced, permitting their agencies to become "dispensing organisms" for Union Nationale patronage.[10] But they were given little choice, and there were just as many people in the Church who warned against the ultimate consequence. By assigning primary responsibility to the welfare institutions and not to the government which had the duty and authority to introduce reforms, the Boucher Commission was turning the situation upside down.

Superficially, the *Public Charities Act of 1921* was the Quebec government's reaction to a temporary crisis, the severe postwar depression. The network of private (in most cases religious) and municipal institutions which sheltered and treated helpless and destitute individuals could not cope with a sudden deluge using traditional sources of revenue. At the same time, it had become clear that neither a recently enacted poor law in the Elizabethan tradition, obliging municipalities to care for indigents residing within their borders, nor the Provincial Secretary's custom of making *ad hoc* grants to individual benevolent institutions, was adequate in the circumstances.[11] Premier L-A Taschereau argued that the Act was an emergency measure which signalled no fundamental change in philosophy. "Voyez-vous par vous-mêmes toutes les affreuses misères à soulager, et dites-moi si le gouvernement n'a pas le devoir impérieux de venir en aide à nos institutions pour leur permettre de réaliser leur oeuvre."[12]

Critics, however, saw far more than an expansion and regularization of subsidies in the legislation. By spelling out categories of assistance in minute detail and creating a Bureau of Public Charities to administer the grants, the Act raised the spectre of increasing state control and the decline of the "moral" aspect of charity. The sensitivity of the Church is a matter of some complexity. It no doubt resulted in part from insecurity about its own ability to provide adequate services, as well as from legitimate fears about the partisan manipulation of provincial assistance. In addition, some Quebec churchmen were in a state of near paranoia after the war because of anticlerical policies adopted in several European Catholic countries. In any case, there resulted a bitter five year dispute pitting the Liberal government against the Roman Catholic hierarchy and its political and journalistic allies, with religious orders frequently caught in the crossfire.[13] Although the government eventually made some minor concessions to religious authorities, other initiatives soon followed.

Provincial authority and activity expanded dramatically in the field of public health under the direction of Dr. Alphonse Lessard, who served simultaneously as Director of the Public Charities Bureau. In fact some of Lessard's health initiatives contained strong elements of social service, such as the temporary removal of children from tubercular surroundings and an educational as well as a treatment campaign against venereal disease.[14] In 1924, the government also passed an adoption law which finally gave legal and emotional protection to children and adopting parents. Although the nuns who operated orphanages and foundling homes had urged some legislation, it caused a new storm of protest from religious militants. Technically, they objected that as originally worded the law did not guarantee that Catholic children would be adopted into Catholic homes; more fundamentally, critics complained that the state was further invading the sacred domain of the family. Henri Bourassa insisted that the legislation "allongera la liste des atteintes

portées à tout ce qui a fait la force et la vitalité de notre ordre social. Elles se sont singu-
lièrement multipliées, depuis quelques années."[15]

By the middle of the 1920s, the reforming zeal of the Taschereau government was
rapidly dissipating. The postwar depression was giving way to a period of industrial expansion, the government did not want to increase its financial commitments unnecessarily,
and Premier Taschereau was anxious for a truce in what he called "religious warfare." For
these reasons and in a classic defence of provincial rights, Taschereau strongly opposed
the federal *Old Age Pensions Act of 1927*. For this he was warmly congratulated in business, ecclesiastical and nationalist circles. However, not everyone in Quebec was satisfied
with the traditional, very restrictive definition of social assistance embodied in the *Public
Charities Act* (effectively, the care of indigents within institutions), or with the virtual
absence of legislation to mitigate the poverty and vulnerability of the urban working class.
In the latter half of the 1920s, voluntary agencies in Montreal began to recognize the
need for a variety of social services "outside walls," and for more effective ways of raising funds necessary to provide them.[16] While the Protestant and Jewish communities
often set the example, as in launching federated appeals and recognizing the profession
of social worker, the parish-based St. Vincent-de-Paul Societies of Montreal began their
own extensive inquiry into the nature of their future services to Catholics.[17] Meanwhile,
organized labour and its sympathizers seized an opportunity to introduce the question of
income security.

This opportunity arose from a combination of circumstances: the provincial government's refusal to participate in the federal old age pension scheme, and a debate concerning
workers' compensation. The non-confessional Montreal Trades and Labour Council
strongly favoured the modest federal initiative, which required provincial governments
to contribute half of a twenty dollar monthly pension for needy persons over seventy
years of age, and to undertake the costs of administration. More surprisingly, support for
Quebec's participation in the scheme came also from Pierre Beaulé, lay president of the
Catholic Labour Confederation.[18] Even the Abbé Fortin, clerical advisor to the catholic
organization, disputed the claim that Quebec had no need of old age pensions. "Il faut être
contre l'étatisme," he agreed, "mais il faut aussi secourir les malheureux. Et aujourd'hui
on est rendu à un état de choses tel qu'il faut prendre des mesures nécessaires pour aider
les indigents." The only way to avoid "statism" was to pay wages which would enable the
working class "d'élever une nombreuse famille et de prendre soin aussi en même temps
de leurs vieux parents."[19] The very fact that Premier Taschereau continued to denounce
Old Age Pensions on philosophical as well as constitutional grounds in 1928 and 1929
indicates his awareness that the plan appealed to many Quebecers.

The government had appointed an inquiry into the system of workers' compensation in
1922, and enacted its unanimous recommendations in 1926. Taschereau at first rejected labour's proposal to remove compensation claims from the courts and transfer the authority
to make awards and the administration of the system to a permanent commission. He was
forced to change his mind, however, when insurance companies suddenly and drastically
increased premiums for the liability insurance employers were required to carry. A commission was created in 1928 to accept liability deposits, make awards and recommend and
enforce improved industrial safety standards.[20] As Taschereau had expected, the existence
of the commission encouraged labour to press for a greatly expanded definition of "risks"

subject to compensation. The argument was disarmingly simple. Seasonal unemployment and poverty in old age were as much "occupational hazards" for the urban working class as were industrial accidents. Politically, this argument was difficult to reject: it proposed a form of old age security without federal intrusion into the constitutional domain of the province and, if workers as well as employers and the government all contributed a share of the "premiums," it was a form of social insurance which did not encourage "reliance on the state." In 1929, growing pressure led Labour Minister Galipeault to admit that "le temps est venu d'étudier le système qui conviendrait pour établir l'assurance social dans cette province.... La loi préférée ... serait une loi contributoire à la mise en oeuvre de laquelle contribueraient le patron, l'ouvrier et le gouvernement."[21] In 1930, Taschereau appointed Edouard Montpetit to chair a royal commission inquiry into social insurance. Thus, although the recommendations of the Montpetit Commission were inevitably influenced by the Great Depression, it must be remembered that the inquiry was launched in response to growing demands and expectations in the preceding decade.

The effects of the Depression were arguably more severe in Quebec than in any other province. Barely able to provide its share of relief under federal unemployment relief legislation, especially when it had to assume a large number of municipal obligations as well, the Quebec government could not seriously consider permanent or more elaborate social security measures. On the contrary, Premier Taschereau emphasized the need for fiscal responsibility and unwisely began denouncing the proponents of reform.[22] Still, the Boucher Report seriously under-estimated the impact of the Depression on clerical, political and public thinking about social assistance. For one thing, the inadequacy of traditional attitudes and existing arrangements was clearly demonstrated. The experience of the St. Vincent-de-Paul societies in Montreal provides a classic example. Since the city had no formal mechanism for administering unemployment relief when the Depression struck, the societies initially agreed to take on the responsibility. As the visible relief agencies, however, the societies found themselves blamed for delays and insufficiencies which they were powerless to control; in fact they became the targets for general discontent and frustration. The laymen and clergy who directed the work of the societies concluded that their original mission, charitable work of the parish level, could be permanently damaged by the loss of prestige. In 1933 they withdrew their services, forcing Montreal City Council to establish its own relief administration.[23]

From a number of quarters, meanwhile, came proposals for reform linked to the realities of the prevailing economic system. The Papal Encyclical *Quadragesimo Anno* (1931) received far more prompt attention in Quebec than had the first great social encyclical, *Rerum Novarum*, after 1891. Now that the Pope had declared governments responsible for protecting the economically weak members of industrial society, rejoiced Father J-P Archambault of the Ecole Sociale Populaire, Quebec clergy need no longer fear being accused of "meddling in politics" simply because they called for social reform.[24] Study sessions organized by Archambault produced the *Programme de Restauration Sociale*, whose reformist content historians often ignore because of the ultimately conservative motives of the authors. There were actually two versions of the *Programme*. The first, written by priests and published in the spring of 1933, called in general terms for a redistribution of wealth in favour of the masses through such state initiatives as accident, sickness, old age and unemployment insurance, crop and other kinds of farm insurance, minimum wage laws related to the cost of living and special grants for large families and the very poor.[25] The second *Programme* published in late 1933 was a more comprehensive document co-authored by lay leaders of the Catholic Action movement. The section on labour legislation, written by union official Alfred Charpentier, called for a contributory social insurance scheme, old age and needy mothers' allowances, an experimental family allowance system, salaries sufficient to support average-sized families, a law requiring employers to pay wages before dividends, a minimum wage for day labour, slum clearance and increased bargaining rights for unions.[26] In the same year, Cardinal Villeneuve publicly invited the state to elaborate a program of social reform based on papal teaching.[27] All of these demands reinforced the recommendations of the Montpetit Commission, which had exceeded its original terms of reference in a series of reports submitted in 1931 and 1932. In addition to regulatory laws protecting workers and wider provincial support for charitable institutions, Montpetit proposed such direct support programs as needy mothers' and family allowances, old age pensions, unemployment insurance and subsidized health insurance.[28] Even before the second *Programme de Restauration Sociale* appeared, various proposals for income security had reached the political arena. The election platform of the opposition Conservatives in 1931 promised "collective insurance" and increased compensation for accidents at work, general minimum wage legislation, allowances for large families and pensions for the blind, for widows and for orphans.[29] These policies were reconfirmed at the 1933 leadership convention which chose Maurice Duplessis to succeed Camillien Houde, however much Duplessis downplayed them afterward. On the Liberal side, Premier Taschereau's continuing rejection of the more far-reaching Montpetit Commission recommendations was apparently decisive in driving Action libérale reformers out of the party.[30] The leader of the group, Paul Gouin, was an unsigned co-author of the second *Programme*, which was adopted almost verbatim as a platform by his new political party, the Action libérale nationale (ALN). The same platform was supposedly that of the electoral alliance between Gouin and Duplessis in 1935.

Although Taschereau agreed to implement old age pensions only as a form of deathbed repentance, and Duplessis enacted practically none of the social legislation contained in the ALN platform,[31] it would be wrong to conclude that the desire for improved social assistance simply vanished. Duplessis' decision to call a provincial election in 1939 on the issue of Canadian participation in the Second World War was almost certainly an attempt to divert attention from the record of his government. In fact, several of the deceived reformers returned to the Liberal fold for the campaign and one of them, Oscar Drouin, played a central role in the reforms of the Godbout administration. While better known for the introduction of compulsory education and female suffrage and for the nationalization of Montreal Light, Heat and Power Company, the wartime Liberal government also laid the groundwork for an expanded role in social assistance. Without directly challenging the domain of the private institutions, Godbout responded to an acknowledged lack of coordination by creating a Ministry of Social Welfare. At the same time, he extended the needy mothers' allowance and established family courts to deal with juvenile delinquency and other family problems.[32]

Godbout only hinted at an expanding role for the new Department;[33] his immediate dilemma was created by federal initiatives. The Report of the Rowell-Sirois Commission, the ensuring transfer of constitutional authority over unemployment insurance to

Ottawa, and the introduction of Family Allowances were anathema to traditional nationalist opinion in Quebec and vindicated Duplessis' prophesies. Yet Godbout and his colleagues probably favoured the new forms of state intervention and believed they were in tune with public expectations. They were undoubtedly less enthusiastic about the expansion of federal authority, regarding it simply as inevitable in the context of wartime fiscal centralization while dreading the eventual political consequences. It is interesting to speculate what would have happened if the Godbout government had not borne the brunt of French Canadian anger over conscription, and instead been re-elected in 1944. For although the "official" social thought of Quebec remained fundamentally different from that of English Canada, practically speaking the gap in terms of public expectations of the state had closed dramatically by the end of the Depression. Despite their distrust of federal authority, after all, Quebec voters supported the welfare state policies of the federal Liberals as strongly as they did the provincial rights platform of the Union Nationale during the postwar decade. And if Godbout was prepared to defy the Roman Catholic hierarchy over education and female suffrage, he was perfectly capable of expanding the state's role in social assistance in response to demonstrated needs. Like Jean Lesage fifteen years later, he would undoubtedly have profited from autonomist sentiment in conflicts with Ottawa: even the Tremblay Royal Commission admitted implicitly that the vacuum in provincial social policy was contributing to the expansion of federal authority during the late forties and early fifties.[34]

Of course 1945 was not 1960. Neither the bureaucratic expertise and ambition, nor the provincial financial resources, nor what Jean-Louis Roy refers to as "social knowledge" were nearly as strong as they would become.[35] Conversely, the "private" sector might have resisted change far more effectively at an earlier stage. Still, it has become almost a commonplace that the Quiet Revolution was not really very revolutionary: rather, it was a period when public policy and institutions caught up with social and economic change.

This is especially true in the case of social assistance. The inadequacies of the prevailing structure and philosophy were widely recognized, and a public desire for social security measures had already been created by the end of the war. In fact some proponents of reform during the 1930s were considerably more radical than the Boucher Committee, in that they explicitly linked social injustice with the economic system. Of course Boucher and his colleagues knew that poverty and insecurity were rooted in the system, but their response was not to challenge the system. The "bureaucratic revolution" they proposed would not fundamentally alter the course of Quebec history; it would merely cure fifteen years of stubborn neglect, while fulfilling the ambitions of a class whose presence, training and outlook were the product of a perfectly normal evolution.

Notes

1. Government of Quebec, *Report of the Study Committee on Public Assistance*, Quebec, 1963, 27, 117 [Hereafter, *Report*].
2. Ralph Heintzman, "Image and Consequence," *Journal of Canadian Studies* 13:2, (Summer, 1978): 2.
3. See the remarkably perceptive contemporary analysis by Hubert Guindon, "Social Unrest, Social Class and Quebec's Bureaucratic Revolution," *Queen's Quarterly* LXXI:2, (1964).
4. *Report*, 27–28.

5. Ibid, 29–33.
6. Ibid, 107–09.
7. Ibid, 110–15.
8. Ibid, 117.
9. Ibid, 27, 30.
10. Conrad Black, *Duplessis* (Toronto, 1977), 687–88.
11. B.L. Vigod, "Ideology and Institutions in Quebec: The Public Charities Controversy 1921–1926," *Social History* XI:21 (May 1978): 168–69.
12. *Le Devoir*, 14 avril, 1921.
13. Vigod, "Public Charities."
14. B.L. Vigod, "Responses to Economic and Social Change in Quebec: The Provincial Administration of Louis-Alexandre Taschereau 1920–1929," Ph.D., Queen's University, 1975, 306–16.
15. Ibid, 291–97; Bourassa citation from *Le Devoir*, 7 mars, 1924.
16. Serge Mongeau, *Evolution de l'Assistance au Québec* (Montreal, 1967), 49–50.
17. Robert Rumilly, *La Plus Riche Aumône: Histoire de la Société St. Vincent de Paul* (Montreal, 1946), 134–48.
18. *Canadian Annual Review*, 1928–29, 386–87; Confédération des Travailleurs Catholiques du Canada, *Procès Verbal*, 1926, 34–35; *La Vie Syndicale*, février, 1928.
19. *L'Evénement*, 18 janvier, 1928.
20. Quebec, *Report of the Investigation Commission on the Compensation in Labour Accidents*, Quebec, 1925; *Canadian Annual Review*, 1927–28, 414–15; Roger Chartier, "La réparation des accidents du travail et la commission du salaire minimum des femmes," *Relations industrielles*, janvier, 1963.
21. Confédération des Travailleurs Catholiques du Canada, *Procès Verbal*, 1929, 15–16.
22. B.L. Vigod, "The Quebec Government and Social Legislation During the 1930s: A Study in Political Self-Destruction," *Journal of Canadian Studies*, 14:1 (Spring, 1979): 62–65.
23. Robert Rumilly, *Histoire de la Province de Quebec* XXXIII, 150–51, 176.
24. "Avant Propos," *Ecole Sociale Populaire*, No. 232–233, mai–juin, 1933, [Hereafter ESP].
25. L. Chagnon, "Directives sociales catholiques," *ESP*, No. 232–233 mai–juin, 1933.
26. "La question ouvrière," *ESP*, No. 239–40, décembre 1933–janvier 1934.
27. *Action Catholique*, 28 avril, 1933.
28. Commission des assurances sociales de Québec, *Rapports*, 1932–33. Recommendations summarized in Mongeau, *Evolution de l'Assistance* ..., 60–62.
29. Jean-Louis Roy, *Les Programmes Electoraux du Québec* (Montreal, 1971, Vol. II), 246.
30. Patricia G. Dirks, "The Origins of the Union Nationale," Ph.D., University of Toronto, 1974, 226.
31. The exceptions were modest allowances for blind persons and needy mothers. Duplessis' *Fair Wage Act* became a cruel joke on labour, since it was used to restrain wage increases.
32. The immediate cause of action, according to Mongeau, *Evolution de l'Assistance* ..., 70–72, was a scandal regarding health conditions in commercial daycare facilities; this provoked a wide ranging Inquiry whose recommendations were heeded.
33. It had been established partly to administer a new health insurance program and partly "d'étudier et de resoudre de façon pratique les graves problèmes du bien-être social ..." Roy, *Programmes Electoraux* II, 319.
34. Quebec, Royal Commission of Inquiry into Constitutional Problems, *Report*, Quebec, 1956, e.g., Vol. I, 258–60. See also René Durocher et Michèle Jean, "Duplessis et la Commission royal d'enquête ...," *Revue d'histoire de l'Amérique française*, 25:3 (décembre 1971): 354–55.
35. Jean-Louis Roy, La *Marche des Québécois: Le Temps des Ruptures 1945–1960* (Montreal, 1976).

7

A New Taxpayer for a New State

Charitable Fundraising and the Origins of the Welfare State*

SHIRLEY TILLOTSON

FOR STUDENTS OF Canada's welfare history, the transition from crisis in the 1930s to a new order in the 1950s is a key moment in the development of the welfare state. And it is rightly characterized as a time of expansion in government's (and especially the federal government's) responsibilities for financing welfare programs (in the largest sense, including health and social services). (See Figure 7.1.) But at the same time public spending on welfare was expanding, charitable donations to the Community Chests were also increasing. In 1959, the collections of these federated fundraising appeals, forerunners of today's United Ways, were somewhat more than eight times their level in 1931.[1] (See Figure 7.2.) In the same period, GNP at market prices grew to slightly *less* than eight times the 1931 level. (See Figure 7.3.)

These data on donations in relation to GNP and government spending may seem to contradict those of economist Samuel Martin, who has contributed significantly, in *An Essential Grace*, to the history of the financing of what he calls "humanistic services."[2] His data show that personal donations to humanistic services declined between 1937 and 1957, from 1.2 percent of GNP to 1 percent. But, as he admits, his data are derived from a number of broken data series, including, for example, taxation statistics available only after 1946. The Community Chest data, while suffering some minor gaps, are consistent in kind throughout the 1931 to 1958 period to which I attend in this essay. Also, Martin's data count somewhat different things than do mine. He includes, for example, donations to church building funds or to the Queen's University alumni fund, whereas the data on the Community Chest collections show only donations to health and welfare charities. So the increases in donations to the Chests were increases in giving to charities that supported families and cared for the ill and the isolated. Measured by the collections of the Community Chests, this kind of privately funded agency continued to benefit from increasing personal donations from Canadians throughout the 1930s, 1940s, and 1950s.

During these three decades, new government spending on health and welfare was in part financed by increasing income taxation (and, after 1951, the Old Age Security tax, counted with income tax in the federal Taxation Statistics).[3] In 1931, individual income tax collections (shown in Figure 7.4) were $26.5 million, and Community Chest donations

---

* This is an adapted version of Shirley Tillotson, "A New Taxpayer for a New State: Charitable Fundraising and the Origins of the Welfare State," in Raymond B. Blake, Penny E. Bryden and J. Frank Strain, eds., The Welfare State in Canada: Past, Present and Future (Toronto: Irwin Publishing, 1997) 138–55.

Figure 7.1. Government Health and Welfare Spending

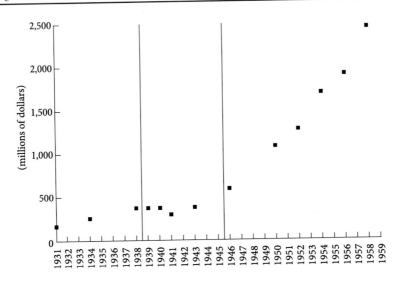

The thinner vertical lines mark the period of World War II.
Source: Dennis Guest, *The Emergence of Social Security in Canada* (Vancouver, 1985).

Figure 7.2. Community Chest Collections, 1931–58

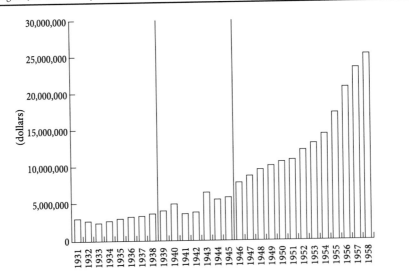

The thinner vertical lines mark the period of World War II.
Source: *Canadian Welfare*, various years. Data for 1938 and 1955–56 are estimates only.

Figure 7.3. GNP at Market Prices

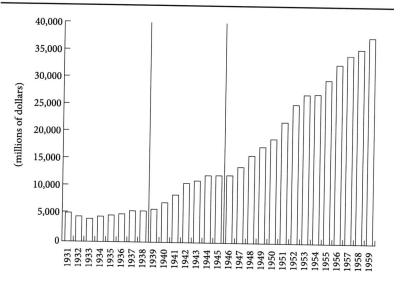

The thinner vertical lines mark the period of World War II.
Source: F.H. Leacy, *Historical Statistics of Canada*, 2nd ed., F-13.

Figure 7.4. Income Tax Collections, 1931–58

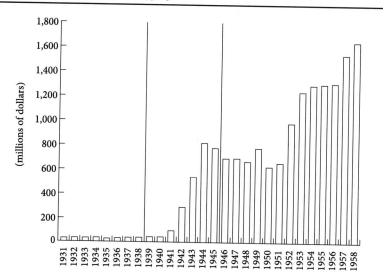

The thinner vertical lines mark the period of World War II.
Source: Department of National Revenue, *Taxation Statistics* and W. Irwin Gillespie, *Tax, Borrow and Spend: Financing Federal Spending in Canada 1867–1990* (Ottawa, 1991).

$3 million. By 1959, individuals' tax payments had multiplied to almost $1.5 billion, fifty-six times their 1931 level. At $25 million, Chest donations at the end of the fifties were only 2 percent of income tax collections and, again, only eight times their Depression-era size. But in the period of highest income taxation, after World War II, charitable giving grew faster than tax collections. The 1959 personal tax collection was only 2.2 times that of 1946, whereas charitable donations through the Chest movement grew more than threefold in the same period.

The significance of these data seems quite clear. In the early years of the welfare state, at least, increases in government spending and one of the main types of tax collecting that financed it do not seem to have deterred or impaired Canadians' charitable impulses. Some fiscal conservatives today call for reduced taxation and greater community involvement in caring and giving, and claim government welfare services have fostered selfishness and individualism.[4] In this paper, I want to put the psychological logic underpinning that claim in question by suggesting that, in the 1930s, 1940s, and 1950s, quite another relationship existed between government welfare provision and private generosity. Rather than being *replaced* by tax paying, charitable giving helped prepare the way in public culture for income tax paying as a feature of citizenship in the welfare state. In effect, the Chests helped shift the political limits on governments' ability to tax.

In particular, the Chest helped prepare the political ground for the great increase in the 1940s in the numbers of payers of *income* tax. Taxation historian W. Irwin Gillespie has argued that the taxpayer is not "a hapless, helpless victim of a rapacious government that taxes indiscriminately." Rather, taxpayers' ability to oppose taxation has shaped government's choices about what kinds of taxation to use.[5] If Gillespie is right, then part of taxation history must be an inquiry into the formation of taxpayer opposition—what produces it and, as well, what allays it. It is this latter question—what allayed or reduced opposition to tax paying, and specifically, to income tax paying by lower income groups— that the study of the Community Chest's fundraising practices can help answer. By a nation-wide, decades-long campaign of public education, the Community Chest movement helped create a new conception of the taxpayer for a newly expanded state.

The "Chest Idea"

The Community Chest movement, or the "federated appeals" as they were more generically known, emerged in the early twentieth century. Montreal's and Toronto's "Financial Federations" began in the latter years of World War I, another three "Chests" or "Federations" began in the 1920s, and another four in the 1930s. By 1939, nine cities (including all Canada's major centres) had federated fundraising appeals. The World War II years and after saw a great flurry of federation of Canadian charities' fundraising appeals, so that by 1949, there were 47 Canadian cities with a Community Chest.[6]

The "Chest idea" was that all the charities making public appeals in any given city would unite to make one common appeal each year.[7] Doing so would not only use with maximum efficiency the publicity dollars of each charity; it would also use more efficiently their human resources. Businessmen sitting on management boards and office staffs in the various agencies would be saved the work of planning, managing, and recordkeeping for many separate, small campaigns. Door-to-door canvassers, mainly women, would make the circuit once a year, rather than repeatedly. In short, each dollar collected would come at a lower price in collecting costs (usually, costs in volunteer labour).

The federated appeal would be able to avoid labour-intensive fundraising methods that were not only inefficient, but also risky and irritating. The risky ones were those that depended on sales to generate revenue; teas, dances, and fairs did not always succeed in making much money, but they did always consume volunteer energies. The annual appeal was meant to reduce the need for mounting this type of risky event. The annual appeal was also meant to reduce the irritation induced by some aspects of uncoordinated fundraising. Vancouver retail merchants, for example, complained of two such aspects. One was that "hours" in their business days were being used up in listening to representatives of individual charities soliciting their firms' support. Another was that retail businesses suffered particularly from the presence in store foyers and downtown streets of "taggers." "Taggers" were women soliciting donations for charity, giving out little lapel labels to each donor. Shoppers routinely had to run a gauntlet of taggers. Merchants wanted this to stop. It was bad for business and not, they believed, especially effective for fundraising. From a business perspective, then, un-coordinated appeals were not only wasteful of human energies and publicity dollars, they were also a positive nuisance.

The single annual appeal had yet another advantage in the eyes of its advocates. It was a "businessman's movement."[8] Early appeals stressed in their publicity the importance of business expertise in managing fundraising campaigns and ensuring that funded agencies budgeted and accounted properly for the expenditure of the appeal funds. "Leading businessmen" or a "Businessmen's Council" or the Board of Trade figured prominently as organizers of the united appeals. They made "exhaustive inquiry into the finances of each of the institutions," to provide assurances that charities were not duplicating each others' work or otherwise spending irresponsibly the public's donated dollars.[9] Such scrutiny, they felt, would promote more giving by overcoming perceptions of inefficiency or even of fraud.

Not only were the Chests to be more efficient, they were also intended actually to increase charitable giving. Of course, an image of efficiency itself was supposed to invite donations. A second source of greater giving, it was hoped, would be the public's happiness with the reduced number of solicitations. A third anticipated incentive to donating, and perhaps a more probable one, was that the coordinated blitz of publicity for the united appeal would heighten public awareness of charitable agencies' welfare work. Each campaign included press releases and advertisements describing the work of member agencies, and provided an occasion for a concentrated flurry of service club speeches and public luncheons, explaining welfare needs and celebrating the work of the member agencies. Whether this method of promotion was more or less effective than earlier, independent fundraising campaigns probably varied for different member agencies. Undeniably, though, the Chest campaign provided publicity resources that the smaller charities had otherwise lacked. Finally, the fourth hope for increased giving, and in my view the most realistic one, was that an appeal organized with the business-like methods of a "modern" sales campaign would actually contact more donors, and successfully elicit contributions from a larger population. Systematic record-keeping, co-coordinated publicity, team organization, and a military-style chain of command provided fundraisers with data for strategic planning and the means to motivate and support canvassers.

Comparison of the Chest Idea with Taxation Philosophy and Practices during the Interwar Years

The Chest movement's attempt to change the culture of charitable fundraising and giving was inspired by and indeed was part of larger, contemporaneous changes in the culture of public administration. The thinking behind the Chest was cut from the same cultural cloth as contemporaneous thinking about taxation. To understand why that was so, we need to recall that, as Paul Pross has argued, the interwar years saw a symbiotic growth of government bureaucracy and private interest groups.[10] Mediating that symbiosis was a shared language of communication.[11] The development in Canada of one aspect of that shared language has been described by Doug Owram in *The Government Generation*. There, he demonstrates the increasing use of social science methods by both the state and social agencies.[12] Another, further aspect of the shared language or common public culture that linked the growing state to civil society was disseminated and promoted by the expanding Community Chests. One might call this shared language "tax talk." It was a set of views about responsible fiscal management and reasonable social obligation that shaped practices in the collecting of both taxes and charity dollars. A business organization, the Citizen's Research Institute of Canada (CRIC), was an important interest group promoting these values on the taxation side.[13] This tax talk was predominantly a language of business expertise, but it could be and, in fact, was given a collectivist, social democratic inflection in the fundraising practices of the Community Chests. I have identified five areas in which taxation and fundraising languages overlapped: cost-effective collection, accounting controls, use of "ability to pay" measures, and base-broadening. In the last of these four areas, fundraising innovations preceded their parallels in income taxation.

(A) Cost-effective collection

To begin, let us take the Chest movement's argument that a single appeal was the most cost-effective means of collecting for charity. Reducing costs of collection made for the largest possible net amount of charity dollars available for their intended use. Similarly, governments choosing means of raising revenue weighed the cost of collection against the amounts a tax might raise. For instance, one of the arguments advanced in favour of the particular form of the 1920 manufacturer's sales tax, and indeed in favour of sales taxes generally, was the low cost of the administrative methods involved in collecting such taxes. The tax collectors were the manufacturers and wholesalers who handled the taxed goods, and the returns they submitted required only about three dozen additional inspectors and auditors in the Department of National Revenue.[14] By contrast, the chief argument against some other tax practices has been that the expense of their administration exceeds the revenue they might generate. For example, tax authority Gwyneth McGregor concluded, on the basis of an analysis of income tax in Canada between WWI and the late 1950s, that government's practice of distinguishing between employees and the self-employed for the purpose of allowing employment expenses could be explained only on the grounds of administrative difficulty and expense. To reduce these, waged and salaried workers' employment expenses, unlike those of the self-employed, were built into the standard personal deduction. This distinction in methods saved "the Revenue" the cost of checking itemized employment expenses for millions of employee tax returns.[15]

Awareness of the cost of collections in determining taxation methods is also apparent in the Taxation Division's publication, in their 1946 *Taxation Statistics*, of data showing Cost of Collections since 1917.[16]

In other ways, too, progress in tax reform was judged by the CRIC tax experts in terms remarkably like those by which the Chest appeal was justified. In taxation discourse, experts worried about the "chaotic condition" of taxation discussed in the CRIC's 1938 report to the Rowell-Sirois commission. The CRIC pointed out, for example, that several provinces might seek to collect death duties from one estate. In many provinces, individuals were required to complete two completely separate income returns (one provincial, one federal). Taxpayers were irritated and public money was wasted when both federal and provincial governments had to audit the securities transactions on which tax was collected.[17] Such multiple taxes were problematic for some of the same reasons that multiple charitable appeals were. Donors, especially large donors, were no happier being dunned by multiple charity appeals than they were about double taxation. One of the reasons both of these "inefficient" types of collection were considered objectionable is that multiple tax assessments, like multiple campaigns, were costly.

In a 1937 Vancouver canvasser training pamphlet, the fundraisers made explicit the analogy between the cost of collecting taxes and donations. After giving in proportional terms the costs of the fundraising methods it wanted to disparage, the Welfare Federation pamphlet continued:

> Even the government spends a large amount of money to collect our taxes from us; the exact percentage is unknown, but the costs of the income tax department, assessment offices, finance departments, etc. (The Finance Department is comparable to the [Welfare] Federation) can safely be estimated as costing not very far short of 10% of the total revenue of city or province. In other words, the Federation, in using only 6 cents out of every dollar received and passing on 94 cents direct to service, is operating at a lower cost than any other revenue raising device, not excluding taxation departments of government.[18]

When Community Chest promoters argued for a cheaper cost of collections, then, they were thinking in the same way public administrators did in planning tax collection. And at least some of them thought that federated fundraising was better than taxation, because it was administratively cheaper.

(B) Accounting controls

Secondly, the call for particular kinds of managerial expertise was another theme that linked discussion of charity fundraising and taxation in the interwar years. In particular, tax experts and the Community Chest managers agreed that in each of their areas of operation, sound practice required better accounting controls. Indeed, the authorities on taxation and the promoters of business-like fundraising were sometimes the same people. For example, Horace L. Brittain was director and secretary of the Citizen's Research Institute of Canada, which had organized annual Canadian Tax Conferences since 1923. He also played an active role in the creation of Toronto's Federation for Community

Service.[19] In the 1930s, Brittain's Citizen's Research Institute created a Taxation Enquiry Fund to finance the *Special Study of Taxation and Public Expenditure in Canada*, by Dr. W.H. Wynne. In 1937, Wynne was credited with assisting in the economic research the Royal Commission on Dominion-Provincial Relations, whose report would help frame fiscal policy in the 1940s and 1950s.[20] We also find some of the leading men of the federated charities active during the 1930s in the Associated Property Owners of Vancouver, an organization devoted to scrutinizing city finances and exposing extravagant spending.[21] Dominion Comptroller Watson Sellar brought his expertise to the board of the Protestant Community Chest in Ottawa in the same period.[22] Like the leading businessmen on the Chest Board, he readily moved from promoting proper financial controls in the spending of public money to doing the same for the spending of Community Chest funds.

Wynne's *Special Study of Taxation* furnishes examples of this common language of fiscal accountability. He criticized public spending in the same technical terms that Chest budget committees brought to their assessments of charitable agencies. One of Wynne's criticisms was that neither provinces nor municipalities used real revenue-expense accounting. Indeed, municipalities facing a revenue shortage had to "slash rather than prune" public spending because they kept no "real expense records." The need for such records, Wynne pointed out, was not only to prevent "peculation" (although that was one good reason). More important was "providing the information necessary for administrative and public control."[23] Public trust required accounting controls. As Michael Piva and Bruce Curtis have shown, colonial Canadian governments had once relied on the good character of public officials more than on routine audit and control mechanisms.[24] Similarly, in Wynne's view, some municipalities (and even provinces) in the interwar years of twentieth century Canada were still operating as though to require expense records was to impugn the character of officials.

Charities, like nineteenth-century colonial governments, had relied on the prestige of their Boards to produce confidence in their spending. When the Community Chest movement promised a business-like audit of all member agencies' accounts, they were promising, as an inducement to charitable giving, the same kind of enhancement in administrative control that tax experts were calling for in government as a prerequisite of legitimate taxation. Budget committees on Community Chests queried agency Board representatives about particular items in their budgets. In Ottawa, the threat of expulsion was used to force a popular Catholic agency, run by nuns, to adopt business-style budgeting.[25] And some agencies were actually removed from one federation because their expense records failed to meet proper standards. In 1931, this was the reason that the Vancouver Welfare Federation ousted from its ranks the Original Great War Veterans Association, as well as the Western Association for the Blind, and the Tuberculous Veterans.[26] What the comparison of these innovations in fundraising and the CRIC's criticism of municipal government suggests is that business people viewed both the public sector and charities as being in need of business expertise. While this view was not new in the interwar years, its expression in the institutional form of the business-directed federated appeals was both new and significant. By way of the Chest movement, across the country in major, and later, in minor cities, charitable fundraising became a widespread means of promulgating to a wide audience the gospel of accounting controls as a necessary part of public spending, whether of charity dollars or tax dollars.

(C) "Ability to pay": The link between income and obligation

Third, and most important, of the elements in the common public culture I am sketching here were the means that the Chests used in their attempts to increase the numbers of charitable donors. More than efficiency in collections and controls in accounting, the methods adopted to implement this feature of the Chest idea prepared the public to contemplate with a degree of acceptance the expanding incidence of personal income taxation, especially in lower income cohorts, in the 1940s. The campaign to induce more people to give to the Chests linked income and social obligation in ways that would also appear in discussions of just taxation in the interwar years.

The links of income and obligation in conceptions of tax in the interwar years may be read from the parliamentary debates incited by R.B. Bennett's 1931 federal budget and from changes in the administration of taxation in subsequent years. To put the budget debate in context, we need to realize that, in 1931, paying income tax was still clearly an experience of the middling salary earner, the highly-paid, and the rich. Wage earners did not often earn more than the $3,000 that for a married, childless household head was tax exempt in 1930. The 1931 census's income distribution figures for wage earning families showed only 4.48 percent were headed by someone with a *taxable income* of $2,950 or more (i.e., $5,950 or more). Nonetheless, when, in 1931, the exemption level for income tax was dropped to $2,400, more relatively low income citizens joined the "elite" ranks of the taxpayers. An economic aristocracy among wage earners, these 52,857 men and 213 women probably all numbered among the 63,276 Canadians who paid tax on *taxable* incomes of less than $2,000. This lowest rank of income taxpayers, many of them solidly middle-class in income level, were 38 percent of the country's total 166,972 income tax payers in 1931.[27] A tax impinging on so few Canadians was hardly a major revenue source. In 1931, personal income tax supplied only 6.61 percent of the federal government's revenue requirements. Over half of those requirements were fulfilled instead by taxes on consumption—sales and excise taxes and customs duties.[28] Quite properly, then, the debate over Bennett's 1931 budget focused primarily on the impact of the customs tariff.

But many speakers commented on the income tax provisions of the budget, too.[29] Even though their remarks showed what can most kindly be called "confusion" about the incidence of income tax, the MPs also revealed common sense assumptions about the social identities of taxpayers. Among the ranks of the official Opposition, only William Motherwell appears to have grasped the structure of the (admittedly limited) data available from the Department of National Revenue and Bennett's budget speech. He alone seems to have appreciated that Bennett's budget actually *cut* income taxes for "the small salaried man" whose taxable income was between $3,000 and $8,000. More importantly, Motherwell realized the full import of income tax *increases* to taxable incomes between $9,000 and $137,000. In this range, as he realized, there were conceivably some millionaires whose taxable income had been carved into a smaller shape by means of ingenious tax deductions.[30] There were well over 15,000 taxpayers in this very wealthy group, and under Bennett's budget, they were all going to pay more taxes. The rich certainly felt some bite from the 1931 Bennett budget.

But most of Bennett's opponents focussed on the tax reductions Bennett proposed to give to a small number of the fabulously wealthy: either the "25 millionaires" or the 523 individuals whose taxable income was greater than $50,000. These were the happy souls whose reduced tax bills under Bennett's new income tax scale gave the 1931 budget its name as "the rich man's budget." The image of these few plutocrats was arrayed as the symbol of unjust tax privilege against the sufferings of "the poor man," whose cup of tea would now cost more in light of a three percent increase in the sales tax. In this rhetoric, the income tax payer appeared as a figure of privilege, contrasted to the downtrodden ordinary man or woman, the payer of sales tax.

Bennett's critics were right to deplore his government's reliance on increased consumption taxes, regressive forms of taxation that ate away at the pennies and nickels of the poor. But it is equally clear that the moral and symbolic meaning of taxation informed the debate more than did real information about tax incidence.

J.S. Woodsworth's intervention was especially striking in this respect.[31] After noting the fact that most Canadians earned too little to pay income tax, he then pointed out how few taxpayers there were in the "under $2,000" taxable income class and how little income tax they paid. He went on to offer the figures for the much larger total sums paid by the wealthy and by corporations. "We are told this country belongs to the people," he then said, clearly about to puncture a myth, "and yet, when we come to matters of taxation we find the taxes are loaded upon only a few people." At this point, it would seem, very oddly, that Woodsworth was deploring the burden of income tax carried by the rich. However, with no apparent regard for consistency, he went on to aver bitterly that "this government is nothing more or less than a vast debt collecting agency operating to collect from the poor people or the people of moderate means moneys to be turned over to the wealthy people." In context of comments on the income tax, this view was simply wrong. Although the *sales* tax did indeed collect disproportionately from the poor and the middling sort, the *income* tax did not.

Woodsworth's remarks were those of a man completely unused to dissecting the impact of income tax. This should not be surprising, for the income tax in the 1920s had been, in fact, more or less a rich man's tax and a rich man's "burden." A tribune of the poor, such as Woodsworth, would have had little reason ever to think of it. When we consider the Chests' effect on public culture, a key focus must be the perception of income tax as a rich man's tax, outside the obligations and taxpaying experience of most working class and many middle class Canadians. The fundraising campaigns of the Community Chests would contribute to changing that perception, both by imitating the methods of the income tax and by enlarging the scope of their application.

The model of charitable giving in the Chest idea mimicked in two ways the model of income taxation. One was the use of a progressive scale of giving, tied to income. Figure 7.5 shows one such scale.[32]

Worth noting is that the lowest annual income registered on this (and other, similar scales) is $2,000, also the lowest threshold in the income cohorts into which data on income tax paying were divided. The concept of obligation increasing with greater wealth is also clearly present in the scale. The rate of recommended donation increases with income, albeit slightly less steeply than did rates of income tax owed in Bennett's 1931 budget.[33]

In using this scale, the Chest might be seen to have described charitable giving, like income tax paying, as a rich man's or woman's activity. But to complement the graded scale, the chest also made appeals to industrial workers.[34] And these appeals were tied to income: the suggested donation for those with incomes under $2,000 was a day's pay. In this way, admittedly somewhat loosely, the link between income ("ability to pay" in tax discourse) and obligation to give was maintained. Like the income tax payer, and unlike the sales tax payer, the donor to charity in the Chest method consciously paid what he or she "owed," knowing that that amount represented something about himself or herself individually.

(D) Base-broadening

The Chest's main purpose was to increase charitable giving, and its main method of doing so was to increase the number of donors. In this aspect of their fundraising, federated appeals anticipated a development that would come in the actual income tax system only during World War II. This "base-broadening" approach to maximizing revenue was what Mark Leff described as the tax reform approach advocated by some left-of-centre American tax reformers in the 1930s.[35] Within fundraising, the emphasis of base-broadening was on coming to the aid of the "unselfish few." (This seems likely to have been the discourse within which J.S. Woodsworth spoke when he lamented the loading of social obligation on the shoulders of a few.) Like fundraisers, the advocates of broadening the income tax base hoped both to relieve some tax payers of a disproportionate burden and to generate more revenue for social services. Unlike fundraisers, though, these social democratic American reformers were mainly interested in relieving the many, not the few. Specifically, they hoped to relieve lower income people from the weight of accumulated small consumption taxes.

Figure 7.5. Targeted Relationship of Annual Pay to Community Chest Contributions

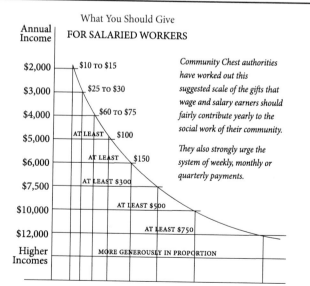

Source: City of Vancouver Archives, J.S. Matthews files, subject "Vancouver Welfare Federation," newsclipping, *Vancouver Sun*, 6 Nov. 1935. The *x*-axis percentages read as follows: 1/2 to 1%, 1%, 1 1/2%, 2%, 2 1/2%, 4%, 5%, 6%.

For these tax reformers, the $2,000 income level was politically important. In the categories identified by economist Henry Simons, for example, the point of base-broadening and the reduction of consumption taxes was to make the tax burden fall "mainly on people with incomes ranging from $3,000 to $20,000" rather than "largely on people below the $2,000 level."[36] The "common sense" income tax payer seems to have been the one whose income was greater than $2,000. This income level had a similar meaning for the Chest fundraisers, too. In both taxation and fundraising, then, the middle and upper income classes had obligations based on the enjoyment of wealth.

But in pursuit of a larger donor base, the Chest also appealed to those with lower incomes, on different grounds. The "pitch" to these potential new donors—the elevator operator, the waiter, the sales clerk, the packing clerk—was that giving to the Community Chest was part payment for the services the Chest provided.[37] For example, in a solicitation to all of Vancouver's "helping hands," the fundraisers created a fictive voice of "tired, unaided domestic hands" who replied "Yes, indeed, I want to do my tiny share, for did not the Welfare help my little girl last year when we were unable to give her the care she needed so badly?" and "tough, calloused, work-thickened hands" expressed appreciation for the summer playgrounds for the kids, and promised, "It won't be much, but I'll do me little bit."[38] Small donors, no doubt many of them wage earners, did indeed come to form the majority of givers to the federations. For example, by 1938, 82 percent of Halifax's donors came from the under $5 cohort. Base-broadening efforts in the interwar years succeeded, elsewhere, too. In Ottawa, it was a point of pride that by 1937 they "had introduced into giving to charity some 18,000—19,000 people who never gave to charity before."[39] Vancouver's multiplying of its donor base by a factor of nearly six, from 4,200 to 25,000 between 1931 and 1935 could not have been achieved without the contributions of working class men and women, the stenographers, railway workers, clerks, and printers whose names appeared in the published donor lists.[40] They were responding to publicity campaigns that represented them, as not only fulfilling obligations to the community, but also as helping to pay for social services they themselves or their families would use.[41] In addition to citizen responsibility and personal altruism, working class men and women were expected to give partially in anticipation of direct benefit as users of social services.[42]

By presenting working class donors as both contributors to and users of services, this rhetoric began to recast the class relations of social services. Working class donors were grouped with the helpers, and not the helpless. They were being offered, as an image of their place in a system of collective care, the citizen as consumer, whose responsibility consists in paying part of the price of the services they use. Fundraising that used this model of the citizen would appear in other cities in the 1940s and 1950s. By then, all three cities would use the slogan "Everybody gives, everybody benefits."[43] These frequent representations of the citizen as consumer belong with the triumph of a universalist vision of welfare in the post-war period. But, as the 1935 ad from Vancouver indicated, the notion of charitable giving as mutual aid, where responsibility and benefit were intertwined, was part of the fundraisers' appeal to working class Canadians even in the 1930s. It would become in the postwar years part of the cultural logic by which working class participation in income tax paying would be legitimated. The territory that fraternal societies' insurance schemes had occupied, with their fulsome rhetoric of mutual responsibility, would be occupied by the soon-to-be equally celebrated collectivism of social insurance.[44] Giving to federated charities was a stop along the way.

From the 1920s to the 1950s, these co-coordinated fundraising appeals broadcast this message of citizen responsibility to Canadians across the class spectrum. In a campaign conducted every year in nine major Canadian cites, charitable giving was linked to the concept of income-based obligations to support a community-wide provision of social services. Chest fundraising educated the mass of Canadians, and not just social élites, in the ways of a modern, rationalized system of funding social services. In this way, the Community Chests promoted awareness of welfare services and perceptions of social obligation that applied just as readily to income tax paying for the welfare state as they did to charitable giving.

Of course, the similarities between the practices and conceptual basis of giving to charity through the Chest and those underpinning the paying of income tax should not blind us to the fact that these two ways of meeting social obligations have been deemed opposite, with every dollar that is turned over to the state lost to use in private charity.[45] The Community Chests' efforts to create an awareness of welfare need and of the cost of a wide variety of social services was *not* primarily intended to create demand for publicly funded services. Indeed, one of the B.C. businessmen involved in the Chest's early years argued (with the Chest director's endorsement) that supporting private charity was a crucial defense against communistic appropriation of private wealth (i.e., against high and progressive income taxes).[46] Furthermore, the head of Catholic charities in Quebec warned that "state charity" might make Canadians "oblivious to the duty and joy of private charity."[47] On the left, advocates of a systematically redistributive welfare state correctly saw that some advocates of private philanthropy hoped to forestall tax-funded services.[48]

But intentions do not wholly determine outcomes. It is important, therefore, to understand that there were not only conflicts, but also connections between income taxation and private uses of the welfare dollar. A joke in a 1945 Calgary labour paper played on the overlap between the taxation and welfare discourses:

> Officials of the Income Tax Division received the following acknowledgement of a blank [i.e., a tax form] received by a citizen: 'Dear Treasury—I received your application blank, but I already belong to several good orders and do not care to join your income tax at this time.[49]

Ruefully, this joke acknowledged that the income tax system occupied the same ground in a worker's life that private welfare spending did. And evidently, the humorist had some doubts about being forced to join the impersonal "order" that was the welfare state. But he understood quite clearly that income taxation was to the welfare state as private insurance systems had been to an earlier, individual-centred welfare regime. The Chest fundraisers' methods had been an attempt to make more collective, to socialize, the process of providing protection against hardship. As a result, their campaigns, as one Vancouver social worker claimed, promoted the work of social agencies, not only to charitable givers but also to "those who contributed through taxation."[50]

This social worker was right in her conclusion about the Chests' effects, because of the common values and practices embodied both in Community Chest fundraising and in the conception of a broad-based income tax for a welfare state. I have suggested that some aspects of these common values and practices were cost-effective collections, accounting controls, obligation based in ability to pay, and breadth of participation. The latter, furthermore, was grounded in part in a sense of obligation based in anticipated benefit rather than purely a spirit of altruism. These were parts of the emerging public culture from which came both increases in a certain kind of charitable giving and legitimation in the 1950s for increased income taxation.

Conclusion

My argument in this paper has not been meant to prove that there has never been at any time *since* the 1950s a diminution in private charitable giving. Martin's data (1985) show a drop in charitable giving between 1957 and 1978 from 1 percent of GNP to 0.6 percent. These years also saw growth in spending on health and welfare from 5 percent of GNP to 18 percent of GNP and, between 1965 and 1970, a striking increase in individual income tax collections. These three phenomena may very well have been connected. But the line of argument I have pursued here does provide historical evidence to suggest that the psychological underpinning to connect these phenomena need not be resentment at increases in income tax paying or apathy about need induced by public provision. When, during the 1930s, 1940s, and 1950s, Canadians paid increasing proportions of their earnings in income tax, and state-funded services blossomed, the federated charities also prospered and expanded. This suggests that the willingness to give is not simply the result of a zero-sum calculation about disposable dollars, where more dollars to the tax-man means fewer to charity. Nor must the generous charitable giver be cast as the free and morally heroic opposite to the grudging and coerced taxpayer. In the Community Chest's methods of fundraising, charitable giving was described in ways that highlighted the similarities, and not the differences, between the taxpayer for the welfare state and the giver to good causes. In an unintended way, the Chests were fundraising for the welfare state, and not just for private charities. The story of the Community Chest in the period I have discussed here thus recalls to mind a vision of a mutually reinforcing relation, rather than a competitive one, between public and private provision for welfare needs. Something of that vision is worth recapturing.

Notes

1. Community Chest giving was, of course, only one kind of charitable giving. Others may have grown or declined on a different pattern. One advantage of the Community Chest data on giving is that it is a nearly complete and readily available data series for the 1931–1959 period, published by the Canadian Welfare Council in their journal, *Canadian Welfare*.
2. Seymour Martin, *An Essential Grace: Funding Canada's Health Care, Education, Welfare, Religion and Culture* (Toronto: McClelland and Stewart, 1985), 27–30.
3. W. Irwin Gillespie, *Tax, Borrow, and Spend: Financing Federal Spending in Canada, 1867–1990* (Ottawa: Carleton University Press, 1991), 215, Chart 10–1; Canada, Dept. of National Revenue, Taxation Division, *Taxation Statistics*.
4. See, for example, William Gairdner, *The War against the Family* (Toronto: Stoddart, 1992), 84–85. Somewhat less bluntly anti-statist variations on this analysis have been offered by Robert

Fulford, "The Way We Were," *Saturday Night*, March 1985, 5–6, and the Editors of the *Globe and Mail*, in "Beyond public and private," 28 September 1995.

5. Gillespie, 179–80.

6. "With the Federation Cities" *Canadian Welfare* 8, 5 (1933), 13–20; "Results of 1948–49 Community Chest Campaigns," *Canadian Welfare* 24, 8 (1949), 29. This paper is part of a larger project in which I draw on the records of three cities—Vancouver, Halifax, and Ottawa—to discuss the distinctively modern characteristics of federated fundraising and the relationship of this innovation to the development of tax-funded social services in Canada.

7. This paper's discussion of the "Chest Idea" draws on the records relating to the initial organizational efforts in the 1920s of the Halifax and Vancouver federated appeals. These are mainly to be found in two collections: Nova Scotia Archives and Records Management (NSARM), MG20, Records of the United Way of Halifax-Dartmouth and City of Vancouver Archives (CVA), Vancouver Board of Trade, Add. mss. 300. In the first of these two collections, the key documents are in vol. 1717, a scrapbook. See especially the clippings for May 1925. For the second of these two collections, the key documents are in vol. 5, 319, report by W.C. Woodward, chairman of the Retail Merchants' Bureau of the Vancouver Board of Trade, 4 May 1922; vol. 146, insert at 44 "Minutes of meeting of Organizations called to receive a report prepared by the special committee re: Community Chest," 26 June 1923; vol. 8, insert at 487, "Minutes of a Special meeting of the Council of the Vancouver Board of Trade," 8 November 1928; and "Expert Urges Chest System of Charities," *Vancouver Star*, 13 August 1929, 7. Some of the same themes appear in the origins of Toronto's Federation for Community Service, described in Gale Wills, A marriage of convenience: business and social work in Toronto, 1918–1957 (Toronto: University of Toronto Press, 1995).

8. Additional emphasis on this point may be found in the National Archives of Canada (NAC), Canadian Council on Social Development (CCSD) Papers, vol. 158, file "CWC Divisions—Community Organization, 1935–37," D.J. Thom, K.C., President of Regina Community Chest, to Marjorie Bradford, secretary for community organization, CWC, 26 November 1936; NSARM, MG 20, vol. 1713, minutes of the Halifax Board of Trade, "Associated Charities Fund," 17 November 1921; NAC, CCSD Papers, vol. 158, file "CWC Divisions—Community Organization, 1935–37," D.J. Thom, K.C., President of Regina Community Chest, to Marjorie Bradford, secretary for community organization, CWC, 26 November 1936; "Twenty-Five Years in Toronto," *Canadian Welfare* 18, 4 (1942), 8–9.

9. The quotation is from NSARM, MG 20, vol. 1717, "Community Chest Will Carry On To Finish," news clipping, May 1925.

10. A. Paul Pross, *Group Politics and Public Policy*, second edition (Toronto: Oxford University Press, 1992), chapter two.

11. By a "language" here, I mean a set of practices and concepts linked by a characteristic set of logical associations (equivalencies, causalities, implications).

12. (Toronto: University of Toronto Press, 1986).

13. For an indication of its importance, see the list of prominent insurance executives, major newspaper publishers, wealthy industrialists, and notable professional men listed as directors in the CRIC's submission to the Rowell-Sirois Commission. For a description of the organization's purposes, see Eric Hardy, *Empire Club of Canada Speeches 1949–1950* (Toronto: The Empire Club of Canada, 1950), 266.

14. Gillespie, 120 and H.R. Kemp, "Dominion Taxation. 1. The Sales Tax," *Canadian Forum* 3 (July 1923), 298.

15. Gwyneth McGregor, *Employees' Deductions under the Income Tax: A comparative study of their treatment in the United Kingdom, the United States and Canada* (Toronto: Canadian Tax Foundation, 1960), 19–21.

16. Canada, Department of National Revenue, Taxation Division, *Taxation Statistics* (1946), 9.

17. *Submission to the Royal Commission on Dominion-Provincial Relations* (Toronto: Citizens' Research Institute of Canada, 1938), 60–62.

18. CVA, Mayor's papers, series 483, file 33–D–6–1, stencilled canvasser training pamphlet for Vancouver Welfare Federation, 1937.

19. "Horace L. Brittain," *The Canadian Who's Who*, 1936–37, 123.

20. Dr. Wynne's connection to both organizations is documented in the covering letter published with the Citizen Research Institute's *Special Study of Taxation and Public Expenditure in Canada* (1937) and in the final report of the Royal Commission on Dominion–Provincial Relations (Book I, 14). My thanks to Jessica Squires for clarification on this point: see Squires, "Ideological Formation and Liberal "Consensus": Reading the Rowell-Sirois Commission" (M.A. Thesis, Dalhousie, 2003).

21. CVA, J.S. Matthews clippings file, subject heading "Associated Property Owners of Vancouver," "Property Owners Re–Elect Board," 9 Feb 1934; "Rap Trustees for Increase," 4 May 1932; "City Finance Position Shows No Improvement," 20 July 1936. For board of directors listings for the Vancouver Chest, see CVA, Add. mss. 849-2, vol. 617-A-3.

22. "Watson Sellar," *Canadian Who's Who*, 1936–37, 980–81; Sellar was a member of the Ottawa Protestant Chest's first budget committee: Records of the United Way of Ottawa-Carleton, minutes of the Board of Directors and Budget Committee, 22 June 1933. These records are held at the office of the Ottawa-Carleton United Way. His importance in the Ottawa Chest is apparent from his having attended a uniquely important meeting of the fundraising and social work élite of anglophone Ottawa on 29 December 1932: NAC, CCSD Papers, vol. 44, file 215, meeting to discuss the developments which were taking place between the City and the Ottawa Welfare Bureau.

23. Wynne, *Special Study of Taxation and Public Expenditure in Canada* (Citizen's Research Institute of Canada, 1937), 50.

24. Michael Piva, "Government Finance and the Development of the Canadian State," and Bruce Curtis, "Class Culture and Administration: Educational Inspection in Canada West" in Allan Greer and Ian Radforth, eds. *Colonial Leviathan: State Formation in Mid–Nineteenth Century Canada* (Toronto: University of Toronto Press, 1992), 265–67, 116–19.

25. Records of the United Way of Ottawa-Carleton, Special meeting of the Roman Catholic Executive Committee to discuss the Joan of Arc Institute, minutes, 8 June 1938.

26. CVA, Add. ms. 849-2, vol. 617-A-3, file 1, minutes, 18 September 1931.

27. J. Harvey Perry, *Taxes, Tariffs, and Subsidies: A History of Canadian Fiscal Development*, vol. 2 (Toronto: University of Toronto Press, 1955), 698; *Census of Canada* 1931, Table 38, 686–87.

28. Gillespie, 280.

29. Discussion of the income tax appears in Canada, House of Commons, *Debates*, on the following dates in June 1931: 4, 5, 9, 10, 15, 17, 18.

30. Canada, House of Commons, *Debates*, 15 June 1931, 2621–22.

31. Canada, House of Commons, *Debates*, 9 June 1931, 2460.

32. CVA, J.S. Matthews clippings files, subject "Vancouver Welfare Federation," 6 November 1935. This scale was used during Howard Falk's tenure as Executive Director, and Falk had been in on the design of federated fundraising appeals in Winnipeg and Montreal. Halifax also used such a scale, as described in NSARM, MG 20, vol. 1713, minutes 1923–1962, "Constitution," article 8, section 6, 20 January 1927.

33. Canada, House of Commons, *Debates*, 1 June 1931, 2176–77.

34. Shirley Tillotson, "Class and Community in Canadian Welfare Work, 1933–1960," *Journal of Canadian Studies* 32, 1 (1997), 63–92.

35. Mark Leff, *The Limits of Symbolic Reform* (Cambridge: Cambridge University Press, 1984), 102–19.

36. Henry C. Simons, *Personal Income Taxation* (Chicago: University of Chicago Press, 1938), 219, quoted in Leff, 107.

37. For further detail on donor participation in these groups, see Tillotson, "Class and Community," table 1.

38. CVA, J.S. Matthews clippings file, subject "Vancouver Welfare Federation," E.S. Roberts, "Our Whole Town's Working," *Vancouver Province*, 26 October 1935.

39. Records of the United Way of Ottawa-Carleton, meeting of Division Chairmen and Campaign Committee, minutes, 9 December.

40. Vancouver *Sun*, 1, 2, 3, 6, 7, 8, 12 November 1935, pages 20, 22, 11, 20, 7, 17, and 17. A sample of these lists, sampled randomly from a fixed starting point, was identified by occupation in the Vancouver City Directory. In 1935, the lists included only donors of $5 or $6 and up. This threshold means that these lists would have heavily understated working class individuals' donations. Nonetheless, 20 percent of the 1935 donors could be classed as wage earners. I thank Russell Johnston for his diligent work as my research assistant, in constructing this sample and searching the city directories.

41. For a sample of a Chest campaign aimed at working class donors, covering their awareness of need from a wage earner's perspective and their sense of responsibilities, see a series of captioned photos of wage earners in the Vancouver *Sun*: a cook, 14 October 1937; warehouse truck driver, 15 October; business girl, 16 October; milkman, 18 October; fireman, 20 October.

42. Another example of this theme can be found in newspaper coverage of the 1940 campaign in Vancouver. In a report of the campaign's progress, the increase in new donors was mentioned. To illustrate, the report quotes a woman who says "Until this year I never knew what Welfare meant but I know now because the Preventorium saved two of my children from tuberculosis." "Larger Donations Mark Services Fund Campaign," Vancouver *Sun*, 30 October 1940, 28.

43. The slogan was used central in the campaigns for 1947, 1948, 1949, and 1950. For use in the late 1940s campaign advertising, see Ottawa *Journal*, 7 October 1947, 18, and 19 October 1957, 9; NSARM, vol. 1718, clipping of Robert Simpson Co. sponsored Chest ad, 19 October 1948, clipping of Chest display ad, 1 October 1949, clipping of display ad that appeared in the *Herald* and the *Mail*, 11 October 1950; NAC, ISN 132568, Red Feather campaign ad, CBC Montreal (slogan is featured in the Wayne and Shuster ad). By 1953, it was incorporated into the Red Feather logo in both Canada and the U.S.: Ottawa-Carleton United Way, Ralph Blanchard to John Yerger, 21 September 1953, insert in 1953 minutes book. In a 1953 campaign post-mortem, one Vancouver fundraiser regretted it hadn't been used more intensively in the campaign just finished: CVA, Add. mss 849-2, vol. 617-B-2, 61, Board of Directors meeting, minutes, 27 October 1953. But it continued to feature nationally in publicity materials. A national United Appeal commercial used it in 1956, and by 1959, a social worker reviewing the fundraising strategies for recreation agencies referred to it as one of nine commonplaces of the business: NAC, ISN 236411, commercial featuring Alex Barris, Archives of Ontario, RG 65, series C3, box 38, file 1137, Report of the 14th Ontario Recreation Association conference, speech by Florence Philpott (consultant to the United Community Fund and the Community Chest).

44. Historian David Beito notes social insurance seemed to some to be an extrapolation of the logic of fraternalism, but he deplores fraternalism's loss of ground to what he considers the impersonal and morally empty tax-funded insurances. David Beito, *From Mutual Aid to the Welfare State: Fraternal Societies and Social Services, 1890–1967* (Chapel Hill: University of North Carolina Press, 2000), 228-29, 231, 234.

45. Martin, 194–95, reports survey results indicating some Canadians hold this view.

46. NAC, CCSD Papers, vol. 13, file 59 "CWC Division—Community Organization 'Publicity and Fund Raising' 1934," Text of broadcast by Robert Cromie on behalf of the Community Chests of Canada, 13 October 1934.

47. NAC, CCSD papers, vol. 13, file 59 "Community Organization, 1933–34, Radio Broadcasts," 8 October 1933.

48. NAC, CCSD Papers, vol. 13, file 59 "CWC Division—Community Organization 'Publicity and Fund Raising' 1934," Charlotte Whitton to Philip Fisher, 31 August 1934; CVA, United Way of the Lower Mainland, minutes binder labelled 1933–35, Budget committee report, 18 February 1934.

49. *The Call* 1, 4 (15 April 1945), 7.

50. CVA, Add. mss 849-2, Mrs. Walter [Alma Gale] Mowatt, "History of the Community Chest and Council of the Greater Vancouver Area," typescript, 1951, 35.

II

TRIUMPH TO REFORM

Triumph to Reform

THE 1940 ROWELL-SIROIS Commission set the stage for the initial triumph of Canada's welfare state. It recommended that the federal government assume control from the provinces over income, corporate and inheritance taxes, and in return, provide unemployment insurance, assume much of the provincial debt, and pay grants to the provinces to raise all parts of the country to minimum standards. With Ottawa requiring unprecedented tax revenues to fight the war, provincial governments essentially had no choice but to accept the deal, though, as some insisted, only for the duration of the conflict.

In 1941, Ottawa began paying unemployment insurance (UI), though initially only 42 percent of workers qualified. But UI quickly turned out as the thin edge of the wedge. Extensive and effective state planning to organize for the war and to control wartime inflation convinced more Canadians that continued government intervention in peacetime would provide for greater security and benefits, including in offsetting an expected post-war economic downturn. By 1943, Prime Minister King and his government were convinced that it could hesitate no longer on introducing substantial measures for postwar planning and social security. That year, the Liberals unveiled the Marsh Report, which recommended better Unemployment Insurance and Old Age Pensions, and, most significantly, the introduction of Family Allowances, Canada's first universal social program. Riding a wave of popular support for such initiatives, in 1945, the federal government introduced the White Paper on Income and Employment, in which it accepted prime responsibility for maintaining minimum standards for all Canadians, and the Green Book, in which it proposed—and achieved for years over objections from several provinces—continued control over tax fields.

Momentum for social welfare programs slowed during the conservative 1950s, but the 1960s proved as seminal as the war years. A buoyant economy provided the federal government with money to spend, and the ideological milieu exuded enthusiasm to promote greater social justice. In 1965, the Canada Pension Plan was introduced, initially covering 92 percent of those aged 65 and older. The initiative also sparked talk about Cooperative Federalism as the Pearson government avoided constitutional wrangling with a more nationalist Quebec—with the advent of its Quiet Revolution—by allowing the province to opt out of the CPP, keep the federal funds, and create its own pension plan so long as it was of comparable quality. The Canada Assistance Plan, which was introduced the next year, saw the federal government offer to cover half the costs—with no spending cap—for several social welfare programs funded solely by the provinces, and permitted provincial governments to maintain their management of these programs as long as certain standards were respected. Also in 1966, Ottawa introduced Medicare, and by 1 July 1968, all the provinces were on board to jointly fund a program that provided Canadians with free access to most physician and specialist services.

However, the following decade saw the pendulum shift toward retrenchment. Sharp oil price hikes in 1973 ushered in a period of high inflation and unemployment that sapped government revenues, and rapidly raised the national debt. Over the last half of the 1970s, Ottawa first froze, and then cut, Family Allowance rates, and tightened qualifications for those applying to receive unemployment insurance. Cap-less joint funding by the federal government under the Canada Assistance Plan was replaced with per capita block grants to the provinces, a formula that provided less money, but with the trade-off of greater provincial control. By the end of the 1970s many expressed concern over Ottawa abandoning its role in assuring minimum social standards for Canadians—concerns that grew louder over the 1980s with the rise of neo-Conservatism and its targeting of supposedly "bloated" and "wasteful" social welfare programs and "financially disastrous" government debt.

The first three articles that follow outline aspects characterizing the early development of Canada's modern, federal-led, welfare state. Jeff Keshen presents a federal government determined to avoid repeating mistakes that left many World War I veterans disillusioned and often destitute. He portrays Canada's Veterans Charter as providing servicemen of the Second World War with unprecedented opportunities to thrive in civilian life through programs that included extensive vocational retraining, free university education, and very generous terms to start farms or businesses. Centering on the roots and formative years of the Family Allowance program, Raymond Blake writes that though the motivations behind its introduction were far from purely altruistic, still for many Canadians, the extra money was crucial, sometimes providing them with the means to purchase things as basic as decent clothing for their children. Richard Lund carries the story of unemployment insurance forward to the 1960s when a strong economy and a rather pervasive liberal ethos combined to produce unprecedented expansion of this program, but also spiraling costs.

The two articles that follow on Canada's First Peoples show that government social welfare was not always greeted with great enthusiasm. To Aboriginal Peoples, such intervention was long associated with promoting assimilation, a theme Frank Tester advances in his examination of interaction during the 1950s and 1960s between federal social workers and the Inuit of the Eastern Arctic. Although federal and provincial governments backed way from the goal of assimilation in more recent years, and spent substantial sums to assist First Peoples, still, as Peter Hudson and Shirley Taylor-Henley write with respect to Child and Family Services during the 1980s, the methods employed to assist recipients often seemed best suited to white society.

The final three articles focus on efforts to deliver social welfare most efficiently and effectively, goals that became more pressing over the 1970s and 1980s as governments faced more claimants, but also increased pressure to cut their deficits. Patricia Evans presents an essentially negative portrayal of strategies adopted by the Mulroney government to reform social welfare. She writes, for instance, that though the wealthy and middle class were hit hardest by decisions to replace universal Family Allowances with a Child Tax Credit and to apply clawbacks to the Canada Pension Plan, there occurred no redistribution of income to the poor. Meanwhile, developing more cost-efficient means of providing health care certainly rose to the top of government agendas during the 1970s and 1980s, as, for instance, Canadians were living longer and placing increased strain upon the system. Joel Baum's contribution examines the care of seniors in the context of a shift that occurred in Ontario during the 1970s from independent to chain nursing homes. Contrasting with the rather widespread assumption of chains as providing less personal and compassionate care, Baum's largely mathematical-based analysis reveals them as being not only more cost-effective, but also as furnishing comparable, if not superior, treatment. Finally, Francois Rivest, Pascal Bosse, Silviu Nedelca, and Alain Simard analyze patient access to physicians in Quebec where the provincial government imposed differentiated fee schedules for graduating doctors to convince them to set up shop in more remote, and generally poorer, areas. Examining the results over 20 years ending in 1991, the authors conclude that though access did not deviate significantly on the basis of social class, regional deviations remained. While producing complaints about a two-tiered health care system, government defenders countered by pointing to substantial improvements made over time, and by claiming that generally, good quality care was provided in remote areas, especially considering the exorbitant costs of servicing such locales.

As the Mulroney years drew to a close many spoke of Canada's welfare state as approaching a crossroads. To some, that translated into a choice between reasserting a sacred trust where the federal government in particular committed itself to guaranteeing a social minimum for all, or returning to the selective, penurious and often cruel practices that prevailed before the Second World War. But to others, the future pointed to very different challenges and choices: namely to making the hard, but necessary, decisions about spending priorities and cuts to social programs so governments could continue to provide decent services to those truly in need, while maintaining their financially solvency and a competitive Canadian economy.

Further Readings

Bacher, John, *Keeping to the Marketplace: The Evolution of Canadian Housing Policy*. Montreal and Kingston: McGill-Queen's University Press, 1993.

Bryden, Kenneth, *Old Age Pensions and Policy-Making in Canada*. Montreal and Kingston: McGill-Queen's University Press, 1974.

Bryden, P.E., *Planners and Politicians: Liberal Politics and Social Policy, 1957–1968*. Kingston and Montreal: McGill-Queen's University Press, 1997.

Canada, *Royal Commission on Dominion–Provincial Relations*. Edited and introduced by Donald V. Smiley. Toronto: McClelland and Stewart, 1963.

Canada, *Dominion-Provincial Conference on Reconstruction: Proposals of the Government of Canada, August 1945*. Ottawa, King's Printer, 1945.

Cassidy, Harry Morris, *Public Health and Welfare Reorganization: The Postwar Problem in the Canadian Provinces*. Toronto: Ryerson Press, 1945.

Granatstein, J.L., *Canada's War: The Politics of the Mackenzie King Government, 1939–1945*. Toronto: Oxford University Press, 1975.

Haddow, Rodney S., *Poverty Reform in Canada, 1958–1978: State and Class Influences on Policy Making*. Montreal and Kingston: McGill-Queen's University Press, 1993.

Harding, Jim, ed., *Social Policy and Social Justice: The NDP Government in Saskatchewan during the Blakeney Years*. Waterloo: Wilfrid Laurier University Press, 1995.

Ismael, Jacqueline S. and Yves Vaillancourt, eds., *Privatization and Provincial Social Services in Canada: Policy, Administration and Service Delivery*. Edmonton: University of Alberta Press, 1988.

Johnston, Patrick, *Native Children and the Child Welfare System*. Toronto: Canadian Council on Social Development in association with James Lorimer & Co., 1983.

Leman, Christopher, *The Collapse of Welfare Reform: Political Institutions, Policy, and the Poor in Canada and the United States*. Cambridge, Mass: MIT Press, 1980.

Lemieux, Denise and Comeau, Michelle, *Le Mouvement Familial au Québec, 1960–1990. Une Politique et des Services pour les Familles*. Sainte-Foy: Presses de l'Université du Québec, 2002.

Marsh, Leonard Charles, *Report on Social Security for Canada*. Toronto: University of Toronto Press, 1943.

McBride, Stephen, *Not Working: State, Unemployment and Neo-Conservatism in Canada*. Toronto: University of Toronto Press, 1992.

Miller, J.R., *Shingwauk's Vision: A History of Native Residential Schools*. Toronto: University of Toronto Press, 1996.

——. *Skyscrapers Hide the Heavens: A History of Indian-White Relations in Canada*. Toronto: University of Toronto Press, 2000.

Naylor, C. David, *Private Practice, Public Payment: Canadian Medicine and the Politics of Health Insurance, 1911–1966*. Montreal and Kingston: McGill-Queen's University Press, 1986.

Neary, Peter and J.L. Granatstein, eds., *The Veterans Charter and Post-World War II Canada*. Montreal and Kingston: McGill-Queen's University Press, 1998.

Pal, Leslie A., *State, Class and Bureaucracy: Canadian Unemployment Insurance and Public Policy*. Montreal and Kingston: McGill-Queen's University Press, 1988.

Rooke, Patricia and R.L. Schnell, *No Bleeding Heart: Charlotte Whitton, A Feminist on the Right*. Vancouver: University of British Columbia Press, 1987.

Rose, Albert, *Regent Park: A Study in Slum Clearance*. Toronto: University of Toronto Press, 1958.

Taylor, Malcolm G., *Health Insurance and Canadian Public Policy: The Seven Decisions that Created the Canadian Health Insurance System and their Outcomes*. Toronto: Institute of Public Administration of Canada, 1987.

Tillotson, Shirley, The *Public at Play: Gender and the Politics of Recreation in Post-War Ontario*. Toronto: University of Toronto Press, 2000.

Vaillancourt, Yves, *L'Evolution des Politiques Sociales au Québec, 1940–1960*.Montréal: Presses de l'Université de Montréal, 1988

8

A New Beginning

"The Veteran's Charter"*

BARELY HAD THE Second World War begun than planning for its end was put in motion. One month into the war, Canada's minister of pensions and national health, Ian Mackenzie, a former vice-president of the Great War Veterans' Association, was already advising Prime Minister King to begin planning for demobilization and rehabilitation. It had to be done differently this time. Mackenzie and the many key players who came together to devise and manage the series of programs that in 1946 became known collectively as the Veterans' Charter were of the opinion that the paltry support that government programs offered Canadians who had fought in World War I had significantly magnified their problems in readjusting to civilian life, leading disgruntled and angry veterans to aggravate postwar social instability. Informal estimates made in Winnipeg in May 1919, for example, suggested that as many as half of the veterans sided with organized labour in the general strike, which authorities saw as a Communist conspiracy to seize power.[1] Others, too, were worried. *Maclean's* magazine was moved to write as early as December 1939, "Without definite, well-worked out plans for the post-war employment of men who ... have served the country we shall be faced with a repetition of the upheaval which followed the last war."[2]

Indeed, early that month, while Canada's 1st Division was still preparing to depart for England, the planning commenced. The passage of PC 4068.5 created, under Mackenzie's direction, the Cabinet Committee on Demobilization and Re-establishment to identify problems relating to the eventual discharge of men and to determine how they might best be minimized.[3] However, most of the real work was handed over to an advisory subcommittee composed of deputy ministers and experts drawn from the civil service, the military, and the private sector.[4] Instrumental in setting direction was its executive secretary, Robert England, a twice wounded Great War veteran and a former director of the Canadian Legion Educational Service. England maintained that the government had to "learn some ... lessons ... in regard to the thoroughness ... of [previous] rehabilitation plans," which he described as "meagre."[5] The other key figure on the subcommittee was the associate deputy minister of pensions and national health, Walter S. Woods. A former member of the Canadian Expeditionary Force who had been wounded in 1915,

---

* This chapter was first published in Jeffrey A. Keshen, *Saints, Sinners and Soldiers: Canada's Second World War* (*Vancouver*: University of British Columbia Press, 2004), chapter 10.

Woods had served after the war as president of the Calgary branch of the Great War Veterans' Association, and as a director with the federal government's Soldier Settlement Board (which placed veterans on farms). In 1930 he became the first chairman of the War Veterans' Allowance Board, which, under his direction, moved toward greater compassion, especially in awarding pensions for long-term burnout cases.[6]

The work of these two committees was primarily responsible for the Post-Discharge Re-establishment Order on 1 October 1941, which significantly appeared just when the federal government was stepping up efforts to attract recruits. Men were promised on honourable discharge a tax-exempt gratuity of $7.50 per month for time they had served in the Western Hemisphere, and $15 per month for time overseas (a scale triple that paid to British servicemen).[7] They also received a tax exempt rehabilitation grant of one month's pay and a clothing allowance voucher initially set at $35 ($100 by war's end) for those with at least six months' military service. For veterans who did not claim other benefits, such as retraining, more cash was available, up to a level matching the gratuity, in the form of a tax-free re-establishment credit intended to help them purchase, furnish, or equip a home or business.

Several other pieces of legislation soon flowed from the Re-establishment Order, which was also designed to guarantee veterans the right to: "(I) re-enter their former employment ... (II) find new employment ... (III) train for new work ... or (IV) finish their education."[8] The 1942 *Reinstatement in Civil Employment Act* affirmed healthy veterans' right to resume their premilitary jobs, or comparable posts with their former employers, at a rate of pay equivalent to what they would have earned had they not enlisted.[9] Veterans could claim new federal unemployment insurance benefits for up to one year during the first eighteen months after discharge. Grants and subsidized loans were made available to those who wished to start up a business, to enter commercial fishing, or, under the 1942 Veterans Land Act, to farm full-time or start a maximum two-acre hobby farm. Self-employed veterans who struggled financially before revenue started flowing in could apply for an awaiting returns allowance, which paid, for up to one year, from $44.20 monthly to a single veteran with no dependants to a maximum of $120.40 monthly to a married man with six dependent children under seventeen years old. The 1942 *Vocational Training Co-ordination Act* provided such allowances to any veteran who decided to retool at the government's expense, an opportunity that, after the Great War, had been available only to those whose injuries significantly compromised their likelihood of finding work. Qualified veterans could obtain free university education with the same living allowance for a period equivalent to their time spent in the military, and provision was made for others to participate by obtaining a high school diploma in as little as six months under a special accelerated program.[10]

In March 1944 the Department of Veterans Affairs (DVA) was created to better coordinate these and other programs, including pensions and medical care, which had formerly involved several government ministries. Under Mackenzie's direction, the DVA quickly grew to mammoth proportions, with over 12,000 employees by the end of 1946. Even with the availability of unemployment insurance and family allowances, DVA benefits and pensions dwarfed all other federal social welfare costs, accounting for expenditures of $1.842 billion out of $3.621 billion between 1944 and 1948 inclusive (Figure 8.1).[11]

Figure 8.1. Veterans Benefits and Other Federal Social Welfare Expenditures, 1943–50

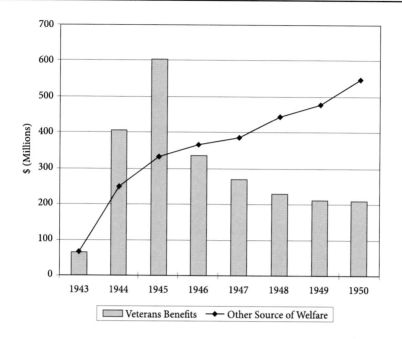

Source: K.A.H. Buckley and M.C. Urquhart, *Historical Statistics on Canada* (Toronto: Macmillan, 1965), 207.

Public opinion strongly supported such generosity. Two-thirds of those polled in mid-1942 agreed, for example, that veterans of this war should receive better treatment than their counterparts had a generation earlier.[12] The generous approach to veterans' benefits was also linked to the expanding influence of the new bureaucrats and advisors recruited by the federal government to help direct the war effort and peacetime reconversion. Many subscribed to the Keynesian strategy of priming the economy to generate spending that would offset the economic trough anticipated after the war.[13] Keynesian economics also drew strong public support, as surveys made it clear that Canadians feared the return of Depression-level unemployment and the emergence of social unrest after the war. Many indicated their intention to turn to the CCF if the Liberals did not introduce more comprehensive peacetime planning and social security—of which veterans' benefits were part—to ensure postwar stability and opportunities.

The King government was also concerned by the attitude among servicemen that the Prime Minister was antimilitary and even a coward for not serving in the Great War himself, despite having been nearly forty in 1914 and in no shape for military service. Many accused him further of abandoning Canada's fighting men by his determined resistance to conscription for overseas duty. Military morale reports also showed dissatisfaction over the paucity of information servicemen had received about veterans' programs, a situation that generated much cynicism and pessimism. A survey of 900 soldiers in May 1943 revealed that only 21 percent were optimistic about their postwar prospects, and 30 percent foresaw hard times, while the rest refrained from speculating.[14] Another poll taken early the following year by the Canadian Youth Commission among 159 servicemen in Canada from all three service branches showed that 40 percent backed the CCF, 37 percent the Conservatives, and just 12 percent the Liberals.[15]

During the final two years of the war, not only did the federal government improve several programs for veterans—increasing, for instance, living and awaiting returns allowances by $15 to $18 monthly, depending on the number of dependants involved[16]—but it also intensified efforts to publicize DVA benefits throughout the ranks. The Air Force and Navy were most inclined to support this effort, believing it would raise morale. In 1944 each of these services appointed over 100 counsellors to meet with men and familiarize them with their postwar options. The army was more cautious, as several high-ranking officers believed that such information would distract men from the still formidable task of defeating the enemy, or perhaps make them hold back in battle to ensure that they would live to enjoy DVA benefits.[17] Still, from around D-Day onward, military publications such as the *Maple Leaf* printed stories detailing in generally positive tones the different programs being instituted. By the end of 1944 all service branches were distributing DVA literature such as the pocket-sized sixty-page booklet *Back to Civil Life*—of which over a million copies were printed—which outlined in laymen's terms the essentials of all the benefits to which veterans were entitled.[18]

The National Film Board helped out with several short, upbeat instructional clips such as the 1945 three-minute entry *Getting Re-established: School and University Opportunities*. Its most substantial entry, *Welcome Soldier*, a fifteen-minute film that appeared in late 1944, opens with a scene of men being transported home on a railway passenger car. Amid singing and good-natured ribbing, a few ponder their prospects after discharge. The film then cuts to a boardroom of "experts" ready to implement many "carefully constructed" DVA plans, after which men are shown proceeding smoothly through the demobilization machinery, quickly obtaining the cash rewards to which they are entitled and then receiving sage advice from counsellors.[19] Assistance also came from the CBC. Among its radio shows broadcast overseas was the eight-part series *Honourable Discharge*, in which DVA personnel answered letters sent in by servicemen as a means of further explaining the particulars of the various programs.[20]

The DVA was indeed getting its message across. A survey taken in December 1944 among 7,000 army personnel overseas indicated that 52 percent considered themselves "adequately informed" about veterans' programs compared to 32 percent who still wanted more information.[21] More men were giving thought to how they would take advantage of DVA benefits. Another survey taken that month among 12,000 soldiers both overseas and in Canada revealed that 4 percent wanted to finish high school, 11 percent favoured university education, 26 percent thought of vocational training, and 11 percent hoped to start a farm—figures that the Department of National Defence interpreted to show a "very clear tendency ... to improve ... upon pre-enlistment status."[22] The general outlook among men regarding their postwar plans was growing more positive as yet another poll taken among soldiers in late 1944 showed that 54 percent believed "things [would] be better" or "comparable" for them following the conflict, as opposed to just 15 percent who were pessimistic.[23] Meanwhile, although the June 1945 federal election revealed continuing anger among servicemen toward Mackenzie King, the promotion of veterans' benefits no doubt helped the Liberals avert a political catastrophe among this group who, according to one straw poll, ended up giving the party a narrow margin of support: 35 percent, compared to 32 percent for the CCF, 26 percent for the Conservatives, and 7 percent for other parties.[24]

Although the Liberals survived at the ballot box, the government still faced the daunting responsibility of reintegrating about 7 percent of the country's population into civilian life. Their first task was to bring home the half-million servicemen stationed outside of Canada in a timely manner. For this too Ottawa began planning early, to avoid the problems that followed the Great War. Then, shortages of transatlantic shipping space and railway cars in Canada, along with inadequate recreational facilities established overseas, had resulted in delays and boredom, and greatly contributed to several violent outbursts among those awaiting repatriation. It was also predicted that greater efforts would be needed to convince men that the demobilization process was fair. After the Great War, the method had not been clearly articulated, and bitter rumours of favouritism arose, especially since such tasks as maintaining supply flows and administering repatriation sometimes created the need to keep certain types of personnel overseas, and led to the seeming inequity of less-essential battalions being sent home before many longer serving troops.

Back in early 1941 the Canadian government had begun reserving shipping space to transport men home as soon as the shooting stopped. Also, the Advisory Committee on Demobilization and Rehabilitation proposed that repatriation be conducted according to a point system closely conforming to the "first in first out" principle. In February 1944, with the war clearly turning against Germany, each of Canada's three service branches set up a Demobilization Directorate to work with the new Directorate of Reorganization and Demobilization, whose job was to apportion transatlantic shipping space. Arrangements were also made with Canada's railway companies to reserve nearly all existing sleeper cars and to convert an additional 100 cars to the role of transporting veterans back to their homes.[25]

However, the destructive impact of Germany's U-boat campaign had made shipping space difficult to acquire. Britain's War Office announced in March 1944 that during the first six months after the conflict Canada could expect to transport home 90,000 men, just 60 percent of its goal. Ottawa lobbied hard to raise that number, but at war's end, with most of the US navy still occupied in the Pacific and the United States also wanting to move its troops out of Europe, estimates for the summer of 1945 remained pegged at 15,000 Canadians per month. Japan's surrender in August then freed up much of the US fleet, so that by the fall Canadians were being repatriated at the rate of some 1,000 per day. By March 1946 the process was essentially complete, with fewer than 25,000 troops remaining overseas.[26]

After years away, men were extremely impatient to return home. While they waited, they needed to be kept active and content. Military duties were reduced to a minimum, and leave facilities were abundant. Thousands heeded the advice of the Legion's Educational Service to use their time taking correspondence courses to prepare themselves for civilian life. Still, military censors reported that men complained bitterly in letters home that some of their compatriots had already departed for Canada despite having fewer points and were likely snapping up the best jobs. On the surface, the process governing demobilization seemed straightforward: two points for each month of service in the Western Hemisphere and three points for each month further afield. However, there were several exceptions. Priority was given to repatriating the wounded, POWs, and men with family emergencies. A 20 percent bonus was added to the score of married men, widowers, and those with dependent children. Thousands with the skills critically needed in the postwar economy, such as experienced construction workers, moved up in the queue. Between May and August 1945, those in Europe who had volunteered to fight against Japan were first given a month's leave to Canada, which became permanent after the dropping of the atomic bomb.[27]

Men were assured that delays caused by loopholes in the point system that allowed exceptions to the "first in first out" principle were minimal. Yet, as the mouthpiece for servicemen, the *Maple Leaf* became so vociferous in its criticisms of such exceptions that Lt.-Gen. G.G. Simonds, then general officer commanding Canadian forces in the Netherlands, fired its editor, J.D. McFarlane.[28] Impatience over repatriation played a role in a July 1945 uprising among Canadian troops in Aldershot, although other contributing factors were bad food, overcrowded barracks, and a history of strained relations between locals and Canadian soldiers. Some 800 windows in town were smashed and eight Canadians were arrested, ultimately receiving jail sentences ranging from twenty-eight days to seven years.[29] This harsh response, and also the ensuing improvements in the pace of demobilization, helped prevent other such incidents. Still, authorities were sometimes reminded of the potential for trouble, as when in January 1946, RCAF ground crew in Odiham, England, staged a brief sit-down strike to protest meagre rations and "their retention overseas." The threat of fines and the loss of gratuity payments quickly ended the demonstration.[30]

When finally on their way back to Canada, nearly all veterans approached their homecoming with relief, excitement and, it seems, considerable optimism. One survey among army personnel about to be repatriated showed that 64 percent believed that through military service they had "gained greatly or a good deal" in confidence and 48 percent felt they had acquired superior leadership qualities. These traits were often subsequently verified, as many veterans who had overcome obstacles during the war ultimately became less self-doubting and more successful in civilian life. Among this group was Eddie Goodman, who went on to become a prominent lawyer and political organizer for the Conservative party and who maintained that much of his confidence derived from the knowledge that he had been "tried in battle and not found wanting."[31]

However, some had misgivings as they prepared to return home, admitting to their loved ones that difficult times might lie ahead. Even a Protestant chaplain thought it advisable to tell his family to expect some "rough edges" because he had "lived with a lot of rough and ready fellows" and had "seen ruined towns by the score ... and hundreds of poor, dirty children, dozens of dead bodies and many sorrowful things."[32]

Wishing to avoid replicating the problems experienced by many Great War veterans, the government made personnel available to prepare men for their return to civilian life.

Over the first ten months of 1945, some 700 new army education officers joined the counsellors appointed earlier by the air force and navy to give lectures not only on veterans' benefits but also on topics such as "Canadian Civics" and "Canada since 1939."[33] Their talks, as well as sermons from padres, also often warned men not to idealize home and family life, for they realized that such pipe dreams could lead to a profound sense of letdown and disillusionment. Men were advised, for instance, to "allow" for the fact that "for three, four or five years," their wives or girlfriends had had to "make decisions and live ... life without [their] daily help and presence."[34] The clear implication was that many wives would not easily accept the submissive homebound role anticipated by numerous men longing for tradition and tranquility after so much strain and suffering, and who, while in the military, had often developed an even more dominant attitude toward females.

Advice was also offered to Canadian civilians, particularly women, on how best to deal with returning servicemen. Contrasting with the wartime pattern in the mass media that generally ignored the disturbing ways in which the war might have affected the outlook and conduct of men, more columns began cautioning civilians that those they were preparing to welcome home were often not the same people they remembered, nor would they live up to the cheery correspondence they had typically sent. *Chatelaine* warned its female readership: men "who ha[ve] faced death and danger ... will return wounded in soul, if not body."[35] Parents were advised that though "he may look like a kid ... he'll be very adult ... with years of responsibilities behind him," and might react against coddling. Still, to build the confidence of veterans, wives and future wives were urged to "cultivate patience" and to offer a "secure [and] reassuring environment."[36] Several accounts stressed the need for women to vacate traditional male jobs to make room for veterans so they could more easily re-establish their "natural role" as breadwinner.[37]

Local groups stood ready to assist veterans. They included more than 700 Citizen Repatriation and Rehabilitation Committees, which were managed by local political, religious, business, labour, and other community leaders, and which attracted over 25,000 volunteers. Besides organizing official welcome home ceremonies, these committees helped veterans to better understand and access DVA programs, to find acceptable employment, and to locate decent accommodation in overcrowded cities.[38] For instance, the Edmonton committee advertised in newspapers and over the radio its "work-pile," for which employers were asked to list jobs suitable for the "more seriously disabled veteran." The Vancouver committee arranged for volunteers from the Board of Trade to give a sixteen-session course for veterans on how best to utilize the money made available by the DVA to start a business.[39]

Official homecomings were typically joyous and often spectacular events. Even with a point system in effect, for administrative convenience large groups of men usually returned home at the same time; also, despite casualties and remusterings, a notable number from the same battalion, squadron, or ship had usually served for a comparable length of time. Although the shifting of personnel over the years meant that most regiments had lost their territorial base, this never seemed to dampen the enthusiasm or size of welcoming crowds. In Windsor, for example, such a throng turned out to see the returning Essex Scottish Regiment that the troops could hardly march up Ouellette Avenue.[40] Inside large train stations or auditoriums, family and friends, many of whom had travelled considerable distances to be present, were organized alphabetically according to the man for whom they waited so as to be more easily found. Sometimes barricades were toppled in the excitement as long-separated loved ones spotted each other. Initially, veterans were treated like celebrities. He had "never been [so] drunk ... never eaten so much food ... never danced so much and never [been] kissed by so many pretty local girls," recalled one man of his first night home.[41]

Ultimately, most veterans reintegrated in their communities. Many silences speak for those who easily or through force of will put the war behind them; there were hundreds of thousands like Bill Irvine of Winnipeg, who said that within two weeks of returning home he "simply got a job and moved on."[42] But for many the reintegration process was difficult, and sometimes traumatic. Even some whose military career had never taken them outside of Canada had difficulties. As noted by the army's Pacific Command, "These soldiers have been subjected to several years of propaganda glorifying their ... comrades [overseas] ... [and] this has left its mark in many places, resulting in a form of inferiority ... and creating a sense of futility."[43] Numerous veterans found their former home community disturbingly alien. It was one thing to read or hear about places being radically transformed during the war, but quite another to confront first-hand a city whose population had as much as doubled, or a rural area or small town that had experienced huge out-migration. Severe shortages of living space frequently forced veterans, often with new families, to live with parents or accept overpriced and tiny hovels, situations that often led to bickering at home and much resentment toward the community at large.

A sense of deflation often followed the initial euphoria of reunions as people returned to their everyday routines.[44] Some veterans became despondent, feeling a lack of importance, direction, and comradeship. They had left behind buddies with whom they had gone through hellish experiences, shared every secret, and entrusted their lives. Trying to recapture those feelings and bonds, several came to spend inordinate amounts of time conversing and drinking, often excessively, in Legion halls.[45] Such places beckoned because many veterans could not reconnect with civilians, who had been sheltered by geography and sanitized information. Moreover, after having lived in close quarters with people from different regions and social and ethnic backgrounds, and after having seen and experienced so much, veterans were known to dismiss civilians, sometimes curtly, as self-serving and parochial. Their complaints over things such as high taxes or rationing were considered trivial, and their willingness to gouge and grasp in postwar black markets "grotesque."[46] This perception of pampered and selfish civilians had also been cultivated during the war by news reports of labour strikes, which many servicemen condemned as resulting "in more of us dying so that they can make good wages."[47] Indeed, by war's end, organized labour felt it essential to stress to those being demobilized that, during the conflict, civilians had worked record hours and that strikes had been declared only as a last resort and had rarely affected war production. Labour leaders realized that some companies eagerly courted veterans because they hoped they would rally against unions and work toward their decertification, though it quickly became apparent that few veterans, despite possible resentment, were inclined to do anything to jeopardize decent wages and benefits.[48]

The DVA also found it necessary to beseech employers to show compassion and patience toward those who had sacrificed and had been through so much. A number of employers avoided hiring veterans, regarding them as having too many problems, such as difficulty settling down into workplace routines or a lack of initiative because they had taken orders all the time. Meanwhile many veterans grew frustrated and angry because they returned to their former jobs expecting more than the junior positions they had left years earlier, or a raise far greater than the amount that reflected the wage freeze that had been in effect since late 1941. Following such a momentous time in their life, many veterans had trouble accepting jobs that they found meaningless or stultifying. It was particularly hard for officers and NCOs who had led men into battle to stomach such disappointments, especially when they found themselves taking orders from civilians who had not fought.[49]

Of course, reintegration also involved reassuming family life. In countless cases, the lack of commentary reflected successful reunions or people who managed in varying degrees to work through their difficulties. Eager to make up for lost time, veterans and women were soon marrying and producing children in record numbers. Interviews with unmarried servicemen showed that they linked marriage with the process of re-establishing themselves as civilians and with the sense of "home" and "security" after such perilous times.[50] Moreover, many Canadian women, in light of the thousands of young men killed overseas and the thousands returning with war brides, became more eager to avert spinsterhood, and hence less choosy.[51]

Although about 70 percent of veterans were single, tremendous attention and concern still focused on the reconstitution of spousal relations and stable nuclear families. Marriage and family were both perceived as having been under siege in recent years, and things seemed to grow worse after the war as long-separated couples often had trouble reuniting. In 1946 divorces in Canada stood at 7,683 and the next year they reached 8,199, in comparison to just 2,068 in 1939. Spousal and family desertion also increased sharply, as indicated by the rise in charges of "nonsupport of families and neglecting children" from 2,442 cases in 1944 to 3,148 in 1945. Some men returning from combat were apparently unprepared to resume family responsibilities.[52] Convinced that many divorces and desertions had resulted from ill-conceived "quickie" wartime marriages, some worried that the postwar rush to the altar would exacerbate these problems. Shortly after the conflict, *Saturday Night* columnist Anne Fromer wrote that many people were putting less thought into their marriage than they would into "raising hogs [or] growing roses."[53]

Social service agencies and churches began marriage counselling programs. Starting in mid-1945, the University of British Columbia's Extension Department offered a Marriage and Family Life course to help "iron out the wrinkles in the lives of newlyweds, and smooth the path ahead for the husbands, wives and children who have to face the rocky days of the postwar era."[54] Others, however, responded to the greater incidence of marital difficulties following the war by proposing less restrictive grounds for divorce; the Canadian Legion, for example, said it was wrong to force veterans to stay in bad marriages. Some small changes did occur. In 1945 Prince Edward Island created its first divorce court, a measure that related to increasing applications for divorce and growing anger, especially among veterans, over the time and money it took to obtain a parliamentary decree to annul a marriage. In February 1946 the Toronto Liberal MP Col. David Croll argued in Parliament that the prevailing rules governing divorce forced too many couples into choosing between ongoing unhappiness or committing fraud by hiring a private detective to take pictures of a staged extramarital affair. Although Croll's resolution for "amendments to ... enlarge the grounds for divorce" was defeated, the Ontario provincial government, seeking to unclog the higher courts, that year passed a measure permitting more accessible and less intimidating county and divisional courts to handle divorces.[55]

Throughout the first postwar decade, the annual divorce rate remained two and-a-half to three times higher than in 1939.[56] But divorce only slowly became a more accepted part of Canada's social landscape; undoubtedly the postwar rate would have been far higher if, as one veteran said, divorce had not remained "such a dirty word." After years apart, many couples found themselves estranged. They had lived very different lives; had been transformed, sometimes radically, both physically and psychologically; and with the passage of time had often felt their love fade or had become habituated to the absence of the other. Many men, grown accustomed to doing what they wanted on leave time, found it difficult to consider the feelings of a wife or family. If there had been an exciting extramarital wartime affair, postwar disappointment in the marriage would likely have been more keenly felt. A number of couples, perhaps most commonly those who had married after a quick wartime romance, even had trouble recognizing one another at first. Far more problematic with such unions, however, was the difficulty of settling into a more mundane routine with a person who, under day-to-day scrutiny, did not appear nearly as dashing or exciting as remembered, and, as was often discovered, still remained very much a stranger.[57]

In this regard, much concern was expressed over Canada's 47,783 war brides, most of whom arrived in 1945 and 1946. Some were shocked to see their husband out of uniform for the first time. Some, however, never saw their husbands at all because they were abandoned. One woman in Halifax remembered meeting a war bride in tears because her husband had telegraphed from Vancouver to say he had changed his mind.[58] Many war brides were distraught by Canada's frigid climate, or life on isolated farms or in dismal flats in overcrowded cities that, with the possible exception of Montreal and Toronto, seemed small and culturally barren. They also had other challenges: adapting to strange food and often to a strange language, living with in-laws, and sometimes, as well as meeting locals eager to help, confronting those who accused them of stealing Canadian men.[59] Most of these women toughed things out and, contrary to many dire predictions, their marriages actually had a high success rate. What kept them in Canada? Besides loving their spouse and expecting some hardships in their new life, it was not financially easy to leave—and home would hardly have seemed enticing, considering the devastation they had left behind overseas. Moreover, many did not want to improve upon pre-enlistment status, admit a mistake and run back home, especially since most had been warned against these marriages in the first place. At the end of 1945, by which point nearly 10,000 war brides had arrived in Canada, only twenty-nine had applied to return home, and in January 1947 the assistant national commissioner of the Canadian Red Cross, a group much involved in the transport of war brides to their new homes, stated, "Our impression [is] that the percentage of shattered romances among these couples is negligible."[60]

The tendency to idealize did make things difficult for many postwar couples. The serviceman who "remember[ed] his wife as a beautiful dream girl," or the wife who thought of the "dashing man in uniform" was quite often disappointed. It took time to adjust to a person who was "older [and] tired ... with a most unusual vocabulary and strange attitudes toward some of life's values."[61] Friction frequently developed after many men came back looking far more grizzled and often with a shocking propensity for profanity, cigarettes, and liquor. One woman remembered that only two weeks after her husband returned home—during which he got drunk every night—she threw him out, adding, "It didn't matter to the kids, because by this time their hearts were like stone to him."[62]

Some women felt worn out after having been left with children during the war, having had difficulties coping financially with the dependants' allowance, or juggling home life, the workplace, and volunteer labour. They sometimes resented their husbands because their letters had given such a positive impression of the grand old time they had had while in uniform.[63] A number of women had grown in confidence and become far more self-sufficient, and now resisted a subservient role within the so-called traditional family structure. However, one survey of nearly 200 Canadian soldiers taken shortly before their demobilization showed that by a margin of 56 to 21 percent, they agreed with the statement, "A woman's place is in the home."[64] Consequently, soon after the war a number of veterans talked resentfully about wives or sweethearts having "grown too independent." One former soldier angrily berated his wife because after "earning good money ... she didn't like doing kitchen work any more."[65]

Another complicating factor was that wartime infidelity, or signs of it, sometimes came to light: one veteran returned home to find books on the shelf inscribed, "To my darling May, from John."[66] Many marriages survived only because people purposefully avoided probing about behaviour during their separation. To men returning home, one syndicated advice columnist urged, "If you have a secret that would make one who loves you unhappy to know, bury it in your soul ... The war ended one phase of your life. You are starting another."[67] But such information was not always so easy to conceal. Sometimes news of a paternity suit launched overseas reached the alleged father in Canada. Men treated for venereal disease (VD) shortly before their discharge had their names sent to provincial boards of health for a follow-up examination; even though the notice was sent in the proverbial plain envelope with no return address, the contents no doubt still became known to some spouses.[68] Some people unfortunately learned that their loved one had strayed only because they too contracted VD. With the return home of servicemen, aggregate recorded cases of VD in Canada rose from 38,772 in 1944 to 40,528 in 1945 and to 41,556 in 1946.[69]

The challenge of re-establishing relationships with children became a major cause of family strain in a number of cases. For many children, their father's return was a joyful day indelibly etched into their memory. André Bernard, only three-and-a-half years old when his father—a man he knew only from a mantelpiece photograph—came home, remembered leaping into his arms at first sight, thrilled to no longer have just a "cardboard daddy." But many children were unsure about how to greet a man so long absent from their lives, and with whom, typically, they had exchanged few letters during the war. They had often grown used to a father's absence and upon his return saw him as a competitor for a mother's love and attention. "He always felt like a stranger [who] had come and taken over my life and my mother's house," said one man who for some time after the war called his father "Mr. Palmer."[70] Children who had engaged in hero worship had to adjust to the reality that few returning fathers could meet their expectations. Bitterness was known to develop when a veteran attempted to re-establish fatherly authority, sometimes in a military manner. "I didn't like the way my dad ran our home like an army barracks," said one woman whose diagnosis was that her father never shook off his former role as a sergeant-major. There were also those such as Jean Little, who did not understand why her father regularly "blew up" for little or no apparent reason.[71]

What Little's father displayed was a classic symptom of the lasting effects of battle neurosis, which has since become known as post-traumatic stress disorder (PTSD). Such men had an especially tough time reintegrating. Their numbers were substantial, though precise figures are impossible to arrive at since most cases went undiagnosed.[72] Compared to the general population, victims of PTSD showed a greater propensity toward irritability, argumentativeness, and violent outbursts. More often, they were plagued by restlessness, insomnia, and nightmares.[73] They were more easily startled and unsettled by loud noises and had trouble concentrating, sustaining conversations, and coping with pressures and responsibilities. Many complained about debilitating physical pain. A 1945 study by Canada's Army Medical Corps of 740 men discharged with severe battle exhaustion said that 19 percent claimed recurrent stomach troubles, 14 percent problems with their legs or feet, 11 percent respiratory ailments, and 8 percent heart troubles. However, doctors could find no physical evidence to explain—nor prescribe effective medicine to treat—such problems, which led to growing frustration and anger among such veterans, and often to resentment from families who began to suspect malingering. Compounding the situation, and constituting one of the most glaring shortcomings of DVA programs, was the decision, effective until 1959, to deny a pension for "neuropsychiatric ailments." The rationalization that there was no visible disability to assess further stigmatized, infuriated, and alienated these men.[74]

Readaptation problems were also particularly marked among former POWs, especially those liberated from the Japanese. POWs in captivity for at least six months were placed at the front of the queue for repatriation to Canada. Once judged physically able, they were moved to reception camps such as the No. 4 Canadian General Hospital in Aldershot. There, back pay and medical examinations were attended to, and staff were on hand to help explain DVA programs and bring men up to speed on key events that had transpired in Canada during their absence. However, such staff often later observed that many of these men should have been held back longer before returning to a country and a life from which they had been so completely cut off. Moreover, to fulfill promises to get POWs home as soon as possible, medical examinations were sometimes cursory, and POWs themselves frequently concealed or dismissed what they thought were minor ailments. These complicities led to much bitterness later on: men judged healthy on discharge were refused pensions for conditions that showed up subsequently. Indeed, this policy was maintained until 1969 toward those who had been held by the Japanese, despite abnormally high instances among this group of debilitating disorders such as crippling pains in the feet and legs.[75]

Disaster also fell on many households because POWs had had endless time to dwell upon and unrealistically romanticize home life. Many who had obsessed about women but had not seen one for years seemed to have forgotten how to act in their presence, even if they were their spouses. One POW greeted his wife with a timid handshake. Civilians were also jolted to find once-robust men mere shells of their former selves, both physically and spiritually. Like victims of PTSD, POWs often suffered from recurring nightmares, "shot nerves," and an inability to hold down steady work. Having been so controlled by and dependent on their captors, they often proved unable to deal with responsibilities or make decisions. In reflecting why, like so many other POWs, he had come back so "cold-hearted" and drained of emotion, one former captive of the Japanese simply explained, "I saw a man sit on a can for five days and just drop dead—[he] shit himself to death."[76]

Despite notable difficulties in reintegrating, Canadian Second World War veterans were generally perceived to be less embittered or alienated than Great War veterans had been, nor were they considered as great a risk to social stability. This difference can be largely attributed to the fact that the challenges and pains associated with reintegration were not generally made worse by stingy government support, as they had so often been after the First World War. Of course, the Veterans Charter could not guarantee that all couples separated by the war would successfully reunite, that the minds of the battle-fatigued would be soothed, that POWs would return to full physical and psychological health, or that children would gravitate to their returned fathers. With DVA programs, "as with everything else in life," remarked one veteran, "there were winners and losers."[77] On balance, and with good reason, the Veterans Charter came to be seen as a key factor in accounting for far more happy endings.

Upon formal discharge, veterans turned in their kit (except for one full uniform), had a final medical and dental examination, registered with the federal government's National Employment Service, had a preliminary discussion of their options with a DVA counsellor, and received their discharge pay (any back pay, the rehabilitation grant, the first monthly installment of their gratuity, and the clothing allowance voucher). By late 1945 the DVA was contending with the discharge of up to 70,000 veterans per month.[78] Such a record, Mackenzie told the press, was the result not only of careful planning but also of the dedication of DVA employees, just over half of whom were Second World War veterans themselves. Such men, he stressed, regularly worked extra hours without complaint to process their former comrades as quickly as possible.[79]

As a politician and head of the DVA, Mackenzie understandably minimized snags and complaints. Other sources told a different story. A September 1945 account in *Maclean's*, for instance, compared the DVA's main office in Montreal to a Depression-era "soup kitchen" with men waiting on wooden benches for hours to register, and then waiting again while their files were retrieved. Those who applied for pensions were promised a decision within a month, but it often took three.[80] However, much was forgiven because overall a compassionate approach was in evidence. DVA counsellors, in both preliminary and more in-depth interviews if requested, were instructed to make it clear that veterans had the right to pursue any program they qualified for. Departmental guidelines said that counsellors were to "advise" on choices. Although some decisions were no doubt made under pressure, they were ideally to be reached in a "cooperative" spirit considering the best interests of the veteran in light of individual qualifications, physical condition, interests and aptitudes (which were sometimes gauged through testing), and the likely demands of the job market.[81]

Approximately two-thirds of veterans chose to forgo free vocational retraining or university education, or the chance to start a farm or business with DVA assistance, and opted instead for maximum cash payouts. A Canadian private returning home after two years' service in the Western Hemisphere and three years overseas qualified for a $720 gratuity—roughly 40 percent of a year's pre-tax salary for a civilian male worker—and a re-establishment credit equal to that amount to acquire, repair, modernize, or furnish a home or business. By 31 March 1951, the DVA had approved 98.2 percent of requested re-establishment credits, worth $267.8 million. With such cash at their disposal, veterans had by 1947 committed themselves to purchasing some $200 million in new accommodation. Low required down payments as specified under the 1944 *National Housing Act* were helpful, as was the assistance of the Central Mortgage and Housing Corporation in obtaining buyer-friendly mortgage rates.[82]

According to a September 1945 analysis, 27 percent of veterans returned to pre-enlistment employers and 6 percent to farms or businesses that they or their families owned or managed, while 24 percent sought out new jobs.[83] Unlike the period immediately after the Great War, the employment market was favourable. The release of women workers created many vacancies, but more significant was the buoyant postwar economy. Pent-up consumer demand was strong, and the money available from wartime savings, postwar income tax cuts, and the new social programs—namely family allowances and veterans' benefits—created an invigorated spending stream. Moreover, with the Department of Reconstruction arranging for corporate tax breaks, low-interest loans, and other incentives to help business and industry retool, reconversion to peacetime production moved ahead expeditiously. Between 1945 and 1947 inclusive, Canada's civilian labour force increased from 4,447,000 to 4,862,000. Even with a flood of some 600,000 servicemen entering the civilian job market in the first year after the war, some 86 percent had obtained jobs within two months after their discharge.[84] Moreover, the government took a stance in stark contrast to its prewar position, when it had derided the unemployed for opting for the dole, and encouraged veterans to take advantage of "out of work" benefits if they weren't satisfied with resuming their prewar employment or had difficulty finding a job.[85]

Under what became known as Canadian Vocational Training (CVT), the DVA spent $75,260,723 by 31 March 1951 to prepare 81,418 former service personnel for over 100 occupations.[86] Entry into CVT could be pursued any time within eighteen months after discharge, though the deadline was flexible for those with a war related injury. Veterans who had partially used their re-establishment credit could still take a shorter course, for depending on the vocation, training lasted between a month and a year. Classes were held evenings and weekends in public schools or technical institutes, during the day at centres established under the War Emergency Training Programme, or on the job where companies were required to pay a minimum of 80 percent of the normal wage for the job. If necessary, the DVA made up the difference to the allowance received by those in training facilities, which by 1944 ranged from $60 a month for single trainees to $138 for those with a spouse and six dependent children under seventeen. Such support could be further supplemented by a spouse earning up to $75 per month, as well as by the trainee obtaining an extra $40 per month through part-time work, thus allowing the more industrious to secure quite an acceptable income.[87]

About 90 percent of those who started CVT courses completed them successfully. By late 1946 their unemployment rate was about half that of veterans in general.[88] Assessing the program six years after the war ended, a DVA study produced 80,110 names, or approximately 96 percent of the participants. Of those it could trace, only 10.2 percent were classed as having had "unsatisfactory results," a figure composed of those who had not finished their program, had left the country, or were deceased. Otherwise, 59.4 percent were employed, and 7.3 percent were self-employed in a position for which they had trained; 15 percent were employed in a job unrelated to their training but still indicated job satisfaction; 1.3 percent were taking further training; 2.8 percent were classed as "awaiting placement" because they had recently finished further courses; 1.8 percent had rejoined the military; and 2.2 percent were unemployed or, especially in the case of women, at home.[89]

Among veterans who wanted to work for themselves, 16,685 had received an awaiting returns allowance by 1947 to help them start a business. Moreover, under the 1947 *Veterans Business and Professional Loans Act*, the federal government earmarked $25 million to help protect banks against financial loss by making low interest and high-risk loans to veterans.[90] Still more extensive was the assistance directed toward those who desired to farm. Under the *Veterans Land Act* (VLA), applicants could qualify for a loan of up to $4,800 to buy land and buildings, and up to $1,200 to obtain livestock, feed, seed, and equipment. The veteran was required to make a 10 percent down payment, but payments to the government were to be based on two-thirds of the amount loaned under the VLA. The rate was fixed for twenty-five years at just 3.5 percent interest, thus requiring a monthly government payment of only $16 on a property worth $4,800. Once the veteran made payments for ten years and demonstrated that the farm was profitable, the balance of the debt to the government would be waived. Moreover, after complaints from veterans that in several parts of the country $4,800 was inadequate to purchase good-quality property, the federal government on 13 April 1945 amended the rules to allow some or all of the $1,200 designated for supplies and equipment to be used for land and buildings.[91]

The VLA was not only more generous, but also far more successful, than the Soldier Settlement scheme created for Great War veterans. That scheme had essentially been a pure loan program under which the federal government selected the vast majority of the land, which was designated only for full-time farming. Much of the property was badly isolated and of poor quality, and not surprisingly the failure rate was high. By contrast, under the VLA most veterans picked out their own property, though the DVA hired agricultural experts to inspect the land to ensure that it was worth the price and was of suitable quality for the type of farming being proposed. Also, prospective full-time farmers were screened to ensure that they were in good physical shape and had adequate experience for such work. The physically disabled were often not able to avail themselves of this opportunity, but veterans who were judged to simply require greater knowledge of farming could qualify at the government's expense by taking a course (usually for six weeks) offered at a number of institutions across the country, or by spending a specified amount of time working on a farm approved by a VLA official. A veteran who chose to do neither could still start a hobby farm for which no experience was necessary, an option that was also successfully pursued by a number of physically handicapped veterans.[92] Despite some complaints about the interference of VLA bureaucrats, about two-thirds of farm applications were approved by the end of 1946: 14,366 full-time farms, 9,468 hobby farms, and 343 commercial fishing operations, which were also administered under this program. By November 1947, expenditures under the VLA, at some $400 million, approximately quadrupled the amount spent by the Soldier Settlement Board.[93] Ultimately, VLA farms topped 60,000, and most seem to have done quite well, as by 1955 their average worth was judged to have doubled (not to mention that many of these farms later became part of housing subdivisions, making their owners—or their heirs—quite a windfall).[94]

Probably the most high-profile DVA program, in that it opened up a world still generally seen as being for the privileged, was free university education. In 1918 the National Conference on Canadian Universities had proposed a modest "loan-grant program" to help veterans enter academe, but Prime Minister Robert Borden rejected it as too expensive. By contrast, between September 1942 and March 1951, Ottawa spent $137,801,657 to provide 53,788 veterans with a university education. Just over half took a degree in general arts, though the number of Canadians with professional degrees also dramatically increased as 18.5 percent of veterans went into engineering, 10.2 percent into commerce, 6.9 percent into medicine and dentistry, and 2.8 percent into law.[95]

As with CVT, a veteran could access this program if he or she qualified within eighteen months after discharge. Universities helped out by admitting veterans with a junior or senior matriculation. Because the school year lasted eight months, veterans obtained government support for 1.5 years of academic study for each year of military service. However, as Mackenzie emphasized, even if a veteran had not been in uniform long enough to qualify for the full program, "a good student" would receive funding to complete a degree and, if "outstanding," could get support to pursue postgraduate study.[96]

At the peak implementation of this program, veterans constituted some 40 percent of Canada's university population. Every institution received veterans, though numbers varied according to size, offerings, reputation, and location.[97] Canadian universities, which had hitherto been rather quaint and cloistered institutions, were propelled toward "reinvent[ing] themselves" into larger, more comprehensive, and accessible places. Increased federal and provincial funding was provided to rapidly expand classroom space and to hire more faculty. As of 30 June 1950, for example, in addition to covering the tuition costs of veterans, Ottawa had provided $3.86 million to the University of Toronto and $2.51 million to the University of British Columbia. With additional millions from the provincial government, UBC built new science and agriculture buildings and a new library wing, and established faculties of medicine, pharmacy, and law to cope with the needs and demands—as well as the space requirements—of a student body that rose to nearly three times the university's recommended capacity of 1,500.[98]

The university program may have been the DVA's most prestigious, but the conditions for students at many schools were anything but glamorous. To deal with the flood of students, many institutions adopted a trimester system—starting courses in January, April, and September—and scheduled classes from 8 a.m. to 10 p.m.[99] At McGill University, Principal F. Cyril James's economics class ballooned from 52 students in 1944 to 295 in the fall of 1945. Makeshift arrangements often became necessary. That year, McGill established Sir William Dawson College in what was formerly the RCAF's No. 9 Observer Training School; and the University of Toronto, in order to teach some 3,000 engineering students, began renting from the federal government a series of buildings formerly used as a shell-filling plant in Ajax, twenty-five miles from its main campus. Army Nissen huts were built on campus at several universities to serve as classrooms and student housing. The University of Alberta temporarily housed veterans in the city's main ice-skating rink.[100] Moreover, veterans often complained they could not get by on the monthly government living allowance, which was meant to cover room, board, books, and other educational supplies. Some emphasized that lack of money, more than shortage of living space, forced student veterans, often with families, to jam into small flats and even to double up with other families, thus making it exceptionally difficult to study and introducing great marital strain.

Such issues figured prominently at the inaugural convention of the National Conference of Student Veterans held in Montreal on 27 and 28 December 1945. Attending in Mackenzie's place, Maj.-Gen. E.L.M. Burns, the DVA's director general of rehabilitation, rejected resolutions for a higher allowance and for free books. Government support, Burns argued, could be supplemented by spousal income, by part-time work, and by special low-interest loans for up to $500 a year.[101] He also pointed out that if preferential treatment was given to veteran university students, other veterans would be resentful or force the government to similarly augment support for all DVA recipients, which he insisted Ottawa could not afford.[102] Not articulated to the delegates was the belief of many DVA officials that if allowances were kept relatively modest, only serious, hard-working veterans would seek university education. Indeed, those who failed a course and a supplementary examination were cut off from government support, although it was decided in 1947 that such students could requalify if they funded themselves for an academic year and passed all their subjects.[103] Ultimately, most veterans coped financially, though the situation was more serious than the DVA acknowledged. For instance, in an October 1946 press release the department stressed that only nine veterans had dropped out claiming poverty; however, 841 others had discontinued their studies because they said they wanted to find a job, a notable proportion of whom undoubtedly had financial difficulties.[104]

Other challenges for student veterans involved adapting to the classroom setting and to the solitude and self-discipline required for studying and essay writing. A February 1945 DVA analysis of thirty-two veterans attending the University of Toronto with an average of twenty months' military service reported that twenty-two often "felt restless," eighteen had "trouble concentrating," and seven experienced "difficulty ... remembering."[105] That year the university established a psychiatric service for veterans having trouble coping. Indeed, many university administrators and professors were reluctant to accept large numbers of veterans, believing that far too many would prove ill-prepared, too agitated, battle-hardened, hard drinking, disruptive, and inclined to "swinging the lead." Yet, although there was some suggestion that professors were reluctant to be hard on or fail veterans, the results from ex-servicemen surprised and in some cases astonished the skeptics. Most veterans were determined to make the most of this golden opportunity. Desiring to finish as quickly as possible, many avoided paid work during the summer so they could squeeze in an extra term. Professors often came to praise the keenness of this group; one at McGill said that "twenty in a class of 200 would set tone." At the University of Toronto, the failure rate for veterans in the 1945–46 academic year, at 12 percent, was half that of the general student body. That same year, seventeen of twenty Canadian Rhodes Scholarships were awarded to veterans, and in universities across Canada twice as many veterans as non-veterans passed with honours.[106] The following year, 77 percent of veterans passed unconditionally, and only 13 percent lost their funding. About half of those who failed repeated their courses at their own expense, and between 1948 and 1952, of 2,962 such cases, 2,604, or 87.9 percent, managed to requalify for DVA funding.[107]

University education also meant better incomes. By 1949 the average salary of a veteran graduate was $2,400, about 20 percent higher than the norm for male workers, and with time this differential likely increased. While some veterans were returning to university studies that had been interrupted by the war, for many, given their social background, the DVA opened the door to opportunities that had not seemed possible before their enlistment. An October 1945 survey by the Department of National Defence revealed that some two-thirds of those entering university with the help of the DVA had never before attended such an institution.[108] Of course, a number had enlisted straight out of high school, but there were many examples like the Manitoba veteran who returned home with a grade five education, and yet in 1951, after completing an accelerated high school course and university studies, graduated as an engineer. "Where would I have been if there hadn't been a war?" remarked another veteran who went on to become a lawyer. "[Maybe] riding the boxcars looking for work ... or ... a two-bit clerk ... with no future."[109] In 1951, as it had done with the CVT program, the DVA followed up those whose university studies it had supported. Of the 44,063 identified (approximately 81 percent of participants), only 8.5 percent fell into the "unsatisfactory" category, compared to 57.8 percent who were employed, and 6.7 percent who were self-employed, in their field of study; 10.2 percent who were in another but still—according to the respondents—satisfactory line of work; 11.4 percent who were still in school; 3.3 percent who were in the military; and 2.1 percent who were either unemployed or at home.[110]

Perhaps the DVA's greatest challenge was to re-establish those who returned home with debilitating injuries. For Great War veterans in this group, ongoing disputes and bitterness over pensions considerably compounded their difficulties. Pension commissioners, few of whom were veterans, had acted in accordance with their cost-conscious superiors and commonly denied compensation unless an injury was incontestably related to military service. Moreover, only about 5 percent of claimants had been awarded the highest possible annual rate—which for noncommissioned personnel ranged from $600 to $900, depending on marital status and the number of dependants. By contrast, 80 percent received less than half of the maximum, largely because it was reasoned that a modest pension would encourage a man to triumph over his handicaps and not become a permanent public charge.[111]

This is not to suggest that pensions were not a source of discontent in the Second World War. Those discharged during training were typically denied support for an injury because it was claimed that it predated their enlistment. Although this was often the case, clearly an exceedingly stringent approach was applied, for by July 1941, only 687 of 12,786 applications had been approved.[112] Following the war, many veterans who had hidden what they mistakenly thought to be small ailments in order to expedite their discharge, or whose injuries were missed by doctors performing examinations during the demobilization process, were denied support. Many pension recipients, as well as the Canadian Legion, complained that average awards were too low, as was the scale paid for different types of injuries, such as 40 percent of the maximum rate for the loss of an eye or 70 percent for a leg.

Still, compared to the pensions paid to Great War veterans, or even to the average annual male salary of some $1,750 in 1945, post-Second World War pensions do not come across that badly. Annual amounts ranged from, at the 10 percent disability level, $756 for a single to $1,574 for a married veteran with six dependent children under seventeen, up to, at the 100 percent level, from $1,260 to $2,364.[113] And compared to the treatment of their Great War counterparts, the handling of Second World War pensioners was far less adversarial. Veterans could obtain free advice from the DVA's Pension Advocate's Office when making a claim or when appealing an award. By the end of 1945, pension boards, which were increasingly staffed by veterans, provided some support in 86.3 percent of cases. Ottawa also raised the award level for several categories of injury shortly after the war and allowed more cases of maximum coverage by adding together, rather than averaging out, claims for multiple injuries thought to overlap.[114] Moreover, as long as an injury remained evident, the pension was paid, whether or not the veteran worked or even earned a lucrative salary.[115]

To treat such veterans medically, the DVA was by 1948 running thirty-four new hospitals or wings of existing institutions, seven occupational health centres, four facilities for paraplegics, three for those with tuberculosis, and nine to provide long-term care. The department recruited doctors who had served with the military and were thus familiar with battlefield injuries, and it linked its facilities with university medical faculties so as to turn them into teaching and research centres. In several areas, veterans reaped the benefits of recent and dramatically improved procedures, such as new ways of treating spinal cord injuries, for which the mortality rate plunged to 10 percent as compared to 80 percent following the Great War.[116]

Key to the economic and, in many cases, the psychological rehabilitation of the wounded was the DVA's Casualty Rehabilitation Section. It arranged for retraining, assisted with the acquisition of benefits and, when the veteran was ready, help in finding employment and often a place to live. Created in January 1945, its first director was the blinded veteran Maj. Edward A. Dunlop; many, including Mackenzie, thought he would serve as an "inspiration" to the injured. Dunlop strongly opposed directing the disabled into simple, sheltered jobs, a policy largely applied after the Great War and which, he said, led to low pay and disillusionment. A tireless and impressive campaigner, Dunlop often spoke before business and industrial associations, stressing, for example, that only 5 percent of jobs "require[d] all a man's physical capacity." His department sent employers, among other materials, literature containing plenty of photographs of rehabilitated veterans performing a wide array of workplace tasks.[117] Whenever possible, press releases from the Casualty Rehabilitation Section cited studies to reinforce this message. A survey of 125 "large companies" that hired disabled workers, conducted in 1945 by the American Society of Safety Engineers, found that 66 percent indicated that the disabled worker's productivity was as high as, and 24 percent that it was higher than, that of the able-bodied, results that Dunlop attributed to employees being more grateful for, and hence more dedicated to, their jobs.[118]

Dunlop's approach of aggressively emphasizing that veterans like himself could always triumph over disabilities undoubtedly pushed some men into the workplace before they were ready and exaggerated the expectations of some employers. Of course, men who were no longer in DVA medical facilities represented a cost saving to the government. But more important to those like Dunlop was that a veteran's successful rehabilitation and ultimate happiness required that he achieve a strong sense of self-worth, a key ingredient of which, Dunlop insisted, was the ability to hold down a job and, if married, to perform to some extent the breadwinner role. In attaining this goal, and in providing higher incomes to the injured and their families, Dunlop and the various others involved from the DVA were remarkably successful. As of 1948, 65.3 percent of the 29,361 veterans who had returned home with "serious wounds" were employed, while 24.8 percent were still retraining. Another study completed two years later observed that of Canada's 5,093 veterans with a pensionable disability rated between 1 and 24 percent of the maximum award, 89.5 percent were employed; of the 9,912 rated between 25 and 49 percent, 87 percent had jobs; of the 6,312 rated between 50 and 74 percent, 83.7 percent worked; and of the 7,328 rated between 75 and 100 percent, 61.4 percent were gainfully employed.[119]

Over the years, the DVA certainly found itself the target of grievances. The Canadian Legion persevered with its campaign for higher pensions. Not until 1992 did the federal government respond to persistent lobbying and change its position about former merchant marines being nonmilitary personnel with no right to compensation for their exclusion from veterans' benefits. At the time of writing, Canada's Native veterans are still seeking redress for what they claim was prejudicial treatment by the DVA.[120] Yet overall, Canada's Second World War veterans have expressed satisfaction and gratitude more strongly than anger and protest. Servicemen may have distrusted and even despised Mackenzie King, but his government provided what likely still stands as the most generous welfare and benefit package in Canadian history. While the Veterans Charter could not cure the heartache that came into many homes after the conflict, it is no understatement that it provided millions of Canadians with a new beginning and, at least in financial terms, a better life. Moreover, by enacting legislation such as the *Reinstatement in Civil Employment Act*, and by furnishing valuable skills, education, first-rate medical care, and a variety of special grants and loans, the government did much to reinstate veterans as breadwinners. In many cases, this meant a return to the traditional gendered order that many deemed essential, particularly after a period seen to be plagued by family instability and moral decline.

Such programs were inspired by the desire to do better for veterans than in 1918, a desire in part stimulated by the fear of disgruntled ex-servicemen emerging as a destabilizing social force, and further supported by a widespread determination that the postwar period not see the type of instability that had followed the Great War or the reassertion of Depression-like conditions. In this light, the Veterans Charter can be viewed as a part of an overarching campaign by Canadians to realize greater progress and stability out of the Second World War, a resolve that encouraged several other social initiatives and ultimately contributed greatly to the lasting impression of the Second World War as the "good war."

Notes

1. National Archives of Canada (NAC), MG30 C181, Robert England papers (RE) vol. 2, file 1940–44, Address by Ian Mackenzie, 6 Dec. 1940. For details on programs for Great War veterans see Desmond Morton and Glenn Wright, *Winning the Second Battle: Canadian Veterans Return to Civilian Life, 1915–1930* (Toronto: University of Toronto Press, 1987). On the roles played by veterans in the Winnipeg strike see D.C. Masters, *The Winnipeg General Strike* (Toronto: University of Toronto Press, 1950), and David J. Bercuson, *Fools and Wise Men: The Rise and Fall of the One Big Union* (Toronto: McGraw-Hill Ryerson, 1978).

2. *Maclean's*, 1 Dec. 1939, 2.

3. Also on the committee were the ministers of public works, national defence, agriculture, and labour. NAC, MG27 III B5, Ian Mackenzie papers (IM), vol. 60, file 527-61(4), PC 4068.5, 8 Dec. 1939.

4. Dean Oliver, "Canadian Demobilization in World War II," in The *Good Fight: Canadians in the Second World War*, ed. J.L. Granatstein and Peter Neary (Toronto: Copp Clark Longman, 1995), 370.

5. RE, vol. 2, file 1940–43, "New Veterans and Old Fictions," 1942.

6. Woods went on to become the first deputy minister of veterans affairs. Walter Woods, *Rehabilitation (A Combined Operation), Being a History of the Development and Carrying out of a Plan for the Re-Establishment of a Million Young Veterans of World War II by the Department of Veterans Affairs and its Predecessor the Department of Pensions and National Health* (Ottawa: Queen's Printer, 1953), vi.

7. The Western Hemisphere was defined as "the continents of North and South America, the islands adjacent thereto and the territorial waters thereof including Newfoundland, Bermuda and the West Indies." J.L. Granatstein and Peter Neary, eds., *The Veterans Charter and Post-War Canada* (Montreal and Kingston: McGill-Queen's University Press, 1998), 259.

8. NAC, RG38, Department of Veterans Affairs records (DVA), vol. 364, file "General Clippings, 1943-52," clipping from *Saturday Night*, 22 April 1944, n.p.

9. A veteran had to reapply to his former boss within three months of being honourably discharged and could be denied his old job only if he had originally held it after another and longer-serving veteran who also reapplied. RE, vol. 2, file 1938–44, *Reinstatement in Civil Employment Act*, 1942; *Canadian Unionist*, July 1941, 27.

10. Morton and Wright, *Winning the Second Battle*, 94, 134; *Veteran*, Feb. 1919, 2; NAC, RG24, Department of National Defence records (DND), vol. 12,278, file 26–37, Routine Order 2080, n.d.; RE, vol. 2, file 1940-43, Report on General Advisory Committee on Demobilization and Rehabilitation, Nov. 1941.

11. Ottawa *Citizen*, 30 Aug. 1945, 2; Jane Ursel, *Private Lives, Public Policy: 100 Years of State Intervention in the Family* (Toronto: Women's Press, 1992), 224.

12. *Public Opinion Quarterly*, 1942, 665.

13. See J.L. Granatstein, *The Ottawa Men: The Civil Service Mandarins, 1935–1957* (Toronto: University of Toronto Press, 1982), chapter 6; J.L. Granatstein, *Canada's War: The Politics of the Mackenzie King Government, 1939-1945* (Toronto: Oxford University Press, 1975), chapter 7; and Doug Owram, *The Government Generation: Canadian Intellectuals and the State, 1900-1945* (Toronto: University of Toronto Press, 1986), chapters 9–11.

14. Directorate of History and Heritage, Department of National Defence (DHH), 113.3 R4003 V1(D1), Unit Survey, May 1943.

15. *Canadian Forum*, Aug. 1944, 100.

16. DVA, vol. 272, Press Release No. 54, 28 Nov. 1944.

17. Dean F. Oliver, "Public Opinion and Public Policy in Canada: Federal Legislation on War Veterans, 1939–46," in *The Welfare State in Canada: Past, Present and Future*, ed. Raymond B. Blake, Penny E. Bryden, and J. Frank Strain (Toronto: Irwin Publishing, 1997), 198.

18. *Khaki* 1, 20: 3; DVA, vol. 183, file 31-8-44, Memo to Governor General, 17 March 1944.

19. NAC, RG36-31, Wartime Information Board records (WIB), vol. 11, file 6-3-5, Rehabilitation Information Committee, Film Sub-Committee, Report, 19 March 1945; National Film Board (NFB), *Welcome Soldier*, 1944.

20. More popular was the satirical Johnny Home Show, which started broadcasting weekly soon after D-Day. Starring Johnny Wayne and Frank Shuster of the No. 1 Canadian Entertainment Unit, it presented a humorous take on the trials and tribulations servicemen might face after returning home, including with the DVA bureaucracy. Some officials criticized the show for "celebrating two shiftless smart-alecs," but most military and government authorities accepted it as a morale booster. WIB, vol. 9, file 6-3-5-8-1, Canadian Broadcasting Corporation, Rehabilitation Programs Committee, Report 3, 11 Dec. 1944, and file "Johnny Home Show."

21. Dean F. Oliver, "Awaiting Return: Life in the Canadian Army's Repatriation Depots, 1945–1946," in *The Veterans Charter and Post-War Canada*, ed. J.L. Granatstein and Peter Neary (Montreal and Kingston: McGill-Queen's University Press, 1998), 41.

22. DHH, 113.3 R4003(D1), Rehabilitation: A Survey of Opinions Among Army Personnel Awaiting Discharge, Dec. 1944.

23. IM, vol. 64, file 527-132, OR Feelings Concerning their Post-War Welfare, Nov. 1944.

24. *Canadian Forum*, July 1945, 80.

25. C.P. Stacey, *Six Years of War: The Army in Canada, Britain and the Pacific* (Ottawa: Department of National Defence, 1966), 432; Oliver, "Canadian Demobilization," 367–386.

26. C.P. Stacey, *Official History of the Canadian Army in the Second World War, vol. 3, The Victory Campaign: The Operations in Northwest Europe, 1944-1945* (Ottawa: Department of National Defence, 1960), 617; Stacey, *Six Years of War*, 433-434; Oliver, "Awaiting Return," 36, 51-52; WIB, vol. 17, file 9-6-2-1, Department of National Defence (Army), Public Relations Future Release, 4 July 1945.

27. NAC, RG19, Department of Finance records (FN), vol. 4031, file 129-W-1-23, clipping from *Consumer Facts*, Sept. 1945, n.p.; DND, vol. 10,508, file 15 A21.009(D68), "After Victory in Europe," May 1945, n.p.; J.L. Granatstein and Desmond Morton, *Victory 1945: Canadians from War to Peace* (Toronto: HarperCollins, 1995), 141–42; Michael Stevenson, "The Industrial Selection and Release Plan and the Premature Release of Personnel from the Armed Forces, 1945-1946," in *Uncertain Horizons: Canadians and Their World in 1945*, ed. Greg Donaghy (Ottawa: Canadian Council for the History of the Second World War, 1996), 115–32.

28. DHH, 312.023(D1), Field Censor's Report, 6 June 1945; Oliver, "Canadian Demobilization," 379.

29. DND, vol. 12,705, file 272/7; Oliver, "Awaiting Return," 44-45.

30. NAC, RG2, Privy Council records (PC), Cabinet Conclusions, 6 Jan. 1946.

31. IM, vol. 64, file 527-132, OR Feelings Concerning Their Post-War Welfare, Nov. 1944; J.L. Granatstein, Canada's Army: Waging War and Keeping the Peace (Toronto: University of Toronto Press, 2002), 309.

32. York University Archives, Jack Lawrence Granatstein papers, box 4, file 67, Rev. J.A. Falconbridge to Laura and James, 19 Sept. 1945.

33. WIB, vol. 17, file 9-6-2-1, Postwar Planning Information, n.d.; WIB, vol. 14, file 8-14b, WIB Lecture Sheets, n.d.; IM, vol. 57, file 527-14(b), Speech by Mackenzie, 31 Dec. 1945; DND, vol. 12,279, file 27/45, Memo from General H.D.G. Crerar, n.d.; Oliver, "Awaiting Return," 41, 46-47.

34. DND, vol. 10,513, file 215 A21.009, Address entitled "Going Home," Aug. 1945; Glenbow Institute (GB), MU6222, file 3, Report Centre, 11 Jan. 1945.

35. *Chatelaine*, May 1944, 9.

36. Susan M. Hartmann, "Prescriptions for Penelope: Literature on Women's Obligations to Returning World War II Veterans," *Women's Studies* 5, 3 (1978): 223–39; *Canadian Home Journal*, May 1944, 8–9, and Aug. 1945, 2–3.

37. Edward C. McDonagh, "The Discharged Serviceman and His Family," *American Journal of Sociology* 51, 5 (1946): 452.

38. NAC, MG30 I311, Montreal Soldiers' Wives' League papers (MSWL), vol. 3, file 64, Brigadier G.B. Chisholm, "Women's Responsibility for Mental Reestablishment of Soldiers," 13 Nov. 1944; DVA, vol. 372, News Release No. 77, 24 March 1945, News Release No. 85, 23 May 1945, and News Release No. 243, n.d.

39. WIB, vol. 18, file "Edmonton," Minutes of Monthly General Meeting of the Citizen's Rehabilitation Council of the City of Edmonton, 18 Dec. 1944; DVA, vol. 372, News Release No. 172, n.d.

40. Granatstein and Morton, *Victory 1945*, 160.

41. Barry Broadfoot, *The Veterans' Years: Coming Home from the War* (Vancouver: Douglas and McIntyre, 1985), 14.

42. Bill Irvine, interview by author, Edmonton, 20 Nov. 1992; Magda Fahrni, "Under Reconstruction: The Family and the Public in Postwar Montréal, 1944–1949" (PhD diss., York University, 2001), 188.

43. DHH, 322.009(D217), Morale Report, Pacific Command, 20 July 1945.

44. WIB, vol. 14, file 8-14-6, pt. 2, Attitudes of Army Personnel Recently Returned from Overseas, 20 Nov. 1944.

45. Bill McNeil, *Voices of a War Remembered: An Oral History of Canadians in World War Two* (Toronto: Doubleday, 1991), 241–42; Donald F. Ripley, *The Home Front: Wartime Life at Camp Aldershot and in Kentville, Nova Scotia* (Hantsport, NS: Lancelot Press, 1991), 188.

46. *Canadian Forum*, May 1945, 38-39, and Aug. 1945, 105.

47. *Khaki* 3, 23: 3; *Khaki* 3, 25: 3.

48. NFB, "Getting the Most out of a Film," a filmed discussion appended to the NFB's movie, *Welcome Soldier*; Fahrni, "Under Reconstruction," 172–73.

49. WIB, vol. 14, file 8-14-E, OR Feelings Concerning their Post-War Discharge, n.d.; Broadfoot, *Veterans' Years*, 212.

50. Instructive in this regard is an American study that tracked representative samples of veteran and civilian males between 1945 and 1950. It discovered that in every age cohort, veterans married far more quickly. John Modell and Duane Steffey, "Waging War and Marriage: Military Service and Family Formation, 1940-1950," *Journal of Family History* 13, 2 (1988): 212; FN, vol. 4031, file 129-W-1-23, Rehabilitation Trends, Montreal, Nov. 1945.

51. Eleanor Taylor, interview, Eastern Townships Research Centre, Lennoxville, QC, Special Media Collection, Oral History of Eastern Townships, Anglophone Women during World War II.

52. *Canada Year Book, 1946*, 1113; *Canada Year Book, 1947*, 283; Fahrni, "Under Reconstruction," 147.

53. *Saturday Night*, 23 Feb. 1946, 29.

54. Mona Gleason, "Psychology and the Construction of the 'Normal' in Postwar Canada, 1945–1960," *Canadian Historical Review* 78, 3 (1997): 456; NAC, MG28 I95, Young Men's Christian Association papers (YMCA), vol. 50, file "Divorce in Canada 1936-49," unidentified clipping entitled "Social Welfare Groups Consider Action to Combat Divorce," n.d., n.p.

55. YMCA, vol. 50, file "Divorce in Canada 1936-49," clipping from Ottawa *Citizen*, 7 Feb. 1946, n.p.; Archives of Ontario, RG4, Attorney-General records, 615/1946; Wendy Owen and J.M. Bumsted, "Divorce in a Small Province: A History of Divorce on Prince Edward Island from 1833," *Acadiensis* 20, 2 (1991): 98–101.

56. *Canada Year Book, 1955*, 224.

57. Broadfoot, *Veterans' Years*, 121, 141, 144-145; McDonagh, "Discharged Serviceman," 452.

58. Joyce Hibbert, *The War Brides* (Toronto: Peter Martin Associates, 1978), 103; Broadfoot, *Veterans' Years*, 133.

59. Some charged that the war brides were like prostitutes, having "hung around ... [military] camps" to lure Canadian servicemen so they could leave behind the misery of war-ravaged Britain or Europe. Vancouver *Sun*, 25 Aug. 1945, 4; Ben Wicks, *When the Boys Came Marching Home: True Stories of the Men Who Went to War and the Women and Children Who Took Them Back* (Toronto: Stoddart, 1991), 118–19; *Canadian Home Journal*, May 1945, 68.

60. MSWL, vol. 3, File 54, Press Release, 15 Dec. 1945; WIB, vol. 8, File 2-26, L.B. Connery to W.S. Durdin, 13 Jan. 1947.

61. McDonagh, "Discharged Serviceman," 454.

62. Broadfoot, *Veterans' Years*, 412.

63. Sheila Waengler, interview by author, Toronto, 12 Aug. 1999.

64. WIB, vol. 14, File 8-14-E, OR Feelings Regarding their Post-War Welfare, 7 Feb. 1945.

65. Mary Turner, interview, 2 March 1983, NAC, Audiovisual Division, Tape R-8550; Diane G. Forestell, "The Victorian Legacy: Historical Perspectives on the Canadian Women's Army Corps" (PhD diss., York University, 1985), 171.

66. Jean Bruce, *Back the Attack! Canadian Women during the Second World War—At Home and Abroad* (Toronto: Macmillan, 1985), 161; Broadfoot, *Veterans' Years*, 140.

67. Vancouver *Sun*, 23 Aug. 1945, 19.

68. DND, vol. 10,924, File 239 C1.7(D19), First Cdn Army, Medical Instructions, 28 July 1945; W.R. Feasby, *Official History of the Canadian Medical Services, 1939–45*, vol. 2 (Ottawa: Queen's Printer, 1956), 114; Archives of Alberta, 68.145, Department of Public Health, Annual Report, 1945, 61.

69. Statistics Canada, *Incidence of Notifiable Diseases by Province, Number of Cases and Rates, 1924–68* (Ottawa: Statistics Canada, 1968), 86-91.

70. William Horrocks, *In Their Own Words* (Ottawa: Rideau Veterans Home Residents Council, 1993), 226; Wicks, *When the Boys Came Marching Home*, 91.

71. *Canadian Home Journal*, July 1945, 5–7, 22; Patricia Galloway, ed., *Too Young to Fight: Memories from Our Youth during World War II* (Toronto: Stoddart, 1999), 91.

72. During the war the army discharged 8,018 men for various "mental, nervous and psychotic" disorders, though these were only the most serious cases. E.L.M. Burns, *Manpower in the Canadian Army, 1939–1945* (Toronto: Clarke, Irwin, 1956), 113.

73. Turner, interview.

74. DND, vol. 2093, File 54-27-7-391, "Psychoneurotics Discharged from the Canadian Army," excerpt reprinted from the *Canadian Medical Association Journal*, vol. 52, 1945, n.p.; Terry Copp, "From Neurasthenia to Post-Traumatic Stress Disorder: Canadian Veterans and the Problem of Emotional Disabilities," in *The Veterans Charter and Post-War Canada*, ed. J.L. Granatstein and Peter Neary (Montreal and Kingston: McGill-Queen's University Press, 1998), 153–54.

75. In 1952, from the sale of Japanese assets in Canada authorized under the formal peace treaty between Japan and the Allies, these Canadian POWs were provided with a lump sum payment of one dollar per day of captivity, on average $1,360. In 1958 they received another fifty cents per day. In 1964 the Canadian Pension Commission undertook an analysis of the "Hong Kong veterans" that revealed abnormally high rates of "optic atrophy, neurological, muscular and minor circulatory defects of the feet and legs ... and coronary artery disease." In 1969 all those held by the Japanese were given a minimum pension of 50 percent of the maximum pension award. In 1987 the War Amps of Canada argued before the United Nations Human Rights Commission to have the Japanese pay these men restitution, but were "stonewalled" by Tokyo. Finally, in December 1998 Canada's federal government provided another $24,000 in compensation to each of the 350 surviving POWs held by the Japanese, and to the widows of former prisoners. Dave McIntosh, *Hell on Earth: Aging Faster, Dying Sooner. Canadian Prisoners of the Japanese during World War Two* (Toronto: McGraw-Hill Ryerson, 1997), 250–55, 258; War Amps of Canada, "Government Pays Hong Kong Claims on Humanitarian Basis," 11 Dec. 1998, <www.waramps.ca>; Jonathan F. Vance, *Objects of Concern: Canadian Prisoners of War through the Twentieth Century* (Vancouver: UBC Press, 1994), 221–25.

76. Daniel Dancocks, *In Enemy Hands: Canadian Prisoners of War, 1939-1945* (Edmonton: Hurtig Publishers, 1983), 281; Joyce Hibbert, *Fragments of War: Stories from Survivors of World War II* (Toronto: Dundurn Press, 1985), 111; DND, vol. 12,631, File 224/18, Lt.-Col. A.T.M. Wilson, RAMC, "Report to the War Office on the Psychological Aspects of the Rehabilitation of Repatriated Prisoners of War," Feb. 1944.

77. Cliff Humford, interview by author, Edmonton, 24 Oct. 1992.

78. Metropolitan Toronto Library, Baldwin Room, untitled pamphlet distributed by Rehabilitation Wing, No. 2 District Depot, n.d.; DVA, vol. 372, News Release No. 138, 18 Oct. 1945 and News Release No. 147, n.d.

79. Many other DVA employees were seconded from the Department of Labour or had a background in adult education or personnel service. DVA, vol. 272, Memo entitled "Training of Rehabilitation Counsellors," n.d.; DVA, vol. 372, News Release No. 63, 27 Nov. 1944.

80. DVA, vol. 272, News Release No. 200, n.d.; Granatstein and Morton, *Victory 1945*, 161-62.

81. DVA, vol. 183, File 61-28, clipping from *Rehabilitation News*, 30 April 1945, n.p.

82. Walter Woods, *Rehabilitation*, 63-64, 70-71; RE, vol. 2, File 1938-44, Notes on War Service Grants Act, n.d.; NAC, RG27, Ministry of Labour records, vol. 2349, File 22-5-14, Memorandum on Progress of Veteran Rehabilitation, 1947.

83. DVA, vol. 272, News Release No. 147, n.d.

84. Eighteen months after the war, that figure rose to over 95 percent. DVA, vol. 272, News Release No. 255, 21 Nov. 1946, and News Release No. 259, 3 Jan. 1947; Robert Bothwell and William Kilbourn, *C.D. Howe: A Biography* (Toronto: McClelland and Stewart, 1979), chapter 12; Granatstein and Neary, *Good Fight*, 452.

85. Said Ian Mackenzie on this point, "We don't want our ex-servicemen and women spending their gratuities for a purpose for which the out-of-work benefit was designed." DVA, vol. 272, News Release No. 162A, n.d.

86. Woods, *Rehabilitation*, 107; DND, vol. 12,278, File 27-1, Bulletin on Vocational Training for Ex-Service Personnel, 1944.

87. IM, vol. 58, File 527-41(3), "Vocational Training on Civvy Street."

88. DVA, vol. 272, News Release No. 261, 16 Jan. 1947; Walter Woods, *Rehabilitation*, 87.

89. Woods, *Rehabilitation*, 109.

90. DVA, vol. 272, News Release No. 259, 3 Jan. 1947, and News Release No. 260, 15 Jan. 1947.

91. DVA, vol. 272, News Release No. 80, 13 April 1945; DND, vol. 12,278, File 26–37, pamphlet entitled "The Veterans Land Act," March 1944.

92. Some men qualified overseas while awaiting their repatriation to Canada, as the army ran an agricultural school in Dordrecht, Netherlands, between 29 July and 15 December 1945. Oliver, "Awaiting Return," 53; DND, vol. 12,278, File 27-1, Bulletin on Vocational Training for Ex-Service Personnel, 1944; IM, vol. 60, File 527-61(4), Second Report of the Veterans Land Act for the Fiscal Year Ended 31 March 1944; Morton and Wright, Winning the Second Battle, 148, 204.

93. *Canada Year Book, 1947*, 1147; DVA, vol. 272, News Release No. 252, n.d.; DVA, vol. 364, File "General Clippings," clipping from Winnipeg *Tribune*, 13 Nov. 1947, n.p.

94. DVA, vol. 364, File "General Clippings," clipping from Red Deer *Advocate*, 17 Nov. 1954, n.p.

95. DVA, vol. 364, File "General Clippings," clipping from *Financial Post*, 5 Oct. 1946, n.p.; Woods, *Rehabilitation*, 107-109.

96. As of February 1951, of the 9,000 veterans who started university without enough credited military service to cover the time necessary to complete their degree, 6,068, or 67.4 percent, had been granted an extension of funding. P.B. Waite, *The Lives of Dalhousie University: The Old College Transformed, 1925–1980* (Montreal and Kingston: McGill-Queen's University Press, 1998), 148; DVA, vol. 272, News Release No. 256, n.d.; Peter Neary, "Canadian Universities and Canadian Veterans of World War II," in *The Veterans Charter and Post-War Canada*, ed. J.L. Granatstein and Peter Neary (Montreal and Kingston: McGill-Queen's University Press, 1998), 122, 124, 128–29.

97. For example, during the 1947–48 academic year, just 48 veterans enrolled at Bishop's University compared to 6,858 at the University of Toronto. Neary, "Canadian Universities," 139–41.

98. *Saturday Night*, 14 April 1945, 14; Vancouver *Sun*, 31 Aug. 1945, 11, and 15 Sept. 1945, 5.

99. *Canada Year Book, 1948-49*, 322-323.

100. Neary, "Canadian Universities," 119, 127–28; DVA, vol. 364, File "General Clippings," unidentified and undated clipping; PC, vol. 2637, Cabinet Conclusions, 2 Aug. 1945; L.G. Thomas, *The University of Alberta in the War, 1939-1945* (Edmonton: n.p., 1948), 58; Martin Friedland, *The University of Toronto: A History* (Toronto: University of Toronto Press, 2002), 373.

101. The maximum total that could be borrowed was $2,000. Each loan was interest-free for the first year and calculated at 5 percent per annum thereafter. Walter Woods, Rehabilitation, 95; DVA, vol. 364, File "General Clippings," undated and unattributed article entitled "Mackenzie Replies to Student Vets' Brief"; Broadfoot, *Veterans' Years*, 143–44.

102. For details on this dispute and militancy among several veterans, especially those from McGill University, see Neary, "Canadian Universities," 135–37.

103. Also, the government allowance could be reduced if a veteran skipped classes. However, this rule was hard to enforce given the large number of students in many courses. DVA, vol. 364, File "General Clippings," clipping from *Varsity Magazine*, 8 Nov. 1949, n.p.

104. DVA, vol. 364, File "General Clippings," clipping from *Financial Post*, 5 Oct. 1946, n.p.

105. WIB, vol. 14, File 8-14-E, Report of a Survey of Thirty-Two Ex-Service Personnel Attending the University of Toronto, 20 Feb. 1945.

106. Waite, *Lives of Dalhousie University*, 148; DVA, vol. 364, File "General Clippings," unidentified and undated clipping, and clipping from *Financial Post*, 5 Oct. 1946, n.p.; Friedland, *University of Toronto*, 372.

107. Neary, "Canadian Universities," 128-129.

108. Granatstein, *Canada's Army*, 204; DHH, 113.3 R4003(D1), "Rehabilitation: A Survey of Opinions among Army Personnel Awaiting Discharge," prepared by Coord 2, Adjutant-General Branch, Oct. 1945.

109. Broadfoot, *Veterans' Years*, 56, 184, 192.

110. Woods, *Rehabilitation*, 109.

111. Morton and Wright, *Winning the Second Battle*, 153, 220; Desmond Morton, "'Noblest and Best': Retraining Canada's War Disabled, 1915–1923," *Journal of Canadian Studies* 16, 3/4 (1981): 77; *Canada Year Book, 1920*, 688.

112. *New Advance*, July 1941, 20–21.

113. Within these ranges, officers above the rank of lieutenant received higher rates. DVA, vol. 183, File 31-8-44, Memo to the Governor in Council, 17 March 1945.

114. For example, just weeks after VJ day, the pension rate for total deafness went from 50 to 80 percent of the maximum award. DVA, vol. 272, News Release No. 30, n.d., and News Release No. 153, 22 Nov. 1945; IM, vol. 11, File 3-125, Speech by Mackenzie, 11 Dec. 1945.

115. For any pensionable injury, veterans had the right to free medical treatment in perpetuity. All veterans received free medical care for one year following their discharge, during which at least some initially overlooked war-related and pensionable injuries were discovered. For veterans with an annual income below $1,200, free treatment at DVA facilities continued past the one-year point for a number of ailments. In 1953, after many complaints, the DVA introduced a sliding scale of medical coverage for those earning between $1,200 and $2,500 per annum. DVA, vol. 364, File "General Clippings, part 2, 1953–55," clipping from Blyth *Standard*, 20 Oct. 1954, n.p.; DVA, vol. 272, News Release No. 205, n.d.; DND, vol. 12,278, File 26-37, Department of Pensions and National Health News Release, 1 Jan. 1944.

116. DVA, vol. 272, News Release No. 139, n.d., and News Release No. 193, 23 March 1946; DVA, vol. 362, File 1946-62, clipping from *DEE-VEE-AYE*, vol. 2, No. 9, Oct. 1947, 1.

117. DVA, vol. 372, File "DVA New-Rel," Casualty Rehabilitation, n.d.; YMCA, vol. 272, File 8, *Rehabilitation: Read All about It*, 1945, n.p.

118. Industrial Canada, July 1945, 318-19; RE, vol. 2, File 1940-44, Employment of Canada's Disabled, pt. 1.

119. *Canada Year Book, 1948-49*, 1160; Woods, *Rehabilitation*, 370.

120. See Senate of Canada, *The Aboriginal Soldier after the Wars: Report of the Senate Standing Committee on Aboriginal Peoples* (Ottawa: Queen's Printer, 1995). Another dispute concerned veterans who were mentally unable to care for themselves and housed long-term in DVA institutions. On their behalf, a class action suit was launched in 1999 claiming that the DVA, in the administration of their pensions, failed to fulfill its fiduciary responsibilities as trustee because it did not secure any interest on these funds. In July 2003 the Supreme Court of Canada ruled in favour of the federal government. *Joseph Patrick Authorson v. the Attorney General of Canada*, Ontario Superior Court, File No. 99-GD-45963; *National Post*, 18 July 2003, A6; DVA, vol. 364, File "General Clippings," clipping from New Glasgow *News*, 24 Feb. 1954, n.p., clipping from Prince Rupert *Examiner*, 11 March 1955, n.p., and clipping from Lethbridge *Herald*, 19 July 1955, n.p.

9

In the Children's Interest?

Change and Continuity in a Century of Canadian Social Welfare Initiatives for Children*

RAYMOND B. BLAKE

Introduction

THE MOST RECENT statistics on child poverty in Canada are alarming. Campaign 2000, a coalition of more than 70 community groups across the country dedicated to eradicating child poverty, claimed in its 2004 report that the level of child poverty had risen in 2002 after five straight years of decline. Fifteen years after the federal government vowed to end child poverty, more than 1.06 million children—nearly one-sixth of all children in Canada—continue to live in poverty. Recent reports of child poverty have surprised and shocked many Canadians, especially as the federal government continues to parade surveys before the nation telling Canadians that their country is consistently rated by the international community to be among the best two or three countries in the world in which to live. In partial response to the depressing and shattering statistics on poverty, all levels of government in Canada have promised to make children and lower income families the primary focus of their social policy initiatives. Hence, there is considerable talk in Canada about a "children's agenda," and in the 2004 Throne Speech, the Liberal government promised a series of program directed at children, noting that "The future of our children is, quite literally, Canada's future."

Children have figured prominently in many of the major initiatives in Canadian social policy throughout the twentieth century.[1] Such programs as mothers' allowances, introduced in most provinces by the 1920s, family allowances in 1945, and, more recently, the federal initiatives with the Child Tax Benefit and the National Child Benefit which have targeted income support programs to children and families most in need of government assistance have all had, invariably, children as their primary beneficiaries. Through these, and other programs, the state has directed billions of dollars toward children. That being the case, one must wonder why, after nearly a century of provincial support for children and a half-century of direct federal support, child poverty has proven so persistent in Canada, and why both levels of government feel compelled on the eve of the millennium,

---

* This chapter was first published as "In the Children's Interest? Change and Continuity in a Century of Canadian Social Welfare Initiatives for Children" in *Journal of Indo-Canadian Studies*, Volume 1, 1 (2001): 113–37. It has been updated for this edition.

to yet again make children a priority in their social policy initiatives. Clearly, state initiatives in child welfare policy have not come anywhere near eliminating child poverty.

This essay argues that while there have been fundamental shifts in Canadian social policy towards children throughout this century, there has also been much continuity. In the first quarter of the century, the state offered assistance to children in one of two ways: those at the lower income level, usually single mother-led families, received mothers' allowance; those at the higher end were permitted income tax deductions for dependent children. This arrangement continued until the 1940s when Ottawa introduced family allowances. In 1978, family allowances were tied once again to income and, in 1992, universal family allowances were dropped in favour of the more selective, income-test child tax benefit. These particular measures represent profound and fundamental change. This paper shows that despite the public pronouncements of governments over the last decades of social policy for children, children have often reaped only collateral benefits of programs supposedly designed to improve their lives. Social security measures supposedly directed towards children have frequently served interests other than children and that may explain in part the persistence of child poverty in Canada. If there was a time when the state was concerned about the welfare of children it was after the Second World War, but family allowances were introduced for a variety of other reasons as well. The more recent changes to family allowances were driven by the need to reduce government expenditure, deal with constitutional problems, promote economic growth and encourage parents to participate in the market economy. The various programs did not have as their primary goal the elimination of child poverty.

Early Years

Mothers' allowances, introduced in most provinces between 1916 and 1920, were one example of a government initiative where children were largely incidental to the program.[2] The issue of mothers' allowances had less to do with mothers and children than it did with the type of society that the middle class proponents of the program envisioned for Canada. The changes created by urbanization, industrialization, and increased immigration in Canada in the first years of the twentieth century frightened many in the middle class. During this period of upheaval, middle-class reformers focused primarily on the family, which they believed was being threatened from all sides. They sought to regenerate their society, which involved imposing their middle-class standards on everyone; they also made a concept of the reconstructed family a pivotal part of the social reform movement. The outbreak of the Great War in 1914 gave added impetus to their cause, as the high casualties on the battlefields of Europe threatened even further the institution of the family. There was, moreover, considerable concern over high infant mortality and an increase in juvenile delinquency during the war. Improvements in home life and improved care for mothers, which would result in children who were physically and morally fit, would regenerate the nation and prepare for the new world order that would blossom with victory.[3]

When Ontario initiated an inquiry into the benefits of mothers' allowances in 1919, many loosely involved in the social services network condemned infant mortality and juvenile delinquency which had become increasingly associated with single-parent families.

They also condemned institutions as inadequate to deal with the problems faced by children. "The family remains the unit of society and nothing compensates the child for the lack of a mother's care," the report concluded. "And, with homes intact and mothers there to care for their children, there would be less of juvenile waywardness and crime."[4] Even Charlotte Whitton, the conservative assistant secretary of the Social Service Council of Canada, concluded in her *Report of the New Brunswick Child Welfare Survey* that, "Every orphanage must face the fact that the consensus of opinion in all modern social work is that the best institutions in the world are no substitute for the family home.... Every normal child in an institution represents a failure of the community."[5] There was a move, then, in the early twentieth century away from a reliance on institutions such as orphanages and industrial schools as a way to "compensate for the shortcomings of inadequate, usually poor families" to one where the nuclear family was reconstructed as the "unequalled environment for optimal child development."[6] In other words, the normal, natural place for children was in the home. Those who administered the Canadian Patriotic Fund to support families whose fathers joined the war after 1914 believed it was their mission to preserve and improve the family during the years of war. Some historians have suggested that the volunteers associated with the CPF who worked closely with families "were the direct predecessors, sometimes the initiators, of public welfare programs."[7]

The middle-class concern with society and the efforts of the Canadian Patriotic Fund led in part to the introduction of mothers' allowances. It should be clear that mothers' allowances were designed for children, not mothers, and it was never questioned that the primary object was conservation of the family as an important national institution. Although the regulations and eligibility requirements varied as the provinces initiated and funded the program,[8] each province enacted similar rules: one, only needy widows with two or more children qualified for the allowances; two, eligibility ended when children left school; and three, recipients had to be deemed fit and proper mothers. The provinces continued to insist on the difference between "deserving" and the "undeserving" poor; as a result, unmarried and divorced mothers were generally denied benefits. The allowance permitted mothers to create, through state assistance, a health, happy and normal home life for their children. Together with other legislation such as compulsory schooling and a series of factory laws and the federal government's Division of Child Welfare in 1919, mothers' allowances were an attempt not only to create a better life for young children but also to create an ordered and stable society in Canada.

Early Attempts at Family Allowances

While many advocated the "rights of children" and the state's obligation to provide for the fatherless child, there were opponents to such initiatives. Much of the opposition was to mothers' allowances. A great deal of this opposition came from private charity organizations: these organizations did not relinquish their belief that public aid to mothers for their children would encourage dependency—hardly the responsible use of the public funds.[9] Such views persisted and were used against family allowances when they were first debated by a parliamentary committee in 1928.[10] Social workers such as Charlotte Whitton, by then director of the Canadian Council on Social Welfare, maintained that workers were paid sufficiently to support their children without government assistance.[11] Moreover, she argued, family allowances infringed on individual rights, and any sort of initiative to enact such misguided schemes "would impugn dangerously" upon the sanctity of marriage, and reduce it to one of "economic relations, capable of financial exploitation." Such state interference, she warned, might reduce women to mere slaves and employees of the state, and "ultimately result in the entire subversion of the present position and privileges which [women] enjoy in almost all the provinces of Canada."[12] In fact, she argued that the introduction of family allowances would undermine the basis of family responsibility and ruin the country as federal assistance would encourage those of limited intelligence and those with a "mental defect" to have even larger families and "bring more unfit children into the community already heavily burdened in caring for this class of dependent child."[13]

When it presented its report to the House of Commons on 31 May 1929, the Standing Committee on Industrial and International Relations steered a safe course, noting that family allowances were new for Canada and required further study. Ottawa allowed the matter to lapse, however.[14] An investigation by the Government of Quebec in 1932 did little more to advance the case for family allowances. It concluded that there is "no equity and social justice" in the salary paid to the workers who had larger families, but it unanimously recommended that "for the moment there is no opportunity of taking legal measures instituting officially family allowances in this province." Moreover, like Charlotte Whitton and other social workers of the period, the Montpetit Commission feared that it was not only impossible but also dangerous for the state to assume a greater role in the family which might then become little more than an agency of the state. And, of course, in the midst of the Great Depression, the Commission concluded that any movement towards family allowances would be virtually impossible given the economic difficulties of the period.[15]

The Great Depression: Watershed Era

Those ideas expressed by the critics of family allowances would all change within a decade. The Great Depression largely discredited many of the traditional ideas of rugged individualism and made it patently obvious that the "old system" was bankrupt of ideas. The foundations of the democratic political system were everywhere under seize, and even Mackenzie King remarked after his 1930 electoral thrashing that, "the old capitalistic system is certain to give way to something more along communist lines."[16] That did not happen in Canada, of course, but the decade witnessed a change in the attitude of governments and Canada's two longstanding political parties largely because of the growing influence of a group of intellectuals and progressive reformers who believed that Canada's social and economic policies had to be reformed to deal with a chaotic world.[17] They dismissed the classic nineteenth-century liberalism and the notion of the state as an organic expression of society; rather, they saw the state "as a mechanism to be used as necessary for the promotion of social well-being," which they defined "in terms of material standards of living" and not in spiritual or moral terms as an earlier generation of intellectuals saw it.[18] The intellectual community—which found influence in all three political parties by the mid-1930s—believed that there must be an "evolutionary method of social reconstruction." At the beginning of the Great Depression, their views generated debate in universities and other intellectual circles, but through the 1930s many of the intellectuals engaged in political activities so that by the 1940s many of their ideas were widely accepted. In his victory speech following the triumphant return of his Liberals to power on 14 October 1935, Mackenzie King championed the dawn of a new era where "Poverty and adversity, want and misery are the enemies which Liberalism will seek to banish from the land."[19]

Social Security Arrives

The Second World War also accelerated the acceptance of those new ideas. Governments everywhere realized that the transition from war to peace had to be made without a return to the problems of unemployment and want that had characterized the pre-war period. On 4 September 1941, King told an audience in London that governments everywhere must work to eliminate the fear of unemployment and the sense of insecurity that workers face when their capacity to meet the needs of their family was threatened. "Until these fears have been eliminated," he told Canada's labour leaders, "the war for freedom will not be won. The era of freedom will be achieved only as social security and human welfare become the main concern of men and nations." The specifics of social welfare, he admitted, would have to be spelled out in due course but the "new order" he envisioned for Canada would include as a "national minimum," full employment, adequate nutrition and housing, health insurance, and social security.[20]

Mackenzie King was not alone in recognizing the need for greater social security as part of the new world order of which he often spoke. In fact, he might have been merely echoing the chorus that was resonating throughout the Allied Nations. "It [social security] is on the tip of every man's tongue," penned a contributor for *Saturday Night* and, "All the United Nations' war leaders have declared it as a leading social objective of this war."[21] President Franklin D. Roosevelt of the United States, the New Deal reformer, advocated greater social security for the postwar world, for instance. He had told the American Congress in January 1941 that international security rested upon four essential human freedoms. Only when each nation could provide an acceptable standard of living for its people would there truly be freedom. Other leaders expressed similar sentiments.[22] Roosevelt and British Prime Minister Winston Churchill reiterated these principles in the Atlantic Charter on 14 August 1941: "[We] desire to bring about the fullest collaboration between all nations in the economic field with the object of securing, for all, improved labour standards, economic adjustment and social security." In fact, many of the Allied Nations felt a certain irony and embarrassment that they had to call upon their citizens to fight and die for their country, which had previously shown little interest in their welfare. There was a growing realization then, as early as 1941, that social security was rapidly becoming synonymous with socially progressive countries. The ideas of social security had become transnational and the public debate, particularly in Canada, had been informed by growing support in Britain for social security, and family allowances in particular (which had been first introduced in Grenoble, France during the Great War). Since then, Australia and New Zealand as well as several other European countries had established family allowances.[23]

Social security was nothing new to Prime Minister Mackenzie King. When he joined Roosevelt at the White House for dinner on 5 December 1942, the President discussed the

British report on reconstruction, *Social Insurance and Allied Services*—popularly known as the Beveridge Report after its author Sir William Beveridge—released a few days earlier in London. King was impressed when Roosevelt said that they should "work together on the lines of social reform in which we had always been deeply interested." Of course, King pointed out that much of the program Beveridge recommended could be found in *Industry and Humanity*.[24]

Shortly after the release of Beveridge's report, the Committee on Reconstruction (which the government had established in 1941) had Leonard Marsh, its young research director, undertake a similar study for Canada. The *Report on Social Security for Canada* proposed a "comprehensive and integrated social security system for Canada, set our priorities for implementation of the different proposals, dealt with decisions respecting administration and constitutional jurisdiction, and with financial considerations."[25] The *Report* demonstrated how thinking about social welfare had changed in Canada since the Great Depression. It paid particular attention to the needs of children. Marsh believed that "children should have an unequivocal place in social security policy." Children's allowances are a clear part of the policy of a national minimum—of the direct attack on poverty where it is bound up with the strain imposed by a large family on a small income. Marsh also believed that family size had a profound impact on whether or not families could adequately maintain themselves on the income they received. He realized that the maintenance of children was a continuous requirement, at least until children reached adolescence. Moreover, since wage levels were not always sufficient to provide for large families, family allowances were a logical complement to any social insurance scheme that intended to establish a national minimum standard of living. Marsh dismissed the concern over family allowances that had been expressed by social workers nearly a generation earlier that cash grants to families would encourage the "wrong" parent to have larger numbers of children.

Not surprisingly, Marsh's *Report on Social Security for Canada* generated considerable excitement and newspaper and magazine copy in Canada; the Wartime Information Board noted that in the first week following the release of the *Report*, more than 160 newspapers made it the subject of their editorials. It was welcomed as Canada's Beveridge Report and endorsed by a large number of editorial writers and such organizations as the Canadian Association of Social Workers.[26] Not all of the commentary was positive, however. The Ottawa *Morning Journal* expressed misgivings over the projected costs of Marsh's recommendations. It wondered if the Canadian economy could sustain the price tag of $900 million. The Toronto *Telegram* agreed, claiming that if implemented the Marsh *Report* would "bankrupt the country and precipitate chaos."[27]

Family Allowances

At the same time that the Marsh Report was being debated publicly, the King Cabinet had to deal with the increasing discontent among disgruntled workers throughout the summer of 1943, while at the same time struggling to maintain the government's wage stabilization policy (which had been implemented early in the war as a means to control inflation). Senior civil servants picked up on the transnational idea of family allowances and began to discuss the possibility of having the government introduce them as a social security measure, as an alternative to wage increases for the growing number of disaffected workers whose wage rates were controlled by government agencies. They agreed that wage rates had to increase or some alternative had to be found to achieve the same ends.[28] They were fully aware that the King Government was committed to fundamental social and economic change after the war,[29] and hoped to use that commitment to deal with the labour problem. For instance, the Governor of the Bank of Canada, Graham Towers, told W.C. Clark, the deputy minister of finance that "Children's allowances are the most direct and economic method of meeting the current strong demand for relaxation of wages control in respect of the lower wage rates." He reminded Clark that the government was determined to introduce a "reasonable minimum of [social] security after the war"; and while he would have preferred to see family allowances introduced then, he realized that this particular social security measure would meet the "legitimate needs" of labour by placing more money in the hands of workers while allowing the government to keep the rate of inflation under control.[30] The principle of children's allowances, he pointed out, was not new or revolutionary. In fact, the government was already paying an allowance of $108 for each child in the form of an income tax credit to wage-earners who made more than $1,200 per year: in other words, those who made less than the threshold and desperately needed the assistance, but did not get it. Like others, Towers also suggested that the introduction of family allowances would enhance Canada's prestige internationally as well as safeguard its economy at home. Moreover, he saw a measure of efficacy in Canada's adoption of family allowances: Canadian wartime controls had become an example to those in the United States who wanted to control inflation, he told Clark. Children's allowances, "would be striking proof that Canada intended to push ahead with progressive policies after the war. It might have appreciable influence in strengthening the hand of like-minded administrations in other countries," Towers concluded.[31]

Family allowances were not introduced as a wage stabilization program, even though the National War Labour Board later recommended the immediate introduction of family allowances as a means of maintaining the government's wage control legislation. Editorial writers also warned the government not to link family allowances to the issue of wages. Indeed, King insisted that the two issues be kept separate; the Cabinet had not discussed family allowances when he announced the government's new labour policy in a radio broadcast on 4 December 1943. In fact, family allowances would not be implement for another nineteen months.[32] Moreover, it seemed somewhat unlikely that the government would respond to the short-term crisis by committing itself to spending between $140 and $200 million—the anticipated costs of family allowances—annually and perhaps in perpetuity when it could have offered workers other forms of direct payment such as cost of living bonuses and wage incentives. And, given the growing radicalization of workers at the time, they would not be satisfied with the government's promise to introduce family allowances at some in the distant future.

Meanwhile, Mackenzie King and the Liberal party were growing worried about the increasing popularity of the opposition parties, both of which seemed to be attracting considerable popular support and threatening to outflank the Liberals with their emphasis on social security. Yet, King did not embrace social policy simply because the Co-operative Commonwealth Federation slipped past the Liberals in a public opinion poll and won a number of by-elections in 1943. The Liberals and the Conservatives—which had become the Progressive Conservatives only a short time earlier to reflect their new and progressive policies—adopted new policies as had the CCF. This was because new ideas and policies had been pushed to the forefront by the growing national and international interest in the ideas of social security and other policies during the Second World War. The Liberals were worried about the political successes of the CCF in the early 1940s, but for King the setbacks came from the lack of party organization, not government policy. Yet, not even he could ignore the fact that both the other parties had included social security as part of their platform.[33]

When the National Liberal Federation met in Ottawa in late September 1943, it was clear to King that the party had to make social security one of its primary concerns. Even though he had made a commitment to social security in the 1943 Speech from the Throne and through a variety of Liberal policies ranging from old age pensions to unemployment insurances, he believed that Canadians needed to be reminded again of the "task of Liberalism."[34] The party reaffirmed its commitment to social security and recommended that the government consider a program of children's allowances to provide adequate support to the upbringing of children and for the maintenance of family life. It also wanted a "national scheme of social insurance" that would offer protection "against the privations resulting from unemployment, accident, ill-health, old age and blindness."[35] The Liberal party left the convention confident that its political agenda—just like the CCF and the Conservatives—finally included social security measures.[36]

King saw family allowances as one of the most important items on the legislative agenda as his Cabinet prepared for the 1944 parliamentary session. He believed that family allowances for larger families went "to the very root of social security in relation to the new order of things which places a responsibility on the State for conditions which the State itself is responsible for creating."[37] And, of course, King was aware that the latest statistics showed that far too many children in Canada died before reaching their first birthday. In 1941, 60 out of every 1000 babies born alive died before the age of one.[38] Statistics also suggested that nearly one-third of Canadian children were born into families where the family income was insufficient to adequately cloth and nourish them. Moreover, a 1943 government report found than Canada had more than a half million undernourished children.[39] Although King realized that the debate on family allowances would create "great diversity" within the Cabinet, he saw the issue as one where he could leave his distinctive stamp.[40]

King, the consummate politician, was right. Throughout the early 1940s, Canadians expressed a strong demand for progressive government, one that was less inclined to leave the fate of their country after the war to the mercies of the unregulated free enterprise system. Martin Cohn and Elisabeth Wallace noted this trend in an opinion piece for the April 1943 issue of *Canadian Forum*: "Social Security," they wrote, "is, with just cause, a popular slogan ... and good propaganda. A constructive welfare program is of cardinal importance to any party interested in the fundamentals of good government, and not least to a socialist party." In fact, the political parties competed with each other to present progressive measures for the postwar in the fields of social security, rehabilitation of service personnel, and the promise of full employment; the ideas traditionally associated with the left had become mainstream, it seems. These views were reflected in the attitudes and idea expressed by many of King's ministers.[41]

The Cabinet turned to family allowances on 6 January 1944 as part of its larger discussion on post-war social security—what King described as "help to those who are unable to help themselves."[42] He noted as soon as the debate began on the government's legislative agenda for the upcoming session that the "one question on which there seems to be great debate is Family Allowances." Yet, when King raised the issue of social security at a meeting of Cabinet on 12 January, he found a number of his powerful Cabinet colleagues, including the minister of finance, J.L. Ilsley, the minister of munitions and supply, C.D. Howe, and the minister of mines and resources, T.A. Crerar, opposed to the idea of greater social security.[43] He had encountered similar opposition in 1940, when he began discussions on the unemployment insurance bill, but he pressed forward and enacted legislation over the wishes of some of his ministers.[44]

At Cabinet on 13 January which King subsequently declared "as one of the most impressive and significant of any I have attended ... I had let it be understood we would settle the Government's policy on Family Allowances which goes to the very root of social security in relation to the new order of things which places a responsibility on the state for conditions which the state itself is responsible for creating."[45] In the absence of the minister, W.C. Clark (the deputy minister of finance) presented the case for family allowance. He began by pointing out that the wage system takes no account of the size of the family and, frequently, workers are not able to provide sufficiently for their families. Too often, married workers were simply not earning enough to support their families. Family allowances, he told the Cabinet, "represent by far the simplest, wisest, and cheapest way of providing the supplementary family income." Clark also reminded the Cabinet that if family allowances were implemented immediately they would not only deal with the inadequacy of the family incomes of wage-earners but would also help the government to maintain its wage stabilization and price ceiling polices. Clark told the Cabinet that family allowances would remove the discriminatory feature of the income tax system against families in the lowest income groups as Canadians with higher incomes were permitted to claim an allowance of $108 for each dependent child. Likewise, soldiers had been paid a dependants' allowance during the war, and Clark suggested that there will be considerable pressure after the war to continue the allowance. Moreover, family allowances might help alleviate the problem many families were having with housing and help improve the level of education in Canada. He suggested that family allowances would help Canadians feel a greater affinity with their government.[46]

The Cabinet debated the issue at length. King told Cabinet that modern society had changed dramatically and that "the present war was all a part of the struggle of the masses to get a chance to live their own lives." He reminded the Cabinet that it had already agreed to press forward with social security. King left no doubt with the Cabinet where he stood on the issue with phrases such as "equality of opportunity," "a minimum of welfare for all children," and "children's allowances as a natural policy for the Liberal party." He also pointed out those social security measures, such as family allowances, might be necessary to save liberal democracies such as Canada.[47] King's long defence of family allowances was largely unnecessary as Cabinet support was nearly unanimous—a point that King himself realized and even acknowledged in the meeting.[48] Despite what King may have thought privately, an improved social security system by early 1944 was widely accepted in Canada,[49] demonstrated perhaps by the unanimous passage of the legislation enacting family allowances later that summer.

Implementation of Family Allowances

Family allowance cheques were sent to mothers. There had never been much doubt that they would be in all of the English-speaking provinces, but Louis St. Laurent, the minister of justice and King's Quebec lieutenant, had worried that designating mothers as the recipients in Quebec might create additional problems for the Liberal party where there was already considerable disenchantment over the issue of conscription. However, with the provincial election won, King said that the government should be consistent and paid family allowances to mothers in all provinces, including Quebec.[50] Thérèse Casgrain, the popular Quebec feminist, wrote to King that to not pay the cheques to Quebec mothers would humiliate them as well as further threaten Canadian unity.[51] The Canadian Federation of Business and Professional Women's Clubs also wanted the cheques paid to mothers across the country. The Quebec legislature also passed a resolution urging that cheques be sent to mothers in Quebec.[52] A Gallup Poll of Canada found that 77 percent of Canadians wanted mothers to receive the family allowances cheques; even in Quebec, the survey found that only 25 percent of those polled wanted fathers to receive family allowances.[53]

Not surprisingly, family allowances were an immediate success if the letters Canadians wrote to King, Claxton and the department of national health and welfare can be taken as an indication of the immediate reaction to the receipt of the first monthly cheques.[54] Many letters reveal that parents were able to purchase clothing and footwear and food, as well as to provide for the health of their child. Others welcomed family allowances because it allowed them to outfit their children for school. In fact, the increase in school attendance was almost immediate and the provinces found that the family allowances were very helpful in enforcing school attendance regulations. The *Family Allowances Act* stated that the allowances would not be paid where children of school age did not attend school.[55] The *Financial Post* report on 4 August 1945 of its survey of 210 parents in Toronto supported what parents had written in their letters. All indications are, the *Post* concluded, "there appears to be very little reason to fear that the baby bonus once it has become accepted routine every month, will drive people either into the beer parlours or away from their own responsibilities." To ensure that they did, Claxton announced in the fall of 1945 that his department would commence an education program for mothers in receipt of the family allowance. A good parental education program that helped mothers spend their family allowances wisely and one that promoted good nutrition and child care practices, he believed, would benefit the whole nation and, at the same time, remove the necessity of spending money on policing parents.[56] Family allowances put millions of dollars into the hands of parents; by 1957, for instance, it injected about $520 million into the economy and was paid to approximately 6.4 million children.

Politics, Federal-Provincial Relations, and Family Allowances

As personal incomes rose throughout the 1950s, family allowances became less important to Canadian families, but they became increasingly important to some provincial governments that tried to wrestle the control of social programs from the federal government. In fact, after 1960 political factors exerted considerable influence over family allowances.

The Quebec Quiet Revolution that began in the 1960s—when Quebec started to question its place in the Canadian Confederation—foreshadowed the end of the trend toward a highly centralized federation that had originated during the Great Depression as first Quebec, and then some of the other provinces, began to demand an increasingly greater role in social security matters. Quebec wanted greater control of social security policy, when it argued that its social philosophy differed from that of the rest of Canada because of its religious convictions, culture, and the social traditions of its populations. Beginning in the later 1960s, income security programs such as family allowances had become central to constitutional change, issues driven largely by Quebec. The provinces believed that provincial jurisdiction over family allowance policy would enable them better than the federal government to direct resources in concert with a variety of provincial programs designed to improve the welfare of children and poor families. After all, the provinces argued, social welfare was primarily a provincial matter.

Even so, the issue of social justice was not dead even if it was on its last leg. After all, Prime Minister Pierre Elliot Trudeau was elected to create a just society. Moreover, Canadians became alarmed in the late 1960s to the early 1970s about the persistence of poverty. Pushed in large part by the American war on poverty, Canada rediscovered its poor despite major improvements in the welfare state since the 1940s. There was considerable discussion on several levels about the most effective ways to use the income security programs.

Reforms to Family Allowances

In 1970, the federal government released a white paper, *Income Security for Canada*, in response to the growing dissatisfaction with the existing income security system and the desire to get more money into the hands of those most in need. What emerged was a growing attack on the principle of universality and a resurgence of the residual concept in social security policy whereby assistance was apportioned on the basis of need. There was a growing recognition that universal family allowances were not a very good policy instrument for increasing the flow of support to the poor because "you had to raise everyone's family allowance in order to raise the family allowance of the poor." The probability of that happening during the period of fiscal restraint which began in the early 1970s was slim. Yet, there was considerable opposition to abandoning the principle of universality. Moreover, any changes to family allowances would mean that virtually 1.5 million women who did not work outside the house would lose the only cheque they received independently of their husbands. Despite the opposition to reform, it was difficult for Parliament to oppose redistribution of wealth in favour of the poor. Somewhat half-heartedly, the federal government introduced the measures to direct a greater portion of Family Allowances to those in the greatest need and abolish universality to tie benefits tied to income, but the plan failed in 1972.

The first major reforms to the Family Allowances program came in 1974. The Liberal government remained committed to the principle of universality. Yet, the changes show clearly how family allowances and other social programs had become linked to Ottawa's constitutional battles with the provinces. The 1974 legislation gave the provinces the option to exercise considerable power over family allowance by permitting them to vary the basic family allowance benefit. The family allowance benefits were increased to $20 per child per month, indexed to inflation and made them taxable. By 1974, the federal government was paying annually more than $1 billion to 7.25 million children, but the total net yearly payment as a percentage of individual incomes have fallen to 1 percent from more than 2 percent in 1945.

The changes to family allowances as well as the appointment of Marc Lalonde to the Health and Welfare portfolio suggest that the federal Liberals were committed in the early 1970s to meaningful social security reform, but two things intervened to prevent them from following through on their agenda: i) mounting fiscal crisis; and ii) the election of the Parti Québécois. The fiscal crisis meant that governments looked to spend less on social programs as the whole concept of the welfare state came under attack in most western nations. And, of course, the PQ coming to power in Quebec meant that Canada turned from social policy review to an increasing preoccupation with keeping Quebec in Canada.

Still, Ottawa realized that it had to constrain expenditure while it attempted to help those most in need of government assistance. In 1977, it introduced a $50 Child Tax Credit for families earning less than $26,000 annually, but this did little to redistribute income to the poor who paid little in taxes.[57] The following year it significantly revised family allowances, introducing several changes that then Minister of Finance Jean Chrétien described as "one of the most significant policy reforms of the decade."[58] In an attempt to reduce government expenditure and challenge limited resources to lower-income families, Ottawa reduced family allowances payments by 23 percent from $312 to $240 annually. It replaced the $50 Child Tax Credit with a $200 Refundable Child Tax Credit for families earning less than $18,000, though its value was reduced by 50 percent of family income in excess of $18,000.[59]

The Mulroney Tories would make radical changes to family allowances. Even so, the Liberals had started to move away from the principle of universality in 1979, when they introduced a Refundable Child Tax Credit of $200 a year to ensure that a greater portion of the new child-oriented benefit went to low and moderate income families rather. The Liberals opted for the Child Tax Credit rather than modify the existing family allowance program, but they created the precedent of using the tax structure to redistribute income to the poor—a significant break with Canadian tradition of universality.

End of Universal Family Allowances

With the election of the Mulroney Conservatives in 1984, the federal government was supposedly committed to balancing the budget and cutting the deficit. Michael Wilson said that all existing social programs would be reviewed to ensure that they were sufficiently sensitive to the changing needs of Canadian society. In November 1984, Prime Minister Mulroney hinted about the fate of family allowances when he asked a Vancouver audience, "Does the man who earns $500,000 a year as bank president need to collect family allowances?" The Conservatives made it clear that they wished to reduce the universal family allowances in favour of more selective, income-tested ones. Not surprisingly, the Conservative government eliminated universal family allowances in 1992 in favour of a new Child Tax Benefit that combined family allowances and the refundable tax credits into a single tax-free monthly payment determined on the basis on the family income tax returns. It also included additional monies for low-income working families. Hence, in December 1992, universal family allowance that had been introduced in July 1945 was eliminated in favour of a selective, income-tested supplementation for children. Canada's best known universal social welfare program was dead and was replaced by the Child Tax Benefit that provided monthly tax-free payments to nearly 85 percent of all Canadian families with children. By 1997, Ottawa paid more than $5.1 billion in CTB annually. Families with net incomes of less than $25,921 received the maximum benefit of $1,020 annually, but it was reduced once net family incomes exceeded that amount and reached zero at an income of about $66,600 for one- or two-child families. In addition, the Child Tax Benefit included a Working Income Supplement which provided benefits up to $500 per year per family at a cost of $250 million annually.[60]

By 1996 with the governments in Canada was making considerable progress on controlling their deficits, the federal government embarked upon a series of initiatives to renew the federation, though the federal government had called several years earlier in its social security review to retarget social assistance to society's most vulnerable, including action to address child poverty. Similarly, the *Report to Premiers on the Ministerial Council on Social Policy Reform and Renewal* released in March 1996, proposed "the possible consolidation of income support for children into a single national program, jointly managed by both orders of government, with options for either federal or provincial/territorial delivery of benefits."[61] Momentum for social welfare reform continued to grow; and at the June 1996 first ministers' conference, the premier and the prime minister decided to place child poverty on the national agenda. When the premiers met again a few months later, they (with the exception of the Premier of Quebec) asked their ministers to work on an integrated child benefit program with the federal government. In the 1996 Speech from the Throne the government committed itself to "renew and modernize Canadian federalism so that it meets the needs of Canadians in the 21st century." An important aspect of that renewal was to enhance social solidarity in Canada by "persevering and modernizing the social union so that the Canadian commitment to a caring and sharing society remains truly Canada-wide in scope."[62] One of the primary areas of concern was to improve the prospects for poor children; the government maintained that "children are our future, so there is no better place for Canadians to invest." Yet, under the system existing prior to 1997, child benefits were often reduced when parents left social assistance or welfare to enter the workforce. Both levels of government realized that children should not be penalized when their parents took a job.[63] While a variety of government programs provided various forms of support to families with children, the whole system had inadvertently created a "welfare wall" that made it difficult for parents to move from welfare to work. In other words, the existing system created significant financial disincentives to leave social assistance.

National Child Benefit

To deal with this dilemma, the federal government proposed a National Child Benefit initiative to reduce child poverty and help parents to return to work without losing their child benefits. Through this initiative, the federal, provincial, and territorial governments hoped to "extend and simply income support for low-income families with children and invest more in services for children." This meant moving child benefits out of the welfare system, so that when parents leave social assistance, they keep these benefits for their children. In 1998 Ottawa created the Canada Child Tax Benefit (this is the federal component of the NCB) by combining the existing $5.1 billion Child Tax Benefit and Working Income Supplement, the $250 million committed in the 1996 budget plus the $600 million in the 1997 budget.[64] The new program totalling $6 billion would provide considerable support to all low-income families across Canada and was billed as a substantial down payment on "an important national project." The CCTB amount payable to each family is determined through the income tax system based on the previous year's family income and is automatically adjusted in July of each year. However, there are two components to the CCTB: the first, a base benefit, is available to families with incomes up to $66,721 and the NCB Supplement which is available to families with incomes of up to $25,931.[65] Pierre S. Pettigrew, the minister of Human Resources Development, admitted that the National Child Benefit System would not eliminate child poverty, but he believed that "it would improve the living standards of thousands of Canadian children."[66]

Moreover, the National Child Benefit System was an attempt to implement structural reforms to how governments responded to the needs of low-income families with children. Underlying this, there was an attempt to promote attachment to the workforce by ensuring that families would be better off as a result of finding work than relying on social assistance. Increased federal expenditure on programs for children and low-income families resulted in substantial savings for most provinces. It allowed them to redirect provincial resources toward improved income support and children's services for low-income working families; in fact, when the National Child Benefit initiative was first established, the provinces agreed that all social assistance savings would be reinvested to benefit low-income families with children. By 1999, the provincial and territorial governments had reinvested more than $450 million in improved benefits and services for low-income families with children in such areas as income supplements for the working poor, child-care support, early intervention programs, and supplementary health benefits.[67] In fact, there has been considerable pressure for such programs from such bodies as the Caledon Institute and the C.D. Institute. As the *Globe and Mail* recently noted "Just giving poor families more money will not do: helping unprepared parents of any income to understand what good child-rearing practices are, and to support them in the home is essential" to the children's agenda.[68] Interestingly, this ideology is not unlike that from nearly a hundred years earlier, which led to mothers' allowances.

The recent revisions in social policy for children mark a fundamental change in Canada's welfare state. One can argue that from the end of the Second World War to the late 1960s, Canada's social security system was built on the notion of collective responsibility designed to ensure that all Canadians enjoyed a social minimum.[69] Now, however, the state has come to see social policy as a tool for promoting economic efficiency and growth, and less as a means of protecting its citizens. Employment insurance and job retraining, for instance, are more concerned with helping Canadians respond to marketplace opportunities than with protecting them from the insecurities that often accompany economic cycles. Likewise, recent changes in social policy for children are more concerned with governments acting to promoting economic growth and help their citizens participate in the market economy than with governments acting as a protector of children. At the same time, though, the state has maintained a measure of its paternalistic role, even if this is currently done on an individual basis rather than a collective one. Social security has been directed to the most vulnerable and to those most in need of assistance.

Conclusion

As with so many federal initiatives in recent years, the National Child Benefit was an attempt to show that Canadian federalism is flexible and that it works. As Minister of Human Resource Development Pierre Pettigrew liked to point out, the program "was a step forward in Canadian federalism, with the federal, provincial and territorial governments seizing on a good idea, setting common objectives and working as partners to secure better lives for our children."[70] The program was heralded as a way to reduce overlap and duplication through closer harmonization of program objectives and benefits and through simplified administration. It was hoped that the co-operative approach would build a stronger federal foundation for all low-income families with children and provincial-territorial investment would provide complementary programs targeted at improving work incentives and services for low-income families with children. This approach to children's issues would ensure a national uniform and basic level of income support for children across the country while providing for provincial-territorial flexibility and innovation.[71] And, for Ottawa, this initiative was a major step forward in investing in children and in renewing the country.

Family allowances were the first social security measure in Canada to be paid to all. It was the start of the Canadian principle of universality in social programs. While family allowances have been an important part of Canada's welfare state, it has also been used for purposes other than social welfare; it was introduced for economic, political, and cultural reasons in 1945 and because it was the current international trend. Since then, it has been tied more recently to constitutional matters and as a means of appeasing the provinces clamouring for a more decentralized federation. Cuts to social programs have been a way for governments to demonstrate that they are putting our fiscal house in order. Cuts to social programs have been easy when only 17 percent of Canadians see that maintaining social programs should be the government's top priority, and many Canadians believe that too many social programs are abused. Even so, while many have talked recently of the dismantling of Canada's welfare state and the social safety net, it might be suggested that if we can learn anything from the case of family allowances it is that Canada's social programs must evolve and change as Canada changes. What some see as the sundering of universality and the welfare state with the demise of family allowances in 1992, the recent changes in income support for children can be seen as a new approach to social welfare and the new welfare state in Canada. Universality is not a sacred trust and governments have decided for now, at least, that they must direct limited resources to those most in need as they strive to show that the Canadian federation still works more than 130 years after it was created.

Notes

1. Since the 1970s there has been considerable discussion in Canada of what many have called the "crisis of the welfare state." The discussion can be summarized briefly: Canada created, incre-

mentally, a welfare state in the postwar period based on the loosely defined notion of "welfare" liberalism whereby Canadians accepted a positive role for the state in the economy and society. Canadians were promised an equality of opportunity as the ideals of universality became entrenched in the delivery of social programs as governments moved away from the residual approach to social welfare which left the individual to provide for herself. However, as the postwar economic boom collapsed in the 1970s, the Canadian welfare state was restructured in an era of retrenchment. The right argued that social spending had gotten out of control, precipitating a fiscal crisis and creating dependency rather than self-reliance among the citizenry. The left, on the other hand, saw the "crisis of the welfare state" and the retrenchment through cuts to social spending as the dismantling of the Canadian welfare state. There has been a move in Canada, it was argued, from "welfare" liberalism where the state protected its citizens from economic fluctuations, to "economic" liberalism where the state believes that it must help and encourage its citizens to participate fully in the market economy. Recent reforms saw Ottawa target social security benefits such as family allowances to those most in need (even if recipients are employed in the workplace); there was a move away from the social democratic notion of universality in social programs. These social policy measures have been either trumpeted or criticized—depending on one's position on the ideological spectrum—as a major transformation of or fundamental change to Canada's social security system.

2. For an overview of mothers' allowances, see Dennis Guest, *The Emergence of Social Security in Canada* (Vancouver, 1991), 49–61, and Veronica Strong-Boag, "'Wages for Housework': Mothers' Allowances and the Beginning of Social Security in Canada," in Raymond B. Blake and Jeff Keshen, eds., *Social Welfare Policy in Canada: Historical Readings* (Toronto, 1995), 122–36.

3. Strong-Boag, "Wages for Housework," 124.

4. Quoted in Strong-Boag, "Wages for Housework," 126.

5. Charlotte Whitton, *Report of the New Brunswick Child Welfare Survey* (Fredericton, 1929), 191–92.

6. Strong-Baog, "Wages for Housework," 122–23.

7. R.C. Brown and Ramsay Cook, *Canada, 1896–1921: A Nation Transformed* (Toronto, 1974), 222–23.

8. The federal government first contributed to the provincial mothers' allowances schemes in 1966 when it introduced the Canada Assistance Plan, which was intended to consolidate all the federal-provincial programs based on means test or needs into a single, comprehensive program of benefits that would meet financial need regardless of cause.

9. Peter Bryce, "Mothers' Allowances," *Social Welfare* 1, 6 (1919): 131–32.

10. National Archives of Canada, William Lyon Mackenzie King Papers, Series J1, vol. 154, Lebel to King, 14 May 1928.

11. *Select Standing Committee on Industrial and International Relations*. Report, Proceedings, and Evidence, 52, 55.

12. *Select Standing Committee on Industrial and International Relations*. Report, Proceedings, and Evidence, 56.

13. *Select Standing Committee on Industrial and International Relations*. Report, Proceedings, and Evidence, 69.

14. King Papers, Series J4, volume 211, file 2018, Copy of Hansard, 22 Nov. 1932.

15. *The Labour Gazette*, August 1932, 861–62.

16. King Diaries, 15 April 1931.

17. The following is based largely on Doug Owram, *The Government Generation: Canadian Intellectuals and the State, 1900–1945* (Toronto, 1986), 160–91.

18. Owram, *The Government Generation*, 171.

19. Quoted in House of Commons Debates, 27 Jan. 1939.

20. Mackenzie Papers, vol 41, file G-25-15, The Rt. Hon. W.L. Mackenzie King, Prime Minister of Canada, Address to the American Federation of Labour 1942 Convention, 9 Oct. 1942.

21. *Saturday Night*, 15 August 1942, 12.

22. Mackenzie Papers, "Watchman—What of the Night," address delivered by Ian Mackenzie to the Canadian Club, Quebec City, 20 June 1941.

23. *Saturday Night*, 14 June 1941, 14–15.

24. King Diaries, 5 Dec. 1942.

25. See Leonard Marsh, *Report of Social Security for Canada* (Ottawa, 1943).

26. Toronto *Globe and Mail*, 17 March 1943.

27. National Archives of Canada, John Bracken Papers, vol. 65, file Social Security S-452, Whitton to Bracken, 17 March 1943.

28. King Papers, vol. 273, file 2753(2); Robertson to King, 8 June 1943.

29. Department of Finance, vol 3392, file 04747P-1, "Memorandum for Dr. MacKintosh. Re: Your List of Post-War Economic Problems," 27 January 1943.

30. It is worthwhile noting that McTague, who was appointed national chair of the PC party in 1944, later remarked in a speech to the Seigniory Club in Toronto that "There is little use talking glibly about family allowances being a substitute for wages. No one suggests that they are. They represent a measure of social security for people whose status really requires it." See *Toronto Star*, 2 June 1944.

31. Department of Finance, vol 304, file 101-53-114, vol 1, Towers to Clark, 13 June 1943, and the enclosed memorandum, "The Case for Children's Allowances."

32. See Kitchen, "Wartime Social Reform."

33. *Saturday Night*, 27 March 1943.

34. Quoted in J.L. Granatstein, *Canada's War*, 270–71.

35. King Papers, Series J4, vol. 302, file 3123, Memorandum for the Prime Minister prepared by Claxton, 7 Oct. 1943.

36. King Papers, Series J1, vol. 339, King to Crerar, 5 Dec. 1943.

37. King Diaries, 13 Jan. 1944.

38. *Saturday Night*, 31 October 1942,

39. *Saturday Night*, 12 July 1943, 20–21.

40. King Diaries, 6 Jan. 1944.

41. King Papers, Correspondence Series, vol 345, J.A. MacKinnon to King, 19 November 1943.

42. King Diaries, 13 Jan. 1944.

43. King Diaries, 12 Jan. 1943.

44. See Granatstein, *Canada's War*, 253.

45. Pickersgill, *The Mackenzie King Record*, 632–33.

46. Department of Finance, vol. 304, file 101-53-114, vol. 1, Bryce to Avison, 12 Jan. 1944. Attached to memo is copy of memorandum which was prepared for Ilsley on Children's Allowance.

47. King Diaries, 13 Jan. 1944, and Claxton Papers, vol. 62, file J.W. Pickersgill, Claxton to Pickersgill, 12 Jan. 1944.

48. King Diaries, 13 Jan. 1944.

49. See Oliver, "Public Opinion and Public Policy in Canada: Federal Legislation on War Veterans, 1939–46," 207.

50. National Archives of Canada, Canadian Federation of Business and Professional Clubs, vol. 8, file Family Allowances, Thornton to Davidson, 19 Apr. 1945, and reply, 23 April 1945.

51. King Papers, Series J1, vol. 379, Casgrain to King, 8 June 1945. After the government announced that it would pay Quebec mothers, Casgrain wrote King, "I want to thank you with all my heart for having spared the women of Quebec from a most humiliating and most unnecessary discrimination." Casgrain to King, 3 July 1945.

52. *Ottawa Citizen*, 3 July 1945.

53. Department of National Health and Welfare, Acc. 85-86/343, box 38, file 3301-3-516, Gallup Poll of Canada, 18 Aug. 1999.

54. King Papers, Series J1, vol. 397, Wilson to King, Aug. 1945.

55. National Archives of Canada, Brooke Claxton Papers, vol. 167, file Family Allowances, Extracts from letters, 15 Nov. 1945, and *Toronto Daily Star*, 20 Dec. 1945.

56. *Toronto Daily Star*, 20 Dec. 1945.

57. House of Commons, *Debates*, 31 Oct. 1978, 652.

58. House of Commons, *Debates*, 31 Oct. 1978, 652.

59. Andrew F. Johnson, "Restructuring Family Allowances: 'Good Politics at No Cost,'" in Raymond B. Blake and Jeff Keshen, eds., *Social Welfare Policy in Canada. Historical Readings* (Toronto, 1995), 366–79.

60. Department of Finance, *Working Together Towards a Child Benefit System* (Ottawa, 1997), 4.

61. The "social union" initiative is the umbrella under which government will concentrate their efforts to renew and modernize Canadian social policy. Children in poverty has become one of the first priorities of building a strong social union.

62. Privy Council Office, *Renewing the Canadian Federation: A Progress Report* (Ottawa, 1996), 2.

63. Department of Finance, *Working Together Towards a Child Benefit System* (Ottawa, 1997), 1.

64. As an interim step towards the new benefit system, the 1997 budget promised to enrich and restructure the Working Income Supplement by providing benefits for each child rather than a single benefit per family. The maximum benefit was increased from $500 per family to $605 for the first child, $405 for the second, and $330 for each additional child.

65. Government of Canada, *National Child Benefit Progress Report: 1999* (Ottawa, 1999), 4–5.

66. Department of Finance, *Working Together Towards a Child Benefit System* (Ottawa, 1997), 1–2.

67. See *Globe and Mail*, 15 May 1999. In 1997, for instance, the provinces combined provide various social assistance program s worth approximately $2 billion in benefits for children.

68. *Globe and Mail*, 9 Oct. 1999 and 21 May 1999.

69. See Keith Banting and Ken Battle, eds., *A New Social Vision for Canada? Perspectives on the Federal Discussion Paper on Social Security Reform* (Kingston, 1994).

70. Department of Finance, *Working Together Towards a Child Benefit System* (Ottawa, 1997), 2.

71. Government of Canada, *National Child Benefit Progress Report: 1999* (Ottawa, 1999), 1.

10

Income Maintenance, Insurance Principles, and the "Liberal 1960s"

Canada's Unemployment Insurance Program, 1961–1971*

L. RICHARD LUND

HISTORIANS HAVE quite correctly emphasized the crucial importance of the Second World War in the development of the Canadian welfare state, but they have not yet generally acknowledged the equal if not greater significance of the 1960s in this process. The core programs of the welfare state, the Canada Pension Plan, medicare, the Canada Assistance Plan, and the Unemployment Insurance (UI) program, all assumed most of their current characteristics between 1964 and 1971. During this period, a belief in the need for the federal government to expand the welfare state predominated to a virtually unprecedented degree among Canadian policy makers, and even apparently among the general population.

The UI program is particularly well-suited to illustrate the power of this liberal climate of opinion because in the early 1960s the scheme was on the verge of bankruptcy. The government of John Diefenbaker faced intense pressure to return the insurance fund to financial health, so it appointed a Committee of Inquiry which concluded that the best way to stabilize the program was to eliminate many of the liberalizations which had crept into the plan since its inception. However, despite these pressures Ottawa refused to cut back UI and eventually decided to expand the program in accordance with the dominant liberal beliefs about social policy in the 1960s. The limits of these beliefs, however, were also evident in Canada's reformed UI program. While new legislation essentially created a universal income maintenance plan, the federal government deliberately incorporated some of the basic characteristics of the old insurance scheme into the new program in order to make it more acceptable to all concerned. The 1960s had significantly altered Canada's approach to social policy, but some beliefs remained unchanged and the very structure of the new UI plan reflected this fact.

Canada's first UI program, implemented by the Liberal government of William Lyon Mackenzie King in 1940, was a limited measure based on fairly strict insurance principles. As with commercial insurance, clients paid premiums or contributions for protection against a clearly defined contingency; if that contingency occurred and all premiums had been paid, the client received compensation from an insurance fund at a previously speci-

---

* This material was first published in Jack Granatstein, Gustav Schmidt, and Penny Bryden, eds., *Canada at the Crossroads? The Critical 1960s* (Bochum: Brockmeyer, 1994).

221

fied rate. In the case of Canada's UI plan, claimants unable to find suitable employment received benefits if they were capable of and available for work, and had made at least 180 daily contributions to the insurance fund during the previous two years. Actuaries determined the amount of compensation claimants received by calculating which rates would ensure that contributions from employers, employees, and the federal government exceeded benefit payments over the long term.[1] In contrast to income maintenance or welfare programs, through which the state distributed assistance largely on the basis of need, claimants' actual economic circumstances had no effect on whether or not they qualified for UI benefits, or how much they received. The program did compensate claimants with at least one dependent at a rate almost 18 percent higher than the rate for those without dependents,[2] but the government framed virtually all other aspects of the plan in strict accordance with insurance principles.

This approach best served the goals and reflected the attitudes of Mackenzie King's government. Mindful of the social and economic chaos which followed World War One, King recognized that UI could play an important role in preventing similar instability after the Second World War. As the Department of Finance argued, UI could help stabilize the economy in Keynesian fashion. Contributions would soak up excess purchasing power during the prosperous war years and accumulate in the form of a large surplus in the insurance fund. Jobless Canadians drawing on this surplus during the expected postwar recession would help keep purchasing power up and therefore lessen the impact of the downturn.[3]

From the Prime Minister's perspective, an insurance program also had the advantage of partially placating, without making an open-ended commitment, the steady agitation which had developed during the Great Depression for the federal government to assume some permanent responsibility for the relief of unemployment. King had never accepted that Ottawa should assume total responsibility for the jobless. In fact, he had been angered by growing support within the civil service for federal responsibility.[4] The Prime Minister, however, found UI acceptable because it allowed him to make only a limited commitment. An actuarially sound plan, in general, could only offer coverage to wage earners in the urban industrial sector of the economy, subject to short term cyclical unemployment. Those who found themselves unemployed too regularly, such as seasonal workers, could not be insured because their frequent claims would deplete the insurance fund. On the other hand, Canadians wealthy enough to withstand a jobless period on their own or those with long term job security, such as teachers and civil servants, did not require the protection of UI. The original Act therefore covered only 42 percent of the labour force; the provinces, much to King's delight, retained responsibility for relieving unemployment among the remaining 58 percent, in addition to those within the insured population who had exhausted their UI benefit rights.[5]

The fact that the insurance plan would permit a significant number of workers to draw benefits before turning to provincial and local relief, the Prime Minister hoped, would relieve Ottawa of the burden of providing the provinces with massive emergency funding during future periods of high unemployment.[6] The always fiscally conservative King did not relish the thought of again making relief expenditures like the $32 million he had been forced to approve during fiscal year 1938–39. The prospect of annually remitting to the UI fund an amount equal to 25 percent of the total contributions made by employers and employees, was much more acceptable. In fact, during the war Ottawa's share amounted to little more than $11 million annually.[7] This sum seemed likely to increase only in proportion to growth in the size of the insured population, as long as the program did not stray from its original goal of being self-financing over the long term. In order to ensure that it did not, the government created the Unemployment Insurance Commission (UIC), a non-partisan semi-autonomous board to administer the Act in accordance with insurance principles.

In addition to allowing Ottawa to meet its financial goals, an insurance based scheme also enabled the government to fulfil its limited social objectives. King, in aiding the unemployed, had no intention of waging a war on poverty or initiating the kind of limited redistribution of wealth inherent in an income maintenance program. His government and indeed most Canadians still assumed that it was each individual's own responsibility, not the state's, to improve his/her standard of living and position in society through hard work and self-reliance. UI could prevent some wage earners from slipping into destitution during a temporary involuntary jobless spell, but it should not, many felt, do anything more.[8]

Indeed it did not. The program, for example, had little if any redistributive effect. It did not collect contributions from the most prosperous members of the labour force to finance benefits for the least prosperous; the Act included Canadians who faced a moderate risk of unemployment but, as previously mentioned, excluded groups subject to frequent joblessness, those enjoying long term job security, and salaried employees earning more than $2000 per year. Even among individuals fortunate enough to be insured the redistributive effect was limited. Because benefits paid to claimants depended upon the number of contributions they had previously made, those who had worked the most steadily in the two years before making a claim received the largest amount of aid; claimants who had worked the least and therefore required the most assistance actually received the fewest benefits, if they were able to qualify at all.[9] The plan's graded system of benefits and contributions also worked to the disadvantage of the most needy claimants.[10] Actuaries warned that flat rate benefits might be high enough to undermine the incentive for low income earners to go back to work. Graded benefits, on the other hand, reduced the incentive for medium and high income jobless workers to accept less lucrative employment, but few federal officials seemed concerned. Apparently, it was much more important to preserve the work ethic among Canada's low income earners.[11] Hence, Canada's original UI plan, reflecting the limited goals and conservative attitudes of the King government, did little to alter the existing distribution of wealth within the labour force.

The UI program remained largely unchanged while Mackenzie King was in office, but the St. Laurent and Diefenbaker governments, in response to changing economic conditions and public demands, gradually inserted a greater element of income maintenance into the insurance plan. They increased benefit rates, eased qualifying conditions during the winter months in particular, and extended coverage to some originally excluded high risk groups. These liberalizations, combined with growing unemployment in the late 1950s reduced the surplus in the UI fund from almost $900 million in late 1956 to less than $185 million by early 1961. Amid growing controversy and warnings that the insurance fund was on the verge of bankruptcy, Prime Minister Diefenbaker appointed a committee of inquiry to determine how Canada's UI scheme could be returned to financial health.[12]

The Gill Committee, named after its chairman, Ernest C. Gill, tabled its report in December 1962. It recommended that Ottawa restore the dominance of insurance principles within the UI plan by eliminating many of the elements of income maintenance which had crept into the program since 1948. Only through such decisive action, the report concluded, could the UI fund be stabilized and the future of the program be guaranteed.[13] Soon after winning the election of April 1963, however, the new government of Lester B. Pearson decided not to act immediately on the Gill Committee's advice, even though the condition of the insurance fund continued to deteriorate. Allan MacEachen, the Minister of Labour, acknowledged that UI had to be reformed, but he argued that owing to the sweeping nature of the Gill recommendations and the importance of UI to so many Canadians, he had to study the report further before he could determine the most prudent course of action. In the meantime, MacEachen committed the government to lending money to the UIC if the insurance fund lapsed into a deficit position, which it did briefly in 1963 and 1964.[14]

John R. Nicholson, who succeeded MacEachen as Minister of Labour in 1965, continued to suggest publicly that the government was still considering acting on the Gill proposals, but in private he instructed the interdepartmental committee considering changes to the UI act to "start afresh ... [and] look at the total adequacy and needs of our Unemployment Insurance Programme in the light of present circumstances and probable future needs."[15] The Gill recommendations were simply too stringent, too controversial for a government which did not enjoy the luxury of a Parliamentary majority. Among other things, Gill advocated more rigorous qualifying conditions for all claimants and the elimination of special seasonal benefits payable each winter. A later study revealed that the Gill plan would have denied these seasonal benefits to approximately 106,000 claimants. Of that total, one third would have received aid for the entire winter from a new national jobless assistance program financed from general tax revenue, which Gill had also recommended. However, two thirds would have received this aid for only a portion of the winter season or not all. Obviously such changes would have greatly disturbed workers who had paid UI contributions for many years in expectation of a certain level of benefit when they were without work. A new national assistance scheme, carrying with it the stigma of charity, in all likelihood, would have satisfied few former UI recipients.[16] Hence, implementation of the Gill proposals held out the possibility of arousing more opposition than most minority governments would care to face.

Fortunately for Pearson, lower unemployment during and after 1964 allowed the insurance fund to recover somewhat, which reduced the pressure to act.[17] Study of the UI issue could now proceed at a leisurely pace as the government addressed more pressing matters on its social policy agenda, such as the Canada Pension Plan, the Canada Assistance Plan, and the *Canada Health Act*. However, after these important pieces of legislation had all been passed and the unemployment rate began to creep up again in 1967, Pearson had little choice but to address the UI issue.[18] His government had promised a major overhaul of the insurance program numerous times since 1963, and although the fund had once again accumulated a surplus of more than $200 million, it was certainly not healthy enough to withstand another period of relatively high unemployment similar to that from 1958 to 1962.[19] Consequently, Cabinet decided in early 1968 to implement some temporary reforms in an effort to meet immediate needs, while the UIC and Department of Labour worked out the details of a new UI plan.[20] This process culminated under the Trudeau government with a 1970 White Paper, entitled "Unemployment Insurance in the 70s," and a new Act a year later.

While both the Pearson and Trudeau governments spent a great deal of time studying the specifics of how to reform the UI program, neither spent much time debating the general direction that reform should take; both wanted to expand coverage to virtually the entire work force and increase benefit rates substantially in an effort to enhance the income maintenance aspects of the scheme. Pearson took a number of steps in that direction with his temporary reforms which increased benefits, extended coverage to paid workers in agriculture and horticulture, and lifted the coverage exclusion for some highly paid salaried employees.[21] The Trudeau government's 1971 UI Act moved the program even further in the direction of income maintenance and away from insurance principles.

This approach was a result of the social, economic, and political conditions which prevailed between 1963 and 1971. The circumstances which had made insurance principles preferable to the King government no longer existed. Low unemployment and a booming economy during the 1960s ironically heightened interest in social problems to an unprecedented degree and produced a liberal attitude towards state activism. In particular, the persistence of poverty in the midst of plenty garnered a tremendous amount of attention, and not just from social activists. Mainstream and elite sources, in fact, also declared themselves to be "against poverty." The Economic Council of Canada, for example, a think tank of economists established in 1963 to advise the government, expressed considerable conviction on this issue with the following comments in its annual review for 1968:

> Poverty in Canada is real. Its numbers are not in the thousands, but the millions. There is more of it than our society can tolerate, more than the economy can afford, and far more than existing measures can cope with. Its persistence, at a time when the bulk of Canadians enjoy one of the highest standards of living in the world, is a disgrace.[22]

In response, Ottawa appointed a Special Senate Committee on Poverty. Pearson had already, in addition to the major social reforms previously mentioned, established a special planning secretariat in the Privy Council Office to co-ordinate the dozens of federal anti-poverty initiatives and help create new programs to wage what became known as the "War on Poverty."[23] Yet the Progressive Conservative (PC) leader, Robert Stanfield, did not question the government's growing expenditures on social programs; instead he accused the Liberals, particularly Prime Minister Trudeau, of ignoring the poor. Stanfield also managed to overcome opposition from the right wing of his party and secure official PC support for a Guaranteed Annual Income program, along with a resolution calling for all social programs to be administered "in a humane and compassionate manner."[24] The climate of opinion in Canada at this time clearly favoured the expansion of the welfare state to alleviate poverty and create more equality of opportunity. Preventing destitution was no longer enough.

The buoyant economy of the 1960s further reinforced this atmosphere by increasing confidence in the government's ability to finance social programs and thereby undermining the influence of the old fiscal conservatism. Therefore, one of UI's original roles as a bulwark against total federal responsibility for the unemployed became less important during this period. Indeed, whether or not Ottawa should be responsible for supporting the jobless was no longer an open question. In 1956 the St. Laurent government had felt secure enough financially to offer the provinces grants equalling almost 50 percent of unemployment assistance costs. So whether through UI or the *Unemployment Assistance* (UA) *Act*, the federal government bore considerable responsibility for supporting jobless Canadians, and virtually no one questioned the appropriateness of this commitment. During the Gill Committee hearings, for example, even business representatives took great pains to point out that they recognized Ottawa's moral obligation to provide aid to Canadians unemployed through no fault of their own; their submissions questioned only what constituted the most effective and appropriate means of delivering that assistance.[25] In this context, the King government's strategy of using a strict adherence to insurance principles as a means of limiting federal moral and financial responsibility for joblessness became irrelevant.

A number of other factors after 1968 gave the Trudeau government further incentive to expand and enhance Canada's UI program. First of all, the Prime Minister had frequently promised a "just society" during the 1968 election campaign, and although he never really specified what he meant by this term, it nevertheless created expectations of continued social reform.[26]

Unemployment also became a major political issue again as it steadily increased from 3.6 percent in 1966 to 5.9 percent in 1970, the worst rate of all major industrialized nations.[27] In addition, constitutional discussions with the provinces carried out between 1968 and 1971 forced Ottawa to justify its role in the social policy field. Quebec desired the freedom, without financial penalty from Ottawa, to establish its own provincial social security system. The province's Minister of Social Affairs, Claude Castonguay, wanted to create a global integrated system in Quebec which would replace all existing federal or partially federally funded social programs.[28] In response, the Trudeau government defined the general purposes that its social initiatives would serve and also reviewed some of its major programs to ensure that they furthered those goals and satisfied the public.[29]

Canada's UI plan, still exhibiting the lingering influence of its original insurance principles, did not meet either of these criteria satisfactorily. Polls in 1968, for example, showed strong majority support, in all regions of the country and within all occupational and income groups, for UI reforms such as increased benefits and broader coverage.[30] In fact, this liberal climate of opinion was so powerful that it produced an ideological revolution within the UIC. The Commission, which heretofore had perceived the defence of insurance principles as its "raison d'être," by the mid-1960s began to question its stance on this issue.

Internal studies become sharply critical of the Commission's rigid adherence to insurance principles. The UIC's inflexibility had produced a system unconcerned with the needs of claimants and unable "to provide adequate compensation on a fair basis for those who are out of work." The program had to be reformed not only to better meet these income maintenance needs but also to become an integral part of a welfare state with "a comprehensive social development strategy." Rather than simply preserving insurance principles and ensuring financial stability within the UI program, the Commission now had to consider its actions within the larger context of Ottawa's general effort to provide all Canadians with adequate income maintenance and the opportunity to develop to their full potential.[31] By 1968, the Commission as a whole accepted that the insurance scheme did not serve the purposes envisioned for UI by Canadians and the federal government.

The UIC, therefore, actively participated in the drafting of the 1970 White Paper and the new Act which followed.

As the times demanded, income maintenance rather than insurance principles predominated in the new program. Both the Commission and the government made a greater effort than ever before to set benefit rates at levels commensurate with the actual needs of claimants. Benefit payments under the old Act had been so meagre that they did not provide unemployed Canadians with much security. In 1965, for example, a claimant with a family of four required a weekly income of $58 to stay above the poverty line, yet the maximum UI benefit paid at the time was $36 per week and the average was only $24.55. This situation only deteriorated as time passed because the government did not adjust benefit rates annually to counteract the effects of inflation. Ottawa did increase benefits in 1968, but only to a maximum of $53 per week, which was still below the 1965 poverty line. Even after these increases, weekly UI payments to claimants represented, on average, only 43 percent of their previous earnings.[32] The new Act, therefore, substantially increased benefits to 66.6 percent of previous earnings in the early weeks of a claim, and to 75 percent for claimants with dependents. In recognition of the fact that as time passed expenses became harder to defer and the needs of the unemployed increased, the new program extended the higher "dependent benefit rate" to all claimants after they had been without work for more than 27 weeks. The new maximum weekly benefit rate of $100 compared favourably with the 1970 poverty line of $85. While the Act did not guarantee all claimants a benefit rate in excess of this level, it did ensure benefits substantially higher than in the past.

The maximum benefit duration remained the same at 51 weeks, but the new scheme contained easier qualifying conditions; rather than requiring a minimum of 30 weekly contributions during the 2 years preceding a claim to establish minimum entitlement, the UI Act now demanded only 8 contributions during the previous 12 months. In general, claimants had to make fewer contributions to qualify for the same duration of benefit payments as in the past. Trudeau's Minister of Labour, Bryce Mackasey, openly acknowledged that one of the government's goals was to pay insurance benefits "more on the basis of need than length of time in the work force."[33]

Other areas of need met by the new UI program included loss of income due to sickness and pregnancy. Prior to 1971, the UIC estimated that 70 percent of the working population possessed sickness insurance coverage in a variety of private plans which offered benefits ranging from generous to grossly inadequate; the remaining 30 percent of the labour force had no protection from such a contingency. Pregnant women had even less security. Surveys indicated that about 90 percent of employees in Canada lacked access to maternity benefits and therefore faced termination or an unpaid leave of absence if they became pregnant. Even the fortunate few who had some protection generally could collect benefits for a maximum of only 6 weeks. The 1971 UI Act, in combination with private insurance plans, ensured that all Canadians covered by the program were eligible for up to 15 weeks of sickness and maternity benefits.[34] Although insurance principles and financial considerations demanded that only loss of income due to unemployment be covered, the federal government decided that it was more important to fill this gap in the Canadian welfare state.

The way in which the Trudeau government chose to finance these more generous benefits also indicated a retreat from insurance principles. Employers and employees continued to make contributions, but most now paid slightly less for more generous coverage. This decrease was, in part, a consequence of the inclusion of high income Canadians and more low risk groups in the new UI program, but to an even greater degree it was the result of increased federal funding. No longer did Ottawa merely contribute an amount equal to 25 percent of total employer and employee contributions. Instead, while private sector contributions financed sickness, maternity, and some unemployment benefits, the government made an open ended commitment to assume the costs of all benefit payments attributed to a national or regional unemployment rate over 4 percent. The government chose 4 percent because it was the average rate of unemployment in Canada over the last decade, and as Bryce Mackasey argued, a jobless rate above this level, "is beyond the direct control of the employer and employee ... [so] it is logical the government should assume the responsibility of paying ... [these costs]."[35] With this new method of financing, Ottawa's costs increased astronomically from $87 million or 17 percent of total benefit payments in 1969, to $1.205 billion or 64 percent of benefits paid in 1972.[36] Government experts had expected Ottawa's share of UI costs to increase, but not quite as much; a higher than anticipated unemployment rate accounted for much of this discrepancy.[37] Nevertheless, by design, UI was now an income maintenance scheme financed from general tax revenue to a much greater degree than in the past.

The new UI program, in addition, reflected the government's desire to reduce disparities in wealth. The UIC divided the country into 16 regions and when the jobless rate in one of these areas exceeded the national average by more than 1 percent, the Commission paid benefits to claimants in that region for a longer period of time than in the rest country. In addition to using this method to redistribute income between regions, the Act also attempted to "redistribute income ... [and] equalize opportunity between individuals across the country."[38] The government extended coverage to more high risk, low-income groups like agricultural workers, and at the same time brought almost 1.2 million formerly excluded low-risk, high-income workers into the plan. This group included nurses, teachers, police officers, armed forces personnel, civil servants, and salaried employees earning more than $7800 per year. Coverage of the labour force became virtually universal, increasing from little more than 60 percent in 1967 to 96.3 percent in 1971.[39] The government justified its actions by arguing that it was "only reasonable ... that those less fortunate, who are out of work temporarily, should be given protection by those in a better position."[40]

Some of these newly covered Canadians, particularly teachers, expressed "deep resentment" at being included in the UI plan. They felt that their chances of being unemployed and having to collect UI benefits were remote if not nonexistent, so their contributions to the plan constituted, in their eyes, "grossly unfair," "discriminatory," and "selective taxation of an inequitable kind."[41] While in all likelihood these opponents of universality never represented a majority of low-risk, high-income workers,[42] the vehemence of their resistance and the support of the Canadian Teacher's Federation challenge to the government's UI reforms, posed a potentially serious challenge to the government's UI reforms.

The Minister of Labour, Bryce Mackasey, responded by reiterating his belief that the more fortunate members of society should help the less fortunate, and by suggesting that no one was completely immune to the threat of unemployment any longer. Technological, economic, and social change, the Minister argued, now proceeding at an unprecedented pace, rendered the labour market for skilled workers and professionals more volatile than in the past. David Weatherhead, the chairman of the House of Commons Standing Committee on Labour, Manpower, and Immigration, pointed out that teachers, for example, would likely soon face a growing problem of declining enrolment and have to grapple with labour-saving educational technology such as closed circuit television. Under such circumstances, he suggested, they would be quite foolish to consider their jobs completely secure for the next 20 years.[43]

The government's argument was effective in undermining opposition to universality because some skilled and professional workers actually had experienced considerable hardship prior to 1971 as a result of facing unemployment without UI coverage.[44] A woman from Penticton, British Columbia, for example, wrote to the Minister of Manpower and Immigration, Jean Marchand, in February 1968 about her husband who had lost his job in June 1967. He had contributed to the UI plan since 1941 and collected benefits only once for 3 weeks in 1953. However, in 1960 when his salary exceeded the earnings ceiling, he received notification than he no longer qualified for coverage. His wife "experienced a certain feeling of insecurity ... [but it] was partially dispelled by the thought that his job was reasonably secure." Unfortunately, that did not turn out to be the case; after spending the previous 6 months borrowing against life insurance policies and selling personal belongings to make ends meet, this disillusioned Canadian vowed that she would "never be so complacent again." Her salary from the BC government was not nearly enough to support her husband and 2 children, and their situation was not yet desperate enough to apply for welfare. They could not sell their house because rent would be more expensive than their mortgage payments. One of her children required glasses but she simply did not have enough money to purchase a pair. She felt "at a loss as to what to do next," and asked the Minister if he honestly felt that such an ordeal "should be necessary in a country like Canada?"[45] Many Canadians at the time would have answered no to this question. Universal UI coverage, which could make unemployment less traumatic than the situation described above, consequently received considerable public support.[46]

Universality had the additional advantage of bringing more Canadians into manpower offices to take advantage of the various services offered. Ottawa had expanded training programs during the 1960s because the increasing pace of technological change created a need for a more skilled work force, and because labour shortages in some skilled occupations had become a surprisingly serious problem. The economy seemed to be producing enough jobs but a lack of training apparently prevented Canadians from enjoying the full benefits of this boom. Hence, in 1966 the Pearson government created the Department of Manpower and Immigration in order to ensure co-ordination between federal job placement, counselling, retraining, and mobility programs previously administered by the UIC and the Department of Labour. In the past, national employment offices had placed more emphasis on the short term goal of finding jobs for UI claimants to keep the drain on the insurance fund to a minimum. The new Department of Manpower and Immigration was supposed to ensure a greater emphasis on the long term development of the labour force. The UI Act of 1971 took this process a step further by making it a basic objective of the insurance plan to "provide an efficient pipeline to manpower programs and other services designed to improve the employment potential of the individual."[47] UI had become a part of the full service welfare state of the 1960s and early 1970s. Integration of social programs was an important national objective at this time because the piecemeal approach, which saw dozens of programs serving many different, sometimes even contradictory goals, had received much criticism in recent years. To achieve the desired integration, Ottawa had to construct its major programs in accordance with similar principles, among the most important of which in the 1960s was universality. Policy makers believed that by offering protection to everyone, rather than just to those who needed assistance the most, universal social programs would not only bring greater economic security to a larger proportion of the population, but also create a sense of community solidarity; theoretically, universality could prevent the unfortunate divisions, so common prior to the 1960s, between those who received help and those who financed it. Universality in the UI program, in addition to philosophic unity, created greater administrative compatibility between the insurance scheme and Ottawa's other major social programs.[48]

In making UI a universal program with the ability to meet all of the goals demanded of it by Canadians and government officials, Ottawa had little choice but to transform a plan formerly based on insurance principles into what was essentially an income maintenance scheme. The federal government, however, did preserve some characteristics of the old program. While hardly sustaining insurance principles, the new UI Act maintained at least the appearance of an insurance plan; employers and employees still made contributions, no one received benefits until after a two week waiting period, and although weakened considerably, the connection nevertheless remained between claimants' eligibility for benefit, their contribution history, and their previous earnings. In fact, at every opportunity federal officials stressed that the new program was still an insurance scheme. Bryce Mackasey, for example, ignored the obvious elements of income maintenance in the new legislation and argued that, "there is no welfare in the proposed plan since anyone who is to draw benefits must be attached to the labour force, have paid contributions, be unemployed for a period of at least two weeks, and be subject to the conditions of being available and capable and seeking work." His comments merely reflected the government's deliberate strategy, pursued since drafting of the new program began, to prevent UI from being labelled a welfare scheme.[49]

Ottawa chose this approach despite the fact that pursuing income maintenance goals behind a facade of insurance to some degree undermined those ends. For example, paying benefits based on the number of previous contributions and previous earnings, although to a lesser degree than in the past, still meant that those who needed help the most received less aid than those who had enjoyed the most steady and lucrative employment. Benefits based on a percentage of previous earnings also did nothing to alleviate the inadequacies of the wage system; those with wages below the poverty line collected UI benefits, when jobless, that were even further below the poverty line. Ottawa accepted such problems because implementation of program alternatives which could have provided aid more in accordance with actual need presented a number of practical difficulties, unlike UI.

Unemployment assistance, for example, paid from general tax revenue to those who lacked the means to support themselves, was unpopular because many people considered it to be charity. UI benefits had much less of a stigma attached because claimants had paid for this protection through their contributions, which conferred upon workers certain clearly defined rights to compensation when unemployed. A 1968 poll indicated that the vast majority of Canadians were aware that employer and employee contributions financed UI, but only a third of the population knew that the federal government also contributed to the insurance fund. In addition, a majority of respondents indicated that they preferred private funding to state support for the UI scheme.[50] Insurance contributions gave Canadians a sense of paying their own way, but non-contributory unemployment assistance usually only brought the unwanted feeling of relying on the charity of others.

In 1966, Ottawa tried to change this situation somewhat with the Canada Assistance Plan (CAP), which consolidated and expanded many existing public assistance programs. In regard to UA, the plan increased the level of aid available, attempted to define legal rights to this assistance, and tried to establish avenues for claimants to appeal the decisions of provincial and local officials, which previously had been final. The provinces, however, did not co-operate in these efforts and Ottawa failed to force the issue. Jobless aid under the CAP remained discretionary. Consequently, despite new higher levels of public assistance, UI benefits paid as a right remained highly preferable.[51] By 1970, even the government admitted that the CAP had failed to become a viable alternative to UI. In fact, Bryce Mackasey openly proclaimed that one of the purposes of the new UI Act was to "postpone the unhappy day when too many Canadians have to go on [CAP financed] welfare."[52]

Constitutional considerations also provided an incentive for Ottawa to maintain the appearance of insurance. As a result of a constitutional amendment passed in 1940, the federal government had complete jurisdiction over UI, but unemployment assistance fell within provincial jurisdiction. Ottawa, however, had used its spending power to establish a presence in this field in 1955; the federal government paid approximately 50 percent of UA costs as long as each province met certain minimum criteria in administering the program. Obviously national standards were more difficult to maintain when the provinces, as opposed to just the federal government, had constitutional jurisdiction. Such a situation also forced Ottawa to pursue laborious negotiations with the provinces in order to establish any new shared cost program or to reform an existing one.[53] A jobless aid plan which maintained the appearance of insurance and sole federal jurisdiction, therefore, was a more preferable option than unemployment assistance.

In addition to UA, the other major alternative to UI discussed at the time was Guaranteed Annual Income (GAI) program. Such a scheme received consideration during the 1960s from many groups, including the Progressive Conservative Party and the Special Senate Committee on Poverty, which would eventually endorse a GAI plan and criticize Ottawa's piecemeal approach to social policy.[54] A GAI program, however, had the same constitutional drawbacks as UA, and produced even greater concerns about costs. In addition, such a scheme would have forced the government, against its better judgement, to confront the basic conflict between preserving the motivation to work and ensuring an adequate standard of living for all citizens. While Canadians had come a long way during the 1960s in their willingness to provide citizens in need with the help they required, "Canada as a nation," according to the Canadian Welfare Council, had "by no means agreed on the philosophical question of whether we should provide at least an adequate standard of living for all members of our society as a matter of right."[55] Indeed, confidence that everyone would continue to work even if they were guaranteed a minimum annual income did not seem high enough to support such a program. The principle of less eligibility could not be abandoned so easily.

Even the new UI program, in the opinion of most business groups, promised benefits on such generous terms that it would seriously undermine the incentive for Canadians to work. For this reason, an editorial in the *Globe and Mail* went so far as to call the plan "immoral and stupid."[56] This opposition, however, never gathered much momentum because the majority of Canadians seemed to want more generous benefits, and the Trudeau government only had to point to the insurance aspects of the new program to convince most people that the incentive to work had been preserved;[57] benefit rates were always less than each claimant's previous earnings level, and because the plan maintained at least some relation between work history and eligibility for benefits, those who worked most steadily at the highest paying jobs were rewarded for their efforts. However, without these insurance aspects in the plan, business attacks would have stood a much better chance of success, even in such a liberal era.

Insurance contributions gave UI benefits the aura of being earned, so the question of whether or not claimants deserved as much in benefit payments as they qualified for did not seem particularly important. Many people raised this question, however, in regard to assistance payments not "earned" with contributions, because no one had a right to charity; some people deserved it, others deserved little, and no one deserved so much of it that they would be tempted not to try to earn a living for themselves. Taxes could have been viewed, like UI contributions, as earning citizens the right when unemployed to reasonably generous aid from government coffers, but not enough Canadians made this connection. The relatively liberal attitudes about poverty and state social activism which developed in the 1960s had limits. Certainly to a much greater degree than in the past, Canadians were sympathetic to the plight of less fortunate members of society; these attitudes, however, did not produce a widespread rejection of the notion that aid from non-contributory public assistance programs constituted a form of charity. Hence, the political situation dictated that the new UI Act, offering relatively generous aid to the unemployed, maintain some of the characteristics of the original plan based on insurance principles.

In implementing a UI program in 1940, Mackenzie King wanted to help ensure a stable post-war economic situation, limit Ottawa's moral and financial responsibility for the unemployed, and provide some aid to a portion of Canada's jobless, without violating the principle of less eligibility or undermining the labour force's existing system of rewarding individual initiative. Insurance principles served these limited goals well. Although the plan drifted towards income maintenance between 1948 and 1960, serious financial difficulties in the early 1960s suggested a return to more stringent insurance principles was in the offing. Indeed, the Gill Committee advised Ottawa that the most prudent course of action was to eliminate many of the liberalizations which had crept into the UI program since 1948.

Financial considerations alone, however, were not enough to justify a return to strict insurance principles. The Pearson government chose not to act on the Gill Committee's recommendations for fear of arousing strong public opposition. A modest recovery by the insurance fund and lower unemployment permitted Pearson to study his options at a leisurely pace until 1967. At that time, the completion of a number of other major social reforms, along with gradually increasing joblessness, forced the government to address the issue of UI.

This process begun by Pearson culminated under Trudeau with a new UI Act in 1971, which transformed the program into an income maintenance scheme; benefit rates reflected the actual needs of claimants and funding depended on general tax revenue to a much greater degree than in the past. The circumstances which had once made insurance principles a desirable option no longer existed. In the liberal 1960s, UI had to serve different goals. Above all, the new program had to meet the actual needs of Canadians who had suffered an interruption in earnings due to joblessness, sickness, or pregnancy. In addition, the government hoped the reformed UI scheme would redistribute wealth between regions and individuals, contribute to community solidarity rather than aggravate divisions between "haves" and "have nots," and direct claimants to manpower programs and other services designed to improve their employment prospects over the long term. Ottawa also aimed to have the new UI scheme operate not within its own narrow context, as in the past, but in the larger context of Ottawa's general effort to provide all Canadians with adequate income maintenance and greater opportunity through a full service welfare state.

The 1971 UI Act, however, also retained some of the characteristics of the old program based on insurance principles; employees and employers still made contributions, and each claimant's contribution history remained the main criteria by which eligibility for benefit was determined. These attributes preserved little more than the appearance of insurance and in the process undermined the cause of income maintenance to some degree, but the federal government felt it had little choice in the matter. The contributory nature of UI ensured Ottawa sole jurisdiction over the new program and removed the stigma of charity which made public assistance unpopular. A plan with insurance characteristics also did not violate the principle of less eligibility in the way that a Guaranteed Annual Income scheme would have. While Canadians in this era were sympathetic towards state activism and the plight of the less fortunate members of society perhaps more than anytime before or since, these liberal attitudes nevertheless had limits; concern about preserving the work ethic still tempered Canadians' desire to ensure a reasonable standard of living for all citizens. Providing income maintenance behind a facade of insurance, therefore, was the most effective way for the federal government to meet the social policy goals demanded by the liberal 1960s, and at the same time remain within the limits also prescribed by that era.

Notes

1. *Report of the Committee of Inquiry into the Unemployment Insurance Act* (Ottawa: Queen's Printer, 1962), 20; National Archives of Canada (cited infra NAC), Liberal Party Papers, vol. 1025, file "Labour," "Remarks by the Hon. John R. Nicholson, Minister of Labour, at the Conference 'Social Security Today and Tomorrow,'" 17 July 1967, 4.

2. Even this one concession to the actual needs of the unemployed was quite limited. This special rate did not escalate with the number of dependents a claimant had; a family with nine children had to live on the same rate increase as a family with only one child. The costs of an escalating "dependent rate" would have been too high for the insurance fund to bear, and such a system also would have violated insurance principles by "overinsuring" wage earners with large families; benefit payments for such individuals likely would have been so high as to reduce their incentive to find employment. *An Explanation of the Principles and Main Provisions of the Unemployment Insurance Act* (Ottawa: Unemployment Insurance Commission, Revised, January 1953), 16; Gary Dingledine, *A Chronology of Response: The Evolution of Unemployment Insurance from 1940 to 1980* (Ottawa: Employment and Immigration Canada, 1981), 14.

3. NAC, Unemployment Insurance Commission (cited infra UIC) Records, acc. 90-91/132, vol. 2, file "Arthur MacNamara," "Radio Address of Hon. Norman A. McLarty, Minister of Labour," 15 May 1941, 3–5; Dingledine, *Chronology*, 8; James Struthers, *No Fault of Their Own: Unemployment and the Canadian Welfare State, 1914-1941* (Toronto: University of Toronto Press, 1983) 197–203; Liberal Party Papers, vol. 1025, file "Labour," "Remarks by the Hon. John R. Nicholson, Minister of Labour, at the Conference 'Social Security Today and Tomorrow,'" 17 July 1967, 7.

4. *Final Report of the National Employment Commission* (Ottawa: King's Printer, 1938), 27; Struthers, *No Fault of Their Own*, 181–84.

5. Dingledine, *Chronology*, 9–11; UIC Records, acc. 90-91/132, vol. 2, file "Arthur MacNamara," "Radio Address of Hon. Norman A. McLarty, Minister of Labour," 15 May 1941, 3–5; *An Explanation of the Principles and Main Provisions of the Unemployment Insurance Act* 13–14; NAC, Treasury Board Records, acc. 80-81/248, file 8508-4, "Proposals For Correcting Some Factors That Have Been Weakening the Unemployment Insurance Scheme, Increasing the Drain on the Fund and Leading to Abuse," UIC, 28 June 1960, Appendix C.

6. Struthers, *No Fault of Their Own*, 199.

7. Struthers. *No Fault of Their Own*, 220; UIC, *Annual Report*, 1942 (Ottawa: King's Printer, 1942) 27; 1943, 25; 1944, 27; 1945, 31.

8. Treasury Board Records, acc. 80-81/248, file 8508-4, "Proposals For Correcting Some Factors That Have Been Weakening the Unemployment Insurance Scheme, Increasing the Drain on the Fund and Leading to Abuse," UIC, 28 June 1960, 2.

9. *Report of the Committee of Inquiry into the Unemployment Insurance Act*, 21.

10. The Act established 7 earnings classes with different benefit and contribution rates so that generally, the higher one's income, the more one had to pay in contributions and the more one was eligible to receive in benefits. Dingledine, *Chronology*, 11–14.

11. Struthers, *No Fault of Their Own*, 200–202.

12. L. Richard Lund, *Unemployment Insurance and Seasonal Workers in Canada, 1940-63*, M.A. Thesis, University of Western Ontario, 1991, 150–57; UIC, *Annual Report*, 1956, 26; 1961, 29.

13. The Gill report did recommend broader coverage of low risk groups and more generous weekly benefit rates, but the net effect of all the proposals was to cut back the UIC program. *Report of the Committee of Inquiry into the Unemployment Insurance Act*, 9–17.

14. *Canadian Annual Review for 1963*, ed. John T. Saywell (Toronto: University of Toronto Press, 1964), 189; Dingledine, *Chronology*, 44–45; UIC Records, vol. 56, file "July 1964," "Minutes of the Meeting of the Unemployment Insurance Advisory Committee" (cited infra: UIAC), 16 July 1964.

15. UIC Records, vol. 56, "Minutes of the Meeting of the UIAC," 20 July 1966: vol. 60, file "Changes to UI," "Report to the Minister of Labour by the Interdepartmental Committee on Changes to the Unemployment Insurance Programme," 25 March 1966, 1.

16. UIC Records, vol. 60, file 'June 1965', "Studies by Committees of Unemployment Insurance and Compensation," UIC, Committee No. 1, Report No. 1, June 1965, 2–5, 7–8; *Report of the Committee of Inquiry into the Unemployment Insurance Act*, 9–17.

17. The unemployment rate was 7.1% in 1961, 4.7% in 1964, and 3.9% in 1965. F. H. Leacy, Ed., *Historical Statistics of Canada* (Ottawa: Statistics Canada, 1983), D491–497; UIC Records, vol. 58, file "UIAC Reports and Minutes 1967," "Actuarial Report to the UIAC," Z. Jarkiewicz, 11 July 1967, 15.

18. Leacy, *Statistics*, D491–497.

19. Lund, *Unemployment Insurance*, 162.

20. UIC Records, acc. 90-91/132, vol. 2, file 500M, "Minutes of the Meeting of the UIAC," 24 July 1967; acc. 81-82/142, vol. 17 file 170-3-2-1 pt. 1, "Memorandum to Cabinet," 1 February 1968.

21. UIC Records, acc. 90-91/132, vol. 2, file 500M, "Minutes of the Meeting of the UIAC," 24 July 1967; acc. 81-82/142, vol. 17 file 170-3-2-1 pt. 1, "Memorandum to Cabinet," 1 February 1968.

22. Economic Council of Canada, *Fifth Annual Review* (Ottawa: 1968), 1.

23. *Canadian Annual Review for 1965*, 17, 321–2; NAC, Department of National Health and Welfare Records, vol. 2110, file 21-1-2 vol. 3, "Fighting Poverty—in 1966"; Liberal Party Papers,

vol. 755, file "Speakers Guide," "Liberal Campaign, October 1965, Speakers Notes No. 4," D-17 to D-31.

24. NAC, Progressive Conservative (cited infra: PC) Party Papers, vol. 398, file "Election 1965— Policy," "PC Policy Handbook," 1968; *Canadian Annual Review for 1969*, 15–17, 35.

25. UIC Records, acc. 90-91/132, vol. 2, file 200M parts 2, 4, and 5, "Committee of Inquiry into the Unemployment Insurance Act: Proceedings of the Public Hearings," vol. 2, 15 Nov. 1961, 154, 224, 246, vol. 4, 17 Nov. 1961, 501, 518–521, 541, vol. 5, 18 Dec. 1961, 596, 601, 633, 657.

26. Leslie A. Pal, "Revision and Retreat: Canadian Unemployment Insurance, 1971–1981," in *Canadian Social Welfare Policy: Federal and Provincial Dimensions*, ed. Jacqueline S. Ismael (Kingston and Montreal: McGill-Queen's University Press, 1985), 78; Treasury Board Records, vol. 1352, file 9720/456-1 Pt. 10, "A Proposal for Updating the Unemployment Insurance Programme," UIC, 21 July 1969, 14.

27. *Canadian Annual Review for 1968*, 286, 303–4; *Canadian Annual Review for 1969*, 392; *Canadian Annual Review for 1970*, 389; *Canadian Annual Review of Politics and Public Affairs*, 1971, ed. John T. Saywell (Toronto: University of Toronto Press, 1972), 29, 38–40, 314; Leacy D491–97.

28. Dennis Guest, *The Emergence of Social Security in Canada* (Vancouver: University of British Columbia Press, 1980), 178–185; *Canadian Annual Review of Politics and Public Affairs*, 1971, 42–45.

29. See *Income Security and Social Services*, Government of Canada Working Paper on the Constitution (Ottawa: Queen's Printer, 1969); *Income Security for Canadians* (Ottawa: Department of National Health and Welfare, 1970); and *Unemployment Insurance in the 70's* (Ottawa: Department of Labour, 1970).

30. UIC Records, vol. 71, file "Project Team," "Personal Factors in Public Opinion towards Unemployment Compensation," B. Portis, C. Michael Lanphier, and Malcolm Golden, Oct. 1968, 3, 5, 31, 31a, 42.

31. UIC Records, vol. 60, file "May 1965," "The Reform of Unemployment Compensation in Canada," K.V. Parkhurst, Chief, Research Division, UIC, May 1965, 8–20; acc. 90-91/132, vol. 2, file 500G. "Summary of Brief to Special Senate Committee on Poverty from UIC," 26 May 1969; Treasury Board Records, vol. 1352, file 9720/456-1 Pt. 10, "A Proposal for Updating the UI Programme," UIC, 21 July 1969, 7–8, 13–14.

32. UIC Records, vol. 60, file "May 1965," "The Reform of Unemployment Compensation in Canada," K.V. Parkhurst, May 1965, 15; acc. 90-91/132, vol. 2, file 500G. UIC to Special Senate Committee on Poverty, 26 May 1969, Appendices D and E; Dingledine, *Chronology*, 47; Treasury Board Records, vol. 1352, file 9720/456-1 Pt. 10, "A Proposal for Updating the UI Programme," UIC, 21 July 1969, 10; *Unemployment Insurance in the 70s*, 10.

33. Dingledine, *Chronology*, 53–56, 62–67; *Unemployment Insurance in the 70's*, 8, 10; House of Commons, Standing Committee on Labour, Manpower, and Immigration, Minutes of Proceedings and Evidence, vol. 10, 15 Sept. 1970, 13; UIC Records, vol. 39, file 528-5 pt. 3, "Canadian Welfare Council Staff Submission on 'Unemployment Insurance in the 70s' to the House of Commons Standing Committee on Labour, Manpower, and Immigration," Oct. 1970, 7–9.

34. *Unemployment Insurance in the 70's*, 10; UIC Records, acc. 81-82/142, vol. 22, file 194-5 pt. 2, "Report to the UIC Regarding Proposals in the White Paper to the Extent These Would Affect Private Sickness and Maternity Wage Loss Replacement Plans," William M. Mercer Limited, 20 Jan. 1971.

35. Standing Committee on Labour, Manpower and Immigration, "Minutes of Proceedings and Evidence," vol. 10, 15 Sept. 1970, 11–12; Dingledine 61, 68.

36. *Canada Year Book*, 1974 (Ottawa: Ministry of Industry, Trade and Commerce, 1974), 338, 771; UIC, *Annual Report*, 1969.

37. Pal, "Revision and Retreat," 81.

38. *Income Security and Social Services*, 60; Dingledine, *Chronology*, 53–56, 62–67.

39. Only the self-employed, some casual workers, and citizens of other countries remained excluded from coverage. *Unemployment Insurance in the 70s*, 17; UIC Records, vol 58, file "UIAC Report and Minutes, 1967," "Actuarial Report to UIAC," Z. Jarkiewicz, 11 July 1967.

40. UIC Records, vol. 34, file 528-1 Pt. 13, "Should Contribute to Jobless Fund," Canadian Press clipping.

41. UIC Records, vol. 34, file 528-1 Pt. 8, Bay Roberts, Newfoundland resident to Department of the Attorney General, 23 Sept. 1968; Edmonton, Alberta resident to Prime Minister, 20 June 1968; Toronto, Ontario resident to Minister of Labour, 3 May 1968; Ottawa, Ontario resident to Chief Commissioner of UIC, 12 Nov. 1968; pt. 13, Windsor, Ontario resident to Bryce Mackasey, 10 May 1970; Principal of Timmins High and Vocational School to Jean Roy, MP, 2 Dec. 1969; Virden, Manitoba resident to Bryce Mackasey, 6 May 1970; vol. 39, file 528-5 Pt. 1, Canadian Teachers Federation Brief to Standing Committee on Labour, Manpower, and Immigration, 13 Oct. 1970.

42. UIC Records, vol. 71, file "Project Team," "Personal Factors in Public Opinion towards Unemployment Compensation," Portis, Lanphier and Golden, Oct. 1968, 3, 5, 31, 31a, 42.

43. House of Commons, *Debates*, 19 April 1971, 5038–9, 20 April 1971, 5081.

44. UIC Records, vol. 34, file 528-1 pt. 13, Winnipeg, Manitoba resident to Bryce Mackasey, 9 May 1970; Calgary, Alberta resident to UI Policy Committee, 23 April 1970; vol. 39, file 528-5 pt. 3, "Public Service Alliance of Canada."

45. UIC Records, vol. 34, file 528-1 pt. 8, Penticton, British Columbia resident to Minister of Manpower and Immigration, 14 Feb. 1968.

46. UIC Records, vol. 71, file "Project Team," "Personal Factors in Public Opinion towards Unemployment Compensation," Portis, Lanphier and Golden, Oct. 1968, 5.

47. *Unemployment Insurance in the 70's* 5, 8; *Canadian Annual Review for 1964*, 404; *Canadian Annual review for 1965*, 302, 316; *Canadian Annual review for 1966*, 252; *Canadian Annual Review for 1967*, 298.

48. Guest, *Social Security*, 148; Liberal Party Papers, vol. 1025, file "Labour," "Remarks by the Hon. John R. Nicholson, Minister of Labour, at the Conference 'Social Security Today and Tomorrow,'" 17 July 1967, 6, 9–12.

49. UIC Records, vol. 39, file 528-5 pt. 1, Bryce Mackasey to Richard Doyle, Editor of the *Globe and Mail*, 25 Sept. 1970; *Unemployment Insurance in the 70's*. 8; Treasury Board Records, vol. 1352, file 9720/456-1 Pt. 10, "A Proposal for Updating the UI Programme," UIC, 21 July 1969, 5.

50. UIC Records, vol. 71, file "Project Team," "Personal Factors in Public Opinion towards Unemployment Compensation," Portis, Lanphier and Golden, Oct. 1968. 5, 8, 14; acc. 90-91/132, vol. 2, file 200M pt. 5, "Committee of Inquiry into the UI Act: Proceedings of Public Hearings," vol. 5, 18 Dec. 1961, 620.

51. Rand Dyck, "The Canada Assistance Plan: The Ultimate in Cooperative Federalism," in: *Canadian Public Administration*, vol. 19 (Winter 1976), 588–89; Guest, *Social Security*, 155–59.

52. Standing Committee on Labour, Manpower and Immigration, "*Minutes of Proceedings and Evidence*," vol. 10, 15 Sept. 1970, 11.

53. Pal, "Revision and Retreat," 78; UIC Records, acc. 81-82/142, vol. 17, file 170-3-2-1 Pt. 1, UIC to Cabinet, 1 Feb. 1968.

54. Guest, *Social Security*, 166–68; PC Party Papers, vol. 398, file "Election 1965—Policy," "PC Policy Handbook 1968"; *Canadian Annual Review for 1969*, 15–17, 35.

55. UIC Records, vol. 39, file 528-5 pt. 3, "Canadian Welfare Council Staff Submission on 'Unemployment Insurance in the 70s' to the House of Commons Standing Committee on Labour, Manpower, and Immigration," Oct. 1970, 22.

56. Standing Committee on Labour, Manpower and Immigration, *Minutes of Proceedings and Evidence*, vol. 12, 17 Sept. 1970, 87–91, 99; vol. 18, 30 Sept. 1970, 75–77, 80–81, 85–6; vol. 20, 6 Oct. 1970, 8–10; *Canadian Annual Review of Politics and Public Affairs*, 1971, 358; UIC Records, vol. 39, file 528-5 pt. 1, "Not a Chosen State," *The Globe and Mail*, 24 Sept. 1970.

57. Pal, "Revision and Retreat," 80–81.

11

Integrating the Inuit

Social Work Practice in the Eastern Arctic, 1955–1963*

FRANK JAMES TESTER

IN A SHORT period between 1955 and the mid-1960s, what may have been the most dramatic process of social change ever experienced by any group of people in the world occurred in the Canadian Eastern Arctic. From scattered camps along the Arctic coast and the Keewatin interior, many Inuit moved to settlements where trading posts and church missions had been located for decades. The reasons for this consolidation are many. They include a dramatic decline in the price of Arctic fox pelts—virtually the only source of cash income for Inuit in the region.[1] Subsequently, Inuit became increasingly dependent upon family allowances and welfare, both of which were administered by the Royal Canadian Mounted Police (RCMP) and trading company officials, usually the manager of a Hudson's Bay Company post. This contributed to Inuit travelling to and remaining in the vicinity of these settlements. In some cases, Anglican and Catholic churches played a role in encouraging settlement around missions where Inuit children were schooled by priests and nuns.

Another reason for the movement to settlements was directly related to the introduction of social workers to the Eastern Arctic. The creation of the Department of National Health and Welfare in October 1944 was followed by the development within the department of the Indian and Northern Health Services Branch. In 1946, the service placed an x-ray machine on board the RMS *Nascopie* making its rounds of northern settlements as part of the annual Eastern Arctic Patrol. The tuberculosis epidemic subsequently identified was to change Inuit social relations forever, as were other diseases for which Inuit were immunologically ill prepared.[2] By 1954, about 450 Inuit TB patients had been evacuated to southern sanatoria. In 1958, Walter Rudnicki, head of the welfare division of the Arctic administration, reported that "from 800 to 1,000 Eskimo patients were admitted yearly to southern hospitals, mostly in Ontario, Manitoba and Alberta" (NAC, 1958a, p. 14).[3]

The task of coordinating this movement of people and dealing with rehabilitation and repatriation to home settlements was the initial reason for hiring northern social workers. Furthermore, many patients, once repatriated to the North, were deemed to be no longer capable of camp life. In 1957 and 1958, two rehabilitation centres were created, one in Rankin Inlet on the west coast of Hudson's Bay and another at Iqaluit (Frobisher Bay). These centres were designed to deal with this problem and the more general one of train-

---

* This chapter was first published as "Integrating the Inuit: Social Work Practice in the Eastern Arctic, 1955–1963," *Canadian Social Work Review*, 11, 2 (1994): 168–83.

ing Inuit for settlement life. Finally, not all movements were voluntary. Inuit relocated to the high Arctic in 1953 and within the Keewatin district following a number of deaths from starvation in the winter of 1957–58 had little choice but to go along with plans already made for them.[4]

Social Integration and Social Work Practice

During the period in question, there were no more than a half-dozen social workers in the Eastern Arctic and only several of these had formal social work training. The Ottawa-based director of field staff was a trained social worker. In addition to these few social workers, welfare teachers—teaching staff who performed some welfare-related functions along with the RCMP—were located in some settlements. By 1957 there were also 12 northern service officers with a community development role located in the larger settlements of the region.

The notion of integrating Inuit with Canadian society developed parallel to the decline in the Arctic fox trade. Previously, Arctic administrators—including the RCMP, which had a major responsibility for Arctic administration well into the 1950s—took a decidedly "Tory" approach to managing the Inuit. They were to be left alone; to be encouraged to pursue their traditional lifestyles relatively free of outside interference. Men like Henry Larsen, Head of the Arctic Division of the RCMP, berated even the Hudson's Bay Company for trapping Inuit within a wage-dependent economy. However, by the mid-1950s, the question was no longer whether Inuit should be integrated but rather "how" and "how fast."

By the early 1960s, following a period of conflicting directions in the development of Inuit policy, the direction had been set: "to give Eskimos the same rights, privileges, opportunities and responsibilities as all other Canadians—in short, to enable them to follow the natural life of Canada" (NAC, 1962d, p. 3). "Integration" was seen as a benevolent and desirable objective of aboriginal policy. The underlying logic permeated government thinking, as typified by the following quote from R.A.J. Phillips, at the time Assistant Director of Plans and Policy within the Department of Northern Affairs:

> The course now being followed is integration. The word "integration" is used in different ways by different people. My meaning is that Eskimos become part of the Canadian whole, benefitting by the achievements of our civilization, making their contribution to it.... One way with which all of you will be familiar is in the realm of art, where Eskimo stone sculpture has won world renown.... Integration may cost us money, and throw pitfalls before the Eskimos, but they and we can win by it. (NAC, 1959c, p. 2)

This approach to aboriginal policy was clearly consistent with a liberal world view, the notion of individual rights and of "no special status"—best exemplified by the White Paper on Indian Affairs which the Trudeau administration was to introduce in 1969.

Fears about the corrupting influence of the welfare state on Inuit independence highlight the contradictions found in the policy of assimilation. On one hand, Inuit were expected to integrate with a modern industrial wage economy. On the other, while participating, they were not to become dependent on the state when it failed to meet their basic needs. The fear was that Inuit would lose the ability to look after themselves, thus recreating a situation that was seen to be a problem for Indian administration. This sentiment was expressed clearly by L.H. Nicholson, Commissioner of the RCMP in the late 1950s and a territorial councillor:

> Now what are the dangers faced in the transition period? Surely the greatest one is that we will upset these people psychologically; give them the wrong ideas and the view of what is important in our way of life. Already we can see in some places a drop in their native characteristic of sturdy independence and a growth of objectionable habits, such as readiness to hang about settlements and live on handouts—government and other—petty thievery, and in the case of women, prostitution. (Nicholson, 1959, p. 23)

Social workers were to play a key role in the efforts to integrate Inuit with mainstream Canadian society. To describe the activities of these new helping professionals as addressing the social implications of rapid change is to be concerned solely with obvious functions. Beneath these activities lay the other important and often taken-for-granted role of integration.

In working for the assimilation of Inuit with mainstream Canadian society, social workers carried with them their own relatively unexamined cultural biases. Reporting on a visit to Inuit camps in May 1958, social worker Phyllis Harrison described her guide and his father's camp as follows:

> Our guide was not the community's most up-and-coming man.... On our return trip we spent one night in his father's camp, which left much to be desired in cleanliness as well as comfort. I bring this up simply to point out that the attributes he did display were those of an ordinary Eskimo and not an outstandingly progressive one. (Harrison, 1959, p. 111)

"Progress" was clearly to be measured by non-Inuit criteria. The norm for the new Inuit culture which social workers were helping to create was to be a nuclear family, wage-earning husband, and wife who cared for the home and family in a setting with standards of health and hygiene matching those of middle-class Canadians. Another piece produced by the same social worker is revealing of this agenda:

> Why did white people find it so important to keep houses clean? Why make a fuss about spring mud—it would soon go away.... How odd to expect neighbours' children to knock before walking into a house. Eskimo children had always been free to visit in any house they chose—it was their right, you didn't tell them they couldn't come in because their feet were muddy.... And time! At camp, there'd been nothing to divide time except night and day, hunger or the urge to sleep. Now two shiny clocks ticked busily—a sign of her over-anxiousness, not to forget when it was time for school—or Anawakaloo to go to work.

> In spite of these things, Kelougah and Anawakaloo never turn back. They've inherited from their fathers the spirit to cope with any challenge, with any hardship. They are learning many new things from the white men. But—they have something to teach too—how to be courageous and se-rene—when everything seems to go wrong. (Harrison, 1962, p. 16)

The deconstruction of this modernist discourse reveals a style which, unfortunately, still dominates much social work practice. The attempt to locate a very clear, value-laden agenda within a seemingly inoffensive verbal style—thus giving the appearance of "ob-jectivity" while giving credit to someone within a culture that the author is attempting to change—is transparent. The attempt to give credit by noting courage and serenity is patronizing at best, and the rhetorical question that introduces the passage could just as easily have been a positivistic statement.

In assimilating Inuit, the role of social workers was critical. The site of practice was not merely that of transforming external and symbolic realities (housing, clothing, food, modes of transport) but on changing internal dynamics (forms of social organization, social attitudes, and personal relationships). Three areas in which social workers exercised this role are examined: child welfare and adoptions, medical services and rehabilitation, and attempts to deal with the social and personal chaos created by the abuse of alcohol.

Redefining Family: Social Work and Traditional Adoption Practices

In the early 1950s, the state moved to regulate Inuit adoption practices. In Inuit culture, children are not regarded as narrowly belonging to a nuclear family and the practice of traditional adoption was widespread.[5] Adoption served other useful purposes. Inuit also used it to redistribute income within traditional family groupings.

As the crisis with the Eastern Arctic fox fur trade developed, family allowances be-came an important, and in many cases the only, source of income. Despite the rhetoric that Inuit should have the same rights and privileges as other Canadians, family allow-ances were paid to Inuit "in kind." This gave the state and its experts *de facto* control over elements of Inuit diet and, in particular, affected child-rearing practices. Inuit mothers were encouraged to feed their babies the pablum made available as one of the foods on the approved list of goods. They were provided with powdered milk and wire whippers for its preparation. In the Western Arctic, Inuit were even issued canned tomatoes.[6]

With a family allowance system in place, by sharing children with older parents or childless couples, families provided for those who would otherwise have been destitute. It was not a practice that welfare workers condoned, as revealed by the following report from the welfare teacher in Inukjouak:

> It seems to me to be in the best interest of the Eskimos for the RCMP to issue Family Allowances, but in the case of adopted children, and children whose parents are in hospital, as well as in instances where it is definitely proved that the Family Allowances clothing is being used by adults instead of by the children, for the welfare teacher to decide what is to be issued, and to take

charge of clothing issued so as to make sure that the child to whom it is issued will get it. (NAC, 1953, p. 3)

This subversion of state policy did not go unnoticed, and the northern administration moved to regulate traditional adoption (NWT Archives, 1956). It was feared that access to family allowances (as was claimed to be true of "relief") would contribute to Inuit indigence and Inuit "hanging about in settlements" when they should be on the land making a living. That there was little or no living to be made from the land still had not occurred to many northern officials—many of whom were based in Ottawa.

The solution to the problem was to attempt to regulate adoption. The result was to introduce Inuit to a court system and procedures firmly grounded in Canadian law, cultural norms, and practices. The following example of an attempt in 1959 by the social worker in Iqaluit to impose such practices on adoption proceedings is worthy of note. In this case, the social worker was upset by the behaviour of Justice Sissons of the Territorial Court. In preparing a case for the court, the social worker learned that the judge liked to bring together both the adopting and the natural parents for a "fatherly chat." She reported the following to Walter Rudnicki, head of the welfare division:

> The practice of a fatherly chat is not to be condemned in itself, and certainly to date as parents themselves have picked their own adoption homes, confidentiality is not an issue at present. However, if we are to develop good adoption practices I think we should try to establish as early as possible the court procedure we would hope to see handling adoptions if and when we have adoption of children needing homes going through the hands of the Welfare Officer to approved adoption home [sic] with which the real parents have no contact. (NAC, 1959a, p. 3–4)

Justice Sissons was ultimately to thwart these efforts. In 1961 he ruled that "adoption by Eskimo custom" was to be regarded as legal in every respect.

However, social administrators remained opposed to practices that undermined the Canadian cultural (and legal) bias for individual rights and the concept of children as "property" within Canadian legal jurisprudence:

> What criteria are to be applied, and by whom, in determining the existence of a so-called "neglect" situation in Eskimo custom adoptions and under what circumstances, if any can our Welfare Officers acting on behalf of the Superintendent of Child Welfare become actively involved in the case?... [T]he common good of the extended family or the group, seems to prevail over what we call the natural rights of the individual, in this case, the mother. (NAC, 1961, pp. 2–3)

In this case, the social worker's cultural bias for the "natural rights of the individual" was clearly to inform her practice among a group of people whose practices were grounded in another—and collective—tradition.

Medical Rehabilitation: Redefining Inuit Life

As noted, Walter Rudnicki, hired in December 1955, was the first professional social worker employed by the Arctic division of the Department of Northern Affairs and National
Resources. Interviewed in 1990, he indicated that his first job was to deal with the chaos
that developed as Inuit were relocated to southern sanatoria for treatment of tuberculosis.[7] The disruption of family and community life caused by this epidemic provided the
state with additional reasons for intervention—with humanitarian intent. Working within
the confines of the dominant ideology of the time, social workers may have believed their
actions were consistent with Inuit welfare. In practice, however, medical evacuations to
southern sanatoria provided new opportunities for the imposition of a modernist agenda.
This agenda is reflected in adoption policies and practices, the cultural biases inherent in
questions used by social workers to interview Inuit, and the stated purposes of the rehabilitation centres established to deal with ensuing medical problems.

Children, their education and integration were especially important to this agenda:

> A nine year old Eskimo boy on discharge from Moose Factory Hospital
> last year was sent to the Fort George residential school. His parents at Port
> Harrison had no knowledge of this arrangement and had assumed the boy
> was under continuing treatment. The boy was located after they had begun
> to make enquiries as to his whereabouts.
>
> Last summer, a five-year-old Eskimo girl was removed by a Fort Smith
> man from the Charles Camsell Hospital. He later reported to us that he had
> spoken to the child's mother and stated that she had agreed to this arrange-
> ment. As the Department had not participated in this plan, we have no idea
> as to what the wishes of the mother actually were. (NAC, 1956, p. 1)

Given the infectious nature of tuberculosis, children born to Inuit women in southern
sanatoria were removed and placed in non-Inuit foster homes. Thus, social workers in
Hamilton, Brandon (Manitoba), and Montreal, where the sanatoria were located, became
involved with a population about which they knew virtually nothing. Some of these children, as evidenced by the correspondence above, disappeared in the child care system.

Welfare workers hired by the department were sent to investigate the manner in which
southern children's aid societies were providing for Inuit infants and young people released from hospital who might be awaiting the discharge of a parent. A welfare worker
was hired to accompany the Eastern Arctic Patrol. The welfare services identified by the
director of the welfare division, Walter Rudnicki, were intended to address the social
chaos caused by the epidemic. On board the *C.D. Howe*, the welfare worker was to:

1) complete a social summary on each Eskimo evacuated to hospital;
2) evaluate how the hospitalization of an Eskimo—and especially a breadwinner or
   mother—would affect the family;
3) supervise the handling of tape-recorded messages and distribution of photographs
   to relatives in hospital;
4) follow up patients discharged in previous years;
5) report on any chronic welfare problems in the settlements visited so the Welfare
   Section could take subsequent action. (NAC, 1957, pp. 3–4)

However, the cultural biases of the administration and the modernist agenda are revealed by the questions welfare workers were asked to complete. These included details about the "Eskimo's estimated level of ability" and if the "Eskimo [was] a breadwinner, ... his or her efficiency" (NWT Archives, 1957a, p. iv).

The problems of rehabilitating patients and of repatriating them to their families led to the development of a rehabilitation centre at Iqaluit and another at Rankin Inlet. The programs run in these centres were for "persons out of hospital and those coming in from the land, including adult education in a general sense: housekeeping, child care, etc., with the objective that all rehabilitants learn what they could and move on, either to total self-sufficiency or their own optimum level" (Department of Northern Affairs and National Resources, 1963, p. 15). Activities included "organized hunting and fishing" (*Canadian Welfare*, 1962, p. 113).[8]

While these centres were badly needed and helped meet the material needs of Inuit, they also played a very obvious role in attempting to change the non-material or socio-psychological dimensions of Inuit culture, as revealed by the following comments by another northern welfare worker: "The Chairman asked for discussion about what the Rehabilitation Centre should hope to achieve. Mr. Zukerman mentioned its use on behalf of those who need to learn good work habits, i.e., punctuality and regular attendance, saving of money, how to get along with their employers" (*Canadian Welfare*, 1962, p. 113).

The disruptions caused by these epidemics and movements of people were considerable. Many Inuit, sent to the south for treatment, never made it home. Others were discharged with inadequate clothing for a northern environment. In some cases, young people being sent north were landed in the wrong community. Given the nature of travel at the time, they had to wait until the following year when the *C.D. Howe*, completing its annual Arctic patrol, could take them to their home settlements. Cultural biases and language barriers acted as compounding factors for social workers on the *C.D. Howe*, as the following report reveals:

> An evaluation of the Welfare Officer service at this point suggests *the very great importance of the social worker being able to communicate with the Eskimo in his own language*.... Such details as sorting out family relationships and exploring the resources for help within the relatives are very hard to obtain from the Eskimo, and all the more so when he is stunned by the thought of evacuation. In more than one case the [welfare officer] was not satisfied that a completely accurate report of the Eskimo's circumstances was obtained. For example, in the case of a child to be evacuated, where two interpreters had been involved ... three different persons in the camp were named at different times to be the child's adoptive mother. (NWT Archives, 1957b, pp. 5–6)

The disruption of family and community life caused by medical evacuation did not go unchallenged. In many settlements, Inuit used the clergy as a means of getting the message to public servants that evacuations to the south were destructive of northern families and communities. Subsequently, Donald Marsh, Anglican Bishop of the Arctic, hounded the government throughout the 1950s about improving communication between those evacuated to the south and their northern relatives. As noted, this contributed, in 1955, to the hiring of the first social worker in the department, Walter Rudnicki.

Regulating Desire: Alcohol and Sexuality in Frobisher Bay

An important development affecting the practice of social work in the Eastern Arctic was a decision in April of 1959 by Mr. Justice Sissons of the Territorial Court that Inuit were entitled to consume alcohol as was any other Canadian citizen. The basis for this little-appreciated decision was that, subject to a 1939 Supreme Court decision, Inuit were a federal responsibility.[9] Therefore, they were not subject to the discriminatory provisions of section 24 of the Northwest Territories Liquor Ordinance (NAC, 1959b, pp. 1–2). Previously, the northern administration had enacted a policy of restricting Inuit access. Paradoxically, the effect of recognizing a special relationship between the Crown and Inuit was, in this case, to give them, *de facto*, the same individual rights of citizenship afforded other Canadians within a liberal democratic tradition.

Subsequently, unrestricted access to liquor was to become a major concern of social workers and welfare administrators in Iqaluit and throughout the Eastern Arctic. The situation that developed highlights the contradictions of the policy of assimilation. With regard to alcohol, if Inuit were to have the same rights and privileges as other Canadians (even, as it turned out, if they did not want them), the resulting social disintegration was to become a major factor restricting their capacity to participate in Canadian society. Social workers were not only given responsibility for dealing with the ensuing social problems, but for finding a solution to Inuit drinking.

The impact of this change in status was immediately apparent. Statistics comparing indictable and summary conviction offences for Iqaluit with those for the rest of the country told the story.[10] For Canada as a whole, the rate per thousand for indictable offences in 1959 was 4.96. For Iqaluit in 1961, the figure was 109.0. For summary conviction offences the comparable figures were 30.96 and 393.0 respectively (NAC, 1962a, Table 2).

Social workers were responsible for dealing with alcohol-related behaviour. This was seen to include promiscuity on the part of Inuit females (but never non-Inuit men), dealing with delinquent behaviour, preparing histories for the many cases brought to court, and casework directed at Inuit with alcohol-related personal problems. Not surprisingly, the later was decidedly ineffective.

Attempts by northern social workers to regulate Inuit sexuality are illustrative of the internal contradictions they faced in trying to make a policy of assimilation work. At Iqaluit the concern was with the relationship between Inuit "girls" and non-Inuit men. There existed a policy of discouraging non-Inuit employees of government and other interests in the community from forming relationships with "Eskimo girls." In the case of Inuit women, integration was embedded with patriarchal values:

> It should be noted that this policy has not been applied uniformly to all Eskimo girls.... These exceptions have been made for selected girls who have been considered by their selectors to be more sophisticated and more socially acceptable. I hope, but I am far from certain, that it was the intention of those who supported the policy to assist the process of integration by

gradually admitting more and more Eskimo girls into this "select" group as they "qualified" for entrance. (NAC, 1958b, p. 2)

Asked to deal with girls who were "fraternizing with members of the U.S. Air-Force," the female welfare officer in Iqaluit was not as inclined to make a special case out of their behaviour as were male administrators. The men produced memos on the subject which included headings like "Immoral Activities—Frobisher Bay" (NAC, 1958c). The welfare officer asked to deal with the situation reported:

> Consider, that in their own culture many Eskimo marriages materealize [sic] out of the simple arrangement of living together. Also, sex is a fact of life to be met as simply and honestly as hunger or thirst. I doubt if much self denial practised [sic]. There is only a narrow margin between these girls [sic] behaviour and that of many other women of this community.... [I]f pre-marital relations are the ground work for marriage (and every one of these girls says she wants a non-Eskimo husband) then as far [as] they can see, they are headed straight for marital bliss. (NAC, 1959c, p. 3)

In the case of Inuit, the regulation of desire seems to have been primarily a concern of male administrators.

Despite being caught in an impossible situation—helping Inuit to help themselves to become good Canadian citizens (as defined by the colonizing culture)—northern social workers often advocated a greater Inuit role in community decision-making. These initiatives were intended merely to extend liberal democratic decision-making to northern communities and, eventually, Inuit councils. Ultimately, however, they were to give impetus to new forms of resistance and to practices that contributed to Inuit demands for self-government. Attempts to deal with the alcohol problem are illustrative.

In July 1960, a Branch Committee of the Arctic administration was established to deal with the problem. This evolved into the Committee on Social Adjustment in the Arctic. In addition to members of the RCMP and the Indian and Northern Health Service, social workers were well represented. Participants included Walter Rudnicki, Chief of the Welfare Division, and "Bud" Neville, the Superintendent of Welfare. The committee met for the first time on December 13, 1961. Five meetings were held between that date and 27 April 27 1962. Members heard every conceivable analysis and prescription for dealing with the problem. In many cases, the same factors identified as causes were put forward as solutions. Inuit were suffering from the social upheaval that accompanied rapid social change. The solution? According to Dr. Willis of the health service, it was anything that sped progress toward bringing the two cultures together. According to Bud Neville, inequality was the source of the problem, and the solution lay in improved housing and economic betterment (NWT Archives, 1961, pp. 4–5).

With the assistance of his field staff, Walter Rudnicki, as chair of the committee, pushed toward what was ultimately seen as a partial solution. Whether or not the proposals developed constituted much of a remedy is perhaps less important than reinforcement of the idea that, increasingly, Inuit themselves should be consulted and even have control over such matters.

Harold Zukerman, the welfare officer in Iqaluit, was asked to prepare a report on the use of liquor by Inuit. In the document he submitted on 29 March 1962, in addition to an exhaustive list of the impacts that excessive drinking was having on the community, he intimated two solutions. One was to eliminate over-the-counter beer sales. The other was to introduce a two- to three-week waiting period for the purchase of beer, similar to one already in place for liquor. He noted that: "The Eskimo people ask why the white man allows them to buy beer if they did not want the Eskimo people to drink.... Some Eskimo people feel that no liquor or beer should be sold the Eskimo people and at least there should be no beer store" (NWT Archives, 1962, p. 5). Clearly, Inuit were prepared to reject the legal and liberal notions of equality that had been forced upon them in the name of "progress." To do so was clearly seen by many to be in their own best interests.

These suggestions were formalized and, with Rudnicki in the chair, it was agreed that not only would the Commissioner of the Northwest Territories be asked to implement the suggestions put forward by Zukerman, but that the administrator for the Eastern Arctic be asked "to refer the measures to the Eskimo Council for an expression of opinion" (NAC, 1962b, p. 3). Opinion is what they got. "Angnaituk had at the moment asked and was wondering why in the world did the white people make this liquor and beer for when there was no use for it.... He said that liquor was one of the useless things in the world for anyone to use because it only causes people a lot of trouble" (NAC, 1962c, p. 3).

Resistance and Change: Challenging the State Agenda

As the historical records reveal, much day-to-day social work practice involved the delivery of conventional services in very unconventional circumstances. Services were dominated by the hegemonic discourse of the day. Inuit were to be made full citizens and were to participate as equals within Canadian society. Canadian society was advanced as "civilized," with much to offer a more primitive people who could no longer survive as they had for thousands of years. Not only was change inevitable, it was to be guided by the hands of helping professionals, among them social workers. Much casework was trapped within this reality.

Similarly, much social development practice and community work shared the state's agenda of assimilation. However, the liberal democratic ideals of social development practice contained contradictory elements and unrealized possibilities. In the 1960s, the creation of settlement councils and Inuit associations gave opportunity to dissenting voices.

A 1959 report on the role of northern service officers in community development described their role as follows. "Changes in their way of life are inevitably bringing problems to many Eskimo people. The task of guiding Eskimos during this difficult transition period falls upon an increasing staff of Northern Service Officers and trained Social Workers" (NWT Archives, 1959, p. 1). Guided integration was thus the aim of community work. The northern service officer was:

> expected to get to know [Inuit], to gain their confidence, respect, friendship and cooperation and to help them to help themselves. To accomplish this he assists the Eskimos in social and political development by organizing group effort and community life, encouraging broad participation in local decision

and action and working toward responsible and articulate pulbic [sic] opinion. (NWT Archives, 1956, pp. 3–4)

What might happen if Inuit did not like the direction in which they were being guided was never considered. However, the voice of resistance was beginning to be heard.

The movement of people through the region for medical and other reasons had, by the early 1960s, created an entirely different configuration of population than had existed in the region a decade earlier. Resistance to non-Inuit ideas about addressing the resulting problems is clearly evident from the following record of a speech given by John Ayaruark of Rankin Inlet. Mr. Ayaruark was attending the tenth meeting of the Committee on Eskimo Affairs, held in Ottawa in 1959. His remarks were made in the presence of every important bureaucrat in the department as well as the Minister of Northern Affairs and Renewable Resources, Alvin Hamilton, and Prime Minister John Diefenbaker:

> Referring specifically to Rankin Inlet, Mr. Ayaruark described it as a settlement populated by people from many scattered places, speaking different dialects, some of whom, particularly from inland Keewatin, were confused and unsettled by their new environment. He pointed out that, like the white man, *the Eskimo had his own ideas about what he wanted to do with his life and his homeland, and the wishes of the Eskimo people should be respected* [emphasis added]. (NWT Archives, 1959, p. 7)

The modernist agenda of integration was entirely assumed within the liberal—and what were believed to be humanitarian—precepts of the day. Ultimately, resistance to this guided integration was considerable, giving rise, in the Eastern Arctic, to Inuit Tapirisat of Canada, committed to the struggle for Inuit rights and self-determination; conflict over the devolution of power from the Territorial Government to settlement councils, in the case of mining exploration in the Baker Lake area, the challenging of federal jurisdiction (Herchmer, 1980, pp. 2–8; Tester, 1980, pp. 9–12); and, ultimately, to the Nunavut self-government agreement for establishing, in the Eastern Arctic, "a new Nunavut Territory, with its own Legislative Assembly and public government, separate from the Government of the remainder of the Northwest Territories" (Minister of Indian Affairs and Northern Development and Tungavik, 1993, Article 4.1.1, p. 23).

Conclusion

The 1950s was a period of late modernism characterized, in Canada, by a profound conviction in the correctness of liberal euro-Canadian values. Consistent with the ethic of high modernism, the role of northern social workers was to bring all the benefits, rights, and privileges of modern civilization to a "primitive" people. The benefits of Canadian society were assumed, as were the legal, social, and institutional forms that accompanied them. In the North, these heavy assumptions clashed with a culture which, while decimated by historical experience, pursued personal and collective forms of resistance that challenged state-mandated objectives and, at the field level, social work practice.

Notes

1. From a high of $36 in 1945, Inuit received as little as $3.50 for the same pelt in 1949. See Tester (1993), p. 112.
2. These included outbreaks of typhoid in the 1940s and an epidemic of poliomyelitis in the Keewatin district in 1949. Regular outbreaks of measles, influenza, and infantile diarrhea in a population lacking immunological resistance to such diseases contributed to a high infant mortality rate and left others permanently disabled. See Hildes (1960), pp. 1255–57.
3. The Northwest Territories (NWT) Archives are located in the Prince of Wales Northern Heritage Centre, Yellowknife, N.W.T., and the National Archives of Canada (NAC) are in Ottawa, Ontario. In a few cases, box numbers are not indicated for documents from the Stevenson Collection as the author was given permission to examine the collection and to take copies prior to it being properly catalogued.
4. These relocations and a detailed discussion of the many contributing factors are found in chapters 3 and 4 of Tammarniit [Mistakes]: Inuit Relocation in the Eastern Arctic by Frank Tester and Peter Kulchyski (1994).
5. In 1960, a paper by W. E. Willmot reporting on research conducted at Inukjouak (Port Harrison), Quebec, suggested that 16% of all children in the community were adopted. The author also noted that children were commonly adopted not because they did not have a home but rather because the adopting couples wanted a child (Willmot, 1960, p. 50).
6. For a complete discussion of family allowances, their administration, and the rationale behind the policy of issuing them "in kind," see Tester & Kulchyski (1994), especially pp. 71–94.
7. Interview held with Walter Rudnicki, former head of the Welfare Division, Department of Northern Affairs and National Resources, Ottawa, December 9, 1990.
8. This article was prepared by editorial staff of the Department of Northern Affairs and National Resources. It is illustrative of the close relationship between the state and the social work profession. Then, as now, the state designated a hegemonic role for many social workers. In the 1950s, their role was to inculcate in both Inuit and other Canadian populations the idea that what was being done for the Inuit was in their best interest, while in fact the prescribed direction served nicely the objectives of a state committed to capitalist development of the country, including the North.
9. For a thorough discussion of this case, see Kulchyski (1994), chap. 2.
10. This may not, of course, be entirely true. The likely element of discrimination against Inuit offenders by law enforcement officers and the courts must be taken into account in interpreting the data. Indictable offences included breaking and entering, theft, assault, indecent assault, and forgery. Summary convictions included liquor violations, common assault, and causing wilful damage. It appears from the reports prepared on this situation that alcohol was involved in virtually all of the summary convictions for common assault and wilful damage. In settlements where there was virtually no access to alcohol, RCMP annual reports make it clear that such problems were uncommon.

References

Canadian Welfare (1962, May 15). "Arctic Welfare Services." Canadian Welfare 38, no. 3, 111–13.

Department of Northern Affairs and National Resources (1962). "Minutes of the Second Arctic District Conference," Ottawa, February 19–22.

Harrison, P. (1959). "Social Work Goes North." Canadian Welfare 35, no. 3, 110–15.

Harrison, P. (1962). "Eskimos in Transition." North 9, no. 5, 14–16.

Herchmer, H. (1980). "'Caribou Eskimos' v. The Canadian Legal System." Northern Perspectives 8, no. 3, 2–8.

Hildes, J.A. (1960). "Health Problems in the Arctic." Canadian Medical Association Journal 83, no. 24, 1255–57.

Kulchyski, P. (1994). Unjust Relations: Aboriginal Rights in Canadian Courts. Toronto: Oxford University Press.

Minister of Indian Affairs and Northern Development and the Tungavik (1993). *Agreement Between the Inuit of the Nunavut Settlement Area and Her Majesty the Queen in Right of Canada.* Ottawa: Indian and Northern Affairs Canada.

National Archives of Canada (NAC) (1953, November 30). "Welfare Teacher's Report for November 1953," RG 85, vol. 1269, file 1000/304, pt. 2.

National Archives of Canada (1956, October 17). "Memorandum for Mr. W. Nason, Chief, Legal Division. Re: Child Welfare," RG 85, vol. 1473, file 251-1, pt. 5.

National Archives of Canada (1957, February 12). "Memorandum for the Director: Welfare Services—'C.D. Howe'," RG 85, vol. 1275, file 201-1, pt. 35.

National Archives of Canada (1958a, May 26). "Minutes of the Ninth Meeting of the Committee on Eskimo Affairs," RG 85, vol. 1514, file 1012-1, pt. 7.

National Archives of Canada (1958b, July 11). "Memorandum for the Chief, Arctic Division, Eskimo Welfare—Frobisher Bay," RG 85, vol. 1064, file 1009-16, pt. 1.

National Archives of Canada (1958c, December 10). "Memorandum for Mr. Cunningham, Immoral Activities—Frobisher Bay," RG 85, vol. 1064, file 1009-16, pt. 1.

National Archives of Canada (1959a, April 22). "Memorandum for Mr. W. Rudnicki," Ottawa Ontario. RG 85, vol. 1064, file 1009-16, pt. 1.

National Archives of Canada (1959b, April 24). "Memorandum for the Administrator f [sic] the Arctic: A Judicial Decision Affecting Federal and Territorial Relations as Applied to Eskimos," RG 85, vol. 1064, file 1009-16, pt. 1.

National Archives of Canada (1959c, April). "The Canadian Eskimo," National Commission on the Indian Canadian of the Canadian Association for Adult Education, Bulletin VI, remarks by R. A. J. Phillips to a conference on the Canadian Eskimo, RG 85, vol. 1003-2-7, pt. 3.

National Archives of Canada (1961, December 11). "Memorandum for the Director, Adoption of Peesee," RG 85, vol. 1947, file A-560-1, pt. 1.

National Archives of Canada (1962a, January 16). "Court Statistics—Frobisher Bay," RG 85, vol. 1947, file A-540-1-2.

National Archives of Canada (1962b, May 11). "Committee on Social Adjustment," Minutes of the Fifth Meeting, RG 85, vol. 1947, file A-560-1-3.

National Archives of Canada (1962c, June 6). "Minutes of the Community Council Special Meeting, Frobisher Bay, N.W.T.," RG 85, vol. 1947, file A-560-1-3.

National Archives of Canada (1962d, October 4). "Statement regarding earlier objectives of Canadian Government Policy with respect to Eskimos," RG 85, vol. 1961, file A-1012-1, pt. 1.

Nicholson, L.H. (1959). "The Problem of the People," *The Beaver*, Outfit 289, 20–24.

Northwest Territories (NWT) Archives (1950, July 7). "Eskimo Adoption Procedure," Ottawa, Alex Stevenson Collection, N92-023, Box 10.

Northwest Territories Archives (1956, December 28). "Material from Arctic Division for the Minister's use," Alex Stevenson Collection, N92-023.

Northwest Territories Archives (1957a, June 17). "Memorandum for Mr. W. Rudnicki," Ottawa, Alex Stevenson Collection, N92-023.

Northwest Territories Archives (1957b). "Report of the Welfare Officer of the Eastern Arctic Patrol, 1957, Quebec to Churchill Section," Alex Stevenson Collection, N92-023.

Northwest Territories Archives (1959, April 17). Taken from an item with the handwritten title "Mr. Stevenson's copy, Arctic Administration Activities and Plans for 1959," Alex Stevenson Collection, N92-023.

Northwest Territories Archives (27 December 1961). "Committee on Social Adjustment in the Arctic," Minutes of the Second Meeting, Alex Stevenson Collection, N92-023.

Northwest Territories Archives (29 March 1962). "Report on the Use of Liquor by the Eskimo People at Frobisher Bay," Alex Stevenson Collection, N92-023.

Tester, F.J. (1980). "And the First Shall Be Last: Some Social Implications of the Baker Lake Decision." *Northern Perspectives* 8, no. 3, 9–12.

Tester, F.J. (1993). "Serializing Inuit Culture: The Administration of 'Relief' in the Eastern Arctic, 1940–1953." *Canadian Social Work Review* 10, no. 1, p. 109–23.

Tester, F. J., & P. Kulchyski (1994). *Tammarniit: Inuit and Relocation in the Eastern Arctic, 1939–1963.* Vancouver: University of British Columbia Press.

Willmot, W.E. (1960). "The Flexibility of Eskimo Social Organization." *Anthropologica* 2, no. 1, 48–59.

12

First Nations Child and Family Services, 1982–1992

*Facing the Realities**

PETER HUDSON AND SHARON TAYLOR-HENLEY

THE 1980s USHERED IN a period which appeared to represent a dramatic break with past policies with the establishment of a number of First Nations child and family services, which assumed responsibility for a major service previously delivered (or contracted to a non-profit, non-aboriginal agency) by the provinces. Of 592 First Nations communities in Canada, 207 currently have service agreements enabling some form of control over child and family services. In Manitoba, for example, seven First Nations agencies have been established with powers and authority very similar to those of the non-profit Children's Aid Societies. The arrangement has been called the delegated authority model because it implies the granting of provincial authority to these agencies.

We take for granted the principle of aboriginal control. A wealth of literature documents the need for this development (for example, Johnston, 1983). Nothing noted here is intended to question this. In order to consolidate and build on these very positive gains in the area of child and family services, however, the focus of debate needs to turn from repetitious arguments about the need for First Nations control to a serious discussion of issues of implementation. These are many, and include the objections of First Nations leaders to the constitutional implications and service development constraints of the delegated authority model. Some have been discussed previously (Taylor-Henley & Hudson, 1992), but an implementation issue that has received only brief attention to date (for example, see Armitage, 1993, p. 169) is the degree of difficulty of the task assumed by the First Nations agencies and an apparent reluctance to confront it.

Stagnation and Setback

A period of rapid expansion and progress of First Nations child and family services agencies from the early to late 1980s has been followed by a period of stagnation. Very few new agreements have been effected since 1987, when Indian and Northern Affairs Canada (INAC) conducted a review of the costs of these services (INAC, 1987). In Manitoba agreements have never been renewed. Existing arrangements have simply been continued

---

* This chapter was first published as "First Nations Child and Family Services, 1982–1992: Facing the Realities," *Canadian Social Work Review* 11, 1 (1994): 89–102.

through annual contribution agreements. Even more disturbing has been the widespread criticism directed at the performance of the agencies in the discharge of their obligation to protect children, to the extent that their credibility has been questioned (*Winnipeg Free Press*, January 23, 1993). General inattention on the part of key stakeholders to the many issues involved in implementing these services has been a major factor inhibiting the ability of the new systems to move smoothly and continuously forward.

Degree of Difficulty Issue

An examination of the enormity of this task begins with the political climate within which the First Nations child and family service agencies came into being. The new agencies were created following a ground swell of criticism levelled at the manner in which the non-aboriginal agencies were conducting their mandate to protect children (Hudson & McKenzie, 1981; Kimmelman, 1983). The analysis suggested that the interventions of the provincial agencies contributed to high rates of admissions of aboriginal children into care, their placement away from the communities, and the frequently reported poor outcomes for these children. In addition the agencies were seen to be assaulting sovereign communities, and their actions were seen as tantamount to cultural genocide.

This analysis is true as far as it goes, and the polemic that accompanied it served its purpose in providing leverage for at least a partial control of child and family services in some First Nations communities. However, although the whole child welfare system, including the law, the regulations, and the courts, not just the workers and their agencies, acted inappropriately in responding to the conditions encountered during the so-called "sixties scoop,"[1] the system was not itself responsible for those conditions or the pressing social needs associated with them. These conditions still prevail. If the analysis remains static, placing all blame on the child welfare system and assuming that aboriginal control will solve the problem, then the new agencies are being set up to fail. Unless the existing analysis is expanded to include an acknowledgement of these conditions and their roots, the First Nations agencies will remain a classic example of what Havemann (1989) referred to as "indigenisation," whereby communities administer unto their own misery.

Severe social and economic damage and widespread pathologies have arisen directly out of the colonized and marginalized status of aboriginal people within Canada. In terms of socio-economic status, volumes of studies over the past 30 years, from the Hawthorne report (1967) to the Penner report (1983) as well as census data up to 1991, have all documented a similar discouraging story. Aboriginal Canadians, when compared to non-aboriginal Canadians, are seen to be overrepresented in the ranks of the unemployed, to have lower rates of participation in the labour force, to rely more heavily on transfer payments, and to have much lower individual and family incomes as well as much lower educational achievement.

Also well documented are the related, if not consequent, indices of social morbidities. Research in progress by the authors regarding the needs of Ojibway adolescents indicates that alcohol abuse is so pervasive that it invariably features first on any list of community problems. Several other indices are intertwined with alcohol abuse in a complex matrix in which causes and effects are almost inseparable. Violent deaths occur three times oftener than the national average. Suicide rates are over twice the national average. Life expectancy for First Nations people is lower both for men and women than for the general population, and aboriginal people tend to require acute medical care more often. Infant mortality rates are twice the national average (INAC, 1989b). Very specific to the task of the child and family services is the apparent pervasiveness of violence in all its forms directed especially against women and children. In one medium-sized First Nations community, no less than 50 children have recently been involved in disclosures of sexual abuse that has persisted over a long period of time, sometimes intergenerationally (*Winnipeg Free Press*, July 23 & 24, 1992). A caregiver in another First Nations community informed us that until recently an estimated 80 percent of all young women had been victims at least once and often routinely of gang rape, and that many of the victims had come to accept such incidences as a normal part of growing up in the community.[2]

The available data do suggest that the socioeconomic conditions of First Nations people relative to the rest of Canadians have improved somewhat over time. Life expectancy, incomes, labour force participation, and post-secondary education enrolment have all improved in the last 20 years (INAC, 1989a). Such trends are cause for hope that, through conscious and planned policies and action, change can occur. The movement to First Nations control of secondary school education, as well as funding for post-secondary education (unfortunately now threatened), has undoubtedly contributed to higher enrolments of First Nations people. Without hope for and evidence of change, there would be no point to our call for further advances in the planning and delivery of child and family services. Such change requires as clear and accurate an analysis of the obstacles and difficulties to be faced as possible. One such obstacle is that, despite these encouraging signs, the problems that the First Nations child and family services are expected to "treat" are of considerably greater proportions than even those of their "mainstream" counterparts, which also have unrealistic expectations placed upon them by the community.[3] The almost total breakdown in many communities of the balance between those available to give and capable of giving help and those in need places an extraordinary burden upon the newly organized formal system of First Nations child and family services.

First Nations' Reluctance to Confront

As we have implied, if these realities are not squarely faced, no basis exists to move out of the period of stagnation. For First Nations people, a reluctance to confront these has its roots in criticism of what they perceive to be the preoccupation of non-aboriginal people with the socioeconomic status and social morbidities of aboriginal people. LaRocque, to take one of many examples, in discussing stereotypes of aboriginal people, refers to their being perceived by non-aboriginals as "social problems." She argues that such preoccupations have provided a negative label for a whole group of people and discount the heterogeneity of that group. More importantly she argues that such preoccupations have a "blaming the victim" quality, which completely ignores the reasons based in oppression and dispossession that would explain why aboriginal communities might experience such problems in greater proportions than the rest of the population (LaRocque, 1984). Subsequent authors argue further that such a preoccupation with pathology results in services that violate a first principle: the need to seek and build on strength (McKenzie &

Hudson, 1985). Confronting the realities of some of the widespread pathologies evident in many communities, while recognizing their strengths and resources, is a very difficult line to walk. In the past, as well as in many circles in the present, error has been on the side of preoccupation with pathology. For the moment, it is sufficient to state that speaking of the pathology has an aspect of "political incorrectness" that inhibits a systematic and sustained problem-solving process.

Some cultural characteristics within the aboriginal communities interact with the political economy of the reserve system, as well as the larger regional and national politics of First Nations which compound these inhibitions. For example, there is said to be some reluctance to speak of evil because of the belief that it then becomes a self-fulfilling prophecy. This comment is made especially in relation to sexual abuse and suicide. Dr. Clare Brandt tells the story of a 13-year-old girl who committed suicide after telling many people in the community about her intentions. Afterwards, these mostly quite caring people said that they did not want to talk to her about it because to do so would have made it happen (Canadian Psychiatric Association, 1989, p. 132). It reinforces a universal tendency to deny, such as the "don't feel, don't talk, don't trust" prescription internalized by victims and survivors of various kinds of abuse (Hodgson, 1987).

In addition, the deeply rooted value of non-interference can easily be understood as a taboo against acting to change pathological situations. In contemporary culture it may sometimes take on a fatalistic quality (Canadian Psychiatric Association, 1989, pp. 139–140). Finally, the very nature of some of the pathologies at the community level block confrontation. A recent study refers to the breakdown in communal caring that occurred in some communities from the 1950s to the 1980s following any period of rapid and usually negative change, such as a forced relocation or the destruction of a local economy. Reference is also made to the incipient violence that emerged in these communities at the same time, making people otherwise willing to care (for example, for the children of others) fearful of reprisal should they do so or speak out (Timpson, 1993). First-hand testimonies from the people in the communities themselves speak of what has been called the conspiracy of silence and the real fear of consequences, such as harsh criticism or even physical violence, which can be visited upon those who break it (Canadian Psychiatric Association, 1987, pp. 75–76, 83–84).

A further inhibition at the community, regional, and national levels has less to do with culture as with political aspiration. Large amounts of energy of the leadership at all levels, but particularly the chiefs, have gone into advancing the cause of self-government. Conceptually, it is easy enough to separate recognition of the right to self-government and its actual exercise. In practice such separation is less obvious. Non-aboriginal people are quick enough to point to alcohol abuse, child sexual abuse, and violence as evidence of "unreadiness" for self-government. Armitage (1993) quotes one First Nations spokesperson who expressed exactly these sentiments in cautioning against providing statistics and information to the government and media who use the information against First Nations people (p. 168). Even First Nations people have expressed doubts about self-government when they look at social, political, and economic conditions currently prevailing in many of the communities (see, for example, *Winnipeg Free Press*, March 29, 1992).[4] Thus, those who currently speak for First Nations people in an official capacity have much invested in showing their communities to the rest of Canada in the best possible light and downplaying the very real problems, especially the social ones, which are the most difficult to attribute to external forces.

Federal Reluctance to Confront

The federal government, too, has been reluctant to confront the full reality of the enormous task faced by the First Nations agencies; not surprisingly, this is motivated by cost containment policies. The case begins with noting the continuing failure of the federal government to endorse unambiguously the notion of aboriginal inherent right to self-government. Boldt and Long examine a series of policies and actions of the federal government over the past 10 years, ranging from land claims, to natural resources, to social services, and argue that this failure is attributable to the knowledge on the part of federal officials that such recognition would imply an admission of guilt and complicity in the appalling damage done to the economic and social fabric of First Nations communities. They conclude: "For the Federal government Indian special status constitutes a political, economic, social, legal and administrative liability of growing proportions and complexity—a liability it wants to be rid of" (Boldt & Long, 1988, p. 42). The second part of our case refers specifically to federal policy with respect to child and family services. A document prepared in 1989, but still current, outlines principles for agreements affecting child and family services, a central one of which is that they "will be in accordance with provincial legislation" (INAC, 1989c). This prescription is absolutely unnecessary even given the current constitutional impasse. There has been a longstanding debate about the extent of the meaning of section 91(24) of the *Constitution Act* (1867), which refers to federal responsibility for "Indians and lands reserved for Indians," and Section 88 of the *Indian Act*, which states that provincial responsibility holds unless specifically mentioned in the *Act* (social services are not mentioned), but it has never been resolved. There are no legal obstacles in the way of the federal government interpreting Section 91 more broadly than it has in the past or than it is doing now. This is clearly a matter of political will.

The relationship between this odd championing of provincial rights on the part of the federal government and its preoccupation with deficits and cost-cutting seems to be clear. Certainly the possibility that ongoing provincial authority could lead at some future date to provincial assumption of a greater proportion of the costs as well cannot have been overlooked by INAC officials, the minister, and cabinet. This argument is consistent with what others have seen as the main thrust of federal Indian policy in the past 10 years (for example, see Long & Boldt, 1988, pp. 9, 44). The recent refusal by the federal government to accept billings for Social Allowances paid to Status Indian people living off reserve stands as an example. It would also be consistent with a more general current federal strategy of offloading (see, for example, National Council on Welfare, 1991). It would be inconsistent with a commitment to advance self-government. A less than happy conclusion, but a believable one, would be that cost containment is of higher priority than First Nations self-government in federal government circles. In any event the policies and trends at both the macro level of the constitutional process and the micro level of First Nations child and family services are hardly conducive to an honest and full appraisal by federal officials of the depth of the problems faced by the communities and the service agencies.

Specific evidence for this reluctance begins with budget allocations which show that, while there has been a rapid increase in allocations to First Nations agencies, these have not kept pace with service demand, even closely. For example, there was an increase in INAC expenditures to the new agencies between 1981 and 1986 from $33.7 million to $72.4 million (INAC, 1987, p. 33). At the same time, however, the number of hours of service provided by the agencies increased by 600 percent, and days of care provided increased nearly 200 percent (INAC, 1987, p. 35). During 1989 and 1990 one of the Manitoba First Nations agencies received no increase in its operating budget (BDO Ward Mallette, 1991, p. 34). That year the agency reported an increase of 52 percent in abuse investigations. The following year this increased a further 35 percent (Manitoba Family Services, 1992, p. 85).[5]

Finally we come to the most recent federal proposals for a funding formula. The formula does have some strengths. It would make INAC's treatment of each agency fairer and more equitable, since the formula would apply in the same way to each. It does appear to have some built-in allowances for differing degrees of difficulty faced by each community in the provision to scale payments to indices of socio-economic well-being in the community, but these are not well formulated. It also guarantees, for the time being at least, that no agency would receive less than the previous year's allocation even if the formula would so indicate.

What is disturbing is that, despite these positive aspects, the proposal moves in exactly the opposite direction to that called for by any realistic appraisal of the depth and breadth of the problems in most of the First Nations communities. Funding is to be directed solely towards "child centred" activities "such as child abuse and neglect prevention" (BDO Ward Mallette, 1991, p. 7). Commenting on this provision the consultants' report states:

> It is beyond the ability of these organisations to eliminate the causes of child abuse and neglect.... Given the critical nature of the role of these organisations in the current communities, it is vital that the services be comprehensive and delivered in a highly competent manner. They will necessarily cover a wider scope of activity than their urban counterparts who have available to them, a range of alternate services. (BDO Ward Mallette, 1991, p. 10)

This narrowing of the mandate of child and family services to only last-resort measures to protect the health and safety of a child judged at risk is consistent with a similar trend, similarly motivated by cost containment, in the funding by provincial governments of mainstream child and family services. As the above quotation indicates, however, the consequences of this trend are even more serious for the First Nations agencies. This typically non-aboriginal design of social welfare services is flawed in two important respects. First, it flies in the face of culturally appropriate ways of caring. Secondly, it assumes that social problems are exceptional, as opposed to epidemic; as we have seen, the latter is the case in many First Nations communities.

The Way Ahead

So far we have argued that neither the First Nations child and family service agencies, nor the communities, nor the federal government is fully facing up to these widespread difficulties for different reasons. The full promise and effectiveness of the agencies cannot be realized until these problems are more realistically assessed and planned for. A discussion about treatment and healing illustrates this point.

Distinguishing between treatment and healing flows directly from the comments about the narrowness with which the new federal funding proposals interpret the mandate of the agencies. Rix Rogers distinguishes between these two words as follows:

> Victims of child sexual abuse are not responsible for the exploitation they have suffered. While they need to come to grips with their feelings of power-lessness and of being violated, it must be understood that the emphasis must be on healing rather than treating. Treatment in its simplest sense implies the presence of illness. Not all victims are ill, but all are hurting and need an opportunity to heal. (Rogers, 1990, p. 80)

A simple chart expands on this distinction. Generally speaking, the treatment approach, as it is characterized here, conforms to non-aboriginal ways of caring. The healing approach conforms to aboriginal ways. In terms of this distinction, the aboriginal ways, far from being obsolete, remain appropriate, given the realities of many First Nations communities. Healing is required in addition to treatment.

Table 12.1. Distinction Between Treatment and Healing

Treatment	Healing
1) Implies very severe symptoms and pathologies requiring intensive therapy.	1) Implies lesser pathologies requiring "life tasks" approaches.
2) Implies focus on the individual.	2) Implies focus on the whole community.
3) Implies relatively short term (e.g., three months) in residential treatment centre.	3) Implies relatively long term.
4) Often partialized to focus on specific problem or symptoms.	4) Implies the need to work with the whole person, as well as the whole community. This includes the spiritual dimension (Hodgson, 1987). In fact the person can only be helped within the context of his or her community.

There are a few examples in which an emphasis on healing a whole community have demonstrated success or at least promise. As early as the mid-seventies, 100 percent of the Alkali Lake First Nations community was affected by alcoholism. Ten years later it had moved to 95 percent sobriety. This was accomplished by envisioning the community as the source of both the problem and the solution: seeing it as a therapeutic community. In action this involved a mixture of changing expectations of what was acceptable behaviour (band councillors and other officials were required to model total sobriety); converting the recently sober into helpers in the process, thereby reinforcing their continued sobriety while expanding community involvement; sanctions (for example, threat of court action if an offender in an alcohol-related offence declined the offer of help); and supports (such as periodic community celebrations of people's ongoing sobriety or return from treatment).[6]

In the Hollow Water First Nations community a program known as Community Holistic Circle Healing has been established. This program consists of a network of paid caregivers in the community along with volunteers who provide support for those who disclose incidents of sexual abuse. Among other steps in the process is a special gathering at which the abuser, the victim(s), people from the families of each, the network personnel, and significant others in the community are present. The offence is openly discussed in the circle, and the abuser is encouraged to acknowledge the offence and the harm done. Towards the end some conclusions are reached about the appropriate restitution, called a Healing Contract. The progress of the contract is followed and a cleansing ceremony is held to recognize its fulfilment and the restoration of harmony and balance. It is envisaged that periodic celebrations will be held to recognize in a more general way the healing and cleansing of community members. Peer support groups are used to protect and heal the victim as well as the abuser and "passive" family members. The non-aboriginal court system may be used as a last resort in the event of non-compliance on the part of the abuser (Taylor-Henley & Hill, 1990).

These two brief examples illustrate a number of relevant points. First is that they are responses to social problems which are epidemic. While doubts may be expressed at the effectiveness of such experiments as the Hollow Water Circle,[7] they present more promising alternatives to the treatment model, which is based on problems being exceptional. In Alkali Lake and Hollow Water, not a person in the community has been untouched in some way by the problems to which the programs attempt to respond. Abusers had been victims; many children are currently victimized; whole families are involved in some way, and many adults who are neither currently abusers nor victims are survivors. Secondly, the fact that the programs in these communities, especially Alkali Lake, are cited so often suggests that they are exceptions rather than the rule. Hundreds of other First Nations communities suffer from the same epidemics, and yet programs such as these are few and far between.

Given the degree of difficulty described, a massive effort is required to begin the process of restoration to well-being. Without it, or, still worse, without even recognition of the extent of the problem, the First Nations child and family service agencies and their workers are left highly vulnerable. They are being held accountable for the many children at risk in their communities and for conditions not within their power to alter. An otherwise very sympathetic judge, who recently conducted an inquest into the death of a ward of one of the agencies, demonstrated this vulnerability by faulting in large part the lack of training and experience of the workers.[8] This was indeed a problem, but it was also evident that social and political conditions in the community were such that, even if all the workers had possessed graduate degrees, the death would still quite likely have occurred (Manitoba Family Services, 1992). While vigilance is needed in the areas of competence of service and monitoring of children in need of protection, faulting the agency when something goes wrong in these circumstances is akin to blaming someone's death on a handful of physicians caught in the middle of a cholera epidemic.

Criticisms levelled at the non-aboriginal agencies for their pre-1980s performance are not misplaced, but the role of the social, economic, and political conditions that they encountered, rooted in what Wotherspoon (1993) has called First Nations' marginalized status in the capitalist economy (pp. 87–94), has not been fully acknowledged as a factor in high rates of apprehensions of children. The First Nations agencies that assumed their role need to account for the same conditions and root causes. Such accounting calls for a much broader and expanded role for the First Nations child and family service agencies, which would include initiatives directed towards the healing of whole communities. If the communities are reluctant to admit the extent of the damage in their midst, and non-aboriginal governments are complicit for fear of acknowledging the full extent of their responsibilities, the development of such approaches is inhibited. The "conspiracy of silence" in some First Nations communities and the philosophy behind federal funding formulas and provincial legislation encourage approaches only appropriate to exceptional problems. They discourage approaches that deal with widespread structural problems and pathologies. Breaking through the denial is a necessary first step to further progress. Tentative beginnings have been made by the Assembly of Manitoba Chiefs in its "Plan of Action for Community Healing" (AMC, 1991) and in the establishment of a Task Force on Child and Family Services commissioned jointly with the province of Manitoba. Although the results are yet to be seen, this is cause for optimism. We still await some sign of movement from the federal party.

Notes

1. The term "sixties scoop" was coined by Patrick Johnston (1983) to refer to the large numbers of Status Indian and other aboriginal children who were removed from the care of their parents or sometimes extended family caregivers during the two decades between 1960 and 1980.

2. Personal interview, May 1993. Permission not given to name the informant or the community.

3. This theme also has applicability in non-aboriginal communities and in non-aboriginal child and family services. Marilyn Callahan (1993), for example, states: "Probably the most significant outcome of this [case] approach to work is that it encourages a sense of individual responsibility and obscures the impact of social conditions. It is clear in the critical incidents that circumstances well beyond the control of the worker may actually determine the outcome of any investigation. Workers are expected to carry out their jobs in the face of inadequate resources, and clients often live in inadequate housing in chronically depressed neighbourhoods and suffer constant poverty" (p. 77).

4. Many of these aboriginal critics have been women concerned that the reality of self-government would consolidate the power of men in the communities, who at best would ignore the concerns of women and children and at worst would be among the perpetrators. Many of the critics are women living in urban areas or otherwise one step removed from reserve politics.

5. The escalation in service loads and budget allocations was partly a result of transfers from provincial caseloads. Thus, increasing. demand for service arising out of community pathology is exaggerated in these figures. By the same token, some of the rising expenditures are taken from funds diverted from payments previously made to the provinces on behalf of First Nations children, rather than new money.

6. This story has been told in a variety of sources, both print and audiovisual. The immediate source for this version is Hodgson (1987).

7. For example, the evaluation report of the program revealed that the women in the community were sceptical about the efficacy of the final stage of the process: reconciliation and forgiveness. Their related concern was with lack of follow-up and protection for women and children who had disclosed. The men in the community did not share these concerns (Taylor-Henley & Hill, 1990, pp. 16–17).

8. Space does not permit a discussion of training and education programs for First Nations service providers, but the points raised in this article also apply to these. Most existing programs do not acknowledge the serious problems facing communities. They therefore tend to be unrealistic in what they can accomplish. Dismal retention rates attest to their failure (Hull, 1987). Programs that recognize the need to heal the healers—a need argued by Hodgson (cited in Martens, 1988, pp. 128–129)—and that provide the necessary supports and flexible time lines show greater success (McKenzie & Mitchinson, 1989).

References

Armitage, A. (1993). "Family and Child Welfare in First Nations Communities." In B. Wharf, ed., *Rethinking Child Welfare in Canada*, pp. 131–171. Toronto: McClelland & Stewart.

Assembly of Manitoba Chiefs (AMC) (1991). "Special Chiefs Assembly on Family Violence: Community Healing," Brokenhead, Manitoba, 16 December.

BDO Ward Mallette (1991). "Critique of the Proposed Federal Funding Formula for Child and Family Services." Draft document, BDO Ward Mallette, Winnipeg.

Boldt, M., & A. Long (1988). "Native Indian Self-Government: Instrument of Autonomy or Assimilation?" In A. Long & M. Boldt, eds., *Governments in Conflict*. Toronto: University of Toronto Press.

Callahan, M. (1993). "The Administrative and Practice Context: Perspectives from the Front Line." In B. Wharf, ed., *Rethinking Child Welfare in Canada*, pp. 64–97. Toronto: McClelland & Stewart.

Canadian Psychiatric Association (1987). "Family Violence: A Native Perspective." Conference Proceedings, CPA, Section on Native Mental Health, London, Ontario.

Canadian Psychiatric Association (1989). "The Native Parent in a Changing World." Conference Proceedings, CPA, Section on Native Mental Health, Thunder Bay.

Hawthorne, H.B. (1967). *A Survey of the Contemporary Indians of Canada*. Ottawa: Indian Affairs Branch.

Havemann, P. (1989). "Law, State and Canada's Indigenous Peoples." In T. Caputo et al., eds., *Law and Society: A Critical Perspective*. Toronto: Harcourt Brace Jovanovich Canada.

Hodgson, M. (1987). "Indian Communities Develop Futuristic Addiction Treatment and Health Approach." Unpublished paper, Nechi Institute, Edmonton.

Hudson, P., & B. McKenzie (1981). "Child Welfare and Native People: The Extension of Colonialism." *Social Worker* 49, no. 2.

Hull, J. (1987). *An Overview of the Educational Characteristics of Registered Indians in Canada*. Ottawa: Indian and Northern Affairs Canada.

Indian and Northern Affairs Canada (INAC) (1987). *Indian Child and Family Services in Canada: Final Report*. Ottawa: Child and Family Services Task Force.

Indian and Northern Affairs Canada (1989a). *Basic Departmental Data*. Ottawa: INAC.

Indian and Northern Affairs Canada (1989b). *Highlights of Aboriginal Conditions 1981–2001: Part II, Social Conditions*. Ottawa: INAC.

Indian and Northern Affairs Canada (1989c). *Indian Child and Family Services Management Regime Discussion Paper*. Ottawa: INAC.

Johnston, P. (1983). *Native Children and the Child Welfare System*. Toronto: James Lorimer in association with the Canadian Council on Social Development.

Kimmelman, E. (1983). *No Quiet Place: Report of the Review Committee on Indian and Metis Adoptions and Placements*. Winnipeg: Province of Manitoba.

LaRocque, E. (1984). "Three Conventional Approaches to Native People in Society and in Literature." Saskatchewan Library Association, Mary Donaldson Memorial Lecture.

Long, A., & M. Boldt, eds. (1988). *Governments in Conflict*. Toronto: University of Toronto Press.

Manitoba Family Services (1992). *Annual Report 1991–92*. Winnipeg: Queen's Printer.

Martens, T. (1988). *The Spirit Weeps*. Edmonton: Nechi Institute.

McKenzie, B., & P. Hudson (1985). "Native Children, Child Welfare, and the Colonisation of Native People." In K. Levitt & B. Wharf, eds., *The Challenge of Child Welfare*. Vancouver: UBC Press.

McKenzie, B., & K. Mitchinson (1989). "Social Work Education for Empowerment: The Manitoba Experience." *Canadian Social Work Review* 6, no. 1, 112–125.

National Council on Welfare (1991). *Funding Health and Higher Education: Danger Looming*. Ottawa: NCW.

Penner, K. (1983). *Indian Self-Government in Canada: Report of the Special Committee*. Ottawa: Queen's Printer.

Rogers, R. (1990). *Reaching for Solutions: The Report of the Special Advisor to the Minister of National Health and Welfare on Child Sexual Abuse in Canada*. Ottawa: Queen's Printer.

Taylor-Henley, S., & E. Hill (1990). "Treatment and Healing, An Evaluation: Community Holistic Circle Healing." Unpublished paper, University of Manitoba.

Taylor-Henley, S., & P. Hudson (1992). "Aboriginal Self-Government and Social Services: First Nations–Provincial Relationships." *Canadian Public Policy* 18, no. 1, 13–26.

Timpson, J. (1993). "Four Decades of Child Welfare Services to Native Indians in Ontario." Doctoral thesis, Wilfrid Laurier University.

Winnipeg Free Press (1992, March 29). "Native Rebels Meet in Bid to Get Self-Government Stalled."

Winnipeg Free Press (1992, July 23). "Abuse Probe Stuns Police."

Winnipeg Free Press (1992, July 24). "Abuse Report Too Hot, Shelved. Author Says Study Revealed Epidemic."

Winnipeg Free Press (1993, January 23). "Aboriginal Agencies under Gun."

Wotherspoon, T., & V. Satzewich (1993). *First Nations: Race, Class and Gender Relations*. Scarborough, Ont.: Nelson.

13

Eroding Canadian Social Welfare

The Mulroney Legacy, 1984–1993*

PATRICIA EVANS

Introduction

IN THE LAST DECADE, Canadian social programmes have been threatened by the same pressures that confront other industrialized nations. These include the impact of two recessions, the challenge to maintain competitiveness in the face of globalization, and mounting concern over the levels of government spending and debt. During the same period, Canada has also experienced rising levels of unemployment, increasing numbers of single mothers, and the aging of the population. As in other English-speaking countries, the conflicting pressures to spend more *and* to spend less have not resulted in overall reductions in social spending, but they have led to significant changes to the social policy landscape.

Although frequently grouped with the United States as a liberal and residual welfare state, Canada's social welfare tradition is differentiated by universal components (health care, old age pensions, and until recently, family allowance), more comprehensive unemployment insurance, and greater attention to the strategy of income supplementation. Unlike Britain or the United States, Canada in the 1980s did not produce a new-right movement of the strength of Thatcherism or Reaganism to provide the ideological spearhead to attack social spending. Instead, the 1984 decisive victory of the Progressive Conservative government led by Brian Mulroney was won on a platform that promised both to attend to the deficit and to maintain and improve social programmes as a "sacred trust." The discourse of the new right never emerged in its more extreme forms, but ultimately, this did not prevent major incursions into Canadian social programmes. The changes, though significant, were often accomplished, with little fanfare or outcry, in small and incremental steps.

The direction of policy during the Mulroney years was made clear in the first major address of the Minister of Finance, Michael Wilson in November 1984 (Canada, 1984). Economic growth was to be achieved by buttressing the private sector through de-regulation, removing counter-productive subsidies and reducing the federal deficit. The twin principles of social and fiscal responsibility were to guide the "improvement and redesign" of social programmes. Social responsibility meant that, "wherever possible, and to a greater extent than is the case today, scarce resources should be diverted first to those in greatest

---

* This chapter was first published as "Eroding Canadian Social Welfare: The Mulroney Legacy, 1984–1993," *Social Policy and Administration* 28, 2 (1994): 107–119.

need" (Canada, 1984: 71). This emphasis on targeting led to the eventual elimination of family allowance and increased the fragility of universality in other social programmes. Fiscal responsibility equated with the principle that "the best income security is a job, and that government expenditure must be allocated to provide immediate employment opportunities" (Canada, 1984: 71). Over time, this translated into efforts to move income support recipients into the labour market by cutting unemployment insurance, by targeting them for short-term employment programmes, and by increasing provincial interest in participation requirements as a condition of benefits.

Restoring "fiscal flexibility" was the third objective to impact directly on Canadian social programmes during the Mulroney years. This was to be achieved by reducing expenditures rather than increasing revenues, and federal transfer payments to individuals and the provinces became the target for deficit reduction: "The challenge over time, will be to limit the growth of these transfer programs in an equitable, effective and enduring way" (Canada, 1984: 67). The pursuit of fiscal flexibility has sharply reduced the federal presence in social programmes in what is very likely to prove an enduring change.

This article assesses changes to Canadian social welfare during the years of the Mulroney government, which ended in June 1993 with the election of his successor, Kim Campbell, the first woman to serve as Canada's Prime Minister. In particular, the three themes of "social responsibility," "fiscal responsibility," and "fiscal flexibility" are examined for their impact on the contours of the Canadian social welfare landscape. The Canadian experience illustrates how a government, committed to bolstering market forces, has "become adept at obscuring the real impact of what it is doing by couching changes within the context of a progressive principle" (Muszynski, 1992: 171–72).

Social Responsibility: The Quiet Death of Family Allowance

The principle of "social responsibility," spelled out in the first major policy speech from the Department of Finance in 1984, translated into the strategy of "targeting," a term that became increasingly familiar during the Mulroney years. While targeting is often regarded as "newspeak" for leaner and meaner welfare provisions, the income supplements that Canada instituted in the 1960s account, in part, for the low incidence of poverty among the elderly, by comparison with their US and UK counterparts (Hedstrom and Ringen, 1990: Table 4.6). This, however, was not the approach to targeting that the Mulroney government had in mind. Instead, the principle of "social responsibility" translated into cut-backs to universal benefits to children and the elderly. In announcing a review of these programmes, the Minister of Finance announced that it "will help to ensure that Canada's social safety net remains one of the most comprehensive and fair in the world, as well as efficient and well-directed, in a period when government's financial capacity is heavily constrained" (Canada, 1984: 71). Although family allowance was called a "sacred trust" in 1984, a slow and gradual process began in 1985 which culminated in its elimination in 1992. The process illustrates, in the context of English-speaking countries, a distinctive feature of Canadian targeting. Unlike Britain or Australia, Canadian family allowance became a taxable benefit in 1973, and it was the tax system which ultimately sheltered the unobtrusive but effective changes that showed "considerable political subtlety" (Banting, 1991: 33) and were aptly labelled the "politics of stealth" (Gray, 1990).

The May 1985 budget spelled out the first steps in targeting. Child and elderly benefits would no longer be fully indexed, and automatic increases would only "kick in" after inflation exceeded 3 percent. The value of these benefits would therefore quietly and gradually erode over time. However, the seniors mounted such a successful protest that the government was forced to restore full indexing to their benefits. Whereas the children's lobby was not as well organized, the value of the benefit much smaller, and children's benefits remained partially de-indexed. The reversal of policy on elderly benefits was viewed as a major defeat for government and it is generally agreed that an important lesson was learned: change must be slow and skillfully managed (Johnson, 1987; Rice, 1987). Just how well the lesson was learned became apparent over time.

In 1989, a surtax was imposed on the family allowance and on the old age pension. This additional tax-back began at incomes over $50,000, and the full value of benefits was recovered in the case of family allowance at $55,240 and $76,332 for the pension. An independent but government-funded citizens' advisory group commented, "This 'clawback' on child and elderly benefits is the most significant change in social policy in a generation because it marks the end of universality, a fundamental and long-standing principle of Canada's system of social benefits" (National Council of Welfare, 1989: 1). Although the clawback initially affected 14 percent of all families with children, it was estimated that the proportion would double over the next eight years (Battle, 1990). Despite some positive changes that were also introduced at this time, overall spending on child benefits declined between 1984–1990 by 21 percent, in constant dollars (Drover, 1992). Although upper-income families sustained the greatest losses and the welfare poor benefited, middle-income families experienced significant declines in benefits, and the working poor lost benefits they could ill afford (National Council of Welfare, 1990, Appendix B). In addition, these changes to child benefits occurred in the context of an increasing tax burden on lower-income families (Battle, 1990).

The 1989 clawback effectively ended the universality of family allowance, because some families had their entire benefit taxed back. Also gone was a recognition of the costs and value of children and the commitment to horizontal equity that Canadians had first made in 1945 with the institution of family allowance. But the formal and explicit abolition of family allowance occurred on 1 January 1993, with a major restructuring of child benefits which amalgamated family allowance, an additional income-related supplement, and a flat-rate child tax credit into a monthly income-tested benefit, called the Child Tax Benefit.

The desire to target the new Child Tax Benefit was not accompanied by a commitment to vertical equity. The poorest of families, those dependent upon social assistance, gain nothing because the value of the new integrated benefit is virtually identical to the previous patchwork of benefits.[1] The working poor are now eligible for a supplement to a maximum of $500 a year per family, but it begins to disappear when net income reaches $21,000 (Caledon, 1992). This threshold is lower than Canada's widely used, but unofficial poverty line, which was set at $23,792 for two adults and two children for 1991 (Statistics Canada, 1993b). The levels of benefits and thresholds for the Child Tax Benefit, and the earned-income supplement, are also only partially indexed.[2]

The Canadian experience in targeting child benefits, and the slow death of family allowance, indicates the dilemmas of maintaining universal benefits in a climate of fiscal restraint. Universal entitlements reinforce the idea of social citizenship and equality of status, but, on their own, cannot do much to reduce income inequality. Yet if the original transfer and/or its post-tax benefit is kept low in the interests of more general redistributive objectives, universal benefits may lose their capacity to promote either social solidarity or social protection. Canadian family allowance was worth about a dollar a day per child but it would have been inconceivable in 1984 to abolish what Mulroney then termed a "sacred trust." However, its slow demise through a series of complicated and poorly understood "technical" changes, suggests that in the end, Canadians were left not certain as to whether there was much left to defend. While efforts to increase the selectivity of social welfare benefits are apparent in a range of industrialized countries (Taylor, 1990), the Canadian experience in dismantling universality in child benefits is unique among the English-speaking countries.

Work Incentives: Fiscal Responsibility or Fiscal Response?

Fiscal responsibility, announced the Finance Minister in 1984, meant that government spending must ensure that Canadians who could work had the opportunities to do so, rather than rely on income support programmes. In the context of a firmly conservative agenda that combines deficit reduction as a major priority and a commitment to market forces to drive employment growth, it is not surprising that the supply side of the labour market, individuals and their "human capital," became the identified problem, rather than the lack of jobs. The responses came in two major initiatives that reflect the "stick" and the "carrot" of work incentives. The "stick" emerged as cutbacks to Unemployment Insurance (UI), while the second initiative, the expansion of employment opportunities appears, at first glance, more positive.

The Minister of Finance's 1984 statement echoed a theme from the previous Liberal government: Unemployment Insurance provisions were too generous and required a major overhaul. In 1990, major changes were introduced that reduced the amount of benefits in payment by increasing the number of weeks of employment that could be required as a condition of benefit, and decreasing the length of the benefit period.[3] The disqualification period for "voluntary job-leavers" was extended and their benefits were reduced. But perhaps the most significant change was the withdrawal of approximately $2 billion in federal funds, leaving UI entirely financed through employers and employee premiums. The federal government had effectively distanced itself from the financial consequences of those of its own policies which had served to increase unemployment, such as free trade, high interest rates and value-added tax. In addition, only $800 million of the $2 billion saved was redirected to training and, overall, the training budget did not increase (Campbell, 1992).

In April, 1993, further changes were made to restrict UI benefits, and "voluntary" job-leavers and individuals fired for misconduct were cut off from benefits entirely. Although sexual harassment, child care problems, and hazardous conditions of employment are recognized in the legislation as legitimate reasons for leaving employment, there is considerable concern about the interpretation of these provisions, and the level of proof that will be required for substantiation. Benefit levels for *all* new claimants were also reduced from 60 percent of insurable earnings to 57 percent. These changes will increase the provincial social assistance caseloads, and it is hardly surprising that the most vociferous opposition should have come from Quebec, where 20 percent of the working age population are UI or welfare recipients (Gherson, 1993). These cuts in social protection, and the shift from the relatively better support available through UI to the very low levels of social assistance, are made at a time when Canadians are most vulnerable. Unemployment increased from 7.5 percent in 1989 to 11.3 percent in 1992 (Statistics Canada, 1993a) and the jobs that are available are increasingly divided into those that demand a high level of skill and provide good wages, and those that offer part-time, temporary and insecure employment (Ternowetsky, 1990; Betcherman, 1992).

The federal moves in employment training initially appear more progressive. However there is little question that Canadian spending on labour market programmes is low. A recent OECD survey indicated that Canada spends three times as much on income maintenance as it does on labour market programmes, an imbalance that places it first out of nine countries (Demers, 1992). The 1985 Canadian Jobs Strategy (CJS) did target training to the most disadvantaged, including social assistance recipients, but paid less attention to direct job creation (Prince and Rice, 1989). The CJS did not even inject new money into the training area, but financed new programmes by cancelling old ones (Campbell, 1992). The CJS emphasis on short-term on-the-job training, rather than on longer-term skill development, may respond to the requirements of the low-paid and expanding service sector, but it is unlikely to meet the needs of those individuals who must be able to move from entry-level jobs into higher-skilled and better paid employment if they are to support their families (Cohen, 1992).

Meanwhile federal policies have increased the pressures on provincial budgets, and concern to reduce the costs of social assistance has grown. This is, of course, the climate that encourages the "stick" rather than the work incentive "carrot," and Canada is not alone in its interest in US-style workfare (Ogburn, 1986; Walker, 1991). Because "work-for-welfare" programmes have never been eligible for federal cost-sharing, the US influence is most evident in the broader strategy of workfare that links benefits to participation in a variety of employment-related activities (Evans, 1993).[4] Benefit levels in Quebec's new Work and Employment Incentives Programme, for example, vary according to whether an individual is regarded as participating or not participating, available or not available, for employment programs (National Council of Welfare, 1992b). A recent widely "leaked" document from the left-leaning Ontario NDP government indicated that they are considering a plan that would require social assistance recipients to engage in "opportunity planning" or risk a reduction in their benefits (Ontario, 1992).

The trend of tying benefits to participation in employment-related activities raises particular issues for single mothers, who comprise an important component of provincial social assistance caseloads. While Canadian policy has been more concerned to move single mothers from social assistance to employment than is the case in Britain, these efforts generally have not been as aggressive, persistent, or regressive as has been true in the United States (Evans, 1992). Nonetheless, single mothers remain the target for work incentives in the Canadian social assistance system and when efforts to move them into employment are not matched by efforts to ensure the availability of jobs or child care, the thin line between the positive and negative ends of the work incentive spectrum is easily crossed. Ontario is now considering a work requirement for single mothers and Alberta has altered its work requirement to include all mothers whose youngest child is aged two or more (Ontario, 1992; National Council of Welfare, 1992b). Ironically, this emphasis on single mothers' employment is occurring at a time when the federal government has abandoned its earlier plans to provide a national child care programme, and is actually "capping" contributions to the programmes that fund provincial child-care subsidies.

The traditional notion of the Canadian "safety net" is being replaced with a vision of social programs that serve as a "springboard" into employment. Yet, while few would argue with the statement "that the best income security is a job" (Canada, 1984: 71), the actions of the Mulroney government have done little to contribute to this objective. Although the permeability of the Canadian economy to outside influences imposes a constraint on achieving full employment, it does not, by itself, explain the continuing high rate of unemployment (O'Connor, 1989). The experience of the low-employment countries such as Sweden and Austria, suggest the political, rather than the economic, nature of the decision to pursue full employment (Demers, 1992; Mishra, 1990), but these are possible lessons yet to be learned. As Robert Campbell (1992: 29–30) suggests, "Neither unemployment nor the globalization challenge has affected the Mulroney's government's broad monetary and fiscal policies—both of which remain divorced from counter-cyclical or employment-generating goals."

Fiscal "Flexibility": The Fading Federal Presence

The federal role in Canadian social programmes historically has reflected both fiscal and political imperatives. The *1867 Act of Confederation* gave the provinces jurisdiction over social welfare, but assigned the federal government the power to raise revenue. This imbalance between responsibility to provide, and ability to pay, is mediated through cost-sharing arrangements that fund social programmes, and equalization payments that redress inequities between richer and poorer provinces. As in many countries, the broad foundations for social welfare were laid in the prosperous postwar period, a time (in this case) of federal economic and political dominance. However, federal economics are now dominated by a concern to reduce social spending, the free trade agreements that Mulroney has vigorously pursued are accompanied by pressures to harmonize social policies, and constitutional discord challenges the political authority of the federal level of government. During the Mulroney years, these have combined to recast the federal role in the Canadian welfare state.

The Mulroney government's pursuit of "fiscal flexibility" has resulted in significant reductions in cost-shared social programmes. Not surprisingly, this has sharply exacerbated the ongoing tension between federal and provincial governments with respect to two major cost-sharing provisions, Established Program Financing (EPF) and the Canada Assistance Plan (CAP). The federal portion of spending on post-secondary education, hospital and medical care (EPF), is delivered through a transfer of both taxing power and cash payments to the provinces. Every budget since Mulroney took office in 1984 has held the rate of the EPF increase below that prescribed by the GNP and population-based formula. In 1990, a freeze on EPF rates was announced that will last until 1995, by which time it is estimated that federal spending will provide a smaller per capita contribution to health care and post-secondary education than when EPF was first established in 1977

(National Council of Welfare, 1991). The federal contribution is also structured to phase out the cash payments portion, casting serious doubt about it's future ability to uphold national standards in social programs. An important leverage to the *Canada Health Act* (1984) had been the threat of withholding cash transfers to a province that fails to comply with the ban on "extra-billing" by doctors and hospital user fees.

Restoring fiscal flexibility was also the rationale for limiting the federal contribution to the CAP, the cost-sharing programme that funds provincially designed and administered social assistance programmes and social services for those "in need." Up until 1990, the costs of these programmes were shared equally by federal and provincial levels of government. Concern about the open-endedness of this funding led to the 1990 "cap on CAP," when the federal government limited CAP increases to five percent in the country's wealthiest provinces (Ontario, Alberta, and British Columbia). Ontario, hard hit by the recession, has fared particularly badly. Between 1989–90 and 1991–92 the numbers on social assistance grew by 31 percent and the total expenditures increased from $2.5 to $5.1 billion. The costs for fiscal year 1992–93 are estimated at $6.2 billion (Ontario, 1992) and the federal government's share, once 50 percent, is expected to account for only 28 percent (National Council of Welfare, 1992b).

The federal role in social programs has also been buffeted by the same general trends toward economic globalization that confront other countries, but there are distinctive aspects. Canada's relatively small population, strung out along its southern border, makes it particularly susceptible to US influence. The 1988 Canada–US Free Trade Agreement, and the upcoming 1994 North American Free Trade Agreement, which will include Mexico, have increased concern about the "Americanization" of economic and social policy. While the impact of these agreements on social policy is controversial, they can hardly help but exacerbate the tendency to "harmonise" the more generous aspects of Canadian policies to ensure a level-playing field (for discussion, see Drover, 1988).

The federal government's role in social programmes is also under pressure from the constitutional issues that have dominated the Canadian political agenda in recent years. The latest round of constitutional discord began in 1980 with the defeat of the sovereignty-association vote in Quebec, and was quickly followed in 1982 by Pierre Trudeau's repatriation of the Canadian Constitution that occurred without Quebec's signature.[5] A set of constitutional amendments, known as the Meech Lake Accord, was intended to remedy this situation, but some provinces objected to the "distinct society" clause, designed to bring Quebec on board.

The Charlottetown Accord, the most recent chapter in the Canadian constitutional saga, served as a lightning rod for an array of malaises and tensions that existed, not only between Quebec and what became known as the ROC (Rest of Canada), but also amongst regions, between notions of individual versus collective rights, and between different levels of government. The Accord was praised as offering a genuinely creative approach to resolving these differences and ensuring Canadian unity, and it was also condemned as the blueprint for the break-up of the country. The major social policy concern focused on the Accord's constitutional entrenchment of a more limited federal role in social programs. Responsibility for labour market training was to devolve to the provinces, and provinces would, for the first time, be able to opt out of any new Canada wide cost-shared programme, with financial compensation. It was not clear how much the Accord, if passed, would have exacerbated the forces of decentralization. But it is clear that its overwhelming defeat in provincial referenda in October, 1992, neither protects the federal role in social programmes nor guarantees the status quo. The fiscal and political forces that have been powerfully eroding the federal presence in social programmes, show no sign of abating.

Assessing the Mulroney Legacy

The Mulroney era ended in June 1993, with several of the traditional indicators of economic "well-being" in decline. The economic and social policies of the Mulroney government had reduced the capacity of both the labour market and social programmes to protect the incomes of Canadians. The unemployment rate averaged 11.3 for 1992, which, except for 1983, was the highest in twenty-five years (Statistics Canada, 1993a: 236). The growing polarization between good and bad jobs that had occurred over the previous two decades was continuing to expand while the shift from full-time to part-time employment, and the increase in short-term layoffs, bore witness to important changes taking place in the structure of employment (Betcherman, 1992; Yalnizyan, 1992). These trends have been particularly important in the traditional female job sectors, and have especially important implications for the ability of the growing number of single mothers, the majority of whom live in poverty, to support themselves and their families through paid work.

Family poverty, which had decreased between 1984–1989, is once again on the increase. Between 1990 and 1991, the last year for which information is available, the overall family poverty rate increased from 12 to 13 percent.[6] While very young families improved their position somewhat, the incidence of poverty for families headed by individuals between 25 and 34 years old jumped from 15 to 19 percent. By comparison, the position of single mothers deteriorated only slightly, but their rates were already extraordinarily high. In 1991, six of every ten single mothers were poor (Lochhead, 1993). The United Nations, in an unusually sharp statement, recently rebuked Canada for failing to address its continuing high levels of child poverty (York, 1993).

The Mulroney government's general agenda included the trio of deficit reduction, fiscal restraint, and increasing international competitiveness through deregulation, private sector initiatives and the liberalization of trade. This was accompanied by a social welfare agenda that targeted benefits, paid greater attention to the stick than the carrot in work incentives, and limited federal contributions to cost-shared programmes. All of these directions are completely consistent with a neo-conservative agenda, but in the Canadian case, the "logic" of the economic market, appeals to vertical equity, and an incremental, and often technical, approach to change substituted for the "bombastic discourse" (Lightman and Irving, 1991) of the overt ideological attacks on social spending that took place in the US and Britain. The evidence presented in this article suggests that the Canadian social welfare landscape has suffered significant erosion since Brian Mulroney took office in 1984, and since 1989 its pace has quickened and its effects have been more severe.

The slow strangulation and final elimination of family allowance raises serious questions, in Canada at least, about the future of universality in income transfer programmes. It remains in a formal manner in the old age pension: although all continue to receive it, some will have it entirely taxed back. The gradual demise of the Canadian family allowance illustrates the way that the objectives of solidarity and citizenship, that have traditionally been associated with universal programmes, can so easily recede in favour of the more explicitly redistributive goals of targeted programs. The low levels of the new Child Tax Benefit indicate that universality can disappear without any increased commitment to re-distribution if the changes are incremental, couched in the language of reform, and poorly understood. Furthermore the fragility of universality is not limited to income support programmes. Medicare seems likely to be the next area to witness a slow but fundamental transformation. Although it was the Mulroney government in 1984 that implemented leg-islation designed to eliminate "extra-billing" by doctors, the possibility of user-fees is now regularly discussed, and provinces are beginning to "de-insure" some medical procedures that are considered to be non-essential.

The specific contours of the social welfare landscape as they relate to work and welfare issues are also shifting. The Unemployment Insurance programme has been significantly tightened and there is accumulating evidence that work-conditioning in social assistance is increasing (National Council of Welfare, 1992b). In response to deficit concerns, the federal fiscal presence in social programmes is fading while political pressures for decen-tralization provide an additional rationale for a failure to provide leadership in the social policy field. The "Americanization" of Canadian social policy is occurring, but the forces that are levelling the social welfare field extend well beyond free trade.

As governments across the major industrialized nations confront the imperatives of global markets and respond to mounting deficits, social programmes are tailored to fit leaner budgets. With the possible exception of the Great Depression, there has not been a time in recent history when the integration of economic and social policy was more im-portant. During the nine years of the Mulroney government, however, social programmes have become increasingly identified as the problem, rather than part of the solution. The challenge of reorienting the Canadian economy to expand its productive and high wage sectors is consistent with increasing, rather than decreasing employment security, and preserving social welfare is critical, rather than antithetical, to the task of economic re-newal (see Muszynski, 1992). The legacy of the Mulroney government, however, has so severely depleted the vital nutrients necessary to sustain the social welfare field that its ability to provide a protective base for its citizens has been seriously weakened. It will be the task of future governments to regenerate the terrain of Canadian social welfare, and work in ways that increase, rather than erode, the capacity of social welfare programmes to contribute positively to the social and economic challenges ahead.

Notes

1. The only exception is for families with more than two children who receive a small additional benefit of $75 per year for each additional child.
2. In contrast, reducing poverty was an important objective and outcome of Australia's efforts to target child benefits. When the Hawke government began to income-test family allowance in 1987, it also introduced an income supplement to working poor families with children that was very generous by Canadian standards, increased the child portion of social assistance benefits, and in 1990, fulfilled their promise to fully index *all* child-related benefits (see Brownlee and King, 1989).

3. The 1990 changes increased the qualifying weeks from 14 to 20 for all workers, except those in areas of high unemployment, and reduced the range of the benefit period from 46–50 weeks to 35–50 weeks.

4. One of the few conditions for CAP cost-sharing is that eligibility must be determined on financial need alone. Work requirements can be part of the process of determining need, but once need is established, there can be no additional barriers to receipt (Lightman, 1990).

5. The 1982 Constitution included the Canadian Charter of Rights and Freedoms. The equality clause (s. 15) has been invoked to change maternity into parental leave and extend access to adoptive parents and biological fathers. Concerns about a Charter challenge also led to the Ontario abolition of the "man in the house" rule which automatically disqualified single mothers from social assistance if they were living with a man who had no legal obligation toward her or her children. However, those that hoped that the Charter would serve as an important force for reform in social assistance have been disappointed (Ellsworth and Morrison, 1992; Hasson, 1989).

6. This rate is based on *Statistics Canada*'s low income cut-offs (1986 base) and is adjusted each year in line with the rate of inflation. The low income cut-off "is based on the proposition that the proportion of a family's income spent on food, clothing and shelter declines as that income rises. It is set at the level ... where families on average spend 56.5 per cent of their before-tax income on those three items." Economic Council of Canada (1992) *The New Face of Poverty*, Ottawa: Economic Council of Canada.

References

Banting, K. (1991). "The Canadian Welfare State: Crisis and Continuity," in *Policy Choices: Political Agendas in Canada and the United States*, edited by K. Banting, School of Policy Studies, Queen's University, pp. 29–46.

Battle, K. (1990). "Clawback: The Demise of Universality in the Canadian Welfare State," in *Social Effects of Free Market Policies*, edited by I. Taylor, New York: St Martin's Press, pp. 269–96.

Betcherman, G. (1992). "The Disappearing Middle," in *Getting on Track: Social Democratic Strategies for Ontario*, edited by D. Drache, McGill-Queen's University Press, pp. 124–35.

Brownlee, H. and A. King (1989). "The Estimated Impact of the Family Package on Child Poverty," in *Child Poverty*, edited by D. Edgar, D. Keane and P. McDonald, Sydney: Allen & Unwin, pp. 123–45.

Caledon Institute of Social Policy (1992). "Child Benefit Primer: A Response to the Government Proposal," Ottawa: Caledon Institute of Social Policy.

Campbell, R. (1992). "Jobs ... Job ... Jo ... J ...: The Conservatives and the Unemployed," in *How Ottawa Spends: The Politics of Competitiveness, 1992–1993*, edited by F. Abele, Ottawa: Carleton University Press, pp. 23–55.

Canada (1984). *New Direction for Canada: An Agenda for Economic Renewal*, Ottawa: Department of Finance, November 8.

Cohen, M. (1992). "The Feminization of the Labour Market: Prospects for the 1990s," in *Getting on Track: Social Democratic Strategies for Ontario*, edited by D. Drache, McGill-Queen's University Press, pp. 105–23.

Demers, M. (1992). "Responding to the Challenges of the Global Economy: The Competitiveness Agenda," in *How Ottawa Spends: The Politics of Competitiveness, 1992–1993*, edited by F. Abele, Ottawa: Carleton University Press, pp. 151–90.

Drover, G., Editor (1988). *Free Trade and Social Policy*, Ottawa: Canadian Council on Social Development.

Drover, G. (1992). "Supporting Canada's Children: A Response," paper prepared for the Four Nations Social Policy Conference, Penn State University, September 15–17.

Ellsworth, R. and I. Morrison (1992). "Poverty Law in Ontario: The Year in Review," *Journal of Law and Social Policy* 8 (Fall): 1–53.

Evans, P. (1993). "From Workfare to the Social Contract: Lessons from Recent US Welfare Reforms," *Canadian Public Policy* 16 (March): 54–67.

Evans, P. (1992). "Targeting Single Mothers for Employment: Comparisons from the United States, Britain, and Canada," *Social Service Review* 66, 3 (September): 378–98.

Gherson, G. (1993). "Tories ready to rejig costly welfare state," *Financial Times* (Toronto), January 16, 1993.

Gray, G. (1990). "Social Policy by Stealth," *Policy Options* 11, 2 (March): 17–29.

Hasson, R. (1989). "What's Your Favourite Right? The Charter and Income Maintenance Legislation," *Journal of Law and Social Policy* 5 (Fall): 1–34.

Hedstrom, P. and S. Ringen (1990). "Age and Income in Contemporary Society" in *Poverty, Inequality and Income Distribution in Comparative Perspective*, edited by T. Smeeding, M. O'Higgins and L. Rainwater. Washington, DC: Urban Institute Press, 1990, pp. 77–104.

Johnson, A.W. (1987). "Social Policy in Canada: The Past as it Conditions the Present," in *Future of Social Welfare Systems in Canada and the United Kingdom*, edited by S. Seward, Halifax, Nova Scotia: Institute for Research on Public Policy, pp. 29–70.

Lightman, E. and A. Irving (1991). "Restructuring Canada's Welfare State," *Journal of Social Policy* 20 (January): 65–86.

Lightman, E. (1990). "Conditionality and Social Assistance: Market Values and the Work Ethic," in *Unemployment and Welfare: Social Policy and the Work of Social Work*, edited by G. Riches and G. Ternowetsky, Toronto: Garamond Press, pp. 91–105.

Lochhead, C. (1993). "Family Poverty in Canada, 1991," *Perception* 17, 1 (March): 21–24.

Mishra, R. (1990). *Welfare State in Capitalist Society: Policies of Retrenchment and Maintenance in Europe, North America and Australia*, Toronto: University of Toronto Press.

Muszynski, L. (1992). "A New Social Welfare Agenda for Canada," in *Getting on Track: Social Democratic Strategies for Ontario*, edited by Daniel Drache, McGill-Queen's University Press, pp. 170–185.

National Council of Welfare (1989). *1989 Budget and Social Policy*, Ottawa: National Council of Welfare, September.

National Council of Welfare (1990). *Fighting Child Poverty*, Ottawa: National Council of Welfare, April.

National Council of Welfare (1991). *Funding Health and Higher Education: Danger Looming*, Ottawa: National Council of Welfare, Spring.

National Council of Welfare (1992a). *Poverty Profile, 1980–1990*, Ottawa: National Council of Welfare, Autumn.

National Council of Welfare (1992b). *Welfare Reform*, Ottawa: National Council of Welfare, Summer.

O'Connor, J. (1989). "Welfare Expenditure and Policy Orientation in Canada in Comparative Perspective," *Canadian Review of Sociology and Anthropology* 26, 1 (February): 127–50.

Ogburn, K. (1986). *Workfare in America: An Initial Guide to the Debate*, Social Security Review, Background Discussion Paper No. 6, Canberra, Australia: Department of Social Security.

Ontario (1988). *Transitions*, Report of the Social Assistance Review Committee, prepared for the Ministry of Community and Social Services, Toronto: Queen's Printer.

Ontario (1992). "Social Assistance Reform: Proposed Program Model," Ontario: Ministry of Community and Social Services, November 25.

Prince, M. and J. Rice (1987). "The Canadian Jobs Strategy: Supply Side Social Policy" in *How Ottawa Spends, 1987–1988: Restraining the State*, edited by M. Prince, Toronto: Methuen, pp. 247–75.

Rice, J. (1987). "Restitching the Safety Net: Altering the National Social Security System," in *How Ottawa Spends, 1987–1968: Restraining the State*, edited by M. Prince, Toronto: Methuen, pp. 211–36.

Statistics Canada (1993a). *Historical Labour Force Statistics, 1992*, Cat. 71–201, Ottawa: Supply and Services.

Statistics Canada (1993b). *Income After-Tax, Distribution by Site in Canada*, Cat. 13–210, Ottawa: Supply and Services.

Taylor, I., editor (1990). *Social Effects of Free Market Policies*, New York: St Martin's Press.

Ternowetsky, G. (1990). "Unemployment Research, Social Work Education, and Social Work Practice: The Declining Middle and Expanding Bottom," in *Unemployment and Welfare*, edited by G. Riches and G. Ternowetsky, Toronto: Garamond Press, pp. 303–22.

Walker, R. (1991). *Thinking About Workfare: Evidence from the USA*, London: HMSO.

Yalnizyan, A. (1992). "Full Employment—Still a Viable Goal?," in *Getting on Track: Social Democratic Strategies for Ontario*, edited by Daniel Drache, McGill-Queen's University Press, pp. 78–101.

York, G. (1993). "UN body chastises Canada on poverty," *Toronto Globe and Mail*, 29 May 1993, p. 1.

14

The Rise of Chain Nursing Homes in Ontario, 1971–1996*

JOEL A.C. BAUM

> Running a nursing home used to be a good livelihood for a widowed nurse. After this year, it's a business. *Toronto Star*, 16 Mar. 1972

SINCE 1971, the year before mandatory province-wide licensing was imposed and hospital insurance was extended to cover nursing-home residents, the number of nursing homes operating in Ontario has declined 31 percent, from 483 to 335. During the same period, the number of nursing-home beds has increased 29 percent, from 24,184 to 31,304, raising the average number of beds per home from 50 to more than 90. Historically, the industry consisted of small owner-operated homes. Since 1971, however, many of them have closed and have been replaced by a smaller number of larger, professionally managed chains. Chains are collections of similar service organizations (location is often the only difference) linked together by common ownership. The ties among a chain's components, which can almost always operate without the chain, are horizontal, although typically there are centralized parts with vertical links to components. In 1971 there were 32 chain-owned nursing homes (7 percent) operating 2,016 beds (8 percent) in Ontario. Twenty-five years later, 144 (43 percent) of Ontario's nursing homes, operating 16,934 beds (54 percent), were components of a chain.

This dramatic transformation, a significant development for nursing-home operators and residents alike, is widely held to have been triggered—albeit inadvertently—by provincial nursing-home policy (Tarman 1990). This view has not been tested systematically. Did government regulatory and funding policy in Ontario bring about the nursing-home industry's metamorphosis? Was it the inevitable result of advantages inherent in the chain organizational form that have favored its rise during this century across diverse service industries: in retailing, food service, hospitality, banking, and, more recently, business, professional, and health and human services? Or did it result from the combination of these factors? To address these questions, I examine the roles of Ontario government policy and features of the chain organizational form in explaining the transformation of Ontario's nursing-home industry.

The growth and acquisition patterns of chains are inherently interesting because they underlie the rise of an organizational form that is coming to dominate every service in-

---

* This chapter was first published as "The Rise of Chain Nursing Homes in Ontario, 1971–1996," *Social Forces*, 78, 2 (1999): 543–83.

dustry (U.S. Census of Business, various years) but that has received little attention from organizational researchers. Recently, researchers have begun to examine the implications of these relationships for chains' components (e.g., Baum & Ingram 1998; Darr, Argote & Epple 1995; Ingram & Baum 1997), but, reflecting the general neglect of the topic of relational dynamics, only one study has examined the dynamics of chain relationships (Ingram & Baum 1998).[1] Framed more generally, this study tackles an overlooked question in organization studies: researchers have attended much more to the consequences of relationships between organizations than to the processes by which those relationships are determined (Walker 1998). My analysis contributes to improving our understanding of the processes by which chains grow, form relationships through acquisitions, and come to dominate an industry.

The basic approach to the dynamics of chain relationship formation (through acquisition) adopted in this study is derived from Mitchell's (1994) study of acquisition and divestment in American medical product markets. Mitchell's key insight for the present study is that the sale of an organization is likely to occur when there is an alignment of the interests of a buyer and seller. This view clarifies the tension in the status of an organization as either independent or chain-affiliated. For a chain relationship to form, the owner of an independent organization must be willing to sell it at a given price and a chain must be willing to buy it at that price. The likelihood of a chain and an independent operator agreeing on a price depends on their perceptions of the relative profitability of the organization as independent or chain-affiliated. Thus, if an independent nursing home would be more profitable as part of a chain, for example, because it would benefit from the economies of scale and reputation of the chain, then a sale to a chain (at the right price) would be in the interests of both buyer and seller. My overarching view of the growth of chains and the dynamics of their relationships, then, is that the likelihood of acquisitions is higher when the characteristics of the nursing home are such that it could be more effectively operated as part of a chain.

In the section that follows, I characterize "organizational forms" as novel combinations of goals, authority relations, technologies, and market strategies and situate chains as an organizational form within the definition. Then, after reviewing Ontario government nursing-home policy and its impact on industry structure, I identify three complementary theoretical explanations drawn from organization theory for chain components' advantage over independent nursing homes: (1) economies of scale, market power, and resource access, (2) reputation, and (3) multimarket contact. Finally, I present a detailed empirical analysis of the two main processes underlying the independent-to-chain transformation in Ontario from 1971 to 1996: (1) failure rates of independent and component nursing homes and (2) the acquisition rate of independent nursing homes by chains.

Organizational Forms and Their Evolution

A useful basis for understanding differences between organizational forms is the distinction between core and peripheral organizational features. Core features include goals, authority relations, technologies, and market strategy (Hannan & Freeman 1984) and vary in the ease with which they can be changed. At one extreme, goals are at the innermost core of organizational forms and are the hardest to modify. At the other extreme, market strategies are relatively less deep in the core and are easier to change. All other attributes are peripheral features.

Organizational forms constitute polythetic groupings, in that members of the form share common core features but may differ with respect to peripheral features (McKelvey 1982).[2] Hence, forms are defined in terms of their core features, and one form differs from another primarily according to each's core features. The core features comprise a four-dimensional space in which new organizational forms appear or disappear over time. An advantage of focusing on core features is that they provide a parsimonious set of relatively stable dimensions on which organizational forms differ. These four features can also help show how an organizational form is connected to ancestral forms and direct attention to processes by which discontinuities in configurations of goals, authority, technology, and market strategies arise (Baum 1989).

The rise of new forms can properly be viewed as an organizational counterpart to biological speciation (Lumsden & Singh 1990; Romanelli 1991).[3] Speciation is an important form of variation by which new organizational entities come into existence, and it plays a vital role in the evolution of organizational diversity. New organizational forms are novel recombinations of goals, authority relations (including governance structures), technologies, and client markets (Rao & Singh 1999). The emergence and character of new organizational forms is shaped both by the creation of new resource spaces (Hannan & Freeman 1989; Schumpeter 1950) and by the characteristics, creativity, and competition among existing organizations (Lumsden & Singh 1990).

Novel organizational forms matter because they create organizational diversity. The ability of societies to respond to social problems may even hinge upon the diversity of organizational forms, and, in the long run, in a fluid environment, diversity can be maintained or increased by the rise of new forms (Hannan & Freeman 1989). Moreover, new forms are vital engines of evolution—indeed, an important piece of organizational change, at the macrolevel, consists of the replacement of existing organizational forms by new ones (see Schumpeter 1950). Furthermore, since new organizational forms are structural incarnations of beliefs, values, and norms, they emerge in tandem with new institutions and foster cultural change in societies (Stinchcombe 1965). For these reasons, where new organizational forms come from is one of the central questions of organization theory (Baum 1989; Singh 1993).

Some examples of new organizational forms include the multidivisional form, health maintenance organizations (HMOs), biotechnology firms, and Internet retailers. The multidivisional form was primarily novel in terms of authority relations, although the various divisions functioning as independent companies were enabled to address broader scope than its predecessor, the functional organization form. HMOs represented a radical departure in health care delivery primarily because of the salience of their goal of cost containment, but differences in authority relations and markets served are evident as well. Biotechnology firms embodied novelty primarily in the application of new technologies to new and existing markets and in their novel interorganizational arrangements. Internet retailers were novel mainly in their use of electronic commerce, novel authority relations, and virtual existence.

The chain form is novel in terms of authority relations, geographic market scope, and strategy of standardization. Chains are collections of service organizations, all doing substantially the same thing, which are linked together into a larger "superorganization" (Ingram & Baum 1997). Often, the only differentiation among a chain's components, which are almost always capable of operating without the chain, is their geographic location. The relationships between a chain's components are horizontal, although typically there are centralized parts that have vertical relationships with components, such as a distribution facility. The essence of the chain strategy, standardization, generates benefits of economies of scale and reputation (Ingram 1996b; Ingram & Baum 1997). In diverse service industries from retailing to food, small, family-managed organizations have been replaced by large, professionally managed chains. Chains now dominate or are coming to dominate service industries in general (U.S. Census of Business, various years). At the same time, service industries are increasingly important to economies around the world. Although perhaps the most successful organizational form of the twentieth century, chains are rarely studied and little systematic research has examined their rise (an exception is Ingram 1996a).

Regulation and Government Funding of Nursing Homes in Ontario

The *Ontario Health Survey Committee Report* (1950) provided the first detailed review of Ontario nursing homes. It called for provincial licensing of nursing homes as a means of reducing variations in care and curbing the further proliferation of substandard homes. Similar concerns were raised by the Welfare Council of Toronto, the United Church of Canada, and the United Senior Citizens of Ontario, which all recommended universal provincial licensing and insurance and funding of more nonprofit homes. Even the Associated Nursing Homes Incorporated (ANHI)—predecessor to the Ontario Nursing Homes Association (ONHA)—acknowledged that the level of care in some homes was alarming and saw a variety of advantages to becoming "licensed government suppliers." Despite this convergence of interests, the government did not act, fearing it would lose control of industry expansion and program costs.

Eventually, the *Nursing Homes Act* of 1966 was passed, stipulating that all Ontario nursing homes were to be licensed by the Department of Health, but local municipalities were left to interpret and enforce the regulations. The extension of hospital insurance was deemed unnecessary for raising the standard of care. Even without funding, the Act raised the status of nursing homes as health care providers. It also restricted competition to homes able to afford the new regulations, increasing the closure rate of smaller homes. Government funding, many believed, was now inevitable (Bruchovsky 1970). In anticipation, several large nursing homes were built (several with more than 200 beds), especially in urban areas. Most of these remained half empty until April 1972, when hospital insurance was extended to cover nursing-home residents.

The 1972 act transferred responsibility for regulatory enforcement from municipalities to the provincial Ministry of Health (formerly the Department of Health). It also provided extended-care insurance for nursing-home residents under the Ontario Health Insurance Plan (OHIP). Residents paid $3.50 per day toward their care and accommodation, and OHIP paid a $9.00 per diem subsidy. The province also took control of the number and geographic distribution of beds, enabling it to offer extended-care insurance within its own regional and budgetary constraints. A systematic effort was to be made to distribute beds equitably across the province so that rural and urban areas would have access to nursing-home care at a rate of 3.5 beds per 1,000 people. The Act also included a grandfather clause excluding homes built before 1972 from complying with many of the regulations (Scully 1986).

Nursing homes were required to provide extended care for at least 75 percent of their beds. The low per diem subsidy made it difficult for many independent homes to afford licensing standards. A 1973 amendment prevented homes from offsetting the cost of providing extended-care services by charging extra fees to their residents above the government fee schedule. To increase revenues, some homes began levying charges for necessary services such as laundry and transportation not covered under extended-care fees. To cut costs, some homes began accepting only the least problematic, and least costly, residents and lowering wages for employees (Social Planning Council 1984).

The closure of independent homes and their absorption by chains, combined with the government-imposed bed shortage, moderated competition—nursing-home beds were in demand regardless of the quality of service offered. Chains, able to afford to operate under provincial standards, expanded by purchasing licenses from closing independents and by acquiring others. With their greater resources, chains were also able to compete more effectively for new licenses by offering a larger variety of services than independent homes to a government interested in improving nursing-home care at the lowest possible cost (Tarman 1990). Nursing-home chains flourished similarly in the U.S. after the passage of Medicare and Medicaid (Light 1986).

Ultimately, the government was left heavily reliant on for-profit, chain nursing-home care, but it was wary that further regulatory limits on nursing-home profitability would exacerbate the bed shortage. As Baum (1977) noted, "The ultimate weapon of government, to close the [nursing] home, is too powerful; it would destroy the very people the law is intended to protect" (70). The government also opposed calls to make nursing homes nonprofit fearing that without the profit incentive many homes would close, and strong criticism greeted its decision to keep confidential the inspection reports on homes' regulatory compliance: how could good nursing homes be chosen without data necessary to assess them? The public questioned the quality of nursing-home care that resulted from cost-cutting measures, low-paid staff, and the rise of chains in a noncompetitive environment (Tarman 1990).

By 1980, concerns about profit orientation and quality of care remobilized interest and lobby groups. Concerned Friends of Ontario Citizens in Care Facilities was formed with the aim of raising the quality and emotional care in institutional facilities. In 1984 the Social Planning Council of Toronto published an influential report, *Caring for Profit*, reflecting the concerns of many public-interest groups about the inherent tension between human service delivery and profit making. A Canadian Medical Association task force (CMA 1984) similarly concluded:

> When an institution becomes the only answer for the care of an elderly person, it must be ... run on a principle of loving care, not tender loving greed. It is recommended therefore that all jurisdictions move as quickly as possible

towards the elimination of for-profit institutions and establish nonprofit facilities. (36)

The 1987 Act responded to these criticisms by establishing a residents' bill of rights, forming residents' councils, and requiring the Ministry of Health to hold a public meeting before renewing, transferring, or granting a license. It also required operators to file detailed financial statements disclosing all revenues and expenditures and making the licensee accountable for violations of the act. Critics charged that it was symbolic politics aimed at placating the public and appeasing operators with a generous financial subsidy.[4] Tarman (1990) concluded, "The case of Ontario nursing homes may ... illustrate that the for-profit 'public agent' presents an unworkable solution for a public sector concerned about both quality of care and costs" (88).

Despite the marked increase in government intervention since 1966, through regulations and the provision of nursing-home insurance, today many issues that existed in the 1950s remain unresolved. Quality and accountability of care and accessibility to nursing homes remain problematic. Economic restraint during the 1970s led government to rely on for-profit nursing homes. This reliance has prevented government from playing a stronger role in the promotion of better-quality care, fearing that further regulation and enforcement would jeopardize industry profitability. Those same economic restraints, which resulted in low per diems and restricted bed supply, forced for-profit nursing homes to apply controversial methods to provide services and make a profit, and they appear also to have fostered the rise of nursing-home chains.

The foregoing overview points to the extended-care per diem subsidy as the element of Ontario nursing-home policy affecting most directly differential survival of independent and component homes. The per diem sets the basic fee paid for nursing-home services covered under the extended-care plan. Nursing homes are required to provide extended care for at least 75 percent of their beds and are prevented by law from offsetting the cost of providing extended-care services by charging their residents more than the government fee schedule. As a result, the per diem is a key determinant of revenues and profitability and ultimately of the viability of *all* nursing homes.

> *Hypothesis 1a*: Increases in the extended-care per diem lower nursing-home failure rates.
>
> *Hypothesis 1b*: Increases in the extended-care per diem lower chains' acquisition rate of independent nursing homes.

Small, independent nursing homes were likely to be most severely affected by low per diems. Compared to large independent or component homes, small independents may lack (1) economies of scale and the scope needed to lower costs, (2) internal resources, including larger administrative staffs focused on strategic needs, and (3) capital for restructuring or expansion to accommodate new regulatory and environmental demands (see, e.g., Banaszak-Holl, Zinn & Mor 1996).

> *Hypothesis 1c*: Increases in the extended-care per diem lower failure rates most for small, independent nursing homes.[5]

Possible Sources of Chain Components' Survival Advantage

Strategic rationales for chains, which can be viewed as related diversification in which operating units are not merged, include (1) economies of scale, market power, and resource access, (2) reputation, and (3) mutual forbearance.

Economies of scale, market power, and resource access

Although it is widely held that nursing-home chains capture economies of scale or, more accurately, advantages of "multiunit operation" by standardizing services, advertising, administration, operating procedures, equipment, and buildings across multiple facilities, empirical evidence is mixed. Several early studies found that chain ownership did not influence nursing-home costs (Birnbaum et al. 1981; Meiners 1982). Other, more recent studies report significant cost differences among ownership classes even after controlling for factors known to be associated with nursing-home cost functions such as payer mix, case mix, occupancy, and quality. Cohen and Dubay (1990), using 1983 national U.S. data, found that chain facilities reported lower costs, although not at the expense of quality. Arling, Nordquist, and Capitman (1987) found that chain facilities in the Virginia nursing-home industry had the lowest operating costs of all facility types. McKay (1991) found that chain facilities in Texas exhibited lower costs at intermediate and high levels of output (patient days) but higher costs at low and very high output levels.

One explanation for these mixed findings is inattention to chains' spatial arrangements (Ingram 1996a, b; Luke, Oscan & Olden 1995). Spatial compactness (i.e., proximate geographic location of a chain's components) can reinforce advantages of multiunit operation by making centralization of purchasing and other functions possible and by increasing possibilities for integrating complex technical, administrative, and strategic knowledge successfully into the organization's activities (Ingram 1996a, b). Not all scale advantages are equally dependent on geographic concentration, however (Luke, Oscan & Olden 1995). For example, economies in management support systems are achievable regardless of whether the chain is geographically concentrated. Compact chains do, however, offer significant opportunities for improving the efficiencies of production, for example, by specializing individual facilities to provide wider-ranging and more sophisticated care or by eliminating excess capacities.

Spatially compact chains also acquire greater local market power (Ingram & Baum 1997). The role of power in motivating interorganizational relations is well developed in resource dependence theory (Pfeffer & Salancik 1978), which predicts that organizations alter their power relations with other organizations on which they are dependent by expanding vertically, horizontally, or through diversification. Horizontal relations are predicted in response to competitive interdependence. These advantages of scale and market power at the chain level should result in lower costs for components of large, spatially compact chains. Moreover, chains' resources may buffer their components—especially small components, which typically experience the greatest difficulty raising capital, hiring skilled personnel, and handling the costs of government compliance—from environmental uncertainty and competition (Aldrich & Auster 1986; Baum & Oliver 1991).

In the context of regulated standards, a low extended-care per diem subsidy and government control of industry growth limited competition in Ontario to homes able to afford the capital outlay required to meet provincial standards. Under these conditions, "nursing home chains, experts in economies of scale, will benefit most" (Yonson 1981:18). Thus, component nursing homes, with their access to their chains' economies of scale, market power, and resources, may be more likely to survive, with components of larger, more spatially compact chains experiencing the greatest benefit. In that they are focused on achieving standardization and economies of scale, I also expect chains to be more likely to acquire large nursing homes than small ones. Consistent with this prediction, Ingram and Baum (1998) found that U.S. hotel chains were significantly more likely to acquire larger independent hotels.[6]

> *Hypothesis 2a*: Components have lower failure rates than independent nursing homes.

> *Hypothesis 2b*: A component's survival advantage increases with its chain's size.

> *Hypothesis 2c*: A component's survival advantage increases with its chain's spatial compactness.

> *Hypothesis 2d*: A component's survival advantage decreases with its size.

> *Hypothesis 2e*: Chains' rate of acquisition is higher for larger independent nursing homes.

Reputation

Contract-failure theory suggests that because nonprofits are prohibited from distributing profits to their owners, they will be perceived to be more trustworthy, since their owners have less incentive to take advantage of underinformed consumers (Hansmann 1980). Consequently, nonprofits are typically viewed as ideologically and operationally distinct from and superior to for-profits, more oriented toward community responsiveness and involvement, noncompetitive behavior, cooperative activities, social image, and the fulfillment of social and cultural needs (DiMaggio & Anheier 1990; Hansmann 1987; Weisbrod 1988). Thus, in nonprofit sectors a normative impetus away from competition often prevails (Halliday, Powell & Granfors 1987). As a result, nonprofit nursing homes are lauded as meeting community needs, often with innovative approaches to managing the care of the people they serve, without regard for profit (Banaszak-Holl, Zinn & Mor 1996; Weisbrod & Schlesinger 1986). Although nonprofits may not typically engage in vigorous competition, they may nevertheless be formidable competitors as a result of their high social legitimacy (Baum & Oliver 1996).

In contrast, for-profit entrepreneurs are often charged with downgrading service quality and underinvesting in facilities and innovation (Banaszak-Holl, Zinn & Mor 1996). Such indictments can undermine for-profit nursing homes' viability by raising questions about the quality of services they provide, decreasing their access to government resources, and constraining their ability to compete aggressively with nonprofit rivals without damaging their own public image. Empirical evidence in health and human services tends to support these characterizations (e.g., Aaronson, Zinn & Rosko 1994; Banaszak-Holl,

Zinn & Mor 1996; Baum & Oliver 1996; but see Kane & Kane 1990; O'Brien, Saxberg & Smith 1983; Vladeck 1988).

For Ontario's nursing homes, these perceptions were heightened by (1) the historical predominance of for-profit nursing homes[7] and (2) nondisclosure of nursing-home compliance reports compiled by the Ministry of Health (Tarman 1990). Given the inaccessibility of nursing homes' compliance reports to the public, a new resident at a nursing home typically is uncertain about the quality of care and service—and is wary of for-profit care. Standardization, the essence of the chain strategy, helps reduce uncertainty about a component's care quality by reference to the corporate reputation (Dranove & Shanley 1995). Standardization across a chain's components raises consumers' perceptions of the chain's components' reliability, the capacity to produce a given quality of service repeatedly (Ingram 1996b). Accountability is also higher, because interdependence puts pressure on each component to maintain and enhance its chain's standards—poor care in any component can damage the entire chain's reputation (Ingram 1996b). These constraints increase beliefs in the trustworthiness and accountability of chain components, reducing search and monitoring costs for families of residents. A reputation for reliability and accountability, in turn, enhances components' survival chances (Hannan & Freeman 1984) and may also help allay concerns about nursing homes' for-profit status.

Although not all chains try to develop such reputations, many do, and affiliation with one that does should benefit its components. Of course, securing such benefits depends on consumers being able to identify components as members of a chain that they trust. Naming patterns differentiate chains that can provide a reputation benefit to their components from those that do not (Ingram 1996b). Chains that give components names that link them to each other thus meet a necessary condition for building a reputation: the ability of customers to recognize various components as members of the same chain.

> *Hypothesis 3a*: A component's survival advantage increases with the proportion of components in its chain with the same name.

The strength of such reputation effects is likely conditioned by two factors. First, Mauser (1998) suggests that perceptions based on indirect performance indicators such as profit orientation and chain membership will be strongest when numerous organizations are present, which makes it more difficult and costly for consumers to determine the reputation of a particular provider. Consequently, if consumers use profit orientation and chain membership as signals of expected behavior of nursing homes, they are likely to be especially important in urban areas where numerous providers are concentrated.

> *Hypothesis 3b*: A component's survival advantage increases more with the proportion of components in its chain with the same name in urban areas.

Second, the reputation of the chain form in the nursing-home industry no doubt influences the benefits associated with individual chains' efforts to promote a standardized product and image (Delacroix & Rao 1994). The absence of a track record is an absolute obstacle to the creation of an organizational form's reputation. Each independent instance of a form increases its visibility and facilitates its development of a track record, for example, by creating consumer awareness, by familiarizing government authorities with the form, and by providing financial institutions opportunity to assess its creditworthiness. Later entrants can free ride on the record established by early entrants into government and community relations (Baum & Oliver 1992). As at the level of the individual chain organization, the visibility and reputation of the chain form in a given field depends on the degree to which chains in that field use common naming strategies. Thus, the potential benefits of reputation building by individual nursing-home chains likely depends on the degree to which *other* nursing home also use common naming strategies. This form-level reputation effect of the diffusion of common naming strategies is also expected to stimulate the growth of chains and thus to increase the rate of independent nursing-home acquisition by chains.

> *Hypothesis 3c*: A component's survival advantage from the proportion of components in its chain with the same name increases more as the proportion of other chains' components with the same name increases.

> *Hypothesis 3d*: Chains' acquisition rate of independent nursing homes increases as the proportion of other chains' components with the same name increases.

Public concerns about the legitimacy of for-profit care also suggest that nonprofit homes will make less attractive acquisition targets since such actions may be viewed as excessive competitive aggression against socially preferred nonprofits, potentially damaging a chain's reputation. Moreover, nonprofits' tendency to orient toward community responsiveness, noncompetition, cooperation, and the fulfillment of social needs (see DiMaggio & Anheier 1990; Hansmann 1980) implies that nonprofit operators will be less likely to consider being acquired by a chain as a viable option.

> *Hypothesis 3e*: Chains' rate of acquisition is lower for nonprofit independent nursing homes.

Multimarket contact

Components of chains may also benefit from mutual forbearance arising from multimarket contact—their joint presence in more than one distinct geographic market (Bernheim & Whinston 1990; Edwards 1955; Simmel 1950). Multimarket contact between competitors is widely held to result both in less vigorous competitive interaction in all markets in which they meet and in more predictable competitive behavior. Cooperation in such cases is thought to be attractive because the opportunity for retribution and the severity of punishment for violating agreements—implicit or otherwise—are greater than if the firms met only in one market. Multimarket rivals can benefit if they each stake out certain markets and then mutually forbear from competing with one another. Multimarket competition theory can thus be viewed as an extension of oligopoly theory that stresses cross-market conjectural variations. One firm meeting another in more than one market anticipates a potential reaction by the other firm in all the markets in which they meet to an action undertaken in any one of them.

Multimarket contact also facilitates adoption of collusive strategies by increasing the potential for future interfirm interaction. Recent empirical studies of multimarket competition in economics (Cotterill & Haller 1992; Evans & Kessides 1994; Hughes & Oughton 1993), strategic management (Baum & Korn 1999; Gimeno & Woo 1996), and organization theory (Barnett 1993; Baum & Korn 1996) robustly support predicted effects of multimarket contact on rivalry. Multimarket contact among nursing-home chains may, by limiting competitive aggression and stabilizing competitive relationships, increase the survival chances of their components. When two nursing homes confront each other in such a manner, they may therefore hesitate to contest a given market vigorously. As a result, multimarket contact among nursing-home chains may, by lowering competitive aggression and stabilizing competitive relationships, increase the survival chances of their components.

> *Hypothesis 4a*: A component's survival advantage increases with the degree to which its chain has multimarket contact with competitors that operate in that component's market.

If multimarket contact reduces the level of rivalry and stabilizes competitive relationships among chains, it may also lower chains' rate of acquiring independent nursing homes, since such actions may be interpreted by competitors as aggressive market expansion or entry behavior. Consistent with this idea, Cotterill and Haller (1992) show that U.S. supermarket chains were less likely to enter local markets when other supermarket chains already served the market.

> *Hypothesis 4b*: Chains' nursing-home acquisition rate in a market declines with increases in the multimarket contact among chains in all markets.

Notably, if nursing-home chains with widespread multimarket contact forbear from competing aggressively with one another, they may be more aggressive toward single-market competitors that cannot retaliate (Barnett 1993) and with whom they cannot reach forbearance agreements (Baum & Korn 1999). Thus, a second effect of multimarket contact among chains may be that chains engage in more intense rivalry with independent, single-market competitors. Thus, if mutual forbearance with a chain's multimarket competitors leads it to target its competitive energies toward independent, single-market competitors, then as the degree of multimarket contact among chain nursing homes increases, independent nursing homes may experience higher rates of failure. Given the socially preferred status of nonprofits and concerns about the legitimacy of for-profits, however, targeting for-profit independent nursing homes for aggressive competition may be less damaging to a chain's reputation.

> *Hypothesis 4c*: Independent for-profit nursing homes' failure rates increase with the level of multimarket contact among the chains that operate in their market.

Methods

The data for this study include information on all 557 independent and chain nursing homes operated in Ontario between January 1971 and December 1996. I used two archival sources to compile these data: the Ontario Ministry of Health (MOH) licensing records, which contain detailed information—recorded by day, month, and year—for all nursing homes in Ontario starting in 1971, and the *Ontario Hospitals' Association Directory*, published annually since 1968. Because much detailed organizational data are missing prior to 1971, this study begins in 1971, even though archival sources begin in 1968. Nevertheless, the study covers the entire period of government funding and mandatory licensing, which began in 1972.

In 1971, 479 of the nursing homes in the sample—447 independents (94 percent) and 32 components (6 percent)—were already in operation; thus, the life histories for these homes were left-censored (i.e., the nursing homes were founded and did not fail before the study period). With available archival information, I was able to confirm founding dates for all left-censored nursing homes. During the study period, 82 nursing homes were founded, 17 by chains. A nursing home was defined as founded in the year it was first licensed by the MOH. The 32 nursing-home chains that operated—at one time or another—in Ontario between 1971 and 1996 acquired 159 independent nursing homes. The maximum number of components (beds) operated by a single chain was 28 (4,022) by Extendicare; the mean was 10 (1,255).

Of the nursing homes operating in Ontario in 1971, 226 (40.6 percent) had ceased operations by the end of 1996 (161 independents and 65 components). Failure was defined as the delicensing of a nursing home and its cessation of nursing-home services. Changes in name or independent owner were not counted as failures, because the organization itself continued to provide nursing-home services. This treatment corresponds to common practice in organizational mortality studies (Baum 1996). Therefore, the final sample for the analysis included 557 nursing homes, of which 226 failed. The number of independent and component nursing homes and the number of nursing-home beds operated in Ontario in each year from 1971 to 1996 are shown in Figures 14.1 and 14.2, respectively.

Market definition

Although not nearly as localized as markets for hospitals (cf. Luft & Maerki 1984; Luke 1991; Succi, Lee & Alexander 1997) or child care (cf. Baum & Oliver 1996), as with most health and human service organizations that provide services on their premises, nursing-home markets are segmented geographically. Geographic segmentation is driven by the desire of nursing-home residents to remain in their own communities and by the transportation costs of residents' families. As a result, the location of a nursing home strongly influences where residents come from. Consequently, specification of local market areas is an important prerequisite to the definition of several of this study's theoretical and control variables (e.g., multimarket contact).

Various approaches to market definition have been used in studies of health and human service organizations. Two general approaches are available: (1) an individual organization perspective and (2) an overall market perspective. In each perspective, market definitions can be based on geopolitical boundaries, distance between organizations, or consumer-origin data. The market definition germane to a given study depends on the research issue at hand (Luft et al. 1986), but the analysis of competition is likely to be robust across specifications (Garnick et al. 1987). I take a market-level perspective to be appropriate for studying multimarket contact and employ census district boundaries to

Figure 14.1. Number of Ontario Nursing Homes

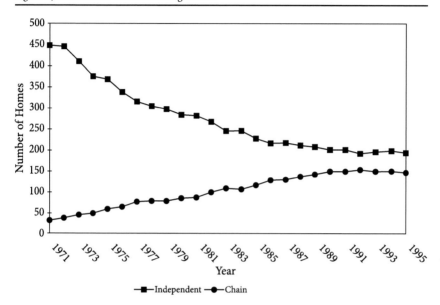

Figure 14.2. Number of Beds in Ontario Nursing Homes, 1975–1995

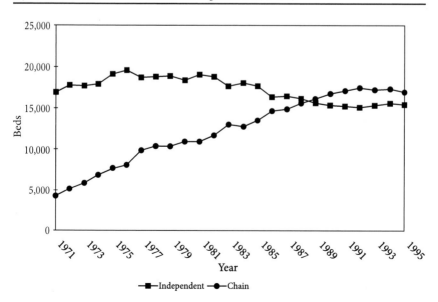

approximate local markets. My approach is similar to county boundaries frequently used to represent the market for health care services in the U.S. (Banaszak-Holl, Zinn & Mor 1996; Farley 1988; Joskow 1980; Nyman 1985, 1987, 1989; White & Chirikos 1988; Zinn 1993, 1994). In the U.S., patterns of funding and patient origin support the county as a reasonable approximation for the nursing-home market (Gertler 1989).

In Ontario, census districts provide an equally useful market definition for several reasons. First, these boundaries are highly salient to industry participants: the Ministry of Health communicates and bases its bed allocation decisions using ratios of nursing-home beds to population at the census district level. Second, the geographic area of a census district is negatively correlated to its population density. This correlation results in market definitions that accommodate the typically larger market areas served by health service organizations in more sparsely populated (rural) counties (Phibbs & Robinson 1993; Succi, Lee & Alexander 1997). Thus census district measures overcome the major problem of organization-centric, fixed-radius definitions, which tend to overestimate the degree of competitiveness in urban markets and to understate it in rural markets (Garnick et at 1987). Third, census districts correspond to yearly population data, making it possible to compute nursing-home supply and demand at the same level of aggregation.

Markets defined by census district do have their limitations, however (see Morrisey, Sloan & Valvona 1989). They do not account for organizational characteristics (e.g., size and services offered) that may affect the size of a nursing home's market area (Phibbs & Robinson 1993; Succi, Lee & Alexander 1997). Nor do they adjust for cross-boundary competition between homes located at or near the edges of census districts, which may systematically bias market definitions for these homes.[8] These weaknesses notwithstanding, census districts should provide a reasonable approximation of nursing-home markets in Ontario, capturing the major rivals with which the average nursing home competes.

Dependent variables and analysis

The dependent variables I study are the likelihoods at any point in the life of a nursing home of (1) failing and (2) become part of a chain if it is independent. Event-history models estimate over time the instantaneous risk of an event occurring and are therefore the appropriate method to use for this analysis (Tuma & Hannan 1984). My empirical estimation and control variable specification follow closely current ecological event studies (e.g., Baum & Oliver 1991; Hannan et al. 1995; Ingram & Baum 1997, 1998; Miner, Amburgey & Stearns 1990). Consequently, my baseline model specifications are comparable to other current work in this area.

Modeling failure of independent and component nursing homes and acquisition of independent homes poses two estimation problems. First, chain-level variables (e.g., spatial compactness, multimarket contact) are undefined for independent nursing homes. Consequently, it is not possible to estimate coefficients for these variables on the pooled sample of independent and component nursing homes. I therefore estimate models for the pooled sample and independent and component nursing homes separately to test the study's hypotheses.

Second, for the component nursing-home failure analysis, data from each chain's multiple components are pooled. Consequently, if a chain makes decisions regarding several components simultaneously, event-history analysis treats these interactions as independent Fortunately, this problem, also known as the "common actor effect," can be understood as one of model misspecification (Lincoln 1984). If the statistical model incorporates all essential chain-level characteristics that influence component failure, no unobserved effects of cross-sectional interdependence would remain. Although the models I estimate include a range of important chain-level variables, they are still likely to suffer from some degree of omitted variable bias. Therefore I estimated exponential models that account for unobserved heterogeneity to adjust for systematic biases resulting from model misspecification.

More formally, I estimate nursing-home failure and acquisition rates using $r_{jk}(t)$, the instantaneous rate of failure (acquisition), as the dependent variable. I modeled the hazard rate using the following specification of an exponential model with a multiplicative gamma-distributed error term to account for unobserved heterogeneity:

$$r_{jk}(t) = a_{jk} / (1 + d_{jk}a_{jk}t)$$
$$a_{jk} = \exp(A^{(jk)}\alpha^{(jk)})$$
$$d_{jk} = \exp(D^{(jk)}\delta^{(jk)}),$$

where a is the constant transition rate of the underlying exponential model; d is the variance of the gamma mixing distribution; $A^{(jk)}$ and $D^{(jk)}$, the first component of each of the covariate (row) vectors, are assumed to be constants equal to one; and $a^{(jk)}$ and $d^{(jk)}$ are the model parameters to be estimated (Blossfeld & Rohwer 1995). Almost all the independent variables in which I am interested change over time. Time-varying covariates are incorporated into event-history models by splitting the observations (in this case, the life histories of nursing homes) into spells and updating covariates in each spell (Blossfeld & Rohwer 1995). I applied this approach by splitting the life histories of nursing homes into one-year spells and for each spell setting covariates to their value at the beginning of the year. Each spell is treated as right-censored unless the home fails or is acquired. I used TDA 5.7 (Rohwer 1995) to estimate the vectors of parameter estimates a and d by the method of maximum likelihood. Because the degree of left-censoring is high (especially for independent nursing homes), in a supplementary analysis I estimated coefficients using Cox's partial likelihood model, which is unrestrictive in its assumptions about time dependence (Guo 1993). In the Cox models, which do not account for unobserved heterogeneity, estimates do not differ greatly from exponential models, and comparison of model log-likelihoods indicates that exponential models with unobserved heterogeneity provide a better fit with the data.

Independent variables

GOVERNMENT FUNDING (HYPOTHESES 1A–C)

I used the time-varying (1986) constant-dollar value of the extended-care per diem to test for the main effects of government funding predicted by hypotheses 1a-b. Figure 14.3 shows the value of the per diem over time in both 1986 and nominal dollars. To test for differential effects of the per diem on small, independent nursing homes (hypothesis 1c), I included an extended-care per diem × nursing-home size interaction in the independent nursing model. I defined nursing-home size as the natural logarithm of the number of beds a home operated at the start of each year. I used a component dummy variable, coded 1 while a nursing home was owned by a chain and 0 otherwise, to assess the basic qualitative difference in survival prospects of component and independent nursing homes predicted by hypothesis 2a. I included two time-varying measures of own chain's size to test hypothesis 2b, which predicted lower failure rates for components of larger chains: (1) the number of nursing homes a component's chain operated and (2) the natural logarithm of the number of beds a component's chain operated. These variables capture a chain's "total productive capacity," which Winter (1990) suggests most accurately reflects the differential competitive strength of larger organizations. To differentiate between market-specific and more diffuse scale and market power effects, I computed each chain size variable the focal component's census district and all other census districts separately. To ensure mutually exclusive variables, I subtracted the focal component's size from its chain's census district size.

I tested hypothesis 2c, which predicted lower failure rates for components of geographically concentrated chains, using own chain's spatial compactness, computed on the basis of the Hirschman-Herfindahl index (Adelman 1969), updated at the start of each year. This index computes spatial compactness as the sum of the squared proportions of a chain's components in each census district in which the chain operated. For example, spatial compactness for a chain operating 10 nursing homes, one in each of 10 census districts, is $[10 \times (1/10)^2] = .1$. For a chain operating 10 nursing homes in three census districts—eight in one, one in the second, and one in the third—it is $[(8/10)^2 + 2 \times (1/10)^2] = .66$. Figure 14.4 shows the trend in mean spatial compactness of Ontario nursing-home chains over time. To test hypothesis 2d, I estimated a component × nursing-home size interaction, where nursing-home size and component are as defined above. I used the same interaction in the acquisition rate analysis to test hypothesis 2e, that chains are more likely to acquire large nursing homes.

Figure 14.3. Per Diem Rate of Ontario Nursing Homes, 1971–1995

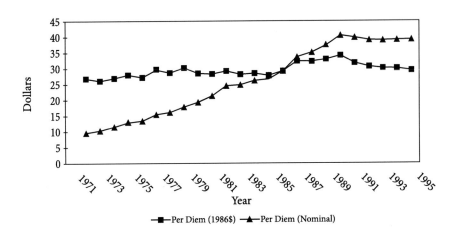

REPUTATION (HYPOTHESES 3A-E)

To test for main effects of potential reputation benefits (hypothesis 3a), I defined own chain's name concentration as the time-varying proportion of a chain's components that have the same name as the focal component (Ingram 1996b). Greater name concentration implies greater potential benefits of pursuit by a chain of a reputation strategy. Figure 14.4 shows the trend in chains' mean name concentration. To examine whether membership in a chain pursuing a reputation strategy was more beneficial in concentrated urban areas (hypothesis 3b), I interacted name concentration with a dummy variable, urban location, coded 1 for nursing homes located in census metropolitan statistical areas (CMSAs) and 0 otherwise. To test hypothesis 3c, which predicts that the benefits of pursuing a reputation strategy depend on the degree to which other chains also pursue such a strategy, I estimated an own chain's name concentration × other chains' name concentration interaction. I measured other chains' name concentration as the sum of proportions of other chains' components that share a common name at the start of each year. Since prior research suggests that such industry reputation effects may vary by level of analysis (Hannan et al. 1995), I computed this variable at both provincial and census district levels and subtracted census district name concentration from the provincial score and each component's name concentration from its census district score. I also used the other chains' name concentration in the acquisition analysis to examine whether chains' acquisition rate of independent homes increases with the "reputation" of the form (hypothesis 3d). Finally, to test hypothesis 3e, that chains' rate of acquisition is lower for nonprofit independent nursing homes, I included nonprofit orientation, measured using a dummy variable coded 1 for nonprofit nursing homes and 0 for profit-oriented homes, in the acquisition analysis.

MULTIMARKET CONTACT (HYPOTHESES 4A-C)

I tested hypothesis 4a using a measure of own chain's census district multimarket contact and hypotheses 4b-c using a measure of census district multimarket contact. I defined

Figure 14.4. Spatial Compactness of Ontario Nursing Home Chains, 1971–1995

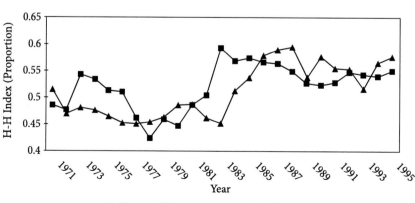

own chain's census district multimarket contact as the number of multimarket competitors (i.e., a competitor the focal chain meets in *more* than one market) that chain *i* meets in census district *m* at the start of each year. Census district multimarket contact was defined as the number of multimarket competitors in census district *m* at the start of each year. Mean values for these variables are plotted over time in Figure 14.5 tested hypothesis 4b, which predicts that chains' rate of acquisition of independent nursing homes declines with increases in multimarket contact among chains in a market by including census district multimarket contact in the acquisition rate analysis. Finally, to examine whether multimarket contact among chains leads them to engage in more intense rivalry toward for-profit independent competitors (hypothesis 4c), I included component × own chain's census district multimarket contact and nonprofit × own chain's census district multimarket contact interactions in the analysis to differentiate the effects of census district multimarket contact on component and nonprofit and for-profit independent nursing homes.

Control variables

Many other factors may influence the fates of nursing homes. Accordingly, in addition to the variables described above, the analysis controls for a variety of additional nursing-home characteristics and nursing-home industry-specific environmental factors.

NURSING-HOME CHARACTERISTICS

I defined nursing-home age as the number of months since the date of a nursing home's founding and nursing-home size as the natural logarithm of the number of beds a home operated at the start of each year. Nonprofit orientation was measured using a dummy variable coded 1 for nonprofit nursing homes and 0 for for-profit homes. Notably, there were no government-run nursing homes, nonprofit nursing homes were infrequently run by religious or charitable orders, and all chain components were operated on a for-profit basis.[9] Replacement facility was also measured as a dummy variable, coded 0 unless a nursing home closed its original facility and transferred its license and residents

Figure 14.5. Multimarket Contact among Ontario Nursing Homes, 1971–1995

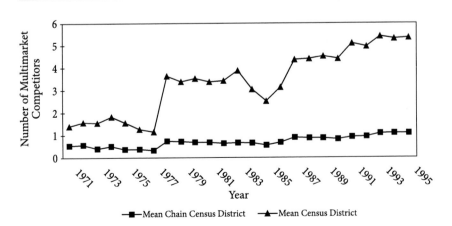

to a new facility constructed to meet provincial requirements. The dummy variable was coded 1 as of the date the new facility opened. These events were not treated as failures and foundings since the original organization continued to operate in the new facility. Several studies have demonstrated that human service organizations' linkages to the institutional environment can reduce failure rates by conferring legitimacy and more specific resources (Baum & Oliver 1991; Singh, House & Tucker 1986). Therefore, I controlled for the effects of nursing homes' linkages to two important institutional actors: (1) membership in the Ontario Nursing Homes' Association (ONHA), and (2) Accredited Care Center (ACC) status, which affords eligibility for extended-care benefits under the Health Insurance Act. Last, I included a left-censored variable, coded 1 for nursing homes founded before 1971, to examine whether such nursing homes, which were excluded from meeting regulatory standards of the *Nursing Homes Act*, had systematically distinct acquisition and failure rates.

ENVIRONMENTAL CHARACTERISTICS

I also controlled for several factors influencing competition and the demand for nursing-home services at the census district level. I operationalized competition among and between independent and component nursing homes using mass dependence (Barnett & Amburgey 1990). Component (independent) nursing-home mass was measured as the natural logarithm of the total number of beds (i.e., the total productive capacities of the independent and chain segments of the industry) in a census district at the start of each spell. Each component (independent) nursing home's number of rooms was subtracted from the total component (independent) census district mass, so the mass variables reflected the number of beds operated by other component (independent) nursing homes in the same census district. To test for differential competitive effects among and between independent and component nursing homes, I included mass × component dummy variable interactions.

The competitive effect of adding nursing-home beds depends on the potential demand at the time the capacity is added. If potential demand is not measured explicitly, then the competitive effect of increasing the number of homes or beds is assumed to be constant over time. It is crucial to my test of hypothesis 6, therefore, to incorporate time-varying information on the potential demand for nursing-home services. I controlled for this potential demand using the population aged 65 or older in a nursing home's census district. I also included measures of the mass (natural log of the number of beds) of homes for the aged operated by local municipalities and charitable foundations. These facilities represent the major government-sanctioned and government-supported competing form of long-term institutional care for the elderly in Ontario.

Results

Appendixes A and B present means, standard deviations, and bivariate correlations for all independent and control variables for the independent and component samples, respectively. The tables indicate a moderate degree of multicollinearity among some of the explanatory variables, which can result in less precise parameter estimates (i.e., larger standard errors) for the correlated explanatory variables but will not bias parameter estimates

(Kennedy 1992). Although moderate multicollinearity does not pose a serious estimation problem, it may result in conservative tests of significance for correlated variables, making it difficult to draw inferences about the effects of adding particular variables to the models. Therefore, I estimate and test the significance of groups of variables in comparisons of a series of hierarchically nested regression models and examine coefficients' standard errors for inflation to check that multicollinearity is not causing less precise parameter estimates (Kmenta 1971).

Table 1 shows estimates for the failure and acquisition analyses. Model 1 presents coefficients for the pooled sample, model 2 for independent nursing-home failure, model 3 for component nursing-home failure, and model 4 for chains' acquisition of independent nursing homes.

The estimates support hypotheses 1a, b, and c. Coefficients for the extended-care per diem are significant and negative in all four models, indicating that independent and component nursing-home failure rates and chains' acquisition rate of independent nursing homes all declined as the per diem increased. The significant positive extended-care per diem × nursing-home size interaction coefficient in model 2 indicates that the decline in the failure rate resulting from increases in the per diem was greatest for smaller nursing homes. For example, the failure rate for an independent 25-bed nursing home declined 7 percent ($e^{-.244 \times 1 + .056 \times \ln 25}$) for every one real-dollar increase in the per diem; for a 50-bed independent home, the decrease was only 2.5 percent ($e^{-.244 \times 1 + .056 \times \ln 50}$). This interaction is not significant in either model 3 or model 4, however. Thus, smaller independent homes were neither more nor less likely to be acquired as a function of the per diem, and small component nursing homes did not benefit more from per diem increases.

The main effect of being a component is significant in model 1, supporting hypothesis 2a. And the effect is large: component nursing homes were, ceteris paribus, 78 percent ($e^{-1.501}$) less likely to fail than independent nursing homes. In model 3 this global effect of chain membership is disaggregated to disentangle the underlying sources of chain components' survival advantage. Surprisingly, none of the four own chain's size variables is significant. Thus, in contrast to hypothesis 2b, component survival chances do not improve with the size of the component's chain. Supporting hypothesis 2c, however, the significant negative coefficient for own chain's spatial compactness indicates that the failure rate is significantly lower for components of spatially compact chains. These results highlight the importance of chains' spatial arrangements for achieving advantages from multiunit operation. The effect is again large: a .25 increase in own chain's spatial compactness (the observed range is .2–1) would lower a component's failure rate by 26 percent ($e^{-1.210 \times .25}$).

The component × nursing-home size interaction in model 1 is not significant, failing to support hypothesis 2d, which predicted that small nursing homes would benefit more from chain membership. However, nursing-home size coefficients in models 2 and 3 are consistent with this prediction: while independent nursing homes suffered a liability of smallness, component homes did not. Hypothesis 2e is supported by the significant positive coefficient for nursing-home size in model 4, and the magnitude of this effect is very large. For example, a 75-bed independent nursing home was 87 percent more likely to be acquired than a 50-bed home ($e^{.195 \times \ln 25}$).

Supporting hypothesis 3a, the main effect of own chain's name concentration in model 3 is significant and negative—components of chains that share a common name with more other components in the same chain have significantly lower failure rates. The significant negative coefficient for the own chain's name concentration × urban location interaction in model 3 supports hypothesis 3b, which predicted that the benefits of name concentration are significantly greater in urban settings. The sizes of these effects are substantial. Based on the coefficients in model 3, the failure rate for a nonurban component that shared a common name with 50 percent of the components in its chain had a failure rate 65 percent lower ($e^{-2.150 \times 0.5}$) than that of a component that did not share a common name with any other member of its chain. In an urban location this advantage increases to 90 percent ($e^{-2.150 \times 0.5 - 2.378}$).

Hypothesis 3c is also supported by the significant negative coefficients for the own chain's name concentration × other chains' name concentration interactions for both the focal component's census district and other census districts. Thus, the benefits to a component of its chain pursuing a reputation strategy depends on the degree to which other nursing homes also use common naming strategies, contributing to the increased visibility and reputation of the chain form. For example, the entry of a chain whose components all shared a common name (i.e., name concentration = 1) to a component's census district would increase the benefit of its own chain's pursuing a 50 percent common name strategy (i.e., name concentration = 0.5) (relative to a component that did not share a common name with any other member of its chain) from 65 percent ($e^{-2.150 \times 0.5}$) to 84 percent ($e^{-2.150 \times 0.5 - 1.572 \times 1 \times 0.5}$).

There is no support for hypothesis 3d; the coefficients for other chains' name concentration are not significant at either census district or provincial levels. Hypothesis 3e, which predicted lower acquisition rates for nonprofit nursing homes, is, however, supported by the significant negative coefficient for nonprofit orientation in model 4. Again, the effect is large: nonprofit independent nursing homes were 82 percent ($e^{-1.707}$) less likely to be acquired by a chain than their for-profit counterparts.

The significant negative coefficient in model 3 for own chain's multimarket contact in a component's census district supports hypothesis 4a; as a chain's level of multimarket contact increased in a given census district, the failure rate of its components in that census district declined. Each additional multimarket competitor a chain had in a component's census district lowered the component's risk of failure by 34 percent ($e^{-.410}$). The significant negative coefficient for census district multimarket contact in model 4 also supports hypothesis 4b, which predicted that chains' rate of acquisition of independent nursing homes would decline with increases in multimarket contact among chains in a market. In this case, each additional multimarket competitor in a census district lowered an independent nursing home's risk of being acquired by a chain by approximately 10 percent ($e^{-.101}$).

The significant positive coefficient for census district multimarket contact and the significant negative coefficients for its interaction with the nonprofit and component dummy variables in model 1 support hypothesis 4b; as the level of multimarket contact in a given census district increased, the failure rate of for-profit independent nursing homes increased ($\beta = .104$), the failure rate of nonprofit independent nursing homes decreased ($\beta = .104 - .151 = -.047$), and component nursing homes in that census district were largely unaffected ($\beta = -.115 = .008$). The significant coefficients for census district multimarket contact and its interaction with the nonprofit dummy variable in model 2 and the insignificant coefficient for census district multimarket contact in model 3 parallel the estimates for model 1. Thus, it appears, supporting hypothesis 4c, that multimarket contact among nursing-home chains leads them to forbear from competing aggressively with one another and to be more aggressive toward single-market, for-profit (but not socially preferred nonprofit) competitors that cannot retaliate.

Table 14.1. Maximum-Likelihood Models of Nursing-Home Failure and Acquisition

	Model 1	Model 2	Model 3	Model 4
	All Nursing Homes	Independent Nursing-Home Failure	Component Nursing-Home Failure	Independent Nursing-Home Acquisition
Nursing home				
Nursing-home age	.000	.000	.013**	−.011*
(in months)	(.000)	(.000)	(.005)	(.005)
ln (no. nursing-home beds)	−2.600***	−3.328***	2.601	.195*
	(.597)	(.614)	(3.750)	(.118)
Nonprofit orientation	−1.803*	−1.829*	—	−1.707*
	(.952)	(.949)		(.907)
Replacement facility	−1.217**	−1.988**	.871	.525*
	(.389)	(.615)	(.833)	(.301)
Urban location	.356*	.352*	.886	−.077
	(.201)	(.207)	(.773)	(.204)
Left-censored	.086	.074	−.782	1.343***
	(.141)	(.144)	(1.057)	(.329)
ONHA link	−.514***	−.508***	.832	−.113
	(.124)	(.146)	(.743)	(.176)
ACC link	−.863**	−.630*	−2.602*	.481
	(.343)	(.367)	(1.237)	(.326)
Government funding				
Extended care per diem	−.262***	−.244***	−.340*	−.184***
	(.037)	(.042)	(.160)	(.047)
x ln (no. nursing-home beds)	.039*	.056**	.076	−.022
	(.021)	(.022)	(.062)	(.026)
Chain				
Component	−1.501**	—	—	—
	(.592)			
x ln (no. nursing-home beds)	.462	—	—	—
	(.501)			
Other CD ln (own chain's	—	—	.272	—
no. beds)			(.557)	
Other CD own chain	—	—	−.120	—
no. components			(.196)	
CD ln (own chain's no. beds)	—	—	.259	—
			(.275)	
CD own chain's	—	—	.056	—
no. components			(.493)	
Own chain's spatial	—	—	−1.210**	—
compactness			(.488)	

Table 14.1. Maximum-Likelihood Models of Nursing-Home Failure and Acquisition *(cont.)*

	Model 1 All Nursing Homes	Model 2 Independent Nursing-Home Failure	Model 3 Component Nursing-Home Failure	Model 4 Independent Nursing-Home Acquisition
Name concentration	—	—	-2.150^{*}	—
			(1.074)	
x Urban location	—	—	-2.378^{*}	—
			(1.382)	
x CD other chains' name concentration	—	—	-1.572^{***} (.462)	—
x Other CDs other chains' name concentration	—	—	$-.059^{**}$ (.024)	—
Own chain's CD multimarket contact	—	—	$-.410^{*}$ (.248)	—
Competition				
CD multimarket contact	$.104^{**}$	$.132^{***}$	.054	$-.101^{*}$
	(.032)	(.032)	(.152)	(.052)
x Component	$-.093^{*}$	—	—	—
	(.042)			
x Nonprofit	$-.151^{**}$	$-.182^{**}$	—	—
	(.057)	(.071)		
ln (CD no. independent beds)	$.314^{*}$	$.351^{**}$	.221	.192
	(.144)	(.148)	(.406)	(.162)
x Component	-.130	—	—	—
	(.196)			
ln (CD no. component beds)	.009	.009	1.989^{*}	$.100^{*}$
	(.044)	(.044)	(1.070)	(.057)
x Component	$.434^{*}$	—	—	—
	(.212)			
Environment				
CD other chain's name concentration	$-.102^{*}$	-.072	$-.473^{*}$	.022
	(.059)	(.059)	(.293)	(.042)
Other CDs other chains' name concentration	-.005	-.004	$-.088^{*}$	.009
	(.007)	(.007)	(.038)	(.012)
CD population > 65	.036	-.065	1.374	$.408^{*}$
	(.259)	(.271)	(.992)	(.249)
CD square miles	-.087	-.112	.533	$.169^{*}$
	(.108)	(.111)	(.423)	(.099)
ln (CD no. homes-for-the-aged beds)	-.067	-.041	-.652	$-.443^{*}$
	(.218)	(.228)	(.936)	(.203)
Constant	3.778	4.876^{*}	-14.480^{*}	-1.260
	(2.318)	(2.370)	(7.606)	(2.145)
δ	-13.390	-13.279	-14.100	-12.016
Log-likelihood	-791.21	-716.96	-49.34	-608.70
df	23	19	24	18
Spells	9,637	7,072	2,565	7,072
Events	226	161	65	159

Note: Standard errors are in parentheses.
$^{*}p < .05$ $^{**}p < .01$ $^{***}p < .001$

Several of the control variables also influenced nursing-home failure rates significantly. Large, nonprofit, and replacement independent nursing homes were significantly less likely to fail, while those located in an urban setting were more likely to fail. Older, but not larger, component nursing homes were more likely to fail, suggesting that chains buffer their components from liabilities of "newness" and "smallness." Younger and replacement independent nursing homes were more likely to be acquired by chains. ONHA links raised survival chances for independent nursing homes, while ACC links raise survival chances for both independent and component homes. Although independent nursing homes faced competition from component homes in markets characterized by high levels of multimarket contact among chains, mass-dependent competition was localized between independent and component homes. Consistent with the idea that visibility and reputation benefits of the chain form depend on the degree to which chains in that field use common naming strategies, other chains' name concentration raises the survival chances of component but not independent nursing homes. Surprisingly, neither independent nor component nursing-home failure rates were affected by either the size of the population over 65 years of age or the presence of municipal and charitable homes for the aged, nursing homes' primary competition. In contrast, coefficients for these variables are all significant in the expected directions in model 4, the acquisition analysis.

Discussion and Conclusion

This article began with a question: What factors shaped the dramatic transformation of the Ontario nursing-home industry from independent to chain ownership after 1971? Was it triggered by Ontario government policy, as typically claimed? Was it the inevitable result of advantages inherent in the chain organizational form that have favored its rise to dominance in diverse industries of the twentieth century? Or was some combination of the two responsible? The results of this study indicate that government policy did indeed play a significant role in triggering the transformation, but results also reveal powerful advantages inherent in the chain organizational form that have also been very influential.

As rhetoric would have it, the initially low extended-care subsidy per diem hastened the demise of many independent nursing homes in Ontario and contributed to the acquisition by chains of many more. In addition, however, components of nursing-home chains—especially components of spatially compact chains—were more likely to survive. Indeed, nursing-home chains might be viewed as "white knights" that made it feasible for the industry to continue to operate under severe austerity measures imposed by provincial authorities. Consistent with mutual forbearance arguments, multimarket contact among rival chains improved their components' survival chances. Mutual forbearance among chains also appears to have led them to direct their competitive energies toward independent for-profit (but *not* nonprofit) competitors that cannot retaliate in multiple markets. In addition to these survival advantages of chain membership, chains' tendency to acquire nursing homes with high survival value (e.g., large replacement facilities) appears to have accelerated the independent-to-chain transition. However, fear of multimarket retaliation and the emergence of mutual forbearance among chains appears to have had the opposite effect.

Historically, there has been a widely held belief in the idea that multimarket contact increases the ability of organizations in any single market to achieve and sustain tacitly collusive arrangements. A critical premise underlying this belief is that organizations engage in mutual forbearance simply by virtue of their operating in more than one of the same product or geographic markets (Korn & Baum 1999). Organizations' members are assumed to comprehend the benefits of actively managing the structure of relationships with competitors across their jointly contested markets, and, by corollary, mutual forbearance is anticipated wherever organizations meet in multiple markets. Although research in organization theory, IO economics, and strategic management generally supports this idea, the assumption that organizations' members are guided by a "multimarket mentality" needs to be tempered by the reality that organizational learning from observation and experience is difficult (Levinthal & March 1993; Levitt & March 1988). Chains, however, appear particularly well suited to experiential and vicarious organizational learning (Baum & Ingram 1998; Ingram & Baum 1997, 1998). Future research on how organizational and interorganizational learning shapes the evolution of multimarket contact and mutual forbearance among chains would enrich our understanding of their success by treating the emergence of mutual forbearance among chains as a history-dependent learning process that accompanies the growth of chains and the rise of the chain form.

There are also advantages of chain reputation. Belonging to a chain having more homes with the same name significantly and substantially increases chances for component survival. Thus, by establishing reputations, chains—and the chain form more generally—appear able to raise their trustworthiness and accountability in the eyes of consumers. Whether this trust is justified is open to question, however. For example, although it is not surprising to discover that an independent gas station waters down its gasoline, it is surprising to discover that a gas station operated by a major oil company has done so. We are surprised because, since such behavior at any station can damage the entire company's reputation, we expect the oil company to put pressure on each station to maintain and enhance its company's reputation. In this example, however, organizational performance is quite easily ascertained. In the case of nursing homes, performance in resident care is far more difficult to discern, which is why nonprofits are typically preferred. So, in the nursing-home field it is widely debated whether consumers' perceptions are being used to chains' advantage rather than residents' welfare (Tarman 1990). Are chains "substitutes" for nonprofits? My findings indicate quite clearly that they are not and suggest instead that chains complement nonprofits. For-profit independents were far more likely to be acquired by chains, and while mutual forbearance among nursing-home chains raised the failure rate of for-profit independent nursing homes, it did not affect their independent nonprofit counterparts. Thus, Ontario nursing-home chains displaced *only* for-profit independent homes. Notably, by displacing independent for-profit nursing homes, the rise of chains served to reduce the intensity of local competition nonprofits faced from for-profits.

Taken together, my results, which indicate that the net effect of chain affiliation is to lower failure rates, are compatible with prior studies of chain component failure (Ingram & Baum 1997; Baum & Ingram 1998) and more generally with what Miner, Amburgey, and Stearns (1990) refer to as "partial selection" resulting from organizational buffers. Rather than simply outcompeting independent nursing homes, nursing-home chains grow and component homes become more numerous because they have lower rates of failure. In this sense, my findings are broadly consistent with ecological research on the effects of interorganizational linkages on organizational failure (Baum & Oliver 1991; Miner, Amburgey

& Stearns 1990; Singh, House & Tucker 1996). My detailed data on chains allowed me to dimensionalize their relationships, however, and to examine the processes underlying the benefits of interorganizational affiliation. My study differs in another important way as well from past work on interorganizational linkages and organizational failure. Most past work has examined relations between organizations and regulatory agencies, community organizations, or political parties. Although these represent important connections between organizations and their environments, these relationships are nondefinitive. In contrast, the relations examined here between component nursing homes and chains create a distinct organizational form.

Over the past 20 years, organization theorists have explored why one form of organization rather than another succeeds in an industry. One organizational form that has succeeded across diverse service industries this century is the chain organizational form. Yet only recently has this form begun to receive significant attention from organization theorists. The results of this study shed light on how organizational, industrial, and institutional factors shaped the rise of chain nursing homes in Ontario over the last three decades. First, I provide an example (perhaps common) of how government regulation and funding facilitate the rise of chains in human services by increasing the advantages associated with economies of scale and increasing chains' rate of acquisition of independent organizations. Second, I offer a rationale for expecting the rise of chains in health and human services where nonprofits are often the socially preferred form. And third, I show how mutual forbearance usefully informs our understanding of chains' competitive advantage over independent organizations. Thus, my study of the reconfiguration of the Ontario nursing-home industry provides a needed window not only into this important industry, but also into this century's most successful organizational form—the chain— which has come to play such a central role in modern society.

Notes

1. Like this study, Ingram and Baum (1998) ask the question, What characteristics of independent organizations and their environments make them potential targets for acquisition by chains? Acquisition research in organization studies has typically asked a different question: what organizational and environmental factors make organizations more likely to be acquisitive? Therefore, the primary focus of the acquisition literature in organization studies has been on the acquirer, and far less attention has been paid to potential targets of acquisitions.
2. There is considerable disagreement on how to define organizational forms, and multiple definitions premised on different approaches to organizational classification can be found in the literature. For more detailed discussions of organizational forms and their classification, see Baum 1989; McKelvey 1982; Rao and Singh 1999; Rich 1992; Romanelli 1991.
3. Romanelli (1991) identifies three perspectives on the evolution of new organizational forms: (1) organizational genetics, which focuses on random variation, (2) environmental conditioning, which conceives variation as environmentally constrained, and (3) emergent social systems, which emphasizes embedded social-organizational interaction as a source of new forms. Romanelli characterizes the organizational speciation view as an environmental conditioning approach.
4. The *Long-Term Care Act of 1993*, abandoned after a government change, similarly aimed to provide holistic service delivery through multiservice agencies that combined responsibilities of care and placement coordination with existing professional services and community groups. Among the Act's aims were to "simplify and improve access to the continuum of community

service" and to "promote the efficient management of human, financial, and other resources involved in the delivery of community services."

5. I do not advance a parallel acquisition hypothesis here since, as discussed below (see hypothesis 2e), I do not typically expect chains to acquire *small* independent nursing homes. Nevertheless, the acquisition equation controls for this possibility.

6. It is also possible that the features of chains may affect the likelihood of acquiring independent nursing homes. Unfortunately, it is not feasible to include chain features as explanatory factors for nursing-home acquisition in an analysis such as mine. The reason is that the set of chains that may acquire a nursing home is unbounded, including not only all chains operating in Ontario, but even chains operating elsewhere and chains that are only "potential," since nursing homes can be acquired by new chains. Because I cannot define the set of chains that might acquire a nursing home, I cannot use chain characteristics to explain nursing-home acquisition.

7. In 1971 92 percent of 483 nursing homes (86 percent of 24,184 beds) were for-profit; in 1996, 83 percent of 335 nursing homes (89 percent of 31,304 beds) were for-profit.

8. Notably, as long as nursing homes are in general located along census district boundaries, this specification error introduces a conservative bias in market definition.

9. The homogeneous character of nonprofit nursing homes is likely a result of the historical and regulatory distinction between nursing homes studied here and homes for the aged, operated exclusively by charitable foundations and municipal governments. Effects of competition from homes for the aged are controlled in the models.

References

Aaronson, William E., Jacqueline S. Zinn, and Michael D. Rosko. 1994. "Do For-Profit and Not-for-Profit Nursing Homes Behave Differently?" *Gerontologist* 34:775–86.

Adelman, S. 1969. "Comment of the 'H' Concentration Measure as a Numbers Equivalent." *Review of Economics and Statistics* 51:99–101.

Aldrich, Howard E., and Ellen R. Auster. 1986. "Even Dwarfs Started Small: Liabilities of Age and Size and Their Strategic Implications." Pp. 165–98 in *Research in Organizational Behavior*. Vol. 8, edited by B. Shaw and L. Cummings. JAI Press.

Arling, Greg, Richard H. Nordquist, and John A. Capitman. 1987. "Nursing Home Cost and Ownership Type: Evidence of Interaction Effects." *Health Services Research* 22:255–69.

Banaszak-Holl, Jane, Jacqueline S. Zinn, and Vincent Mor. 1996. "The Impact of Market and Organizational Characteristics on Nursing Care Facility Service Innovation: A Resource Dependency Perspective." *Health Services Research* 31:97–109.

Barnett, William P. 1993. "Strategic Deterrence among Multipoint Competitors." *Industrial and Corporate Change* 2:249–78.

Barnett, William P., and Terry L. Amburgey. 1990. "Do Larger Organizations Generate Stronger Competition?" Pp. 78–102 in *Organizational Evolution: New Directions*, edited by Jitendra V. Singh. Sage.

Baum, Daniel J. 1977. *Warehouses of Death: The Nursing Home Industry*. Don Mills, Ont.: Burns and MacEachern.

Baum, Joel A.C. 1989. "A Population Perspective on Organizations: A Study of Diversity and Transformation in Child Care Service Organizations." Ph.D. dissertation, University of Toronto.

———. 1996. "Organizational Ecology." Pp. 77–114 in *The Handbook of Organization Studies*, edited by Stewart R. Clegg, Cynthia Hardy, and Walter R. Nord. Sage.

Baum, Joel A.C., and Helaine J. Korn. 1996. "Competitive Dynamics of Interfirm Rivalry." *Academy of Management Journal* 39:255–91.

Baum, Joel A.C., and Christine Oliver. 1991. "Institutional Linkages and Organizational Mortality." *Administrative Science Quarterly* 36:187–218.

———. 1992. "Institutional Embeddedness and the Dynamics of Organizational Populations." *American Sociological Review* 57:540–59.

———. 1996. "Toward an Institutional Ecology of Organizational Founding." *Academy of Management Journal* 39:1378–427.

Bernheim, B. Douglas, and Michael D. Whinston. 1990. "Multimarket Contact and Collusive Behavior." *Rand Journal of Economics* 21:1–26.

Birnbaum, H., C. Bishop, A.J. Lee, and G. Jensen. 1981. "Why Do Nursing Home Costs Vary?" *Medical Care* 19:1095–107.

Blossfeld, Hans-Peter, and Gotz Rohwer. 1995. *Techniques of Event History Modeling: New Approaches to Causal Analysis.* Lawrence Erlbaum.

Bruchovsky, A. 1970. "Nursing Homes Plan to Grow with 'Good Quality Care.'" *Financial Post*, 21 Mar.

Canadian Medical Association. 1984. *Health, A Need for Redirection: A Task Force on the Allocation of Health Care Resources.* Ottawa.

Cohen, J.W., and L.C. Dubay. 1990. "The Effects of Reimbursement Method and Ownership on Nursing Home Costs, Case Mix and Staffing." *Inquiry* 27:183–200.

Cotterill, Ronald W., and Lawrence E. Haller. 1992. "Barrier and Queue Effects: A Study of Leading U.S. Supermarket Chain Entry Patterns." *Journal of Industrial Economics* 40:427–40.

Darr, Eric D., Linda Argote, and Dennis Epple. 1995. "The Acquisition, Transfer and Depreciation of Knowledge in Service Organizations: Productivity in Franchises." *Management Science* 42:1750–62.

Delacroix, Jacques, and Hayagreeva Rao. 1994. "Externalities and Ecological Theory: Unbundling Density Dependence." Pp. 255–68 in *Evolutionary Dynamics of Organizations*, edited by Joel A.C. Baum and Jitendra V. Singh. Oxford University Press.

DiMaggio, Paul J., and Helmut K. Anheier. 1990. "The Sociology of Nonprofit Organizations and Sectors." Pp. 137–59 in *Annual Review of Sociology*. Vol. 16, edited by W. Richard Scott and Judith Blake. Annual Reviews.

Dranove, David, and Mark Shanley. 1995. "Cost Reductions or Reputation Enhancement as Motives for Mergers: The Logic of Multihospital Systems." *Strategic Management Journal* 16:55–74.

Edwards, Corwin D. 1955. "Conglomerate Bigness as a Source of Power." Pp. 331–59 in *Business Concentration and Price Policy*. National Bureau of Economics Research conference report. Princeton University Press.

Evans, William N., and Ioannis N. Kessides. 1994. "Living by the 'Golden Rule': Multimarket Contact in the U.S. Airline Industry." *Quarterly Journal of Economics* 109 (2):341–66.

Farley, B. 1988. *Trends in Hospital Average Length of Stay, Case Mix, and Discharge Rates, 1980–85.* Department of Health and Human Services Publication No. (PHS) 88-3620. Hospital Studies Program Research Note 2. Public Health Service.

Garnick, Deborah W., Harold S. Luft, James C. Robinson, and Janice Tetreault. 1987. "Appropriate Measures of Hospital Market Areas." *Health Services Research* 22:69–89.

Gertler, Paul J. 1989. "Subsidies, Quality and Regulation in Nursing Homes." *Journal of Public Economics* 39:33–53.

Gimeno, Javier, and Carolyn Y. Woo. 1996. "Hypercompetition in a Multimarket Environment: The Role of Strategic Similarity and Multimarket Contact in Competitive De-escalation." *Organization Science* 7:322–41.

Guo, Guang. 1993. "Event-History Analysis for Left-Truncated Data." Pp. 217–43 in *Sociological Methodology*, vol. 23, edited by Peter V. Marsden. Blackwell.

Halliday, Terence C., Michael J. Powell, and Mark W. Granfors. 1987. "Minimalist Organizations: Vital Events in State Bar Associations, 1870–1930." *American Sociological Review* 52:456–71.

Hannan, Michael T., Glenn R. Carroll, Elizabeth A. Dundon, and John C. Torres. 1995. "Organizational Evolution in a Multinational Context: Entries of Automobile Manufacturers in Belgium, Britain, France, Germany, and Italy." *American Sociological Review* 60:509–28.

Hannan, Michael T., and John Freeman. 1984. "Structural Inertia and Organizational Change." *American Sociological Review* 49:149–64.

——. 1989. *Organizational Ecology.* Belknap Press.

Hansmann, Henry. 1980. "The Role of Nonprofit Enterprise." *Yale Law Journal* 89:835–901.

——. 1987. "Economic Theories of Nonprofit Organizations." Pp. 27–42 in *The Nonprofit Sector: A Research Handbook*, edited by Walter W. Powell. Yale University Press.

Hughes, Kirsty, and Christine Oughton. 1993. "Diversification, Multi-Market Contact and Profitability." *Economica* 60:203–24.

Ingram, Paul. 1996a. *The Rise of Hotel Chains in the United States, 1896–1980.* Garland.

———. 1996b. "Organizational Form as a Solution to the Problem of Credible Commitment: The Evolution of Naming Strategies among U.S. Hotel Chains, 1896–1980." *Strategic Management Journal* 17:85–98.

Ingram, Paul, and Joel A.C. Baum. 1997. "Chain Affiliation and the Failure of Manhattan Hotels, 1898–1980." *Administrative Science Quarterly* 42:68–102.

———. 1998. "Interorganizational Learning and the Dynamics of Chain Relationships." Paper presented at the Academy of Management Meetings, San Diego, Calif, Aug.

Joskow, Paul L. 1980. "The Effects of Competition and Regulation on Hospital Bed Supply and the Reservation Quality of the Hospital." *Bell Journal of Economics* 11:421–48.

Kane, R.L., and R.A. Kane. 1990. "The Nursing Home: Neither Home nor Hospital." Pp. 216–48 in *Introduction to Health Services*, 2d ed., edited by Stephen J. Williams. Wiley.

Kennedy, Peter. 1992. *A Guide to Econometric Methods.* 3d ed. MIT Press.

Kmenta, Jan. 1971. *Elements of Econometrics.* Macmillan.

Levinthal, Daniel A., and James G. March. 1993. "The Myopia of Learning." *Strategic Management Journal* 14:94–112.

Levitt, Barbara, and James G. March. 1988. "Organizational Learning." *Annual Review of Sociology* 14:319–40.

Light, Donald W. "Corporate Medicine for Profit." *Scientific American* 225:38–45.

Lincoln, James R. 1984. "Analyzing Relations in Dyads." *Sociological Methods and Research* 13:45–76.

Luft, Harold S., and Susan C. Maerki. 1984. "The Competitiveness of Hospital Markets." *Contemporary Policy Issues* 3:89–102.

Luft, Harold S., James C. Robinson, Deborah W. Garnick, Susan C. Maerki, and Stephen J. McPhee. 1986. "The Role of Specialized Clinical Services in Competition among Hospitals." *Inquiry* 23:83–94.

Luke, Roice D. 1991. "Spatial Competition and Cooperation in Local Hospital Markets." *Medical Care Review* 48:207–37.

Luke, Roice D., Yasar A. Ozcan, and Peter C. Olden. 1995 "Local Markets and Systems: Hospital Consolidations in Metropolitan Areas." *Health Services Research* 30:555–67.

Lumsden, Charles J., and Jitendra V. Singh. 1990. "The Dynamics of Organizational Speciation." Pp. 145–63 in *Organizational Evolution: New Directions*, edited by Jitendra V. Singh. Sage.

Mauser, Elizabeth. 1998. "The Importance of Organizational Form: Parent Perceptions versus Reality in the Day Care Industry." Pp. 124–36 in *Private Action and the Public Good*, edited by Walter W. Powell and Elisabeth S. Clemens. Yale University Press.

McKay, Niccie L. 1991. "The Effect of Chain Ownership on Nursing Home Costs." *Health Services Research* 26:109–18.

McKelvey, Bill. 1982. *Organizational Systematics: Taxonomy, Evolution, Classification.* University of California Press.

Meiners, Mark R. 1982. "An Econometric Analysis of the Major Determinants of Nursing Home Costs in the United States." *Social Science and Medicine* 16:887–98.

Miner, Anne S., Terry L. Amburgey, and Timothy Stearns. 1990. "Interorganizational Linkages and Population Dynamics: Buffering and Transformational Shields." *Administrative Science Quarterly* 35:689–713.

Mitchell, Will. 1994. "The Dynamics of Evolving Markets: The Effects of Business Sales and Age on Dissolutions and Divestitures." *Administrative Science Quarterly* 39:575–602.

Morrisey, M.A., F.A. Sloan, and J. Valvona. 1989. "Defining Geographic Markets for Hospital Care." *Law and Contemporary Problems* 51:165–94.

Nyman, John A. 1985. "Medicaid Reimbursement, Excess Medicaid Demand, and the Quality of Nursing Home Care." *Journal of Health Economics* 4:237–59.

———. 1987. "Excess Demand, the Percentage of Medicaid Patients and the Quality of Nursing Home Care." *Journal of Human Resources* 23:76–91.

———. 1989. "Analysis of Nursing Home Use and Bed Supply, Wisconsin 1983." *Health Services Research* 24:511–38.

O'Brien, J., B.O. Saxberg, and H.L. Smith. 1983. "For-Profit or Not-for-Profit Nursing Homes: Does It Matter?" *Gerontologist* 23:341–48.

Ontario Health Survey Report. Vol. 1 1950. G. Davis, Chairman. Toronto.

Pfeffer, Jeffrey, and Gerlad R. Salancik. 1978. *The External Control of Organizations: A Resource Dependence Perspective*. Harper & Row.

Phibbs, Ciaran S., and James C. Robinson. 1993. "A Variable-Radius Measure of Local Hospital Market Structure." *Health Services Research* 28:313–24.

Rao, Hayagreeva, and Jitendra V. Singh. 1999. "Types of Variation in Organizational Populations: The Speciation of New Organizational Forms." Pp. 63–77 in *Variations in Organizational Science: In Honor of Donald T. Campbell*, edited by Joel A.C. Baum and Bill McKelvey. Sage.

Rich, Philip. 1992. "The Organizational Taxonomy: Definition and Design." *Academy of Management Review* 17:758–81.

Rohwer, Gotz. 1995. TDA (Transition Data Analysis) 5.7 [computer software]. Florence: European University Institute [producer and distributor].

Romanelli, Elaine. 1991. "The Evolution of New Organizational Forms." Pp. 79–103 in *Annual Review of Sociology*. Vol. 17. Annual Reviews.

Schumpeter, Joseph A. 1950. *Capitalism, Socialism, and Democracy*. Harper.

Scully, D. 1985. "History of Nursing Homes in Ontario." *Ontario Nursing Home Journal* 1:22–25.

——. 1986. "History of Nursing Homes in Ontario." *Ontario Nursing Home Journal* 2:12–15.

Simmel, Georg. 1950. *The Sociology of Georg Simmel*, translated and edited by Kurt H. Wolff. Free Press.

Singh, Jitendra V. 1993. "Density Dependence Theory—Current Issues, Future Promise." *American Journal of Sociology* 99:464–73.

Singh, Jitendra V., Robert J. House, and David J. Tucker. 1986. "Organizational Legitimacy and the Liability of Newness." *Administrative Science Quarterly* 31:171–93.

Social Planning Council, Metropolitan Toronto. 1984. *Caring for Profit: The Commercialization of Human Services in Ontario*. Christa Feller, Project Director. Toronto.

Stinchcombe, Arthur L. 1965. "Organizations and Social Structure." Pp. 153–93 in *The Handbook of Organizations*, edited by James G. March. Rand McNally.

Succi, Melissa J., Shoou-Yih D. Lee, and Jeffrey A. Alexander. 1997. "Effects of Market Position and Competition on Rural Hospital Closures." *Health Services Research* 31:679–99.

Tarman, Vera I. 1990. *Privatization and Health Care: The Case of Ontario Nursing Homes*. Toronto: Garamond Press.

Tuma, Nancy B., and Michael T. Hannan. 1984. *Social Dynamics: Models and Methods*. Academic Press.

Vladeck, Bruce C. 1988. "Quality Assurance through External Controls." *Inquiry* 25:100–107.

Walker, Gordon. 1998. "Strategy and Network Formation." Pp. 149–65 in *Disciplinary Roots of Strategic Management Research* (*Advances in Strategic Management*, vol. 15), edited by Joel A.C. Baum. JAI Press.

Weisbrod, Burton A. 1988. *The Nonprofit Economy*. Harvard University Press.

Weisbrod, Burton A., and Mark Schlesinger. 1986. "Public, Private, Nonprofit Ownership and the Response to Asymmetric Information: The Case of Nursing Homes." Pp. 133–51 in *The Economics of Nonprofit Institutions: Studies in Structure and Policy*, edited by Susan Rose-Ackerman. Oxford University Press.

White, J., and A. Chirikos. 1988. "Measuring Hospital Competition." *Medical Care* 26:256–62.

Winter, Sidney G. 1990. "Survival Selection, and Inheritance in Evolutionary Theories of Organization." Pp. 269–97 in *Organizational Evolution: New Directories*, edited by Jitendra V. Singh. Sage.

Yonson, D. 1981. "Growth in Old Age: Nursing Home Firms Lively, Yet Ignored." *The Financial Times of Canada*, Feb. 2:18,26.

Zinn, Jacqueline S. 1993. "The Influence of Nursing Wage Differentials on Nursing Home Staffing and Resident Care Decisions." *Gerontologist* 33:721–29.

——. 1994. "Market Competition and the Quality of Nursing Home Care." *Journal of Health Politics, Policy and Law* 19:555–82.

Appendix 14.A. Descriptive Statistics and Bivariate Correlations—Independent Nursing Homes

Variable	1	2	3	4	5	6	7	8	9	10	11	12	13	14	15	16	17
1. Nursing-home age (in months)	1.00																
2. ln (# nursing-home beds)	-.04	1.00															
3. Nonprofit orientation	-.01	.02	1.00														
4. Replacement facility	-.05	.17	.02	1.00													
5. Urban location	.02	.14	.05	-.04	1.00												
6. Left-censored	.13	-.18	-.08	-.36	.01	1.00											
7. ONHA link	-.02	-.13	.00	.14	.03	.00	1.00										
8. ACC link	.04	.32	.02	.24	.01	-.15	.28	1.00									
9. Extended care per diem	.02	.25	.06	.18	-.03	-.14	.12	.25	1.00								
10. CD multimarket contact	.01	.28	.05	.07	.29	-.13	.10	.25	.20	1.00							
11. ln (CD # independent beds)	-.01	.14	.00	-.03	.41	-.03	.10	-.03	-.04	.45	1.00						
12. ln (CD # component beds)	-.03	.20	.03	.08	.48	-.10	.11	.14	.15	.54	.47	1.00					
13. CD other chain's name concentration	-.01	.22	.04	-.02	.38	-.09	.06	.06	.12	.70	.58	.67	1.00				
14. Other CDs other chains' name concentration	.03	.37	.11	.34	-.08	-.25	.19	.58	.55	.27	-.18	.15	.03	1.00			
15. CD population > 65	-.01	.18	.02	-.07	.33	-.08	.06	.07	.03	.65	.66	.50	.79	-.03	1.00		
16. CD square miles	-.01	.04	-.03	-.05	-.05	-.09	-.05	.02	.03	-.08	-.12	-.12	-.08	.06	-.08	1.00	
17. ln (CD # homes-for-the aged beds)	-.03	.16	.01	.00	.49	-.07	.08	.03	.03	.54	.73	.66	.75	-.06	.81	-.10	1.00
Mean	146.7	3.91	.05	.20	.64	.36	.74	.25	27.01	2.16	6.23	4.28	1.64	44.79	41,762	7,496	6.40
Standard deviation	634.8	.69	.22	.40	.48	.48	.44	.43	7.44	3.94	.99	2.69	2.26	17.14	69,698	38,910	1.13

Note: The sample of independent nursing homes contained 7,072 yearly observations.

Appendix 14.B. Descriptive Statistics and Bivariate Correlations—Component Nursing Homes

Variable	1	2	3	4	5	6	7	8	9	10	11	12
1. Nursing-home age (in months)	1.00											
2. ln (# nursing-home beds)	-.04	1.00										
3. Replacement facility	-.23	-.06	1.00									
4. Urban location	-.08	.47	-.01	1.00								
5. Left-censored	.46	-.04	-.30	-.03	1.00							
6. ONHA link	.22	.01	.07	-.02	-.01	1.00						
7. ACC link	.47	.08	.08	-.05	-.03	.31	1.00					
8. Extended care per diem	.28	-.05	.13	-.07	-.06	.19	.33	1.00				
9. Own chain's spatial compactness	.11	.13	-.18	.00	-.07	.13	.12	.00	1.00			
10. Own chain's name concentration	-.07	.37	-.10	.17	-.03	.08	.01	-.07	.44	1.00		
11. Own chain's CD multimarket cont.	.11	.20	.04	.20	-.07	.10	.24	.12	.14	.10	1.00	
12. Other CD ln (own chain's # beds)	.05	.38	-.17	.15	-.10	.17	.25	.05	.55	.35	.25	1.00
13. CD ln (own chain's # beds)	.08	.39	-.02	.18	-.04	.11	.11	.21	.09	.19	.25	.31
14. Other CD own chain's # comps.	.12	.11	-.06	.02	-.16	.21	.32	.13	.56	.16	.22	.86
15. CD own chain's # components	.05	.08	.04	.02	-.04	.06	.05	.18	.03	.01	.08	.25
16. CD multimarket contact	.18	.25	.06	.30	.03	.06	.22	.15	-.09	.02	.66	-.01
17. ln (CD # independent beds)	-.02	.23	.02	.31	.07	-.07	-.09	-.07	-.21	.02	.29	-.20
18. ln (CD # component beds)	.07	.51	-.03	.49	.00	-.01	.09	.08	-.04	.14	.44	.13
19. CD other chain's name conc.	-.04	.37	-.04	-.33	-.02	-.04	-.03	.04	.03	.27	.33	.13
20. Other CDs other chains' name conc.	.52	-.11	.02	-.19	-.10	.33	.66	.50	.06	-.11	.15	.11
21. CD population > 65	-.01	.35	-.06	.29	.02	-.05	.01	.04	-.08	.09	.26	.02
22. CD square miles	.06	-.06	-.09	-.20	.01	-.07	-.01	-.01	.13	.09	-.15	.10
23. ln (CD # homes-for-the-aged beds)	-.04	.40	-.07	.47	.00	-.07	-.07	.01	-.07	.12	.32	.02
Mean	154.6	4.62	.27	.73	.20	.89	.59	29.40	.56	.50	.76	6.71
Standard deviation	105.7	.63	.44	.44	.40	.32	.49	3.92	.48	.39	.96	.97

Appendix 14.B. Descriptive Statistics and Bivariate Correlations—Component Nursing Homes *(cont.)*

Variable	13	14	15	16	17	18	19	20	21	22	23
13. CD ln (own chain's # beds)	1.00										
14. Other CD own chain's # comps.	.21	1.00									
15. CD own chain's # components	.81	.26	1.00								
16. CD multimarket contact	.19	-.06	.04	1.00							
17. ln (CD # independent beds)	.04	-.33	-.10	.49	1.00						
18. ln (CD # component beds)	.35	-.01	.27	.68	.45	1.00					
19. CD other chain's name conc.	.27	.01	.27	.60	.45	.82	1.00				
20. Other CDs other chains' name conc.	.12	.27	.11	.15	-.24	-.02	-.15	1.00			
21. CD population	.21	-.11	.13	.64	.51	.69	.77	-.12	1.00		
22. CD square miles	-.04	.12	.10	-.16	-.26	-.15	-.07	.00	-.12	1.00	
23. ln (CD # homes-for-the-aged beds)	.21	-.13	.12	.59	.60	.77	.74	-.24	.81	-.16	1.00
Mean	4.68	10.07	4.88	3.85	5.67	6.08	2.62	54.96	49,367	8,251	6.56
Standard deviation	1.54	7.81	2.40	4.71	1.72	.99	2.30	14.55	76,172	31,479	1.09

Note: The sample of component nursing homes contained 2,565 yearly observations.

15

Access to Physician Services in Quebec

Relative Influence of Household Income and Area of Residence*

FRANÇOIS RIVEST, PASCAL BOSSÉ, SILVIU NEDELCA, AND ALAIN SIMARD

Introduction

THE CURRENT APPROACH to health care taken by Canadian provinces and territories—their biggest budget expenditure—is very much inspired by earlier efforts in Saskatchewan. That province's New Democratic Party (NDP) government set up a universal hospital care program in 1947, followed 15 years later by a medical (physician) care program. The government saw this as the major piece in order to make health services more accessible in an equitable fashion.

The adoption of framework legislation by the federal government on hospital insurance (1957)[1] and on medical care (1966)[2] resulted in the adoption of concomitant laws in the provinces that provide a broader context than the specific policies of the province of Saskatchewan. In this step-by-step approach the much greater challenge of moving into the provision of physician's services—the medical care program—was underlined by both the federal and Quebec governments holding highly publicized commissions of inquiry in order to prepare public opinion (Canada 1964; Quebec 1967, 1970–72). Each of these actors expressed concerns for accessibility and equity while at the same time raising an effort to broaden the issue.[3]

Our goal is to draw a portrait of the situation in Quebec as of 1991. To this end, the Régie de l'assurance maladie du Québec (RAMQ) gathered data on a very large number of households from its own files, supplemented by data from two Quebec government departments: Health and Revenue. Two aspects of social equity interest us: equity in terms of income and regional equity.

From a policy analysis perspective, Quebec is of special interest in that the government's response to income and regional accessibility issues has generally been more pronounced than elsewhere. From November 1970 (launch of medical insurance in Quebec) to 1991 (year under study), no user fees were charged for physician services (medical care), hospital stays,[4] or outpatient consultations in hospitals, unlike in other provinces where certain types of user fees exist or have existed (Canada 1983).

---

* This chapter was first published as "Access to Physician Services in Quebec: Relative Influence of Household Income and Area of Residence," *Canadian Public Policy* 25, 4 (1999): 453–481.

Moreover, the removal of major financial constraints in Canada to the consumption of physician services by households has made regional equity in the dispensation of such services a much more politically sensitive issue. In fact, there is now widespread concern about this in all provinces. The three largest and most populous provinces (British Columbia, Ontario, and Quebec) have all adopted administrative or legislative measures addressing the issue of the provision of physician services. The measures adopted by these three provinces give a good idea of the range of possibilities open to governments. On the one hand, Ontario and Quebec were relatively quick to bring in financial incentives for doctors to set up practice in rural and remote areas. Ontario's system has been dealt with in detail by Andersen and Rosenberg (1990). The incentives put in place by Quebec will be presented in a later section.

On the other hand, two of these provinces (Quebec and British Columbia) have also gone much further and have adopted measures to restrict access by new doctors to urban centres. In 1985, British Columbia gave itself the power to restrict "the issuance of practitioner/billing/payment numbers to new physicians under the medical insurance plan unless there was demonstration of need for the physician" (Crichton, Hsu and Tsang 1994, p. 253). This measure, however, was contested in the courts and declared unconstitutional by the British Columbia Court of Appeal. Quebec adopted less restrictive control measures in 1982 (described later). Although they led to discontent among newly graduated physicians, they were not legally contested, at least not as of this writing.[5]

Considering the more generous response of Quebec to problems of equity, we might expect the province to be a benchmark in terms of how income and regional disparities in physician service consumption should be handled. It is in Quebec that these disparities, if any, should be the least flagrant. We thus propose Quebec as a case study, and hope that this will encourage others to clarify the issue based on new data, and thus make it possible to draw comparisons with other provinces. A description of the research and results will be preceded by a review of the literature.

Previous Research

A number of researchers had examined access to physician services in Canada before the introduction of government insurance programs. Badgley (1991) conducted an interesting review of the research by individuals and groups as well as the reports ordered by the commissions of inquiry that preceded the introduction of medical care insurance. The Hall Commission took a particular interest in the percentage of the population covered by group and individual insurance policies. It also published a monograph on *Physician Resources in Canada* (Judek 1964), which contains a chapter (Chapter 4) dealing specifically with the provincial and regional allocation of physician resources in the early 1960s. This issue did not have to be re-examined by the Castonguay-Nepveu Commission, which spent relatively little time on the question of accessibility. It focused more on epidemiology and the extent of public demand for health services. The conclusion that it was the right time for the government to take control of medical services was so unanimous that neither commission felt it worthwhile or necessary to conduct an empirical examination of data on the actual consumption of physician services by individuals and households in view of socio-economic variables that were said to influence it.

Household Income

With the adoption of a medical insurance program by Quebec seemingly imminent and inescapable, a group of university researchers in Montreal set up a research project to evaluate the impact of the program (we will call it the Enterline-McDonald study) on the number of physician visits in a given period of time.[6] The study was a sampling survey of some 5,500 households in the Montreal area (number of completed questionnaires). The study therefore did not provide any information about regional disparities, but was useful in terms of income disparity because the households were asked to indicate an annual range of income. The great usefulness of the study arises from the fact that there were two surveys that closely overlapped the official launch of government medical insurance on 1 November 1970. The first was conducted in 1969–70 and the second in 1971–72.

This piece of good luck meant the results of the study were widely disseminated. Within a year and a half (May 1973 to September 1974), three articles were published in the respected *New England Journal of Medicine* (NEJM) (Enterline et al. 1973a, 1973b, McDonald et al. 1974), and a fourth in *Medical Care* (McDonald et al. 1973). Among the NEJM articles, the second (Enterline et al. 1973b) dealt more specifically with income-based accessibility.

The main conclusion of the second NEJM article was that the introduction of medical insurance did not cause an increase in demand but led to a transfer in consumption from rich to poor households. This assertion is supported by the data in Table 2 of the article (Enterline et al. 1973b), indicating that the poorest households (< $3,000/year) accounted for the greatest increase in the number of visits, rising from an estimated 6.6 visits per person per year to an estimated 7.8 in 1971–72 (percent change, +18.2). On the other hand, more affluent households ($15,000+) saw consumption drop from 5.3 visits to 4.8 (percent change, –9.4).

A certain transfer in consumption is very plausible, but we believe that the size of the percentage changes (+18.2 and –9.4 percent) should have led the authors to probe further and to provide a more detailed explanation. In the case of low-income households, the *Medical Care* article revealed that "nearly a third of the families making under $3,000 per year" were covered under the *Quebec Medical Assistance Act* (McDonald et al. 1973, p. 272), which was adopted in 1966 in the wake of the Canada Assistance Plan (itself adopted in 1965). With this legislation, the province bypassed the municipalities and other local authorities, and took on direct responsibility for the medical expenses of income-security recipients. This meant unimpeded access by income-security recipients to the physician of their choice, with no need to seek authorization before or after a visit. It would therefore be unlikely that this group experienced any increase in medical visits with the advent of universal medical insurance in 1970.[7] The reported increase in the under $3,000 group would thus have to be concentrated among those not on income security, meaning that the real percentage increase for these households could have been well over 30 percent.[8]

The decrease in the number of visits by households earning over $15,000 is equally surprising (–9.4 percent). Had some of these households previously visited doctors for no good reason? Apparently not. Physicians interviewed (for another part of the study) generally surmised that the advent of medical insurance had increased, not decreased, the percentage of visits without reasonable cause (Enterline et al. 1973a, p. 1154). Could these more affluent households, 85 percent of which had private health insurance coverage (McDonald et al. 1973, Table 1), have been subjected to more physician-initiated requests to return, and could the adoption of universal medical insurance have eliminated this bias?

A new survey of Montreal households was conducted in 1974 by a team led by Siemiatycki, Richardson and Pless (1980). This study also examined the link between income and "volume of care (is) expressed as the percentage of persons who had seen the doctor in the past two weeks" (ibid., p. 11). The selection of residences (households) was restricted to five federal electoral districts with a total population of some 400,000. There were 1,559 randomly selected households, which were distributed into three income categories. The results of the study (Table 1) indicated that, "in 1974, differences between economic classes in rates of doctor visits were very small, with marginally higher rates among the poor" (ibid., p. 12). These results were thus similar to those observed by Enterline-McDonald at the time of their 1969–70 survey (Enterline et al. 1973b).

Interestingly, Siemiatycki, Richardson and Pless asked for the records of those households from the Enterline-McDonald study residing in the five federal electoral districts covered by their study. The overall comparisons (no breakdown for income) between these two groups of households were reported. They showed a constant increase in the rate of visits to doctors: from 12.4 percent who had seen a doctor "in the past two weeks" in 1969–70, to 13.4 percent in 1971–72, to 19.7 percent in 1974 (Siemiatycki, Richardson and Pless 1980, p. 12).

In the late 1970s, Health and Welfare Canada and Statistics Canada set up the Canada Health Survey (CHS), (see Canada 1981), which was to be a recurrent survey with representative samples from each province. However, they were only able to complete the initial 1978–79 survey. The sampling objective was 12,000 households (40,000 individuals). There were two indicators of health-services consumption. The first one was similar to that from the two studies just mentioned. Each person from all sampled households was asked whether they had consulted with a physician over the last two weeks (q. 13),[9] Then the questionnaire shifted to the previous 12 months as a reference period and asked whether and how often the interviewee had seen a physician during that period (q. 15). Finally, the interviewers also inquired about the estimated income of each individual in each household (q. 73).

Broyles et al. (1983) published an analysis of this data set. Declared incomes were divided into quintiles. The reference period chosen for the DV was "the year" (ibid., p. 1041). Two distinct analyses were performed by the authors. The first one was to differentiate between users and non-users by way of a discriminant analysis. The second one involved only the users (participants). The DV was "number of visits" and the method was weighted regression. Results from the first analysis indicated that "the respondent's *family income* [our italics] failed to contribute significantly to the discrimination of users from nonusers" (ibid., p. 1047). As for actual frequentation (number of visits) among users, the authors discovered that "poor persons (i.e., members of the first and second income quintiles) used significantly more care than *individuals* [our italics] earning a high income" (ibid., p. 1050). The results were thus mixed, since income had no impact on participation but did on consumption. It should be mentioned that, as written, the article is not clear as to what income was used for the second analysis (consumption). It appears that individual income was used and not household income as was the case in the discriminant analysis (users versus non-users).

Area of Residence

The CHS was also the first sufficiently large-scale study to allow the influence of the area of residence to be analyzed. The sampling plan divided the regions and the larger provinces into three categories: large cities, smaller urban areas, and rural areas. Broyles et al. found that participation increased with the size of the area of residence (1983, p. 1047). As for consumption, however, it seems, if we look at the partial coefficients in Table 10 of the article (ibid., p. 1051), that area of residence was not significant at an alpha level of 0.05.

One of the studies mentioned by Badgley (1991) appears to be quite relevant with regard to the question of region. It is a study of Saskatchewan, published in 1990 and dealing with the changes to different health-services programs over an eight-year period: 1977–78 to 1985–86. The study broke down the increases recorded in each program based on certain cost factors and socio-demographic variables. On the rural-urban question, the main conclusion of their review of "physician services" was that the cost per person for residents of urban areas rose by 130.84 percent (from \$79.84 in 1977–78) while the increase was 120.63 percent in rural areas (up from \$67.85).[10]

The Anderson-Rosenberg study (1990) mentioned in the introduction contained no consumption data as such. The "indirect analysis" they used was based on physician-to-population ratios in Ontario's 52 counties. Although the authors noted a drop in ratios in northern counties during the 1956–86 period (Table 15.4), the same trend was seen in southern Ontario, with the result that the same discrepancies remained. And, just as Judek showed in 1964, north–south differences were strongly accentuated when only specialists were examined (Anderson and Rosenberg 1990, see p. 42).

In 1990 the province of Ontario conducted its first Health Survey (OHS). Apparently modeled on the CHS, this survey interviewed some 60,000 people composing the sample of households selected about their use of health services over the previous 12 months. A study by Rosenberg and Hanlon (1996) using these data was published in 1996. Following through from the questionnaire used, this study shares many similarities with that of Broyles et al. Rosenberg and Hanlon were in a position to examine both area-of-residence and income variables and they also subdivided their DV by introducing a distinction between general practitioners (GP) and specialists use. Furthermore, in the logistic regression framework they used, they experimented with three ways of dichotomizing GP use (*i•* non-users vs. users; *ii•* 0–1 visit users vs. 2+; *iii•* 0–4 visits users vs. 5+ visits) and two ways for specialists (the first two from GPs).

The income variable was reproduced as in the three categories used by the OHS (*i•* below poverty line; *ii•* above poverty, less than \$50,000; *iii•* \$50,000+) with few details given except that the threshold for the poverty line took into account family size and income (?), while the model's equation makes it clear that the *individual's* income was used (see Rosenberg and Hanlon 1996, pp. 977–78). By contrast, Broyles et al. used family income even though they, as Rosenberg and Hanlon, used the individual as the unit of analysis. As for area of residence the latter devoted much effort to building a variable that is a construct based on a set of four indicators measured in each of Ontario's 48 census divisions. These indicators included population density for one, while the others are all related to medical resources.[11] Seven ordinal levels of "Health Service Environment" were created out of these indicators, from "Metropolitan Toronto" down to census divisions characterized as "Low Density Rural."

The authors provide results (Table 15.4a and 15.4b) only from their first categorization of DVs (i.e., non-users versus users). As for general practitioners use, income is reported as significant with p=0.01. However, in a section entitled "Discussion" the authors mention that the parameter estimate (p.e.) for this IV changed sign when using any of the other two methods of dichotomizing the DV (see Rosenberg and Hanlon 1996, p. 982). The other independent variable of interest here (IV), the more sophisticated Health Service Environment variable, was not significant (p= 0.60).

Both of these IVs though do end up with significance levels standing at p = 0.0001 when the authors look into specialist services only. We understand this result can only be attributable to the substantial number of people who, over the course of one year, are in a position to visit one or more specialist without seeing a GP. Significant main effects though should always be tested for interactions; this is not reported as having been done despite the study's most sufficient sample size (close to 36,000 individuals).

Government Action in Quebec with Regard to Regional Accessibility

The fact that interest in researching regional accessibility is more recent does not mean the issue is any less relevant or important. Indeed, the geographic distribution of healthcare facilities and medical practitioners was a major postwar concern for the federal and provincial governments. At the time, the federal government freed up major funding under the National Health Grant Program—matched on a dollar-for-dollar basis by the provinces—for the construction of health-care facilities and the opening of new medical schools (Brown 1983). Four new medical schools were set up under the program in locations that seemed to indicate a desire by decision-makers to make physician training available outside the main urban centres: McMaster University (Hamilton, ON, 1965), Université de Sherbrooke (Quebec, 1966), Memorial University (St. John's, NF, 1967), and the University of Calgary (Alberta, 1970).[12]

As mentioned previously, specific measures aimed at the apportionment of doctors were also implemented in the three largest provinces after the setup of medicare. The same year the program was launched in Ontario (1969), the province also adopted the Underserviced Area Program (see Anderson and Rosenberg 1990). As for Quebec, it launched its medicare program in 1970, but did not initially seem overly concerned by the issue. In fact, the report from the Castonguay-Nepveu Commission (Quebec 1967, 1970–72), which had an enormous influence on the health department at the time, scarcely mentioned it.

However, the increase in demand for health care created by the new program, which came on top of any increases owing to the capital expenditures of the 1950s and 1960s[13] and to the hospital insurance program, made itself felt very quickly. The low medical staffing levels in the regions created more difficult conditions for medical practitioners, which in turn scared away newly trained physicians. In any case, doctors seemed to be doing very well in urban centres where demand was also increasing and any restrictions on the number of licences issued for hospital practice had not yet even been considered.

From what can be gleaned from documents of the time, the initial response by the Ministère de la santé (then called the Social Affairs Department) was to promote the development of community health centres (CLSCs) in rural and remote areas, supposedly to attract general practitioners.[14] To deal with the lack of specialists—for whom the CLSCs were not designed—the department tried a formula whereby visiting or travelling physicians were available part-time and were reimbursed for their travel and living expenses. It also tolerated the fact that hospitals occasionally used their budgets to provide monetary incentives to attract specialists, temporarily or on a regular basis, to their facilities.

Without abandoning these indirect, piecemeal responses to the problem of disparities in physician resources, in 1975 the Government of Quebec added a first, official incentive measure along the lines of what Ontario was already offering: an annual scholarship program for medical students who agreed to practise in remote regions for a number of years equal to the number of scholarships received. Three years later, in 1978, the government adopted a new incentive measure, the Incentive Fee Program for Psychiatrists, to promote a better apportionment of this type of specialist throughout Quebec.[15]

Then, faced with the persistent lack of medical personnel in the regions coupled with the more general, recurring problem of program cost overruns, the government adopted a bill in December 1981 giving it the power to institute a general, compulsory measure: differential remuneration based on where physicians practised. The regulations adopted under the bill cut fees for *new* doctors—whether general practitioners or specialists, and whether paid by fee-for-service or salaried—to 70 percent of the normal scale for the first three years of practice if they chose to work in specific urban centres (Montreal, Quebec City, and Sherbrooke are the locations of the four medical schools in the province).[16] On the other hand, all physicians (*new* and *existing*) practising in remote regions received 115 percent (general practitioners) or 120 percent (specialists)[17] of the regular scale for their services. This situation remained unchanged in 1991.[18]

This universal control measure, however, did not result in the government's abandoning the incentive measures (scholarships, etc.) it had previously set up. In summer 1982, the government concluded new multi-year agreements with the two medical federations (general practitioners and specialists) introducing three new incentive measures to encourage physicians to set up practice in remote regions:

- quarter-based ceilings on general practitioners income were abolished for those practising there;
- 20 working days a year of professional resourcing with allocation for income loss, and refund of living and travelling expenses[19] (maximum of 80 days over their stay in designated regions); and
- a rather small subset of the "designated" regions were identified as "isolated territories." Physicians practising there are entitled to a pay bonus plus some outing expenses (annual, renewable). Their moving expenses are also covered.

Physicians agreeing to practise in any of these designated regions are entitled to these measures as a right (as long as the collective agreement between the physicians and the government is standing). In 1984 the ministry adopted a new incentive measure which is on the model of the scholarship program for medical students. It is made up of yearly contracts or agreements between the ministry and individual applicant physicians. Those willing to practise in designated regions can apply for an installation bonus (subjected to a maximum of $25,000) and in the following years they can apply for a retention bonus. These bonuses are paid on a yearly basis and the amount given may depend on the exact location of the applying physician, his future plans and, of course, budgetary availability on the part of the ministry. It should be said that as a quid pro quo to adopting this new incentive measure, the government eventually passed legislation to forbid any public health-care facility from paying bonuses and monetary incentives directly to physicians in order to attract them.

A study of the impact of differential remuneration and incentive measures on where new general practitioners choose to practise was published in 1993 (Bolduc, Fortin and Fournier 1993, p. 23). The study, based on data for all newly trained GPs during the 1967–88 period concluded that both sets of policies had an impact on their location choices. A larger proportion of them than before set up practice in non-central regions. However, the study did not take into account the comparative work output of these new GPs compared to the earlier ones, and neither did it take into account the number of years actually spent there.

The situation in outlying areas thus remains relatively fragile, and it is far from certain that the incentive and control policies will truly succeed in ensuring the inhabitants of these regions a level of service comparable to that available to people in more populated areas. The longer distances that people have to travel to receive care and the general shortage of specialists—which surely have an impact on demand—are both obstacles to regional equity.

Table 15.1. Evolution of Supply and Demand for Physician Services, Quebec, 1972–1991

| Year | Demand for Services | | Supply of Services |
	Estimated Number of Persons Eligible	Mean Number of Visits to Doctor Per Person[*]	Number of Physicians Having Claimed Fees[*]
1972	6,122,131	5.6	7,723
1991	7,154,591	8.6	13,029
Rate of increase for whole period	+16.9%	+53.6%	+68.7
	(combined rate: +79.6%)		

Note: [*]From total number of visits under fee-for-service data only and covering "medicine and surgery" (but not laboratory medicine or salaried positions).

Sources: RAMQ, *Statistiques annuelles 1972*, Tables B-1 (p. 33) B-4 (p. 45) and P-1 (p. 74). RAMQ, *Statistiques annuelles 1991*, Table 1 in Introduction (p. 28–29) and Tables 3 and 4 in the chapter on physician services.

The Research Project

Two concerns led RAMQ to set up this particular research project: *accessibility based on income*, the original problem predating government-insured health care, and *accessibility based on area of residence*, a more contemporary concern brought to the forefront by the disappearance of financial constraints to physician consultations.

Research evidence on the income factor is rather sketchy. As a result, the coefficients obtained are never very strong. Enterline-McDonald and Broyles et al. suggest a somewhat redistributive vision (favourable to low-income households); Siemiatycki, Richardson and Pless a zero-sum result; and Rosenberg and Hanlon a non-redistributive interpretation. As for the area-of-residence factor, Broyles et al. indicate that it has a significant impact on participation, but not on consumption, whereas Rosenberg and Hanlon find it has no impact on consultation rates for general practitioners, but does affect those of specialists.

Moreover, although Quebec has specific policies on these issues (total lack of user fees and controls on the supply of doctors), Quebec's specificity has not been fully exploited in research. The Enterline-McDonald and Siemiatycki et al. studies do not permit any variation in area of residence variables. They also cover a period when the program was still in its infancy. As shown in Table 15.1, there was a significant increase in consumption between 1972[20] and 1991, and it is worthwhile to look at how the increase was distributed.

The RAMQ research project was designed to shed new light on these issues with the help of Quebec data. The study period selected was the 1991 calendar year (January to December). This period was chosen because it marked the tenth year of differentiated fee schedules, but predated the effects of Bill 120,[21] which was passed in 1991. The project team was aware that the Ministère du revenu du Québec (MRQ) had undertaken work to set up a household unit database for planning purposes (Loignon, Paré and Veillette 1990). As a result, and despite the literature review suggested above, the greatest outside influence on project design probably came from the MRQ. The department's influence bore especially on the first two from the following nine characteristics of the study design.

The Unit of Analysis

Like most studies reviewed earlier, we felt that the unit of analysis for the project should be the household. Normally, consumption of medical services is more likely to be similar for members of any given household due to factors such as age, schedules, the presence of children, lifestyle, the contagious nature of certain illnesses and diseases, etc.

This unit is also highly appropriate for looking at collective factors such as region of residence because all household members by definition live under the same roof. The same goes for the income issue, since overall household income is a more accurate indicator than individual income of the real financial situation of any dependents (the economically inactive, students, etc.) in a given household. In short, the household unit seemed a useful tool to help us further our understanding of the consumption of services.

Types of Households

Working with household units constituted a real challenge since RAMQ does not have a household file. Its eligibility verification database—the Beneficiaries Identification File (BIF)—is an individual one, and it was this database, as it existed on 1 July 1991, that was used to create a household file. Home address information (after standardization) and "family ties" declarations from individual files were compiled to create household units, which were classified according to the same typology used by MRQ for its household file. In essence, the typology was as follows:

Table 15.2. Main Household Types

Single Individuals
Married Couples
Common Law Couples
Single Parent Households

However, RAMQ quickly broadened the categories to more accurately reflect household composition. The goal was to make each household category a relatively specific blocking factor. The first category in Table 15.2 (Singles) was therefore subdivided into two: persons living alone and those sharing accommodation with unrelated individuals.[22] The other categories were also subdivided according to the number of children in the household:

- 0, 1, 2, 3 or 4 children or more for married and common-law couples.
- 1, 2 or 3 children or more for single parent households.

Finally, five other categories were added for households where the oldest member (designated as "head of household") was 65 or over. See Appendix (Table 15.A.1) for the complete household typology, including codes.

By incorporating an age threshold, the typology sought to take into account life-cycle trends and the particular circumstances of elderly households relative to health-care expenditures. At the beginning of adult life, people go to work to become independent, form couples, and subsequently have one or more children. By age 65 their working lives are generally over and their children have left home.[23] Couples find themselves on their own again, their incomes decrease and they make, or soon start to make, heavier demands (and sometimes much heavier demands) on the health-care system.

To look into the issues of income and region-based accessibility, the team next needed information on these two variables.

A Typology of Regions

Our objective was to take representative samples from each territorial unit selected for the study. The 16 administrative regions that existed in 1991 were appropriate divisions for a sampling operation. Figure 15.A.1 (see Appendix) is a map of the health regions. They are identical to the administrative regions, with the exception of Administrative Region 10, which has been subdivided to include two extra zones where northern native populations control their own Regional Health Boards (the Inuit in region 17 and the James Bay Cree in region 18).

The fee schedule zones delineated by the Health Department (French abbreviation: MSSS, for Ministère de la santé et des services sociaux) indicate that even though fee schedules may vary within a given territory, reduced and bonus fee zones never coexist within the same health region.[24] The most critical regions in view of the summary grouping discussed in the paragraphs below are those that combine reduced and regular fee zones, given the demographic characteristics generally associated with reduced fee zones. This combination is found in three health regions: Quebec City area (03), Beauce-Appalaches (12), and the Eastern Townships (05). Of the three, only Quebec will be considered as having across-the-board reduced fees (for new physicians) because of its population and supra-regional importance, which are much greater than Sherbrooke (region 05) or Levis (region 12, on the south side of the St. Lawrence River across from Quebec City).

For the purposes of our analysis, we will therefore consider region 03 as a central region where reduced fees are standard, like Montreal (06) and Laval (13). At the other extreme are what we call the peripheral or remote regions where no major urban centres exist. A clockwise examination of the map in the Appendix (Figure 15.A.1) reveals that these include region 08 in the west, as well as regions 10, 18, 17, 09, 11, and 01—all areas where bonus fee schedules apply.[25] In terms of differentiated fee scales then, we have a situation where half of the health regions incarnate centre-region extremes (i.e., regions where either reduced or bonus fee schedules apply throughout the entire territory).

The eight other regions are "mixed" to varying degrees, that is, none are entirely designated as regular fee zones. In some of them, regular fee schedules co-exist with reduced fee zones, which, in addition to regions 05 and 12 mentioned earlier, is the case for those regions surrounding the central regions of Montreal (06) and Laval (13), that is, regions 14, 15, 16.[26] In other regions (from left to right, regions 07, 15, 04, and 02), regular fee schedules co-exist with bonus fee schedules paid in northern sections.

The Regions: Clarifications on the Consumption of Physician Services

The research project required an additional clarification on the concept of regions, specifically the link between region and the dependent variable (consumption of physician services). As a general rule, medical services data sets compiled by administrative bodies such as Health Insurance Boards and Health Departments are based on the concept of *health professional's region* (health professional's billing address).[27] However, for this study, it was important to compile data on services by *user region (of residence)*, a concept perfectly adapted to interregional user mobility.[28] Details on this aspect are available upon request.

Household Income

In sampling surveys, cost considerations usually severely limit the number of questions on the topic of household income. It also tends to generate higher non-response rates than other socio-demographic variables. In other words, household income as declared by survey respondents (self-reported income, widely used in surveys such as those mentioned earlier, CHS and OHS) remains a fragile variable.[29]

The MRQ agreed to provide for each household in the sample the 1988 household income decile ranking for each social insurance number (SIN) holder. MRQ had defined household income as *the sum of the gross incomes of each individual in the household having filed a tax return*. Decile rankings were established on the basis of the total population for all households identified by MRQ for the 1988 tax year.[30]

The Sampling Process

The RAMQ BIF generated 3,274,561 households. A stratified sample (20 household types x 16 regions = 320 strata) of 139,120 was drawn. The initial sampling objective was 470 households per strata. Given the predominance of salaried positions among physicians in northern Quebec and the difficulties of applying a household typology developed for southern Quebec to native populations, health regions 17 and 18 were dropped, reducing the sample to 136,919.

Validating Household Composition

RAMQ decided to use the information provided by MRQ to validate the composition of the households it had generated using the technique mentioned earlier. This exercise solely targeted SIN holders and the rule followed was very simple: nothing in the SIN information provided by MRQ could contradict the household portrait drawn by RAMQ. For study purposes, only those households with concordant data from both agencies were retained, despite the three-year lag between the MRQ and RAMQ files.

Here, in summary form, are the results of the matching process:

Table 15.3. RAMQ-MRQ Matching: Results

Household Sample		(N)	(%)
Households without SIN holders	(Group D)	3,225	2.4
Households with SIN holders			
Absent from MRQ	(Group C)	19,932	14.6
Included in MRQ			
Concordant	(Group A)	92,924	67.9
Non-concordant	(Group B)	19,838	14.5
Total		136,919	100.0

The 92,924 concordant households represent a "response rate" of 67.9 percent.[31] The breakdown of households in groups A, B, C, and D varies according to household type (hh_type). For example, the proportion of non-concordant households (B) is higher among couples, particularly common-law couples. However, Group A households form the majority in every category of hh_type. Unlike survey research, the RAMQ project has the particularity of providing as much information on non-respondents as on respondents, to the extent that household makeup as established by RAMQ is correct. The representativeness of Group A was fully assessed in relation to the dependent variable (consumption of medical services). The comparison revealed no dramatic deviation when the size of groups was sufficient. A non-respondent adjustment factor was established.

General Model

The dependent variable (DV) is physician-services consumption per household. It has been defined somewhat differently than in the other empirical works reviewed earlier. Dollar costs of each service as measured by the negotiated doctor-government fee schedule was preferred to number of visits, which equalizes all visits, whether they be for a minor office examination or for some inpatient surgical procedure. All fee-for-service visits were counted in even those performed in hospitals or in outpatient clinics. Services performed in public clinics such as the CLSC and those of other salaried physicians were estimated.

To make the model, the more general non-users were attributed a cost of $0 and kept along all participating households. No distinction was made between GPs and specialists services. To enhance comparability, total physician-services consumption per household was divided by the number of people in the household. Such a fully metric dependent variable enabled the use of a linear explanatory model, that is, a model that breaks down the variation in DV values into effects specific to a given set of independent variables. The general explanatory model takes the following form:

CONSUMPTION (unit: household) = Constant + Effect (HOUSEHOLD_TYPE)
+ Effect (REGION) + Effect (INCOME) + Error

The two sampling stratification variables (type of household and region) are nominal categorical variables. An analysis of variance (Anova) is normally used when categorical variables are combined with a metric DV. This technique allows interactions with the model to be introduced without creating problems, which is usually essential. In general, it also allows the original DV scale (here Cdn $) to be used.

Because that amounts to increased variance some measures to reduce heteroscedasticity were taken. Among these was the withdrawal of northern health regions 10, 17, and 18 (which had been combined together), plus withdrawal of type 45 households (common-law couples with four children or more), thus reducing total sample size from 92,924 to 88,708 households. These measures reduced somehow heteroscedasticity without, of course, providing a perfect solution. With an Anova, heteroscedasticity may lead to an underestimation of the probability levels for the null hypothesis (Tabachnick and Fidell 1996, pp. 80–82). To counterbalance this possibility, and also to make allowance for the design effect that must be applied to the estimates of consolidated sampling strata in a non-epsem design, we opted for an alpha threshold level of $\alpha=0.01$ in this study.

A Framework for Anova Tables

We mentioned at the beginning of this paper that we had obtained the cooperation of the Health Department. It agreed to provide us with the number of days in hospital in 1991 for each person in the household sample, as recorded in Med-Echo.[32] This piece of information was put to the same treatment as the DV: days hospitalized were aggregated by household, and a mean number of days hospitalized per person per household was calculated.

There is widespread agreement that hospitalization is generally associated with greater consumption of health services. At the very least, the number of days hospitalized may serve as a proxy variable to take into account the health status of a household.[33] We will thus examine the analysis of variance results according to certain rates of use of hospital services. In this way we will be able to verify whether the observed thresholds of the F ratio of the model remain stable as the variance of the observations increases. Four "days hospitalized" categories were defined:

- 0 days hospitalized,
- ≤ 1 day,
- ≤ 10 days,
- All "days hospitalized" categories confounded.

Tests on the complete model showed that the total number of categories of the three independent variables exceeded machine limitations. The only variable for which it was possible to reduce the categories without reducing the sample was the Income variable. Consequently, adjacent deciles were consolidated into quintiles. In this format, we were able to test the model fully. This consolidation theoretically leads to a loss of explanatory power for the Income variable insofar as there is variation lost that is not offset by the accompanying loss of degrees of freedom (df).

Results

Anova tables

Table 15.A.3 in the Appendix summarizes all the relevant data in the Anova tables obtained for each of the predefined categories of days hospitalized per household. The top of Table 15.A.3 presents the results for the saturated model, that is, the three independent variables and the interactions. The bottom of the table presents the analysis of variance, but only those effects determined to be significant by the saturated model, that is, the consolidated significant terms arising from the tests of the model. We will not comment on these consolidated results. Let us recall first that the evaluation of factors and interactions using the GLM-SAS procedure is conservative.[34]

The data from the saturated model show that R^2 remains stable ($\cong 0.08$) as more households are added, whatever the number of days hospitalized (d ≤ 1 day, d ≤ 10 days, d = all). Overall, the observed means for physician services increase by $100, from $163.57 per person for non-hospitalized households to $263.46 per person when all hospitalization lengths are included. The variation in the model increases even more because the root mean square error goes from $232.78 to $448.21 (see Root Mean Square [MS] Error entry).

To examine the results of the saturated model, let us begin with the simplest situation: unhospitalized households. In this case, only the effects of Region and Type of Household are significant. The Type of Household variable needs scarce comment: the factorization it creates with regard to the age of heads of households would most likely lead to a significant probability threshold. The result of the Region variable, on the other hand, is in agreement with what has been observed in studies that were reviewed above. Lastly, the Income variable is not significant, which is also in agreement with previous studies.

The simplicity of the model of non-hospitalized households is, however, perturbed when hospitalized households of any type are included. As soon as households which have experienced one day or less of hospitalization are included, a portion of the increased variation in DV is channelled to the simple effects of the Region and Type of Household factors, of which the F ratios are slightly reinforced. However, another portion diffuses to the interaction between these two factors, which becomes significant at close to $p \leq 0.01$. The addition of households with hospital stays longer than one day reinforces the Region*Hh_Type interaction, which then reaches a threshold of $p \leq 0.0001$. A significant interaction raises questions about the general scope of the main effect of variables involved in the interaction. The Region*Hh_Type interaction implies that the variation in the mean cost of health services between two given regions, for example, will be significantly different from the others in at least one of the categories of households studied.

The significant interaction between the Region and Type of Household variables is the main change the model undergoes when it has to make allowances for hospitalized households of any sort. The model remains stable with regard to the Income variable because neither the main effect of this variable nor any of the interactions associated with it become significant.[35]

Without being restricted to what is significant or not, there are a number of interesting nuances regarding the main effects of the three independent variables when households with hospitalizations exceeding one day (d ≤ 10 days, d = all) are included. The addition of these households lowers the F ratio for the Region variable, doubles it for the Household variable (from 29.8 to 59.2), and causes a perceptible increase in that of the Income variable (from 0.24 to 1.73) without, however, making it significant.

As households that are large consumers of physician services are added and as the variance of DV increases that portion of the variation attributable to Region increases at a lower rate than the error or residual, while the opposite occurs with Type of Household and Income.

Why do the F ratios of these two variables increase? Very simply because of their relationship with age, the most powerful predictor variable for health costs. In the model we are proposing, there are two age-linked variables: one is Type of Household. As may have been noted, this variable has two dimensions: household composition (notably adult-child distribution) and the age of the head of the household, which is dichotomized at 65 years of age. The age effect of this variable becomes much more important with the inclusion of longer hospitalizations because the cut-off point (65) is evidently very relevant. More often than not, households headed by people aged 65 or over are the ones most responsible for the consumption of physician services associated with longer hospitalizations.

The other variable related to age is household income. Indeed, the two are not independent. Those older head of households that enter into the equation when hospital stays exceeding one day are included have a greater tendency to be in the lower quintiles (1 and 2) in terms of Income. This explains why the F ratio of the Income variable rises to a significance level of $p = 0.14$ after being close to 1. The Income variable is thus simply piggybacking on the Age variable. It cannot, however, become significant ($p \leq 0.01$) because the relation between age and income is not linear. Lower quintiles also recruit a larger than expected number of younger households (under 30 years of age, for instance), which are low consumers of physician services.

In a nutshell, the Type of Household variable more directly channels the relation between age of head and physician costs. On the other hand, the Region variable is unaffected by age (and its Hh_Type variable representation), and retains a significant F ratio for all categories of days hospitalized.

Examination of means

Tables 15.A.4(a) and (b) in the Appendix present the weighted means of physician services per person recorded for each category of independent variable (or factor) and for all four predefined categories of days hospitalized. The analysis of variance involves essentially comparisons and contrasts of these means. In terms of regions, we observe that Montreal (06), Laval (13), and Quebec City area (03) occupy the first three positions in all categories of days hospitalized. Quebec City area and Laval are tied on second rank only when longer length of days hospitalized are considered. The situation of remote regions (01, 08, 09, 11) is not as clear cut. Their means are situated toward the bottom of the rankings but the rankings lose their cohesion when the longest length of days hospitalized (> 10 days) is included.

The range for physician mean cost for the Region variable, which is approximately $100 per person, is perhaps slightly over-evaluated. As the title of Table 15.A.4 makes clear, these costs were not calculated upon standardized data. Despite the large samples taken, there is some variation in the mean age of the head of household, and this variation tends to increase when longer hospital stays are included. This is precisely what happens to Montreal when all hospitalizations are taken into account. Its mean age increases to 1.4 and 1.8 years above that of regions 03 and 13 respectively, and so its mean cost difference from them also increases. An average age comparable in Montreal would probably decrease the observed mean for physician services by a few dollars.

While this age differential plays against region 06 at the upper end of the Region scale, the same cannot be said for region 01 at the lower end of it. Mean age of head of household in that region is higher than that in the other three remote regions (08, 09, and 11). Mean costs in region 01 though is systematically the lowest. The only possible explanation for this, if it is not real behaviour, would be that of the correction factor for salaried physician services. While it was developed using universal data, the databank used was very recent at the time, and some unidentified element may have caused an underestimation of salaried activities in region 01 in 1991. Thus at approximately $100, the range in mean costs for the Region variable may be at a maximum.

As for Types of Households (Table 15.A.4(b)), placing the means in descending order first of all draws out the importance of the age of the head of the household. We provide data on the Age*Hh_Type relationship in Table 15.A.5. Household_Types 12, 22, 51, and 61—all headed by someone 65 or over—occupy the first four ranks, and the mean costs separating them are relatively small. Types 31 and 52 are *ex aqueo* in fifth place. The mean age of Type 31 heads of household is relatively high, indicating the presence of couples that are on their own following the departure of their children. Type 52 households have heads 65 and over but still have one or more dependent children, which lowers their mean costs (per person) for physician services.

The composition of the 13 remaining types of household (those with head under 65) has a more pronounced impact on mean costs. For purely illustrative purposes, we propose a distribution of the total range of the Type of Household variable between that portion attributable to age (that is difference in mean cost attributable to the hh_type being headed by someone 65 or above, or headed by someone under 65) and that attributable to household composition (see bottom of Table 15.A.4(b)). We can see that the latter range is approximately $60 for non-hospitalized households and raises to approximately $95 when all households are considered. The portion attributable to age is larger and varies more under the effect of longer hospitalizations.

As we saw earlier, when a household member is hospitalized, the Region*Type of Household interaction becomes significant. The classification of Regions or Types of Household may then vary. Following a verification, we can confirm that these variations are relatively minor. Moreover, the main effects of these factors remain significant.

Parameter estimates

To be able to compare the categories of independent variables by taking the model into account, the "parameter estimates" (p.e.) applicable to each of these categories were determined. In attempting this, we ran into the problem of the heteroscedasticity of the DV. The transformation of the DV, in order to bring its distribution more in line with a normal distribution, became vital. The log transform was applied $[DV = log_e(DV+1)]$.

The parameter estimates from a "core model" have been obtained, that is, the three independent variables (IVs) only, not taking into account the significant Region*Hh_Type interaction we get when DAYSHOSP > 0. Income has been included since its inclusion did not appear to impact in any noteworthy manner the p.e.'s for the two significant IVs in the model. Region 05 (Eastern Townships) was selected as the base category for the Region IV. Single individuals under 65 years of age living alone (Hh_Type 11) were selected for Hh_Type, and Quintile 3 (median quintile) for Income.

Results from the SAS output are given in Table 15.A.6. The "parameters estimates" for all the levels of each IV can be interpreted as a percentage variation of the predicted value from the predicted base category in the transformed metric of the DV variable.

Results for the Region IV confirm the expectations created by the previously observed means (Table 15.A.4). Regions 01, 08, 09, and 11 obtain a negative p.e., with a $p < 0.01$ threshold with respect to region 05, while central regions 03, 06 and 13 obtain a positive coefficient, also with a $p < 0.01$ threshold. The coefficients of all the other regions are not significant at $p < 0.01$. These results are summarized in Table 15.4.

Table 15.4. Region Variable: T-test Probability (at α:0.01) and Sign of the Parameters Estimates (Reference Category: Region 05)

Level of Significance	Regions
Non-significant	02, 04, 07, 12, 14, 15, 16
$p < 0.01$ with negative p.e.	01, 08, 09, 11
$p < 0.01$ with positive p.e.	03, 06, 13

The results (p.e.'s) for the Type of Household IV do not agree as well with the observed mean costs. While the mean of Type 11 households seems middle of the road, all parameter estimates for other levels, except one, are positive, which implies higher consumption. The p.e.'s of all types of households with heads 65 or over (types 12, 22, 51, 52, and 61) as well as type 31 households obtain elevated p.e.'s (defined as p.e. > 1.0), just like type 42 households (common-law couples with one child), which is unexpected. The only negative p.e. is that of type 21 (single individuals under 65 sharing accommodation with unrelated individuals). It should also be noted that all p.e.'s for Hh_Type levels are significant at a convincing level ($p < 0.0001$).

As a final comment, let us digress briefly on the Income variable. In its log form, this IV is still not significant in Anova table results (results not shown), but we can see from Table 15.A.6 that two categories break through at a significant level from the third quintile: these are the fourth and fifth quintiles. Contrary to expectations given by the means costs displayed in Table 15.A.4, these p.e.'s are positive (> 0) and significant at $p < 0.0001$. These would indicate that taking into account the Region and Hh_Type variables (but not the interaction), people from better-off households would be getting a bit more physician services than those from other quintiles.

Conclusions and Discussion

The goal of this research project was to study the relationship between accessibility and physician services insurance. We know that this insurance program was designed with great expectations regarding accessibility. The provision of private medical services could be a serious obstacle to low-income people. The physician services insurance program drawn up by the federal government was designed to be the definitive response to this problem. It thus ensured universal coverage, portability (between provinces), and promised fair and equal treatment for all. Provincial governments remain in charge of managing the program and paying for professional services, which gives them effective control over the program.

We examined the situation in Quebec using data for 1991. Although the legislation promotes access to medical services as an individual right, many external and/or collective factors may impact the exercise of this right. These external factors are above all influenced by the preferences of medical professionals since they are in a monopoly situation. The importance of these external factors may be weighed by examining certain features of households. We first wanted to know whether the socio-economic situation of households, as estimated by income, still plays a role in consumption rates, as it supposedly did before the intervention of the federal government. The other external factor of interest to us is region of residence.

Our study first emphasizes that there is a great deal of variation in physician services consumption by households. During a given year, a certain percentage of households do not consume medical services (10.2 percent of our sample), while others are large consumers. The program thus implies that significant transfers occur, which, of course, argues for some form of insurance. Despite the large variability of the observation units (households), significant differences emerged regarding certain collective factors.

Obviously, as might be expected, the physician services program makes allowances for providing many more services to households with head 65 or over than for households headed by people under this age threshold. There is thus an intergenerational redistribution or transfer in the program (on an annual basis, of course).

By taking this factor into account in a very summary form (dichotomy based on the age of heads of households), and by holding constant household composition, the model tested did not produce a significant result for the household Income factor. Thus, by making allowances for the intergenerational transfer, the study cannot detect any differences between households based on income (quintiles), even by including households with long-term hospitalizations. The overall situation in Quebec in 1991 seems to be identical to what Siemiatycki observed in 1974 in the central sectors of the Island of Montreal that he had selected for his study.

The effect of another collective factor was tested on the amount of medical services consumed by households: region of residence. In 1991, after 20 years of universality, including ten years of preferential rates to promote the establishment of doctors in remote regions, significant differences between regions were still observed. Regional mean costs can be approximately ranked in the predicted order, with central regions (Montreal, Laval, and Quebec) at the top and peripheral regions at the bottom of the scale. This significant result with the Region variable was obtained, moreover, using a relatively unrefined geographic detail, that is, administrative regions. Almost all the non-central administrative regions studied were created around one or more urban centres. A more refined indicator of geographic remoteness with regard to hospital and medical resources would most probably increase the significance of this factor.

Although we do not have any valid longitudinal data on the consumption of medical services, it seems that this factor did not remain static between 1971 and 1991. As Evans indicated in a text published in 1978 (pp. 194, 206), the disappearance of cost restraints in the provision of medical services first resulted in an increase in the "geographic cost." Relatively major urban centres were better equipped to deal with the increased demand for medical services resulting from the free government insurance plan because they already had enough physicians and others, either newly graduated or transient, were moving to these urban centres. Physicians remaining in remote regions did not benefit from a sufficient infusion of new blood to meet the increasing demand. Their workloads increased to such a point that it had a negative impact, on the recruitment of new doctors. During the 1980s, however, when the Quebec government injected new money to consolidate and improve physician establishment programs, and to introduce a tangible difference in salaries (+20 percent), the situation began to improve. The number of physicians in peripheral regions has increased. Data from 1991 most certainly show an improved situation over that existing five to ten years earlier.

Despite this improvement, it must be acknowledged that in 1991, consumption in remote regions was still not on a par with central regions. Special government measures thus helped lessen or correct the geographic cost related to program universality, but were not able to erase the relative consumption deficit that in most likelihood predated the measures. It should be emphasized that we are talking here of consumption, because the deficit in terms of real costs (per person) would be lower, perhaps even non-existent. The data in our study have been standardized so as to not reflect the differential rates introduced in 1982. Furthermore, the study does not take into consideration additional government expenditures for bursaries, establishment costs, travel and training costs, etc. granted to physicians in remote regions. Similarly, it does not take into consideration higher regional administrative costs such as the large number (with respect to population) of regional boards, a situation that is perhaps justifiable to some extent by the time and energy devoted to attracting physicians or physicians-in-training. However, it must be acknowledged that the government's discourse does make reference to a notion of virtual equality of all residents in terms of the provision of physician services. When we look at consumption data though, which reflect probabilities of use, we see that they are not identical.

The study by Rosenberg and Hanlon suggests that these differences in consumption may be due to services provided by specialists. Unfortunately our data have not been compiled in a way that allows us to verify and quantify this aspect. However, this suggestion remains highly plausible given the concentration of specialists in large urban centres. There might thus possibly be a "qualitative" component in the regional differences, if we accept that specialists are trained to provide greater quality and/or more complex care.

However, even in terms of services provided by general practitioners, there is no certainty that serving remote regions through a system of rotating, recently graduated doctors who go to these regions to begin their careers and honour their contractual agreements with the government, will provide the same quality of service to households in these remote regions. In medicine, as in most trades and professions, experience can be a precious commodity and an efficiency factor that is difficult to replace. Remote regions may have the impression that they are training grounds for young general practitioners who then leave and give central regions the benefit of their newly acquired experience.

With this in mind, it would thus be desirable for the Quebec government to promote measures, or strengthen existing ones, that give general practitioners in remote regions the same support structures as physicians in central regions, whether through telemedicine, visiting specialists, etc. Obviously such initiatives generate additional costs, and it would be relatively easy to come up with a few more of these. Since physician services provided in remote regions are already more costly, any new investments would undoubtedly have to meet stricter criteria of desirability.

To compensate for the fact that households in remote regions enjoy fewer physician services, some researchers, including Anderson and Rosenberg (1990, p. 43), have suggested the use of paramedical or auxiliary personnel. The danger inherent in such an approach is that it strengthens the image of a two-tiered system. Why would such an approach only apply to remote regions? Indeed, with the benefit of hindsight, Quebec is in a perfect position to understand the problems with this approach because, while it devoted lots of time and effort to preparing and planning an ambitious *réforme des professions* which was supposed among other benefits to lay the foundations for sharing responsibilities between health-care professionals in a more equitable fashion, the Rochon Commission concluded that the reform clearly had produced no concrete results in this area (Quebec 1988, pp. 262–95). The observation by Evans seems apropos even today: "Public programs to extend access to the existing system of service provision tend to validate that system and create yet further vested interests supporting it" (1978, pp. 204–05).

So even high-powered planning and regulation has had its shortcomings. By and large physicians have been shielded from economic pressure to delegate more routine work to auxiliary personnel. For their part Quebec physician organizations have been centering on the global, highly centralized bargaining process with the government and none of them have ever given any consideration to such delegation, even for peripheral regions. Trying to regulate the supply of services by decreeing differential physician pay scales in favour of remote regions and at the expense of starting physicians in densely populated areas was undoubtedly seen as a more viable option for the government. However, it does not appear to have brought along entirely comparable levels of consumption even in the context of an increasing physician workforce.

What is government left to do if it wants to improve further the situation without increasing the overall costs of the program? Increasing the pay differential does not appear to be an option. Following the retirement packages for physicians brought forward by the government in 1996 and the tight controls and even narrowing of admissions in Quebec's School of Medicine which have been going on for a number of years, regions or hospitals that were once thought to be sheltered from shortages have begun experiencing some of them.

One approach to the problem is to admit that households in remote regions are faced with higher non-price barriers with regard to the physician services program (Evans 1978, p. 193). How then can governments bound by universality clauses deal with this situation? It is hard to think of any further remedies without any revision of those universality clauses including at first level the ban on any out-of-pocket expenditures for medical services. The personal income taxes and employers payroll taxes that finance the program are the same over all Quebec's territory even though households from remote regions cannot compete in consumption with households from central regions. Would it not be possible then to balance the probabilities of use by introducing a point-of-service charge for households in central regions (with clearly some exceptions like accidents, newborns' care, birth defects, mental-health care, etc.)? Given the lack of significance of the Income variable, the number of households whose point-of-service charge would have to be subsidized might be manageable. It is not our intention to go any further in the presentation of details of such a proposition. Our aim here is only to sort out for discussion some of the results of this study. Simply put, the point is whether universality as we now know it could be maintained only where consumption is lowest, and thus possibly deemed to be the most essential?

The RAMQ authorized use of the data for an independent publication. We thank them for this. We also thank the editor and the referees who provided valuable assistance. However, we alone bear responsibility for any errors or misinterpretation remaining.

Notes

1. Official title of the law: the *Federal Hospital Insurance and Diagnostic Services Act*.
2. The *Medical Care Act* was adopted in December 1966. Budgetary considerations prevented it from coming into force in 1967, Canada's Centennial Year, and it was delayed until 1968. For a brief survey of the development of health-care insurance in Canada, see Brown (1983, pp. 24, 31–54).
3. Both commissions took pains to present the initiative from a very broad, systemic perspective, where intervention was also justified by the evolution of society, the health-care sector, and demographic growth, as well as the resulting need for increased medical and professional personnel.
4. Except, of course, for stays in private or semi-private rooms when the use of such rooms is not medically required and is requested by the patient.
5. Coupled with the effects of ceilings on physicians' incomes, and especially the ceiling established in July 1997 on the number of individuals (patients) general practitioners could see on any given day without their fees being amputated (that ceiling was abolished a year later in July 1998), the controls came under much criticism in 1997–98, not only from young doctors but also from the press and some political figures in the Montreal area, where effects from this decree were exacerbated by the ice storm.
6. This is roughly speaking the dependent variable (DV) from all research papers that will be reported upon in this section. Variations will be indicated as requested. The observation period from the Enterline-McDonald study was two weeks and the DV included telephone calls.
7. Unless income-security recipients feared disapproval from doctors (for reasons of social bias maybe, because the fee schedule had been negotiated and endorsed by the profession) and restrained themselves accordingly. This aspect would have been interesting to verify because the only additional benefit they received from universal medicare was that of being brought into the mainstream and no longer having to disclose their socio-economic status.
8. This would have been a substantial increase given that free or low-cost care was available in hospital emergency rooms, usually conditional on a means test. Moreover, beginning in 1961, "Quebec's universal hospital insurance plan ... included payment for emergency room care within 24 hours of an accident" (Steinmetz and Hoey 1978, p. 133).

9. The survey also inquired about visits to other health professionals such as dentists, nurses, etc.

10. Percentage increases calculated by us from data presented in Table III.2 (Saskatchewan 1990, p. 29). Later analysis of the rural-urban factor showed different patterns of increase depending on whether visits were to general practitioners or to specialists (see pp. 80–82).

11. These three indicators were the number of physicians, the number of chronic and acute care hospital beds, and the number of in-hospital full-time nursing equivalents (Rosenberg and Hanlon 1996, p. 977).

12. List based on Crichton et al. (1994, p. 69). This brought the number of medical schools in Canada up to 16 from 12, and none have been added since.

13. The National Health Grant Program was terminated in 1970.

14. Physicians working at community health centres, called CLSCs, are paid a salary and as a result generally earn less than their colleagues, who are paid fee for service. They benefited, however, from the fact that they generally worked days (at least until 1991), did not work on weekends, had set hourly schedules and did not have to pay overhead.

15. The fate of this program is not known. It does not appear any more in official documents.

16. However, 12 of the 31 specialties recognized by the agreement between the government and the specialists were excluded from this measure. Faculties of Medicine wishing to employ new graduates in some capacity (teaching or research) could also exempt a certain number of young physicians from the measure.

17. There were no exemptions in this case. Physicians in all 31 recognized specialties were eligible.

18. For general practitioners and emergency doctors though, a government decree that has been in force since September 1993 abolished the penalty for new graduates working in the emergency rooms of facilities in Montreal, Laval, Quebec City, and Sherbrooke.

19. Living expenses are subjected to some norms and travelling expenses are covered for a maximum of four trips a year. Resourcing does not have to actually take place in Quebec.

20. The first year RAMQ annual statistics were published in stabilized format.

21. Bill 120 notably gave the minister of health the power to determine how many physicians had the right to practise in hospitals and other public facilities for each region and specialty.

22. Whenever ten single individuals or more were found living at the same address, the household was declared "collective" and excluded from the study. A total of 10,397 collective households were identified.

23. Using a detailed household typology therefore provides clues as to the head of the household's age. For a household to be classified in the "couple with three children" category, chances are very good that the head of the household is under 65.

24. There is only one, relatively minor exception to this empirical rule: Region 15 (Laurentides). In the northern part of this region (main town: Mont-Laurier, population app. 8,000), doctors in public facilities (hospitals, community health centres) are on bonus pay whereas those working in private clinics in the southern portion (main towns: Sainte-Thérèse, Saint-Jérôme, Boisbriand, Mirabel, etc.) are on reduced fees.

25. The limited number of residents in northern regions 17 and 18 made it necessary to group them with region 10 for sampling and study purposes.

26. However, in these latter three regions, fees are not reduced when patients are seen in public facilities (hospitals, community health centres).

27. In practical terms, this corresponds to the region where the service was performed.

28. In 1991, the average portion of fee-for-service per region attributable to users from other regions was 16 percent province-wide (*Statistiques annuelles 1991*, p. 48–49). Of course, this percentage varies widely from one region to another (but is stable over time).

29. Quebec has its own version of this type of study: the Enquete Santé Québec, started in 1987 and planned to be a quinquennial instrument.

30. To better situate household socio-economic status. another governmental collaboration could have been sought, that of the Ministry of Education in order to add an education variable such as the most recent diploma obtained by the head of the household. However, a universal diploma file does not exist in any readily accessible form. Furthermore, a variable of this type gives rise to risks of collinearity given the relation between education and income.

31. The response rate is strictly defined given that we have included households without SIN holders: response rate = [households in groups] A/(A+B+C+D).

32. The information gathered by Med-Echo involves stays in short-term hospitals. Med-Echo provided almost universal coverage of these hospitals in 1991.

33. It would admittedly be a rough indicator though because, for one thing, the overall rate of hospitalization varies somewhat among regions.

34. With the usual non-orthogonal data of survey research, some part of the variation is attributable to more than one variable. This was resolved by using Type III estimable functions to evaluate the effects. They produce minimal sums of squares (SS), that is, SS that result when a variable is added last to the model (*SAS/STAT Users Guide*, p. 964).

35. However, conceptually, it is legitimate to think that the hospitalization of economically active people (who are generally under 65) in a household may negatively impact their incomes. In the present study, the three-year lag between the observation period (1991) and the income estimation period (1988) might attenuate any possible negative relationship between Income and DV in households whose heads are under 65. To clarify this situation, we examined the cross-tabulations of Household Income (Quintiles) and Days Hospitalized variables controlled by the Age of the head of the household (< 65; ≥ 65). These tables rather point to a systematic link between income and long hospitalization (> 10 days), a systematic link that may be caused by the true age of the head of the household. Households with head under 65 having had long hospitalizations in 1991 were strongly represented in Quintiles 1 and 2. Thus, three years previously (in 1988), their incomes were already under-average, generally speaking. This association decreases substantially in households whose heads are 65 or over.

Appendix

Table 15.A.1. RAMQ Household Typology

(Effective codes are the two-digits numbers)

1. Single individuals living alone
   11   Under 65 years of age
   12[*]   65 or older
2. Single individuals sharing accommodation with unrelated individuals
   21   Under 65
   22[*]   65 or older
3. Married couples with head under 65

31	No children		34	With 3 children
32	With 1 child		35	With 4 children or more
33	With 2 children			

4. Common-law couples with head under 65

41	No children		44	With 3 children
42	With 1 child		45	With 4 children or more
43	With 2 children			

5. Married couples where head (or both spouses) is 65 or older
   51[*]   No children
   52[*]   With children
6. 61[*]   Common-law couples where head (or both) is 65 or older[**]
7. Single parents (with no restriction as to age)
   71   With 1 child
   72   With 2 children
   73   With 3 children or more

Notes: child = dependent person under 25 years of age.
[*] Household types headed by a person 65 or older.
[**] In Hh_type 61, occurrences of children are possible.

Table 15.A.2. Quebec's Health Regions

01 Lower Saint Lawrence	07 Ottawa Valley	13 Laval
02 Saguenay-Lake Saint John	08 Abitibi-Temiscaming	14 Lanaudière
03 Quebec City area	09 North Shore	15 Laurentides
04 Mauricie-Bois Francs	10 North-of-Quebec	16 Montérégie
(Trois-Rivières)	11 Gaspé-Magdalen Islands	17 Nunavik
05 Eastern Townships	12 Chaudière-Appalaches	18 James Bay Cree Lands
06 Montreal	(Beauce)	

Note: Map follows.

Figure 15.A.1

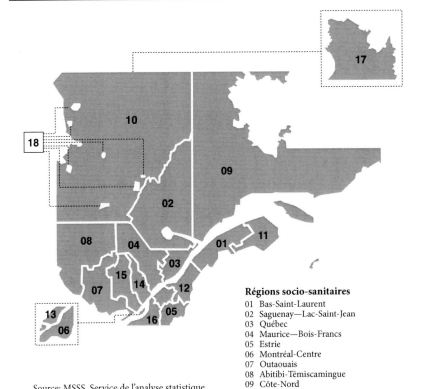

Source: MSSS, Service de l'analyse statistique.

Régions socio-sanitaires

01 Bas-Saint-Laurent
02 Saguenay—Lac-Saint-Jean
03 Québec
04 Maurice—Bois-Francs
05 Estrie
06 Montréal-Centre
07 Outaouais
08 Abitibi-Témiscamingue
09 Côte-Nord
10 Nord-du-Québec
11 Gaspésie—Îles-de-la-Madeleine
12 Chaudière-Appalaches
13 Laval
14 Lanaudière
15 Laurentides
16 Montérégie
17 Nunavik
18 Terres-Cries-de-la-Baie-James

Table 15-A.3. Anova Tables, Saturated and Significant Terms Only Models, According to Length of Hospitalization

Saturated Model

Summary statistics (by hospitalization group):

	o Day Hosp (Not Hosp.)	<= 1 Day Hosp.	<= 10 Days Hosp.	All Hosp. Included
N*	65618	76685	86350	88708
Mean Cost	163.57$	178.83$	220.12$	263.46$
R square	0.073	0.072	0.082	0.083
RootMSError	232.78$	239.43$	294.69$	448.21$

List of Terms	Degrees of Freedom (df)	o Day F Ratio**	o Day Prob	<=1 Day F Ratio**	<=1 Day Prob	<=10 Days F Ratio**	<=10 Days Prob	All Hosp. F Ratio**	All Hosp. Prob
Overall	1421	3.55	0.0001	4.12	0.0001	5.34	0.0001	5.58	0.0001
Region	14	8.1	0.0001	12.39	0.0001	8.82	0.0001	4.26	00001
Household_Type	18	25.4	0.0001	29.82	0.0001	57.57	0.0001	59.17	0.0001
Reg*Housh. interact	252	0.97	0.605	1.21	0.0124	1.46	0.0001	1.58	0.0001
Income (quintiles)	4	0.15	0.963	0.24	0.9132	1.53	0.1916	1.73	0.1396
Region*Income	56	0.32	1	0.47	0.9998	0.40	1.00000	0.38	1
Household_Type*Income	72	0.44	1	0.55	0.9992	0.64	0.9927	0.61	0.9964
Reg.*Hh_type*Income	1005	0.67	—	0.72	1	0.87	0.9989	0.79	1
Error df:		64196		75263		84928		87285	

Significant Terms Only Model

Summary statistics (by hospitalization group):

	o Day Hosp (Not Hosp.)	<= 1 Day Hosp.	<= 10 Days Hosp.	All Hosp. Included
R Square	0.053	0.058	0.068	0.071
RootMSError	232.79$	239.48$	294.69$	448.26$

List of Terms	Degrees of Freedom (df)	o Day F Ratio**	o Day Prob	<=1 Day F Ratio**	<=1 Day Prob	<=10 Days F Ratio**	<=10 Days Prob	All Hosp. F Ratio**	All Hosp. Prob
Overall	see Model df at bottom	114.37	0.0001	16.46	0.0001	22.21	0.0001	23.87	0.0001
Region	14	54.49	0.0001	15.49	0.0001	10.94	0.0001	5.35	0.0001
Household_Type	18	157.38	0.0001	62.05	0.0001	106.53	0.0001	137.62	0.0001
Reg*Housh. interact.	252	—	—	1.61	0.0001	1.83	0.0001	1.99	0.0001
Model df:		32		284		284		284	
Error df:		65585		76400		86065		88423	

Notes: * Because of unequal probability sampling given Ns are not appropriate to estimate rate of hospitalization among households.
** All F ratios for terms in the model are computed from Type III sum of squares (SS).

Table 15.A.4(a). Mean Individual Physician Services Cost According to Length of Hospitalization and the Three Factors Studied, Quebec, 1991

			Length of Hospitalization				
0 Day Hosp (Not Hosp.)		<= 1 Day Hosp.		<= 10 Days Hosp.		All Hosp. Included	

Factor: REGION

Region	Mean Cost	Region	Mean Cost	Region	Mean Cost	Region	Mean Cost
	$		$		$		$
6	194.45	6	211.04	6	250.22	6	301.79
13	185.04	13	200.67	13	237.92	3	274.59
3	168.06	3	180.36	3	224.68	13	273.78
7	162.06	16	177.87	16	221.10	5	257.02
16	159.09	7	171.98	15	210.62	11	254.01
15	155.38	15	169.47	7	209.60	16	253.61
5	152.22	14	166.05	5	209.00	12	246.93
14	150.20	5	164.97	12	208.69	4	246.64
12	148.16	12	161.63	14	202.34	15	243.05
11	130.00	4	148.35	8	189.16	9	236.68
4	128.69	11	143.28	4	188.95	7	236.05
2	126.93	2	136.99	11	184.91	14	230.79
8	117.47	8	134.12	9	183.11	8	219.72
9	115.61	9	131.91	2	179.20	2	218.74
1	94.30	1	106.58	1	150.69	1	195.71
Factor's range:	$100.14		$104.46		$99.53		$106.08

Factor: INCOME

Income	Mean Cost	Income	Mean Cost	Income	Mean Cost	Income	Mean Cost
	$		$		$		$
Quintil1	179.46	Quintil1	192.94	Quintil1	245.26	Quintil1	336.09
Quintil5	162.37	Quintil5	178.36	Quintil2	225.54	Quintil2	292.66
Quintil4	160.41	Quintil2	176.84	Quintil3	215.62	Quintil3	249.05
Quintil3	159.80	Quintil4	176.35	Quintil4	211.83	Quintil4	237.63
Quintil2	159.34	Quintil3	173.18	Quintil5	210.74	Quintil5	226.19
Factor's range:	$20.12		$19.76		$34.52		$109.90

Table A4(b). Mean Individual Medical Services Cost According to Length of Hospitalization and the Three Factors Studied, Quebec, 1991

Length of Hospitalization							
o Day Hosp (Not Hosp.)		<= 1 Day Hosp.		<= 10 Days Hosp.		All Hosp. Included	
Factor: HOUSEHOLD_TYPE							
Hh Type	Mean Cost	Hh Type	Mean Cost	Hh Type	Mean Cost	Hh Type	Mean Cost
	$		$		$		$
12	288.06	12	308.55	61	399.29	12	519.50
61	265.42	61	295.52	51	391.99	61	518.72
51	262.89	51	288.09	12	385.01	22	517.08
22	261.72	22	273.33	22	334.16	51	501.09
31	177.30	31	199.10	52	262.54	31	297.90
52	170.92	52	190.53	31	259.34	52	295.79
11	155.78	42	184.65	42	223.89	42	231.35
42	151.22	32	168.55	71	211.64	11	222.24
71	148.72	71	165.52	32	202.63	71	221.99
32	145.88	11	164.12	41	199.66	41	217.88
41	141.44	41	159.94	11	190.31	32	211.77
21	136.97	72	152.19	72	178.33	21	208.85
72	132.82	43	151.59	43	177.58	72	183.38
43	125.09	21	146.03	21	173.38	43	181.48
33	124.07	33	144.42	33	164.84	33	168.49
44	110.89	44	141.35	44	160.87	44	163.02
73	107.82	73	131.90	73	154.23	73	159.77
34	107.00	34	129.94	34	144.77	34	146.08
35	97.32	35	120.06	35	134.33	35	136.87

Factor's range: $190.74 $188.49 $264.96 $382.62

Age-related range (first entry for hh_type – first entry under the line)

$132.29 $123.91 $175.40 $288.15

Household composition-related range (first entry under the line – last entry)

$58.45 $64.58 $89.56 $94.48

Table 15.A.5. The Age * Household_Type Relationship
Mean Age and Standard Deviation of Head of Household by Household Type

Hh_Type	N Obs	Mean Age	Std Dev
Households Without Any Hospitalization (N=65618)			
11	4603	36.9	12.3
*12	3228	73.8	6.6
21	4099	35.3	11.6
*22	2721	74.7	7.1
31	4775	54.0	9.0
32	4007	43.0	9.6
33	4539	40.4	6.6
34	4258	41.0	5.9
35	3573	41.5	5.7
41	2863	37.7	11.2
42	2544	37.3	8.3
43	2854	37.7	6.6
44	2353	38.9	6.3
*51	4213	71.6	5.5
*52	1958	67.7	3.1
*61	2440	71.9	6.1
71	3836	39.0	9.7
72	3733	38.4	7.2
73	3021	38.6	6.3
All Households (and All Hospitalizations) (N=88708)			
11	5030	37.2	12.4
*12	4111	74.1	6.5
21	4467	35.6	11.8
*22	3490	75.1	7.1
31	6229	53.6	9.6
32	5486	42.1	10.0
33	6138	39.9	6.9
34	5956	40.5	6.2
35	5341	41.0	5.9
41	3547	37.7	11.3
42	3863	36.4	8.5
43	4392	37.0	6.8
44	3755	38.2	6.4
*51	6283	72.2	5.7
*52	2861	67.9	3.2
*61	3788	72.5	6.4
71	4862	38.4	9.8
72	4926	37.7	7.3
73	4183	38.0	6.8

Note: *Head of household is 65 or older.

Table 15.A.6. Dummy Variable Regression for Model with Logarithmic DV and Main Effects Only (Base Categories: Region: 05; Hh_Type: 11; Quintile: 3)

Variable	DF	Parameter Estimate	Standard Error	T for HO: Parameter=0	Prob > T
Intercept	1	3.79490	0.03418	111.021	0.0001
REGION_1	1	-0.45254	0.04579	-9.884	0.0001
REGION_2	1	-0.06713	0.04268	-1.573	0.1158 n.s.
REGION_3	1	0.12914	0.03576	3.611	0.0003
REGION_4	1	-0.08907	0.03771	-2.362	0.0182 n.s.
REGION_6	1	0.19942	0.03200	6.232	0.0001
REGION_7	1	0.03965	0.04249	0.933	0.3508 n.s.
REGION_8	1	-0.18056	0.05011	-3.604	0.0003
REGION_9	1	-0.26155	0.05866	-4.459	0.0001
REGION_11	1	-0.33190	0.05502	-6.032	0.0001
REGION_12	1	0.05279	0.04002	1.319	0.1871 n.s.
REGION_13	1	0.22571	0.04119	5.480	0.0001
REGION_14	1	0.01431	0.04064	0.352	0.7248 n.s.
REGION_15	1	0.07449	0.03921	1.900	0.0575 n.s.
REGION_16	1	0.06850	0.03333	1.995	0.0460 n.s.
TYPE_12[*]	1	1.43059	0.02829	50.569	0.0001
TYPE_21	1	-0.20254	0.01985	-10.205	0.0001
TYPE_22[*]	1	1.16234	0.03207	36.241	0.0001
TYPE_31	1	1.04073	0.02534	41.069	0.0001
TYPE_32	1	0.94717	0.02582	36.689	0.0001
TYPE_33	1	0.82830	0.02380	34.807	0.0001
TYPE_34	1	0.70863	0.03483	20.348	0.0001
TYPE_35	1	0.63705	0.06665	9.558	0.0001
TYPE_41	1	0.74705	0.02879	25.946	0.0001
TYPE_42	1	1.14594	0.03956	28.666	0.0001
TYPE_43	1	0.94011	0.04963	18.941	0.0001
TYPE_44	1	0.85812	0.09570	8.967	0.0001
TYPE_51[*]	1	1.72429	0.02728	63.219	0.0001
TYPE_52[*]	1	1.26080	0.10799	11.675	0.0001
TYPE_61[*]	1	1.69375	0.08132	20.827	0.0001
TYPE_71	1	0.86884	0.03198	27.167	0.0001
TYPE_72	1	0.83763	0.04483	18.685	0.0001
TYPE_73	1	0.72994	0.08272	8.824	0.0001
QUINTIL_1	1	0.04568	0.02008	2.275	0.0229 n.s.
QUINTIL_2	1	-0.03150	0.01891	-1.666	0.0958 n.s.
QUINTIL_4	1	0.09354	0.01837	5.093	0.0001
QUINTIL_5	1	0.11585	0.01874	6.182	0.0001

Notes: [*]Household headed by a person 65 or older.
n.s., non-significant at alpha=0.01.

References

Anderson, M. and M.W. Rosenberg (1990), "Ontario's Underserviced Area Program Revisited: An Indirect Analysis," *Social Science and Medicine* 30(1):35–44.

Badgley, R.F. (1991), "Social and Economic Disparities under Canadian Health Care," *International Journal of Health Services* 21(4):659–71.

Bolduc, D., B. Fortin and M.-A. Fournier (1993), *The Impact of incentive Policies on the Practice Location of Doctors: A Multinomial Probit Analysis*, Cahier 93-05 (Québec: Département d'économique Université Laval).

Brown, M.C. (1983), *National Health Insurance in Canada and Australia* (Canberra: Health Economics Research Unit, Australian National University).

Broyles, R.W., P. Manga, D. Binder, D. Angus and A. Charette (1983), "The Use of Physician Services under a National Health Insurance Scheme," *Medical Care* 21(11):1037–54.

Canada (1983), *Preserving Universal Medicare: A Government of Canada Position Paper* (Ottawa: Supply and Services Canada).

Canada. Hall Commission (1964), *Report of the Royal Commission on Health Services* (Ottawa: The Queen's Printer).

Canada. Statistics Canada and Health and Welfare Canada (1981), *The Health of Canadians: Report on the Canada Health Survey*, Cat. No. 82-538E (Ottawa: Supply and Services Canada).

Crichton, A., D. Hsu and S. Tsang (1994), *Canada's Health Care System*, rev. ed. (Ottawa: Canadian Hospital Association).

Enterline, P.E., J.C. McDonald, A.D. McDonald, L. Davignon and V. Salter (1973a), "Effects of 'Free' Medical Care on Medical Practice—The Quebec Experience," *New England Journal of Medicine* 288(22):1152–55.

Enterline, P.E., V. Salter, A.D. McDonald and J.C. McDonald (1973b), "The Distribution of Medical Services before and after 'free' Medical Care—The Quebec Experience," *New England Journal of Medicine* 289(22):1174–78.

Evans, R.G. (1978), "Universal Access: The Trojan Horse," in *The Professions and Public Policy*, ed. P.S. and M.J. Trebilcock (Toronto: University of Toronto Press).

Judek, S. (1964), *Royal Commission on Health Services: Medical Manpower in Canada*, Hall Commission (Ottawa: The Queen's Printer).

Loignon. N., R. Paré and S. Veillette (1990), "Reconstitution des ménages québécois en 1986 à l'aide des déclarations de revenus de 1986," in *Recueil des textes des présentations du colloque sur les méthodes at domaines d'application de la statistique 1990* (Québec: Bureau de la statistique du Québec).

McDonald. A.D., J.C. McDonald and V. Salter (1974), "Effects of Quebec Medicare on Physician Consultation for Selected Symptoms," *New England Journal of Medicine* 291(13):649–52.

McDonald. A.D., J.C. McDonald, N. Steinmetz, P.E. Enterline and V. Salter (1973), "Physician Services in Montreal before Universal Health Insurance," *Medical Care* 11(4):269–86.

Quebec. Castonguay-Nepveu Commission (1967, 1970–72), *Report of the Committee of Inquiry on Health and Social Welfare* (Quebec: presumed editor, Éditeur officiel du Québec).

Quebec. Rochon Commission (1988), *Rapport de la Commission d'enquête sur la santé et les services sociaux* (Quebec: Les Publications du Québec).

Régie de l'assurance-maladie du Québec (RAMQ): *Statistiques annuelles* selected years (Quebec City: RAMQ).

Rosenberg M.W. and N.T. Hanlon (1996), "Access and Utilization: A Continuum of Health Service Environments," *Social Science and Medicine* (43)6:975–83.

SAS Institute (1990), *SAS/STAT Users Guide*, Version 6, 4th ed., 2 Vols. (Cary N.C.: The SAS Institute).

Saskatchewan (1990), *The Growth in Use of Health Services: 1977/78 to 1985/86*, reported authors: M. Gormley, M. Barer, P. Melia and D. Helston (Regina: Saskatchewan Health).

Siemiatycki, J., L. Richardson and I.B. Pless (1980), "Equality in Medical Care Under National Health Insurance in Montreal," *New England Journal of Medicine* 303(July 3):10–15.

Steinmetz, N. and J.R. Hoey (1978), "Hospital Emergency Room Utilization in Montreal before and after Medicare," *Medical Care* 16(2):133–39.

Tabachnick, B.G. and L.S. Fidell (1996), *Using Multivariate Statistics*, 3d ed. (New York: Harper, Collins College Publishers).

III

NEW REALITIES
IN SOCIAL SECURITY

New Realities in Social Security

In RECENT YEARS, Canadians have accepted that a greater array of social problems require government assistance. Social programs have been developed for issues that were formerly downplayed, ignored, or even treated as criminal matters: these issues include drug and alcohol addiction, spousal and child abuse, homelessness, affordable childcare, and unwanted pregnancy. Yet, while the social welfare system took on increasingly many issues, governments continued to face pressure to practice restraint. By 1995 Canada's accumulated national debt generated interest payments consuming one-quarter of federal revenues. Moreover, passage of the Free Trade Agreement with the United States in 1989, the North American Free Trade Agreement five years later, and the broader trend toward economic globalization, compelled Canada to provide a more business-friendly environment—namely one where the costs of doing business were kept competitively low to prevent an out-migration of capital.

While neo-Conservatism has not been as pronounced in Canada as it has been in the United Kingdom or the United States, since the Mulroney years Canadian governments have nevertheless placed increased emphasize upon deficit cutting, and, when possible, reducing taxes. During the latter half of the 1980s, the principal of universality largely disappeared as Child Tax Credits replaced Family Allowances, and clawbacks were applied to old age pensions. In 1996, Unemployment Insurance was replaced by Employment Insurance: under this new system, it became more difficult to qualify for benefits, and less support was provided over a shorter period of time. The federal government also reduced its participation, and level of funding, in several areas of social welfare and provided more authority to the provinces. While defenders stressed the reduction of constitutional bickering, as well as less administrative overlap and greater cost-effectiveness, critics pointed to gaps in essential programs and differentiated services across the land. Often heard was that governments were abandoning their responsibilities to Canadians, and even more, that they were compromising national identity, namely Canada's strong sense of community (particularly compared to the more individualistic United States).

The first two articles focus on Canadian-American comparisons in the context of social policy, and reach very different conclusions. Keith Banting, writing during the Mulroney years, claims that despite emphasis on deficit cutting and free trade, the plight of the needy remained significantly better north of the border. In a more recent study, however, Garson Hunter and Dionne Miazdyck—who use Saskatchewan as their focus for analysis—contend that the trend with social welfare has been toward "downward convergence" and increasing similarity to America.

The case studies on specific policies that follow also present contrasting perspectives on the direction and status of social programs. Glen Drover notes that by the late 1990s, not only were clawbacks applied to the Canada Pension Plan, but also a move by the federal government to invest a portion of the fund in the private market. Michael Prince's article on the disabled contends that despite obligations under the Charter of Rights and Freedoms to end discrimination on the basis of "physical and mental disability," progress has remained mixed and assistance piecemeal. However, Donald Carter, writing in 1998, predicted that the Charter would significantly expand social policies for same sex couples, namely equal access to spousal benefits, tax breaks, pensions, and adoption rights. This prediction that came true in 2005, with Canada's Supreme Court and its Parliament giving these unions full legal status and rights.

Yet, in recent years, no area of social policy has generated as much concern, debate, and frustration as public health care. With rising drug and treatment costs and an aging population, revenue problems continued worsening, as did doctor shortages, wait times for surgery, and the de-listing of services. To address this situation, on 3 April 2001, the federal government established the Commission on the Future of Health Care in Canada, under the former NDP premier of Saskatchewan, Roy Romanow. While recommending strategic reforms to improve Medicare's efficiency and long-term sustainability, the November 2002 Final Report also advocated extra billions in federal funding. Gregory Marchildon, who served as the commission's Executive Director, contends in his paper that bold action to reinvigorate the public system represents Canada's best option. He presents the retention of the status quo as inviting "death by stealth," American-style private health care as producing radically increased costs and reduced access, and greater provincial control as likely to undermine national standards. Donna Greschner suggests that the future of health care may be decided not only by politicians, but also by the courts. An activist Supreme Court, she argues, could use the Charter's Section 7 (guaranteeing "life, liberty and security of the person") or Section 15 ("equal protection and equal benefit of the law") to declare a patient's right to receive an expanding array of publicly insured medical services; but also she warns that the same sections could justify private health care in light of long delays for several surgical procedures.

In many respects, Canada's social welfare state has been a victim of its success: the more it has achieved, the more demand it has generated. As such, in light of government efforts to produce more balanced budgets, criticism has grown from several quarters over cuts to a number of programs and the downloading of services to lower levels of government, or community groups, with limited resources. Many worry that the trend in recent years has been to move backwards to the piecemeal and often insensitive approach to social policy that typified the pre-Second World War era. Yet, as Yves Valliancourt, François Aubry, Louise Tremblay, Muriel Kearney, and Luc Theriault write, similarities to old structures need not equate to old practices. Focusing on the non-profit and voluntary sector in Quebec, they assert that such groups have not only contributed significantly to the social economy, but have also developed and applied policies better grounded in local conditions and that have empowered and raised the morale of recipients much more than far costlier government initiatives. These authors assert that the debate surrounding welfare has too often reflected a false dichotomy between adherence to the public system or privatization, and that new models are not only possible, but essential. For as they, and a growing chorus of others, argue, innovative thinking will become ever-more necessary in the years ahead given the expanding client base, the demand for quality and sustainable programs, and continuing pressure upon governments to practice financial restraint.

Further Readings

Banting, Keith G., *The Nonprofit Sector in Canada: Roles and Relationships*. Kingston: School of Policy Studies, Queen's University, 2000.

Banting, Keith G. and Stan Corbett, eds., *Health Policy and Federalism: A Comparative Perspective on Multi-Level Governance*. Kingston: Institute of Intergovernmental Relations, Queen's University, 2002.

Battle, Ken and Sherri Torjman, *Ottawa Should Help Build a National Early Childhood Development System*. Ottawa: Caledon Institute of Social Policy, 2000.

Carniol, Ben, *Case Critical: Challenging Social Services in Canada*. Toronto: Between the Lines, 2000.

Drover, Glen, *Free Trade and Social Policy*. Ottawa: Canadian Council on Social Development, 1988.

Fawcett, Gail, *Bringing Down the Barriers: The Labour Market and Women with Disabilities in Ontario*. Ottawa: Canadian Council on Social Development, 2000.

Grady, Patrick, Robert Howse, and Judith Maxwell, *Redefining Social Security*. Kingston: School of Policy Studies, Queen's University, 1995.

Hanvey, Louise and Dianne Kinnon, *The Health Care Sector's Response to Woman Abuse: A Discussion Paper for the Family Violence Prevention Division, Health Canada*. Ottawa: National Clearinghouse on Family Violence, Health Canada, 1993.

Hall, Michael H., Larry McKeown, and Karen Roberts, *Caring Canadians, Involved Canadians: Highlights from the 2000 National Survey of Giving, Volunteering and Participating*. Ottawa: Statistics Canada, 2001.

Heisler, Paul, *Promoting Access to Postsecondary Education*. Ottawa: Caledon Institute of Social Policy, 2002.

Holosko, Michael J. and Marvin D. Feit, eds., *Social Work Practice with the Elderly*. Toronto: Canadian Scholars' Press, 2004.

Kent, Tom, *Social Policy 2000: An Agenda*. Ottawa: Caledon Institute of Social Policy, 1999.

MacLeod, Linda, *Counseling for Change: Evolutionary Trends in Counseling Services for Women who are Abused and for their Children in Canada*. Ottawa: National Clearinghouse on Family Violence, 1990.

Mendelson, Michael, and Pamela Divinsky, *Canada 2015: Globalization and the Future of Canada's Health and Health Care*. Ottawa: Caledon Institute of Social Policy, 2002.

Mendelson, Michael, *Aboriginal People in Canada's Labour Market: Work and Unemployment, Today and Tomorrow*. Ottawa: Caledon Institute of Social Policy, 2004.

Pomeroy, Steve, *Toward a Comprehensive Affordable Housing Strategy for Canada*. Ottawa: Caledon Institute of Social Policy, 2001.

Quarter, Jack, *Canada's Social Economy: Co-operatives, Non-Profits and Other Community Enterprises*. Toronto: James. Lorimer, 1992.

Rachlis, Michael, *A Review of the Alberta Private Hospital Proposal*. Ottawa: Caledon Institute of Social Policy, 2000.

Richards, John, *Retooling the Welfare State: What's Right, What's Wrong, What's to be Done*. Toronto: C.D. Howe Institute, 1997.

Riches, Graham, *Food Banks and the Welfare Crisis*. Ottawa: Canadian Council on Social Development, 1994.

Ross, David P., Mark Kelly, and Katherine Scott, *Child Poverty: What are the Consequences?* Ottawa: Canadian Council on Social Development, 1996.

Puttee, Alan, ed., *Federalism, Democracy and Disability Policy in Canada*. Kingston and Montreal: McGill-Queen's University Press, 2002.

Sayeed, Adil, ed., *Workfare: Does it Work? Is it Fair?* Montreal: Institute for Research on Public Policy, 1995.

Scott, Katherine, *Funding Matters: The Impact of Canada's New Funding Regime on Nonprofit and Voluntary Organizations*. Ottawa: Canadian Council on Social Development, 2003.

Torjman, Sherri, *The New Liberalism: Ideas and Ideals*. Ottawa: Caledon Institute of Social Policy, 2003.

Wesley-Esquimaux, Cynthia C. and Magdalena Smolewski, *Historic Trauma and Aboriginal Healing*. Ottawa: Aboriginal Healing Foundation, 2004.

16

The Social Policy Divide

The Welfare State in Canada and the United States*

KEITH BANTING

The politics of change are perhaps most intense in the domain of social policy. The globalization of economic life, the fiscal weakness of the state, and the vigorous pluralism of domestic society have placed powerful pressures on the structure of social programs in all Western nations, including Canada and the United States. On both sides of the border, popular social programs have been subject to successive waves of retrenchment and restructuring, prompting increasingly polarized debates about the social role of government.

Social policy represents a critical test of the pressures for convergence or even harmonization implicit in more integrated economies. During the postwar decades, Canadians developed a more expansive welfare state than their neighbours to the south, and the ability of Canadians to maintain distinctive social programs has immense political and theoretical significance. Social programs have become an integral part of Canadians' sense of identity, part of their conviction that they have created something different on the northern half of the continent. Not surprisingly, therefore, the scope for continuing to chart a separate course on social issues sparked intense political debates as the country moved towards closer economic integration with the United States in the 1980s. More generally, however, the case of social policy in Canada and the United States has wider theoretical significance, illuminating in interesting ways the degrees of freedom that nation-states retain in a future framed by global economic forces.

Table 16.1. Public Expenditure on Social Programs in Selected OECD Countries, 1990 (Percent of GDP)

EC countries		Outside the EC	
Belgium	25.2	Canada	18.8
Denmark	27.8	Japan	11.6
France	26.5	Norway	28.7
Germany	23.5	New Zealand	19.0
Italy	24.5	Sweden	33.1
Netherlands	28.8	United States	14.6
United Kingdom	22.3		

Source: OECD 1994, tables 1b and 1c.

---

* This chapter was first published as "The Social Policy Divide: The Welfare State in Canada and the United States," in Keith Banting, et al., eds, *Degrees of Freedom: Canada and the United States in a Changing World* (Montreal and Kingston: McGilll-Queen's University Press, 1997), 267–309.

Not everyone is impressed with the differences between the Canadian and U.S. welfare states. Viewed from the perspective of OECD nations generally, the differences may seem limited, as Table 16.1 suggests. Indeed, some analysts consider both Canada and the United States to be archetypal examples of the liberal model of the welfare state, and contrast their programs with the more extensive benefits provided by the social democratic and corporatist systems of Europe (Esping-Anderson 1990; Myles 1995). However, from the perspective of life on the North American continent, especially for the poor and for marginal social groups, the differences between Canadian and American social programs are important. These differences can be seen along three distinct dimensions:

- *Comprehensiveness*. Public social programs have provided significant support for a broader range of the population in Canada than in the United States. The welfare state in the United States is often described as having two tiers (Wier, Orloff, and Skocpol 1988; Orloff 1991). The upper tier consists of social security programs that provide pensions and health insurance for elderly Americans. Throughout most of its life, social security has been sustained by strong public support, powerful bureaucratic champions, and protective congressional committees; as a result, it provides far richer benefits than other programs. In Michael Harrington's words, "The welfare state in the United States is primarily for people over sixty-five" (1984, 85). As we shall see below, these social security benefits are broadly comparable to those received by the elderly in Canada. The lower tier of the American welfare state, however, affords more meagre protection for children and for persons of working age. This tier consists of unemployment insurance, Medicaid, a variety of means-tested benefits such as Aid to Families with Dependent Children (AFDC) and Food Stamps, and the Earned Income Tax Credit (EITC). These programs offer lower benefits, and they leave many poor and vulnerable individuals without protection. In contrast, the Canadian combination of universal health care, a larger unemployment insurance program, child benefits, and stronger social assistance has provided more comprehensive protection for the non-elderly population. Unlike in the U.S. system, the Canadian welfare state is an important component of the lives of average citizens over their full life cycle.

- *Transfers to the poor*. Canadian mythology suggests that the country is more committed than the United States to universality in social programs, and this has certainly been the case in health care. However, in the field of income security, it is Canada that has the stronger tradition of targeting benefits on the poor through income supplements, refundable tax credits, and social assistance. This difference, which began to emerge in the 1960s, has been reinforced by the recent transformation of several universal income-security programs into selective ones. In the United States, however, the universal components of social security continue to dominate, and targeted transfers to the poor are much weaker. A rich menu of means-tested programs exists, each with its appropriate acronym, and considerable controversy swirls around many of them. Nevertheless, benefits tend to be low, and limited resources are channelled through them.

- *Redistributive impact*. Not surprisingly, the combination of more comprehensive coverage and more strongly targeted programs has reduced the levels of poverty and inequality in Canada more effectively than has been done in the United States.

Universal health insurance has a stronger equalizing effect on access to health care, and the tax-transfer system makes a larger dent in the patterns of inequality generated by the market economy. This difference has been particularly noticeable over the last decade, as economic forces generated pressures for greater inequality in both countries.

These differences in the two welfare states lie at the heart of the debate about the scope for distinctive national choices in an integrated North American economy. This chapter explores the issues by analysing the roots of their distinctive approaches, comparing their social programs in greater detail, and examining the extent of convergence in this most sensitive of policy sectors. As we shall see, the pattern is complex. Many social programs in both countries have been weakened significantly by successive rounds of retrenchment and redesign. Yet restructuring is not driving the two systems towards a single model. There has certainly been convergence in some programs, but there has also been divergence elsewhere, accentuating traditional differences between the two countries. Indeed, during the 1980s and early 1990s, the overall gap in total spending on social policy grew significantly, as Figure 16.1 indicates, in part because of higher unemployment in Canada but also because cuts in social benefits in this period were more dramatic south of the border. This expanded difference began to narrow again in the mid-1990s as governments

Figure 16.1. Public Expenditure on Social Programs in Canada and the United States as a Proportion of GDP, 1960–1990

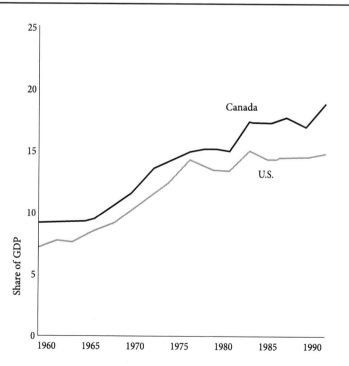

Source: OECD 1994c, Tables 1a and 1b.

began to cut more deeply in Canada. Nevertheless, Canada and the United States continue to travel different paths in social policy, and most components of the two systems are as different in the mid-1990s as they were in the mid-1970s, the high-water mark of the postwar welfare state. Whether this pattern will prove sustainable in the future remains a compelling question. So far, Canada and the United States have been adjusting to economic and social turmoil according to different inner rhythms.

The chapter is organized in four parts. The first examines the economic, social, and political factors that have traditionally sustained distinctive social policy regimes in the two countries. The second part examines the basic health and income security programs in the two countries in greater detail, traces their evolution in recent years, and assesses their redistributive impact. The next part focuses more directly on the extent of convergence and divergence in the two policy regimes, and examines the reasons for the cases of convergence that have emerged. The final section summarizes the conclusions and reflects on the extent to which differences in social policy are likely to persist.

The Roots of Distinctiveness

The different versions of the liberal welfare state that emerged in Canada and the United States are deeply rooted in the economic, social, and political structures of the two societies. The positions of the two countries in the wider global economy, as well as domestic social cleavages such as economic class, language, race, and region, have created distinctive pressures on the social role of the state in each country. These economic and social contrasts have been further sharpened by differences in the political institutions and processes through which Canada and the United States shape and reshape the complex web of programs that constitute the welfare state. Because all the differences point to a stronger social role for government in Canada, it is impossible to weigh the relative contribution of each factor with precision. In combination, however, they have created a firmer foundation for the welfare state in Canada than in the United States.

Position in the global economy

Early studies of the welfare state paid relatively little attention to the international context, preferring to search for the determinants of welfare policy in the social and political forces at work within each country. In effect, the welfare state was seen as the creation of national political economies. This approach understated the importance of the wider international economy even during the postwar years, and it is clearly incomplete today. Each country's position in the larger global economy shapes the context within which the domestic politics of welfare are played out, and international constraints provide more autonomy for domestic choices in some periods than in others.

During the postwar decades, the growth of international trade and the expansion of social expenditures seemed mutually reinforcing. The massive support for reconstruction provided by the Marshall Plan, the progressive liberalization of trade and finance under the General Agreement on Tariffs and Trade (GATT), and the improving terms of trade, especially in energy, all contributed to economic prosperity among Western nations, which in turn helped to finance an impressive expansion of social spending (Keohane 1984; Ruggie 1982, 1994). Growth gave nations considerable latitude in designing their domestic social contracts, especially in the case of larger countries that were not heavily dependent on foreign trade. Smaller nations with comparatively open economies were inevitably more sensitive to the international context even in the postwar years, and these countries tended to adopt more expansive social programs as part of a larger attempt to cushion their societies from economic shocks originating outside their borders (D.R. Cameron 1978; Katzenstein 1984).

The United States and Canada reflected this pattern. As a hegemonic state with little dependence on foreign trade, the United States was largely free to design its social programs in the light of its internal economic and political impulses. The country's larger geopolitical role during the Cold War undoubtedly imposed constraints on the government's response to domestic interests (Krasner 1978), and scholars have searched for evidence that military expenditures acted as a significant brake on American social expenditures in this period. The evidence does not point to a strong effect, however, and the social programs appear to have been shaped primarily by domestic pressures and preferences.[1] In contrast, the role of the state in Canada has always been sensitive to the openness of the economy and international influences. The historical dependence on trade in natural resources, the need to create a transcontinental economy in the face of geographic barriers and a sparse population, and the need to counter powerful American influences contributed to a more central role for public initiative in Canada.[2] In the early life of the nation, state action concentrated on transportation, energy, and economic infrastructure; but as the twentieth century unfolded, the tradition also contributed to a broader consensus on the social role of the state. Moreover, the continued vulnerability of employment in Canada to economic shifts in the global economy contributed more directly to growth in public spending during the postwar years (D.R. Cameron 1986).

Since the late 1970s, the postwar symbiosis between the international economy and the welfare state has broken down. Economic integration on a global and regional basis, intense competition in the international trading system, the associated restructuring of domestic economies, and less stable macroeconomic conditions have generated contradictory pressures on the welfare state. On one hand, change creates victims; hence workers, regions of the country, and sectors of the economy that have been hurt create pressures for increased public spending. On the other hand, global economic changes create pressures to limit expenditures and to redesign social programs in ways that reduce rigidities in the labour market, enhance the flexibility of the domestic economy, and reduce the fiscal burdens on the state. This contemporary emphasis on adaptability stands in tension with the concern for security and protection that was embodied in the historical conception of the welfare state. Thus, pressures rooted in the international economy press simultaneously for expanded social security and fundamental restructuring. Both Canada and the United States have been grappling with these contradictions throughout the 1980s and 1990s.

According to many commentators, globalization also generates a second level of constraint, by narrowing the degrees of freedom that each nation-state has to craft its policy response. According to these interpretations, governments are under powerful pressures to harmonize their economic and social policies with those of their trading partners. Even if full standardization is not inevitable, a process of convergence is seen as restricting the rich diversity of policy regimes that characterized Western nations in the postwar era, largely by eroding the levels of social protection achieved in more generous systems.

This issue takes on a special importance in the case of Canada. Although there is no formal harmonization of monetary policy or mobility of labour on the model of the European Community, Canadian financial markets and trade patterns are tightly integrated with the United States. Not surprisingly, therefore, Canada has engaged in an intense debate about whether its more ambitious social programs are sustainable in the context of an ever closer economic embrace with the United States. The most dramatic clash occurred during the 1988 election, which was fought over the free trade agreement with the United States. Apart from a provision in an annex to the chapter on services, the fight was not over the specifics of the trade agreement itself. Rather, the issue was whether the competitive pressures implicit in closer economic integration with the United States would produce greater convergence in the structure of the two welfare states, with the burden of adjustment falling primarily on Canada.

Two basic arguments were advanced by Canadian critics of a closer economic relationship.[3] On one hand, it was argued that if Canada established social programs and related taxes that *raised* the costs of production above those in the United States, investment would drift south, Canadian business would lobby for lower costs, and Canadian governments would have little choice but to reduce their social commitments. On the other hand, it was argued that if Canada established programs and tax policies that *lowered* the costs of production by socializing costs that are borne by employers in the United States, these programs might be interpreted in the United States as subsidies and could be subjected to countervail and other trade action. In either case, the result would be convergence between the two social policy regimes, with the primary burden of adjustment falling on Canada.

Defenders of closer economic links with the United States during the 1980s insisted that economic integration does not necessitate policy harmonization. After all, they insisted, Canada's distinctive social programs were actually developed over a period when the two economies were becoming more deeply entwined, and the country would continue to be free to pursue more ambitious social goals in a closer North American context. Programs financed by taxes that reduce net real incomes rather than increasing the costs of production would present no problem; and programs that do increase business costs would simply trigger a compensating change in the exchange rate. Moreover, social programs that are generally available in Canada would be immune from such actions under existing laws and the prevailing norms of international trade.

This debate was hardly unique to Canada. Broadly similar concerns about labour standards and environmental issues emerged a few years later in the United States during the debate over the North American Free Trade Agreement (NAFTA). Clearly, the world has changed since the early postwar era, and the consequences of globalization for social policy have become a central concern (to which this chapter returns below).

The pattern of social cleavages

While the international economy shapes the general context within which a country develops its welfare state, social divisions within the country have a more direct impact on the politics of social policy. Three cleavages were particularly important to understanding the differences in the welfare states that emerged in Canada and the United States: economic class; social heterogeneity in terms of race, ethnicity, and language; and regional divisions.

The most common interpretation of the politics of the welfare state sees social policy as a reflection of class divisions. Expansive welfare states tend to be found in countries in which the labour force is highly unionized, the union movement is organized in centralized federations, and labour has close links with sympathetic political parties, whether of a social democratic or confessional variety.[4] Viewed from this perspective, the political foundations of the welfare state are weak in both Canada and the United States. In comparison with other Western nations, especially European ones, unionization is low, the two labour movements have often been divided among different federations, and collective bargaining is decentralized.

Within this broad pattern, however, there are important differences between Canada and the United States. The two labour movements have diverged since the mid-1960s, with union membership declining dramatically in the United States but remaining comparatively stable in Canada. In addition, the two labour movements are animated by different ideological orientations. The predominant tradition in the United States has been an economic unionism that concentrates on the pursuit of the material interests of its members through collective bargaining. While collective bargaining is still the primary function of Canadian unions as well, they espouse a more social unionism, as represented by a social democratic policy agenda and formal links with the New Democratic Party (NDP). The largest labour federation, the Canadian Labour Congress (CLC), places a higher priority on lobbying for social legislation, developing common fronts among unions to fight retrenchment, and establishing coalitions with a wide range of community groups (Haddow 1991). Admittedly, the contrast with the United States can be overstated. The older Congress of Industrial Organizations (CIO) tradition of a wider social agenda continues in the United Auto Workers and other American unions; and in Canada, some unions, such as those within the Canadian Federation of Labour which broke away from the CLC, adopt a more conservative approach. Nevertheless, the different balance within the two labour movements is unmistakable. Organized labour represents a stronger force for comprehensive social protection for the working population north of the border.

Racial and linguistic divisions also shape the politics of social policy. A number of scholars have argued that redistributive policies enjoy greater public support in societies that are relatively homogeneous in terms of language, ethnicity, and race (Wilensky 1975; Gould and Palmer 1988). The differences between Canada and the United States are clear on this dimension as well. The poor are not socially distinctive in Canada; they do not stand out in linguistic, ethnic, or racial terms. The primary fault line in Canadian politics has traditionally been between English- and French-speaking Canadians, but as Table 16.2 illustrates, dependence on social benefits is not significantly higher in Quebec than elsewhere in the country, and it is considerably lower than in the Atlantic provinces. Nor do other ethnic or racial divisions dominate national political discourse over welfare. Certainly, members of certain ethnic and racial minorities are much more likely to be poor; Aboriginal peoples, to take the most striking case, suffer high levels of economic and social distress. Moreover, immigration from the Third World is creating a multiracial society in large urban centres such as Toronto, Montreal, and Vancouver, and is changing the case loads in social assistance and some social housing projects. For example, black families are now significantly overrepresented in the case loads of child-welfare agencies serving Toronto and Montreal.[5] Nevertheless, these changes are not yet powerful enough to give a distinctive ethnic or racial hue to welfare case loads on a nationwide basis, or—more importantly—to the dominant public perception of the poor.

Table 16.2. Per Capita Expenditures on Selected Social Programs in Canada, by Province, 1990–1991

	Unemployment insurance	Social assistance[1]	Total federal social security[2]
Newfoundland	1,244	246	3,790
Prince Edward Island	1,011	253	3,796
Nova Scotia	600	273	3,264
New Brunswick	776	351	3,400
Quebec	536	343	2,396
Ontario	319	352	2,527
Manitoba	307	219	2,922
Saskatchewan	258	199	2,806
Alberta	309	278	2,346
British Columbia	438	293	2,808
Canada	429	320	2,627

Source: Human Resources Development Canada, "Social Security Statistics: Canada and the Provinces," Tables A7.3, A9.3, and A33.3 (unpublished).

1 Includes federal and provincial expenditures.

2 Includes all federal income security and health programs, including transfers to provinces.

In contrast, race has constituted a core feature of the politics of the American welfare state throughout its history. During the passage of the *Social Security Act* in 1935, resistance from southern congressmen and other conservatives led to the exclusion of agricultural and domestic labour, denying coverage to three-fifths of black workers. In addition, southern congressmen led a successful campaign in the name of "states' rights" against national standards in public assistance, leaving southern blacks at the mercy of the local authorities (Orloff 1988; Quadagno 1988). In the 1960s, controversy swirled around AFDC and the Great Society programs. As welfare rolls expanded and new poverty programs were put in place, the profile of the poor became racially charged. Black families represented close to half of AFDC recipients, and Hispanic groups were also increasingly overrepresented (see table 16.3). These trends generated political resentment. Throughout the 1970s, public opinion polls recorded declining support for programs popularly identified with poor blacks, and Republican electoral campaigns in the 1980s capitalized on these tensions. While blacks continued to support redistributive social programs and the Democratic Party, white union members, urban ethnics, and southerners deserted their traditional political home, especially in presidential elections, in part because of its image on race and welfare issues (Skocpol 1991). In effect, the politics of race drove a wedge into the New Deal coalition and politically isolated the welfare poor, with predictable results. During the retrenchments of the 1980s, programs with predominantly African-American and Hispanic clienteles, such as subsidized housing and AFDC, bore particularly heavy cuts (Slessarev 1988). The issue was so powerful that in the 1990s the Democratic Party sought to insulate itself from race-freighted attacks by embracing hard-edged welfare reforms. During the 1992 presidential campaign, Bill Clinton promised to "end welfare as we know it" by cutting off unconditional welfare support after two years.

Table 16.3. AFDC Recipients by Race, 1973–1992

	1973	1979	1986	1992
White	38.0	40.4	39.7	38.9
Black	45.8	43.1	40.7	37.2
Hispanic	13.4	13.6	14.4	17.8
Native American	1.1	1.4	1.3	1.4
Asian	na	1.0	2.3	2.8
Other/unknown	1.7	0.4	1.4	2.0

Source: U.S. Committee on Ways and Means 1994, p. 402.

Race contributes to the difference between Canadian and American social policy at all levels. It influences the definitions through which social problems such as poverty are interpreted. In the United States the debate centres on the "urban underclass," the African-American and Hispanic inhabitants of inner-city ghettos, and intense scrutiny is focused on the social pathologies and behaviour of the poor themselves. In contrast, the term "underclass" is virtually unknown in Canada, where the debate centres far less on the characteristics of poor families. Canadian critics of social programs are more likely to emphasize changes in labour markets and the nature of the incentives implicit in the design of social programs (Myles 1991). At the level of program structure, the politics of race also help to explain the less developed coverage for working-aged population and children in the United States, and the less redistributive character of American income transfer programs.

Regionalism represents a third social division with different implications in the two countries. In the United States, resistance from the South represented a barrier to the expansion of welfare. This opposition was rooted not only in race but also in the region's distinctive economic base. In Quadagno's words, "Two distinct economic formations existed within the boundaries of a single nation-state" (1988, 15). In the first half of the twentieth century, the South was distinguished by the system of sharecropping, which was dominated by the power of landlords; and as sharecropping faded, it was replaced by a low-wage economy in which per capita income lagged significantly behind that of the country's North and West. Moreover, potential constituencies of support for social programs remained hobbled in the South during important phases of the history of the American welfare state; labour was relatively unorganized, and most blacks and poor whites were effectively disenfranchised until the 1960s.

The southern states believed that generous welfare programs would jeopardize their labour arrangements and social institutions. They were among the last to adopt mothers' pensions and child-labour laws earlier in the century, and welfare and unemployment benefits in the region remain low today (Peterson and Rom 1990). In addition, southern representatives in Congress fought the establishment of minimum welfare standards by the federal government, not only in the 1930s but in the decades that followed. In 1970 southerners helped defeat Nixon's Family Assistance Plan (FAP); in the late 1970s they fought the welfare reforms presented by Carter; and in 1988 they defeated the proposal to include a national minimum for welfare benefits in the *Family Support Act* (Quadagno 1990; Pierson 1995).

Canada is also marked by uneven economic development, with Atlantic Canada in particular lagging behind other regions. In contrast with the southern United States, however, Atlantic Canada has embraced national social programs and has come to depend heavily on the large interregional transfers implicit in them. The importance of independent commodity producers in the fishing and lumber industries of Atlantic Canada, and the seasonal nature of much employment there, created a large political constituency in favour of expanded federal income transfers. The region welcomed the extension of Unemployment Insurance to fishermen in 1957, as well as a major enrichment of the program and the introduction of regionally extended benefits in areas of high unemployment in 1971. These changes transformed Unemployment Insurance from a traditional social insurance program into a broad instrument of income supplementation, and its benefits sustain many small communities throughout the region.[6] In contrast to the American South, Atlantic Canada has regarded expansive social programs as a mechanism for protecting traditional occupations and communities from the forces of economic modernization (Banting 1995a). As a result, the region has fought vigorously against successive efforts to retrench the program since the late 1970s. Indeed, the most effective political resistance to cuts in Unemployment Insurance has come from politicians in the poorer provinces rather than from leaders of organized labour (Pal 1988; Smardon 1991). The provincial premiers and MPs from Atlantic Canada have repeatedly fought to protect seasonal workers and to reduce the impact of program changes in their region. The result is that although Unemployment Insurance is a federal program, its benefits are increasingly differentiated on a regional basis. By 1994, for example, the generosity of the program was about 40 percent greater in Newfoundland than the national average (Sargent 1995).

Historically, the primary regional obstacle to the expansion of national social programs in Canada flowed from Quebec, which played a role analogous to that of the American South during the first half of the twentieth century. French-Canadian nationalists resisted federal social programs as a form of cultural imperialism that threatened to undermine the distinctiveness of their society (Banting 1987a). Like the American South, Quebec was unable to halt the emergence of national social programs, but it slowed the pace and helped to preserve a substantial sphere for provincial discretion. However, this similarity disappeared rapidly after 1960, when a reformist Liberal Party won power at the provincial level and launched a sweeping program of modernization which significantly expanded the role of the provincial government in Quebec life (McRoberts 1988; Simeon and Robinson 1990). Quebec nationalism became imbued with a broadly *étatiste* orientation that produced major reforms to the educational system, the expansion of social services, and the adoption of hospital insurance which the province had hitherto resisted.

This Quiet Revolution was critical to national politics during the 1960s and 1970s, when core elements of the Canadian welfare state were put in place. In the federal Parliament, Quebec ministers and MPs began to lead rather than resist efforts to expand social programs; and in federal-provincial negotiations, the Quebec government joined the reformist cause on medicare, contributory pensions, and income supplementation. Admittedly, the transformation of Quebec was a double-edged sword. Quebec nationalists were determined to consolidate control over this expanded welfare state in provincial rather than federal hands. The province insisted that it operate new programs such as the contributory pension plan, and it struggled to recapture jurisdictions lost to the federal government during previous decades, thereby contributing to a constitutional struggle that has endured for thirty years (Banting 1995a). Quebec nationalism has lost much of its statist orientation in more recent times. Nevertheless, during the most important period of welfare innovation in Canada, Quebec helped tip the political balance towards expansion.

In contrast to the distinctive social dynamics generated by class, race, and region in Canada and the United States, the emergence of new lines of social division and new social movements represents an element of greater commonality in the politics of social policy. In both countries, the political mobilization of women, ethnic groups, Aboriginal peoples, the gay community, and others has broadened policy discourse and expanded the social agenda. On both sides of the border, these movements have been broadly support-ive of governmental activism on social issues and have been committed to modernizing core health and social security programs to reflect a more diverse society. This tendency may be more pronounced in Canada, where organizations such as the women's move-ment have emerged as political bulwarks of the welfare state and have formed alliances with like-minded interests. Moreover, the Canadian movements seem to be less coun-terbalanced than their American counterparts by conservative organizations rooted in Christian fundamentalism and traditional conceptions of family life. Nevertheless, the contrasts between Canada and the United States are less dramatic here and have therefore been of less account in shaping the different policy regimes of the two countries.

Clearly, differences in the welfare state in Canada and the United States are deeply rooted in the structures of the two societies. Class, race, and region have interwoven to create a less supportive environment for social policy south of the border.

Political structures

The differences rooted in economic and social structures tend to be amplified by the po-litical structures through which Canadians and Americans make collective choices about social policy. The political institutions themselves and the ideological orientations embed-ded in the party systems are both important in this respect.

Political institutions of the United States represent the classic example of fragmented power, combining congressional government, federalism, and decentralized political parties. As a result, policy innovation requires the construction of often fragile and tem-porary coalitions, a painful process that increases the likelihood that any proposal will be delayed, diluted, or defeated. In contrast, power is more concentrated in Canada by the combination of parliamentary government and cohesive political parties at the national level. Although Canada's federal nature ensures that power is more dispersed than in a unitary state such as Great Britain, its decision making is more concentrated than in the United States, a difference that facilitated the development of social programs.

Institutional complexity in the United States has increased the leverage of conservative political forces. For several critical decades, the congressional and party systems com-bined to give southern politicians a degree of control over the design of social programs that was much greater than the population or economic importance of their region war-ranted. One-party dominance ensured that long-serving conservative Democrats from the South chaired the relevant congressional committees and could manage the legislative process. Although this system did accommodate the incremental expansion of social se-curity after its introduction (Derthick 1979), more radical departures were blocked, as the tangled history of proposals for health insurance illustrates. Only exceptional Democratic majorities, as in the 1960s, could break the log-jam. In the 1990s the fate of the health plan developed by President Clinton confirmed once again the paralysing possibilities inherent in the congressional system.

Other more subtle institutional dynamics have also become visible in contemporary struggles, such as that over urban poverty. Equal representation for each state in the Senate significantly overrepresents rural America, for whom the social devastation of urban centres can seem somewhat distant. In addition, Ferejohn (1983) and Heclo (1986) argue that congressional politics militates against programs that redistribute income in a highly targeted fashion to the poor. The need to build fragile coalitions by spreading benefits widely over many districts militates against targeting programs on the areas of greatest need. In contrast, the concentrated power inherent in Canadian parliamentary institutions and cohesive political parties creates no such additional barriers to redistributive politics.

Federalism represents the only qualification to this general pattern of fewer institutional blockages in Canada. In the United States, federalism contributes to the larger system of checks and balances, but history records few major initiatives in social policy that were blocked primarily by constitutional limits on federal jurisdiction. Indeed, the dominant trend was the steady expansion of the federal role, a pattern that continued until the adoption of Supplementary Security Income (SSI) and the Earned Income Tax Credit (EITC) in 1974 (Pierson 1995). This is not to deny that federalism constrains social programs. For example, there is evidence that average AFDC benefits are depressed by economic competition among states (Peterson and Rom 1990; Marmor, Mashaw, and Harvey 1990). Moreover, the absence of any significant commitment to equalizing the fiscal capacity of the rich and poor states limits the scope for new initiatives at the state level, a constraint that may well loom larger in the future as retrenchment at the federal level and greater reliance on block funding enhances the role of state and local governments (Nathan and Doolittle 1987). Nevertheless, federalism still appears to be a secondary feature of the politics of social policy in the United States.

In Canada, federalism stood as a major barrier in the early history of the welfare state. In 1937 a judicial decision struck down social insurance programs as being beyond the constitutional powers of the federal government, and in 1946 a package of similar proposals foundered on the shoals of wider federal-provincial conflict. During the postwar decades, however, stronger political support for action overcame this barrier. In the field of health care, federalism actually facilitated expansion, as social democrats were able to capture power and introduce path-breaking legislation at the provincial level. Saskatchewan advanced the cause dramatically by introducing a health insurance program that became a model for the country, and then mounting a protracted campaign for national cost sharing of such programs (Gray 1991; Tuohy 1989). In other sectors, however, federalism did represent a constraint. For example, a complex system of federal and provincial vetoes over changes in contributory pensions has effectively insulated these programs from expansionist political pressures and has inclined the federal government to rely on other more limited instruments, such as the income-tested Guaranteed Income Supplement (Banting 1985). Overall, federalism has probably been a modestly conservative factor in the politics of the Canadian welfare state, although the sharpness of the contrast on this dimension with the United States that existed during the 1930s and 1940s has faded.

Thus, even when full weight is given to the complexities of Canadian federalism, the American combination of congressional government, federalism, and non-cohesive political parties diffuses power more thoroughly, amplifying resistance to expansive social programs and especially to redistributive efforts targeted on the poor.

The ideological complexion of the party systems in the two countries reinforces the pattern. Historically, the presence of a social democratic party in Canada added a forceful voice committed to both universal social programs and to targeted assistance for vulnerable groups. Until its serious electoral setback in 1993, the NDP—and its predecessor, the Co-operative Commonwealth Federation (CCF)—exercised an influence in national politics that was much greater than its third-party status might suggest. Not only did the NDP hold power at various times in four provinces, but it was an active participant in national debates in Parliament and the media, and a pressure on other parties, especially the Liberal Party, which borrowed ideas from the left at electorally strategic moments. NDP influence was considerably magnified during periods of minority Liberal governments, when the Liberal Party's hold on power depended on accommodating at least some parts of the left's agenda.

The combination of legislative and party structures in the two countries created distinctive patterns of policy innovation and expansion during the postwar period. As Weaver (1990) points out, reform in the United States came at times of great Democratic strength, whereas in Canada reform often came at times of Liberal weakness. The periods of Liberal weakness were more common than those of Democratic triumph. Large Democratic majorities were limited to brief periods in the 1930s and 1960s, when Social Security, Medicare, and other Great Society programs were passed. In contrast, Liberal vulnerability has been a recurring feature of Canadian politics. The first federal old age pensions were introduced by a minority Liberal government in 1927; Family Allowances were introduced in 1944 by a Liberal government that felt threatened by the sudden strength of the CCF in opinion polls; Medicare, contributory pensions, and the Canada Assistance Plan were all introduced by a minority Liberal government in the mid-1960s; and Family Allowances were tripled in value in 1973 by another minority Liberal government that was dependent on the NDP. These initiatives do not represent the entire history of the Canadian welfare state, but they do constitute one of its important themes.

Ideological and electoral coalitions in the two countries also differed in important ways during the conservative dominance in the 1980s and 1990s. The election of Ronald Reagan represented a realignment in presidential politics. The traditional New Deal coalition had been slowly eroding for over a decade, and the Republicans seized the opportunity to expand their support among southern whites, urban ethnics, white union members, and the fundamentalist religious movement (Wattenberg 1990; Carmines and Stimson 1989; Edsall 1991). The Republican approach to social issues reflected this political base. Changes made during the 1980s to social security—which remained well supported by the public, including Republican voters—reduced the expenditure level that would otherwise have prevailed in the early 1990s by only 8 percent. Programs for the poor and inner cities fared less well; the comparable cut for AFDC was 36 percent, and the figure was 54 percent for programs covered by the social services block grant (U.S. Committee on Ways and Means 1991, 1515). In effect, the politics of retrenchment in the United States sharpened the traditional contrast between the two tiers of its welfare state by rolling back expansions of the lower tier that had crept in during the 1960s and early 1970s.

Canadian conservatism pushed in the opposite direction. Although the Liberal and Conservative parties tend to present broadly similar programs, their party activists lean in different directions. Surveys in the mid-1980s found Conservatives to be more concerned about welfare abuse, less supportive of enhanced funding for child care and the poor, and less sympathetic to universal programs such as Old Age Security (OAS) and Family Allowances (Perlin 1988). This last predisposition proved particularly important in government. Although some reductions implemented by the Mulroney government—such as the freezing of transfers to provincial governments for health care and postsecondary education—cut across the board, the Conservatives accelerated the trend towards greater selectivity. The universal OAS payments were clawed back from upper-income recipients through the tax system; the universal Family Allowances were replaced with an income-tested Child Benefit that eliminated support for middle- and upper-income families; reductions in Unemployment Insurance benefits continued to be much more dramatic in affluent regions than in poor ones; and a cap on the growth in federal support for provincial social assistance was applied only to the three richest provinces (Banting 1992, 1995a).

Thus, ideological impulses embedded in the two countries' party systems differed, not only during the expansion of the welfare state but also in the period of conservative retrenchment. Cuts in the United States fell disproportionately on benefits for the poor, whereas Canadian cuts accelerated an historical trend of targeting benefits on such people.

The Sources of Distinctiveness: A Summary

The contrasts explored here might strike a distant observer as rather subtle, representing minor variations on the major themes of North American life. Cumulatively, however, these differences have provided a stronger base for the welfare state in Canada than in the United States. Historically, Canada's vulnerability to international economic pressures has contributed to a stronger tradition of collective responses to social needs, and core features of domestic life in the two countries reinforce this difference. Not only does organized labour represent a stronger presence in Canada, but social initiatives have been less constrained by racial and regional divisions than in the United States. Finally, political structures amplify these differences. Canadian political institutions provide fewer blocking opportunities to those resisting social programs in general and to income transfers to the poor in particular; and the ideological orientations embedded in the party systems have pushed the two social policy regimes in different directions at critical stages in their evolution.

The social policy regimes

The imprint of these economic, social, and political differences between Canada and the United States can be seen clearly in their social programs. This section examines health and income security programs in greater detail, paying particular attention to the three interrelated differences noted at the outset: comprehensiveness of support, especially for children and those of working age; the strength of selective programs targeted on the poor; and the redistributive impact of social policy on poverty and inequality.

HEALTH CARE

Health care traditionally has provided the most dramatic contrast between Canada and the United States. In Canada, Medicare covers basic hospital and medical services on a universal basis without deductibles, co-payments, or significant user fees. As a result, there is no parallel private sector in basic health care. Private health plans provide supplementary items not covered by the public program, such as semi-private accommodation in hospital, prescription drugs, the additional costs of out-of-country medical care, and dental care. Although the private sector has been growing incrementally as a result of some trimming in public coverage, private expenditures still represent less than 30 percent of total health spending (OECD 1994).

In contrast, public programs in the United States play a more limited role, covering only specific categories of the population. Medicare provides health insurance for the elderly, although those covered must still bear a proportion of the costs of basic care in the form of premiums, deductibles, and co-insurance payments, giving rise to private "Medigap" policies for those who can afford them. Veterans Affairs provides health care for some elderly and disabled veterans. Finally, Medicaid, a means-tested program delivered by state governments, provides health care to less than half of the nation's poor, albeit with considerable variation among states. In 1995, for example, Nevada served 284 Medicaid beneficiaries for every 1,000 poor or near-poor individuals in the state, whereas Rhode Island served 913 per 1,000 (U.S. General Accounting Office 1995a). The rest of the American population must rely on the private sector. However, private coverage is seriously incomplete: approximately 16 percent of the population—some 41 million people, primarily low-income workers and their families—were without coverage in 1992; and many more were seriously underinsured (Aaron 1996). The vast majority of these people must rely on the willingness of doctors and hospitals, especially public hospitals, to provide uncompensated care, largely through cross-subsidies from those who are fully insured. Otherwise, the uninsured must simply do without adequate medical care.[7]

Differences in coverage lead to differences in access. Given the universal coverage in Canada, differences in the utilization of health care among different social groups reflects other factors, such as geographic location. In the United States, however, incomplete insurance coverage adds other inequalities. In 1986 a national survey found that uninsured Americans contacted a doctor two-thirds as often as the insured population and used only three-quarters as many days in hospital (see Figures 16.2 and 16.3). The uninsured are more likely to delay seeking care or to be turned away, leading eventually to more serious illnesses and to hospital admissions that could have been avoided; and when the uninsured do receive treatment for serious problems, they tend to receive less extensive care than insured individuals with similar conditions. Sorting out the consequences for the actual health status of the two groups is difficult, since health is also affected by related factors, such as the poverty of many of the uninsured. Nevertheless, the uninsured are clearly less healthy. One study found that between 1982 and 1986 infants born to parents without health insurance were 30 percent more likely to become ill or die than those born to insured parents. In the words of a major commission, "Lack of health insurance means diminished chances at the outset of life and more illness and disability ahead" (U.S. Bipartisan Commission on Comprehensive Health Care 1990, 35).

The contrast between the Canadian and American systems grew sharper in the 1980s and 1990s. The intense pressure on health-care costs has been a key political issue on both

Figure 16.2. Average Reported Physician Contacts, by Income and Insurance Status, 1986

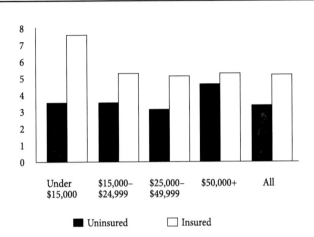

Source: U.S. Bipartisan Commission on Comprehensive Health Care 1990.

Figure 16.3. Average Reported Hospital In-Patient Days, by Income and Insurance Status, 1986

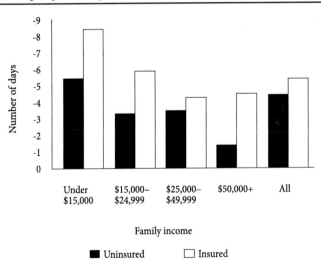

Source: U.S. Bipartisan Commission on Comprehensive Health Care 1990.

sides of the border, but the two countries have responded differently, as Figure 16.4 attests. In Canada, concerns that extra billing by doctors and user fees in hospitals were beginning to undermine universal access led Parliament to adopt—with all-party support—the 1984 *Canada Health Act*, which imposed penalties on provinces that allowed such charges. This prohibition is not without its critics, and in the mid-1990s the federal government was locked in battles with a number of provincial governments—especially Alberta, which wished to expand the role of private clinics. Nevertheless, the 1984 Act has curbed the expansion of fees and user charges. Some provinces have narrowed the range of medical procedures covered by deinsuring such items as cosmetic surgery and newer reproductive technologies, and by refusing to pay the difference between domestic rates and the cost of medical care received by their citizens while visiting other countries (Tuohy 1988, 1994). In general, however, the burden of the substantial financial cuts imposed by provincial governments has fallen on the service providers. As the single payer responsible for financing health care within its jurisdiction, each provincial government is in a strong position to control costs—by setting budgets for hospitals, by supervising capital expenditures for new equipment and buildings, and by negotiating increases in physicians' fees with medical associations. Critics of the Canadian model emphasize that this approach has resulted in a slower adoption of new technologies than in the United States and lengthy waiting lists for some surgical procedures. In the early 1990s a favourite example of the technological gap was the MRI scanner, the magnetic resonance imaging device that represents a major advance in diagnostic science. In 1991 there were approximately fifteen MRIs in Canada but more than two thousand in the United States—an immense gap even when the size of the two countries is taken into consideration.[8] Moreover, Canadians seem to

Figure 16.4. Total Health Expenditures as a Proportion of GDP, Canada and the United States, 1960–1991

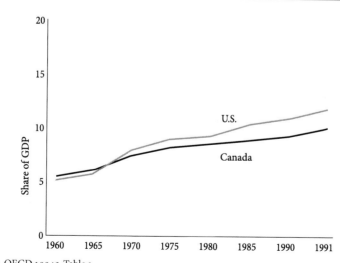

Source: OECD 1994c, Table 2.

accept longer waits for some non-lifesaving operations, such as knee replacements (Coyte et al. 1994). The Canadian version of restraint is thus not without costs. So far, however, broad equality of access has been preserved.

Health-care costs in the United States have not been controlled as effectively, and this failure has further eroded equality of access. The American health-care system is much more pluralistic, with private insurers, employers, and three levels of governments paying for health-care services. As a result, no single unit is as well placed as Canadian provincial governments to manage cost increases, and health expenditures continued their relentless climb throughout the 1980s (R. Evans 1986; R. Evans, Barer, and Hertzman 1991; U.S. General Accounting Office 1991). In this context, employers have responded in two ways. First, they have reduced their health commitments by transferring more of the burden to both current and retired employees through reduced coverage and increased deductibles and co-payments; at the extreme, health insurance has collapsed completely in many small firms. Second, private corporations have been turning to health-maintenance organizations (HMOs) to deliver health care to their employees. These agencies have the power to influence the pattern of care, access to doctors, the salaries and fees paid to service providers, staffing levels in hospitals, and other aspects of health care—all in the name of controlling costs. This transformation of health care in the United States is occurring with breathtaking speed: most working-age, insured Americans are already receiving care through such plans, and the model is expected to incorporate virtually all insured Americans within a few years (Aaron 1996).

Medical coverage under public programs has also eroded in the United States. Although the primary burden of the cuts in Medicare has fallen on the service providers, the elderly have not escaped unscathed. For example, out-of-pocket health spending increased from 7.8 percent of after-tax income in 1972 to 12.5 percent in 1988 (U.S. Committee on Ways and Means 1991, 250); and the 1988 *Catastrophic Health Care Act*, which was designed to protect the elderly from the additional costs of acute health problems, was repealed within a year of its passage. In the case of Medicaid, federal initiatives begun in 1986 did expand eligibility for low-income pregnant women and children, but sharp limits on reimbursement rates reduced the willingness of doctors and hospitals to accept large numbers of Medicaid patients.

The cumulative effect of all the changes is hardly surprising: the uninsured population rose from 24 million in 1980 to 41 million in 1994, and the number with inadequate coverage also continued to grow. In addition, much more stringent payment systems developed both by HMOs and by the public programs have been weakening the capacity of hospitals and others to provide uncompensated care to the growing uninsured population, thus drying up "the balm that has made socially tolerable the abrasive fact that one non-aged person in six is without insurance at any given time" (Aaron 1996, 35; see also U.S. Committee on Ways and Means 1994; and U.S. Bipartisan Commission on Comprehensive Health Care 1990).

Health care thus reflects two central differences between the welfare state in Canada and the United States. The public sector in Canada provides more comprehensive coverage and stronger redistribution of well-being between rich and poor, a contrast that has grown sharper during the 1980s and 1990s.

INCOME SECURITY

Canada and the United States do not form such a sharp contrast in the world of income security. Nevertheless, the Canadian system does provide more comprehensive protection, especially for children and those of working age; it devotes more of its resources to selective programs; and its program structure has a larger redistributive impact. This pattern often comes as a surprise to those accustomed to thinking of Canada as more dedicated to the universal approach. Table 16.4 tracks expenditures on universal and selective transfer programs in the two countries between 1960 and 1992. Canada and the United States started in almost identical positions in the early 1960s. Since then, a growing proportion of Canadian income-security dollars have flowed through selective programs, whereas the American proportion remained stable until the 1980s and then declined. Initially, the Canadian trend reflected the introduction of income supplements, such as the Guaranteed Income Supplement (GIS) and the refundable Child Tax Credit (CTC). Since the 1980s, however, the pattern has also reflected the growth of social assistance programs and, more recently, the transformation of universal programs, such as *Family Allowances and Old Age Security* (OAS), into income-tested benefits. Moreover, table 16.4 probably understates the trend towards selective programs in Canada, since it does not reflect the fact that elements of income testing have also crept into Unemployment Insurance benefits.[9] In contrast, the fiscal dominance of Social Security has remained unchallenged in the United States. Despite the development of the Earned Income Tax Credit, which will be discussed more fully below, selective programs generally have declined as a proportion of income security expenditures. Clearly, the two systems have been travelling different pathways for decades.

Table 16.4. Universal and Selective Expenditures as a Proportion of Total Income Security, Canada and the United States, 1960–1992 (in percent)

	1960	1965	1970	1975	1980	1985	1990	1992
United States[1]								
Universal	79.6	81.2	77.2	75.7	79.1	83.3	83.7	82.2
Selective	20.4	18.8	22.8	24.3	20.9	16.7	16.3	17.8
Canada[2]								
Universal	79.2	72.4	69.2	70.7	62.6	64.5	52.5	48.0
Selective	20.8	27.6	30.8	29.3	37.4	35.5	47.5	52.0

Sources: Calculated from data in Health and Welfare Canada, *Social Security Statistics: Canada and the Provinces* (Ottawa, various years); U.S. Department of Health and Human Services 1994; and U.S. Office of Management and Budget 1995.

1 Universal programs include OASDI, unemployment insurance, workers' compensation, plus public employee retirement benefits and railroad retirement and unemployment benefits not provided through social security. Selective programs include income-tested programs (earned income tax credit) and all means-tested income transfers.

2 Universal benefits include demogrants and all social insurance income transfers. However, family allowances and old age security are considered to be increasingly selective due to the phasing in of the tax clawback of benefits from upper-income recipients. These expenditures are treated as 66 % selective in 1990 and 100 % selective in 1992. Selective programs include both income-tested programs (child benefit, guaranteed income supplement, spouses allowance, and refundable provincial tax credits) and means-tested benefits. Social assistance expenditures in Ontario, British Columbia, and Alberta in 1990 and 1992 are based on estimates.

Underlying this general pattern, however, is a more complex pattern of both convergence and divergence in different programs. A fuller appreciation of these contrasting
trends requires a closer look at the core programs—pensions, unemployment insurance,
child benefits, and social assistance—and at their redistributive impact.

PENSIONS

For the average senior citizen, the role of the state in providing retirement income is quite
similar in Canada and the United States. Public programs provide comparable portions of
the income of those aged sixty-five and over on both sides of the border, as Table 16.5 indicates; and similar benefits flow from the universal programs—the Canada and Quebec
Pension Plans and the OAS in Canada, and in the United States the Old Age Security Income
(OASI), which is a component of Social Security. The biggest difference lies in the more
redistributive character of the benefit structure in Canada. During the late 1980s, close to
half of the entire elderly population of the country, including many who had had average earning records before retirement and who held significant assets during retirement,
received a GIS payment. In the United States, the Supplementary Security Income (SSI) is
a means-tested benefit that has much more stringent income limits and requires individuals to exhaust most of their assets before they can qualify for it.[10] As a result, it reaches a
tiny proportion of the elderly. In 1993, for example, only 6.7 percent of elderly Americans
received any benefit from the program (U.S. General Accounting Office 1995b, figure 1.3).

Table 16.5. Sources of Income of the Elderly, Canada and the United States, 1989[1]

Income source	Canada	United States
Public transfers	40.1	40.9
Private pensions	16.9	17.0
Investment income	26.2	27.5
Other	16.8	14.6

Sources: Canadian Institute of Actuaries 1993, 9; U.S. Committee on Ways and Means 1991, 1107.
  1 Canadian data are for couples in which both are aged 65 or over; U.S. data include both unat-
    tached individuals and couples in which both are aged over 65.

Table 16.6 compares replacement ratios, which measure retirement benefits as a proportion of preretirement earnings for new retirees. As can be seen, the general programs
have comparable replacement capacity, but the GIS significantly enhances the position of
low-income and average retirees in Canada. This table overstates the cross-national difference somewhat because it does not incorporate SSI in the calculations for the United
States. It is difficult to include a means-tested benefit in replacement ratios, since assets
constitute a major consideration in determining eligibility. Nevertheless, the general impression conveyed by the table is undoubtedly correct, since SSI reaches such a small
portion of the elderly population. It is the power of their selective component that distinguishes Canadian retirement benefits from their counterparts south of the border.

The politics of the 1980s and 1990s accentuated this difference. Frontal assaults on major retirement benefits were initially repulsed on both sides of the border, and only more
limited adjustments survived the political process. Nevertheless, the burden of change fell
differently in the two countries. Under changes in U.S. Social Security legislation, the pain

was spread evenly, with the poorest and the richest recipients suffering approximately the same proportionate reduction in their replacement rates between 1981 and 1991 (U.S. Committee on Ways and Means 1994, table 1.7). In contrast, the Canadian system was made more redistributive: the GIS for low-income recipients was significantly enriched in the early 1980s, and the previously universal OAS payment was clawed back through the tax system from high-income recipients at the end of the decade. The 1996 federal budget announced the logical culmination of this process: beginning in the year 2001, the OAS and GIS will be replaced by an integrated, income-tested Seniors Benefit that will provide support to low- and middle-income Canadians only (Canada, Department of Finance 1996). Thus, the traditional differences have been accentuated by the politics of retrenchment in the two countries in the 1980s and 1990s.

Table 16.6. Replacement Ratios: Public Retirement Benefits as a Proportion of Pre-retirement Earnings for New Retirees, Canada and the United States, 1989

	Low earnings	Average earnings	High earnings
United States	57.9	41.7	24.1
Canada:			
without GIS	61.0	44.6	22.3
with GIS	86.5	50.7	22.3

Sources: Ratios for Canada calculated from benefit levels reported in National Council of Welfare 1990, tables 4 and 5; ratios for the United States from Committee on Ways and Means 1990, app.a, table 15.

UNEMPLOYMENT INSURANCE

If pensions have moved consistently in one direction, unemployment insurance has resembled a roller-coaster. The large historical difference between the two systems expanded dramatically during the 1980s, but it began to contract again during the 1990s.

In the United States, unemployment insurance is a federal-state program and is delivered by the state governments. The program is financed exclusively through a payroll tax on employers, with employees making no direct contributions. The federal government imposes a payroll tax on employers and then rebates the revenue to the state governments that operate a federally approved program. The state governments impose an additional payroll tax and can borrow from the federal Treasury if their programs are threatened with insolvency during periods of high unemployment. Federal legislation generally determines what employment is covered, but the states determine the qualification periods, as well as the level and duration of the regular state benefit programs. There is also a federal-state program of extended benefits, designed to be triggered on a state-by-state basis during recessions. In comparison, the Canadian program enjoys the simplicity of being an exclusively federal program, financed by contributions by employers and employees which were supplemented until 1991 from general federal revenues. The complexity of the Canadian program is found in the regional differentials that have been built into both the qualification periods and the duration of benefits, providing enriched support in areas of high unemployment.

After a major expansion in 1971, the Canadian program provided far greater protection to the unemployed than the program in the United States did. Although benefit levels were not dramatically higher, especially after they were trimmed in 1978, coverage in

Canada was broader, work requirements were less restrictive, and benefit periods were longer. For example, maximum benefit periods were normally twenty-six weeks in the United States and fifty-two weeks in Canada. In addition, the Canadian program introduced elements, such as maternity and later paternity benefits, that are not covered in the United States. With this more liberal program structure, unemployment benefits represented a dramatically larger financial commitment for the public sector in Canada. For example, as recently as 1993 unemployment insurance benefits represented 2.6 percent of GDP in Canada, but only 0.5 percent in the United States, a gap far greater than the difference in unemployment rates (Osberg, Erksoy, and Phipps 1994).

The differences between the two programs grew strongly over the course of the 1980s. While the Canadian program suffered only marginal adjustments during the decade, the Reagan administration had a significant impact on unemployment insurance south of the border. Federal legislation virtually eliminated extended benefits, and it began to charge interest on state borrowing from the federal Treasury, which put pressure on the states to revise their programs. Given the weakness of organized labour in most state capitals, the revisions relied much more on benefit restrictions than on increased payroll taxes. According to Burtless, the result was a serious erosion of unemployment insurance that went "virtually unnoticed in the early 1980s at a time when far smaller proportional cutbacks in public assistance, disability insurance and social security caused loud public outcries" (Burtless 1991, 41; see also Hansen and Byers 1990). Whereas approximately 80 percent of the unemployed received benefits during the recession of the mid-1970s, only 26 percent of the unemployed were receiving benefits in 1987 (U.S. Committee on Ways and Means 1991, 483).

The divergence in the 1980s has given way to some convergence since then. Faced with major increases in spending on unemployment benefits during the recession of the early 1990s, Canadian governments of both Conservative and Liberal persuasion have taken slices from the program. In 1991 the federal government's financial contribution ended, shifting the full cost to employers and employees. In addition, the period of employment required to qualify for benefit was increased in 1990 and 1994, and was planned to rise again in 1996. The maximum length of time for which benefits can be received was reduced in 1990 and was to drop again in 1996. And benefits levels were reduced from 60 to 57 percent of insurable earnings in 1993 and were cut further for most beneficiaries to 55 percent in 1994. At the same time, the United States was temporarily repairing some of the damage to its program. After protracted political battles between president and Congress, benefits for victims of the current recession were extended in late 1991 and twice in 1992.

In summary, then, strong divergence in the 1980s has given way to convergence in the 1990s. Canada has withdrawn significant resources from its program in recent years, especially in the more affluent parts of the country. Nevertheless, it is important not to overstate the extent of convergence with the United States. As Figure 16.5 suggests, the differences between the two programs in terms of coverage of the unemployed has remained significant.

Figure 16.5. UI Recipients as a Proportion of Unemployed Workers, Canada and the United States, 1968–1993

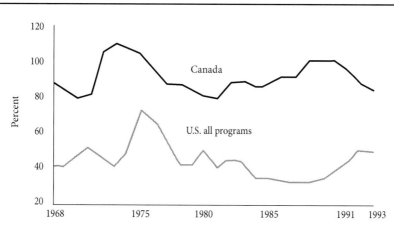

Sources: Calculated from data in Committee on Ways and Means 1994 and from Statistics Canada 1994a and 1994b.

CHILD BENEFITS

The strongest case of convergence is to be found in child benefits. In the mid-1970s the contrast between the two countries was clear. Canada had a universal program of Family Allowances, whereas the United States was the only major industrialized nation with no child-allowance program. Since then, the contrast has disappeared as both countries have experimented with the integration of the tax and transfer systems in order to provide more targeted support for low-income families. By the mid-1990s, the programs in the two countries differed only in their details.

The United States introduced its refundable Earned Income Tax Credit (EITC) for working-poor families with children as part of a wider tax-cut package in 1975. Coverage under the program is relatively narrow because, as a credit against earned income, it provides no support to welfare families who have few earnings. However, benefit levels were boosted significantly in 1986, 1990, and 1993. The final and biggest increase, in 1993, represented one of President Clinton's few victories in the domain of social policy. In 1994 the maximum annual benefits were $2,038 for a family with one child and $2,528 for larger families, and these levels were scheduled to rise to $2,094 and $3,370 by 1996.

Canada has moved in the same direction. The first major step came in 1978, when the federal government introduced the refundable Child Tax Credit (CTC), financed in part by a reduction in the universal Family Allowances. In the years that followed, child-related programs underwent a tortuous series of incremental changes, which culminated in the 1992 budget. The previously universal Family Allowance and the general tax exemption for children were replaced with a single, income-tested Child Benefit that was to be delivered through the tax system. Coverage under the Canadian program is broader than in the United States, since it goes to both the working poor and the welfare poor (although there is an additional supplement for the working poor). However, benefit levels are marginally lower in Canada for most families. In 1994 the maximum annual benefits were

$1,020 per child, with a supplement of $213 for younger children and a supplement of up to $500 for families with employment earnings.

Thus, child benefits in the two countries have clearly converged over the last twenty years. The traditional contrast generated by the Canadian system of universal Family Allowances has given way to variations on a common theme of income-tested benefits delivered through the tax system. Nevertheless, the transition reflects the stronger shift in Canada towards redistribution to the poor. In abandoning its universal Family Allowances and the general tax exemption for dependent children, both of which provided benefits to middle- and upper-income earners in the mid-1970s, the reallocation of benefits towards low-income groups was marked. Moreover, the long-term prospects for targeted support to poor families seem better in Canada; for example, the 1996 federal budget announced a doubling of the supplement for working-poor families (Canada, Department of Finance 1996). In the United States, however, the bipartisan consensus that had sustained the expansion of the EITC had broken down by the mid-1990s, with congressional Republicans proposing significant cutbacks in the program (Weaver 1995; see also U.S. General Accounting Office 1995c).

SOCIAL ASSISTANCE

The pattern in social assistance resembles that in unemployment insurance, with significant divergence during the 1980s fading in the 1990s. Throughout all the turmoil, however, the underlying pattern of recent history has remained one of stronger redistribution towards poor people who live north of the border. Under the terms of the Canada Assistance Plan, which provided federal support to provincial welfare programs from 1965 to 1995, provinces were required to provide assistance to all persons in need. Although the level of support provided to single employable persons has not been overly generous in some provinces, support is provided to all categories of needy people. In contrast, coverage in the United States is much less complete. Traditionally, Aid to Families with Dependent Children (AFDC) has been restricted to single-parent families, with only some states extending partial support to the children in two-parent households when the principal wage earner is unemployed. Single persons and childless couples remain ineligible for AFDC in all states. Income support for these people is limited to Food Stamps (a federal program) and General Assistance (a purely state and local program which provides meagre benefits and does not exist at all in almost half of the states). In addition to differences in coverage, benefit levels have traditionally been higher in Canada. For example, Blank and Hanratty found that in 1986 "even in the least generous province in Canada, the [social assistance] benefit level for single-parent families exceeds the maximum low-income transfers (AFDC and Food Stamps) available in all states except Alaska" (Blank and Hanratty 1993, 197).

These differentials between the two countries grew in the 1980s and the first half of the 1990s. In the United States, AFDC benefit levels have undergone a long-term decline: between 1970 and 1994 the maximum AFDC benefits in the median state declined by 47 percent in real terms, an erosion that has been only partially cushioned by the federal Food Stamps program (U.S. Committee on Ways and Means 1994, table 10.14). This trend reflects the failure to index benefits fully for inflation since the mid-1970s, plus explicit cutbacks in both eligibility and benefits during the last years of the Carter presidency and the early years of the Reagan administration. The pattern of decline accelerated again in the early 1990s. Unlike their Canadian counterparts, budget makers in the U.S. states could not rely on deficit financing. Forty-nine states are required by their constitutions or state law to balance their budgets, and the result was a wave of reductions in AFDC, and especially in General Assistance. In the recession year of 1991, for example, Michigan abolished General Assistance altogether; significant reductions in benefits took place in states as diverse as Massachusetts, California, Maryland, Ohio, Illinois, Maine, and the District of Columbia; and most other states froze benefit levels (Center on Budget and Policy Priorities and Center for the Study of the States, 1991).

Although comparable long-term data is unavailable in Canada, it is clear that the predominant pattern has been different. During the recession of the early 1980s, the three westernmost provinces did in fact reduce welfare rates, but most other provinces maintained their benefits in real terms (Banting 1987b). This record was repeated over the rest of the decade. Although benefits in several provinces declined in real terms, especially in Alberta, other provinces maintained or enriched the real value of their benefits, with particularly strong increases in the big provinces of Ontario, Quebec, and British Columbia. Indeed, Ontario increased its benefits in real terms by approximately 25 percent between 1985 and 1990 (National Council of Welfare 1995). By the mid-1990s, the differential been Canada and the United States had never been greater.

This gap between the two systems seems to be narrowing again in the second half of the 1990s as Canadian governments struggle to reduce their deficits. In 1995 the federal government sharply reduced its transfers to provincial governments for social programs, and it rolled the Canada Assistance Plan into a broader block fund, which gives provinces more discretion in reforming welfare. In addition, the newly elected Conservative government in Ontario effectively eliminated most of the increases of the previous decade with a 21 percent reduction in welfare benefits. Major changes in welfare were also being debated in the United States, including proposals to replace AFDC with a block fund to state governments, similar to the Canadian initiative. However, divided government once again worked its magic. Early in 1996 President Clinton vetoed the Republican's welfare bill, ensuring that the issue would be swept up into the politics of the presidential race.

Table 16.7. Social Assistance Benefits, Canada and the United States, 1994[1]

	Average benefit national $	Average benefit Cdn $
Canada:		
single parent/one child	13,487	13,487
couple/two children	18,289	18,289
United States:		
single parent/two children	7,932	10,708

Sources: National Council of Welfare 1995, table 2; U.S. Committee on Ways and Means 1994, table 10.11.

1 Canadian figures represent the average provincial/territorial benefit, including social assistance, child benefits, and provincial refundable tax credits. U.S. figure represents AFDC and food stamps in the median state. The EITC is not paid to welfare families with no earnings and is not included.

Despite this narrowing of the gap in the mid-1990s, it is important not to overstate the convergence between the systems. As in the case of unemployment insurance, the Canadian programs remain more generous than the American. Coverage is much more comprehensive, with single individuals, childless couples, and two-parent families eligible for support. Benefits also remain significantly higher. Table 16.7 demonstrates the differences in 1994, the most recent year for which data are available. Although the reductions in Ontario have undoubtedly reduced the Canadian average, the differences facing the poor on both sides of the border remain compelling. A comparison of the welfare program in Ontario at the time of the 1995 cuts, with that prevailing across the border in Michigan, concluded that "residents of Michigan may consider what Ontario is facing a walk in the park" (Gadd 1995).

REDISTRIBUTIVE IMPACTS

In view of the more comprehensive coverage and the more targeted programs, it is hardly surprising that Canadian programs have a greater impact than the American on the distribution of income. Comparative studies of trends in both the rates of poverty and the extent of overall inequality confirm that Canadian programs have a stronger redistributive role and that the difference in the two systems grew during the the 1980s and early 1990s. Figure 16.6 tracks the poverty rates in Canada and the United States for families headed by an individual under sixty-five years of age during the period 1969–87, using the Canadian definition of poverty in both countries. Figure 16.7 supplements this basic data with evidence about one subgroup that is particularly vulnerable to poverty—female-headed families. Although the economic and demographic structure of the two countries is similar, the poverty rates have followed different trajectories. Poverty in Canada declined rapidly over the course of the 1970s, from a rate considerably higher than that in the United States to one well below it. Although poverty increased in both countries dur-

Figure 16.6. Canadian and U.S. Poverty Rates

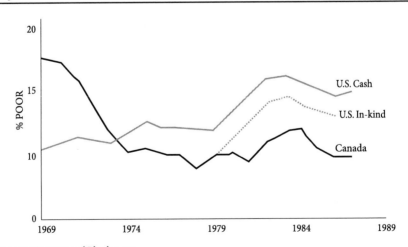

Source: Hanratty and Blank 1992.

ing the recession of the early 1980s, the rate fell back in Canada but remained stubbornly above its pre-recession level in the United States.

An analysis by Hanratty and Blank (1992) demonstrates that the divergence in poverty rates during the 1980s did not flow from demographic or macroeconomic factors but from the different fate of income transfer programs in the two countries. The deterioration of social assistance, unemployment insurance, and other benefits in the United States had unmistakable consequences. Hanratty and Blank estimate that in 1979 Canadian social assistance, Family Allowances, and the Child Tax Credit provided an average combined benefit that was 14 percent more generous than the comparable combination in the United States; by 1986 the gap had grown to 42 percent. This pattern was reinforced by the growing gap in eligibility for, and duration of, unemployment insurance benefits. As a result, "virtually all of the divergence in poverty trends in the two countries may be explained by differences in the share of families who were moved out of poverty by transfers" (Hanratty and Blank 1992, 252). A separate simulation by the same authors concludes that if the United States adopted Canadian income-security programs, the poverty rate would drop significantly (Blank and Hanratty 1993).

The cross-national Luxembourg Income Study points to comparable conclusions for two vulnerable groups, children and the elderly. Table 16.8 examines child poverty. Although the definition of poverty in this analysis differs slightly from that in the studies just cited, the patterns are similar: the redistributive gap between the two countries grew during the 1980s, primarily because of a weakening of the redistributive impulse in the United States. Using the same data set, Coder, Smeeding, and Torrey (1990) examined poverty among the elderly in Canada, the United States, and Australia in 1981 and 1987, and they concluded that changes in transfer programs reduced the number of Canadian elderly living in poverty more than elsewhere. The 1980s, they observed, "saw the low-income elderly in Canada as big winners."

Figure 16.7. Female-headed Family Poverty Rates, Canada and the United States, 1969–1987

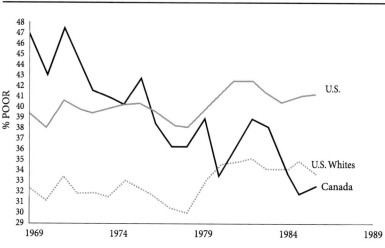

Source: Hanratty and Blank 1992.

Table 16.8. Effect of Taxes and Transfers on Levels of Child Poverty in Canada and the United States in the 1980s (% poor)[1]

	Canada		United States	
	1981	1987	1979	1986
Pre-tax and transfer	15.5	15.7	19.0	22.3
Post-tax and transfer	10.2	9.3	14.7	20.4
Reduction	5.3	6.4	4.3	1.9
% reduction	34.2	40.8	24.2	8.5

Source: Smeeding 1991.
  1 Poverty is defined as 40 percent of median disposable income in each country.

Trends in inequality more generally in the two countries followed similar patterns. The economic pressures of the decade generated greater inequality in the income that individuals and families derived from the market in both countries. The redistributive role of the state, however, was quite different. In the United States, a weakened redistributive impulse in both transfers and taxes could not compensate for the growing inequality in market incomes; no matter what indicator is used, the distribution of final income, incorporating both earnings and government transfers, became less equal throughout the 1980s and early 1990s (U.S. Committee on Ways and Means 1994, 1181–211). In contrast, across the border, the growing inequality in market earnings was offset by the expansion of transfer payments and changes in the tax system, producing a relatively stable distribution of final income (Blackburn and Bloom 1993). Figure 16.8 demonstrates this reality in

Figure 16.8. Changes in Income Inequality among Families, Canada and the United States, 1971–1992

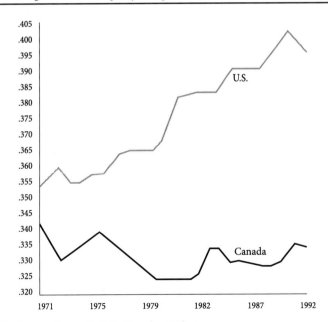

Sources: Karoly 1993, Fig. 2.1; Statistics Canada 1994d, 42.

statistical terms by tracking the Gini coefficients for the level of inequality in total family income from the early 1970s to the early 1990s. The higher the Gini coefficient, the greater is the degree of inequality. As the data reveal, inequality in family incomes rose sharply in the United States but stayed constant in Canada. The divergence in social life in the two countries could not be clearer.

Convergence and Divergence in a Global Economy

As noted earlier, many advocates of an active social role for the state fear that global economic integration is undermining the effective sovereignty of the nation-state and constraining the ability of national governments to maintain distinctive social policy regimes. For Canadians, the issue is whether their distinctive social programs are compatible with even closer integration with the American economy; for Americans, attention focuses on the impact on labour and environmental regulation of NAFTA and economic integration with Mexico.

Although the evidence in this chapter cannot resolve this debate definitively, the patterns of the 1980s and 1990s are clearly relevant. As the preceding discussion has demonstrated, the evolution of social programs in Canada and the United States has created a complex pattern of convergence and divergence during the 1980s and the first half of the 1990s. Perhaps the broadest trend has been incremental divergence, with the traditional differences between the two countries growing more marked in certain areas—for example, in health care, in the broad balance between universal and selective income transfers, in the role of public pensions, and in the redistributive impact of the state. In part, this trend has resulted from program changes in Canada, but the divergence is largely the result of the more rapid erosion of coverage and benefits in the United States, especially during the Reagan-Bush years. Other programs, however, provide a counterpoint to this trend. In the case of social assistance, the strong divergence of the 1980s began to fade in the mid-1990s. Stronger patterns of convergence emerge in child benefits and unemployment insurance, with child benefits representing the most dramatic case of harmonization among the social programs surveyed here.

This complex pattern suggests two major conclusions. First, the persistence and indeed incremental accentuation of the traditional differences in many social programs is testimony to the enduring influence of domestic politics and cultures, even in a global economy, and to the ways in which the policy legacies from earlier generations structure the choices confronting policy makers in difficult times. The growing integration of economies, globally and continentally, still leaves important degrees of freedom for domestic choice.

Second, not all of the cases of convergence in Canadian and U.S. social programs flowed unambiguously from closer economic integration between the two countries. Convergence in the programs of two countries can develop for a variety of reasons:

- *Convergence as a result of parallel domestic factors.* Convergence in policy regimes can emerge because two countries face similar problems and experience similar domestic political responses to them.[11] For example, the fiscal weakness of government has triggered similar political struggles over fiscal policy in the Canadian and American capitals, with powerful implications for social programs. Indeed, the higher levels of public debt in Canada presumably generate proportionately greater pressure on the role of the Canadian state and represent a pressure for narrowing traditional differences in expenditure levels.

- *Convergence as a product of emulation.* The policies of two countries can converge when one country adopts the other's policies not because it is pressured to do so but because it is attracted to that country's experience. For example, during the early stages of the recent health-care debate in the United States, the strengths and weaknesses of the Canadian model were debated by health-care experts, the media, and members of Congress. Similarly, the results of evaluations of experimental training and employment programs for displaced workers in the United States are scrutinized intently by policy specialists north of the border.
- *Convergence as a result of international constraints.* As critics of economic integration have emphasized, policies can also converge because of constraints inherent in the political and economic relations between and among countries, which limit the capacity for autonomous action by individual states. These constraints can arise from international treaties or from the mobility of factors of production, especially capital, in an increasingly globalized economy.

Separating these different dynamics in specific cases is not easy, even in the short term. In the longer term, the task becomes even more difficult because the categories can become conflated when secondary consequences come into play. For example, if close economic links between two countries eventually lead to greater cultural convergence, harmonizing the preferences that citizens bring to their politics, then a subsequent narrowing of policy differences that appears on the surface to reflect emulation or parallel domestic pressures may, in reality, reflect a deeper process of integration. Nevertheless, the distinctions between different sources of convergence do help when examining the recent evolution of social policy in Canada and the United States.

An examination of the two strongest cases of convergence in social policy—child benefits and unemployment insurance—is revealing. First, in both cases the narrowing of the gap between the countries stemmed in part from American decisions to develop the Earned Income Tax Credit and to extend unemployment benefits—and not even the most optimistic Canadian would attribute these changes to pressures inherent in the relationship between the two countries. Second, changes on the Canadian side that contributed to convergence in these policy areas were not driven by bilateral economic integration alone.

Convergence in child benefits has predominantly been a reflection of parallel domestic trends. The remaking of this sector has been a slow process of incremental change rooted initially in a common ideological debate about the nature of poverty and the interaction between tax and transfer systems, a debate which first emerged during the 1960s and 1970s in the form of proposals for a negative income tax. From the beginning, reform efforts on both sides of the border were also fuelled by economic issues, especially concerns about the perverse incentives facing those dependent on traditional welfare programs; in more recent years, these concerns have been reinforced by the impact of globalization and international trade on the prospects for low-skilled and displaced workers in developed nations generally. Nevertheless, parallel ideological development rather than economic integration between Canada and the United States seems to be the predominant factor in the convergence in child benefits. It could be argued that this pattern reflects a broader cultural integration of the two countries that flows with a lag from closer economic links, but such an argument would have to contend with the interest in similar ideas in Britain and other nations during the same period (Banting 1979; Lenkowsky 1986).

Unemployment insurance is more contentious. As noted earlier, changes in the 1990s in both Canada and the United States have narrowed the differences between the two countries. Although there is still a major difference between the two systems, the trend in the 1990s is towards convergence. Concern for economic competition and trade relations between the two countries may have been part of the calculus in Canada, but it was certainly not all-pervasive. In the 1991 changes, for example, the special benefit for fishermen, which has been a source of trade friction with the United States, was retained; regional differentials, which some analysts have argued will be undermined by economic integration with the United States, grew larger rather than smaller; and changes in financing increased rather than decreased employer costs (Smardon 1991). Changes in Canada since then have been driven by fiscal constraints, by a shift in support for the unemployed from income benefits to retraining, and by a desire to reverse some of the major increases in employers' contributions that were imposed earlier in the decade.

It seems more plausible to interpret the changes on the Canadian side as the joint product of domestic conservatism and pressures implicit in the global economy. Most of the cuts have been driven by the priority given by both Conservative and Liberal governments to reduction of the federal deficit; and decisions to cut passive income benefits and transfer the savings to retraining initiatives are consistent with a broader approach to employment programs in a period of rapid economic restructuring. This agenda is undoubtedly reinforced by an assessment of Canada's position both in North America and the world. However, these pressures go well beyond the immediate economic relationship with the United States; they reflect the Canadian version of a debate about labour markets, income support, and training programs that pervades OECD nations more generally.

In general, then, the record of the 1980s and the early 1990s offers only limited support for the proposition that closer economic integration of Canada and the United States will necessitate social policy convergence. Program structures changed, often dramatically, in those years, and in some cases significant damage was done to the social accomplishments of the postwar generation. The level of social protection provided to the average citizen was less generous in both countries in the mid-1990s than in the mid-1970s. Nevertheless, change was not driving both societies more firmly towards a single model of the welfare state. The pattern in many sectors is incremental divergence, and it is arguable that the Canadian and American welfare states are as different in the mid-1990s as they were in the late 1970s. Moreover, where convergence has taken place, it is difficult to establish a simple link to economic integration between the two countries.

Future Prospects

Nations are changing communities. The configuration of economic, social, and political factors that generated different approaches to the welfare state in Canada and the United States during the postwar period and sustained those differences in the 1980s is constantly evolving. There can be no guarantee that the patterns of today will persist into the future. Moreover, predictions in this sector are particularly hazardous, since the various factors that generated distinctive policy regimes during the postwar years are evolving along different trajectories and at different speeds. For example, the continued strength of organized labour in Canada hints at the possibility of even greater divergence in the future. Elsewhere, however, the trajectory of change points to the possibility of convergence. The full effects of economic globalization and closer integration within North America have yet to be felt. As noted earlier, the greater severity of the fiscal crisis facing governments in Canada could reverse the pattern of the 1980s, producing more rapid erosion of benefit levels in Canada than in the United States. And the social policy consequences of the increasingly multiracial nature of Canada, which is narrowing what was once a marked difference between the two societies, may yet generate political dynamics similar to those south of the border.

On the political level, the victory of President Clinton in the 1992 presidential election and that of the Liberal Party in the 1993 federal election in Canada did little to change the trajectories established in the 1980s. In the United States, reforms of health care and welfare represented the centrepoints of the domestic agenda of the Clinton presidency, but the weakness of the Democratic victory in 1992 precluded major change. Clinton won only 43 percent of the popular vote, and the Democratic majorities in both houses of Congress remained weak. The expansion of the EITC in the first budget represented a marginal expansion in the redistributive role of government in the United States, but overall the direction of American social policy has not changed. Indeed, the subsequent shift in control of both houses of Congress to the Republican Party in the 1994 mid-term elections is likely to accentuate the trends established in the 1980s.

Similarly, the election of the Liberal government in Canada in 1993 did not change the overall direction of social policy established by the Conservatives. The priority accorded to deficit reduction is smothering any expansionist impulses that may still beat within the heart of the Liberal Party. The new government's first budget introduced significant reductions in Unemployment Insurance benefits; and the proposals for a broad restructuring of social programs introduced by the Minister of Human Resources Development in the fall of 1994 were largely swept aside by the 1995 budget, which sharply reduced federal transfers that support provincial programs in health, postsecondary education, and welfare, and which eased federal conditions on provincial social assistance programs (Banting 1995b).[12] The future will continue to be shaped by shifts in the partisan context of the federal government. The critical political pressures on the Liberals no longer come from the NDP, which was devastated in the election; instead, they come from two parties that are strongly opposed to an activist social role on the part of the federal government: the Bloc Québécois, the separatist party based in Quebec; and the Reform Party, which replaced the Conservatives on the right and is even more strongly opposed to social engineering on the part of the state. These political pressures, coupled with the depth of the fiscal crisis, are likely to continue to drive federal social policy towards restraint, more targeting of expenditures, and a greater emphasis on retraining rather than on simple income support.

Health care has represented the greatest contrast in the past, and in theory it presents the greatest scope for convergence in the future. However, the failure of the Clinton health plan and the 1994 victory of the Republicans in the congressional elections suggest that American initiatives are unlikely to narrow the widening gap between these two neighbours. If significant convergence is to occur, it is more likely to come from north of the border. In Canada, the fiscal pressures generated by rising health costs and large government deficits are putting serious pressure on the postwar model. The deinsurance of some minor medical procedures and the refusal of some provinces to cover additional health costs incurred when travelling outside of the country are already triggering an expansion of private health insurance, with "medigap-style" policies becoming more common for Canadians who can afford them (Tuohy 1994). The federal Liberal government seems determined to resist the growth of user fees, which is an issue in some provinces, particularly Alberta and British Columbia; however, how successful Ottawa can be as its own financial contribution to health care shrinks remains to be seen. The possibilities for some convergence with the American model are thus real. Yet they should not be overstated. The two health-care systems will remain profoundly different at their core. Whatever the incremental changes, health insurance in Canada will remain predominantly a public system; the death of health reform in the United States confirms that health care there will remain predominantly private.

In income security, the prospects for convergence seem more limited, partly because the contrast is already less marked. However, existing areas of convergence may well be accentuated. For example, differences between the two unemployment insurance systems may continue to narrow, although the tenacity of regional politics in Canada will undoubtedly prevent anything close to full harmonization. The reversal of the trend towards greater divergence in social assistance may also continue, although much depends on the outcome of the battles in Congress over welfare reform. In other income-security programs the prospects are for continued divergence, with Canada maintaining its trend towards a stronger targeting of transfers on low-income families and individuals. For example, the 1996 budget of the federal Liberal government pointed to the future with its announcement that the income-tested Seniors Benefit would be implemented in the year 2001. South of the border, the fate of the Bipartisan Commission on Entitlement and Tax Reform suggests that proposals to apply means tests to universal programs such as social security remain politically controversial. Formed to examine the fiscal pressures on entitlement programs, the commission could not agree on recommendations for action, and the modest proposals advanced personally by the senators who chaired the commission were widely criticized (U.S. Bipartisan Commission on Entitlement and Tax Reform 1994, 1995). The prospects for the late 1990s are thus for continued divergence between the two countries along these traditional lines.[13]

Overall, the record of the 1980s and early 1990s is helpful in warning against the assumption that convergence is necessarily a consequence of economic integration. Predictions of harmonization, whether in the context of the single European market or North American free trade, assume that future policy decisions will be shaped more by international economics than by domestic politics. Although international pressures on the state have clearly grown, narrowing the autonomy of national states in a palpable way, it is important to avoid determinist interpretations. Each nation must adjust to powerful pressures emanating from the global economy, but the global economy does not dictate the way in which each country responds. Policy is also shaped by domestic politics, and different countries respond to a changing world differently. As a result, the equilibrium point is unlikely to be harmonization on a standardized model.

During the postwar decades, Canada and the United States developed different versions of the liberal welfare state, reflecting important differences in the economic, social, and political structures of the two countries. During the last decade, they have been adjusting to a difficult global economy, and Canada has faced the added pressures emanating from the bilateral relationship between the two countries. The result has been a series of shifts in social programs that have altered the trajectory of development in the two welfare states. Many of these changes have done damage to the social protection that was painfully constructed in the postwar decades. But each country has adjusted to its economic context in its own way, subject to the rhythms of its domestic politics, and Canada and the United States continue to travel different paths in many parts of the welfare state. Despite a pervasive globalization of economic life, the nation-state retains important degrees of freedom in charting its course, and politics within the nation-state retains social importance.

Notes

1. Wilensky (1975) argued that defence spending undercut welfare expenditures in the United States during the 1950s and 1960s, but subsequent analyses have found less support for the proposition (Russett 1982; Domke, Eichenberg, and Kelleher 1983; Mintz 1989).
2. Canada's relationship with the international system has been central to virtually every interpretation of the scope of state activity in the country. For a useful summary of this literature, see Laux and Molot 1988, chs. 2 and 3.
3. For the flavour of the debate, see Crispo 1988; Drover 1988; Economic Council of Canada 1988a; Gold and Leyton-Brown 1988; Manga 1988; and Warnock 1988.
4. For a useful survey of this literature, see Shalev 1983. More recent developments in this literature emphasize the nature of coalitions among different classes at critical junctures in this history of the welfare state (Esping-Andersen 1990; P. Baldwin 1990; Gourevitch 1986).
5. The *Globe and Mail* reported that blacks made up 26 percent of families receiving services from the Metro Toronto Children's Aid in 1990 even though they represented only about 7 percent of the population; in Montreal, black children make up 23 percent of those receiving services from the anglophone child-welfare agency, despite making up only 4 percent of the city's anglophone population (*Globe and Mail*, 6 August 1991).
6. Unemployment insurance generates much more substantial interregional transfers in Canada than in the United States not only because of the size of the Canadian program but because of key features of its design. First, the Canadian system has an explicit system of regional differentials both in qualification requirements and in maximum benefit periods, creating a more generous program in regions with high unemployment. Second, the absence of experience rating in the formula determining contributions to the program generates a significant transfer from industries with comparatively stable patterns of employment to industries with highly seasonal employment, which are disproportionately located in the poorer regions. In the United States, state payroll taxes for unemployment insurance vary with the unemployment history of the industry.
7. For a survey of the contemporary patterns of health care in the United States, see the U.S. Bipartisan Commission on Comprehensive Health Care (the Pepper Commission) 1990. For a recent reformist analysis, see Marmor 1994. For a useful comparative survey of the Canadian and U.S. systems, see the U.S. General Accounting Office 1991.
8. An example of the American focus on waiting lists for surgical procedures and the technological gap can be found in a feature-length analysis of the Canadian system in the *New York Times*, 30 April 1991. For a more systematic analysis, see U.S. General Accounting Office 1991.
9. Under changes to unemployment insurance announced in 1995, low-income beneficiaries with children are entitled to special family supplements. In addition, individuals who collect unem-

ployment benefits for part of the year but still have an above-average income for the year as a whole face a "clawback" of their benefit through the tax system; this clawback can reach 100 percent (Canada, Human Resources Development 1995).

10. In determining assets, a number of items such as the individual's home and some personal effects are not included.

11. For example, Overbye 1994 argues that there has been a long-term convergence in pension outcomes among Western nations during the twentieth century, which has been driven by the spread of industrialization and democratic politics.

12. The initial federal proposals for social policy reform, which were released in the fall of 1994 and launched a cross-Canada consultative process, were set out in Canada, Human Resources Development 1994; for commentaries on the proposals, see Banting and Battle 1994.

13. For an alternative view of the significance of the Bipartisan Commission and the prospects for means-testing entitlements in the United States, see Myles 1995.

References

Aaron, H. 1996. "End of an Era: The New Debate over Health Care Financing." *Brookings Review* 13:35–7.

Banting, K.G. 1979. *Poverty, Politics and Policy: Britain in the 1960s.* London: Macmillan.

——. 1985. "Institutional Conservatism: Federalism and Pension Reform." In *Canadian Social Welfare Policy: Federal and Provincial Dimensions,* ed. J.S. Ismael. Montreal: McGill-Queen's University Press.

——. 1987a. *The Welfare State and Canadian Federalism.* 2d ed. Montreal: McGill-Queen's University Press.

——. 1987b. "The Welfare State and Inequality in the 1980s." *Canadian Review of Sociology and Anthropology* 24:309–38.

——. 1992. "Neoconservatism in an Open Economy: The Social Role of the Canadian State." *International Political Science Review* 13:149–70.

——. 1995a. "The Welfare State as Statecraft: Territorial Politics and Canadian Social Policy." In *European Social Policy: Between Fragmentation and Integration,* ed. S. Liebfried and P. Pierson. Washington, dc: The Brookings Institution.

——. 1995b. "The Social Security Review: Policy-Making in a Semi-Sovereign State." *Canadian Public Administration* 38:283–90.

Blackburn, M., and D. Bloom. 1993. "The Distribution of Family Income: Measuring and Explaining Changes in the 1980s for Canada and the United States." In *Small Differences that Matter: Labour Markets and Income Maintenance, in Canada and the United States,* ed. D. Card and R. Freeman. Chicago: University of Chicago Press.

Blank, R., and M. Hanratty. 1993. "Responding to Need: A Comparison of Social Safety Nets in the United States and Canada." In *Small Differences that Matter: Labour Markets and Income Maintenance in Canada and the United States,* ed. D. Card and R. Freeman. Chicago: University of Chicago Press.

Burtless, G. 1991. "The Tattered Safety Net." *Brookings Review* 9:38–41.

Cameron, D.R. 1978. "The Expansion of the Public Economy: A Comparative Analysis." *American Political Science Review* 72:1243–61.

——. 1986. "The Growth of Government Spending: The Canadian Experience in Comparative Perspective." In *State and Society: Canada in Comparative Perspective,* ed. K.G. Banting. Toronto: University of Toronto Press.

Canada, Department of Finance. 1996. *Budget Plan: Including Supplementary Information and Notices of Ways and Means Motion.* Ottawa: Department of Finance.

Carmines, E., and J. Stimson. 1989. *Issue Evolution: Race and the Transformation of American Politics.* Princeton, NJ: Princeton University Press.

Center on Budget and Policy Priorities and Center for the Study of the States. 1991. *The States and the Poor: How Budget Decisions in 1991 Affected Low Income People.* Washington, DC.

Coder, J., T. Smeeding, and B. Torrey. 1990. "The Change in the Economic Status of the Low-Income Elderly in Three Industrial Countries: Circa 1977–1986." Paper for the annual research conference of the Bureau of the Census, Washington, DC.

Coyte, P., et al. 1994. "Waiting Times for Knee-Replacement Surgery in the United States and Ontario." *New England Journal of Medicine* 331:1068–71.

Derthick, M. 1979. *Policymaking for Social Security.* Washington, DC: The Brookings Institution.

Edsall, T.B., with M. Edsall. 1991. *Chain Reaction: The Impact of Race, Rights and Taxes on American Politics.* New York: W.W. Norton.

Esping-Andersen, G. 1990. *The Three Worlds of Welfare Capitalism.* Princeton, NJ: Princeton University Press.

Evans, R. 1986. "Finding the Levers, Finding the Courage: Lessons from Cost Containment in North America." *Journal of Health Politics, Policy and Law* 11:585–615.

Evans., R., M. Barer, and C. Hertzman. 1991. "The 20-year Experiment: Accounting for Explaining and Evaluating Health Care Costs in Canada and the United States." *Annual Review of Public Health* 12:481–518.

Ferejohn, J. 1983. "Congress and Redistribution." In *Making Economic Policy in Congress*, ed. A. Schick. Washington, DC: American Enterprise Institute.

Gadd, J. 1995. "Ontario, Michigan Welfare Standards Show Bold Contrast." *Globe and Mail*, 4 November.

Gould, S., and J. Palmer. 1988. "Outcomes, Interpretations and Policy Implications." In *The Vulnerable*, ed. J. Palmer, T. Smeeding, and B. Torrey. Washington, DC: Urban Institute Press.

Gray, G. 1991. *Federalism and Health Policy: The Development of Health Care Systems in Canada and Australia.* Toronto: University of Toronto Press.

Haddow, R. 1991. "The Canadian Labour Congress and the Welfare State Debate." Paper presented to the Canadian Political Science Association meetings, Kingston.

Hanratty, M., and R. Blank. 1992. "Down and Out in North America: Recent Trends in Poverty Rates in the U.S. and Canada." *Quarterly Journal of Economics* 58:233–54.

Hansen, L., and J. Byers, eds. 1990. *Unemployment Insurance: The Second Half-Century.* Madison, Wis.: University of Wisconsin Press.

Harrington, M. 1984. *The New American Poverty.* New York: Holt, Rienhart, and Winston.

Heclo, H, 1986. "The Political Foundations of Antipoverty Policy." In *Fighting Poverty: What Works and What Doesn't*, ed. S. Danziger and D. Weinberg. Cambridge, MA: Harvard University Press.

Karoly, L.A. 1993. "The Trend in Inequality among Families: Individuals, and Workers in the United States: A Twenty-Five-Year Perspective." In *Uneven Tides: Rising Inequality in America*, ed. S. Danziger and P. Gottschalk. New York: Russell Sage Foundation.

Katzenstein, P, 1984. "The Small European States in the International Economy: Economic Dependence and Corporatist Politics." In *The Antimonies of Interdependence: National Welfare and the International Division of Labour*, ed. J. Ruggie. New York: Columbia University Press.

Keohane, R.O. 1984. "The World Political Economy and the Crisis of Embedded Liberalism." In *Order and Conflict in Contemporary Capitalism*, ed. J.H. Goldthorpe. Oxford: Oxford University Press.

Krasner, S. 1978. *Defending the National Interest: Raw Material Investments and U.S. Foreign Policy.* Princeton, NJ: Princeton University Press.

Lenkowsky, L. 1986. *Politics, Economics and Welfare Reform: The Failure of the Negative Income Tax in Britain and the United States.* Lanham, MD: University Press of America.

McRoberts, K. 1988. *Quebec: Social Change and Political Crisis.* Toronto. McClelland & Stewart.

Marmor, T.R., J.L. Mashaw, and P.L. Harvey. 1990. *America's Misunderstood Welfare State: Persistent Myths, Enduring Realities.* New York: Basic Books.

Morrisette, R., J. Myles, and G. Picot. 1995. "What Is Happening to Earnings Inequality in Canada?" In *Labour Market Polarization and Social Policy Reform*, ed. K.G. Banting and C. Beach. Kingston: School of Policy Studies, Queen's University.

Myles, J. 1991. "Social Structures and Welfare Policies: Perspectives for Canada and the United States." Working Paper 91–8. Ottawa: Department of Sociology and Anthropology, Carleton University.

Nathan, R.P., and F. Doolittle. 1987. *Reagan and the States.* Princeton, NJ: Princeton University Press.

National Council of Welfare 1995. *Welfare Incomes 1994*. Ottawa: Minister of Supply and Services Canada.

Organization for Economic Cooperation and Development 1994. *New Orientations for Social Policy*. OECD Social Policy Studies 2. Paris: OECD.

Orloff, A.S. 1988. "The Political Origins of America's Belated Welfare State." In *The Politics of Social Policy in the United States*, ed. M. Weir, A.S. Orloff, and T. Skocpol. Princeton, NJ: Princeton University Press.

——. 1991. "The American Social Policy Agenda: Constraints on Reform." In *Policy Choices: Political Agendas in Canada and the United States*, ed.

Osberg, L., S. Erksoy, and S. Phipps. 1994. "Labour Market Impacts of the Canadian and U.S. Unemployment Insurance Systems." Discussion Paper Series 94-12. Halifax, NS: Department of Economics, Dalhousie University.

Pal, L. 1988. *State, Class and Bureaucracy: Canadian Unemployment Insurance and Public Policy*. Montreal: McGill-Queen's University Press.

Perlin, G., ed. 1988. *Party Democracy in Canada: The Politics of National Party Conventions*. Toronto: Prentice-Hall.

Peterson, P.E., and M. Rom. 1990. *Welfare Magnets: A New Case for a National Standard*. Washington, DC: The Brookings Institution.

Pierson, P. 1995. "The Creeping Nationalization of Income Transfers in the United States, 1935-94." In *European Social Policy: Between Fragmentation and Integration*, ed. S. Leibfried and P. Pierson. Washington, DC: The Brookings Institution.

Quadagno, J. 1988. *The Transformation of Old Age Security: Class Politics in the American Welfare State*. Chicago: University of Chicago Press.

Ruggie, J. 1982. "International Regimes, Transactions and Change: Embedded Liberalism in the Postwar Order." *International Organization* 36:379-415.

——. 1994. "Trade Protectionism and the Future of Welfare Capitalism." *Journal of International Affairs* 48:1-11.

Sargent, T.C. 1995. *An Index of Unemployment Insurance Disincentives*. Working Paper no. 95-10. Ottawa: Department of Finance.

Simeon, R., and I. Robinson. 1990. *State, Society and the Development of Canadian Federalism*. Toronto: University of Toronto Press.

Skocpol, T. 1991. "Targeting within Universalism: Politically Viable Policies to Combat Poverty in the United States." In *The Urban Underclass*, ed. C. Jencks and P. Peterson. Washington, DC: The Brookings Institution.

Slessarev, H. 1988. "Racial Tensions and Institutional Support: Social Programs during a Period of Retrenchment." In *The Politics of Social Policy in the United States*, ed. M. Weir, A.S. Orloff, and T. Skocpol. Princeton, NJ: Princeton University Press.

Smardon, B. 1991. "The Federal Welfare State and the Politics of Retrenchment in Canada." *Journal of Canadian Studies* 26:123-41.

Smeeding, T.M. 1991. "Cross-National Perspectives on Trends in Child Poverty and the Effectiveness of Government Policies in Preventing Poverty among Families with Children in the 1980s: The First Evidence from lis." Unpublished manuscript.

Statistics Canada 1994a. *Canadian Economic Observer: Historical Statistical Supplement, 1993/94*. Ottawa: Minister of Supply and Services Canada.

——. 1994b. *Unemployment Insurance Statistics* 53, no. 7 (July). Ottawa: Minister of Supply and Services Canada.

Tuohy, C. 1988. "Medicine and the State in Canada: The Extra-Billing Issue in Perspective." *Canadian Journal of Political Science* 21:267-96.

——. 1989. "Federalism and Canadian Health Policy." In *Challenges to Federalism: Policy-Making in Canada and the Federal Republic of Germany*, ed. W. Chandler and C. Zöllner. Kingston: Institute of Intergovernmental Relations, Queen's University.

United States. Bipartisan Commission on Comprehensive Health Care (Pepper Commission). 1990. *A Call to Action: Final Report*. Washington, DC: Government Printing Office.

——. Bipartisan Commission on Entitlements and Tax Reform. 1994. *Interim Report to the President.* Washington, DC: Superintendent of Documents.

——. Bipartisan Commission on Entitlements and Tax Reform. 1995. *Final Report to the President.* Washington, DC: Superintendent of Documents.

——. Committee on Ways and Means. 1991. *Overview of Entitlement Programs: 1991 Green Book.* Washington, DC: Government Printing Office.

——. Committee on Ways and Means. 1993. *Overview of Entitlement Programs: 1993 Green Book.* Washington, DC: Government Printing Office.

——. Committee on Ways and Means. 1994. *Overview of Entitlement Programs: 1994 Green Book.* Washington, DC: Government Printing Office.

——. General Accounting Office. 1991. *Canadian Health Insurance: Lessons for the United States.* Washington, DC: U.S. General Accounting Office.

——. General Accounting Office. 1995a. *Medicaid: Spending Pressures Drive States Towards Program Prevention.* Washington, DC: Government Printing Office.

——. General Accounting Office. 1995b. *Supplementary Security Income: Growth and Changes in Recipient Population Call for Reexamining Program.* Washington, DC: Government Printing Office.

——. General Accounting Office. 1995c. *Earned Income Credit: Targeting to the Working Poor.* Washington, DC: Government Printing Office.

Wattenberg, M. 1990. "From a Partisan to a Candidate-Centered Electorate." In *The New American Political System*, 2d ed, ed. A. King. Washington, DC: American Enterprise Institute.

Weaver, R.K. 1990. "The State and Welfare State in the United States and Canada." Paper for Conference on the New Institutionalism, Boulder, CO.

Wilensky, H. 1975. *The Welfare State and Equality: Structural and Ideological Roots of Public Expenditures.* Berkeley: University of California Press.

17

Current Issues Surrounding Poverty and Welfare Programming in Canada

*Two Reviews**

GARSON HUNTER AND DIONNE MIAZDYCK

I. Race to the Bottom: Welfare to Work Programming in Saskatchewan and its Similarities to Programming in the United States and Britain

1. Introduction

In this article we argue that the modern welfare state in Canada is being redesigned to accommodate the needs of employers during a time of economic restructuring brought about by legislation such as the North American Free Trade Agreement (NAFTA). The research literature suggests that in refashioning welfare program delivery, states have moved from a needs-based eligibility, social entitlement and labour market exclusion programs to models that emphasize selective entitlements, active programming and maximum participation in wage labour (Theodore & Peck, 1999, p. 488). Active welfare programming suggests that national programs for welfare have been replaced by local experimentation in delivery. In the United States this model is viewed as the "work-first approach" to welfare programming (Peck, 2001; Theodore & Peck, 1999) and in England the model is viewed as "Third Way" policymaking (Holden, 1999; Jordan & Jordan, 2000; Callinicos, 2001).

The literature indicates that there are two types of workfare styled programs. The *Human-Capital Development* (HCD) approach involves high-cost training and educa-tion, with job entry that is usually above the minimum wage. The other approach is the *Labour-Force Attachment* (LFA) model that favours a "low-cost work-first, move-people-off-welfare-quickly" solution, with job entry that is usually at or near minimum wage (Peck, 2001). The approach adopted in Canada, and specifically Saskatchewan, is the model most closely aligned with the LFA.

---

* This material was first published as "Current Issues Surrounding Poverty and Welfare Programming in Canada: Two Reviews," Social Policy Research Unit, Faculty of Social Work, University of Regina, 2004.

Evidence suggests that the province of Saskatchewan has followed the United States in welfare programming, while blending United States workfare with ideology borrowed from the *Third Way* approach to produce its own hybrid welfare programming model. Our paper examines the local experimentation of welfare programming in the province of Saskatchewan, and makes comparisons between welfare programming for the vulnerable population of the poor in Saskatchewan to the welfare programming for the poor in the United States and England.

Social assistance programming (welfare) in Saskatchewan has experienced two major changes during the 1990s. One change has been to extend welfare benefits beyond those on welfare to include a growing low-income labour market, and the scaling back of the level of benefits for those in the workfare program.

The Canadian federal government and the provincial government of Saskatchewan argue that the welfare program in Canada needed to change due to the pressures of a global economy. Before we look at the specifics of the move towards workfare in Canada and Saskatchewan, we will explore the nature of the global economy and the validity of the governments' arguments.

2. Social democracy redefined for a global economy

Proponents of the Third Way ideology claim that it is a modern approach to social democracy capable of meeting the challenges of the twenty-first century. Within the current period of neo-liberal dominance wherein market interests are set as the major priority of nearly every government, social democracy is being redefined by Third Way ideologues to fit the trend. Third Way philosophy departs from the traditional social democratic ideals of equality of outcome and government intervention, opting instead to trust the market economy as a tool for constructing a just society. In defending the Third Way, two arguments are used: 1) that government intervention and redistribution were wrongheaded; and 2) that globalization forces us to minimize government spending, to accept a weaker labour position and to cut back social programs. Examples of Third Way leaders are Tony Blair in Britain, Bill Clinton in the United States, Gerhard Schroeder in Germany, Kim Dae-Jung in South Korea and Fernando Henrique Cardosa of Brazil (Callinicos, 2001, pp.1–2). The adoption of the term Third Way would appear to be an unfortunate choice however, as Third Way is a phrase that was employed by fascists during the twentieth century:

> Intellectual fascists were often to term themselves supporters of a "Third Way," neither left nor right, neither capitalist nor communist: they sought to achieve individual prosperity, but linked to communal goals. (Eatwell, 1995, p. 14)

It is not suggested here that the current representation of Third Way ideology is fascist, however it does represent a lack of historical, and critical, thinking on the part of the current Third Way advocates.

A Third Way approach to society is thought necessary by its advocates because of the failure of the adherents of the "Old Left" approach to acknowledge the importance of the market system in the new global economy (Callinicos, 2001). With the economic consequences of global integration, the autonomy of nation-states has been greatly reduced, therefore the economic statism of a particular form of the "Old Left" has been rendered obsolete. Economic statism is an approach that points in the wrong direction, for the economic game has changed.

The second reason that Third Way advocates offer for moving away from the "Old Left" is that globalization is inevitable. Opinions on the consequences of globalization are varied but the common thread in Third Way literature is that social democracy must accommodate this "new reality." The ability of national governments to enact policies are curtailed by globalization (Graham & Al-Krenawi, 2001, p. 417). Commenting on social policy changes in Canada, they write: "As companies compete in an increasingly international marketplace, the demands upon national governments to restrict welfare may grow" (p. 417).

Economic globalization is not a new reality, despite the claims of its advocates. During the formation of modern industrial society in the 1800s, there were few "barriers" to trade such as minimum wages, high taxes, labour standards, production regulations, and trade laws. However, after World War I many countries moved in the direction of protectionist trade policies to secure their own economy (Government of Canada, 2002). The failure of the gold standard as a system of currency regulation caused instability in currency exchange rates. Regulation over trade laws became a more global concern after World War II when they were linked to the rise of instability in Europe (Howse & Mutua, 2000). The International Trade Organization was set up in accordance with the Bretton Woods agreements to help regulate labour and business practices (Howse & Mutua, 2000). At the same time, increased regulation over domestic financial markets allowed governments to control their own economies (McQuaig, 1998). Throughout WWII people watched as state sponsored, wartime programs backed by government spending ignited failing economies (Lightman & Riches, 2001). There was some measure of confidence in government intervention, and Keynesian ideas provided the intellectual rationing that allowed for social program spending (Piven & Cloward, 1997).

The move back to capitalizing on global trade came from the spotlight on the successful export-based economies in East Asia (Midgley, 2000). At the same time, the removal of currency controls with the subsequent rise in capital speculation and the rapid growth of technology have been important influences on the growth of economic globalization (Midgley, 2000). The energy crisis of the 1970s was also an important historical factor. The quadrupling of oil prices and the inability of the U.S. to control the market led to uncertainty and the search for new answers (Clarke, 1997).

For an export driven economy such as Canada, trade is of crucial importance, and in the 1980s the focus of business was to maximize Canada's potential as a trading partner. McQuaig (2001) argues that the impetus for a free trade agreement came from U.S. corporate leaders who were set on ending government protectionism of the service industry and reducing responsibility to meet "performance requirements" (p.55). With very few protectionist measures in place in Canada in the first place, it was obvious that there was more at stake for business to push the NAFTA than simply reducing tariffs. Merrett (1996) argues that the desire "to restructure the Canadian economy along neoconservative lines," that is, to limit the power of labour and reduce the welfare state, was the real reason for originally pushing free trade with the U.S. (p.15).

The NAFTA, signed on to by the participating governments of Canada, Mexico, and the U.S., allows businesses to ask their respective government to seek formal resolutions against other governments if local policies or trade decisions are undesirable to those businesses. "The treaties contain clauses used as levers to extend the agenda of finance capital against state intervention, including measures to decrease of erase welfare statism" (Collier, 1997, p. 89). The process of altering domestic economic and social policies and programs to meet the standards of the business interests creates a harmonization of policy within the trade agreement partners (Swenarchuk, 2001). Harmonization of policy through the inclusion of services and the loss of labour power have been the most obvious affects of the NAFTA.

With the signing of NAFTA, Canada has come under increased pressure to harmonize its social policies with the lower standards of the U.S. and Mexico (Pulkingham & Ternowetsky, 1996). The move away from adequate federal cost-sharing with the provinces for health care, post-secondary education, and welfare has left these programs financed mostly by the individual provinces without enforceable national standards, and has consequently opened the door to privatization and workfare programs. Rather than globalization, economic pressure in Canada has by and large been the product of NAFTA. Peck (2001) comments:

> For all the talk of globalization in Canada, much of the competition the country faces is originating from just south of the border. And just as the North American Free Trade Agreement (NAFTA) has accelerated and deepened the process of economic continentalization, so also it seems that pressures are mounting for a "downward convergence" in social policy. (p.215)

Neo-liberal concerns such as budget deficits and federal funding cuts to social programs, have conveniently provided an avenue for the dismantling of social programs. The inclusion of services as an item to be competitively traded in the NAFTA threatens the existence of programs even if the government chooses to protect them (McQuaig, 2001). Services that are presently non-profit, protected or subsidized by the government can be deemed a trade barrier and challenged under the Chapter 11 clause of NAFTA.

Labour force adjustment is argued as a necessary step to reap the economic benefits of free trade (Stranks, 2001). Free trade challenges union protection of workers against practices such as wage reductions and casualization when they can easily move out of the country (Glenday, 1997). Piven and Cloward (1997) explain that the loss of labour influence stems from the increased ability of capital to exit, changing the balance of power between them. The effect of NAFTA on jobs has been most evident in the manufacturing sector as companies were given the opportunity to relocate to low-wage areas. Manufacturing job losses intensified the recession of the early 1990s, linking the recession directly to free trade (Broad, 1995). Canada has been more affected than the U.S., losing four times more manufacturing jobs (Burman, 1997). Under free trade, protection for workers is limited. The decline of labour organization and labour parties as an influential force is noted as a crucial element to the undermining of the social compact. Industrialization allowed for the growth of class-based labour parties. In the post-industrial economies, the erosion of class-consciousness has limited the electoral power backing social democratic parties.

While the acknowledgment is made that there are fewer jobs available and that wages are stagnant, the solution is to become more competitive. Although high unemployment is seen as structural, the answer is to make the labour force more flexible. The Third Way advocates have accepted the neo-liberal argument that workers need to be prepared for a more competitive market and lower expectations. Workfare schemes increase the desperation of the most marginalized with the promise that economic success is found in competition rather than state intervention (George & Wilding, 1985).

Third Way proponents don't attempt to challenge globalization or strengthen the welfare state in response to it. Callinicos (2001) quotes Clinton and Blair ambivalently touting globalization adages and suggesting that they no longer have the power to change anything. When economic globalization is mentioned in a negative way, there is a sense of powerlessness in Third Way writing. At other times, Third Way advocates argue expressly for the benefits of globalization. With a certain degree of enthusiasm, Third Way leaders have accepted the theories of neo-liberal monetarism and incorporated it into their platforms. Callinicos (2001) points out that the new reality that governments are contending with is not an ethereal new era known as globalization, but the triumph of global capitalism.

However, it is within a context of globalization rather than trade agreements that Third Way ideology has been adapted to Canada. In reinventing themselves, social democratic political parties have felt it crucial to distinguish themselves from the "Old Left" that is tied to trade protectionism (Callinicos, 2001). Canadian politician Chris Axworthy (1999) uses Third Way rhetoric in Canada to argue for workfare, suggesting that the Left was wrong to offer programs based on entitlement alone and, given the new global reality, programs will need to keep pace. The new agenda of the Third Way is to increase labour participation through work participation programs and training and/or supports for workforce participation.

The constraining power of globalization, while obvious, is still a product of government choices that have been made over a relatively short period of time. In their critique of the surrender to globalization, Piven and Cloward (1997) look back historically at similar attempts by capital to limit the power of labour. "Capital has often mobilized politically to change government laws and policies in order to enlarge employer exit options or narrow worker exit options" (p.7). Callinicos (2001) agrees giving historical examples of the pressure labour governments experienced in past attempts to create a universal welfare state:

> The tale of reformist governments defeated by economic constraints notably through the flight of capital on the financial markets is almost as old as social democracy itself...This record at least puts into question the idea that globalization has introduced radically new economic constraints on government action. (Callinicos, 2001, p.27)

The movement towards workfare is not necessitated by a mystical force identified as a global economy, "but from neoliberal politics, from political ideas and political strategies conceived by political actors" (Piven & Cloward, 2001, p. xi). Thus, the shape that globalization has taken has not been benign, but has been an imposition of neo-liberal policies such as deregulation, trade liberalization and privatization by those who have economic power (Callinicos, 2001, p. 7).

3. The expansion of eligible recipients

Just as NAFTA has accelerated and deepened the process of economic continentaliza-
tion, so also it seems that pressures are mounting for a downward convergence in social
policy. During the 1990s, changes to the welfare system in Canada have been similar to
the changes to the welfare system in the United States. The similarities in welfare reform in
the two countries may be more than just coincidence. What we may in fact be experiencing is a closer harmonization between Canadian and American welfare policy.

In 1996, the United States replaced its federal Aid to Families with Dependent Children
(AFDC) welfare program with the *Personal Responsibility and Work Reconciliation Act*
(PRWORA) welfare program. The PRWORA decentralized the controlling influence of
the federal government, with the states now being allowed to develop individual welfare
delivery experiments. Funding under the new Act was provided to the individual states
as block grants. The Act included significant cuts to existing programs and fundamentally
changed the welfare system with the introduction of the Temporary Assistance to Needy
Families (TANF) program (Karger & Stoesz, 1998, pp. 273–74). Under TANF, there is no
entitlement to assistance and the states are free to determine which families receive help.

Canada has followed a similar path. Under the cost-shared Canada Assistance Plan
(CAP), people were entitled to welfare when in need. Provincial welfare officials often
violated that condition of CAP, but nonetheless it was designed as an entitlement program
similar to AFDC in the United States. Also importantly, although provinces experimented
with workfare programs, a condition on the provinces under CAP was that recipients
did not have to participate in training or workfare programs to be entitled to assistance.
In 1996, Canada replaced CAP with the Canada Health and Social Transfer (C.H.S.T.)
program. Gone under the new C.H.S.T. were the national welfare program standards of
need-based eligibility and the voluntary nature of training and participation in workfare
programs. The C.H.S.T. is a block-funded program from the federal government to the
provincial governments. Provinces are allowed to experiment with their own welfare delivery.

Canada's movement towards workfare has more closely followed the example of the
United States than the model in Britain. Jones and Novak (1999) write that unlike Britain,
the United States never established a national universal system of means-tested welfare
(p. 189). They suggest that the individual states opposed the implementation of a national program as an infringement upon state rights, and that under the federal AFDC,
individual states still retained considerable leeway in the delivery of welfare programs
(p. 190). Canada's path has been somewhat similar to the United States in its structuring
of a national welfare program.

Under the *British North America Act* (BNA) (1867), individual provinces in Canada
were given responsibility for what we know today as social services. The *Canadian
Constitution Act* (1982), which replaced the BNA, did not change the constitutional responsibility for welfare. The federal government of Canada did participate in a national
welfare program under CAP, however individual provinces were and are responsible for
welfare. The C.H.S.T. program has promoted the devolution of welfare programming back
to the provinces.

Local experimentation of welfare programming does advantage the national governments in the United States and Canada. The advantage of decentralizing welfare standards

is that reforms at the state or provincial level can allow the advancement of a national reform agenda. Provincial experiments in individual welfare delivery have the advantage of appearing to be local initiatives to local labour situations without restriction from the federal government:

> It would be quite wrong, then, to dismiss local work-welfare experiments as merely local experiments. Self-evidently, they have material effects on "local people," but more broadly, they open up the political and institutional space for extralocal change. Still sensitive about U.S. imports, especially in highly charged fields like social policy, Canadian governments have set about the task of growing their own welfare-to-work programs. (Peck, 2001, p. 232)

For the federal government in Canada, extralocal change is facilitated by the joint federal/provincial Canada Child Tax Benefit (C.C.T.B.) program. Within the structure of the C.C.T.B., the provinces can carry out their own localized workfare experiments under the umbrella of wage subsidy programs for low-income working families. The federal C.H.S.T. program stipulates that provincial savings in welfare expenditures due to increased federal spending are to go towards low-wage subsidy programs for working families with children.[1] Resultantly, local welfare experimentation allows the introduction of wide sweeping welfare changes on a national scale. "This is certainly one of the reasons why local "models" and policy ideas have been so effective in framing, channeling, and levering wider regulatory reform, even if in a conveniently circular fashion they are merely confirming and concretizing the predispositions of national policymakers" (Peck, 2001, p. 232). In Britain and the United States, there have been parallels in the federally orchestrated decentralization and localized experimentation of welfare programming. While accounting for differences between the two countries, Theodore and Peck (1999) identify the commonalities of eliminating federal entitlements, block funding, and work-participation requirements (p. 489). In Canada, the first two have been implemented by the federal government's C.H.S.T. and the cancellation of CAP, and the latter by the provinces and their localized welfare delivery. With the cancellation of CAP, the provincial governments have been allowed to localize their welfare delivery policies and introduce workfare.[2]

In the following section we look at the province of Saskatchewan as a case study of the federal and provincial introduction of workfare. The federal introduction of workfare is examined through the C.C.T.B. program agreement between the federal government and Saskatchewan; the provincial introduction of workfare is examined through the Transitional Employment Allowance (TEA) program in Saskatchewan.

4. Canada Child Tax Benefit

During the summer of 1998, Saskatchewan introduced its version of welfare reform under the program *Building Independence—Investing in Families* initiative (Brochures, Saskatchewan Social Services). This policy initiative included six programs, with three programs designed to address the problem of child poverty in poor working families. The first program was the Saskatchewan Employment Supplement (S.E.S.) which is a monthly payment to supplement income earned by lower income parents; the second program was the Saskatchewan Child Benefit (S.C.B.) a monthly allowance provided for all children of lower income families; the third was the Family Health Benefits (F.H.B.) program which provides limited supplementary health benefits to lower income working families including some dental and drug expense relief. We will first look at the S.C.B. program, and then the S.E.S. program.

The S.C.B. program change to social assistance delivery in Saskatchewan was designed to coincide with changes to the federal government's funding of the existing Child Tax Benefit (C.T.B.) program, and during 1998 social assistance (welfare) reform in Saskatchewan took a limited but nonetheless important policy direction in affixing provincial welfare benefits for children to the Federal Canada Child Tax Benefit (C.C.T.B.) program.

The major piece of legislation enabling the social income transfer program in Canada designed specifically to eliminate child poverty is the Canada Child Tax Benefit (C.C.T.B.). The predecessor to the C.C.T.B. (1997) was the New Integrated Child Tax Benefit (C.T.B., 1993). The social income programs that existed for families with children before the C.T.B. were the universal Family Allowance program and income tax-based measurers including the refundable child tax credit, the non-refundable child tax credit, the equivalent to married credit and the child care expense reduction. Under the Integrated C.T.B. there were three components: the C.T.B.; the equivalent to married credit; and the child care deduction. The previous non-refundable and refundable tax credits and the Family Allowance program were aggregated into the income-tested C.T.B.

In 1997, the C.T.B. program was replaced with the Canada Child Tax Benefit (C.C.T.B.) legislation. Both programs are somewhat similar in their underlying values. The major difference between the two is that the C.C.T.B. program includes all the provinces and territories. The provinces and territories were not part of the federal-only C.T.B. program.

The C.C.T.B. program is divided into two benefits. One is the Basic Benefit provided to families with children, contingent upon the family's level of income. There are maximum levels of family income whereby this benefit is fully phased out. The other benefit is provided under the cost-shared National Child Benefit program (N.C.B.)—a program the federal government shares with the provinces and territories. The federal contribution to the N.C.B. is the National Child Benefit Supplement (N.C.B.S.), which is similar to the previous Working Income Supplement (W.I.S.) program.

The W.I.S. program, which replaced the universal Family Allowance program, was a **per family** benefit provided to low-income working families with children, whereas the subsequent N.C.B.S. is a **per child** benefit provided to low-income working families with children. The N.C.B.S. has been integrated into the basic allowance component of provincial social assistance programs in the provinces and territories (Kitchen, 2001, p. 241). The N.C.B.S. contribution removes children from the basic allowance component of the provincial welfare rolls, with the payments now coming from the federal government's N.C.B.S. contribution to the N.C.B. The provinces, territories, and First Nations contributions to the N.C.B. are to provide programs that support low-income working families with children, whether or not the families receive welfare. Programs that the provinces can provide to low-income families with children could include pharmacare or dental care, child care services, child credit for low-income families (British Columbia, Quebec), an earned income credit (Alberta), a combination of programs (Saskatchewan [S.E.S.;

S.C.B.; F.H.B.] & New Brunswick), and early prevention programs for children at risk. The provincial and territorial contributions to the N.C.B. go under various names in the different provincial/territorial, and First Nations jurisdictions.[3] By agreement with Canada Customs and Revenue Agency, the Saskatchewan provincial basic allowance benefit for children whose families are on welfare is fully integrated as a single payment within the C.C.T.B.

Although the C.C.T.B. is touted as a program to deal with child poverty, it is in actuality an income tested wage subsidization program for low-income working families with children. Although not obvious at first, the C.C.T.B. program's relation to workfare programming is found within its relationship with the provinces. The introduction of this federal income program has tied the amount of assistance the program pays to the labour force status of the family. For families on welfare, the only means of receiving the increased spending of the federal government is to have some form of labour force attachment. For others on welfare without children, there is no increased funding. The federal C.C.T.B. program advances the idea of targeting benefits to those in the labour force, and encourages the provinces to target their savings in welfare expenditures towards benefits for low-income families in the labour force.

Changing the social assistance children's basic allowance payment to a fully integrated single payment within the C.C.T.B. delivered through Canada Customs and Revenue Agency represents significant savings for the province of Saskatchewan. The provincial contribution to the welfare budgets for children has been reduced by the amount of the increase in the federal contribution to the N.C.B. program.

The provincial savings from reduced welfare expenditures under the C.C.T.B. are quite substantial. For example:

> Saskatchewan reinvested a total of approximately $13 million in N.C.B. initiatives in the nine-month period from July 1, 1998 to March 31, 1999. This reinvestment represents $17.2 million on a full fiscal year basis. As a result of further federal investments in the National Child Benefit supplement, reinvestment funds for 1999–2000 and 2000–01 are expected to increase to $21.2 million and $26.6 million respectively. (Government of Canada, 2000, Appendix 2, p. 9)

The federal government estimated that for the fiscal year 1999–2000, Saskatchewan's N.C.B. Initiatives Reinvestment Funds would allot $16.27 million to the Saskatchewan Child Benefit (S.C.B.) (a monthly allowance provided for all children of lower-income families), $2.64 to the Saskatchewan Employment Supplement (S.E.S.) (a monthly income supplement available to lower-income families) and $2.3 million to the supplementary Family Health Benefits program (F.H.B.) which provides limited supplementary health benefits to lower-income working families (Government of Canada, 2000, Appendix 2, p. 10). In Saskatchewan most of the reinvestment of funds from savings due to an increase in federal spending under the C.C.T.B. have gone into the supplement of low-income wages through programs such as the S.C.B. and the S.E.S. programs which provide an income supplement to lower-income families with children. Much of the funds "invested" by Saskatchewan would have been paid out anyway under the old welfare program. As mentioned, the sources of these reinvestment funds are from provincial "social assistance adjustments." Social assistance adjustments are the savings the provinces incur by not passing on the increases in federal spending for children to families on welfare who have no labour force income.

In fact provincial savings on welfare expenditures, due to increased federal contributions through the C.C.T.B., do not need to go to increased spending on families with children on welfare who have no other source of income, presumably the poorest children in Canada. Rather under the C.H.S.T. the money can be used to fund social income programs for the working poor, as has happened in several provinces. Using the funds saved by not passing on the increase in federal expenditures to the poorest families on welfare with no source of income, and using those funds to support families with low-incomes, is entirely in keeping with the intent of the C.C.T.B. program. According to the C.C.T.B. agreement, provincial savings from decreased welfare expenditures are to go to programs designed to assist low-income families with children. An Enriched Canada Child Tax Benefit will "[p]ave the way for provinces and territories to redirect their resources towards improved child services and income support for low-income working families" (Government of Canada, *Budget 1997 Fact Sheets*, p. 2) and, further, will "... promote attachment to the workforce—resulting in fewer families having to rely on social assistance—by ensuring that families will always be better off as a result of finding work" (Government of Canada, *Finance Canada, Budget 1997*, p. 1). The savings incurred by the provinces under the C.C.T.B. are to be directed toward children's services and income support programs for low-income families with children.

Saskatchewan has also made considerable expenditures under the C.H.S.T. under what is referred to as "investment funds." Investment funds are additional expenditures by the provinces within the N.C.B. program. Saskatchewan's initial investments in the N.C.B. program were $19,790,000 for the S.C.B. program, $2,600,000 for the S.E.S. program and $2,030,000 for the F.H.B. program. These additional investments allowed Saskatchewan to completely remove all children's basic allowance from the social assistance program and fully implement the three programs for all low-income working families. The provinces refer to this process as "main streaming," that is, extending programs beyond just those people on welfare.

It should be noted, however, that the increase in federal and provincial spending is not new money. The federal government would have been making these expenditures under the cost-sharing agreement with the provinces under the preceding CAP, which was replaced in 1996 by the block-funded C.H.S.T. program. The federal government would have also made further expenditures through the previous Family Allowance program and its successor, the federal C.T.B. program (Pulkingham & Ternowetsky, 1997, p. 205). The provinces would have made these expenditures under the preceding CAP program and also under the new C.H.S.T. program. As an example, in 1998–999, before the S.C.B. and S.E.S. initiatives, Saskatchewan spent $327,504,000 on income support programs. In 1999–000, after the initiatives, the province spent $348,379,897 on income support programs (Government of Saskatchewan, Saskatchewan Social Services; Annual Reports). Eventually as the C.C.T.B. program "matures" the S.C.B. program should be eliminated due to increasing federal contributions to the N.C.B. program.

As mentioned, the National Child Benefit (N.C.B.) portion of the two-part C.C.T.B. is a social income program shared between the federal government and the provinces, territories and First Nations to assist working poor families with children. Due to the focus of the N.C.B. policy initiative on the work place attachment of the recipient, there is a fundamental flaw with the N.C.B. portion of the C.C.T.B. program. If the program were designed to reduce child poverty, then benefits would increase according to the financial need of families with children (Pulkingham & Ternowetsky, 1997, pp. 206–27). There is no extra money for families whose only source of income is social assistance.

The C.C.T.B. program with the participation of the government of Saskatchewan has linked the level of benefits for children to the labour force attachment of their parents. Those who are employed receive more benefits for their children through government run social programs than those who do not have paid employment. The C.C.T.B. program does not address the employability status of a family on welfare (whether they are actually employable or whether employment exists for them), nor does it account for the unpaid labour necessary to raise a child. All families are considered able to find employment; that is, all families are considered as having an equal chance or right to paid employment, and the level of benefits received is tied to the paid labour status of the family. In effect, this results in a horizontal distribution of resources from the poor families on welfare who have no other source of income and do not benefit from the provincial savings in welfare payments, to the distribution of those provincial savings in the form of small monthly income supplements to working poor families from the S.E.S. program. Under the C.C.T.B. program rights are derived from the marketplace and the family. A family receives benefits for their children dependent upon their attachment to the labour force, and children receive a level of benefit that is calculated in reference to their family's attachment to the market.

Families with children who are low-income earners but not receiving provincial welfare can access a benefit from the S.E.S. program by contacting the Saskatchewan provincial office of the S.E.S. program and making an application to the program over the phone. Examples of the monthly rates for the S.E.S. program in Saskatchewan for the year 2000 are given in Table 17.1 below. If the child is under 13 years of age, the rates are reduced as shown in Table 17.2.

Table 17.1. Saskatchewan Employment Supplement Monthly Rates

Eligible Monthly Gross Income	1 Child	2 Children	3 Children	4 Children	5 Children or more
$250	$31.00	$38.00	$48.00	$50.00	$56.00
$500	$94.00	$113.00	$131.00	$150.00	$169.00
$750	$156.00	$188.00	$219.00	$250.00	$281.00
$1000	$185.00	$222.00	$259.00	$296.00	$333.00
$1250	$157.00	$194.00	$231.00	$268.00	$305.00
$1500	$104.00	$141.00	$178.00	$215.00	$252.00
$1750	$52.00	$89.00	$126.00	$163.00	$200.00
$2000	$36.00	$73.00	$110.00	$147.00	—

Table 17.2. Saskatchewan Employment Supplement Monthly Rates, Supplementary Benefit for Children Under 13

Eligible Monthly Gross Income	1 Child	2 Children	3 Children	4 Children	5 Children or more
$250	$7.00	$9.00	$11.00	$13.00	$14.00
$500	$23.00	$28.00	$33.00	$38.00	$42.00
$750	$39.00	$47.00	$55.00	$63.00	$70.00
$1000	$46.00	$56.00	$65.00	$74.00	$83.00
$1250	$39.00	$48.00	$58.00	$67.00	$76.00
$1500	$26.00	$35.00	$45.00	$54.00	$63.00
$1750	$13.00	$22.00	$31.00	$41.00	$50.00
$2000	$9.00	$18.00	$28.00	$37.00	-

Source: Government of Saskatchewan, Brochure, For Low-Income Working Families, Employment Supplement.

Program checks and audits for the S.E.S. program are made through the income tax system. Beneficiaries of the S.E.S. program report changes in income as they occur, or on a quarterly basis.

The S.E.S. program is designed to primarily assist the working poor, but families with children on welfare can also access the program. Money from work, self-employment, farming and child/spousal maintenance are considered as income for the program. To receive the S.E.S. benefit, gross family income must be at least $175/month. The level of benefit is calculated as a percentage of earnings, with the maximum amount dependent upon the number of children in a family. The maximum benefit level is $315/month with a gross family income of $1,000/month and five children in the family. The federal Indian Affairs Department and First Nations leadership agreed to the creation of a parallel benefit for on-reserve Status Indians. The income supplements of the program are rather modest, and families on social assistance with no other source of income receive no benefit from the S.E.S. program. For a detailed examination of the S.E.S. program and its effect on welfare budgets in Saskatchewan see Hunter (1998).

5. Cutbacks in benefits

The other major change to welfare in Saskatchewan, the localized welfare delivery experiment, has been the introduction of the Transitional Employment Allowance (TEA) Regulations in 2003. While the earlier Saskatchewan Assistance Regulations stipulated that the program was established to provide assistance to "persons in need," the TEA Regulations stipulate that the program was established to provide an allowance to "persons in need who are participating in certain pre-employment programs" or those who would soon not require welfare. It is interesting to note that while changes to Acts must be debated in legislative assemblies and therefore in public, changes in Regulations are done by government Cabinets and do not require introduction into the legislative assemblies for public debate. The TEA program is not considered to be welfare by the government of Saskatchewan. Rather, the program is envisioned as providing people the supports they need to get back to work and become "self-sufficient."

The TEA program is designed as a Labour Force Attachment (LFA) program, with a work-first approach to workfare. With the LFA approach to workfare, any type of employment is considered by the government to be better than welfare. The already meager benefits of the welfare system are reduced for recipients of the TEA program, presumably in an effort to recover some of the costs of the program and make welfare appear less an alternative than any form of employment. Increasingly, the LFA approach to welfare has been the model favoured by provincial governments in Canada (Peck, 2001, pp. 234–35). The LFA approach to workfare is the model most conducive to the interests of the business community, as this approach "fuels working poverty by swelling contingent labor supply and depressing wages; high social externalities; residualizes hardest-to-serve clients" (Peck, 2001, p. 78). It is telling that the social democratic government of Saskatchewan has not adopted the HRD model most identified with social democratic welfare states, but rather has adopted the LFA model most identified with a corporatist welfare state that focuses on a market based workfare formula.

(For a breakdown of the difference in benefits and a comparison of the Regulations between the welfare and TEA programs in Saskatchewan, please refer to Appendix.)

The province does not address the issue of forcing people into a "low wage trap," but problems with workfare policy are an area of concern. Peck (2001) writes:

> While a labor-force-attachment model may gain support due to its lower cost structure, the narrow basis on which such costs are calculated suggests that this path too, is likely to be problematic. "Savings" on welfare costs, calculated on the basis of simply moving people off welfare, do not take account of externalities associated with working poverty or—yet worse—with complete loss of income (where claimants are simply sanctioned off welfare due to some administrative misdemeanor without a job to enter). Welfare "savings" may consequently become simply displaced as "new" costs in the form of increased homelessness, ill health, criminality, or foster care. (pp. 234–35)

Although these may be the consequences of workfare programs, a concern with the well being of the poor is not the focus of government assistance. The program is designed to pressure and maintain a low-wage labour force, and discipline the remainder of the labour force who face tenuous employment situations. "Whether or not conditions in the lower reaches of the labor market really matter all that much for individual enterprises, the presence of no-nonsense, work-orientated welfare system will nevertheless register as emblematic of wider attitudes to labor-market management" (Peck, 2001, p. 72). The amounts of assistance provided by the federal government to deal with low-income working families with the C.C.T.B. program, is criticized by the government funded National Council of Welfare as "token efforts" that "help only a minuscule number of families who are in dire straits" (1999).

6. Third way ideology and social assistance

Third Way literature is laden with talk about the negative effects of government intervention creating dependency upon recipients of welfare, and how state redistribution favoured rights over responsibilities. Third Way scholar, Anthony Giddens, denounces the idea of equality of outcome, advocating instead for equality of opportunity (Callinicos, 2001). Redistribution is deemed passive and hedonistic by Third Way proponent David

Marquand (Lund, 1999). Social democratic models of the "Old Left" did not demand "responsibility" from recipients of welfare. The Third Way approach represents the efforts of center-Left and social democrats of combining the best of the Right and the best of the Left as a new political actor.

Third Way finds its proponents not only on a global or national level, but also on a sub-national level as well. The province of Saskatchewan has also turned to Third Way ideology in the area of welfare delivery. Saskatchewan is often considered an oasis of social democracy in a sea of centrist and right wing government. A social democratic government of Saskatchewan introduced the first hospitalization insurance program in Canada in 1946, and the first medical care insurance program in Canada in 1961. During the 1990s and into the twenty-first century, Saskatchewan continued to elect the social democratic New Democratic Party (NDP) political party to government, albeit a minority NDP government during the 1999 election. The precarious electoral appeal of its social democratic government, and the deteriorated positions of social democratic parties in Europe have not been lost on the NDP. However, Tony Blair's Labour Party experienced electoral success in England during 1997, in part due to its Third Way approach to social policy. The NDP in Saskatchewan has looked to capitalize on the electoral success of other social democratic governments by articulating their social policy adjustments using Third Way justifications.

The clearest indication of the adoption of Third Way justifications for changes to welfare programming in Saskatchewan can be found in an article by Chris Axworthy, who at the time was a Saskatchewan Member of Parliament for the federal NDP and later became Saskatchewan's Minister of Justice under the provincial NDP government. Axworthy is representative of the Third Way approach to welfare in Canada. Axworthy titled his article "A Modern Socialist Approach: R and R for Social Policy" (Axworthy, 1999, Chapter 19). Using the obviously intentional pun of "R & R" to explain welfare programming in Saskatchewan, implying that those on welfare are on some sort of break or holiday and that social policy was on some sort of socialist hiatus, Axworthy lays out, as he sees it, the Rights and Responsibilities (the R and R) of those who receive welfare.

Axworthy envisions the Third Way approach to social policy as a modern approach to modern socialist social policy, a social policy that views as a right, assistance to those who have lost their employment, but places a responsibility on those recipients "to improve their chances of fending for themselves" (Axworthy, 1999, p. 278). Social policy is viewed within a communitarian understanding, where rights extend from being a member of an interdependent community and the responsibilities members have back to that community. The interdependence of community and members is summed up by Axworthy (1999) with the exhortation: "We are, after all, all in this together" (p. 278); the "we" consisting of governments, corporations, the economy, the community and the economy.

Third Way social policy is viewed as a break from the mistakes of the old socialism. Socialist social policy during the modern welfare state was based mostly upon the concept of entitlement, with little to say about responsibility, which Axworthy (1999) derides, observing:

> Not much has flowed from this approach other than entitlement to receive a cheque—no responsibility to prepare for old age, look for work, seek the

skills needed for the workplace, relocate to a job, provide for our children, etc. Worse yet, there has been no empowerment. In fact, in many cases the opposite has been the result—dependencies have been created. (p. 279)

The creation of dependencies should be the opposite of what social programs create, and the Third Way "approach incorporate[s] the truly socialist notion that rights carry with them social responsibility" (Axworthy, 1999, p. 279). Entitlement based social programs creates dependency upon the recipients, they are passive programs that do not work (Axworthy, 1999, p. 283). Axworthy supports his argument using a quote from a similar NDP government at the time in British Columbia: "Welfare isn't working. We need to change from a system that traps people in dependency and poverty to a system that supports people as they move towards independence" (Axworthy, 1999, p. 283).

The continuation of entitlement based social policy without responsibilities is seen to be unworkable. Canada, as well as the rest of the world, must face and adjust to the new global economy (Axworthy, 1999, p. 283). "Social programs must change to keep up with new realities—realities around a changing economy, around unmanageable public debt and around problems with the programs themselves" (Axworthy, 1999, p. 283). The social policy solution to the challenges presented by the new global economy is to give people in receipt of government assistance "the chance to acquire the skills inventory they need for the current workplace and the chance to be as independent as possible—a hand up rather than a handout" (Axworthy, 1999, p. 283).

Therefore, people should have the right to help from the community when they need it, regardless of the cause of that need. This help should be given regardless of the causes that lead to the need, with a caveat:

We need to take on faith their despair and their need for help from their community. But it does not, and should not, end there. We must demand and expect a real partnership. We must demand, in return for this acceptance, for this unquestioning help, a commitment to a return to self-sufficiency. (Axworthy, 1999, p. 281)

The commitment from society is to use government action and policy to ensure that the economy's overarching objective is to move toward full employment, to ensure training, education, and skills upgrading available to those who need them, and "ensure that those who cannot make their own way in the world are entitled to adequate support" (Axworthy, 1999, p. 282). Saskatchewan Social Services (whose name changed in 2003 to Community Resources and Employment) explains:

People have the right to apply for Social Assistance. They also have the responsibility to try to support themselves and their families. They do so by working and by using programs and services that help low-income families. (Education handout in the "About" series)

Regarding recipients, Axworthy does not see that the social-program rights should end with eligibility to help with the responsibility to become self-sufficient, but rather rights, if partnered with responsibilities, could be expanded. "Job training, education and skills upgrading, entrepreneurial training, child care, jobs and other programs that assist Canadians to re-enter the paid workforce should be seen as rights too" (Axworthy, 1999, p. 281). The commitment from recipients of government help then, in their quest for self-sufficiency in response to society's help, is to become employed within the labour market. "For those able to take advantage of expanded, enhanced employment, education and training opportunities, it will be imperative that they do" (Axworthy, 1999, p. 283). Accordingly, work in all its forms is good, the *quality* of that employment not an issue for welfare programmers. To be without employment, apparently is, unless one is rich or disabled, to be outside of the community. The idea that people on welfare are excluded from full citizenship is a conservative concept. Jones and Novak (1999) comment:

> The primary aim of social inclusion and cohesion is therefore to bind the excluded back into the labour market as a solution to the problem. That this may result in their continuing poverty is conveniently overlooked, since it is their inclusion (whether self-imposed or structural) that is the problem rather than their poverty. (p. 188)

Within the logic of state social services in Saskatchewan, citizenship for individuals and families is defined as "job, self-sufficient contributing to society with access to education, health care and security" (Saskatchewan Social Services, 1999). According to Saskatchewan Social Services (1999), this is "A New Way of Doing Business." Seemingly at odds however to the goal of self-sufficiency, if the work is low pay with few or no benefits the government will offer programs that support that work, and hence, the individual or family's community integration. The contradictions of self-sufficiency and individual pursuit of wealth in a market based system as a member of a community, or the additional responsibility and obligations of welfare recipients to the community, are not explained.

For Third Way advocates, global changes and markets have created a need for a shift in social policy programming in the area of welfare. The old way of delivering programs is no longer viable, and social programs need to change. Giddens observes: "The left has to get comfortable with markets, with the role of business in the creation of wealth, and [sic] the fact that private capital is essential for social investment" (Giddens, 2000 quoted in Callinicos, 2001, p. 8). According to Third Way advocates, if state management of the economy was ever a feasible idea it is now certainly a discredited idea. What the Left has to offer in the new economy that separates and defines them from the Right are their values (Callinicos, 2001, p. 8). Through the stressing of community, opportunity and responsibility, Third Way advocates reassert themselves in a globalized economy as an approach that stresses values (Callinicos, 2001, p. 45). Axworthy writes: "What separates socialists from other political ideologies is how we see the world and how we would wish the world to be" (Axworthy, 1999, p. 280).

The stress on values is also present in the statement by former NDP party leader and premier of Saskatchewan, Roy Romanow: "The over-riding question facing Canada today is whether we have the will to continue to maintain the values that will guarantee our common future—our commitment to community, compassion, fairness, sharing and opportunity" (New Directions, 1996, p. 1). Axworthy (1999) observes that the old welfare social policies in Canada were programs "... which do not work for people and which do not reflect socialist community values" (p. 280).

Using values to present the need for welfare changes, Jordan and Jordan (2000) have pointed out that the Third Way use of responsibility and community is misplaced when applied to the economy. "Our first criticism of the Third Way version of responsibility and community is that it extrapolates from the morality of small-scale groups and as-sociations (families, clubs, voluntary organizations) and informal networks, and applies this inappropriately to large-scale societies and the formal rights and duties of citizenship (pp. 4–5). The move toward the inclusion of the morality of small-scale groups into the ongoing development of the welfare system would seem, nonetheless, in keeping with the thrust of capitalist development and the welfare state since World War II.

It has been posited that full membership in a community is dependent upon the pos-session of three sets of citizen rights:

a) *citizen (civil) rights* are those rights concerned with individual liberty and include freedom of speech and thought, the right to own private property and the right to justice;

b) *political rights* are primarily those rights of participation in the political process of government, either as an elector or as an elected member of an assembly;

c) *social rights* cover a whole range of rights, from the right to a modicum of economic security through to the right to share in the heritage and living standards of a civi-lized society. (Sullivan, 1998, p. 74)

Social policy analysts have pointed out that citizenship theory's emphasis on the creation of equality of rights does not imply the creation of material equality (Sullivan, 1998, p. 75). Rather the growth of citizen rights coincides with the growth of capitalism, and the equality of social status as legitimizing social inequalities. Sullivan (1998) in summarizing citizenship rights and justification of inequality writes:

> This is so because they permit individuals to engage in economic struggle for the maximization of profit through the right to buy, own and sell. Political rights may have redressed some of the power imbalance between the social classes in capitalist society but social rights—by peripherally modifying the pattern of social inequality—had the paradoxical, but utilitarian, effect of making the social class system less vulnerable to change. Social rights accord-ed community membership to all—and thus made all citizens stakeholders in capitalist society—without effecting any fundamental redistribution in income or wealth. Social welfare raised the level of the lowest (through in-come maintenance schemes, education, health care systems and the like), but redistribution of resources, where it occurred was horizontal rather than vertical. In the British welfare state, inequality persisted but the possession by all citizens of a package of social rights created a society in which no *a priori* valuations were made on the basis of social class or social status. For Marshall [T. H. Marshall], then, the aims of social policy and service provi-sion include: the incorporation of all as members of the societal community; the modification of the most excessive and debilitating inequalities of British society; but the legitimization of wider and more fundamental inequalities through the process of incorporation. (p. 75, italics in the original)

Incorporation of welfare recipients into the paid labour market is key to Third Way ideology. Incorporation is also key to understanding welfare programs and the function of social policies in the legitimization of inequalities.

Piven and Cloward assert that "the key to an understanding of relief-giving is in the functions it serves for the larger economic and political order, for relief is a secondary and supportive institution" (Piven & Cloward, 1971, p. xiii). These authors maintain that welfare policies are cyclical in nature, that welfare policies expand during periods of civil disorder produced by mass unemployment, and conversely that welfare policies are restrictive at other times to enforce work norms (Piven & Cloward, 1971, p. xiii). Welfare programs are created by governments to deal with dislocations in the work system that lead to mass disorder, and are then retained and maintained to enforce work (Piven & Cloward, 1971, p. xv). Therefore, the two main functions of welfare are to maintain civil order and to enforce work.

What we are experiencing is a restructuring of the welfare state in the delivery of social assistance programs to meet the needs of economic restructuring. The current changes to welfare are not a break from the "old" or Keynesian welfare state, rather "[t]he workfare offensive against the traditional welfare state and its rights-based benefits is an effort to construct a new system of labour regulation, to enforce work under the new conditions of casualisation, falling wages and underemployment that characterises postindustrial labor markets in the mother countries" (Piven & Cloward, 2001, p. x). The old welfare program served the needs of the business community during a time when unemployment was relatively low and workers could expect lifetime employment from an employer and a wage that a family could live on. At that time the welfare state served the needs of business by supplying it with a low-wage labour pool, controlling social unrest during a period on increased expectations from the citizenry and providing a minimum living standard for those who could not work (Piven & Cloward, 1971) and the reproduction of the labour force. With the economic restructuring occurring since the early 1980s and a business community that wishes increasingly to offer flexible employment to workers with low-wages, no security and little in the way of benefits, we see the income support programs of the welfare state adjust. Current welfare programs are now being designed to keep people off social assistance by providing enough of an income supplement so that families do not qualify for welfare, thereby assuring business the labour force most desired for profit in service sector and temporary employment. "Under conditions of falling wages, chronic underemployment, and job casualization, workfarism maximizes (and effectively mandates) participation in contingent, low-paid work by churning workers back into the bottom of the labour market, or by holding them deliberately "close" to the labour market in a persistently "job-ready" state "(Peck, 2001, pp. 13-14). Social policy in Saskatchewan has taken the direction of an increasing number of programs designed to keep workers in the labour force under conditions of low-wages, little or no job security, few if any benefits and short term employment.

It is important to understand the primary function of welfare as a labour market institution, and how welfare interacts with labour market. The actual bottom of income in Canada is not the various provincial minimum wage laws; rather, the bottom is the provincial welfare scales. Workfare conditions the labour market, especially in the area where youth, women and unskilled workers compete for employment. The floor of wages is maintained by the welfare system, however workfare allows wages to fall to meet the standards of the local labour markets. "The shadow of workfare therefore falls far across the labor market itself, where it helps set the terms and the tone of low-wage employment relations" (Peck, 2001, p. 21).

The redesigning of welfare with a more robust focus upon workfare participation of welfare recipients, coupled with an increasing inclusion of the low-income labour force within social welfare programming, represents, to paraphrase Marshall, an extension of the aims of social policy and service provision to include the incorporation of all as members of the societal community; the modification of the most excessive and debilitating inequalities of society; and the legitimization of wider and more fundamental inequalities through the process of incorporation. Welfare programming in Saskatchewan is expanding to cover more and more workers who would not come under the purview of social assistance programs.

With the rush to embrace the labour market as the best social program there is, changes to welfare programming beg the question: what of those who remain on welfare? As what can be considered social assistance programming within a modern welfare state becomes more and more marginalized, what of those people? Jones (2001) identifies them as having the most fragile connection to the labour force due to health, age, disability, education, and the myriad other reasons for being on social assistance. Not only are these people poor, but they are the poorest of the poor in society. "To know something of that service—the treatment of the most impoverished—says a great deal about society's humanity and commitment to social justice" (Jones, 1999). As Saskatchewan, at the time of this writing, has only just introduced its workfare program, it is difficult to say what the outcome might be. However if we look to Britain, Jones (1999) comments that for the most marginalized and excluded people in society, the changes have become "a sort of Poor Law for the twenty-first century."

It also appears that the types of employment to be found by people on TEA in Saskatchewan would be at the low end of the pay schedule. It is unlikely that employers with established labour forces would alter their employment arrangements and hire new employees to take advantage of a government mandated workfare program. Workfare would be more attractive to employers who are in need of temporary, low-wage employees. Accordingly, the shift towards workfare and the development of a mandated contingent labour force meets the recent needs of much of the current job growth that is occurring within the lower paid service sector employment in Canada and the province of Saskatchewan.

Canada and the province of Saskatchewan are very similar to the United States in wage inequality. The United Nations Innocenti Report Card (2000) placed Canada 13th of 14 rich nations for having greatest wage inequality (23.7 percent), only ahead of the United States (25 percent). The province of Saskatchewan has a low wage score of 29 percent (Hunter & Douglas, 2002). Therefore the adoption of a workfare program that most favours a corporatist, market-based approach would make most sense in an employment area such as Saskatchewan.

Saskatchewan has introduced its version of workfare, explaining the changes as a process of expanding citizenship through labour force attachment. It has done so through participation in the federal C.C.T.B. program and provincially through the creation of the

TEA program. Although there are national differences, workfare in Saskatchewan is similar to workfare in the United States, explained with Third Way justifications. Third Way proponents are embracing the best "ideological shell of neoliberalism today" (Callinicos, 2001, p. 8).

References

Axworthy, C. (1999). "A Modern Socialist Approach: R & R for Social Policy." In D. Broad & W. Antony (eds.), *Citizens or Consumers? Social Policy in a Market Society*. Halifax: Fernwood.

Broad, D. (1995). "The Contingent Economy: Manufacturing McJobs?" Working Paper 11, *Social Policy Research Unit*, Faculty of Social Work, University of Regina.

Burman, P. (1997). "Changes in the Patterns of Unemployment: The New Realities of Joblessness." In A. Duffry, D. Glenday, & N. Pupo (eds.), *Good Jobs, Bad Jobs, No Jobs: The Transformation of Work in the 21st Century*. Toronto: Harcourt Brace.

Callinicos, A. (2001). *Against the Third Way*. Cambridge: Polity Press.

Clarke, T. (1997). *Silent Coup: Confronting the Big Business Takeover in Canada*. Toronto: James Lorimer.

Canadian Council for Policy Alternatives (1999). "The WTO: What's the Big Deal?" *Fast Facts*. Canadian Council for Policy Alternatives. Winnipeg, MB. Online at www.policyalternatives.ca.

Eatwell, R. (1997). *Fascism: A History*. London: Penguin Books.

George, V. & Wilding, P. (1985) *Ideology and Social Welfare*. London: Routledge.

Glenday, D. (1997). "Lost Horizons, Leisure Shock: Good Jobs, Bad Jobs, Uncertain Future." In A. Duffy, D. Glenday, & N. Pupo (eds.) (1997). *Good Jobs, Bad Jobs, No Jobs: The Transformation of Work in the 21st Century*. Toronto: Harcourt Brace.

Government of Canada (1997). *Investing in a stronger society: Towards a national child benefit system*. Online at www.fin.gc.ca/budget97/childe/child2e.html.

Government of Canada (1997). *Working together towards a national child benefit System—Budget 1997*. Online at www.fin.gc.ca/budget97/childe/childe.txt.888.

Government of Canada. (2000). *National Child Benefit*. Online at www.nationalchildbenefit.ca/ncb/NCB-progress2000/a2.html.

Government of Canada. (2002). *Key Economic Events, 1944-Bretton Woods Agreement: Developing a New International Monetary System*. Online at www.canadianeconomy.gc.ca/english/economy/1944Bretton_woods.html.

Government of Canada. National Child Benefit. Online at www.ccra-adrc.gc.ca/benefits/ncb-e.html.

Government of Canada. Your Canada Child Tax Benefit. Online at www.ccra-adrc.gc.ca/E/pub/tg/t4114ed-02.html.

Government of Canada. Your Canada Child Tax Benefit. Online at www.ccra-adrc.gc.ca/E/pub/tg/t4114ed-03.html.

Government of Canada. Your Canada Child Tax Benefit. Online at www.ccra-adrc.gc.ca/E/pub/tg/t4114ed-04.html.

Graham, J., & Al-Krenawi, A. (2001). "Canadian Approaches to Income Security." In J. Turner & F. Turner (eds.), *Canadian Social Welfare*. Toronto: Pearson Education.

Holden, C. (1999). "Globalization, Social Exclusion and Labour's New Work Ethic." *Critical Social Policy* 61, Vol. 19(4): 529–38.

Howse, R. & Mutua, M. (2000). *Protecting Human Rights in a Global Economy: Challenges for the World Trade Organization*. Montreal: International Centre for Human Rights and Development.

Hunter, G. (1998). "Less Eligibility Principle and the New Canada Child Tax Benefit." *Canadian Review of Social Policy* 42 (Winter): 120–25.

Hunter, G. & Douglas, F. (2002). "Report Card on Child Poverty in Saskatchewan 2002." *Social Policy Research Unit*, Faculty of Social Work, University of Regina. Online at www.campaign2000.ca/rc/pdf/SKpovertyreportnov02.pdf.

Jones, C. (2001). "Voices from the Front Line: State Social Workers and New Labour." *British Journal of Social Work* 31: 547–62.

Jones, C. & Novak, C. (1999). *Poverty, Welfare and the Disciplinary State*. London: Routledge.

Jordan, B. & Jordan, C. (2000). *Social Work and the Third Way: Tough Love as Social Policy*. London: Sage.

Karger, H. & Stoesz, D. (1998). *American Social Welfare Policy: A Pluralist Approach* 3rd edn. New York: Addison Wesley Longman.

Kitchen, B. (2001). "Poverty and Declining Living Standards in a Changing Economy." In J. Turner & F. Turner (eds.), *Canadian Social Welfare*. Toronto: Pearson.

Lightman, E. S. & Riches, G. (2001). "Canada: One Step Forward, Two Steps Back?" In P. Alcock & G. Craig (eds.), *International Social Policy*. Hampshire: Palgrave.

Lund, B. (1999). "Ask not What Your Community Can Do for You": Obligations, New Labour and Welfare Reform." In *Critical Social Policy* 61 (19:4): 447–62.

McQuaig, L. (1998). *The Cult of Impotence: Selling the Myth of Powerlessness in the Global Economy*. Toronto: Viking.

McQuaig, L. (2001). *All You Can Eat: Greed, Lust and the New Capitalism*. Toronto: Penguin.

Merrett, C.D. (1996). *Free Trade: Neither Free nor about Trade*. Montreal: Institute of Policy Alternatives.

National Council of Welfare (1999). *Children First: A Pre-budget Report by the National Council of Welfare*. Ottawa: Minister of Public Works and Government Services Canada.

Peck, J. (2001). *Workfare States*. London: Guilford Press.

Piven, F. & Cloward, R. (1971). *Regulating the Poor: The Functions of Public Welfare*. New York: Pantheon.

Piven, F. & Cloward, R. (1997). *The Breaking of the American Social Compact*. New York: The New Press.

Piven, F. & Cloward, R. (2001). Forward. In J. Peck, *Workfare States*. London: Guilford Press.

Pulkingham, J. & Ternowetsky, G. (1996). "The Changing Landscape of Social Policy and the Canadian Welfare State." In J. Pulkingham & G. Ternowetsky (eds.), *Remaking Canadian Social Policy: Social Security in the Late 1990s*. Halifax: Fernwood.

Pulkingham, J. & Ternowetsky, G. (1997). "The New Canada Child Tax Benefit: Discriminating between 'Deserving' and 'Undeserving' among Poor Families with Children." In J. Pulkingham & G. Ternowetsky (eds.), *Child and Family Policies: Struggles, Strategies and Options*. Halifax: Fernwood.

Saskatchewan Social Services (1999). *Information: Social Assistance Handbook* [Brochure].

Saskatchewan Social Services (2000). *Annual Report 1998–1999*. Government of Saskatchewan.

Saskatchewan Social Services (2001). *Annual Report 1999–2000*. Government of Saskatchewan.

Saskatchewan Social Services (2003). Jobs First and Transitional Employment Allowance. *About*. Government of Saskatchewan.

Saskatchewan Social Services. "Building Independence—Investing in Families." *Saskatchewan Employment Supplement; Saskatchewan Child Benefit; Family Health Benefits; Provincial Training Allowance; Youth Futures* [Brochures].

Sullivan, M. (1998). "The Social Democratic Perspective." In P. Alcock, A. Erskine, & M. May (eds.), *The Student's Companion to Social Policy*. Oxford: Blackwell.

Stranks, R. (2001). "Trade Liberalization: The Broader Context." In *Trade Policy Research 2001*. Minister of Public Works and Government Services.

Swenarchuk, M. (2001). "Civilizing Globalization: Trade and Environment Thirteen Years On." *Canadian Centre for Policy Alternatives, Briefing Paper Series: Trade and Investment* 2.6 (October).

Theodore, N. & Peck, J. (1999). "Welfare to Work." *Critical Social Policy* 61 (19.4): 485–510.

UNICEF (2000). *The League Table of Child Poverty in Rich Nations*. Florence: UNICEF Innocenti Research Centre.

Appendix I.

	Saskatchewan Assistance Plan (SAP)	Transitional Employment Allowance (TEA)
Eligibility	It is the duty of the local unit to provide assistance: "Subject to any program Act of program regulations, a unit shall provide assistance to **persons in need who are eligible** for assistance." (The Saskatchewan Assistance Act, p.4) "A person who receives program benefits pursuant to an income-tested program shall in accordance with program regulations (b) provide or authorize the release of any information prescribed in the program regulation on the request of the program manager." (The Saskatchewan Assistance Act, p.13)	"The Transitional Employment Allowance program is established to provide a transitional employment allowance to **persons in need who are participating in certain pre-employment programs or who have a reasonable expectation of becoming self-sufficient in a short period of time.**" (The Transitional Employment Allowance Regulations, p. 3) - clients on application must provide the health services numbers and social insurance numbers of the applicant and the applicant's spouse, if any, and give consent to their use to verify the eligibility of the applicant - during confirmation of application clients must consent to "disclosure to the department of personal information with respect to the family unit in the records of government departments and agencies and other bodies for the purpose of determining the eligibility of the family unit to receive a transitional employment allowance..." (The Transitional Employment Allowance Regulations, p.7)
Requirements	- **Clients are expected to participate in First Steps program.** - **Must report** any changes in your situation to your worker while receiving assistance. - Must participate in an Annual Review - Must be involved in employment/transition planning.	Must confirm the application in person within 14 days Category A - **must be participating** in a pre-employment program - **must file a report** every month with any changes to: the family unit, pre-employment program participation, income, place of residence and mailing address, utilities payments and accommodation payments. Category B - must establish that they will be self-sufficient at the end of the eligibility period (month of application plus three months) - **must report** every month with any changes to circumstances that affect eligibility as they occur. (The Transitional Employment Allowance Regulations, p. 12)

	Saskatchewan Assistance Plan (SAP)	*Transitional Employment Allowance (TEA)*
Benefit Amount (Shelter and Basic Allowance)	**Single Employable** $195 (living allowance) + $210 (shelter) = **$405** **Single Parent, one child** $230 (living allowance) +385 (shelter) = **$615**	Single Employable (general living allowance) $405 Single Parent, one child (general living allowance) $615
Utilities	"Payment for utilities for the full month in which eligibility is established may be provided if the need exists. Utility allowances include usual charges as well as costs related to septic systems and garbage pick up where the municipality charges for service.... **The actual monthly cost for basic utilities** in the client's name is provided through electronic billing (SP/SE), to the vendor or to the client upon receipt of a bill or confirmation from the utility company.... **An allowance may be provided based on confirmed utility information.... GST charges are included** for clients who pay their own accounts.... Sharing—**the actual cost of the client's share is provided.**" - provisions can be made if utilities are in the landlord's name.	"A **utilities allowance** may be provided to a client who is eligible for a general living allowance pursuant to subsection (1) if the client pays for any of the following: telephone; electricity; home heating; sewer and water." - utilities must be in applicants name "The amount of a utilities allowance mentioned in subsection (6) is to be **determined in accordance with a schedule of rates** established by the minister in accordance with subsection (8)." (The Transitional Employment Allowance Regulations, p.8) Actual utility rates for TEA - water—min.$20 to max. $54 - telephone—min. $30 to max. $30 - electricity—min.$50 to max.$126 - energy/heating—min.$70 to max. $110 (TEA Rate Schedule)
Laundry	"When a client requires a laundry allowance to pay to use a washer and/or dryer the following rates are provided: one person - $10 a month, etc." (Social Assistance Policy Manual, p. 51-52)	Funds not provided for laundry.
Child Care	Child care is available for approved plans (AA, support groups), employment, training, disability, illness, employment seeking, Fine Option programs, funerals, provincial appeals, and court appearances.	Child care is provided while participating in pre-employment program or if employed. (child care flat rate provided per day as needed).

	Saskatchewan Assistance Plan (SAP)	Transitional Employment Allowance (TEA)
Employ-ment Allow-ances	"To participate in training/employment or approved transition plan programs of the community of residence, **actual cost or mileage rate**."	"Up to **$140 per adult** per application can be used for employment supports including travel." (TEA Rate Schedule)
	"**Actual cost or mileage rate**" to - attend a job interview outside the community of residence within Saskatchewan where a similar opportunity does not exist in the community. - accept confirmed employment/training program outside the community of residence. "Work boots, special clothing, mandatory licenses…fees or permits, Hepatitis B immunization and minor tools may be paid when essential to employment." - $40 for travel if necessary - $50 for vehicle registration if necessary (Social Assistance Policy Manual, p. 61 & 65)	
Income	Eligible for earned income exemptions: - at time of application if disabled or not fully employable. - within 3 months of application for all other recipients	No earned income exemptions.
	Various other types of income exemptions: - portions of rental income - portions of room and board income - Lump sum payments for settlements such as HIV and Residential Schools	Only incomes exempted are: Saskatchewan Child Benefit payments, Saskatchewan Employment Supplement payments, Benefit Adjustment payments, foster care payments or payments for young offenders in open custody.
Other	**Available in SAP but not in TEA:** - Water heater, water softener, service reconnection, wood and water delivery for rural areas - damage deposits - utility deposits and connection fees - back bill payments for utilities - deferral/arrangements with utility companies - special clothing - special diet allowances - travel allowances for medical or funerals - daycare deposits - household equipment - repairs to property - educational expenses for children - transitional training allowance - moving costs	

	Saskatchewan Assistance Plan (SAP)	*Transitional Employment Allowance (TEA)*
Other	**Available in SAP but not in TEA:** - Water heater, water softener, service reconnection, wood and water delivery for rural areas - damage deposits - utility deposits and connection fees - back bill payments for utilities - deferral/arrangements with utility companies - special clothing - special diet allowances - travel allowances for medical or funerals - daycare deposits - household equipment - repairs to property - educational expenses for children - transitional training allowance - moving costs	
Appeals	"Clients have the right to appeal decisions made by department employees." (Social Assistance Policy Manual, p.93) - A client is permitted to appeal when - he was not allowed to apply or reapply for assistance - his request for assistance or an increase in assistance was not decided upon within a reasonable time depending upon the circumstances for each case. - his application for assistance was denied - assistance was cancelled, suspended, varied or withheld - the amount of assistance granted is insufficient to meet his needs - the recipient is dissatisfied with unit policy (Saskatchewan Assistance Regulations, pp. 36 & 37) "When clients request assistance prior to the hearing, minimal assistance may be provided until the appeal is concluded." (Social Assistance Policy Manual, p.94) "Clients may be represented by an advocate." (Social Assistance Policy Manual, p.95). There are certain payments available to advocates. - Child care and travel costs may be covered.	"Clients who are dissatisfied with the decision about their Transitional Employment Allowance have the right to appeal to the local committee. Decisions which can be appealed are: denial of application, amount of allowance, cancellation of allowance, and assessment of overpayment." As well, provincial appeals are permitted after local appeals. (The Transitional Employment Allowance Regulations, p. 13) - There is no interim assistance available pending appeal. - Advocate fees are not covered.

	Saskatchewan Assistance Plan (SAP)	*Transitional Employment Allowance (TEA)*
Termin-ation	Adjustments to allowance or termination **may** occur is there is a change in employment status, income, family composition absence from accommodation, relocation, death, marriage or common law relationship, or leaving the province.	Clients **must** be terminated if they fail to give a monthly report, if they are no longer eligible, they are not able to participate in the pre-employment program, or they fail to participate in the pre-employment program. (The Transitional Employment Allowance Regulations, p. 12)

II. Low Income Cut-Offs (LICO) and Poverty Measurement

1. Introduction

The Low-Income Cutoff (LICO) measure, which is used to analyze the incidence and depth of poverty in Canada, has been the focus of some criticism. Recently, this criticism has been magnified by Statistics Canada's move from using the before-tax income variable to using the after-tax income variable when measuring poverty. Changing from before-tax to after-tax LICO calculations has a dramatic effect on the incidence and depth of poverty. In this review we will examine the LICO and explore the history of the measure in order to present a perspective on its original intent. We will also discuss the criticisms of the LICO measure and suggest its strengths.

The LICO measure was developed in 1961 by Jenny Podoluk, a research coordinator with Consumer Finance Research in the Dominion Bureau of Statistics. The LICO methodology was developed in Consumer Finance Research as a means of examining the low-income population in Canada, as there was no official statistical concept of poverty in Canada (Podoluk, 1968, p. 185). Now, more than forty years later, there is still no official statistical concept of poverty in Canada. The LICO measure stands as the de facto poverty measure in Canada, resulting in recent heightened attention and controversy around this particular measure.

Podoluk suggested that Canada did not have an official poverty measure "… because no minimum standard budgets have been constructed that would allow for a location of points in the income distribution below which income inadequacy might exist" (Podoluk, 1968, p. 185). There were two possible poverty measures conceived of at the time: (1) a poverty measure based upon a fixed income point below which an income was considered inadequate, and (2) a measure based upon a budget approach that took into account family size, age, composition, their place of residence and the price levels in the area. The budget approach, although identified as having weaknesses, was judged to be superior to the fixed income approach. Due to the problem of a lack of minimum standard budgets, a compromise between the two approaches was developed. A strictly fixed income approach was modified with a budget examination of income spent on the essentials of food, clothing and shelter.

Determination of expenditures on essentials was derived from the 1959 Urban Family Expenditure data, Prices Division, Consumer Expenditure. This was the fourth in a series of surveys begun in 1953 (Dominion Bureau of Statistics, 1963, p. 5). The 1959 survey was to be an improvement upon the three previous surveys. It was to be the most comprehensive survey of urban family expenditures since the survey of 1947–48 and would relax the restrictions that had been placed on the 1947–48 survey sample. With the 1959 survey, the sample would be drawn from all urban families and individuals in cities with a population of 15,000 and over.

Farm families were not included in the survey as these families were judged to have different expenditure patterns than their urban counterparts. An examination of family budgets available at the time suggested that there were differences of condition between farm families and non-farm families. Farm families were thought to have less monetary requirements than non-farm families because farm families were often able to produce their own food and other commodities, and were more likely to own their homes (Podoluk, 1968, p. 181). Differential expenditures were a major concern to the drafters of Canada's low-income measure.

Examination of the differences in expenditures and a definition of needs were viewed as necessary to the developers of LICO because they wished to create a relative—as opposed to an absolute—measure of poverty. A relative measure of poverty establishes a standard of living in society, and then decides what level below that standard is unacceptable. The standard of living will change as society's opinion on what constitutes minimum needs changes. In an interesting aside, Podoluk suggested in 1968 that the automobile had joined the list of family needs since the Second World War, rather than just being thought of as a luxury item (Podoluk, 1968, p. 184).

In keeping with the conservative milieu of the post-war era, Podoluk settled on *food, clothing, and shelter* as essential needs. She noted that the decision on what constitutes need was subjective, but also noted: "However, in an affluent society the notion that incomes should provide subsistence and no more is often unacceptable and other budgets have been drawn up to provide what is sometimes called a 'modest but adequate' level of living" (Podoluk, 1968, p. 183).

The 1959 survey of expenditures was much more thorough than food, clothing, and shelter items, however. It also contained detailed average expenditures on a diverse range of items including chrome furniture, china, reading materials, repairs, floor wax, shaves, rogues, and ice. Calculations were performed on the three essential expenditures incurred by 2,000 spending units living in urban centers of 15,000 and over. From the data, it was calculated that, on average, families of different sizes spent about half their income on the three essentials. To arrive at a low-income measure, low-income families were thought to be families who spent most of their income on these essentials. Podoluk added 20 percentage points to the average expenditure rate of fifty percent, and stated that families who spent seventy percent or more of their incomes on the three essentials of food, clothing and shelter might be in "straitened circumstances" (Podoluk, 1968, p. 185). As proposed, the LICO measure was to be a conservative measure of low income and it is still most commonly used as a measure of poverty in Canada.

2. Politics and LICO

A number of criticisms have been made about LICO since 1961. Perhaps the most common is that although it is widely used, it is not a poverty line.

The discussion of poverty, especially child poverty, has come to prominence since the Government of Canada passed a unanimous resolution to end child poverty in Canada by the year 2000. That goal was never reached, nor was there evidence that the government even came close to achieving that end. However, the government is often reminded of its goal and its failure to achieve it by advocacy, community, church, and union groups. The political nature of the debate about poverty was not lost on Statistics Canada when it commented that it was partly due to the government commitment to eliminate child poverty that the LICO measure was under a great deal of public scrutiny (Webber, 1998, p. 7).

Statistics Canada, which produces the LICO data, entered into the debate about using LICO as a poverty measure and reported: "At the heart of the debate is the use of the low income cutoffs as poverty lines, even though Statistics Canada has clearly stated, since their publication began over 25 years ago, that they are not" (Fellegi, 1999, p. 36). As well, "Statistics Canada continues to correct media commentary that portrays low income estimates as a measure of poverty. The Agency often repeats that they are not intended as such" (Webber, 1998, p. 9).

Readers of the work of Jenny Podoluk and her use of the LICO measure she helped to develop are led to a different conclusion than that currently taken by Statistics Canada. In her work, specifically the chapter "Low Income and Poverty," Podoluk explains her reasoning and the methodology employed to develop the LICO measure. As the title of the chapter suggests, she equated low-income with poverty, and she often used the words low-income and poverty interchangeably. How else would it be possible to understand the following:

> There is no existing official statistical concept of poverty in Canada, primarily because no minimum standard budgets have been constructed that would allow for a location of points in the income distribution below which income inadequacy might exist. For purposes of this study, low-income families are defined as those families whose incomes fall into those income groups in which, on average, most of the income received must be spent upon essentials such as food, clothing and shelter. (Podoluk, 1968, p. 185)

Even more telling, she writes in the same chapter: "The incidence of poverty follows a somewhat different pattern among families with male heads than among families with female heads" (Podoluk, 1968, p. 191). Whatever Statistics Canada currently thinks its LICO indicates or was intended to indicate, it was clear to the developers of LICO that it was a measure of low-income and therefore of poverty in Canada.

Much debate also revolves around the use of LICO based upon the before-tax Total Income variable and the after-tax Total Income variable to calculate low-income rates. It is an important discussion. At the essence of this argument is the poverty rate in Canada. Using LICO on the after-tax Total Income variable dramatically reduces the poverty rate. For example, if the before-tax Total Income LICO is used with the 1998 Survey of Labour and Income Dynamics (SLID) data, the poverty rate for all people in 1998 is 16.9 percent, however if the after-tax Total Income LICO is used the poverty rate for all persons in 1998 falls to 12.2 percent (Statistics Canada, 2000).

The argument presented by Statistics Canada for the drop in poverty rates is that using the LICO measure based upon after-tax Total Income reflects the progressive income tax structure of Canada whereby the income disparity in Canada becomes more compressed (Statistics Canada, 2002, p. 135). Some consider the after-tax method to be a truer standard of poverty than the before-tax method (Graham, Swift & Delaney, 2003, p.76). Others see problems with the after-tax method. For instance, the after-tax method only adjusts income for provincial and federal income taxes and not for all the other taxes such as provincial sales tax, GST, EI premiums, etc. (Ross, Scott & Smith, 2000, pp. 35–36) and, low-income people do not pay taxes and taxation rates differ across provinces.[4] In this article however we argue that a major problem with using LICO with after-tax Total Income is methodological. Consider the following example:

According to the *Family Expenditure Survey* (FAMEX) from Statistics Canada, rebased in 1992, an average family spends 35 percent of its income on the essentials of food, clothing, and shelter. Of course, that is what the family would spend of their disposable, after-tax income. This percentage is arrived at by dividing the average family expenditure by the average family income to give a ratio of the number of cents of every dollar spent on essential items:

$$\frac{\text{Average Expenditure on Essentials}}{\text{Average Income}} = \% \text{ Income on Essentials}$$

For the average income, before-tax Total Income was the main income variable available, until 1980, when Statistics Canada began also providing figures for after-tax Total Income (Cotton, Webber & Saint-Pierre, 1999, p. 24). The following example using the 1998 SLID data and the 35 percent (1992) base of expenditures demonstrates the differences in low-income rates: The average before-tax Total Income in Canada in 1998 was $44,736.21 and the average after-tax Total Income was $35,948.98.

The original methodology added 20 percentage points to the average expenditure of 50 percent on essential items, as it was thought that a family spending another 20 percent of their income on essentials would be in "straightened circumstances" best understood as poverty. Rebased to 1992 expenditures, the LICO measure still adds 20 points to the average family expenditures.

The following calculations use the average before-tax Total Income of $44,736.21 and the average after-tax Total Income of $35,948.98 for the year 1998 with the expenditures rebased to the 1992 average family expenditures of 35 percent on necessities ($15,658). 1992 represents the most current rate of expenditures on necessities used by Statistics Canada to calculate the LICOs.

BEFORE-TAX TOTAL INCOME

$$\frac{15,658}{44,736.21} = .35 \text{ (35 cents of every dollar is spent on essentials)}$$

$.35 + .20 = .55$

Adding 20 percentage points to the average expenditure of 35 percent or 35 cents of every dollar on essentials, then a family spending 55 cents of their before-tax Total Income on essentials would be low-income.

$$(.55)(44,736.21) = \$24,605$$

Therefore a family with a before-tax Total Income of $24,605 or less would fall below the LICO measure for low-income (the actual LICO levels take into account family size and geographic location).

Using the same average expenditure data applied to the after-tax Total Income that Statistics Canada is now adopting in its publications, the results are:

AFTER-TAX TOTAL INCOME

$$\frac{15,658}{35,948.98} = .435 \text{ (43.5 cents of every dollar is spent on essentials)}$$

$$.435 + .20 = .635$$

Adding 20 percentage points to the average expenditure of 43.5 percent or 43.5 cents of every dollar on essentials, a family spending 63.5 cents of their after-tax Total Income on essentials would be low-income:

$$(.635)(35,948.98) = \$22,828$$

A family with an after-tax Total Income of $22,828 or less would fall below the LICO measure for low-income.

This is where the methodological shift to using after-tax incomes is shown to be a politically valuable, if unintentional, decision by Statistics Canada. As mentioned earlier, in both examples, the family's actual, disposable income and expenditures do not change. However the family with a gross income of $24,605 spending 55 percent of their income on essentials is no longer in poverty according to the after-tax measure. Only the families spending 63.5 percent of their income on essentials are considered low-income. This effectively lowers the number of people in Canada considered to be low-income.

Presumably the 20 additional points would include a margin for the LICO ratio of net expenditures on necessities with before-tax Total Income. The ratio built with before-tax Total Income has changed to actual expenditures on essentials with after-tax Total Income. If after-tax Total Income is used that is fine, but tax should not be accounted for twice. It is unclear how much of the 20 points should be reduced if after-tax Total Income is used, but it would seem reasonable to reduce the 20 points by the taxation rate. Then only approximately 14 points would be added to the ratio of expenditures to after-tax income. Doing so would make the after-tax LICO rate only slightly less in terms of percentage, than the before-tax LICO low-income percentage rate.

A major concern with the LICO measure is that the level of low-income cutoffs rises over time. The reason the low income cut-off level rises with time is that the ratio of expenditures on necessities is less than the growth in income, therefore people spend, on average, less and less of their yearly income on necessities. As the amount of the family's income spent on necessities declines, the low-income cutoff levels rise. For example, in 1961 when the LICO measure was developed, the average family expenditure on necessities was approximately 50 percent of their pre-tax income. With the 20 percentage points added to the average, low income was defined as families who spent 70 percent or more on necessities. As incomes have increased and the average ratio of expenditures on necessities as a proportion of income has decreased, the low-income cutoff levels have risen. The most current rebasing (1992) of the LICO measure calculated on the average family expenditures on necessities, was established at 35 percent of pre-tax income. If the 20 percentage points are added to that average, low income would be defined as families who spent 55 percent or more on necessities. The climb from 70 percent of income spent on necessities to be considered low income in 1961 to 55 percent of income spent on necessities to be considered low income in 1992 has caused concern (Kerstetter, 2000, pp. 6–8).

The developers of LICO were aware that their poverty measure was relative, and that the level at which people would be considered poor would climb over time. Commenting on the issue, Podoluk (1968) wrote:

> It is because poverty is a relative concept that poverty or low income does not diminish as much as might be expected in view of the real income growth of a country. The extent of change can be evident only if contemporary standards are applied to the income structure of an earlier day. (p. 183)

Explaining why poverty or low income does not decrease as would be expected in terms of income growth that is adjusted for the inflation rate, Podoluk noted:

> Thus, even though the level of living of the poor improves through time, poverty never seems to be eliminated because a wide gap persists between the level of living attained by some segments of the population and those enjoyed by the majority of the community. (p.184)

This quote demonstrates that the developers of LICO knew that it was a relative measure. Additionally, they knew that the low-income, or poverty rate, would not remain fixed at 70 percent; rather, if the income of the majority grew over time then the level of what was considered low income would grow as well. That is what it means to have a relative measure, it is relative to some standard in the community. If the standard of the community changes, then low income should be evaluated in the context of the rising community standard.

There is one major problem with the LICO measure as Podoluk developed it. Podoluk understood the average income as representative of the income of the majority of people, which it clearly is not. Average income is a notoriously poor measure to describe the central tendency of incomes. Income distribution is highly skewed in a positive direction with most incomes falling well below the average. When using the average, or mean value, it is necessary to be cognizant of extreme scores. Averages are sensitive to extreme values, whereby a few extreme high income values can pull the average value well above what most people earn. Therefore as incomes grow at the top of the scale at a faster rate than the rest of the population, the average income will rise while most of the population are little or no better off. It is obvious that as the incomes of the highest earners rise, they will spend less on necessities. Their rise in income will be reflected in the average income, creating a distorted picture of income distribution. That is why income is most often described in terms of median income, or with inequality measures such as the Lorenz Curve and Gini Coefficients. It is the use of average income with LICO however, that gives this measure its strength. The LICO is useful to social research as a reflection of rising inequality in the whole population and would best be used in conjunction with other measures of inequality such as Lorenz curves and Gini coefficients.

As is clear, the LICO measure is a relative measure. With the use of average income in the LICO measure, as income disparity between the wealthy few and most other people continues to grow, the extent of that disparity is captured by the LICO measure. The LICO measure stands as an indicator of the growth of income disparity between the rich and the rest of the population. As the income of the wealthy continues to climb and eclipse the incomes of everyone else, the LICO will provide an indicator of that growing disparity.

Podoluk had her own concerns about the comprehensiveness of an income-based methodology. Her concern was that an appropriate measure needed to account for family size, age composition of the family, place of residence and price levels in the area (Podoluk, 1968, p. 181). Statistics Canada has always varied the level of the LICO to account for family size up to seven members (Ross et al, 2000, p. 15). In 1973 Statistics Canada began setting the level of the LICO to reflect the size of the community, resulting in 35 separate LICO categories. The larger the community population and family size, the higher the income is for the LICO. Age composition of the family has not been accounted for by Statistics Canada. The varying price levels of large urban areas have also not been accounted for. Areas such as Montreal, Toronto, and Vancouver have inflated living costs in comparison with other cities with populations over 500,000 (the largest community size accounted for with the LICO), thus producing a concern about the strength of the categories (Cotton & Webber, 2000, p. 17). As well, the three territories and First Nation reserves are unaccounted for in the LICO methodology, limiting the development of an inclusive understanding of poverty.

Another of Podoluk's concerns was a lack of longitudinal data which could be useful in establishing the length of time families are in poverty. In 1997 Statistics Canada replaced the yearly data from the Survey of Consumer Finances with data from a longitudinal study—the Survey of Labour and Income Dynamics (SLID)—as the source for population data. However, the benefit of the SLID data is limited since it has not been made widely available to social researchers concerned about studying the persistence of poverty. The year 1998 represents the last time the SLID data was made widely accessible to the public.

3. Changes to LICO

Over the years the LICO publishers have tried to reflect the changes in society through rebasing the measure to changing spending practices. The LICO was first rebased in 1973, basing it on the 1969 FAMEX data. Changes occurred again in 1980 when the LICO was rebased to the 1978 FAMEX data and the low-income rates were hence calculated with after-tax income rather than the original pre-tax measure (Cotton et al., 1999, p.24). Now, Statistics Canada has chosen to use after-tax income in their publications:

> The choice to highlight after-tax rates was made for two main reasons. First, income taxes and transfers are essentially two methods of income redistribution. The before-tax rates only partly reflect the entire redistributive impact of Canada's tax/transfer system, by including the effect of transfers but not the effect of income taxes. Second, since the purchase of necessities is made with after-tax dollars, it is logical to use people's after-tax income to draw conclusions about their overall economic well-being. (Statistics Canada, 2002, p. 135)

In 1987 the LICO was rebased to the 1986 data. Shortly after, in 1989, there was a major public consultation reviewing the usefulness and methodology involved in setting the LICOs (Cotton et al., 1999, p. 24). The review brought out concerns about the lack of attention to the issue of depth of poverty and agreed that low-income information should still be published, but that all measures discussed had their weaknesses (Cotton et al., 1999, p. 24). In 1992 the LICO was rebased to the 1992 FAMEX data, which is the measure used today.

4. The market basket measure

The issue about appropriate poverty measures goes beyond the LICO debate. Statistics Canada still holds that the LICO is not a measure of poverty despite Podoluk's original intent and despite the evidence that the rising level of income to expenditure comes not so much from bettering conditions of the poor, but rather from the rising incomes of the wealthy. Other relative measures have been introduced such as the Low Income Measure (LIM) from Statistics Canada, the Toronto Social Planning Council measure, the Canadian Council on Social Development measure, the Croll measure, and the Gallup Poll. Some people argue that provincial welfare rates serve as poverty lines, as they are the absolute minimum income a family should receive. The Montreal Diet is an example of an attempt to formulate absolute measure of poverty, rather than a relative one.

In May 2003, Statistics Canada introduced its own absolute low-income measure: the Market Basket Measure (MBM). The MBM was not produced as a result of requests from a large number of advocacy groups and researchers. Rather, the measure was developed in response to a 1997 request of the Federal/Provincial/Territorial Ministers Responsible for Social Services (Human Resources Development Canada [HRDC], 2003, p. 1). As an absolute measure, the MBM approach is an attempt to determine how much disposable family income[5] is required for a pre-determined, specific basket of goods and services. The HRDC market basket measure includes five types of expenditures: (1) food; (2) clothing and footwear; (3) shelter; (4) transportation; and (5) other household needs (e.g., school supplies, personal care products, telephone, furniture etc.).

The MBM is calculated with a referent family, comprised of two adults (one male and one female) aged 25–49, and two children (a girl aged 9 and a boy aged 13). All other household configurations are calculated using a formula based on the Low Income

Measure (LIM) equivalence scale. A family of four has an equivalence scale value of 2. A single person has an equivalence value of 1, therefore it is postulated by Statistics Canada that a family of four requires twice as much income as a single adult (HRDC, 2003, pp. 34–35). The MBM then establishes thresholds, which are sum of the costs for the pre-determined basket of goods and services for the selected communities and community sizes across the ten provinces. Economic families that are below the MBM thresholds are considered low-income. For the year 2000, the incidences of low income for all persons in Canada were; 13.1 percent using the MBM; 10.9 using after-tax LICO; and 14.7 using before-tax LICO.

A couple of issues with the MBM approach should be raised in the context of the LICO measure. First, although the MBM is considered an absolute approach to poverty measurement, it is actually a relative measure because it must be decided what constitutes a basket of goods and services. Any number of subjective opinions comprises what should and should not be in the market basket. All measures of poverty are relative. However, the larger problem is that the MBM approach does not account for the growing disparity of income. Incomes and wealth of the rich recede further and further from scrutiny as focus is more and more attuned to what is a reasonable MBM basket of goods and services. The relative measures of poverty have the advantage of employing all of the incomes in its methodology and are therefore tied to the growth of income disparity. The MBM based measures determine what level of income is needed for a certain decided-upon basket of goods and services. Growth in income disparity is not required for the calculation of this threshold.

5. Conclusion

The efficacy of poverty measurement as a means of political advocacy has also been challenged. For instance, Ternowetsky (2000, p. 2) comments:

> One important outcome of a poverty-line approach is that it restricts the way we think about poverty. It asks the question "how much is enough" and directs the gaze of our research towards the poor, towards those without sufficient income to fully participate in society. It treats the poor as "residual," as a special category which can be brought back into society and reintegrated into mainstream life through adjustments in income (Rainwater, 1970). This is the most common and widespread method of poverty research. And, it continues. It continues in the face of the mounting evidence that the "normal" outcome of the "normal" functioning of capitalist economies is to simultaneously generate extremes of poverty and wealth (Roby, 1974).

Rather than focusing only on the poor, it might be useful to examine the incomes and wealth of the economic elites and the ongoing growth in inequality. The real strength of the LICO might be its odd but perhaps very useful inclusion of average incomes. The LICO measure, in its design and use of average income reflects the upward movement of capital over time. As such, it could be a useful measure of income inequality if used in conjunction with other inequality measures such as the Lorenz Curve and Gini Coefficient.

Notes

1. The National Child Benefit (N.C.B.) Program of partnership between the federal government and the provinces is only available to low-income working families with children.
2. In April 2004, the C.H.S.T. program was divided into two separate programs. The Canada Health Transfer (C.H.T.) program provides funding and program standards for health care funding while the Canada Social Transfer (C.S.T.) provides funding for post-secondary education and social services funding. The C.H.T. program has established guidelines for funding, however the C.S.T. has no similar guidelines nor program standards. The C.H.T. was developed in response to the uncertainty among the electoral public about the erosion of this program.
3. For further information on provincial programs see Revenue Canada, *Your Canada Child Tax Benefit*, (On-line), Available: <http://www.ccra-adrc.gc.ca/E/pub/tg/t4114ed/4114ed-03.html>.
4. For a more complete discussion of issues with after-tax incomes and the LICO measure see Cotton, C. & Webber, M. (2000).
5. The MBM defines disposable family income as the sum remaining after deducting from the total household income the following: total income taxes paid; the personal portion of payroll taxes; other mandatory payroll deductions such as contributions to employer-sponsored pension plans, supplementary health plans and union dues; child support and alimony payments made to another household; out-of-pocket spending on child care; and non-insured but medically-prescribed health-related expenses such as dental and vision care, prescription drugs and aids for persons with disabilities (HRDC, 2003, p. 4). As such, the MBM definition of disposable household income would appear to more closely reflect available funds than the after-tax LICO.

Works Cited

Cotton, C., Webber, M. & Saint-Pierre, Y. (1999). *Should the Low Income Cutoffs be Updated? A Discussion Paper.* Ottawa: Income Statistics Division, Statistics Canada, Catalogue No. 75F0002MIE – 99009. December 1999.

Cotton, C. & Webber, M. (2000). *Should the Low Income Cutoffs be Updated? A Summary of Feedback on Statistics Canada's Discussion Paper.* Ottawa: Income Statistics Division, Statistics Canada, Catalogue No. 75F0002MIE – 00011, September 2000.

Dominion Bureau of Statistics. (1963). *Urban family expenditures, 1959.* Ottawa: Dominion Bureau of Statistics, Prices Division, Catalogue No. 62-521, March 1963.

Fellegi, I. (1999, pp. 36–37). "On Poverty and Low Income." In *Should the Low Income Cutoffs be Updated? A Discussion Paper.* Ottawa: Income Statistics Division, Statistics Canada, Catalogue No. 75F0002MIE – 99009. December 1999.

Graham, J., Swift, K. & Delaney, R. (2003). *Canadian Social Policy: An Introduction, Second Edition.* Toronto: Pearson Education Canada Inc.

Human Resources Development Canada. (2003). *Understanding the 2000 Low Income Statistics Based on the Market Basket Measure.* Hull, Quebec: Human Resources Development Canada Publications Centre. Catalogue No. RH63-1?569-03-03E.

Kerstetter, S. (2000). "LICOs and LIMs." In *Defining and Measuring Poverty: Prince George Forum, April 3, 2000.* Edited by Goldberg, M. & Pulkingham, J. Prince George: Child Welfare Research Centre, University of Northern British Columbia.

Poduluk, J. (1968). *Income of Canadians.* Ottawa: Census Monograph, Dominion Bureau of Statistics.

Rainwater, L. (1970). Neutralizing the disinherited: Some psychological aspects for understanding the poor. In V. Allen (ed.), *Psychological Factors in Poverty.* Chicago: Markham.

Roby, P. (1974). Introduction: The Poverty Establishment. In P. Roby (ed.), *The Poverty Establishment.* Englewood Cliffs: Prentice Hall.

Ross, D. & Roberts, P. (1999). *Income and Child Well-Being: A New Perspective on the Poverty Debate.* Ottawa: Canadian Council on Social Development.

Ross, D., Scott, K. & Smith, P. (2000). *The Canadian Fact Book on Poverty.* Ottawa: Canadian Council on Social Development.

Statistics Canada (2002). *Income in Canada 2000.* Ottawa: Statistics Canada, Catalogue No. 75-202 XIE, November, 2002.

Statistics Canada. (2000). *People with Low-Income before Tax.* Available online: <http://www.statcan. ca/english/Pgdb/People/Families/famil41a.htm>.

Ternowetsky, G. (2000). *Poverty and Corporate Welfare.* Social Policy Research Unit, Faculty of Social Work, University of Regina.

Webber, M. (1998). *Measuring Low Income and Poverty in Canada: An Update.* Ottawa: Income Statistics Division, Statistics Canada, Catalogue No. 98-13. May 1998.

18

Tilting Toward Marketization

Reform of the Canadian Pension Plan*

GLENN DROVER

Introduction

It's official. Canada is moving into the millennium with a reformed earnings-related Canada Pension Plan (CPP). Like most Canadian reform, the policy shift is subtle and tenuous but it is cautiously tilting toward competitive marketization. The assumption behind the reform, which was legislated in 1998, is that the Canada Pension Plan will be affordable to future generations of young workers and sustainable in the face of an aging population and increasing longevity. The three hallmarks of competitive marketization are: fuller funding, a new investment policy, and changes to benefits and administration. Under the reform, the Canada Pension Plan, initially legislated in 1965, will remain public and mandatory but the change will create a board and an investment policy which are more sensitive to market pressures and less amenable to government interference. Compared to countries which have dumped their public pensions in favour of private mandatory retirement schemes like Chile or optional retirement schemes like the United Kingdom, the Canadian changes are modest but they have received relatively wide spread support from Labour, business and social policy interest groups outside Quebec. Typically, no group is entirely happy with the initiative, some arguing for further marketization, others claiming that the government has weakened its commitment to public provision. But most agree that the reform provides greater public confidence about the financial future of the scheme.

In some respects, the new measures are the result of a statutory review of the Canada Pension Plan which is now required every three years, but fundamentally they are a consequence of pension debates which have been ongoing over two decades. Like most member countries of the Organisation for Economic Co-operation and Development (OECD), retirement support for the elderly of Canada evolved during the early part of the twentieth century and accelerated in importance and in cost during the halcyon years of rapid economic growth during the fifties and sixties. However, since social welfare is constitutionally a responsibility of provincial governments rather than the federal government, a national pension scheme is only possible with the permission of the provinces. Policy changes to the CPP must receive the support of two-thirds of the provinces rep-

---

* This chapter was first published as "Tilting Toward Marketization: Reform of the Canadian Pension Plan," *Review of Policy Research*," 19, 3 (2002): 85–107. Glen Drover, retired, is an Adjunct Professor in the School of Social Work at Carleton University, Ottawa, Canada.

resenting two-thirds of the population of Canada. To some extent, therefore, the review process tends to assure relatively widespread support for changes when and if they come. On the other hand, it also curtails radical or rapid changes of the three tiered provision of Canadian retirement income programs. The CPP is one of those tiers. It is a contributory social insurance scheme which protects against loss of income. The other two tiers are the Old Age Security (OAS) and a Guaranteed Income Supplement (GIS) which provide basic income support and employment based retirement pension plans (RPPs) as well as group and individual registered retirement savings plans (RRSPs) which supplement the CPP on a voluntary basis.[1] In this article, the focus is on the reform of the Canada Pension Plan rather than the other two tiers even though a change in one affects the others. The article examines the CPP in four ways. First, it is placed in an international context. Second, the national context for reform is considered. Third, the technical aspects of the reform are outlined. Fourth, I reflect on the way ahead and offer a conclusion.

International Context

One reason why Canada is tilting toward pension marketization rather than running flat out in favour of privatization is that it already relies on private schemes more heavily than many other OECD countries. Another reason is simply path dependency. Having chosen one policy route in the early post-war period, it takes considerable political will to change path and go in an entirely new direction. To date in Canada, there has been a strong commitment to incremental reform of the CPP rather than wholesale change. Part of the reason for the caution in reducing public pensions in Canada is that by international standards, current (and even projected) contributions and benefits are low. In 1996, when Canadians were contributing 5.6 percent of their earnings toward the CPP, American workers were paying 15.3 percent toward social security (Table 18.1). Because of the lower contributions, Canadian maximum benefits were also 70 percent less than the Americans.

Table 18.1. Comparing the Canada Pension Plan and U.S. Social Security 1996

Social security scheme attributes	CPP (Canadian$)	Social Security (U.S.$)
Combined Worker-Employer Contribution Rate	5.6%	15.3%
Maximum Contributory Earnings	$35,000	$62,700
Maximum Annual Worker Contribution	$893.20	$4796.55
Maximum Annual Employer Contribution	$893.20	$4796.55
Maximum Annual Self-Employed Contribution	$1786.40	$9593.10
Maximum Annual Retirement Pension	$8724.96	$14976.00

Source: National Council of Welfare 1996.

One of the reasons for the large differential in contributions and benefits between Canada and the United States can be attributed to the fact that Canadian retirees also draw upon a flat rate basic benefit (Old Age Security) which supplements the contribution scheme. Hence, the CPP has to be combined with the Old Age Security and sometimes the Guaranteed Income Supplement in order to allow for comparability. When basic income support is taken into account, Canadian workers at the average wage actually have slightly higher benefits than their American counterparts.

However, even when both types of social security expenditures are taken into account, Canadian expenditures are a lower percentage of Gross Domestic Product than many other OECD countries and also replace a low percentage of average wages in comparison with other countries. According to OECD statistics (Table 18.2), they were 5.2 percent and 33 percent respectively in 1995.

Table 18.2. Estimated Public Pension Expenditure and Implicit Replacement Rates 1995 Percent

Country	Expenditure relative to GDP	Implicit replacement rate[1]
United States	4.1	30
Japan	6.6	54
Germany	11.1	46
France	10.6	56
Italy	13.3	49
United Kingdom	4.5	23
Canada	5.2	33
Australia	5.6	30
Austria	8.8	40
Belgium	10.4	63
Denmark	6.8	40
Finland	10.1	65
Iceland	2.5	13
Ireland	3.6	25
Netherlands	6.0	39
New Zealand	5.9	51
Norway	5.2	44
Portugal	7.1	33
Spain	10.0	34
Sweden	11.8	54

Source: OECD 1996.
Note: [1] Implicit replacement rates are calculated as the ratio of average pensions to average wages.

Among the Group of Seven (G-7) countries, Canada was lower than France, Germany, Italy and Japan but slightly higher than the United Kingdom or the United States. In addition, it was lower than all member countries except Australia, Ireland, and New Zealand. Another reason for the caution about change is that Canada has a low percentage of elderly among OECD countries. Hence, the per capita cost of public pensions at a given benefit level is also low. In 1990, among twelve OECD countries, Canada had a lower percentage than any country except Australia and Japan. By the year 2010, it will still to be in the lowest tier with a levelling effect not taking place until the middle of the next century (Table 18.3). Furthermore, administrative costs for public pensions on a per capita basis are relatively low (Table 18.4).

According to a World Bank report (1994), however, there are also some aspects of public pensions in Canada and in other OECD countries which are problematic. Like many public pensions, the CPP is essentially pay-as-you-go. Hence, there are unfunded liabilities which reflect an implicit debt which would have to be met if the CPP were to be closed. In the Canadian case, that unfunded liability is greater than the national debt

Table 18.3. Percentage of Population Over Sixty Years Old, 1990–2050

Country	1990	2000	2010	2020	2030	2050
Australia	15.0	15.3	18.1	22.8	27.7	30.4
Austria	20.2	21.5	24.9	28.9	34.5	33.9
Belgium	20.7	22.5	24.8	28.7	32.2	31.2
Canada	15.6	16.8	20.4	25.9	30.2	30.6
Denmark	20.2	20.4	24.8	28.4	32.1	30.9
Finland	18.4	19.8	24.4	28.7	30.9	29.9
France	18.9	20.2	23.1	26.8	30.1	31.2
Germany	20.3	23.7	26.5	30.3	35.3	32.5
Greece	20.2	24.2	26.5	29.1	32.5	34.4
Iceland	14.5	14.9	17.3	21.4	26.0	29.0
Ireland	15.2	15.7	17.8	20.1	22.9	28.2
Italy	20.6	24.2	27.4	30.6	35.9	36.5
Japan	17.3	22.7	29.0	31.4	33.0	34.4
Luxembourg	19.3	21.2	25.3	29.5	33.0	30.1
Netherlands	17.8	19.0	23.4	28.4	33.4	31.7
New Zealand	15.2	15.9	18.9	22.7	26.8	29.0
Norway	21.2	20.2	22.4	26.0	29.6	30.2
Portugal	18.0	19.8	21.4	24.6	293	33.0
Spain	18.5	20.6	22.4	25.6	30.9	34.2
Sweden	22.9	21.9	25.4	27.8	30.0	28.7
Switzerland	19.9	21.9	26.6	30.5	34.0	31.6
United Kingdom	20.8	20.7	23.0	25.5	29.6	29.5
United States	16.6	16.5	19.2	24.5	28.2	28.9
Simple average	18.6	20.0	23.2	26.9	30.8	31.3
Weighted average	18.2	19.9	23.1	27.0	30.7	31.2

Source: World Bank 1994.

Table 18.4. Comparison of Administrative Costs of Publicity Mandated Pension Schemes

Country	Year	Per member administrative cost/income per capita (percent)	Per member administrative cost in U.S. dollars[1]
Belgium	1986	0.18	20.6
Canada	1989	0.05	10.0
Denmark	1989	0.02	3.9
Finland	1989	0.26	63.7
Germany	1989	0.18	35.9
Italy	1986	0.34	35.6
Japan	1989	0.04	8.3
Luxembourg	1986	0.28	38.1
Netherlands	1989	0.13	20.1
Spain	1989	0.11	10.4
Sweden	1988	0.07	15.5
Switzerland	1991	0.09	28.9
United States	1989	0.05	11.3

Source: World Bank 1994.
Note: [1] The table uses the average exchange rate during each year.

which, at the moment, is larger than all other countries in the G-7 except Italy. The World Bank warns Canada and other OECD countries that current payroll taxes are inadequate either to pay the unfunded liabilities or future obligations. Furthermore, while an implicit debt for public pay-as-you-go pensions schemes is seen by some as a fallacious argument because it does not take into account future growth, it nevertheless is a concern which resonates among the Canadian public, particularly the young. On the other hand, outright replacement of the CPP is also resisted by the Canadian public because the number of active participants in private occupational pensions in Canada as a percentage of the private Labour force is only about 30 percent (Turner and Watanabe, 1995: 111) compared to over 40 percent in the United States, 60 percent in the Netherlands, and 100 percent in France. Therefore, wholesale marketization of the CPP is not only a political challenge but fiscally impractical because of the unfunded liability and the large public debt. Too many people in the country, retired or about to retire, are dependent upon the current system. It cannot be radically altered without widespread disruption.

A more general reason why Canada is leaning toward marketization of the CPP rather than wholesale change is related to the path of welfare reform which the country has followed in the past. Unlike the United States which built social security on Bismarckian social insurance principles, the CPP was built on a foundation of flat rate and income-tested programs. In practice, as Myles and Quadagno (1997) suggest, Canada like many OECD countries can be considered an institutional mix of Beveridge and Bismarck but politically it remains partial to income-tested basic benefits for the elderly coupled with mandatory contributory schemes like the CPP. The first income-tested initiative came with the introduction of the Guaranteed Income Supplement to provide support for the elderly who had few or no CPP benefits. Similarly in the early 1980s when there was considerable pressure to raise CPP benefits in order to increase the earnings-replacement ratio as a way of reducing poverty, the government again turned to the Guaranteed Income Supplement to demonstrate that the issue of poverty could be addressed by simpler means. By the early 1990s, the universal Old Age Security also was subject to income testing through the tax system. In addition, the income tax-back was coupled with de-indexation so that over time the flat rate component declined relative to the income supplement. Similarly, a tax credit for the elderly was recently limited to seniors below an income cut-off.

The use of a guaranteed income principle to provide benefits for the retired has been labelled "Friedman's Revenge" by Myles and Pierson (1997). They also suggest that recent developments in Canada's retirement income system represents a fundamental shift from public to tax expenditures. While the changes have primarily affected the delivery of the basic income support programs, they also provide a basis for the marketization of the Canada Pension Plan because they guarantee a basic income to all seniors below a defined level of income. On the other hand, the advantage of using taxes to offset social security benefits, including benefits from the Canada Pension Plan, is that the system is progressive since all benefits are subject to taxation. A further advantage is that changes in benefits and the income guarantee have largely been funded by transfers within the social security system through cut-backs or claw-backs from high income Canadians. In the future, however, expansion of tax expenditures can only be achieved at the expense of other programs such as the Canada Pension Plan or through further increases in taxes. Hence, while current changes to the CPP are widely touted because they stabilize contributions and provide assurances to current contributors, it is less clear that reform has run its course. Future reform will depend, in part, upon what happens in other OECD countries and close trading partners, particularly the United States.

National Context

The pension system in Canada has its roots in income tested benefits to retired seniors which actually were developed prior to World War II. However, it was only in the 1960s that the Canada Pension Plan was developed. Then as now, the government of the day was headed by the Liberal Party. Then unlike now, the main opposition was the Conservative Party. From the beginning, the two main federal parties took somewhat different positions on pensions, the Liberals emphasizing contributory public pensions and the Conservatives emphasizing basic support along with private pensions. In the federal parliament, the New Democratic Party played a pivotal role in moving the Canadian pension system toward public provision.[2] However, serious limitations in the funding of the Canada Pension Plan, the regressivity of the basic income support programs, and gaps of coverage in the country's private pension plans led to extensive pension debate in the seventies and 1980s. During the debate, many proposals were put forward to reform the retirement income system but conflict between business and labor plus an increasingly lacklustre performance of the Canadian economy and limited political commitment put the push for reform on hold until the late 1980s and early 1990s. Hence, it was not until the past decade that a Conservative government committed to free trade and reduction in the public debt began the slow, difficult task of unravelling universal retirement benefits which have been a part of the Canadian income retirement system since 1951 (Guest, 1980). Prior to the 1990s, there was an age of expansion in the Canadian welfare state including pensions. The late 1980s and early 1990s, under the Conservatives, witnessed the beginning of an age of retrenchment. Moreover, when a Liberal government was re-elected in 1993, the retrenchment policies of the Conservatives were continued and the door was open to a re-examination of the Canada Pension Plan.

In recent years, the stated reasons for the re-examination of the CPP have been changing demographics, the changing labor market, and concerns about the financial solvency of the scheme. Like most countries, Canada is faced with an aging population as fertility rates fall, people live longer, and immigration slows down. In addition, the funding of the Canada Pension Plan is confronted by an age bulge in the Canadian population associated with the baby boomers who were born in the post-war period and who will retire in the first and second decade of the next century. Complicating the general demographics are changes in the labor market (Schellenberg, 1996). Faced with fierce international competition due to globalization and a continental labor market, talented and skilled workers are increasingly comparing job and income prospects in Canada and the United States. Also, the Canadian labor market in the 1990s is increasingly vulnerable due to plant closures in the manufacturing sector, heavy reliance upon the resource sector, growth in contract employment, foreign take-over of companies, and the low value of the Canadian dollar. In addition, levels of productivity are down even though growth rates in the latter half of the 1990s have been above the OECD average. The combined effect of the changes is that Canadian levels of unemployment remain high, jobs are uncertain, laid-off older workers find it difficult to find new employment, total wages and salaries are growing slowly, and workers in general cannot easily save for retirement.

A further complication with the Canada Pension Plan, say the critics, is that it was designed as a pay-as-you-go system when the Canadian labor market was vibrant, when national markets prevailed, when interest rates were low, wages were growing, and birth rates were high. Under current demographic and labor market realities, few of these conditions hold. Hence, the Canada Pension Plan, like most pay-as-you-go schemes around the world, is largely unfunded and the liabilities, as we have seen, exceed the national debt. Moreover, given the shifting demographics, the ability of the plan to finance future beneficiaries will mean much higher rates of contribution. Without reform, young workers currently in the labor market will likely have to pay premiums in excess of real rates of return at the time of their retirement. Not surprisingly, given this prospect, young and not so young workers in Canada feel that the Canada Pension Plan either has to be reformed or phased out. Many of them no longer have confidence that they will benefit from it or that it will even be available to them (Lam, Cutt and Prince, 1997).

On the other hand, there are also misperceptions about the CPP which influence the public policy debate (Dickinson, 1996). The first is that the plan is regressive because benefits for high income workers are more than benefits for low income workers. This in fact is true but the concern is probably misplaced because the objective of the basic income support programs (OAS and GIS) is confused with the objective of the CPP which is income replacement. Hence, people who pay more get more. A related concern is that contribution rates are regressive because low income workers pay proportionately more of their incomes than high income workers because of the low ceiling placed upon pensionable earnings. However, here again, the purpose of the plan is only to provide benefits up to the average wage and on that portion of wages, the taxes are actually progressive because higher income earners pay higher taxes. A third concern is that future workers will have less disposable income than current workers because of the increases required to pay the CPP in the future. That, however, is only likely to happen in very unusual circumstances where there are high rates of tax increases and very limited economic growth. With even modest rates of growth, future standards of living are likely to be higher than current standards. Another concern expressed often in the public debate is that the CPP is approaching bankruptcy because of the problem of unfunded liability and adding to the public debt. However, this concern too is a misunderstanding since a public plan cannot be bankrupt in the legal sense provided future contribution rates cover future obligations. Moreover, "unlike the real national debt, the CPP's unfunded liability has yet to be spent" (Dickinson, 1996: 214).

Given the challenges of underfunding and public misperception, the federal government issued a consultation paper on the Canada Pension Plan in 1996 in co-operation with the provincial and territorial governments (Federal, Provincial and Territorial Governments of Canada 1996). In the report, the government proposed several ways to strengthen the plan. One was to move from a pay-as-you-go system of financing toward fuller funding such that future benefits could be met without ongoing increases in contributions beyond a fixed or "steady-state" premium. A second was to reduce benefits as a percentage of average wages from 25 percent to 22 percent. A third was to extend the years of contributions which would be required to achieve a full pension at retirement.

A fourth was to raise the age of entitlement from 65 to 70. A fifth was to move from fully indexed to partially indexed benefits. A sixth was to increase investment earnings by moving from non-marketable government securities to a diversified portfolio. Still another was to broaden the income base upon which contributions would be made so that the system would be closer, for example, to the United States. With these proposals in tow, the governments consulted across the country and quickly learned that Canadians wanted to preserve and protect the Canada Pension Plan as one of the pillars of the retirement income system but were divided in the way in which they thought that could happen. Spokespeople for labor and low income Canadians stated that the CPP should be expanded. Seniors opposed reductions and restrictions but accepted the need for sustainable funding. Most business and pension professionals called for changes which combined reductions in benefits with increases in contributions but some preferred privatization or full funding (Federal, Provincial and Territorial CPP Consultations Secretariat, 1996).

Table 18.5. Comparing the Existing and Proposed Schedule of Contribution Rates

Year	Existing Schedule Combined Rate %	Proposed Schedule Combined Rate %	Increase or decrease in combined rate percentage points
1997	5.85	6.0	0.15
1998	6.10	6.4	0.30
1999	6.35	7.0	0.65
2000	6.60	7.8	1.20
2001	6.85	8.6	1.75
2002	7.10	9.4	2.30
2003	7.35	9.9	2.55
2004	7.60	9.9	2.30
2005	7.85	9.9	2.05
2006	8.10	9.9	1.80
2016	10.1	9.9	-0.20
2030	14.2[*1]	9.9	-4.30

Source: CPP, Securing the Canada Pension Plan 1997.
Note: [1]The existing legislated 25-year schedule does not go beyond 2016. The chief actuary of the CPP has projected that the rate would have to continue to rise to reach a combined rate of 14.2% in 2030 to cover growing expenditures.

Reform

In the end, the three levels of government decided, in response to public pressure, to take a compromise position. They did not accept the principle of privatization or full funding but they did agree to move toward marketization in the form of fuller funding, new investment policies, and greater accountability to the Canadian public through "arm's length" administration.[3] Fuller funding will be achieved in two ways. First, the contribution rate will rise from 6 percent in 1997 to 9.9 percent in six years (Table 18.5).

By moving quickly rather than slowly, it is intended that the contribution rate will cover the costs of benefits for current contributors plus a proportion of the unfunded liability that built up in the early years of the pay-as-you-go system. Second, the plan will move to fuller funding by moving toward a principle of paying contributions on the full amount of earnings by freezing the low income exemption at the current value of CC$3500 rather than allowing it to increase with average wages. The effect, like de-indexation of benefits, will be to lower the value of the exemption overtime. The effect of fuller funding is that reserve funds of the CPP will grow significantly from two years of benefits to five years of benefits (Canada Pension Plan, 1997). These, in turn, will be used to keep contribution rates at a steady-state provided that returns on investments generate a real rate of return of about four percent (that is, a rate of four percent above the rate of inflation).

Reaching the new investment target will be no mean achievement. Past rates of return have been about half that level. Nevertheless, the new rate is considered realistic because it is based on rates of return in the Quebec Pension Plan which since its inception has operated like the Canada Pension Plan except for the method of investment. In the Quebec Pension Plan, unlike the Canada Pension Plan, surplus funds have been invested in a diversified portfolio in order to generate funds for economic development in the province (Office of the Superintendent of Financial Institutions, 1998). CPP investments, by contrast, have been invested in non-marketable securities of provincial governments and paid back at the prevailing federal bond rate rather than prevailing rates in the capital market. The impact of this policy, as some commentators noted, has been a lower rate of return on the CPP than would have been achieved if the funds had been invested in capital markets. More importantly, it has also meant that the accumulated funds available for distribution in the CPP were estimated to be 21 percent to 26 percent less than they might otherwise have been if the real rate of return were higher than provincial securities (Table 18.6).

Table 18.6. Varying the Real Rate of Investment Return

Increase in the Real Rate of Investment Return	Increase in Accumulated Funds at Age 65
From 1 % to 2%	21.0 %
From 2 % to 3%	22.1 %
From 3 % to 4%	23.2 %
From 4 % to 5%	24.3 %
From 5 % to 6%	25.3 %
From 6 % to 7%	26.2 %

Source: Lam, Prince and Cutt 1996.
Assumptions: 7 percent contribution rate; 40 years of contributions; retirement at age 65.

Coupled with a concern about the rapid increase in the contribution rate over a short period of time (combined with a diversified investment portfolio) is the potential impact on the Canadian capital markets. It is estimated that assets which are currently in the range of CDN$36 billion (1998) will double by the year 2004 and quadruple by the year 2010 (Office of the Superintendent of Financial Institutions, 1998) making the CPP one of the largest players in the capital markets. The sums are so great that they could distort Canada's capital markets where, according to legislation, most of the funds must be invested. To alleviate the concern of finance analysts, the federal government has legislated two new governance structures to ensure sound fund management (*Canada Pension Plan Investment Act* 1997). Under the legislation, the fund will be managed professionally at arm's length from the government by a board of twelve directors drawn from different regions of the country and having proven financial ability. The investment board is accountable to the public as well as to the government and will report regularly on the state of CPP pensions and will be subject to federal-provincial reviews every three years. In addition, the federal government, which will continue to administer the benefits, will model the administration of private pension plans by basing benefits on the average of the last five years of earnings, shortening the application period, improving verification procedures, and minimizing overpayments. The effect of these changes, it is claimed, will reduce administrative costs by nine percent compared to what they would have been otherwise (Canada Pension Plan, 1997). The overall impact of the changes can been appreciated by reference to Table 18.7 where comparisons are drawn between the old and the new CPP in relation to the reserve fund, contribution rates, the exemption level, investment policy, provincial borrowing, age of retirement, and indexation.

Table 18.7. Existing CPP and New CPP Proposals

	Existing CPP	New CPP Proposals
Reserve fund	Equal to two years of benefits and declining	Growing to five years of benefits
Contribution rates	Rising to 10.1 % by 2016	Rising to 9.9 % by 2003, then held steady
	Projected to increase to 14.2 % in 2030	Will not rise above 9.9%
Year's basic exemption	Currently $3,500 indexed to wages	Frozen at $3,500
Year's maximum pensionable earnings (YMPE)	Indexed to wages	No change
Investment policy	Invested in non-negotiable provincial bonds	New funds invested in a diversified portfolio of securities
Provincial borrowing	Provinces borrow at federal rates	Limited provincial borrowings at their own market rates
Normal retirement	Age 65	No change
Early retirement	Starting at age 60	No change
Late retirement	Up to age 70	No change

Source: CPP, Securing the Canada Pension Plan 1997.

The Way Ahead

The introduction of fuller funding and diversified investment have alleviated the most pressing problems of the Canada Pension Plan but they have, according to the critics, not fundamentally changed the scheme. Fuller funding does not mean full funding, only that future expenditures will be brought in line with future revenues without continually increasing the rates. The greater part of the unfunded liability which has built up from the start of the CPP (about CDN$570 billion) remains unpaid. In addition, the "steady-state" contribution rate presupposes favourable economic conditions into the future as well as real benefits which do not substantially increase beyond the rate of inflation. For all these reasons, critics, like William Robson of the C.D. Howe Institute (1996), argue that the CPP remains a pay-as-you-go system in spite of the reform. Hence, he suggests that without termination of the plan, politicians will be tempted again in the future to provide generous pensions in return for meager contributions. Hence, he proposes that the CPP be terminated and replaced by a universal private system based on money purchase accounts like those available in Chile. The big financial challenge of closing down the CPP, as Robson acknowledges, it to pay the unfunded liability.

To solve the problem, he claims that the money which is owed to participants in the current CPP can be paid through further increases in premiums. Second, he thinks that there are few institutional problems in replacing the CPP by money purchase schemes because Canada already has an extensive system of employment based registered retirement pensions and individual, as well as group, based registered retirement savings plans. Third, he claims that private mandatory schemes can, like public pensions, cover all workers and assure portability of funds. Fourth, he argues that inflation protection can be provided either by eliminating restrictions on foreign investments or by the government issuing bonds with guarantees of real rates of interest. Fifth, because of the availability of a basic income security for low income retirees through Old Age Security and the Guaranteed Income Supplement, he is convinced that there would be protection for anyone who for a variety of reasons (sickness, disability, death of a spouse) falls outside the mandatory system. Finally, he argues that the transitional costs from CPP to a new system would be financially manageable if the change were phased in over a period of ten years. An advantage of moving in that direction, aside from having pensions which are fully funded, is that it also positions Canada in international financial markets by relieving governments of accumulated fiscal obligations.

Thomas Courchene (1997), a well-known economist and policy analyst in Canada, also worries about the unfunded liability of the CPP. However, he feels that Robson's solution for eliminating the CPP is inadequate, partly because he attempts to solve the problems within the confines of the scheme, partly because its elimination would reinforce the increasing polarization of incomes through heavy reliance on private pensions. According to Courchene, the problem of the CPP is related to intergenerational equity as much as it is to financial credibility. His solution to intergenerational equity is to introduce age-related premiums to assure that benefits are tied more closely to contributions with younger workers paying less than older workers. His solution to the lack of financial credibility of the CPP and the unfunded liability is to shift the burden out of the public pension onto the tax system. In that way, rather than passing the unfunded liability onto future generations, as we have done in the past, it can be shared by all taxpayers, present and future or by targeting certain taxes which are logically related to retirement. This could include taxes on CPP payment or taxes deferred on subsidized savings such as Register Retirement Savings Plans after the official age of retirement (65), or even a levy of duty and inheritance taxes similar to those which exist in the United States but which to date, Canada has avoided or minimized. By moving in this direction, Courchene seems to support the current reform of the CPP but thinks that the way ahead is to pay down the unfunded liability through general or targeted taxation.

Monica Townson, another economist, disagrees with both Robson and Courchene. Writing for the National Council on Ageing, she defends the Canada Pension Plan and opposes the move toward increasing reliance on private pensions or money purchase plans in Canada (1994). Townson feels that concerns about demography and dependency rates which form the basis for much of the policy debate about pensions for retirees are overstated. Instead of focusing on the dependency rates for the elderly in isolation, she argues that it is necessary to look at the dependency rate for the young and the old together (the total dependency rate). When she does that, she notes that even until the middle of the next century, the projected total rate in Canada will be less than it was in the early period of the twentieth century. With respect to the CPP, she also thinks that in the future, the commitment should be stronger than it is at present, partly because such a commitment reflects a shared commitment to retirees, partly because occupational pension plans in Canada cover less than 50 percent of workers (Townson, 1997). While Townson does not appear to be opposed to fuller funding of the CPP, she is opposed to its replacement by private schemes and to the payment of the unfunded liability on the grounds that the latter is a bogus argument (since it negates the impact of future economic growth and the role of government). Her preference is to put the CPP on a sounder financial foundation by increasing the contribution rate and bringing it closer to the contributions made by American retirees in their social security system. She claims that the CPP could also be funded by placing stricter limits on tax assistance to private retirement savings such as the RRSPs which generally benefit high income Canadians. Another argument she advances in favour of the CPP is that it is more beneficial to women than private schemes because women are in and out of the labor market more than men. In the end, she feels that the future development and provision of public pensions depends less on economics than political commitment. For her, the issue ahead is not financial solvency but ideology and political debate.

Conclusion

In the future, as in the past, reform of Canada's income retirement system, including the Canada Pension Plan, will be undertaken with caution. During the post-war decades, the retirement income schemes were constructed to meet the needs of the elderly for income replacement and income support without diminishing economic development. As a result, they have the burden of protecting the incomes of all retirees in the country while also having an overall impact on savings, investments and growth. Economically, pensions are a major source of funds for capital markets and private development in Canada as they are in other countries. Politically, their beneficiaries represent some of the more powerful political constituencies in the country, and politicians approach questions of reform with considerable care. However, in the future, that care has to be matched by attention, not only to beneficiaries but also to the impact which reform has on Canada's competitive position in the global economy. Just as globalization has fundamentally changed the role of the welfare state so also it has changed the capacity of each country to reform retirement income programs and other social policies in isolation from the changes which are taking place among trading partners. In that respect, the Canada Pension Plan is particularly vulnerable to international pressure because it has a direct impact on labor and capital markets which are themselves increasingly globalized.

Not surprisingly, therefore, the most controversial aspects of the reform of the CPP have been the unfunded liabilities and the move toward fuller funding. Looked at from the perspective of those who defend a pay-as-you-go system of payment, there is little need to move toward fuller funding because future premiums will not be high by international standards. In addition, they argue that a shift to fuller funding undermines the principle of intergenerational equity which is foundational to public provision. On the other hand, those who make the case for full funding say that a pay-as-you-go system is no longer viable in a global economy because it undermines Canada's competitive position by fostering inflexibility in the labor market, reducing the rate of savings, and lowering levels of productivity.

A complication with the ongoing debate is that neither side brings much evidence to substantiate its position and relies heavily on political persuasion or economic logic rather than hard data. Hence, the current reform is a compromise between the two positions, recognizing, at the same time, the need to promote social cohesion and to accommodate, or appear to accommodate, international pressure. Fundamentally, though, what is at stake in the future is the role of the public sector in the provision of retirement income. If the Canadian state is only to provide a regulatory framework for private provision, there will be little room for the CPP. If it serves primarily to assure the redistribution of income rather than intergenerational transfers, again the CPP seems to be largely out of step with the times. If, however, the Canadian state continues to play an important role in promoting intergenerational equity, either because it is necessary to ensure that individuals save sufficiently for retirement or because the private sector is likely to balk at mandatory provision, the CPP will continue to be a third pillar of the Canadian retirement income system. Along with basic income support such as Old Age Security and the Guaranteed Income Supplement as well as private pensions and savings such as Retirement Pension Plans and Registered Retirement Savings Plans, the Canada Pension Plan will be important to future retirees.

Notes

1. The bottom tier, the OAS and GIS, is similar to, but more developed than the Supplemental Security Income (SSI) of the United States or the flat-rate portion of the National Insurance scheme in the United Kingdom. The second tier, the CCP, is similar to, but less developed than the Old Age Security and Disability Insurance (OASDI) in the United States or the State Earnings-Related Pension Schemes (SERPs) in the United Kingdom. Unlike the U.K., beneficiaries cannot contract-out under the CPP. The third tier, the RPPs and the RRSPs, is similar to group or individual savings initiatives like the 401(k) salary reduction plans (which are defined after the section of the Internal Revenue Code which enabled them) and Individual Retirement Accounts (IRAs) of the United States or Individual Savings Accounts (ISAs) of the United Kingdom.

2. The federal government in Canada has been dominated by the Liberal Party since the thirties. Its control over government is however continuously contested. For much of the post war period, the main opposition has been the Conservative Party. Its longest term of office was from 1984 to 1993. During its brief stay in office, it passed the Canada United States Free Trade Agreement and the North American Free Trade Agreement. In addition, it challenged the universal principles of the Canadian welfare state. The unpopularity of these measures virtually wiped the federal Conservative Party from the electoral map. As a consequence, the Conservatives were replaced in large measure by the Reform Party. Two other federal parties

are the New Democratic Party (representing the social democratic left) and the Parti Québecois representing separatist interests in Québec.

3. The Canada Pension Plan protects workers against loss of income due to retirement, disability, and death. Hence, in addition to retirement benefits for contributors to the plan, it provides flat rate benefits to workers who become disabled as well as surviving spouses. Some critics of the Canada Pension Plan feel that these provisions weaken the social insurance principle of the CPP since they substitute income support for income replacement. In this article, the subsidiary debate about these provisions is not addressed. The focus is on the impact of changes for regular retirement pensions. They represent about 65 percent of CPP payments (Canada, 1994).

References

Ascah, L. 1991. *The Great Canadian Pension Debate: Federal and Provincial Pension Reform*. Ottawa: Canadian Centre for Policy Alternatives.

Canada Pension Plan. 1997. *Securing the Canada Pension Plan: Agreement on Proposed Changes to the CPP*. Ottawa: Human Resources Development Canada.

Courchene, T. J. 1997. "Generation X vs. Generation XS: Reflections on the Way Ahead." In Banting, K.G. and Boadway, R. eds., *Reform of Retirement Income Policy: International and Canadian Perspectives*. Kingston: Queen's University, School of Policy Studies.

Davis, E.P. 1995. *Pension Funds: Retirement-Income Security and Capital Markets*. Oxford: Clarendon Press.

Dickinson, Paul. 1996. "Six Common Misperceptions about the Canada Pension Plan." In Burbidge, J. ed., *When We're 65*. Montreal: C.D. Howe Institute.

Federal, Provincial and Territorial Governments of Canada. 1996. *An Information Paper for Consultations on the Canada Pension Plan*. Ottawa: Department of Finance.

Federal, Provincial and Territorial CPP Consultations Secretariat. 1996. *CPP: Report on the Canada Pension Plan Consultations*. Ottawa: Department of Finance.

Guest, D. 1980. *The Emergence of Social Security in Canada*. Vancouver: University of British Columbia Press.

Human Resources Development Canada. 1994. *Basic Facts on Social Security Programs*. Ottawa: Ministry of Supply and Services Canada.

Lam, N., Cutt, J. and Prince, M. 1997. "The Canadian Pension Plan: Retrospect and Prospect." In Banting, K.G. and Boadway, R., eds., *Reform of Retirement Income Policy: International and Canadian Perspectives*. Kingston: Queen's University, School of Policy Studies.

Lam, N., Cutt, J. and Prince, M. 1996. "Restoring the Canada Pension Plan: Simulating the Future and Stimulating the Social Security Debate." In Burbidge, J. ed., *When We're 65*, Montreal: C.D. Howe Institute.

Murphy, M. 1996. "Implications of an Ageing Society and Changing Labour Market: Demographics." In Caledon Institute of Social Policy, *Roundtable on Canada's Ageing Society and Retirement Income System*. Ottawa: Caledon Institute.

Myles, J. and Pierson, P. 1997. *Friedman's Revenge: The Reform of 'Liberal' Welfare States in Canada and the United States*. Ottawa: Caledon Institute of Social Policy.

Myles, J. and Quadagno, J. 1997. "Recent Trends in Public Pension Reform: A Comparative View." In Banting, K.G. and Boadway, R. eds., *Reform of Retirement Income Policy: International and Canadian Perspectives*. Kingston: Queen's University, School of Policy Studies.

National Council of Welfare. 1996. *Improving the Canada Pension Plan*. Ottawa: National Council of Welfare.

Office of the Superintendent of Financial Institutions. 1998. *Canada Pension Plan: Seventeenth Actuarial Report*. Ottawa: Office of the Superintendent of Financial Institutions.

Organization for Economic Co-operation and Development. 1996. *OECD Economic Surveys 1995–1996: Canada*. Paris: OECD.

Robson, W.B.P. 1996. "Putting Some Gold in the Golden Years: Fixing the Canada Pension Plan." *C.D. Howe Institute Commentary* 76.

Robson, W.B.P. 1997. *The Future of Pension Policy: Individual Responsibility and State Support.* Ottawa: British-North American Committee.

Schellenberg, G. 1996. "Implications of an Ageing Society and Changing Labour Market: Labour Market." In Caledon Institute of Social Policy, *Roundtable on Canada's Ageing Society and Retirement Income System.* Ottawa: Caledon Institute.

Townson, M. 1994. *The Social Contract for Seniors in Canada: Preparing for the 21st Century.* Ottawa: National Advisory Council on Ageing.

Townson, M. 1997. "The Way Ahead." In Banting, K.G. and Boadway, R. eds., *Reform of Retirement Income Policy: International and Canadian Perspectives.* Kingston: Queen's University, School of Policy Studies.

Turner, J. and Watanabe, N. 1995. *Private Pension Policies in Industrialised Countries.* Kalamazoo, Michigan: W.E. Upjohn Institute for Employment Research.

Walsh, M. 1997. *Reforming the Canada Pension Plan.* Kingston: Queen's University, Industrial Relations Centre.

World Bank. 1994. *Averting The Old Age Crisis: Policies to Protect the Old and Promote Growth.* New York: World Bank Policy Research Report, Oxford University Press.

19

Canadian Disability Policy

*Still a Hit-and-Miss Affair**

MICHAEL J. PRINCE

A QUARTER CENTURY AGO, a major Canadian study on policies and programs for people with disabilities was aptly entitled "A Hit-and-Miss Affair" (Brown, 1977). Prepared for the Canadian Council on Social Development, the inquiry sought to discover what was happening in services and programs for people with physical disabilities across the country. Looking at the total policy system, Brown found that the network of policies for Canadians with disabilities was not functioning effectively. Gaps in service provision, late referrals and inadequate follow-up programs, insufficient linkages among social programs, and incomplete information systems were among the barriers. Brown concluded her study with two strong impressions: "The first was that there is a lively awareness of the many deficiencies in policies for disabled people in Canada together with a desire for constructive change. The second was a strong sense of frustration that the need to change is not being given an adequate priority at the level where decisions must be made" (Brown, 1977: 548). A growing awareness of the need for change coupled with a strong frustration with inadequate policy action meant that addressing the needs and rights of Canadians with disabilities was a hit-and-miss affair.

This description of the policy setting, I will argue, remains a fair portrayal of Canadian disability programs and services, especially from the perspective of groups of, and for, persons with disabilities. Why has there been relatively slow movement on the disability agenda in Canada in recent decades? To explore this question, this paper examines reports and observations by various disability community groups and parliamentary committees that critique the Canadian government's disability policy record since the early 1980s, spanning the International Year of Disabled Persons of 1981 to the current context in the early 2000s.[1] The slow pace of reform is evident by what I call the "déjà vu discourse" on disability reform and the disability issues circle.

Traditionally, disability studies as a field of inquiry included relatively little analysis of public sector governance and related policy processes. Canadian social science was a clear example of this custom that, happily, is changing with major contributions to problematizing the way people with disabilities and their experiences have been studied or ignored (Bickenbach, 1993; Enns, 1999; Titchkosky, 2000 and 2003; Cameron and Valentine, 2001). A key premise of this article is that matters of governance and public policy are major determinants of the sluggish pace of reform. The paper therefore identifies several interrelated

---

* This chapter was first published as "Canadian Disability Policy: Still a Hit-and-Miss Affair," Canadian *Journal of Sociology/Cahiers canadiens de sociologie* 29, 1 (2004): 59–82.

factors for why we are still a long way from meeting disability policy commitments on the Canadian government's agenda. Foucault's concepts of bio-politics and governmentality are used to inform the analysis and interpretation of this state of affairs. Following Foucault, the paper asks: what is conducting our conduct of people with disabilities in Canada? What, in other terms, is governing the governance of disability issues and claims?

The Significance of Disabilities and Disability Studies: Sociological and Otherwise

Disability is a personal experience and public issue of great significance in Canada. In 2001, an estimated 3.6 million people in Canada, or 12.4 percent of the population, reported some level and type of disability. For the purposes of this national survey, persons with disabilities are those persons with reported difficulties with daily living activities, or who indicated that a mental or physical condition or a health problem reduced the kind or amount of activities they could do.[2] Evidence in Canada and other countries suggests that both the number and severity of disabilities increases with age. As the population ages over the coming decades, the incidence of disability can be expected to increase as well. In the adult population in 2001, among Canadians aged 15 and over, an estimated 14.6 percent reported a disability; of those in the 45 to 64 age group, an estimated 16.7 percent reported a disability; and, among seniors, 40.5 percent reported a disability. Among Aboriginal peoples in Canada, almost one-third of adults report a disability, more than twice the national average (Canada, 2002; Statistics Canada, 2002). Compared to persons without disabilities, adults with disabilities in Canada tend to have lower levels of education, far higher rates of unemployment, lower earnings, and lower household incomes. Persons with disabilities face further serious challenges of accessibility and affordability of housing, health care, transportation, learning, training, and employment opportunities (Rioux and Prince, 2002).

As a field of academic inquiry, disability studies, while multidisciplinary, has a strong sociological foundation, paying close attention to the dynamics and interrelationships among various institutions, groups, and societal practices and processes (Barnes, Oliver and Barton, 2002; Prince, 2001a). Disability studies and disability policies relate directly to central issues in contemporary sociology: stigma, normalcy and the role of the body; the politics of identity, recognition and difference; conceptual and discursive practices of power; and challenges of framing and achieving social change (Goffman, 1963; Kallen, 1989; Morris, 1992; Titchkosky, 2000, 2001 and 2003; Turner, 1986).

In examining the welfare state, the role of bureaucracies, and the struggles for citizenship, disability studies contributes to Canadian perspectives on political sociology, public administration, and social policy (Baer, 2002; Cameron and Valentine, 2001; Prince, 2002; Rioux and Prince, 2002). A political sociology perspective, for instance, recognizes the unequal distribution of power and influence in policy processes and governance regimes. It acknowledges that certain individuals and groups are economically and socially disadvantaged; and, that the politics of policy reform include both the organized mobilization for, and resistance to social change.

A socio-political model of disability fits well with this outlook. This model holds that attitudinal, economic market, legal, and policy barriers, rather than physical and developmental limitations, are the main difficulties preventing people with disabilities from participating fully in society (Oliver, 1990; Finkelstein, 1980; Zola, 1982). In this model, reform concentrates on altering environmental barriers, changing attitudes, and programs, plus advancing human rights. The focus of analysis and action, therefore, is on the state and ruling practices rather than solely, or even primarily, on individuals with disabilities and their families. Thus, disability studies promises empirical and theoretical payoffs for social scientists working in this or other policy domains.

Conceptual Framework: The Governmentality of Disability Policy

Fox and Willis (1989: 1) describe the phrase disability policy as "a convenient and recognizable, though still inadequate way, to characterize interventions that seek to enable people with impairments to live in ways that are personally satisfying and socially useful." From this conventional perspective, as they call it, disability policy is about methods and processes, and about what interventions are available or desirable. Disability is identified as a category of social need and as a threat to personal well-being and family security. Disability policy-making is about formulating programs and providing services for people in need who have disabilities or who are at risk of developing a disabling condition. In turn, disability policy analysis involves describing and explaining the goals, instruments, and processes of these interventions.

By contrast, from the perspective of people with disabilities, disability policy is about addressing results and focusing on "what people aspire, or could aspire, to do." Disability policy-making is, or should be, about "enabling people to function in and contribute to society" and about addressing "what individuals should be enabled to do for themselves and for others" (Fox and Willis, 1989: 3). Thus, policy analysis from this perspective involves examining and assessing the impact of all programs on the aspirations and capacities of people with disabilities, their families and related networks. This can be described as a disability perspective.

While aspects of both the conventional and disability perspectives are evident, the argument presented here is that the traditional perspective still dominates Canadian policies, programs, and popular discourse. Disability policy in Canada traditionally has been, and remains largely today, a dimension of the health, education, social services, and income security fields. But it is more than these programs. Along with providing programs and services, redistributing income, and regulating behaviours, disability policy entails constructing a discourse through the creation of structures and practices. The official delineation of disability policy in terms of vocabulary, scope, and priority is a fundamental part of the governance process.

This article offers a critique of the official textual representation of Canada's disability policy record over the last 20 years, drawing on Michel Foucault's concepts of bio-politics and governmentality. Disability policy is surely an aspect of what Foucault termed bio-politics, that is, to the strategic organization of power and knowledge to manage health problems and needs, among other issues, in the life of individuals and of the population (Foucault, 1980; Tremain, 2001; Titchkosky, 2003). Obvious examples in disability services are the needs of parents caring for children with disabilities for a range of technical and medical supports, personal respite, and other resources.

Governmentality, in Foucault's words, is "the conduct of our conduct" (Foucault, 1980). A central insight of Foucault is that the modern state is not a singular entity nor is it an omnipotent leviathan. People are citizens of a state rather than subjects of a sovereign (Burchell, Gordon and Miller, 1991; Dean, 1999; Martin, Gutman and Hutton, 1988). Though still a powerful institution in modern societies, the state both divides and shares governing power. Sovereignty has given way to governmentality, yielding a network of explicit and hidden power relations. Rules and practices governing individuals operate in and through various state and non-state institutions, organizations, tactics, and procedures. The population is the primary object of political action, with state activities designed at managing the economic life, health, civil order, and social mores of society. With this focus on bio-politics, the state becomes "governmentalized," that is, more administrative in orientation, structure, and work. Power is exercised by inducing people to seek self-improvement and advancement. It is also exercised through a political and bureaucratic rationality depicting, and thus controlling, people by the use of countless categories and sub-categories for the purposes of policy and program eligibility or exclusion (Faubian, 1994). Persons with disabilities are thus constructed as a "unit of the population—deserving special attention, but always with reference to ... the larger social aggregate" (Clifford, 2001:111).

With the administrative state exists a dominant discourse, an organization of knowledge, based on values, interests, and practices associated with the market economy and medical science. These ways of framing issues and labelling people are encoded in files and records across the ensemble of institutions and organizations in society. As we will see, this governing discourse contains strategic accounts of what has happened to date in disability policy reform, what the status quo therefore looks like according to those in government, and what possible actions may lay ahead.

Canada's Disability Policy Record: 1981 to 2001

Frustration and disappointment are two major themes running through studies by advocacy groups, community service organizations, and legislative reports on Canadian disability policy over the past two decades. Repeated reports by parliamentary committees at the federal level, along with reports by national disability organizations, Aboriginal groups, reviews by academics, and children's rights groups tend to be unfavorable (Council of Canadians with Disabilities, 1996 and 1999). They are disapproving of inaction by government on many disability issues, the incomplete implementation of promised reforms, and the apparent inattention by government officials to the adverse effects of other policy decisions on people with disabilities. In addition, groups are critical of the disconnection between children with disabilities and their families from both the broader disability agenda and the National Children's Agenda (Prince, 2002).

"In critical ways," the Standing Committee on Human Rights and the Status of Disabled Persons (House of Commons, 1990a: 5) observed, the "achievements of the 1980s lived up to expectations. Pre-eminent among the advances for persons with disabilities was constitutional recognition. The inclusion of disabled persons in Section 15(1) and (2) of the Canadian Charter of Rights and Freedoms remains an outstanding achievement of Canadian governments—both federal and provincial." In fact, the authors of the achievement were disability groups. The original version of the Charter, proposed by the federal government in October 1980 did not include any reference to "mental and physical disability" as specific grounds of discrimination. The phrase was added to the final version of April 1981 after strong and persistent lobbying by disability organizations, which was supported by other social groups. The successful inclusion of this Charter guarantee of equality came from their struggle (Boyce, et al. 2001). The Standing Committee also said of the 1980s, "we have seen new levels of awareness and sincere, if sometimes, patronizing goodwill. While there have been some noteworthy achievements, progress has overall been modest.... Sadly, the range of issues remains substantially undiminished.... What is plainly needed now is action" (House of Commons, 1990a: 1, 3). In a follow-up report, later that year the Committee frankly stated in reply to a government response to their earlier report: "A convincing message that the government means business is still needed in the area of disability.... Disabled persons are not, and have not been, a priority. Our report also sets out how successive governments have been ineffective in carrying out actions that would demonstrate priority action" (House of Commons, 1990b: 3, 4).

Five years later, the Standing Committee on Human Rights and the Status of Disabled Persons offered a blunt assessment of the 1991–96 National Strategy for the Integration of Disabled Persons, close to winding up at that stage. The Committee concluded that, "the National Strategy was not a 'strategy' but a series of 'tactics.' Consequently, the problems of leadership, coordination, and collaboration for various players within the government remain unsolved" (House of Commons, 1995: 11). Rather than a regime of policy coordination, the federal strategy was seen to be a loose set of marginal programmatic activities. A leading text on Canadian social policy reached a similar conclusion at around the same time: "Canada has no overall framework for social justice for persons with disabilities and, unlike for seniors or the unemployed, has never aspired to build one" (Armitage, 1996: 76).

These critiques and, more importantly, similar criticisms coming loudly from the disability community prompted the federal government to establish a Task Force on Disability Issues in 1996. The creation of the Task Force on Disability Issues was prompted by the federal government's response to the House of Commons Standing Committee report on the National Strategy for the Integration of Persons with Disabilities. The government response put forward the message, echoed by the then Minister of Human Resources Development Canada (HRDC), Doug Young, that there was little if any future role for the federal government in disability issues. This created considerable unrest in the disability community, and among Liberal MPs. This political backlash to Ottawa's apparent retreat on disability policy led to the involvement of the Prime Minister's Office and the idea of creating the Task Force.

A submission to the Task Force by the Council of Canadians with Disabilities argued a position shared by many other groups. The Council stated that Ottawa had abandoned Canadians with disabilities and that disability issues were conspicuously absent from Canada's political agenda (Council of Canadians with Disabilities, 1996). Largely in response to this critique and associated lobbying, in October 1998, the federal, provincial and territorial governments released "In Unison: A Canadian Approach to Disability Issues." Articulating what government officials called a "new approach" to disability issues, the document speaks of governments agreeing to work toward a "holistic and multisectoral approach to reform" (Federal-Provincial-Territorial Ministers Responsible for Social Services, 1998).

In November 1999, a coalition of disability organizations presented to Canadian governments "A National Strategy for Persons with Disabilities: The Community Definition." "In recent years," the coalition noted, "the community of persons with disabilities has witnessed an approach to disability issues which is piecemeal and uncoordinated, favoring 'disability initiatives' and 'special projects' which do not have sufficient scope or depth to achieve the equality promised in the Charter of Rights and Freedoms" (Council of Canadians with Disabilities, 1999: 1). Here the coalition is touching on governmentality, on the way governments in Canada conceptualize their conduct of disability issues. The coalition's concern is that the federal and provincial governments are approaching disability from the conventional perspective (Fox and Willis, 1989) with a series of specific interventions to address specific needs, rather than adopt a human rights and equality perspective.

"In Unison" and related government documents are responding chiefly to persons with disabilities of working age, largely ignoring issues concerning children with disabilities and their families. A November 1999 report from the Canadian Coalition for the Rights of Children entitled "How Does Canada Measure Up?" was sharply critical of the treatment of various groups of children, especially children with disabilities. The Coalition argued that children with disabilities have varying opportunities to live full and decent lives and the supports they need are not considered an entitlement but are framed as a private privilege. Many families of children with disabilities do not receive adequate assistance. Early identification of needs and the provision of suitable services are not universally available, and the right to appropriate education in the most enabling environment is not guaranteed. Parliamentarians have tended to agree with such critiques. In June 2001, a joint report from the Sub-Committee on Children and Youth at Risk and the Sub-Committee on the Status of Persons with Disabilities concluded that, "while progress may be occurring, it is painfully slow and not without setbacks" (House of Commons, 2001: 14).

The Déjà-Vu Discourse on Disability Reform

After two decades of disability policy-making, there is a strong sense that we have been here before. I call this phenomenon the déjà-vu discourse of disability. It entails the official declaration of plans and promises by governments and other public authorities, followed by external reviews of the record, and then official responses with a reiteration of previously stated plans and promises. To illustrate this déjà-vu discourse on disability reform, two examples are presented; first, policies for Aboriginal children with disabilities; and second, the idea of a disability lens for the policy process. Both cases, while briefly presented, exemplify a broader pattern of ideas proposed before by a number of committees and task forces.

Policies for Aboriginal Children with Disabilities

In a follow-up to their Obstacles Report, the House of Commons Special Committee first addressed the matter of native people and disabilities in the early 1980s. The Committee concluded there was considerable evidence to show that "federal departments do not consult among themselves in a systematic fashion when implementing policies and programs which affect Native people." The effect of this non-consultation, the Committee pointed out, was "wasted money and effort on the Government side, and confusion and mistrust on the part of those Native persons whom the efforts are intended to help" (House of Commons, 1981a: 11, 12).

The next parliamentary report on Aboriginal people with disabilities, called *Completing the Circle*, was released in 1993. This report echoed the problems of confusion and mistrust identified in the first report of the early 1980s: "Arbitrary legal classifications, such as those that separate status from non-status Indians, have too often served to confuse and complicate the lives of Aboriginal people with disabilities. Such barriers to progress must be eliminated" (House of Commons, 1993: v). Alluding to the repetitive cycle of policy talk, the Committee noted that, "while some things have changed since 1981, there has been little measurable progress in many areas" and that "over and over again, Aboriginal people with disabilities recounted their skepticism about promises made by the federal government. Talk has been plentiful, but actions have been few and far between" (House of Commons, 1993: 5, 6). Concerns of a lack of cohesive action in the federal government were again mentioned in promoting better lives for Aboriginal people with disabilities (House of Commons, 1993: 18).

"A National Strategy," developed in 1999 by disability organizations, remarked that persons with disabilities within the First Nation, Metis, and Inuit communities "are faced with a confusing web of programs and eligibility requirements. As a starting point, responsibilities and eligibility rules should be reviewed and clarified, in consultation with the community of persons served by these programs" (Council of Canadians with Disabilities, 1999: 5). Once more, we read of the problems of arbitrary program categories, client confusion, and poor coordination within government, jurisdictional challenges, and insufficient consultation with affected communities. Starting in the fall of 2001, the Sub-Committees on Children and Youth at Risk and the Status of Persons with Disabilities, of the federal Parliament, began examining the circumstances of Aboriginal children from birth to age 12, including Aboriginal children with disabilities, which the Sub-Committee calls "both a classic horizontal issue, and an issue in which the most vulnerable members of society "fall through the cracks" of our existing policies and programs" (House of Commons, 2001: 20-21).

A Disability Lens for the Policy Process

The idea of a "disability lens" for the public policy-making processes of the federal government is another case of a proposal oft repeated over the last 20 years but yet to be implemented. The 1981 *Obstacles Report* observed that most federal decisions are taken without regard to their impact upon the lives of children, youth, and adults with disabilities. Accordingly, the Committee recommended that the federal government establish a review at the cabinet level similar to that for the Status of Women, which would ensure ongoing consideration of the concerns of people with disabilities, including children and their families. The government's response at the time was one of general interest and an expressed intention to explore implementing the proposal. Three governments and 14 years later, another parliamentary committee reached a similar finding. "Federal institutions have not succeeded in bringing about the systemic changes that are required to build disability-related concerns into the basic premises that guide policy formulation and programme implementation" (House of Commons, 1995: 5). That Committee recommended that, "all memoranda to cabinet and other relevant cabinet documents should immediately include a mandatory section that assesses the impact of any proposed measure on persons with disabilities" (House of Commons, 1995: 22). Four years later, yet another parliamentary committee found that as ministers outlined their departmental activities to the committee, members "could not but notice the uneven understanding and uncoordinated activities undertaken by the various federal departments." In addition, "many decisions about the nature of initiatives ... fail to take people with disabilities into account." The committee proposed that, "using a disability lens on government policies, programs and legislation could assist in breaking down the barriers between government departments and programs" (House of Commons, 1999: 2). Disability organizations have made a similar plea for an "access and inclusion lens" to be "applied to all activities of all governments, from human resources practices to the broad range of programs delivered" (Council of Canadians with Disabilities, 1999: 4). As of 2003, federal officials were still studying the concept of an access lens and how to introduce it to Ottawa's administrative and policy practices.

Along with being about words, déjà-vu discourse includes a series of practices by various governmental and political actors: actions, inaction, and reactions. In disability policy, governmental practices of déjà-vu discourse have included the following strategies or tactics:

- Stressing gains made on the surface while overlooking the structural gaps;
- Consciously not taking action on further measures, an example of non-decision making;
- Downplaying disability as a human rights issue and, at times, discrediting the use of litigation and the Charter of Rights and Freedoms to advance equality and equity claims; and,
- Promising additional actions, often in unspecified tomorrows, to be taken up, in accordance with the principles of limited government and shared social responsibility, by various institutions and groups.

Laden with values and power relations, this discourse aims to discipline the way people in the general population as well as in the disability community think about what to date has been accomplished, what remains to be done; and to what ends, by what methods and processes, over what time frame, and by whom. For state officials, déjà-vu discourse offers a political and bureaucratic rationality for producing forceful responses to these core questions of governing (Foucault, 1980).

Disability policy analysis, advocacy, and evaluation seem to circle back to the beginning, time and again. Consumer and advocacy groups that have participated over this period have no doubt become more cynical. They also have learned to recast issues and ideas in different ways, tailor analysis and advocacy to shifting contexts, and to come equipped with data where possible. As yet, we have not been able to break free from this déjà-vu discourse to make significant advances in the policy agenda for children with disabilities and their families. Possible ways of overcoming this frustrating circle and advancing a policy reform agenda bring us back to matters of governance.

Governmentality: How the Canadian State Conducts the Conduct of Disability Policy Reform

Why we are still a long way from meeting prior commitments to coordinate reforms and provide concrete resources for children and adults with disabilities? Why is disability not a fundamental policy priority for governments? Why, in other words, are we trapped in a déjà-vu discourse? These are questions regularly posed and examined by legislators, disability advocates and clients—but rarely so by governments. At times, governments touch upon these questions in responses to parliamentary reports and critiques by disability groups and by child and family organizations.

The archetypal position of governments, found in official texts, contains several elements.[3] First, governments claim they do have a vision for disability issues and, more fundamentally, for people with disabilities. This vision is of an inclusive society, as articulated in various documents including "In Unison," the Social Union Framework Agreement, Future Directions, and various Throne Speeches. Federal and provincial governments point out that they have assumed leadership for disability issues over the years. Significant actions taken by Ottawa alone and in conjunction with other governments and sectors, helped build an extensive range of activities for removing barriers and offering opportunities. Consequently, the disability domain looks quite different in the early 2000s than it did in 1981, though deplorable conditions persist. Canadian governments admit that there is much more to do on disability issues in Canada, that the agenda remains unfinished. In a basic sense, it always will be. The policy agenda changes and grows as public attitudes and perspectives on disability evolve, and it adjusts in response to program developments, pilot projects, and court cases, among other factors. Government officials also argue that realizing the vision of citizenship—the full participation of people with disabilities within Canadian society—is a responsibility shared among all sectors, and not the sole responsibility of governments and the state.

Getting people with disabilities on the agendas of governments in the form of plans and strategies is one thing. Receiving serious attention and sustained action by policymakers and officials is quite another. For example, the 1991–96 National Strategy for the Integration of Persons with Disabilities, a deputy ministers committee on issues concerning persons with disabilities was established, but it met infrequently. This coordinating function was delegated to a committee of assistant deputy ministers who, in many cases, further delegated this role to more junior departmental officials. Over time, this invariably led to a diminished commitment by senior management and cabinet ministers to coordinated action across federal government agencies and departments. This official narrative or story line by governments comprises a significant part of the governmentality of disability, involving the use of various techniques by authorities for taking some action, abridging other actions and not taking some action at all in relation to Canadians with disabilities. A close and critical examination of governmental depictions of Canada's disability policy record reveals there has been more advancement in certain jurisdictions, in certain policy sectors, and in certain time-periods than in others. Some progress has been made in the areas of shelter and transportation but relatively less in income maintenance and home support services (Prince, 2001b; Valentine, 2001). Disability organizations, community advocates and parliamentarians mention a number of explanations for this differential pattern and frustrating pace of reform. I have grouped these explanations into five types. These are the public attitudes and lack of information; the relative powerlessness of the disability community; the constraints of the economic context and public finances; federalism in the form of inter-jurisdictional bargaining, buck-passing and suspicions; and bureaucratic factors and weak accountability mechanisms.

Public Attitudes and Lack of Information

Established public beliefs and lack of awareness is one factor noted by government officials among others to account for limited policy reform and social change. Public interest in, and support for disability-related initiatives for children and adults seems favourable, but diffuse. Jenny Morris explains, "The experience of aging, of being ill, of being in pain, of physical and intellectual limitations, are all part of the experience of living. Fear of all these things, however, means that there is little cultural representation, which creates an understanding of their subjective reality" (Morris, 1992: 164). The federal government's strategy paper on disability, Future Directions, has similarly observed that "attitudinal barriers ... still exist among many people who do not understand that persons with disabilities can and do make a positive and meaningful contribution to our society" (Canada, 1999a).

This explanation reflects traditional sociological analyses of disability, which emphasize bodily impairments, normalcy, and stigma (Titchosky, 2000 and 2001). When compared against societal standards of what is regarded as "normal," an image promoted through advertising, the mass media, and general discourse, people with disabilities experience "precarious social identities," resulting at times in segregation, sterilization, disqualification of citizenship rights, and denial of "full social acceptance" (Goffman 1963; Prince 2001b). It must be noted too, that other beliefs such as, "the child is the responsibility of the parent(s)" and that, "women are the primary caregivers in families" are further deep-rooted attitudinal barriers to adequate services for, and properly valued work by families and caregivers (Beauvais and Jenson, 2000). Surveys continue to find that unpaid female family members and friends do most of the caring work, including the provision of disability-related supports (Statistics Canada, 2002).

As well, information about the nature and extent of disability among Canadians, children more specifically, and especially Aboriginal children and youth is outdated, incomplete, or even inaccurate, although there have been some modest improvements in recent years (Canada 2002; Statistics Canada 2002). For close to 20 years now, mental health programs and services for children and youth have been topics of policy discussions in Canada, but we still lack adequate information on the well being of children (Mahon, 2001). Likewise, the state of data on program expenditures for children with disabilities, whether for a specific budgetary year, over time or across jurisdictions, is appalling. We simply do not know how much or little in public resources are devoted to fostering the full inclusion and equal opportunities of children with disabilities.

Policy is often based on the knowledge derived from data. No data, no problems to address. Until quite recently, the Health Activity Limitation Survey (HALS) survey of 1991 was the only national survey on disability topics. A follow-up survey planned for 1996 was cancelled due to budget cuts. After extensive lobbying and discussion, led by the Canadian Institute of Child Health, a survey was done in 2001 called Participation

Activity Limitation Survey (PALS). The change in focus from HALS to PALS and the fact that a new round of current information is presently being generated is an important aspect of the social policy process (Statistics Canada 2002). Also in 2001 an Aboriginal Peoples Survey II (APS) was conducted as a post-census survey, a follow-up to one done in 1991.

Such attitudinal, cultural, and informational features have important public policy implications. As a parliamentary committee noted not long ago, "the Canadian public needs to be educated or disability issues will fall off the public, and political agenda" (House of Commons, 1999: 1). To promote change in the attitudes and awareness of Canadians, the disability community has a necessary part to play, although the public sector has a fundamentally central role in partnership with other sectors. Many attitudinal barriers and cultural biases are embedded in programs, policy designs, administrative data sets, and service delivery systems. The classic paradigm in social policy of the "worthy poor" remains in effect today across many program files, with the result of excluding or segregating disability issues and people with disabilities from the public domain (Rioux and Prince, 2002). This problematic positioning is repeated with the marginal status of disability studies in most universities and think tanks in Canada.

The Relative Powerlessness of Children with Disabilities and Their Families

Bio-politics and the governmentality perspective relate to this explanation by pointing out inequalities in the distribution of power, opportunities, conditions, and life chances. Groups representing children or youth with disabilities are generally far less powerful than business and industry groups and even other social policy groups representing, for example, broader health care or education interests. Some disability studies also call attention to the existence of multiple conceptions of, and organizations for disability. This multiplicity and diversity fragments somewhat the disability movement that can have the consequence of diminishing their effectiveness.

Most disability, family, or parent groups lack regular and easy access to senior government decision makers and, in the aftermath of program cutbacks in the 1990s and more recently, relations of trust between governments and the disability community are weak and in a process of rebuilding. This relative powerlessness reflects the highly marginalized status of children with disabilities and their families, whether measured by income, employment, educational attainment, or the absence of supports and incentives. These multiple dimensions of subordinate status translate into marginal resources and limited capacity for influencing governments and other governance regimes. Moreover, coalition building and networking with other social groups has not been as advanced as might be. Writing in the early 1990s, Brian Wharf commented that, "the powerful social movements—labour, women, and First Nations—have neglected child welfare. In a very real sense children are "the orphans of the major social movements in Canada" (Wharf, 1993: 103). A decade later, this remains the case for children with disabilities.

That policy reform processes generate resistance to the intended social or economic changes is a basic fact of political life. This political truism seems especially the case when a group actively seeks new or enhanced rights of citizenship. Bryan Turner has written that "citizenship provides a challenge to existing patterns of power and authority and there-fore any growth of citizenship will be met with political struggles by dominant groups to preserve their advantages within the status quo" (Turner, 1986: 104). In disability policy, the drive to achieve greater inclusion within school systems, introduce a comprehensive disability income insurance plan, and strengthen human rights provisions have all been met with some resistance by various interests (Morris, 1992; Prince, 2001a).

The Constraints of the Economic Context and Public Finances

For most of the last 20 years in Canada, fiscal austerity, deficit reduction, and public ser-vice downsizing have been profound drivers of the public policy context for all issues, including disability issues. This period was marked also by two serious recessions in the Canadian economy. These events and priority concerns both reflected and reinforced broader shifts in policy thinking (evident across many nations), away from state interven-tion and social issues, and toward market approaches and economic issues. Consequently, "proposals for persons with disabilities have not formed a prominent part of the debate on the future of redistributive social policy. This is partly because their relationship to issues of the global economy is slight, and partly because of the way issues of equity have been sidelined by economic issues" (Armitage, 1996: 77). Part of the reason that children with disabilities have been ignored or insufficiently linked with the wider disability and children's agendas is that when "welfare" left Health and Welfare Canada in 1993 and be-came part of the then newly formed HRDC (and responsibility for disability went with it) the federal government's focus on disability has centred on employability. This emphasis on employability is part of the federal government's broader theme in social policy of "investing in people." Certainly, expenditure implications associated with major program reforms have been and remain a significant factor in government thinking. The great un-stated concern deals with the worry of what economists call the "moral hazard" of social programs, especially insurance programs for certain risks. The theory behind this notion, and hence the worry by officials, is that establishing or expanding programs will give people more of an incentive to self-identify as having a disability and, conversely, less of an incentive to avoid risks that may produce a claim for compensation. This perspective is rarely stated in documents or given emphasis in public by policy-makers. This does not mean, however, that it is not a concern of government bureaucracies. Proponents for reform, however, believe that financial costs to the public purse have been overplayed and used as an excuse to avoid taking responsibility and demonstrating leadership on matters of equality. Emphasizing costs to the public purse tends to ignore the human costs and social benefits, and to downplay the financial costs to private household budgets in caring and advocating for children with disabilities.[4]

Federalism in the Form of Inter-Jurisdictional Bargaining, Buck-Passing, and Suspicions

Delays and inaction in implementing child rights and disability reform plans are partly explained by the need for federal-provincial agreement on a number of recommenda-tions put forward by parliamentary committees, children's groups, disability groups, and government advisers. Inter-jurisdictional agenda setting, planning, and bargaining take time. Also critical is that most disability groups in Canada, even provincial and national associations, feel powerless in dealing with federal/provincial/territorial working groups of officials, lacking the information and capacity to penetrate this labyrinth of intergovernmental relationships.

For international statements of human rights for people with disabilities to have the force of law in Canada, they must be accepted by the federal, provincial and territorial governments and incorporated into various statutes. Evelyn Kallen makes the important point that: "Canada's adoption of the declaration, covenants, and protocol does not automatically update the rules, policies, and laws of every company, organization, and level of government in the country. At every level of Canadian society there are formal regulations and informal practices that are contrary to the principles of human rights. Violations of omission and commission in the innumerable laws and regulations enacted in the past require considerable time and attention in order to be properly redrafted so as to conform fully with international human-rights principles" (Kallen, 1989: 12).

The division of powers associated with federalism presents incredible complications and jurisdictional barriers for Aboriginal peoples of all ages with disabilities. In particular, there is ongoing buck-passing between the two orders of government over which order is responsible for funding and providing services for urban-based Aboriginal children, youth, and adults living in cities rather than on reserves (Prince and Abele, 2000). Moreover, there is a residue of suspicion by provinces toward the federal government because of past federal initiatives that were followed by unilateral cuts in transfers. Thus, in the new post-deficit era, provinces may see an examination of broader reforms as a federal attempt to increase its influence in the disability, health, or family policy sectors, all of which are primarily provincial jurisdiction.

Federalism, to be sure, is a fundamental feature of the regime of public power in Canada. The close and ongoing contact between the two orders of sovereign governments, involving a mixture of techniques and processes in cooperation and conflict, can therefore be regarded as a defining element of governmentality. By and large the population accepts the authority of both the federal state and provincial states, and are compelled to accept the various agreements reached between the political elite of each order on matters of social, economic and fiscal policy.

Bureaucratic Factors and Weak Accountability Mechanisms

The structure and operation of the government is widely and continually cited as a major reason for the delays and modest results in addressing the concerns of Canadians with disabilities. Indeed, this is probably the most oft repeated reason cited by disability groups, child and family organizations, and parliamentarians for the lack of substantial and sustained action on disability issues by government. Governments generally seem unable to deal effectively with cross-departmental or horizontal issues (Savoie, 1999; House of Commons, 2001). And with disability and children, we have two such horizontal issues.

As an early report stated, "the crucial obstacles which prevent the Government of Canada from responding directly, appropriately, and continually to the needs of more than two million Canadians have nothing to do with motivation. They have to do with the systems of communication, organizations and decision-making within the Government of Canada, and within Canadian society in general" (1981a: 5–6). A 1990 report by the relevant standing committee made a related observation: "The absence, within the federal government, of an effective and accountable mechanism for change is one important reason why Canada's commitments to people with disabilities remain only partially fulfilled" (House of Commons, 1990a: 33). A subsequent report on Aboriginal peoples with disabilities was far more critical. It stated the federal government had taken "a strikingly fragmented approach" with responsibility scattered amongst different departments and programs, "turf wars among bureaucrats," and "definitely no concentrated focus on disability." This fragmented focus was "a clear illustration of the ad hoc approach that departments are taking to the needs of people ... with disabilities" (House of Commons, 1993: 13, 17). The Scott Task Force report employed more temperate language, but the message was similar.

Because disability issues cut across the federal government's organizational lines, they often get lost in a bureaucratic shuffle. In some instances, a positive action by one department may be lost because of the inaction of another that unintentionally cancels out the first. In other cases, a department may have the will to act but needs the support and input of others to get the job done. While government departments are able to join forces to meet disability-related goals, it is important to establish clear lines of accountability at the federal level (Canada, 1996: 25).

Parliamentary committee reviews of federal disability policy done in 1999 and 2001 again focus on the processes and structures of government. The committee reported a "lack of departmental responsibilities, an absence of strong program structures, fragmented service development and inconsistent standards" (House of Commons, 1999: 18; House of Commons, 2001). Matters of access and inclusion for children, youth, and adults with disabilities are not routinely a part of legislative and policy and program development. The lack of input by disability and family organizations in setting goals and desired outcomes compounds this problem.

The departmentalized nature of government has a number of dysfunctional consequences. Hierarchies separate policy development from program administration within departments, with the result that departmental managers are accountable for the vertical rather than the horizontal management of programs. The same is the case for planning documents and performance reporting systems. Cross-departmental coordination and accountability are frustrated by the deep-seated reliance on individual departmental portfolios and ministerial responsibilities. The need for a strong government-wide accountability mechanism is again noted: "One of the major problems in implementing disability policies and programs is that no one has ever been clearly accountable for results." The committee acknowledged that even the lead minister for disability issues, presently the Minister of HRDC, has a difficult job since lead ministers cannot force action.

Conclusions

Over twenty-five years ago now, the Canadian Council on Social Development noted that policies and services for people with disabilities was a hit-and-miss affair, a situation reflected in "the excellence of many individual programs and the fragmentation and lack of organization in the system as a whole" (Brown, 1977: 460). From a value stance, this reality was apparent in the incomplete realization of human rights and lack of choices to individuals and families in enjoying a decent and dignified life. "Not the least of the problems of this policy area is that disabled people do not fit neatly into the categories with which people identify, or into which policy-makers decide their activities" (Brown, 1977: 451).

This review of subsequent political and policy debate on disability issues as reflected in parliamentary, governmental, and advocacy group documents yields a similarly disturbing, if not even more discouraging, conclusion. A strong and widespread sense of frustration persists within the disability community in Canada, based on personal experience and engagement with authorities, that the political will to act by the federal and provincial governments, while evident at times through the 1980s and 1990s, has, for the most part, been haphazard.

Foucault's notion of governmentality offers some insights into this case study of Canadian disability policy. The analysis here exposed certain mechanisms by which power is exercised. Policy issues and government track records are framed by those in positions of state authority through discourse technologies that include consultations, statistical surveys, parliamentary studies, action plans, and ministerial speeches. Government structures and programs shape individuals in relation to their particular health status in performing daily living activities. The discourse embodied in such programs and structures link these health issues and conditions to the wider interests of the general population, in which the prevailing culture and "art of government" rest largely on political economy and medical science.

Governmentality as a way of thinking and talking is observable in the déjà-vu discourse of disability. This discourse naturalizes the limited scale and pace of reforms in disability policy and services (Tremain, 2001). More dangerously, the discourse not only perpetuates a pattern of relentless incremental changes but also conceals the erosion and decline in existing programs and benefits to persons with disabilities. The language of shared societal responsibility for addressing disability issues further legitimates a limited role by the Canadian state and places duties on individuals and families themselves as well as on other institutions, most notably the corporate and voluntary sectors.

In these ways we can see how specific governing concepts of disability lie behind the variety of failed, inadequate, and unfinished reforms and endlessly repeated promises to do more. Disability continues to be primarily understood and approached by governments as a category or set of categories of discrete needs. Despite rhetoric to contrary—expressed in official documents of equality, inclusion, and citizenship—disability remains framed by governments and other institutions, such as the health-care industry, rehabilitation, and psychiatry, within a bio-medical paradigm.

According to Foucault, an essential development in the art of modern government was the "introduction of economy into political practice" (Burchell, Gordon, and Miller, 1991: 92). A political economy discourse of resource scarcity or, even in times of budgetary surplus, of fiscal prudence to avoid government deficits again, profoundly circumscribe the scope of debate and the political room to maneuver by disability advocates and client organizations. This discourse of economy is apparent in the priority emphasis given by governments to the employability of adults with disabilities, compared to the lower priority to children with disabilities. It is apparent too in government talk and action concerning the financial sustainability of such disability-related programs as the Canada Pension Plan, workers' compensation, and social assistance. These are powerful arguments, tied to powerful interests that conduct the conduct of others. The findings additionally support the view that as the state became more governmentalized, it became more complex, complicated, and compartmentalized in terms of programs, services, and relationships with the general population and a multiplicity of particular clientele groups. This poses serious problems of public transparency, accountability, and citizen access, problems which political sociology needs to further take up as pressing issues of democracy.

Given disparities in economic and social status as well as the rights and equality discourse of citizenship, reforms are wanted and expected by families, parent groups, youth, disability organizations, other voluntary sector groups, service providers, and Aboriginal communities. Reforms are necessary for addressing gaps, overlaps, and inequities in policies, programs, and services for preschool and school-aged children and youth with disabilities. Major changes are required to move toward a more inclusive and integrated set of governance arrangements. Minor tinkering with programs and structures will simply perpetuate the frustrating pattern of the past generation, with disability issues seemingly trapped in a circle. Fundamental reforms in several arenas are essential for advancing the vision of full citizenship and inclusion for all people with disabilities.

In sociological terms, inclusion is multidimensional. It happens on an everyday or episodic basis, in formal and informal ways, and on interpersonal, organizational, interagency, intergovernmental, and intersectoral levels. In policy terms, integration has an important dualism. First, it means building disability considerations into mainstream programs and policies in all service and practice areas. At the same time, the integration of people with disabilities means supplementing mainstream programs where necessary with complementary services and supports for addressing the additional disadvantages faced by children and adults with disabilities.

Notes

1. The main methods used for this study include a textual and thematic analysis of numerous government, parliamentary and disability community documents over the past 20 years; a review of the academic literature on Canadian social policy; interviews and focused conversations with approximately a dozen key informants inside and outside of government in this policy field in 1999 and 2000; and comments from 20 participants at a Roundtable held in Ottawa in May 2001, sponsored by the Canadian Policy Research Networks. I am grateful to the Roundtable participants, who comprised governmental and advocacy representatives, for their constructive and challenging comments. For more details on the Roundtable, see Prince (2001a).

2. This estimate is likely conservative, since the survey was of the 10 provinces and people living in households and did not include people living in the three territories, First Nations people living on reserves, or people living in institutions such as nursing homes.

3. I generated this list of themes from a survey of federal government documents spanning the last 20 years, typically made in response to parliamentary reports. The relevant documents are listed in the References.

4. A recent parliamentary report endorsed by members from all five federal political parties noted: "We recognize that during a period of cutting costs, administrative measures need to be put in place that contain expenditures but we share the concern of independent policy analysts and disability organizations that the current disability income support programs op-

erated by the federal government, notably the Canada Pension Plan-Disability (CPP-D), has not recognized the fundamental realities of many people who live with a disability" (House of Commons, 2001: 17).

References

Armitage, Andrew. 1996. *Social Welfare in Canada Revisited: Facing Up to the Future*. Toronto: Oxford University Press.

Assembly of First Nations. 1998. First Nation's Position on Disability. Ottawa: Resolution Online at <www.afn.ca/resolutions/1998/con-dec/res71.htm>.

Baer, Douglas (ed.). 2002. *Political Sociology: Canadian Perspectives*. Toronto: Oxford University Press.

Barnes, Colin, Mike Oliver and Len Barton (eds.). 2002. *Disability Studies Today*. Cambridge: Polity Press.

Beauvais, Caroline, and Jane Jenson. 2001. *Two Policy Paradigms: Family Responsibility and Investing in Children*. Ottawa: Canadian Policy Research Networks.

Bickenbach, Jerome. 1993. *Physical Disability and Social Policy*. Toronto: University of Toronto Press.

Boyce, William, Mary Tremblay, Mary Anne McColl, Jerome Bickenbach, Anne Crichton, Steven Andrews, Nancy Gerein, and April D'Aubin. 2001. *A Seat at the Table: Persons with Disabilities and Policy Making*. Montreal and Kingston: McGill-Queen's University Press.

Brown, Joan C. 1977. *A Hit-and-Miss Affair: Policies for Disabled People in Canada*. Ottawa: Canadian Council on Social Development.

Burchell, Graham, Colin Gordon and Peter Miller. 1991. *The Foucault Effect: Studies on Governmentality*. Chicago: University of Chicago Press.

Cameron, David and Fraser Valentine (eds.). 2001. *Disability and Federalism: Comparing Different Approaches to Full Participation*. Montreal and Kingston: McGill-Queen's University Press.

Canada. 2002. Advancing the Inclusion of Persons with Disabilities: A Government of Canada Report, December 2002. Ottawa: Human Resources Development Canada.

——. 1999a. Future Directions to Address Disability Issues for the Government of Canada: Working Together for Full Citizenship. Ottawa: Human Resources Development Canada. Online at <www.hrdc drhc.gc.ca/socpol/reports/disability/conte.shtml>.

——. 1999b. Government of Canada Response to Reflecting Interdependence: Disability, Parliament, Government and the Community, the Sixth Report of the Standing Committee on Human Resources Development and the Status of Persons with Disabilities. Ottawa. Online at <www.hrdc-dhrc.gc.ca/dept/general/response.shtml>.

——. 1996. The Will to Act: Equal Citizenship for Canadians with Disabilities, Report of the Federal Task Force on Disability Issues. Ottawa. Online at <www.proxy.bib.uottawa.ca:3081/hrib/sdskForce/English/report/html>.

Canadian Association of Community Living. 2000. CACL Campaign 2000—Disability and the Federal Government, Support to Families. Toronto: Canadian Association of Community Living. Online at <www.cacl.ca>.

Canadian Coalition on the Rights of the Child. 1999. How Does Canada Measure Up? Toronto: Canadian Coalition on the Rights of the Child. Online at <www.rightsofchildren.ca>.

Council of Canadians with Disabilities. 1996. Federal Leadership on Disability and Citizenship Rights Required. Final Presentation to the Federal Task Force on Disability Issues. Winnipeg. Online at <www.pcs.mb.ca>.

Council of Canadians with Disabilities, with 13 national disability organizations. 1999. A National Strategy for Persons with Disabilities: The Community Definition. Winnipeg: Council of Canadians with Disabilities. Online at <www.pcs.mb.ca>.

Clifford, Michael. 2001. *Political Genealogy After Foucault: Savage Identities*. London: Routledge.

Dean, Mitchell. 1999. *Governmentality: Power and Rule in Modern Society*. London: Sage.

Enns, Ruth. 1999. *A Voice Unheard: The Latimer Case and People with Disabilities*. Halifax: Fernwood.

Faubian, James D. 1994. *Power: Michael Foucault, Essential Works of Foucault 1954–1984*, Vol 3. New York: The New Press.

Federal-Provincial-Territorial Ministers Responsible for Social Services. 2000. Public Report on the Public Dialogue on the National Children's Agenda—A Shared Vision. Online at <www.socialunion.gc.ca>.

——. 1998. In Unison: A Canadian Approach to Disability Issues. Online at <www.socialunion.gc.ca>.

Finkelstein, Vic. 1980. *Attitudes and Disabled People*. New York: World Rehabilitation Fund.

Foucault, Michel. 1980. *Power/Knowledge*. New York: Pantheon.

Fox, Daniel M. and David P. Willis. 1989. "Disability Policy: Restoring Socioeconomic Independence." *The Milbank Quarterly* 67 (Supp. 2, Parts 1 and 2): 1–7.

Goffman, Erving. 1963. *Stigma: Notes on the Management of Spoiled Identity*. New York: Simon and Schuster.

House of Commons. 2001. A Common Vision: Interim Report. Standing Committee on Human Resources Development and the Status of Persons with Disabilities. Ottawa: June 12. Online at <www.parl.gc.ca/IfoComDoc/37/1/HUMA/Studies/Reports/report4-huma-e.htm>.

——. 1999. Reflecting Interdependence: Disability, Parliament, Government and Community. Sixth Report of the Standing Committee on Human Resources Development and the Status of Persons with Disabilities. Ottawa: June 8.

——. 1995. The Grand Design: Achieving the "Open House" Vision. Report of the Standing Committee on Human Rights and the Status of Disabled Persons. Ottawa.

——. 1993. Completing the Circle: Aboriginal Canadians with Disabilities. Report of the Standing Committee on Human Rights and the Status of Disabled Persons. Ottawa.

——. 1990. A Consensus for Action: The Economic Integration of Disabled Persons. Report of the Standing Committee on Human Rights and the Status of Disabled Persons. Ottawa.

——. 1981a. Follow Up Report: Native Population. Report of the Special Parliamentary Committee on the Disabled and the Handicapped. Ottawa.

——. 1981b Obstacles Report. Report of the Special Parliamentary Committee on the Disabled and the Handicapped. Ottawa. Online at <www.hrdc-drhc.gc.cahrib/sddi/documents/obstacles.html>.

Kallen, Evelyn. 1989. *Label Me Human: Minority Rights of Stigmatized Canadians*. Toronto: University of Toronto Press.

Mahon, Rianne. 2001. *School-aged Children across Canada: A Patchwork of Public Policies*. Ottawa: Canadian Policy Research Networks.

Martin, Luther H., Huck Gutman and Patrick H. Hutton (eds.). 1988. *Technologies of the Self: A Seminar with Michel Foucault*. Amherst, Mass.: University of Massachusetts Press.

Morris, Jenny. 1992. "Personal and Political: A Feminist Perspective on Researching Physical Disability." *Disability, Handicap & Society* 7 (2): 157-166.

Oliver, Mike. 1990. *The Politics of Disablement*. Basingstoke: Macmillan.

Prince, Michael J. 2002. "The Governance of Children with Disabilities and Their Families: Charting the Public-Sector Regime in Canada." *Canadian Public Administration* 45(3): 389–409.

——. 2001a. Governing in an Integrated Fashion: Lessons from the Disability Domain. Ottawa: Canadian Policy Research Networks. Online at <www.cprn.org>.

——. 2001b. "Citizenship by Instalments: Federal Policies for Canadians with Disabilities." in Leslie A. Pal (ed.), *How Ottawa Spends 2001-2002: Power in Transition*. Toronto: Oxford University Press.

——. 1992. "Touching Us All: International Context, National Policies, and the Integration of Canadians with Disabilities." in Frances Abele (ed.), *How Ottawa Spends 1992–1993: The Politics of Competitiveness*. Ottawa: Carleton University Press.

Prince, Michael J., and Frances Abele. 2000. "Funding an Aboriginal Order of Government in Canada: Recent Developments in Self-Government and Fiscal Relations," in Harvey Lazar (ed.), Canada: *The State of the Federation 1999/2000*. Kingston: Institute of Intergovernmental Relations.

Rice, James J., and Michael J. Prince. 2000. *Changing Politics of Canadian Social Policy*. Toronto: University of Toronto Press.

Rioux, Marcia H., and Michael J. Prince. 2002. "The Canadian Political Landscape of Disability: Policy Perspectives, Social Status, Interest Groups and the Rights Movement." in Allan Puttee (ed.), *Federalism, Democracy and Disability Policy in Canada*. Montreal and Kingston: McGill-Queen's University Press.

Savoie, Donald J. 1999. *Governing from the Centre: The Concentration of Power in Canadian Politics*. Toronto: University of Toronto Press.

Statistics Canada. 2002. A Profile of Disability in Canada, 2001. Catalogue Number 89-577-XIE. Ottawa. Online at <www.proxy.bib.uottawa.ca:2142>.

Titchkosky, Tanya. 2003. *Disability, Self, and Society*. Toronto: University of Toronto Press.

——. 2001. "'Disability': A Rose by Any Other Name?: 'People-First' Language in Canadian Society." *Canadian Review of Sociology and Anthropology*. 38(2): 125–40.

——. 2000. "Disability Studies: The Old and the New." *Canadian Journal of Sociology*. 25(2): 197–224.

Tremain, Shelley. 2001. "On the Government of Disability." *Social Theory and Practice*. 27(4): 617–36.

Turner, Bryan S. 1986. *Citizenship and Capitalism: The Debate over Reformism*. London: Allen & Unwin.

Valentine, Fraser. 2001. *Enabling Citizenship: Full Inclusion of Children with Disabilities and their Parents*. Ottawa: Canadian Policy Research Networks.

Wharf, Brian (ed.). 1993. *Rethinking Child Welfare in Canada*. Toronto: McClelland and Stewart.

Zola, Irving K. 1982. *Missing Pieces: A Chronicle of Living with a Disability*. Philadelphia: Temple University Press.

20

Employment Benefits for Same-Sex Couples

The Expanding Entitlement*

DONALD D. CARTER

Introduction

THE PAST DECADE in Canada has seen a growing amount of litigation arising from the claims of same-sex couples to employment benefits that opposite-sex couples, including those living in common-law relationships, can claim as of right. Some of this litigation has been initiated before human rights tribunals and arbitration boards, but it has been primarily the courts that have led the way in expanding the entitlement of same-sex couples to employment benefits. This paper analyses this recent jurisprudence and explores its implications for human resource managers in both the public sector and the private sector.

What is somewhat surprising about this recent litigation is that much of it has occurred well after most Canadian jurisdictions had amended their human rights statutes by expressly including sexual orientation as one of the prohibited grounds of discrimination. Why has it been necessary to litigate extensively the entitlement of same-sex couples to employment benefits in the face of these clear statutory prohibitions against discrimination based on sexual orientation? I would suggest that the reason for this litigation is the ambivalence of Canadian society toward homosexuality. Many Canadians, while now prepared to accept that gays and lesbians should be protected from workplace conduct that is openly intolerant of their sexual orientation, are much less willing to affirm homosexuality by regarding same-sex relationships as analogous to opposite-sex relationships. This ambivalence may explain the fact that, while from the outset it was clear that the prohibition against discrimination based on sexual orientation protected gays and lesbians from improper interference in the workplace, it was much less clear whether it also created an entitlement for same-sex couples to certain employment benefits that in the past had been reserved for traditional spousal relationships.

The fact that it has been necessary to resort to extensive litigation to clarify the scope of the prohibition against sexual orientation reflects a division within Canadian society

---

* This chapter was first published as "Employment Benefits for Same Sex Couples: The Expanding Entitlement," *Canadian Public Policy* 24, 1 (1998): 91–106. An earlier version of this paper was presented at the Employment Law '97 conference held in Vancouver, British Columbia on 25 April 1997. The proceedings of this conference, "Employment Law—1997 Update" have been published by The Continuing Legal Education Society of British Columbia.

over the issue of whether same-sex couples should be entitled to the same treatment as heterosexual couples. Clearly there has been a reluctance in certain parts of Canadian society to take the prohibition against discrimination based on sexual orientation to its logical conclusion. While many Canadians appear prepared to tolerate homosexuality by recognizing that gays and lesbians as individuals should not be subject to harassment in the workplace, they appear much less prepared to affirm homosexuality by acknowledging that long-standing same-sex relationships should be recognized as a type of family relationship that would entitle gay and lesbian couples to employment benefits already provided to more traditional families. Indeed this ambivalence is still reflected in many public statutes, including human rights legislation in some jurisdictions, that expressly define marital status as being confined to conjugal relationships involving persons of the opposite sex.[1]

Canadian legislators have been less than eager to resolve this ambivalence and have preferred to remain silent rather than to expand the statutory definition of family arrangements by means of legislative amendment. Recent federal legislation, for example, amended the *Canadian Human Rights Act* by adding sexual orientation as a prohibited ground of discrimination but still left the term "marital status" undefined.[2] The cautious approach of our politicians to such a contentious issue has left the field open to our judges to do by judicial interpretation what our legislators are unwilling to do by legislative amendment.

Only a few years ago Canadian courts appeared to be just as reluctant as our politicians to resolve the contradiction between the express prohibition against discrimination based on sexual orientation set out in human rights legislation and the discriminatory treatment of same-sex couples when it came to the provision of employment benefits.[3] This initial reluctance to affirm long-standing same-sex relationships has now largely disappeared as Canadian courts have begun to give clear judicial recognition to the claims of same-sex couples to be treated in the same manner as more traditional family units in the application of employment benefits. Indeed the courts are now beginning to look to the guarantee of equality set out in the *Canadian Charter of Rights and Freedoms*[4] in order to resolve the legislative contradiction between statutory prohibitions against discrimination based on sexual orientation and other statutory provisions that confine family status to arrangements between members of the opposite sex. What the courts have said is that the right to be protected against discrimination based on sexual orientation is more than just the product of human rights legislation and now must be considered as a fundamental right that arises by implication from the Charter's guarantee of equal treatment under the law. By giving constitutional status to the right to be protected against discrimination based on sexual orientation, and including within the ambit of that right protection for same-sex relationships, the courts have signalled that in some cases at least this right will trump any legislated definition of marital status.

Egan and Nesbit and Its Aftermath

This overriding effect of the right to be protected against discrimination based on sexual orientation has now been recognized in the Supreme Court of Canada's landmark decision in the *Egan and Nesbit* case.[5] In *Egan and Nesbit* the Supreme Court of Canada faced squarely the issue of whether same-sex couples were entitled to the benefit of equal treatment under the law provided by section 15 of the *Canadian Charter of Rights and Freedoms*. Egan and Nesbit had lived together as a same-sex couple since 1948 in a relationship that had the degree of commitment and interdependence that one would find in a traditional heterosexual marriage. Nevertheless Nesbit was denied the spousal allowance under the federal *Old Age Security Act* because his relationship with Egan did not fit within the definition of spouse set out in that statute. This definition had been amended to include persons living in a common-law relationship but the amended definition expressly referred to such persons as being of the opposite sex—the clear effect being to provide less advantageous treatment for same-sex couples.

Egan and Nesbit were not successful in asserting their particular claim but they did succeed in obtaining Charter protection for same-sex relationships. Five of the nine justices of the Supreme Court of Canada were prepared to find that the definition of spouse set out in the *Old Age Security Act* was inconsistent with the Charter's guarantee of equal treatment. One of these justices, however, did hold that the definition, at least at the time of the decision, constituted a reasonable limit under s. 1 of the Charter since it was intended to provide financial assistance to those in greatest need. This latter finding was fatal to the particular claim before the Court since the four remaining justices were not prepared to find any infringement of the Charter's guarantee of equality, viewing preferred treatment for heterosexual couples as relevant given what they considered to be the much larger role that such couples play in child-rearing.

Despite the failure of Egan and Nesbit's particular claim, the case has important implications for future claims from same-sex couples. For the first time a majority of the Supreme Court of Canada was prepared to find that sexual orientation was a personal characteristic that brought same-sex relationships under the umbrella of the Charter's guarantee of equality of treatment. This finding that same-sex relationships are now afforded constitutional protection has particular significance for future claims from same-sex couples asking to be treated in the same way as heterosexual couples. Future claims, because they can now be Charter based, could even prevail in the face of express statutory language that confines family status to opposite-sex couples, leaving the way open to an expanding entitlement to employment benefits for same-sex couples.

The impact of the Egan and Nesbit case can already be seen. In *Vogel v. Manitoba*[6] the Manitoba Court of Appeal considered the claim of a Manitoba government employee, who had been living in a same-sex relationship since 1972, to employment benefits already provided to employees living in a common-law relationship with a person of the opposite sex. Such benefits included a dental plan, a pension plan, an extended health care plan, and a group life insurance plan. The Court, in the light of the *Egan and Nesbit* case, had no difficulty concluding that the different treatment of same-sex and opposite-sex couples where they both held themselves out as common-law couples, could only be discrimination based on sexual orientation. On that basis the matter was referred back to the human rights adjudicator who had initially dismissed the claim in order to be reconsidered in accordance with the decision of the Court. It would appear that the only matter left open to the adjudicator by this decision was whether the qualification of "bona fide or reasonable cause" set out in Manitoba's human rights legislation might be a defence to what was, on its face, improper discrimination based on sexual orientation.

What is interesting about the *Vogel* case is that the Manitoba Court of Appeal clearly recognized the full implications of the Supreme Court of Canada's decision in *Egan and Nesbit*. Once same-sex couples are recognized as being entitled to equal treatment under the Charter, it then becomes much more difficult to justify treating such couples in a manner different from opposite-sex couples in more traditional spousal arrangements, especially now that these benefits are generally extended to opposite-sex couples living in common law arrangements where formal marital status is no longer regarded as a condition of receiving spousal benefits. Clearly employers in Manitoba are now likely to face a high hurdle when faced with the task of establishing "bona fide or reasonable cause" for providing a less favourable package of employment benefits to same-sex couples than to opposite-sex couples living in a common law arrangement. As will be discussed later, however, in the area of pension benefits federal income tax legislation may still provide employers with a sufficient justification to clear that hurdle.

The *Egan and Nesbit* decision has made it clear that the Charter's guarantee of equal treatment under the law extends as far as same-sex couples, but it also has another important effect in those few Canadian jurisdictions which still have not expressly included sexual orientation as a prohibited ground of discrimination in their human rights legislation. Human rights legislation itself is subject to the Charter and its provisions must be consistent with the Charter's guarantees of equal treatment under the law. Now that the Supreme Court of Canada has recognized that sexual orientation falls within the Charter's guarantee of equality as being analogous to the grounds expressly enumerated in that provision, human rights legislation that omits this ground has become constitutionally suspect.

What is important to understand is that the Charter's impact reaches beyond its direct application to government, either as legislator or employer. Employers in the broader public sector and in the private sector, while not subject to the direct application of the Charter, are still regulated by human rights laws that do fall within the direct reach of the Charter. Human rights laws, either at the federal or provincial level, must be read in a manner consistent with the Charter and, as a result, have been reshaped by Charter imperatives. This indirect impact of the Charter, as will be seen, now has important implications for employers in the private sector and the broader public sector.

This reshaping of human rights laws through application of the Charter was occurring even before the Supreme Court of Canada's decision in *Egan and Nesbit*. In the *Haig* case[7] the Ontario Court of Appeal was faced with the issue of whether there was any legal basis for complaints made by former members of the Canadian Armed Forces that they had been the victims of employment discrimination because of their sexual orientation. At that time sexual orientation was not included as a ground of prohibited discrimination in the *Canadian Human Rights Act*. The federal government, however, conceded that by analogy sexual orientation fell within the guarantee of equal protection under the law set out in s. 15 of the Charter. In the face of this concession the Court had no difficulty finding a legal basis for the claim, holding that the failure of the federal human rights legislation to include sexual orientation as a prohibited ground of discrimination was inconsistent with s. 15 of the Charter. This improper omission was remedied by the Court reading this prohibition into the legislation by interpreting and applying the statute as though it actually did contain an express prohibition against discrimination based on sexual orientation.

Now that the Supreme Court of Canada, in *Egan and Nesbit*, has clearly recognized sexual orientation as a ground analogous to those expressly set out in s. 15, the argument that human rights legislation must be brought in line with the Charter would appear to have even more force. In *Nolan and Barry*,[8] Justice Barry of the Newfoundland Supreme Court interpreted *Egan and Nesbit* as clear recognition by the Supreme Court of Canada that homosexuals had been historically disadvantaged and were entitled to protection from discrimination. In his view the omission of this group from the protection of Newfoundland's human rights legislation was a "glaring omission" which itself was discriminatory. The appropriate remedy, according to Justice Barry, was to read sexual orientation into the legislation as a prohibited ground of discrimination.

The Alberta Court of Appeal in the *Vriend* case,[9] however, took a much different view of the omission from Alberta's human rights legislation of sexual orientation as a prohibited ground of discrimination. Vriend had been dismissed from his employment because of his homosexuality. His complaint to the Alberta Human Rights Commission was rejected because discrimination on the ground of sexual orientation was not expressly prohibited by Alberta's *Individual Rights Protection Act*. The matter then moved on to the courts. The Alberta Court of Queen's Bench differed with the Alberta Human Rights Commission and took the same approach as the Ontario Court of Appeal did in the *Haig* case, reading into the human rights statute sexual orientation as a prohibited ground of discrimination and finding a breach of that prohibition. This approach, however, was rejected by a majority of the Alberta Court of Appeal.

The majority of the appeal court held that legislative silence on the matter of sexual orientation must be construed as a legislative choice not to deal with the issue rather than as a legislative choice to create a distinction based on sexual orientation. Given this characterization of the legislative omission, the majority held that Alberta's human rights legislation was not inconsistent with the Charter's guarantee to homosexuals of equal treatment under the law. The dissenting justice, on the other hand, held that legislative silence on the matter did amount to discrimination by the Alberta legislature since it had clearly drawn a distinction between homosexuals who were omitted from the legislation and other victims of discrimination who had been expressly brought within its scope. This distinction constituted a denial of equal benefit and protection of the law contrary to s. 15 of the Charter. Despite this conclusion, the dissenting judge was not prepared to go so far as to read into the Alberta statute sexual orientation as a prohibited ground of discrimination because of a concern about the potential impact of this remedy on the entitlement of homosexuals to employment benefits. Instead she temporarily suspended the declaration of the invalidity of certain sections of the legislation in order to give the Alberta legislature the opportunity to bring its legislation into conformity with the Charter.

The majority decision in *Vriend* is a departure from both the *Haig* and *Nolan and Barry* decisions. Its impact appears to be restricted to Alberta and Newfoundland since human rights legislation in all other Canadian jurisdictions now expressly prohibits discrimination based on sexual orientation. Moreover, in light of the Supreme Court of Canada's clear recognition in *Egan and Nesbit* that the Charter's guarantee of equal protection under the law embraces sexual orientation, it is debatable whether the majority decision in *Vriend* can withstand the test of an appeal to the Supreme Court of Canada.

It should be made clear that *Vriend* has little impact in those Canadian jurisdictions that expressly prohibit discrimination on the basis of sexual orientation in their human rights legislation. The implication of *Egan and Nesbit* for these jurisdictions is that a denial of employment benefits to same-sex couples might very well constitute improper discrimination in violation of the express prohibition against discrimination found in their human rights legislation. As we will now see, the practical impact of *Egan and Nesbit* may only have been to give retroactive judicial approval to an approach that had already been accepted by human rights tribunals and arbitration boards.

Recent Decisions of Human Rights Tribunals

Even before the Supreme Court of Canada spoke in the *Egan and Nesbit* case, human rights tribunals were beginning to grapple with claims for employment benefits from same-sex couples. Of particular interest is the *Leshner* case,[10] a 1992 decision of a board of inquiry appointed under the *Ontario Human Rights Code*. The complainant, Leshner, alleged discrimination based on sexual orientation because his employer, the Ontario government, had failed to provide certain employment benefits to his partner with whom he had lived for ten years. By the time the hearing began, however, the Ontario government had changed its policy by extending employment benefits to same-sex couples except for survivor benefits under the Ontario government pension plan. The apparent reason for this exception was a restriction in the federal *Income Tax Act* that prevented the extension of spousal benefits in pension plans to same-sex couples. At issue before the board of inquiry was whether the Ontario government's reliance on this restriction amounted to improper discrimination under the provincial human rights legislation.

The problem facing the board of inquiry was that the provincial human rights legislation was itself internally inconsistent. Even though the *Ontario Human Rights Code* expressly prohibited discrimination based on sexual orientation, that statute's own definition of marital status was restricted to a conjugal relationship involving two persons of the opposite sex. As well the Code also provided that pension plans in conformity with the requirements of Ontario's *Employment Standards Act* were not considered to infringe the right to be protected from discrimination based on marital status. A majority of the board of inquiry held that, given the restricted definition of marital status in Ontario's human rights legislation, the refusal to provide the pension benefits to Leshner's partner was not because of his sexual orientation but because he was considered to be single, a distinction that was permitted by the exemption of pension plans from the prohibition against discrimination based on marital status. Using this analysis the majority of the board concluded that the refusal to extend pension benefits was not in conflict with Ontario's human rights statute.

At this point, however, the majority proceeded to address the larger issue of whether the *Human Rights Code* might itself be inconsistent with the Charter. It held that the effect of the Code was to deny pension benefits to same-sex couples and this denial amounted to discrimination on the basis of sexual orientation contrary to the Charter's guarantee of equal treatment under the law. Since there was no sound policy reason for this difference of treatment, the distinction created by the Code could not be considered as a reasonable limit. As a remedy the majority of the board directed that the definition of marital status in the Code be read down by omitting the words of "opposite sex" so that marital status could be read as including the status of living with any person in a conjugal relationship outside marriage. By broadening the definition of marital status in this way, the denial of spousal pension benefits to a same-sex partner could only be characterized as improper discrimination based on sexual orientation, rather than marital status, since Leshner's partner could no longer be considered as being single under this broader definition of marital status.

To remedy this unlawful discrimination the board of inquiry directed the employer to create a funded, or unfunded, arrangement outside the registered pension plan to provide survivor benefits and pension eligibility to same-sex partners at a level equivalent to that already enjoyed by unmarried opposite-sex partners. The board further provided that, if the *Income Tax Act* were to be amended to allow survivor benefits in the case of a same-sex conjugal relationship, the employer was required to amend its plan accordingly. If this amendment did not occur within three years of the decision, the employer was obligated to provide a new and separate funded pension arrangement for employees in same-sex relationships.

Following the *Egan and Nesbit* decision human rights tribunals had even more legal support for finding an entitlement of same-sex couples to employment benefits. In *Moore v. Treasury Board of Canada*[11] the Canadian Human Rights Tribunal dealt with two complaints against the federal government based on a denial of employment benefits to a same-sex partner. In both cases there existed a committed long-term relationship analogous to a spousal relationship. It was not disputed that, because of the earlier *Haig* decision, sexual orientation was a prohibited ground of discrimination under the *Canadian Human Rights Act*. The tribunal concluded that the denial of employment benefits to a same-sex partner that were being provided to opposite-sex partners amounted to improper discrimination based on sexual orientation. This discriminatory action, moreover, could not be justified by the fact that the employer was the federal government. Unlike in the *Egan and Nesbit* case the government in this case was not wearing its hat as developer and implementor of social policy but only its hat as employer. In its role as employer, according to the tribunal, the government had no stronger justification for its discriminatory actions than would a private employer.

The significance of this decision is not in the result, which was hardly surprising in light of the previous jurisprudence, but in the remedy ordered by the tribunal. Not only did the tribunal provide a remedy to the two individual complainants but it ordered the federal government to desist from continuing the discriminatory practice in the administration of its employment policies. In addition it required the federal government to prepare both an inventory of all legislation, regulations, and directives that contained a definition of common law spouse that discriminated against same-sex couples and a proposal for eliminating this discrimination. Pension benefit legislation could be excluded from this inventory at the request of the parties but not provisions of the *Income Tax Act* that treat employment benefits for same-sex couples in a manner that discriminates on the ground of sexual orientation. It has been reported that the federal government has now agreed to extend medical and dental benefits to same-sex partners of their employees but is seeking judicial review of the broader remedial order requiring it to eliminate discriminatory treatment of same-sex couples in its laws and policies.

Recent Arbitration Awards

Recent arbitration awards have provided further legal support for the claims of same-sex couples to employment benefits similar to those already provided to opposite-sex couples. Many collective agreements contain non-discrimination provisions that include sexual orientation as a prohibited ground of discrimination. These provisions are the product of collective bargaining rather than legislation and may even provide more comprehensive protection than human rights legislation. What is interesting is that in recent decisions arbitrators have given a broad interpretation to these contractual non-discrimination provisions, affirming the claims of same-sex couples for equal treatment in the provision of employment benefits.

A landmark arbitration award dealing with the entitlement of same-sex couples to employment benefits is the *Bell Canada* case.[12] The grievance brought by two homosexual employees alleged that the employer had violated the collective agreement by failing to provide certain spousal benefits to their same-sex partners. The employer provided such benefits to employees in common-law relationships with persons of the opposite sex but, as a matter of company policy, did not make these benefits available to employees in long-standing same-sex relationships. The union argued that the policy was discriminatory and contrary to both the *Canadian Human Rights Act* and the terms of the collective agreement. At that time the *Canadian Human Rights Act* did not expressly prohibit discrimination based on sexual orientation, but the collective agreement itself contained a non-discrimination provision under which the employer agreed not to discriminate unlawfully against an employee on certain specified grounds, one of which was sexual orientation.

The arbitrator looked first to the human rights legislation, following the reasoning in *Haig* that the Charter required that sexual orientation be read into the *Canadian Human Rights Act* as a prohibited ground of discrimination. He then concluded that, if denial of employment benefits to same-sex couples constituted discrimination on the basis of sexual orientation, it would be contrary to this implied provision in the *Canadian Human Rights Act*. This breach of the statute would then constitute a violation of the collective agreement provision prohibiting "unlawful discrimination."

The union argued that there had been discrimination based on sexual orientation because the grievors had been denied benefits that had been made available to opposite-sex couples living in otherwise identical relationships. The arbitrator accepted this argument, finding that the denial of spousal benefits to employees living in same-sex relationships did amount to unlawful discrimination based on sexual orientation contrary to the non-discrimination provision in the collective agreement. In making this finding the arbitrator rejected the employer's argument that the non-discrimination provision in the collective agreement applied only to employee rights addressed expressly by the terms of the collective agreement, and not to the benefit plans which had not been incorporated by reference into the collective agreement.

The arbitrator viewed the non-discrimination provision as "an independent obligation on each party to deal with employees in a non-discriminatory fashion, whether or not the subject-matter of the discriminatory behaviour is addressed in specific terms of the collective agreement." This obligation extended to the terms of the benefit plans even though these plans did not form part of the collective agreement. The arbitrator allowed the grievance but confined his remedy to a general declaration that there had been a breach of the collective agreement, leaving it to the parties to amend the benefit plans to bring them into compliance with the collective agreement's non-discrimination provision.

The reasoning in the *Bell Canada* award was directly challenged in a subsequent arbitration also arising within federal labour relations jurisdiction. In *Canadian Broadcasting Corp.*[13] the employer submitted that *Bell Canada* was wrongly decided, arguing that a denial of spousal benefits to employees in a same-sex relationship was simply based on their lack of spousal status. The employer argued that an employee in a same-sex relationship did not enjoy legal status as a spouse either under statute law or at common law. The denial of the benefit, therefore, was the result of the application of the general law rather than any discriminatory treatment by the employer. The arbitrator rejected this argument, observing that it was the employee plans themselves that drew the distinction between same-sex relationships and opposite-sex relationships.

In the arbitrator's view this distinction amounted to discrimination based on sexual orientation in contravention of the non-discrimination clause in the collective agreement. The arbitrator saw the denial of benefits as relating directly to the grievor's sexual orientation rather than to his status as an unmarried employee. Because single heterosexual employees, unlike homosexual employees, were eligible for spousal benefits once they entered into a settled relationship, the arbitrator concluded that the only reason for this distinction was sexual orientation.

As in the *Bell Canada* case, the arbitrator also rejected the employer's further argument that the non-discrimination provision did not apply to the administration of benefit plans which were not themselves part of the collective agreement. The arbitrator held the scope of the non-discrimination clause was not confined to the "proscribed discriminatory conduct being evident on the face of the collective agreement or in the administration or application of the collective agreement." The arbitrator was equally unimpressed with the employer's argument that the union was estopped from raising the issue of the entitlement of same-sex couples to spousal benefits because of its failure to grieve on earlier occasions. The grievance was allowed and the arbitrator retained jurisdiction to supervise the implementation of the award.

In response to this award the employer did extend the health care plan, the dental care plan, and the life insurance plan to employees in settled same-sex relationships. As for the pension plan, the employer took the position that in light of the Supreme Court of Canada's decision in the *Egan and Nesbit* case it was not required to extend pension benefits to same-sex couples. This issue was considered in a supplementary award.[14] The arbitrator held in this award that *Egan and Nesbit* did not create any barrier to the extension of the pension plan to same-sex couples in a settled relationship and directed the employer to take the necessary steps to bring its pension plan in line with the collective agreement's prohibition against discrimination based on sexual orientation.

An Alberta arbitrator has given a similarly broad interpretation to an express prohibition against discrimination based on sexual orientation set out in a collective agreement. In his words:

> Sexual orientation encompasses the natural inclination of a homosexual
> person to favour a spousal relationship with a person of the same sex. Sexual

orientation, in my opinion, is not to be viewed as relevant only where the alleged discrimination is directed toward the personal characteristics of an individual homosexual person. One of the direct consequences of such a person's sexual preference is that conjugal relationships, if established, are likely to be with persons of the same sex. This is a matter of sexual orientation. Consequently, discrimination related to such same-sex conjugal relationships is discrimination on the basis of sexual orientation, just as discrimination against a woman on the basis if her pregnancy is discrimination on the basis of sex.[15]

The arbitral jurisprudence now leaves little doubt that collective agreement provisions that proscribe discrimination based on sexual orientation will be given an interpretation broad enough to embrace an entitlement of same-sex couples to employment benefits provided to other couples. This arbitral jurisprudence is only one part of a larger trend that has seen a growing recognition of this entitlement by courts and human rights tribunals as well as arbitrators. Now that the Supreme Court of Canada has recognized that same-sex relationships enjoy constitutional protection there would appear to be no turning back.

Impact on the Workplace

Clearly the *Egan and Nesbit* case represents a watershed in the increasing litigation involving the claims of same-sex couples to benefits already provided to opposite-sex couples. The majority decision in this case has recognized that same-sex relationships enjoy constitutional protection under the Charter's guarantee of equality of treatment. This constitutional status given to these relationships makes it increasingly likely that human rights legislation and other statutes will have to be brought into line to protect and recognize these relationships. If this does occur, then collective agreements and workplace practices will have to conform to this change in the law and employers will no longer be able to deny to same-sex couples the employment benefits they already provide to opposite-sex couples. Indeed some of the larger employers in both the public and private sectors have already anticipated this change and have extended a full range of employment benefits to same-sex couples.

There is no question that this extension of employment benefits to same-sex couples will carry some cost implications. The cost of the recent decision of the federal government to extend medical and dental benefits to same-sex couples has been estimated to be between $1.80 million and $3.7 million annually, assuming that somewhere between 1 or 2 percent of the workforce would apply. This cost, however, does not appear to be particularly large given the size of the federal government payroll.

A more difficult issue for employers will be the extension of pension plans to same-sex couples. At the present time the express wording of the federal *Income Tax Act* disallows their extension to same-sex couples. An Ontario judge has held that this restriction can be justified as a reasonable limit on the Charter's protection of same-sex couples.[16] She concluded that this provision was just one part of "an overall federal retirement income system" and, as such, was indistinguishable from a similar restriction in the *Old Age*

Security Act that the Supreme Court of Canada in the *Egan* case held to be a reasonable limit. It has been reported that this decision is under appeal.

This restriction in the *Income Tax Act* is the last legal barrier to the full extension of employment benefits to same-sex couples. Even though it may be possible to establish separate pension plans for same-sex couples it may be both difficult and costly for employers to establish a pension benefit equivalent to that already provided to opposite-sex couples. The difficulties of extending full pension benefits to same-sex couples was considered in a recent decision of a federal human rights tribunal, *Laessoe v. Air Canada*.[17] The tribunal considered whether Air Canada was justified in refusing to extend pension benefits to same-sex couples after the Supreme Court of Canada's decision in the *Egan* case. The tribunal concluded that the cost and difficulty of providing an equivalent benefit under the present provisions of the *Income Tax Act* and the *Pension Benefits Standards Act* justified the employer's refusal. The answer, according to the tribunal was for the federal government to amend these two statutes rather than to require private sector employers to devise pension arrangements that do not conflict with the present legislation.

It appears that the issue of the provision of pension benefits may be the last remaining hurdle for same-sex couples to clear before they receive the same treatment as opposite-sex couples in the workplace. An easy solution would be for the federal Parliament to remove that barrier through legislative amendment, but whether our politicians would expressly affirm same-sex relationships is still problematical. It appears more likely that this issue of the entitlement of same-sex couples to pension benefits, like all the other claims of same-sex couples, will be resolved through the litigation process rather than legislative action. Canadian legislators have clearly avoided dealing with these issues and have left the field open to the courts to resolve them on a case by case basis. The difficulty with this abdication by our legislators is that litigation is a slower process that often creates uncertainty until a case is authoritatively resolved.

It may still take some time before this process of litigation is completed with a clear affirmation of the right of same-sex couples to all of the employment benefits now provided to opposite-sex couples. Nevertheless employers, whether in the public or private sector, should realize that the present pattern of litigation suggests a trend toward recognizing the claims of same-sex couples. The present pattern of litigation, aimed primarily at government and other large employers, has already produced some important gains. There is every indication that this trend will continue, encouraged by the increasing receptivity of the courts and other adjudicators to the argument that the prohibition against discrimination based on sexual orientation includes within its ambit discriminatory treatment directed at same-sex couples. The direction of this trend suggests that employers should now be looking at how their employee benefit plans might be adjusted to ensure equal treatment for same-sex couples.

Notes

1. See *Human Rights Code*, R.S.O. 1990, c. H-19 as am., s. 10(1).
2. S.C. 1996, c.14, s. 2.
3. See, for example, *Andrews* v. *Minister of Health for Ontario* (1988), 88 C.L.L.C. para. 17,023 (S.C.O.); *Attorney General (Can.)* v. *Mossop* (1993), 93 C.L.L.C. para. 17,006 (S.C.C.).
4. S. 15(1) of the *Canadian Charter of Rights and Freedoms*.

5. *Egan and Nesbit* v. *The Queen in Right of Canada* (1995), 95 C.L.L.C. para. 210-025 (S.C.C.).
6. *Vogel* v. *Manitoba* (1995), 95 C.L.L.C. para. 230-034 (C.A.).
7. *Haig* v. *The Queen* (1992), 92 C.L.L.C. para. 17,034 (Ont. C.A.); see also *Douglas* v. *The Queen* (1993), 93 C.L.L.C. para. 17,004 (Fed.Ct.T.D.).
8. *Nolan and Barry* v. *Her Majesty the Queen* (1995), 95 C.L.L.C. para. 230-027 (Nfld.S.C.T.D.).
9. *Vriend* v. *Alberta* (1996), 96 C.L.L.C. para. 230.013 (C.A.).
10. *Leshner* v. *The Queen in Right of Ontario* (1992), 92 C.L.L.C. para. 17,035.
11. *Moore* v. *Treasury Board of Canada* (1996), 96 C.L.L.C. para. 230-037.
12. *Bell Canada* (1995), 43 L.A.C. (4th) 172, MacDowell.
13. *Canadian Broadcasting Corp.* (1995), 45 L.A.C. (4th) 353, Munroe.
14. *Canadian Broadcasting Corp.* (1996), 52 L.A.C. (4th) 350, Munroe.
15. *Re Board of Governors of the University of Lethbridge* (1995), 48 L.A.C. (4th) 242 at 250, Lucas.
16. *Re Rosenberg and the Attorney General of Canada* (1996), 25 Q.R. (3d) 612 (Ont. Ct. (Gen. Div.)).
17. (1996), 96 C.L.L.C. para. 230-047.

21

Three Choices for the Future of Medicare*

GREGORY P. MARCHILDON

IN AUGUST 2000, the Caledon Institute of Social Policy published a policy memorandum to the Prime Minister on what Tom Kent felt should be done about medicare (Kent 2000). Two years later, Kent followed up with *Medicare: It's Decision Time*, urging the federal government to act before it was too late (Kent 2002). Kent's plea also was directed to the federal Commission on the Future of Health Care in Canada chaired by Roy Romanow, then just three months away from reporting. Kent feared the possibility of the Romanow Commission making "soft" recommendations offering a "range of options" that would let the Canadian government off the hook (Kent 2002: 4). Kent urged a strong report that would "define, firmly and clearly, how to strengthen medicare by modernizing it" and force a hard decision on the future direction of the system (Kent 2002: 5).

When the Romanow Commission delivered its report in November 2002, it made hard recommendations on transfer funding, the *Canada Health Act*, governance, and federal leadership. It urged that transformative changes in primary care, home care, Aboriginal health, prescription drug utilization, and health-care human resources are essential to improving quality, access, and the sustainability of the public health-care system. The report also concluded that a tax-funded, single-payer, universal system was more equitable *and* more efficient than the alternatives. It argued that the introduction of patient-pay mechanisms such as user fees or medical savings accounts would result in higher total health-care costs—even if governments would gain a temporary advantage on their bottom line by offloading part of the financing burden onto patients.

During the Commission's existence, very influential voices—a dissenting minority of Canadians—challenged the efficiency and effectiveness of a single-payer, publicly administered health-care system. However, the overwhelming weight of evidence adduced through the Commission's consultations and research demonstrated the advantages of Canadian medicare—the set of medically necessary hospital and physician services covered under the *Canada Health Act*.[1] This *Act* requires the provinces to operate single-payer, publicly administered health plans for hospital and physician services without user fees, in return for federal transfers to help pay their cost.

The Commission's deliberative consultations demonstrated the clear commitment by the vast majority of Canadians to the values and principles at the foundation of such a system, including universality and equity of access (Maxwell et al. 2002, 2003). In the im-

---

* This material was first published by the Caledon Institute of Public Policy in April 2004.

mediate aftermath of the Romanow report, presumably struck by the strength of public opinion, the dissenters muted their concerns about the desirability of a single-payer, universal system for hospital and physician services as defined under the *Canada Health Act*, even while continuing to encourage private-for-profit delivery within the existing publicly administered medicare system.

Where Are We Today and How Did We Get Here?

More recently, however, the dissenting minority has resumed its attack on Canadian medicare. Some want the *Canada Health Act* changed so that user fees could be introduced, while others argue in favour of a system of variable premiums to be introduced by the provinces and/or the federal government. Some want a return to the past where medicare benefits would be restricted to the very poor, while others want Ottawa to remove itself from medicare so that provinces can experiment without the "constraints" of the *Canada Health Act*. In fact, Premier Klein recently stated that Alberta may be prepared to break with the *Canada Health Act* completely—despite his earlier and explicit commitment to the universality, accessibility, portability, comprehensiveness, and public administration principles of the *Canada Health Act*, in the February 2003 First Ministers' agreement on health care.[2]

On the surface, the 2003 agreement appeared to implement the bulk of the Romanow Commission's recommendations concerning transfer funding and governance. The substance and timing of the Health Accord—so quick following the Romanow report—seemed to signal federal direction and leadership as well as a clear consensus among all the provinces and territories.

But appearances are misleading. Although most Canadians were ready and the political timing ostensibly seemed right, no bold blueprint for the future of medicare emerged from the meeting.

The substance of the Accord actually reflected an extremely limited consensus among the Premiers and the Prime Minister—much less an agreed upon vision and direction for the future of medicare. The weak compromise that emerged out of this closed-door meeting obscured what were in fact sharply competing views on the future of medicare.

To be sure, some progress was made. Existing provincial initiatives in primary health care, home care, and prescription drug coverage were fortified. A tip of the hat was given to improving the state of advanced diagnostics and information technology, including electronic health records. Encouragement was given to public reporting on health system performance and health outcomes. A commitment was made to create a national Health Council by May, although subsequent opposition from Alberta would produce a narrow mandate for the Council and delay its establishment until November 2003, ultimately without the participation of Alberta and Quebec.

However, even this limited progress was purchased at a high price—an increase in federal cash transfers to the provinces, including an immediate $2.1 billion top-up, and a $16 billion investment in a five-year Health Reform Fund, enriched by a further $2 billion, one-time top-up the following year. It was the price that Ottawa felt it had to pay for a few months of peace again.

The money may be enough to avoid medicare becoming the major issue for the federal Liberal government in the coming election campaign. But it did not lever transformative change for medicare.

It did not establish a new transfer funding mechanism that would create a clearer accountability relationship between Ottawa and the provinces, much less allow Canadians to know with any precision the level of the federal contribution.[3] It did not result in a modernization and strengthening of the Canada Health Act that would have permitted a carefully calibrated and fiscally responsible extension of insured services beyond hospitals and physicians. It did not lay down a national platform for home care services throughout Canada.[4] It did not begin addressing the fragmentation of Aboriginal health services and funding. And it did not tie fundamental changes in drug prescription and utilization behaviours and patterns to any extension of public coverage, despite the fragile fiscal sustainability of all current provincial drug plans. These would have been transformational changes in both governance and health-care policy.

So despite Tom Kent's warnings, the Romanow Commission's clear recommendations in these areas and the general public's thirst for change, Canadians are still waiting for a decision on fundamental direction from both orders of government. Deep down, they know that unless their governments arrive at a workable consensus for change, the Canadian brand of medicare is not likely to survive for long. Although accustomed to a certain level of intergovernmental tension—it goes with the territory in our diverse federation—Canadians nonetheless understand that the past decade has been anything but normal when it comes to medicare.

Recent Federal-Provincial Relations and the Damage Done, 1994–2000

From 1994 until 2000, I participated in almost every meeting of Premiers and First Ministers, as well as numerous federal-provincial meetings of Ministers and officials. As Deputy Minister of Intergovernmental Affairs and later as Deputy Minister to the Premier and Cabinet Secretary for the government of Saskatchewan, I represented a "middle" province that traditionally has pursued a meeting point between the more centralist tendencies within the federal government and the more decentralist provinces. From this position, I observed how health care eventually became hostage to a crass struggle over money and power and, at critical points, a much more profound clash between contending visions of the country.

At bottom, however, these titanic clashes between Ottawa and the provinces had precious little to do with medicare itself. As former federal Minister of National Health and Welfare, Monique Bégin, so aptly put it, the crisis that emerged was more a crisis in governance than a crisis in medicare (Bégin 2002). The origins of this crisis lie in the unanticipated consequences of decisions made by both orders of government. One part of the story involves provincial health reforms and cost constraint efforts that squeezed health funding in the early 1990s, resulting in the general public perceiving substantive provincial health reforms as a cover for mere budget cutting. The other part entails the federal government's unilateral decision to change the nature and amount of transfer funding for health care through a series of unilateral reductions in funding by the

Mulroney government in the 1980s and early 1990s, and the introduction of the Canada Health and Social Transfer and across-the-board transfer cuts by the Chrétien government in the mid-1990s.

By 1992, many provinces were initiating real health reforms on the ground in an effort to improve the continuity and coordination of illness care through organizational changes such as regionalization, while placing more emphasis on wellness and prevention. At the same time, however, the provinces put the brakes on health spending to an extent that was unmatched among OECD countries. Measured in constant (1997) dollars, the growth in total public sector health expenditures declined from 4.2 percent in 1991–92 to 1.7 percent the next year, then registered negative growth for four consecutive years: –0.7 percent in 1993–94, –0.2 percent in 1994–95, –0.9 percent in 1995–96 and –0.5 percent in 1996–97.

Then, almost as suddenly, in response to voters angered by long wait lists and deteriorating quality that they perceived to result from the cuts, provincial governments began to pour money back into health care. Real growth in public sector health expenditures ballooned up from 3.0 percent in 1997–98 to 6.2 percent in 1998–99, 6.5 percent in 1999–2000, 6.0 percent in 2000–01 and 6.8 percent in 2001–02. Overall, health-care spending went from feast in the 1980s to famine in the early 1990s and then back to feast by the late 1990s (Commission on the Future of Health Care in Canada 2002: Appendix E).[5] While substantive provincial health reforms combined with stop-go financing were changing medicare on the ground, the introduction of the Canada Health and Social Transfer in the mid-1990s was fundamentally altering the country's fiscal and social policy environment (Yalnizyan 2004). In terms of public health care alone, it produced three major changes.

First, the Canada Health and Social Transfer (CHST) reduced cash transfers to the provinces just as they were ending their fiscal squeeze on health-care expenditures. This meant that the provinces would be drawing on their own revenues in their health spending ramp-up. Second, the CHST eliminated the escalator formula that previously had tied growth in federal cash transfers to growth in the economy. This meant that annual increases would henceforth be subject to episodic, highly charged, and unpredictable negotiations between the provinces and Ottawa. Third, the CHST allowed provincial governments to blame the federal government for the dislocation caused by their own reforms as well as cutbacks in health-care spending.

Despite the fact that the Canada Health and Social Transfer cuts also affected postsecondary education and social assistance/services, the Premiers insisted on referring to the CHST as "health funding." Initially frustrated by the public's lack of sympathy or understanding for their plight, the provinces began to describe their own difficulties in health care (in part caused by their own stop-go financing) as a crisis that could only be fixed through more money from the federal treasury. However erroneous in terms of timing, this was a logic that was easily understood, and the public began to blame the federal government for the deterioration—both perceived and real—in medicare. The Premiers had finally hit on a winning formula to shift at least some blame onto Ottawa.

This blame-shifting became apparent with the signing of the Social Union Framework Agreement (SUFA) in February 1999. When the First Ministers sat down together at 24 Sussex Drive, the ostensible purpose was to finalize and sign a protocol regulating the conduct of both orders of government in terms of social policy. With the exception of Quebec, which chose not to sign, this was done.

In reality, however, the meeting was all about health-care funding. The dynamic was simple—even crude. From the provincial perspective, expenditures—driven by health care—were climbing faster than revenues; a quick transfer shot from Ottawa would make the problem go away for a little while. This was valuable for those Premiers about to call elections, particularly Premier Harris of Ontario who suddenly dropped all his objections to the Social Union Framework Agreement, abruptly ending his alliance with Premier Lucien Bouchard of Quebec. From the federal government's perspective, the provinces would agree to a less decentralizing Social Union Framework Agreement in exchange for more cash—the kind of bargain permitted by the Canada Health and Social Transfer mechanism in which increases were now entirely at the discretion of the federal government.[6] The extra money from Ottawa might also alleviate Canadians' growing concern about the commitment of the federal government to medicare.

Unfortunately for both sides, the fix was temporary. A combination of promised tax cuts and rising health expenditures pushed many provinces into deficit territory, and all blamed Ottawa for under-funding health care in an effort to shift blame. At the Annual Premiers' Conference in the summer of 1999, the provinces demanded more money but the Prime Minister refused, disappointed that the earlier February agreement had not bought more credit and time. Just before the release of the next federal Budget, the Premiers sent an open letter to the Prime Minister demanding "an immediate rescue of Canada's failing health-care system" (Crites 2002: 398). Although rescue did not come in the subsequent 2000 federal Budget, the general public was, after a four-year lag, finally associating the earlier Canada Health and Social Transfer cuts to the perceived crisis in health care. With Ottawa now seen to be as culpable as the provinces, the intergovernmental struggle for the hearts and minds of Canadians began in earnest.

The provinces charged Ottawa with under-funding health care based on a historic 50/50 cost sharing formula, blithely ignoring the impact of a massive transfer of federal tax points to the provinces in 1977. The federal government responded with some misleadingly "clever fiscal arithmetic" of its own, overstating its contribution to provincial social programming including medicare (St-Hilaire and Lazar 2003: 66). Counter-attacking in August with a report called *Understanding Canada's Health Care Costs*, the Premiers called for a cash increase equal to what had been cut with the introduction of the Canada Health and Social Transfer in 1995 (Provincial and Territorial Ministers of Health 2000).

The arguments used by both sides as ammunition in this war—misleading at best, dishonest at worst—simply served to confuse and confound the Canadian public. Further adding to the public's growing anxiety, three provinces—Quebec, Alberta, and Saskatchewan—set up external committees that summer to advise them on health-care reform and financing, leaving open the question of whether at least one report might end up recommending a fundamental break from the basic principles of the *Canada Health Act*.

With the so-called health-care crisis drumbeat growing louder, Prime Minister Chrétien called a meeting of First Ministers to focus on health-care reform and funding for 11 September 2000. The war of words had escalated to the point that the stakes were enormous for both sides. Opening a window for a fall election, Chrétien went into the meeting prepared to increase cash transfers by a considerable amount if the provinces would sign onto an accord linking this money to new investment in medical and advanced diagnostic equipment as well as primary care reform. The provinces went into the meeting expecting a federal cash injection equal to what had been pulled out in the original Canada Health and Social Transfer cuts. Though substantial, the federal offer fell short of expectations, and the fragile unity of the Premiers fractured.

The division among the Premiers was about both money and principle. On money, some believed that continuing the attack on Ottawa while boycotting the conditional federal offer would force the federal government to give cash with no strings attached. On principle, some wanted an unconditional transfer—perhaps in the form of a transfer of federal tax points to the provinces—while others continued to believe that Ottawa should play some role in setting the national dimensions of the health-care system, and were therefore prepared to sign onto an accountability framework.

These conflicting views came to a head very early in the morning. Explaining that Ontario officials had met the night before with officials from Quebec, Nova Scotia, New Brunswick, and Prince Edward Island (Manitoba's role was less clear), Ontario's Premier proposed a much more decentralist approach in which the provinces would have maximum latitude to allocate any additional federal money for health care. Vigorous debate followed as Premiers who knew nothing about the secret discussions the night before fumed.

Taken by surprise, Chrétien temporarily adjourned the meeting in the hope that the provinces left out of the decentralist gambit would pressure Ontario and its allies back to the table with a response more acceptable to Ottawa. At this, Premier Harris of Ontario threatened to leave the meeting permanently. After some acrimonious debate and a further series of private meetings among Premiers and their officials as well as the Prime Minister and some of his key officials, the Premiers of Ontario and Quebec along with the three Maritime Premiers eventually dropped their alternative text, accepting a slightly amended version of the original agreement. In the end, even the decentralist Premiers found the federal cash too difficult to turn down. Nonetheless, the September 2000 agreement was achieved at the high cost of further damaging relations between Ottawa and the provinces, as well as creating deep suspicions and mistrust among the provinces themselves.

As with the February 1999 SUFA deal, the September 2000 agreement turned out to be another temporary fix. Almost immediately afterwards, the provinces most opposed to the agreement began dragging their collective feet on the collaborative work outlined in the Accord and soon started up the familiar drumbeat for more money (with fewer strings attached) from Ottawa. While the September Accord may have allowed the federal Liberals to portray themselves as the defenders of medicare, it did not remove health care as the major irritant in the federal-provincial relationship.

From Romanow to the Present

Ottawa's now perpetual battle with the provinces over health-care funding convinced Chrétien of the need to try to find a more permanent solution in the spring of 2001. He appointed a veteran of the recent federal-provincial wars and a close colleague from earlier constitutional battles, Roy Romanow, as the chair of a new Commission on the Future of Health Care in Canada. As the recently retired Premier of Saskatchewan, Romanow understood the provincial perspective, but also had consistently advocated a more meaningful federal role in social policy (Romanow 1998).

While agreeing on the arm's length nature of the study and consequent recommenda-tions, Chrétien insisted on a November 2002 deadline for its final report—long enough to avoid having to commit any further federal money for 2002, but short enough potentially to implement some of the recommendations within the current term of his government. With the general public, health-care providers, and the provinces all demanding action, few cared that this eighteen month deadline was substantially shorter than normally al-lotted royal commissions: Indeed, it amounted to one-half the time taken by the Hall Commission on Health Care in the early 1960s. Despite this, Romanow insisted on his Commission initiating a major program of research projects as well as conducting the most ambitious, sophisticated, and multi-layered series of consultations ever undertaken by a royal commission.[7]

To manage the Commission's relationship with the provinces and territories and to facilitate their participation in the consultations, an intergovernmental unit was estab-lished.[8] This initiative reflected Romanow's own view that, although the provinces did not have exclusive jurisdiction over medicare, they nonetheless had the primary responsibility for health-care organization and delivery. As such, a royal commission concerning the future of health care in Canada had to be a national—rather than an exclusively federal—enterprise. To emphasize its independence from the federal government, the Commission ran its operations from Saskatchewan rather than Ottawa—the first federal royal commis-sion to do so.

At a minimum, these gestures prevented the Commission from being dismissed by a majority of provinces and territories as just more federal ammunition in the intergovern-mental war. Perhaps not surprisingly, however, Premiers were much more focused on how the Commission might provide some advantage in their own immediate struggle with the Prime Minister. Speaking and meeting with Premiers directly, Romanow was consistently being pressured to reveal his recommendations—particularly those concerning federal funding—well before the final report.

Delivered in November 2002, the recommendations in the Romanow Commission's final report were a curse and a blessing for both orders of government. From the provinces' perspective, the report endorsed their argument that the federal government should live up to its historic funding obligations, which would mean a significant increase in transfers from Ottawa to the provinces. But the Commission also said that federal transfers should be targeted for transformational change and directly attached to funding conditions with-in a modernized *Canada Health Act*. For the decentralist Premiers, this recommendation involved a degree of federal partnership (beyond funding) that they found difficult to swal-low. From Ottawa's perspective, considerable weight was given to the federal role through legislation and conditional transfers, though at the price of exposing the historic decline in federal transfers and the need to bolster the amount of transfers to the provinces.

Moreover, the Romanow report exposed the weaknesses in the arguments on health funding and governance put forward by both sides during their recent battles. It also de-manded that Ottawa and the provinces meet as soon as possible to reach a consensus, repair the damage done, and come forward with a long-term action plan to improve pub-lic health care in Canada.

In the immediate aftermath of the report's release, much of the Canadian media fo-cused on the increase to the federal cash transfer recommended by Romanow. But the media largely ignored the fundamental governance changes and the national health re-form agenda that the Commission put forward as preconditions to any new investment in medicare by Ottawa.[9]

In some quarters, the report was crudely interpreted to be simply a call for more (fed-eral) money to be pumped into medicare.

The Premiers themselves focused on the money and soon coined a phrase—"the Romanow gap"—to dramatize the difference between the Commission's recommendation on federal funding and what Ottawa was actually transferring to the provinces. Contrary to the Romanow report's insistence on restricting the federal share to *Canada Health Act* expenditures, the Premiers inflated the size of the gap by including all provincial and territorial health expenditures including prescription drug plans, home care and long term care in their calculation. Predictably, the federal government responded in kind by throwing into its calculation of the federal contribution a number of non-medicare ex-penditures and transfers.

Thus deployed as a weapon in the ongoing federal-provincial struggle, the so-called Romanow gap, now serves only to create more confusion for the Canadian public. In the February 2003 agreement, the federal government partially filled the Romanow gap. The Premiers took what they could, but made it clear they were disappointed with the quan-tum of money and would soon be back for more.

Three Options for the Future

In these circumstances, there are three main options in terms of the future of medicare. One is to continue with the status quo, with Ottawa achieving temporary truces with the provinces through transferring billions of federal dollars politically calibrated to be the minimum necessary to keep Premiers temporarily at bay, while exerting limited or no leadership on the future direction and governance of the system. The second is for the federal government to get completely out of the medicare business, perhaps with a final transfer of tax points, allowing the provinces maximum freedom and maneuverability in running their respective health plans. The third is for Ottawa to get back in the game in a new and more vigorous way, working with the provinces to establish a new direction for medicare better suited to the needs and pressures of the new century. Each of these op-tions will be examined briefly.

1. The status quo: Death by stealth

The federal-provincial story told above reveals why the status quo is really death by stealth for medicare. Clearly, there are structural incentives that encourage the Premiers to use health care as a weapon against Ottawa to get additional cash in "health" transfers—money that can, in reality, be used for almost any purpose including tax cuts and deficit control. The constant demand by the provinces for more cash will continue because the reforms announced in the First Ministers' agreement of February 2003 do not change these struc-tural incentives; neither does the extra $2 billion one-time cash transfer confirmed in their meeting in January 2004.

The status quo also will allow the current debate over the sustainability of health care to fester, further undermining public confidence in the future viability of medicare.

During the past few years, there has been a concerted campaign by an array of interests opposed to a universal system of medicare to convince Canadians that they no longer can afford the current system. The campaign has been given a real boost by First Ministers who have consistently used health care as a hostage in their larger struggle over taxation and fiscal resources.

The sustainability argument has claimed credence in the rapid growth of health-care costs since 1997. Less commented on is the fact that since 1997 most governments also have introduced significant tax cuts. Given the unpopularity of raising taxes, these tax cuts constitute a quasi-permanent reduction in the revenue stream needed for public services such as medicare in the future. It is also little understood that both public and private health-care costs have grown slightly faster than the rate of economic growth (and therefore government revenues) for at least the past half century. Since 1977, annual health-care expenditures have been growing about 0.8 percent faster than the gross national product of the country (Lazar, St-Hilaire and Tremblay 2004: 172). This fact alone does not constitute a sustainability crisis. But the reasons for this phenomenon need to be understood.

First, health care is a leading sector in the economies of advanced industrial nations, and leading sectors by definition grow faster than most other sectors of the economy. According to economist William Nordhaus, health-care spending—both public and private—has added as much to the growth of the American economy as all other consumer spending combined (Nordhaus 2002). The conventional wisdom is to speak of private health-care spending as a dynamic investment in the economy and public health-care spending as a static consumption of existing resources. The truth is that both types of expenditure are investments that stimulate the economy, but both are also costs to Canadians as investors, consumers, or taxpayers.

The second important point is that health care has all the attributes of what economists call a "superior good." This term means that we tend to spend progressively more on health care as our incomes go up. We do so collectively through the taxes we pay for public health-care services, and as individuals privately paying for services not covered under our public plans. Indeed, higher income is the single most important determinant of higher levels of public and private health spending for all countries (Gerdtham and Jönsson 2000).

This brings us to the question of why current health expenditures are growing faster than the historic average. Two theories have been advanced. One is that we are simply in a period of catch-up after the cutbacks, layoffs and under-funding of the early 1990s that produced growth rates well below the historic average (Tuohy 2002). The other is that this is a permanent ratcheting-up of health-care expenditures for which we must now make new private funding arrangements to relieve the pressure on public resources—although little hard evidence is advanced to explain why the growth trajectory for health-care costs has fundamentally changed (Boothe and Carson 2003). These explanations will be confirmed or denied over the next five years. But right now, we know that simply shifting costs from the public purse to individual pockets is more likely to exacerbate, than to solve, the problem of the total costs for health care faced by Canadians—to say nothing of the new accessibility problems that would be created by such a shift.

Canadians spent just over $120 billion on health care in 2003 or about $3,840 for each man, woman, and child (Canadian Institute for Health Information 2003). Paid for through taxes, insurance premiums, and out-of-pocket, this amount equals about one-tenth of the Canadian economy. It is worth looking more closely at the public and private components of this expenditure.

Health-care expenditures fall into four categories. Medicare services under the Canada Health Act (CHA) come to just over 42 percent of the total. Prescription drug plans and home-, continuing-, and institutional care as well as other non-CHA services provided by the provinces and territories amount to about 25 percent. Direct federal expenditures on Aboriginal health, public health, and other items constitute 5 percent of the total. The private component (non-medicare health services paid by patients, private insurance plans and employee benefit plans) makes up just over 27 percent of the total. Of these components, provincial expenditures on non-medicare services and private expenditures have been growing much faster than medicare expenditures not only since 1997, but since medicare was introduced in the 1960s. Therefore, it is illogical to argue that simply reducing the basket of CHA services, thereby shifting health costs from the public purse to individual pocketbooks or targeted public programs, would reduce overall health costs. On the contrary, it is more likely to do the opposite given the proven administrative efficiencies of single-payer insurance systems over the alternatives (Woolhandler et al. 2003). One way or another, Canadians will pay these costs either through a system that provides access to "medically necessary services" based on need or through a system where access is based on ability to pay.

The solution to the "sustainability problem" offered by the opponents of medicare—that of shifting costs from the public purse to private pockets—is simple but illusory from an economic policy standpoint (Evans 2004). It is also highly inequitable from a social policy standpoint. And it is neither bold nor innovative—"out of the box"—thinking since it generally involves old nostrums such as user fees, co-payments, and health premiums (occasionally dressed up in modern garb such as medical saving accounts) that were the norm prior to the introduction of universal medicare.

Nonetheless, sustainability continues to be equated with the growth in medicare costs—with little or no thought given to the growth in non-medicare costs, whether in the public or the private sector. Proponents of introducing more private health care rarely discuss rising health-care costs in this sector, but cost-shifting in this way will lead to higher personal costs for Canadians. It will also lead to cost escalation in non-universal, non single-payer provincial programs (such as the majority of provincial drug plans) which, in turn, will contribute to further cost-shifting from the provinces to individual Canadians as they try to prevent other priority programs and services such as education from being crowded out.

If we want to see the future in this scenario, we need look no further than the United States where public health care is non-universal and non single-payer, and where Americans bear a much higher burden of personal health-care costs. In the US, per capita total health costs are almost double those in Canada; per capita *public* health-care costs are actually higher than in Canada; and population health outcomes are among the lowest in the OECD. Is health care more fiscally sustainable in the United States than in Canada? Clearly not.

And for those who believe that the United States is so unique a case that it should never be compared to Canada, I would point to the example of Switzerland, which has the most expensive health system in the world after the US. The Swiss private health insurance system is an anomaly among the predominantly publicly insured systems of Western Europe, and its higher costs are a product of the inevitably higher costs associated with multi-payer insurance systems.

2. Tax transfer: Death by execution

One alternative to the status quo is to accept the decentralist provinces' argument that health care is exclusive provincial jurisdiction. This approach would remove Ottawa's influence over medicare by eliminating the *Canada Health Act* and cash transfers.[10]

There are at least two reasons why a future federal government might wish to leave medicare entirely in the hands of the provinces. While federal cost-sharing originally ensured that provincially administered, single-payer systems for hospital and physician care services were adopted by all jurisdictions (including the minority that would have preferred targeted, means-based programs), it could be argued that the federal spending power in health care has outlived its early usefulness. According to this argument, medicare is here to stay as an "established program" and provincial governments, irrespective of their ideological proclivities, will be prevented by their own voters from subverting or eliminating the national dimensions of the system.

Of course, there are no guarantees. In fact, it is unlikely that all provinces would continue to uphold the medicare principles of public administration, universality, accessibility, comprehensiveness, and portability in the absence of transfer funding and the *Canada Health Act*. There would be little incentive to do so. Even now, the principle of portability is not being upheld by Quebec within Canada and by five provinces for out-of-country services (Flood and Choudhry 2004). And even now, the Alberta government threatens to break with the *Canada Health Act* by introducing user fees that are inconsistent with the principle of accessibility.

There is another possible argument in favour of the federal government vacating the field. Ottawa might decide that medicare is no longer worth the candle—that the influence the government of Canada buys through billions of dollars in transfers is just too minimal and the political cost in terms of intergovernmental squabbling just too high.

Indeed, provinces have been demanding greater flexibility for decades, and the tax transfer deal worked out between Prime Minister Trudeau and the Premiers in 1977 was partly in response to their demand for greater freedom. This freedom was offered through a historic transformation of roughly 50/50 cost-sharing of provincial hospital and physician costs to what eventually was intended to be a 25 percent permanent federal tax transfer to the provinces in combination with a 25 percent cash transfer.[11] Has the time now come for Ottawa to move the remaining cash transfer into a final transfer of tax room to the provinces, and forget about the national dimensions of medicare? Transferring the Goods and Services Tax (GST) to the provinces, for example, would give them a sufficiently robust revenue source to fund medicare well into the future (Rode and Rushton 2004).

If nothing else, such a change would produce clarity. Henceforth, the provinces would be solely responsible for medicare—so no more accusations about Ottawa treading on provincial jurisdiction and no more blaming the federal government for the performance of provincial health plans. No more painful meetings between federal and provincial health ministers, except perhaps on items that clearly involve federal jurisdiction (First Nations and Inuit health care, drug safety and regulation, and public health).

However appealing this solution may seem to some, there is evidence that a majority of Canadians would find it unacceptable (Mendelsohn 2001). There are some very good reasons why most people feel this way. With this option, Canadians no longer would be guaranteed the basic contours of a health-care system that most regard as a keystone of their national identity. Without federal cash, and the consequent ability of the federal government to withdraw it, the *Canada Health Act* would be a dead letter law.

Canadians could only accept a tax transfer option if it came with a guarantee. This could only be achieved in one way—by entrenching the current five principles of the Canada Health Act as a right of citizenship in the constitution. Presumably, no federal government would offer a transfer of tax points to the provinces without first getting unanimous agreement from the provinces to support such an amendment to the Charter of Rights and Freedoms. The courts rather than governments would then be entrusted with the responsibility of protecting and preserving the national dimensions of medicare, and governments could not change the medicare pact without a further constitutional amendment.

Even assuming a constitutional amendment to be politically feasible—and this is a very dubious assumption—it may not be desirable for a number of reasons. Canadians would lose their ability to shape the future basic direction of the health-care system acting through democratically elected governments at both levels. With the permanent loss of its spending power on health care, the federal government would be unable to set the broad framework for any expansion of the public health-care system as it did with hospitalization in the late 1950s and primary physician care in the late 1960s. Finally, Canadians would lose the equalization effect of accessing a national revenue base as well as provincial revenues to fund the system, making it even more difficult for poorer provinces with thinner tax bases to deliver health services roughly comparable to those funded and delivered by wealthier provinces.

3. Ottawa as a real partner in medicare

There is a real alternative to the options discussed above and to the demise of medicare as Canadians have come to know it. This would be for both orders of government to agree upon a new medicare pact that draws upon the more positive features of a cost-sharing regime but sheds some of its more negative aspects. Such a pact would be built upon a recommitment to the founding principles of medicare as well as an agreement on its future direction.

In terms of funding, the federal government could create a purely cash-based transfer to the provinces and territories for medicare expenditures. In line with what the public has long accepted as a fair share, this would be 50/50 cost sharing. But the federal government made a tax point transfer to the provinces in 1977, so the more appropriate federal contribution is now 25 percent. This new federal cash transfer should be calculated on the basis of a national average, with provinces receiving a per capita share to avoid any potential skewing of provincial resource allocation simply to lever federal dollars.

While federal contributions and provincial medicare expenditures would be transparent and made available to the public and governments, there would be no need for federal monitoring or micro-managing of provincial expenditures. At the same time, the federal government would share in some of the fiscal risks of medicare by virtue of its permanent 25 percent stake that would make future contributions more predictable. To add to this predictability, an escalator formula could be introduced within the context of a permanent 25 percent contribution target. However, the Canadian public and governments must understand that the provinces should get no more and no less from Ottawa than the 25 percent. This formula would remove the incentive for Premiers to make regular demands on the Prime Minister for more health-care money.

In terms of governance, an agreement among First Ministers concerning principles and direction would give Ottawa the moral legitimacy to modernize the *Canada Health Act*. The discretionary penalty provisions underpinning the five principles that have been so ineffective (as well as irritating to the provinces precisely because of the discretion given to the Minister of Health) could be replaced by the mandatory "dollar-for-dollar" penalties that have worked so well in eliminating user fees and extra billing. Some targeted home care services could be added to the basket of insured services and form part of the federal cash transfer to the provinces in order to encourage some transformational changes in health care on the ground.

At the same time, it would be understood that the provinces should be entirely responsible for administering their own single-payer systems within the principles of the *Canada Health Act*. The provinces have had decades of experience in managing their respective systems and know best how to implement reform, including changes that will ensure that all Canadians have timely access to high quality services in the most cost effective manner. The national dimensions encompassed by the *Canada Health Act* are not a barrier to innovative organization and delivery of medicare. In fact, provinces and provincially delegated organizations such as regional health authorities should be encouraged to experiment as much as they choose within the very broad framework principles of the *Canada Health Act*, rather than be subject to any delivery model designed in Ottawa. This is the federal balance in medicare that can, and should, be achieved in the months ahead.

Despite the corrosive intergovernmental disputes of the last few years, public support for the Canadian model of medicare remains high. Moreover, Canadians want their elected representatives at both the federal and provincial levels to work together in renovating their medicare house for the twenty-first century. Their vision is of a country that is a sharing community, one that works actively to reduce regional disparities in terms of access to quality health-care services (Banting and Boadway 2004). Such a vision requires a meaningful federal role in medicare.

The meeting of the Prime Minister and the Premiers in June 2004 will be pivotal. It will provide an opportunity to put the damage caused by federal-provincial fighting over health-care transfers behind us and agree upon the national dimensions of medicare. The issue is of such importance to Canadians that they should know exactly what their governments are negotiating and the decisions they ultimately make. This is reason enough to televise the proceedings and let some light into a process that has been hidden in the shadows for too long.

On the tactical front, there may never be a better time to attempt such a change. In 2003, new governments were elected in Quebec and Ontario. We now may have two Premiers more willing to work on using a strengthened federation to address some deep-seated federal-provincial problems in medicare. We have a Prime Minister who believes that universal medicare is one of Canada's greatest achievements (Martin 2003). While stating that the Romanow report was "a milestone in the development" of health-care policy in Canada, the Prime Minister also has made it clear to the Premiers that he will not "talk about the Romanow gap" unless they deal with it in the context of "the report in its entirety" (Hansard, Feb. 3, 2004: 41).

Further federal transfer cash should flow only *after* both orders of government agree on the national dimensions of public health care in Canada, a modernized *Canada Health Act*, and the federal government as a real partner in the medicare enterprise. Without such a role, it is difficult to see why Ottawa should continue transferring billions of dollars to the provinces for health care.

Conclusion

Historically, the federal role in medicare has made a profound difference to all Canadians. Universal public health-care insurance would not exist without the federal spending pow-er or the various pieces of legislation setting out the transfer conditions, from the *Hospital Insurance and Diagnostic Services Act* of 1957 and the *Medical Care Act* of 1966 to the *Canada Health Act* of 1984. While Saskatchewan got the ball rolling by introducing hos-pitalization in 1947 and medicare in 1962, national medicare could not have achieved its policy framework consistency nor funding stability without the federal government.

As important to remember, medicare would not exist without brave and visionary acts of personal leadership from Premier Tommy Douglas and Prime Minister Lester B. Pearson. And it cannot be maintained and improved without both provincial and federal nationbuilders. Despite his difficulties as a minority leader and his perceived failings as a strong leader of cabinet, Pearson will always be remembered as a great Prime Minister be-cause he insisted on implementing national medicare in the face of stiff opposition from organized medicine, the business elite and many within his own party. He also strove to find the optimal balance between broad national principles and funding conditions on the one hand, and the breathing room required for the provinces and territories to administer and deliver as effectively and efficiently as possible 13 individual medicare plans on the other hand.[12]

The time has come to remake the social compact concerning medicare. "Muddling through" will be a disaster for the country. The debate over health-care transfer funding will continue to poison federal-provincial relations, forcing other urgent matters into the back-ground, even while it contaminates Ottawa's ability to have a collaborative and constructive relationship with the provinces and territories. This can only lead to further political crowd-ing-out of other important issues demanding federal-provincial collaboration.

Provinces also face enormous challenges on their respective home fronts. Public health care is taking up more and more spending space in provincial expenditure plans. This crowding-out of other program spending is creating considerable hardship for provinces, most of which are either skirting deficits or once again running deficits. They are desperately looking for quick solutions to slow down the growth of health-care expenditures. Some provinces may be tempted to push health-care costs out of the public purse and onto individuals if they lose faith in their political ability to improve the efficiency and effectiveness of their public health-care plans.

National leadership provided by First Ministers could boost confidence. More importantly, it could clarify the national dimensions of medicare and produce a national game plan for a set of transformative reforms that would make the system much more sustainable in the future.

Medicare is too important to continue to be held ransom by both orders of government in an increasingly sterile debate over fiscal transfers. For most Canadians, medicare is an integral part of their citizenship and identity. They want their First Ministers to quit playing the blame game and instead to work at improving medicare on the ground, including reducing waiting times and improving the quality of care. At the same time, they want both orders of government to come up with a common game plan that will address growing costs and ensure the sustainability of medicare for the future. Most want the principle of "access based on need" preserved.

For a vocal minority, however, nothing less than greater privatization and decentralization, attractively dressed up as patient choice, is required to fix medicare in Canada. Though well financed, visible, and powerful, we should always remember that this view is a minority view, and should not be allowed to dictate what the majority of Canadians actually want for themselves and future generations.

Notes

1. The Commission's consultations included 12 all-day regional citizens' dialogue sessions involving almost 500 randomly selected Canadians, televised forums, nine expert workshops, three regional forums, partnered dialogue sessions on individual health policy issues and an internet consultation workbook as well as the more traditional public hearings. The Commission's research included a series of expert roundtables on public-private partnerships (London, UK), co-payments and related options (Paris), health system cost-drivers (Washington, DC) and financing options (Toronto); three major research projects; and 40 externally commissioned researched papers. Many of the latter have recently been published by the University of Toronto Press in a three volume series entitled *The Romanow Papers* edited by Gregory P. Marchildon, Pierre-Gerlier Forest and Tom McIntosh.

2. *Canadian Press*, 20 Feb. 2004. Perhaps the most serious threat to medicare, however, comes from a case currently before the Supreme Court of Canada brought by Dr. Jacques Chaoulli and George Zeliotis that is challenging the legal basis of the single-payer system in Quebec (and therefore all provinces). A long-time advocate of two-tier health care, Chaoulli has been joined on the main constitutional issue by Senator Michael Kirby and some fellow Senators who argue that the rights of Canadians under section 7 of the Charter of Rights and Freedoms are violated if timely access to publicly funded health care is denied through wait lists and they are prohibited at the same time from seeking private health care. The case will be heard in June 2004 and could have momentous consequences for the manner in which medicare has been administered since the 1960s.

3. This is so despite the appearance of creating a dedicated transfer. The Canada Health Transfer referred to in the February 2003 Accord is simply the health portion of the CHST, mixing tax with cash transfers in the same confusing manner. In addition, the transfer can be used for any health or related expenditure, not merely medicare expenditures as defined under the *Canada Health Act*.

4. It did suggest a move towards home care norms by 30 September 2003, although little progress was made by that date or afterwards.

5. Total (public and private) health expenditures per capita (in constant 1997 dollars) tell a similar if less dramatic story. From 1990 until 2003, total health expenditures grew an average of 2.3 percent per year, which is very close to the overall 2.5 percent annual growth rate from 1975 until 2003. But if you split this 13-year period into two, then you discover an annual growth rate of 0.4 percent from 1990 to 1996 and 3.6 percent from 1997 to 2003. See Canadian Institute for Health Information, *National Health Expenditure Trends, 1975–2003*.

6. Although two separate communiqués were issued from this meeting—one on SUFA—and one on health fund funding in order to allow Quebec to avoid signing SUFA on principle while gaining the benefit of the health funding, the other provinces understood that more federal cash for health was conditional on the SUFA agreement.

7. See Appendix C on the external research program (pp. 301-307) and Appendix B (pp. 271-299) on the structure of the consultation processes in the Romanow Commission's final report, *Building on Values: The Future of Health Care in Canada*.

8. This unit also was responsible for the Commission's relationship with the major national Aboriginal organizations.

9. The French-language media in Quebec concentrated on the broader constitutional and federal-provincial implications of Romanow's recommendations.

10. For analyses as to why the constitutional argument concerning exclusive provincial jurisdiction is faulty, see the chapters by André Braën and Howard Leeson in T. McIntosh, P.G. Forest, and G. Marchildon eds. *The Governance of Health Care in Canada*.

11. There has been much huffing and puffing about whether shared cost programming for medicare was ever 50/50, but this was the explicit assumption under the *Hospital Insurance and Diagnostic Services Act* (1957) and the *Medical Care Act* (1966). Moreover, the empirical evidence supports a rough 50/50 split for provincial hospitalization and medicare expenditures (but clearly not for total provincial health expenditures) during the era of cost-sharing. Established Program Financing (1977) introduced additional complications in terms of an imputed amount for the tax transfer and the mixing of hospitalization and medicare expenditures with all other health expenditures as well as postsecondary education.

12. There is an argument, however, that federal direct services to special groups including First Nations (on reserve), Inuit, veterans, and members of the RCMP and Armed forces constitute a 14th medicare system which would be the sixth largest in Canada based upon expenditures.

References

Banting, K. and R. Boadway. (2004). "Defining the Sharing Community: The Federal Role in Health Care." In H. Lazar and F. Saint-Hilaire eds., *Money, Politics and Health Care: Reconstructing the Federal-Provincial Partnership*. Montreal: The Institute for Research on Public Policy and The Institute of Intergovernmental Relations.

Bégin, M. (2002). "Revisiting the Canada Health Act (1984): What are the Impediments to Change?" Speech to The Institute for Research on Public Policy 30th Anniversary Conference.

Boothe, P. and M. Carson. (2003). *What Happened to Health-Care Reform?* Toronto: C.D. Howe Institute.

Braën, A. (2004). "Health and the Distribution of Powers in Canada." In T. McIntosh, P.-G. Forest and G. Marchildon, eds., *The Governance of Health Care in Canada*. Toronto: University of Toronto Press.

Canadian Institute for Health Information. (2003). *National Health Expenditure Trends, 1975–2003*. Ottawa: Canadian Institute for Health Information.

Canadian Intergovernmental Conference Secretariat. (2003). *2003 First Ministers' Accord on Health-care Renewal*. 5 February.

Commission on the Future of Health Care in Canada. (2002). *Building on Values: The Future of Health Care in Canada*. Saskatoon: Commission on the Future of Health Care in Canada.

Crites, V. (2002). "Chronology of Events: January 2000–December 2000." In H. Telford and H. Lazar, eds., *Canada: The State of the Federation, 2001—Canadian Political Culture(s) in Transition.* Kingston: The Institute of Intergovernmental Relations, Queen's University.

Evans, R. (2004). "Financing Health Care: Options, Consequences, and Objectives." In G. Marchildon, T. McIntosh, and P.G. Forest, eds., *The Fiscal Sustainability of Health Care.* Toronto: University of Toronto Press.

Flood, C. and S. Choudhry. (2004). "Strengthening the Foundations: Modernizing the Canada Health Act." In T. McIntosh, P.G. Forest, and G. Marchildon, eds., *The Governance of Health Care in Canada.* Toronto: University of Toronto Press.

Gerdtham, U. and B. Jönsson. (2000). "International Comparisons of Health Expenditure: Theory, Data and Econometric Analysis." In A. Culyer and J. Newhouse, eds., *Handbook of Health Economics,* Vol. 1A. New York: Elsevier.

Government of Canada. (2000). *Backgrounder on Federal Support for Health in Canada.* Online at <www.fin.gc.ca/activty/pubs/health_e.pdf>.

Hansard. (2004). 3 February, p. 41.

Kent, T. (2002). *Medicare: It's Decision Time.* Ottawa: Caledon Institute of Social Policy, May.

Kent, T. (2000). *What Should Be Done About Medicare?* Ottawa: Caledon Institute of Social Policy, August.

Lazar, H., F. St-Hilaire, and J.-F. Tremblay. (2004). "Vertical Fiscal Imbalance: Myth or Reality?" In H. Lazar and F. St-Hilaire, eds., *Money, Politics and Health Care: Reconstructing the Federal-Provincial Partnership.* Montreal: The Institute for Research on Public Policy and The Institute of Intergovernmental Relations.

Leeson, H. (2004). "Constitutional Jurisdiction over Health and Health-care Services in Canada." In T. McIntosh, P.G. Forest, and G. Marchildon, eds., *The Governance of Health Care in Canada.* Toronto: University of Toronto Press.

Martin, P. (2003). *Making History: The Politics of Achievement.* Ottawa: February 15. Online at <www.paulmartin.ca/the-campaign/politics-of-achievement_e.pdf>.

Maxwell, J., K. Jackson, B. Legowski, S. Rosell, D. Yankelovich, P.G. Forest, and L. Lozowchuk. (2002). *Report on the Citizens' Dialogue on the Future of Health Care in Canada.* Prepared for the Commission on the Future of Health Care in Canada.

Maxwell, J., S. Rosell, and P.G. Forest. (2003). "Giving Citizens a Voice in Healthcare Policy in Canada." *British Medical Journal* Vol. 326.

Mendelsohn, M. (2001). *Canadians' Thoughts on Their Health-care System: Preserving the Canadian Model through Innovation.* Study prepared for the Commission on the Future of Health Care in Canada. Online at <www.hc-c.gc.ca/english/care/romanow/hc0038.html>.

Nordhaus, W. (2002). *The Health of Nations: The Contribution of Improved Health to Living Standards.* Working Paper 8818. Cambridge, MA: National Bureau of Economic Research.

Organization for Economic Co-operation and Development. (2003). *OECD Health Data 2003.* Paris.

Provincial and Territorial Ministers of Health. (2000). *Understanding Canada's Health-care Costs.* Final Report, August.

Rode, M. and M. Rushton. (2004). "Increasing Provincial Revenues for Health Care." In G. Marchildon, T. McIntosh, and P.G. Forest, eds., *The Fiscal Sustainability of Health Care.* Toronto: University of Toronto Press.

Romanow, R. (1998). "Reinforcing the Ties that Bind." *Policy Options* (November).

St-Hilaire, F. and H. Lazar. (2003). "He Said, She Said: The Debate on Vertical Imbalance and Federal Health-care Funding." *Policy Options* (February).

Tuohy, C. (2002). "The Costs of Constraint and Prospects for Health-care Reform in Canada." *Health Affairs* 21.

Woolhandler, S., T. Campbell, and D. Himmelstein. (2003). "Costs of Health-care Administration in the United States and Canada." *New England Journal of Medicine* 349.

Yalnizyan, A. (2004). *Paul Martin's Permanent Revolution.* Ottawa: Canadian Centre for Policy Alternatives.

22

How Will the Charter of Rights and Freedoms and Evolving Jurisprudence Affect Health-Care Costs?*

DONNA GRESCHNER

I. Introduction

The *Charter of Rights and Freedoms*, as part of the Canadian Constitution, regulates governments' decisions about health-care services. The *Charter* does not expressly guarantee either a right to health or a right of access to health care. However, its general rights provisions, such as equality rights, cover many aspects of the health-care system. Since the *Charter's* enactment in 1982, persons have brought court actions that use *Charter* rights to challenge health-care policies.

To date, the number of *Charter* challenges to facets of the health-care system is not large, and the majority of them have been unsuccessful. Their impact has been uneven. The most successful litigants have been doctors, who have mobilized *Charter* rights to prevent governmental policies that affected their remuneration and mobility. The least successful plaintiffs have been groups and individuals opposing hospital restructuring, with no victories grounded directly in the *Charter*. Patients have been only slightly more successful at using the *Charter* in their efforts to obtain particular health services at public expense. However, notwithstanding the small number of successful challenges since 1982, *Charter* litigation has the potential to affect significantly the allocation of health-care resources, both the distribution of public money within the current Medicare system and the boundaries between the public and private components of health care. Consequently, health-care reform needs to take into account the imperatives of *Charter* rights.

Part II describes the *Charter's* application in the health-care field. It focuses on the *Charter* rights with most relevance for health-care decisions, summarizing briefly the jurisprudence under sections 7, 15, and to a lesser extent, section 6. Part III examines in closer detail the jurisprudence under section 1 of the *Charter*, and Part IV discusses the

---

* This chapter was first published as "How Will the Charter of Rights and Freedoms and Evolving Jurisprudence affect Health Care Costs?" in Tom McIntosh, Pierre-Gerlier Forest, and Gregory P. Marchildon, eds., *The Governance of Health Care in Canada. Romanow Papers*. Volume 2 (Toronto: University of Toronto Press, 2004): 82–124.

relevance of international jurisprudence. Part V gives an overall analysis of the *Charter's* potential impact on health-care costs.

II. The *Charter* and Health-Care Policies

A. General

Because the *Charter* is an entrenched legal document, people may launch legal actions to change governmental decisions that they believe interfere with their rights. Indeed, people do not bring *Charter* actions for any reason other than to change governmental decisions. Every time a plaintiff succeeds with a *Charter* action, governmental decisions are modified or reversed. Since almost all governmental decisions involve expenditures, a successful court action means that money will be spent in ways different from those that governments had first wanted. Governments faced with a court order that requires expenditures have a number of options with respect to covering the cost. They include the following: divert the money from other components of the health-care system; manage the existing system more efficiently and use the savings to cover the costs of the court order, divert more money into the general health-care budget from other areas of spending; off-load some costs to users; decrease the money paid to providers; raise taxes; or a combination of these and other methods. Regardless of the method it chooses to cover the cost of a remedy, the government's spending decisions are affected. Indeed, the only way that the *Charter* could not affect government spending in some way is if no plaintiffs ever win their lawsuits.

The *Charter's* application to health-care policies brings into play several other general features of *Charter* litigation. First, as with other areas of public policy, the *Charter* shifts a measure of power over health-care reform to judges. They assess the merits of *Charter* claims and determine whether an aspect of the health-care system complies with *Charter* rights. If it does not, they order governments to change the particular rule or practice. When governments first introduced Medicare, beginning with Saskatchewan's legislation in 1962, judicial involvement in the program's design and implementation was minimal. The *Canada Health Act*, sometimes considered the bedrock of Medicare, did not need to consider *Charter* litigation when it was enacted in 1984, as the *Charter* had come into force a mere two years earlier. Now, however, reform initiatives must take into account judicial interpretations of *Charter* rights, and be defensible in a courtroom, not only an operating theatre. Generally, the availability of judicial review based on entrenched rights narrows the range of policy options available to governments (Manfredi and Maioni 2002, 217–219).

Second, the *Charter* has a homogenizing effect. Since constitutional rights apply across the country, an interpretation by one court will influence other judges and policy-makers. Decisions from the Supreme Court of Canada are binding on lower courts, and decisions from provincial appellate courts have persuasive authority. This inescapable feature of *Charter* adjudication has consequences for health-care costs. For instance, a ruling by a court in one province that the province must pay for a particular service means that other provinces will likely have to pay, too. A ruling that a specific reform, such as changing methods of paying doctors, is off limits to one province likely means that no province can introduce it. This tendency toward uniformity reduces sensitivity to local conditions

(Manfredi and Maioni 2002, 219–221), and could dampen the increasing diversity in provincial reform initiatives (Gray 1998, 928).

Third, the *Charter* offers people additional arguments in political debates about health-care policies. Because of the *Charter*, the discourse of rights is an increasingly important component of public policy formation. Even if people do not intend to launch legal actions to vindicate rights, they may resist controversial changes to health-care services as encroachments upon their rights. Or, they may use rights language not as a shield to protect the existing system but as a sword to pressure governments into facilitating changes that they prefer, such as permitting private health insurance or adding particular treatments to the list of insured services. In the same way, governments may be able to justify reforms, or the status quo, as enhancing *Charter* rights. To the extent that deployment of rights language in political debates succeeds in influencing policy outcomes, the *Charter* has an impact upon costs, although in a more intangible and non-quantifiable way than with court actions.

Many features of the health-care system are subject to *Charter* claims:

1. The *Charter* may restrict a government's options for payment and supply of medical services. For instance, doctors in British Columbia successfully argued that their section 7 liberty rights and section 6 mobility rights were infringed by policies allocating billing numbers (*Re Mia* 1985; *Wilson* 1988; *Waldman* 1999). However, the Supreme Court has rejected the interpretations that succeeded in *Re Mia* and *Wilson*, and the New Brunswick Court of Appeal recently rejected a section 6 challenge to a similar billing number policy in that province (*Rombaut* 2001).

2. People have used *Charter* arguments to challenge integral aspects of the Medicare system, such as the prohibition on private health insurance, but thus far unsuccessfully (*Chaoulli* 2002).

3. The *Charter* affects governments' decisions about particular services to include within publicly funded Medicare systems. These decisions may violate section 15 equality rights (*Eldridge* 1997; *Auton* 2000). If courts order governments to pay for these previously uninsured services, they expand the scope of publicly funded services, shifting the balance between public and private funding.

4. The right of parents to choose or refuse medical treatment for their children may be an aspect of their right to liberty in section 7, and, if they decide on religious grounds, their freedom of religion in section 2(a) (*R.B. v. Children's Aid Society* 1995).

5. The involuntary treatment of persons with mental illnesses is subject to section 7 rights of liberty and security of the person (Carver 2002).

6. The *Charter* is implicated in the "right to die with dignity" cases, in which patients assert constitutional rights to choose the manner and time of their deaths (*Rodriquez* 1993).

7. The *Charter* affects the governments' prohibition of particular health services. In *R v. Morgentaler* (1988), the Supreme Court's first involvement with the *Charter* and health care, the Court struck down the Criminal Code restrictions on abortion services as a violation of a woman's right to security of the person.

8. The *Charter* covers the employment relationship between governments and health-care workers. However, not every work relationship in a health-care facility falls within the *Charter*'s purview (*Stoffman* 1990).

9. The *Charter* affects the legal power of professional organizations in the health-care sector to regulate the activities of their members. The courts have struck down bans on advertising by dentists as a violation of freedom of expression (*Rocket* 1990) and a bylaw preventing optometrists from having business associations with other optometrists (*Costco Wholesale* 1998).

Each type of litigation has an impact on costs. For instance, even those decisions that reduce procedural complexities of accessing services, such as *Morgentaler*, will affect costs in several ways. For one thing, complying with procedures always has direct and indirect costs, and changing procedures will alter these costs. In addition, since procedural obstacles often have a deterrent effect, simplifying procedures may increase total cost because more people will obtain the service. However, the most important effects of the *Charter* on health-care costs result from cases in the first three areas. These areas comprise two related categories: structure of payment and delivery of health care, and scope of coverage with respect to publicly insured services (Von Tigerstrom 2002).

The first category involves changes to the methods by which governments pay for health services and provide them. Generally, Canada has a mixed system, with considerable public financing and mostly private delivery. Whether and how to change the mix between the public and private components of health-care financing and delivery is one of the key policy questions of our time. *Charter* rights may be invoked to question the wisdom and constitutionality of proposals that alter the mix or restructure in other ways the institutions of health care. This category includes challenges by doctors to changes in physician management schemes (e.g., *Rombaut* 2001), attempts to enjoin hospital closures (e.g., *Wellesley Central Hospital* 1997; *Ponteix* 1994), and actions to permit private health insurance for services covered by Medicare (*Chaoulli* 2002). The last type of action, if successful, has the potential for causing the most dramatic change to the health-care system, since removing the ban on private health insurance would create a two-tier or multi-tiered system (Schrecker 1998, 143).

The second, related category involves challenges by patients who want the government to pay for more services than those currently covered by the medical insurance plan (e.g., *Cameron* 1999a; *Auton* 2000). Here, again, successful court actions change the mix between public and private funding. These lawsuits usually do not strike at the core of Medicare's principles. Rather, because they ask for public insurance to include more services, they seek expansion of the principles of universality and accessibility. However, that does not reduce their potential to affect significantly the distribution of health-care costs.

Overall, *Charter* actions brought by patients and others have been few in number. Appendix II lists *Charter* decisions that involve, in some aspect or another, health-care services, whether provided in hospitals, clinics, nursing homes or schools. (The table excludes cases involving involuntary treatment of patients, fetal rights, and informed consent.) There are only 33. Even if this number were doubled to compensate for any cases missed by the searches, the total number would not be large. This low number is surprising. Since health care affects everyone and is the largest single budget item for provinces, one would expect more litigation, especially in light of the state of flux in the health-care system.

With these 33 cases, claimants in 11 cases succeeded in obtaining remedies for a *Charter* violation. The rate of success, 33 percent, is in line with the general success rate for *Charter* claims from 1982–98, which most authors calculate at between 30–35 percent (Kelly 1999). Moreover, in several cases in which plaintiffs have successfully proven a violation of a *Charter* right, the government has demonstrated that the violation is a reasonable limit under section 1 (*Cameron* 1999a). Courts have been cautious about judging governments' health-care policies as unreasonable. Further, in several *Charter* actions where plaintiffs obtained remedies, governments did not attempt to raise section 1 arguments (*Re Mia* 1985; *Wilson* 1988). If they had, the results might have been different, and the number of successful challenges even lower.

The impact of these successful cases on health-care costs is difficult to assess because no numbers are readily available. Nevertheless, it is possible to draw tentative conclusions. Overall, of the 11 cases in which courts gave a remedy, the ones with the greatest impact on health-care costs were the doctors' mobility and liberty claims. The provinces' restricted ability to ration physician services likely had financial ramifications in the tens or hundreds of millions of dollars, not only in British Columbia, where the cases originated, but also in other provinces that were considering similar schemes in the late 1980s and early 1990s. At the other end of the cost spectrum, several successful cases likely had a much smaller effect on overall costs: *R. v. Morgentaler* (1988), which involved access to abortion services; and *R. v. Parker* (2000), which concerned access to marijuana for medical purposes. Somewhere in between are cases such as *Lalonde* (2001). *Lalonde* is similar to the doctors' mobility rights cases because it involves structural issues of health-care delivery. On its face it involves a large sum of money because the Ontario government decided not to proceed immediately with restructuring services at the hospital in dispute. However, more precise information is needed to assess the monetary consequences of a failed attempt at hospital restructuring. Whether closure of a particular hospital saves money in the long run depends on several factors, such as the inefficiency of the hospital in question, and whether services are managed efficiently among other hospitals in the area.

With respect to challenges about the scope of insured services, patients obtained remedies in only two cases. In *Eldridge*, the Supreme Court accepted evidence that the cost of providing sign language interpreters was $150,000, which was approximately 0.0025 percent of the provincial health-care budget. Since all provinces now have to provide such a service, the nationwide cost is greater (assuming that some provinces did not provide the service before the court decision), but still not significant. In *Auton*, the British Columbia court ordered Lovaas treatment for autistic children, which was estimated to cost $40,000 to $60,000 a year per child, with treatment ranging from two to five years per child. Unfortunately, the court did not estimate the total cost of the service. Although several provinces already pay for this treatment when recommended by doctors, others do not. On a national basis, the cost implications of this ruling would not be negligible.

Overall, the direct effect of *Charter* litigation on health-care costs has not been large, except with respect to restructuring physician services. However, the future may be quite different. One scholar's comment about the Supreme Court is apt: "Offering predictions about the Court's future use of the *Charter* is a dangerous game" (Kelly 1999, 636). Kelly concludes that the Supreme Court's recent decisions indicate a trend toward minimizing conflict with the legislative branch (636), which would suggest that governments may not need fear too greatly an activist judiciary. On the other hand, studies also show that judges are more inclined to nullify recent policy choices by provincial legislatures (Manfredi and Maioni 2002, 221), which would mean that new provincial policy directions in the health-care field are more susceptible to judicial reversal.

In grappling with the question of future judicial involvement, this paper focuses on the courts' interpretation of the most important *Charter* rights. On the premise that courts rarely change jurisprudential direction overnight, the interpretations accepted to date for *Charter* rights would continue to structure arguments in the near future.

Appendix I reproduces the most relevant *Charter* provisions. Section 15, the equality rights provision, gives everyone the right to equality without discrimination on a number of grounds. Two of the enumerated grounds have direct relevance to the health-care field—physical and mental disability. Section 7 gives everyone the right not to be deprived of life, liberty and security of the person, except in accordance with the principles of fundamental justice. Section 6 states that every citizen and permanent resident has the right to pursue the gaining of a livelihood in any province. If a court rules that a person's rights have been violated, governments may justify the limitation under section 1 as reasonable in a free and democratic society. However, justificatory arguments also come into play in interpreting the scope of rights.

B. Section 15

Claims under section 15 have focused on expanding the scope of insured services. Persons allege that a particular health-care policy, which excludes them from coverage or reduces their share of resources, violates their rights to the equal protection and equal benefit of the law. The potential for claims is theoretically quite broad because one prohibited ground in section 15 is physical or mental disability. Although the courts have not issued an authoritative definition of this ground, it covers illnesses and a wide array of conditions. However, the total number of *Charter* claims under section 15 is very small, and only two, *Eldridge* and *Auton*, have been successful. Courts have been cautious about ordering governments to pay for particular health services.

This conclusion may seem surprising in light of the considerable media attention given to the Supreme Court's unanimous judgment in *Eldridge*. A group of deaf patients argued that the British Columbia government's decision not to fund sign language interpreters for them when they received medical treatment violated their right to equality under section 15. Specifically, they argued that this failure constituted adverse effects discrimination on the basis of physical disability because their inability to communicate effectively with medical personnel denied them the equal benefit of the provincial Medicare program. The Supreme Court agreed and directed the government to provide sign language interpreters where necessary for effective communication.

The *Eldridge* ruling imposes a positive obligation on governments to provide a particular service for patients. However, it does not open the floodgates to constitutional challenges about the scope of "insured medical services." As the Court stressed in its reasons, the inequality was about *access* to insured health-care services. The plaintiffs were not asking for a specific medical treatment that the government had decided not to fund, such as expensive fertility treatments. Rather, they wanted equal access to all the services, and no more than those services that were available to the hearing population. The problem was not the services offered by the government but the fact that the government provided the services in a manner that hearing persons could readily access, but not deaf people. As in the earlier *J.C.* (1992) decision from a lower court about the exclusion of women from prisoners' treatment programs, the *Eldridge* claimants could not access equally services that were generally available to others because of an enumerated ground (disability in *Eldridge*; sex in *J.C.*).

The policy that distressed the patients in *Eldridge* is an example of "rationing by characteristic"—a particular health-care service is insured, but not everyone who can benefit from the service can access it. Governments also engage in "rationing by service"—a specific medical treatment for a particular illness or condition is not funded for anyone. For example, in *Cameron* the province funded some hospital services for infertility, but not *in vitro* fertilization (IVF) or intra-cytoplasmic sperm injection (ICSI). In *Auton*, the province funded some treatment for autistic children, but not the Lovaas treatment preferred by the plaintiffs, who were parents of autistic children. These cases, which involve the scope of coverage, raise different questions. Governments assess a broad range of factors in making such decisions, including the cost of the treatment, its effectiveness in improving the patient's quality or length of life, and social and ethical concerns. Moreover, courts may hesitate to evaluate complex decisions about the clinical effectiveness and other medical standards for highly specialized treatments (Von Tigerstrom 2002, 171). Von Tigerstrom argues that cases involving "rationing by services" are more difficult to resolve, but even if this is the case, one cannot underestimate the complexities of "rationing by characteristics," which may involve a multitude of interconnected assessments.

With respect to "scope of coverage" cases, courts now assess claims in accordance with a general scheme that the Supreme Court articulated after its *Eldridge* decision. In *Law v. Canada* (1999) the Court held that a plaintiff must satisfy the following three steps in order to prove a violation of equality rights:

- The impugned law or policy must draw a distinction between groups of persons on the basis of a personal characteristic, or fail to draw such a distinction for a group already disadvantaged, in a manner that results in substantively differential treatment between the groups.
- The differential treatment must be on a ground that is enumerated in section 15 (such as sex or age) or on a ground that is analogous to an enumerated ground (such as sexual orientation).
- The differential treatment must constitute substantive discrimination, which means that it offends the plaintiff's essential human dignity.

The first two criteria are not too burdensome for plaintiffs who want an expansion of insured services. After all, the plaintiffs are patients who seek treatment for physical or mental health problems. The third criterion presents more problems, as it does generally for plaintiffs with section 15 claims. Not every distinction in health treatment between groups of patients is discriminatory; for instance, the mere fact that governments do not fund IVF or ICSI treatment for infertility is not automatically discriminatory. Patients must also convince a court that the distinction offends their dignity. The Supreme Court has said that such distinctions have "the effect of perpetuating or promoting the view that the individual is less capable or worthy of recognition or value as a human being or as a member of Canadian society, equally deserving of concern, respect, and consideration" (*Law* 1999, para. 88).

The case law to date does not provide clear guidelines to distinguish between exclusions from insured services that offend dignity and those that do not. In *Cameron*, the Nova Scotia Court of Appeal split on whether the non-insurability of IVF and ICSI impinged upon the plaintiff's essential human dignity. A majority of the Court concluded that the exclusion did violate dignity because of historical stereotyping of infertile persons, especially women, and the stigma associated with infertility. By contrast, a minority opinion ruled that the exclusion of some infertility services did not offend dignity, stating that it was "an inevitable consequence of the administration of health care" (*Cameron* 1999*a*, 682). However, the dissenting judge commented that if the government refused to fund any medical treatments for infertility, such a policy would likely offend essential human dignity (683–684).

Although the sparse case law does not permit ready generalizations, it does seem that exclusions justified by cost, risk, safety and low effectiveness will not violate human dignity. However, wholesale delisting of services might well do so. Governments will need to justify exclusions with evidence about the reasons for the exclusion; in short, they will need to prove that the exclusion is supported by sound medical evidence or other cogent reasons that are unrelated to any prejudice or stereotyping about the persons who wish to have the service. In this regard, the third criterion replicates the balancing that takes place in section 1.

In summary, section 15 does present possibilities for patients to challenge decisions about the scope of coverage. Perhaps one reason for the low number of cases in which persons seek more health services is the relative universality, accessibility and comprehensiveness of Canada's existing Medicare system. Anyone in need of medical treatment to preserve life or health is usually entitled to receive it (Jackman 1995; Von Tigerstrom 2002). Thus it is not surprising that *Charter* cases to date have involved expensive uninsured services, such as drug prescriptions (*Brown* 1990) and fertility treatments (*Cameron* 1999, 1999*a*). Consequently, if governments change significantly the current mix of public and privately funded health-care services, section 15 will become more important as a shield to protect existing coverage. In addition, however, the *Charter* may be used as a sword to obtain more insured services, such as pharmaceutical products. With escalating drug costs and increasing reliance on life-saving drugs, it is surprising that major exclusions from Medicare, such as most prescription drugs and home care, have not been subject to more *Charter* challenges.

If the courts do hold that a particular feature of the health-care system violates equality rights, the government may justify the limit under section 1. For instance, in *Cameron* the majority of the Nova Scotia Court of Appeal held that the exclusion of IVF and ICSI treatments from insured services violated section 15, but was a reasonable limit under section 1. Part Ill discusses section 1 in more detail.

C. Section 7

Section 7 protects the right not to be deprived of life, liberty, or security of the person except in accordance with the principles of fundamental justice. Its power as a tool to

challenge health-care policies has been limited because plaintiffs must overcome significant obstacles in proving a violation of section 7.

First, plaintiffs must show that either "liberty" or "security" encompasses health or
health-care services. The courts have not interpreted the rights in section 7 in a manner sufficiently broad to encompass a general right to health, or, except in exceptional
circumstances, a right to access health-care services. With respect to liberty, a majority
of Supreme Court judges has ruled that the phrase covers only freedom from physical
restraint, and not economic liberty, such as the right to engage in contractual relations
(Hogg 2001, 920). With respect to security, the Court has held that it includes the right of
access to health care (R. v. Morgentaler 1988), and the right to refuse medical treatment
for oneself (Rodriquez 1993). Lower courts have ruled that security does not include the
right to have health care of one's choice provided at public expense, such as public funding of drug prescriptions (Brown 1990) or enhanced public funding for nursing homes
(Ontario Nursing Home Assn. 1990). In Nova Scotia recently, a claim under section 7 for
public funding of fertility treatments was curtly dismissed by the trial court (Cameron
1999, para 160), and not pursued on appeal (Cameron 1999a).

Second, even if plaintiffs can prove a deprivation of liberty or security, they must also
show that the deprivation contravened the principles of fundamental justice. The Supreme
Court has interpreted the phrase "principles of fundamental justice" to mean basic tenets
of the legal system, such as the presumption of innocence (Reference Re. Motor Vehicle
Act 1988). These basic tenets clearly include the rules of fair procedure, but whether they
include substantive principles is more debatable. In a recent decision involving child
protection hearings, the Court suggested that section 7 is restricted to situations where
the infringements to liberty or security are "a result of an individual's interaction with
the justice system and its administration" (New Brunswick (Minister of Health and Social
Services) v. G.(J) 1999, para. 65). With health-care services, when plaintiffs challenge governmental decisions about "medically necessary services" or other funding provisions,
they will find proving a violation of these principles exceedingly difficult because generally the health-care system is administrative, not criminal.

One example of criminal prohibitions was the therapeutic abortion committee provisions that the Supreme Court struck down as a violation of section 7 in R. v. Morgentaler
(1988). These provisions made abortion a criminal offence unless the abortion was approved by a cumbersome hospital committee structure. The unusual feature of this
legislative regime was that women seeking abortions and doctors performing them were
guilty of a criminal offence unless they received prior approval from a committee. A woman's access to health services and a doctor's freedom to perform the service were severely
constrained by the most onerous legal sanction—criminal punishment. In this context,
the Supreme Court held that a woman's right to security of the person included the right
to access health-care services without threat of criminal sanction, and that the convoluted
and often elusive committee structure violated the principles of fundamental justice. One
judge, Madame Justice Wilson, went further and held that the Criminal Code provisions
also violated a woman's right to liberty.

The legal rule in Morgentaler was exceptional because it was situated on the overlap
between the criminal law process and the health-care system. A similar example is R. v.
Parker (2000), where the Ontario Court of Appeal struck down the criminal prohibi-

tion against possession of marijuana for people who use the drug for medicinal purposes. However, cases in which a form of health care is subject to severe criminal penalty are rare. In an effort to overcome the stricture of criminal or quasi-criminal sanctions as a condition of section 7 claims, several commentators have argued recently that principles of fundamental justice should encompass administrative procedures, which would include a wide variety of health-care policies (Karr 2000; Hartt and Monahan 2002).

Moreover, in cases where plaintiffs challenge basic tenets of the health-care system, governments may be able to rely on the principles of fundamental justice to defend their decisions because these principles include other *Charter* values, such as equality and human dignity. In *Chaoulli* (2000), the trial judge ruled that the prohibition of private health insurance for services covered by Medicare, while perhaps infringing section 7 rights if the public system did not provide sufficient access to health services, did not contravene the principles of fundamental justice. The prohibition was adopted because allowing a parallel private system would impair the viability of the public system, and adversely affect the rights of the rest of the population. The judge concluded as follows: "[the prohibition is] motivated by considerations of equality and human dignity ... it is clear that there is no conflict with the general values promoted by the Charter" (as quoted in Von Tigerstrom 2002, 166). The trial judge's decision was upheld by the Quebec Court of Appeal (*Chaoulli* 2002).

One underlying reason for the judicial hesitancy about broadly interpreting section 7 is the more general reluctance to include economic interests within section 7. The Supreme Court has ruled that economic rights in the corporate or commercial context do not come within section 7. The courts are afraid of opening section 7 to a host of economic claims. Indisputably, health services are bundles of economic interests, not manna—someone must provide them, and someone must pay for them. At the same time, however, the Supreme Court has left open the question of whether section 7 could protect economic interests that are integrally connected to material well-being (*Irwin Toy* 1989, 1003–1004). Since health care qualifies as essential for well-being in the same manner as food and clothing, it remains possible to protect health care under section 7 notwithstanding its economic aspect. For instance, if people were denied access to emergency medical services because they could not pay for them, their claim of a section 7 violation could receive a sympathetic judicial hearing. Moreover, the Medicare system is extremely popular, and many citizens view it as a fundamental plank of Canadian society. This popularity may assist judges in overcoming their usual reluctance to evaluate and supervise benefits programs. The Supreme Court recently heard an appeal from a Quebec case that raises the issue of whether inadequate social assistance payments violate security of the person (*Gosselin* 1999). Its decision may foreshadow the Court's direction on analogous cases in health care.

In the near future, one can reasonably expect more *Charter* claims that address the phenomenon of waiting lists. Recently, several lawyers have argued, as in the *Chaoulli* litigation, that waiting lists impair patients' psychological health and, in some cases, threaten their lives (Karr 2000; Hartt and Monahan 2002). Further, they argue that the appropriate remedy is private health insurance that covers services now paid for by Medicare. This line of argument is attractive not only to wealthy patients who could afford private insurance, but also to those doctors and other health-care providers who wish to establish private medical facilities. If successful, these arguments would have a major impact on health-care costs; parallel private systems reallocate existing resources and cause an increase in the total budget, as well as raise issues of equity and access (Gray 1998, 910–13). But success for these arguments is not assured. Besides the difficulty of showing a violation of principles of fundamental justice, patients and health-care providers who argue for more private insurance face an additional obstacle. Even if waiting lists violate section 7, the appropriate remedy may be more public funding or better management of waiting lists, rather than creating a system of parallel private health care by removing the ban on private insurance. For instance, since waiting lists for a specific procedure may vary greatly among a group of specialists, it might be appropriate for a court to order publication of wait times for all specialists in the province. Such an order would give patients valuable information on when to choose specialists. What is not obvious, however, is that the remedy for wait times is private insurance; this remedy would only fix the constitutional violation for wealthy people who could afford insurance, and may substantially worsen the constitutional violation of wait times for poor people, who would endure longer wait times because of a drain of medical resources to the privately funded system (Schrecker 1998, 143). As noted above, the government's egalitarian objective in prohibiting private insurance was recognized by the trial judge in *Chaoulli* (2000).

The debates about remedies for correcting wait times illustrate a major difficulty with *Charter* review of health-care policies. The health-care system is fiendishly complicated and simple answers to problems (such as allowing private insurance as a response to waiting lists) could wreak considerable damage to the system, and cause constitutional violations for other groups of people. Judges are not well equipped to deal with the enormous ramifications of changing elements of the health-care system. They may not obtain much help from counsel, who may have neither the expertise or interest in assisting judges in understanding fully the variables and dynamics of health-care policy. For instance, it is distressing that a major article arguing for the unconstitutionality of the prohibition on private health insurance (Karr 2000) does not cite a single study from health economists or policy analysts on the causes of, and remedies for, wait times. The more recent study by Hartt and Monahan (2002) arguing that wait times violate section 7 rights, while referring briefly to several studies about wait times, fails to consider the wider consequences of judges creating a two-tier health system. The complexities of wait times and options for solving them (Lewis et al. 2000) illustrate that assessing health-care policy is a quintessentially interdisciplinary undertaking. Yet judges will be wading into these thorny areas without expertise. For understandable reasons, they may adopt an attitude of extreme caution, if not deference, as they have generally done with health-care cases to date (*Cameron* 1999a; *Chaoulli* 2000, 2002).

One last point must be made about section 7. In several cases, judges have said that violations of section 7 can only be justified under section 1 in exceptional circumstances (*Reference Re Motor Vehicle Act* 1988, 518). In practice this means that the justificatory arguments for limiting rights occur within the interpretation of the section itself (Hogg 2001, 916), defining the scope of "liberty" and "security" and the content of principles of fundamental justice. One example of this practice is the trial judgment in *Chaoulli* (2000).

D. Mobility rights and fundamental principles

Of the other *Charter* provisions that affect the health-care system, mobility rights deserve attention. Section 6 states that every citizen has a right to earn a livelihood in the province. Mobility rights have impaired the provinces' ability to reform their policies of physician management. British Columbia's efforts to rationalize physician services have been particularly hard hit in this regard (*Re Mia* 1985; *Wilson* 1988; *Waldman* 1999).

However, mobility rights may no longer protect doctors' freedom from regulation. The Supreme Court recently issued a major decision about section 6 in which it held that a violation of mobility rights required discrimination on the grounds of provincial residency (*Canadian Egg Marketing Agency (CEMA)* 1998). Consequently, policies that regulate doctors' practices within a particular province do not violate mobility rights, contrary to the holding in *Re Mia* and the trial judgment in *Waldman*, unless the particular scheme distinguishes between doctors on the basis of past or present residency. Most proposals for equitable distribution of doctors do not draw such distinctions, and therefore do not violate section 6. Accordingly, when the British Columbia Court of Appeal heard the appeal in *Waldman*, it applied the *CEMA* decision to hold that only one provision of the scheme violated section 6, although it refused to sever the offending provision and thus struck down the entire law (*Waldman* 1999, para. 51). Recently, when a group of doctors in New Brunswick challenged that province's rationing scheme for physician services, the New Brunswick court applied the *Canadian Egg Marketing Agency* decision to dismiss their claim (*Rombaut* 2001).

One recent case involving a hospital restructuring attracted considerable media attention, but on closer scrutiny it does not herald a new era in judicial regulation of health-care policies. In *Lalonde* (2001) a group of francophone citizens challenged the decision of the Ontario Health Services Restructuring Commission to change the mandate of Hôpital Montfort, the only French-language hospital in Ontario. They argued that the decision adversely affected medical services to their official-language community. The Ontario Court of Appeal held that the Commission must respect the Constitution's fundamental organizing principles, which include protection of minorities, in its restructuring decisions. The Court quashed the decision and remitted the matter to the Minister for reconsideration in accordance with its reasons. The judgment's only novel feature was the ruling that administrative agencies must consider fundamental constitutional principles in addition to *Charter* values. It is a long established principle that governmental agencies, such as health services commissions, must respect *Charter* rights and exercise their discretion in a manner consistent with the *Charter*. The plaintiffs in *Lalonde*, however, could not rely on section 15 because of a line of cases holding that language was not an analogous ground under section 15. Hence they relied instead on the fundamental constitutional principle of protection of minorities. Given section 15's broad scope with respect to enumerated and analogous grounds, cases such as *Lalonde* where plaintiffs must resort to deeper constitutional values in challenging administrative discretion may be quite rare.

III. Section 1

Section 1 serves a dual purpose. It guarantees rights and freedoms, but also permits governments to limit those rights if the limits are reasonably justified in a free and democratic society. In the classic case of *R. v. Oakes* (1986), Chief Justice Dickson established the basic criteria by which to assess whether violation was a reasonable limit. The *Cakes* test is two-fold. First, the government must establish that the impugned law had an important objective. This criterion has proven easy for governments to satisfy. Indeed, there have been virtually no cases in which the test is not met (Hogg 2001, 743). In the context of health care, the government has invariably argued that its objective for a particular policy, such as not insuring particular services or rationing billing numbers, is to protect the viability of Medicare and use its resources effectively. This objective satisfies the first branch of *Oakes*.

The second branch of the *Oakes* test assesses the government's means of achieving its objective. The test is one of proportionality, with three parts. First, the means must be rationally connected to the objective. Second, the means must impair as little as possible the right or freedom; there must not be a less drastic alternative by which to achieve the ends. Third, the means must not have a disproportionately severe effect on persons to whom it applies. Generally, in almost all section 1 cases, the disputes have turned on the second part of this three-pronged test—the least drastic means (Hogg 2001, 743). The language in *Oakes* was quite stringent: the law had to impair the right as little as possible. However, later cases have softened the language considerably. Quite soon after *Oakes*, the Supreme Court recognized that governments needed a margin of appreciation in designing laws, and that courts should give some degree of deference to legislators in crafting policies. Courts now look for reasonable efforts by governments to minimize legislative infringements of *Charter* rights, rather than the least minimal interference. In short, a range of governmental policies, not merely the least drastic, will satisfy section 1.

Generally, courts are more willing to give a margin of appreciation to governments when one of several considerations is present: if the law is intended to protect a vulnerable group, such as children or poor people; if the law reconciles the interests of competing groups; if the law allocates scarce resources; or if the law rests on complex, and often competing, social science evidence (Hogg 2001, 764). Laws regulating the health-care system usually possess all four of these characteristics. Accordingly, in cases involving components of the health-care system, all of these considerations should come into play, resulting in a wide margin of appreciation when governments justify restrictions under section 1.

The wide margin of appreciation for governments is demonstrated in the jurisprudence. Judges understand that health-care budgets are complex and controversial, involving difficult trade-offs. They have been reluctant to second-guess governments about the best way to spend health-care dollars. The majority opinion in *Cameron* (1999a), in ruling that a section 15 violation was justified under section 1, illustrates the general judicial attitude. After reviewing the government's evidence about increases to the health-care budget and federal cutbacks to cost-sharing programs, which resulted in compelling pressures on the Department of Health, it expressed considerable reluctance to find that the government's policies were unreasonable under section 1: "the evidence makes clear the complexity of the health-care system and the extremely difficult task confronting those who must allocate the resources among a vast array of competing claims.... The policy makers require latitude in balancing competing interests in the constrained financial environment. We are simply not equipped to sort out the priorities. We should not second guess them, except in clear cases of failure on their part to properly balance the Charter rights of individuals against the overall pressing objective of the scheme" (*Cameron* 1999a, 667).

With respect to predicting when the government will fail in meeting its burden under section 1, the two "scope of coverage" cases in which courts rejected the section 1 arguments are not especially helpful for drawing generalizations. In *Eldridge*, where the Supreme Court ordered the government to pay for sign language interpreters for deaf patients, it stressed that the cost was minimal. Unfortunately, it did not consider the impact of its ruling on other provinces, who might have different financial circumstances. Nor did it assess the cogency of the evidence about cost, accepting without question an intervenor's somewhat dubious estimate (Manfredi and Maoini 2002, 229). In *Auton*, the rather skimpy discussion of section 1 is unsatisfactory. The court seems to duck the issue of money, noting the cost per child, but not the total amount of the treatment. It apparently regarded the situation as identical to that in *Eldridge*, which was erroneous since the Supreme Court stressed that *Eldridge* involved access to existing services, not adding new ones. In *Auton* it seems that the most important consideration was the court's assessment that the savings created in the long run by assisting autistic children would likely offset the cost of Lovaas treatment.

The exception to this general deference is the doctors' claims that physician management schemes violated their *Charter* rights. Overall, courts have been unusually insensitive to the enormous cost ramifications of invalidating provincial rationing schemes for physician services. Although, as noted previously, the jurisprudential foundations of the doctors' victories are now shaky, the general judicial fondness for doctors' claims may carry over into new challenges brought by doctors to preserve their dominant position within the health-care system. For instance, it is not unrealistic to expect challenges if a regional health authority required all doctors in its area to be paid by capitation or employment contracts, rather than permitting "fee for service" arrangements. Although section 7 does not cover the right to exercise a profession (*Reference Re Criminal Code, Ss 193 & 195.1(1)(c)* 1990, 527), past *Charter* victories by doctors would give their challenges more chance of success than analogous claims by other professions. Nevertheless, the odds of victory in challenging contractual requirements with health authorities would still be low (Flood 1999, 193).

Two clear points emerge from the case law. First, cost is indeed a consideration in section 1 balancing. In its early *Charter* jurisprudence, the Supreme Court stated rather categorically that cost could not justify infringements of rights; in other words, governments could not use money as a reason to violate *Charter* rights (*Singh* 1985, 469). If fair hearings for refugee claimants would cost hundreds of millions of dollars, as did the remedy in the *Singh* case, then the government must pay the bill. However, this rigid view about the role of costs has considerably loosened. With many rights, providing the right to one group without regard to costs may result in another group being denied its rights. Arguably, health-care decision-making is a paradigmatic example of these trade-offs. The courts may ignore the cost of providing a service if it is small (*Eldridge*) but not when it is relatively large (*Cameron*).

Second, there is a great need for cogent evidence. Even with a margin of appreciation and judicial sensitivity to the complexities of health budgeting, section 1 justifications will require evidence that the government considered alternatives to the impugned policy.

This evidence could involve the cost-benefit analysis engaged in by policy-makers, the medical studies that were examined, and any other relevant factors that were taken into account. If governments do not adduce evidence, their likelihood of success under section 1 is greatly diminished. In *Eldridge*, for example, the Court emphasized several times the government's failure to adduce evidence of undue strain on the health-care system if the service was provided (*Eldridge* 1997, paras. 92, 94).

The obligation to produce evidence in an open court about the merits, expense, and risks of different health-care options may have positive benefits for health policy. For one thing, it may deter policy-makers from making decisions based on the decibel level of the group asking for a particular service at a particularly sensitive time, such as immediately before an election. Overall, it may hasten the incorporation of what has been called "evidence-based medicine" into public policy about health care.

However, there remain significant problems with judicial assessments under section 1. In the very nature of adjudication inheres one major problem. telescopic vision. As the litigation in *Eldridge* and *Auton* illustrates, in each case the court assesses only one tiny part of a very large puzzle. And, because it focuses on only one part, that part is magnified. What adjudication usually fails to consider is the opportunity cost of its orders—where else could the money be spent? Yet this is the question that necessarily preoccupies policy-makers. Judicial recognition of the telescopic nature of adjudicatory methods ought to strengthen their caution about reviewing health-care decisions.

IV. International Law

Canada is a signatory to international conventions about human rights. The right to health is firmly embedded in many conventions, albeit with slightly different language in each one (Toebes 1999). These conventions are binding at international law. Canada is obliged to act in accordance with these conventions, but convention rights are not directly enforceable in Canadian courts (Hogg 2001, 689). Nevertheless, they are important to a study about the *Charter* because of the long-standing principle that domestic law should be interpreted in a manner consistent with international obligations. In a recent decision, the Supreme Court emphasized that this principle includes *Charter* interpretation: "[I]nternational human rights law ... is also a critical influence on the interpretation of the rights included in the *Charter*" (*Baker* 1999, para. 70).

This paper will discuss briefly one important convention, the *International Covenant on Economic, Social and Cultural Rights (ICESCR)*, as an example of the right to health in international law. Article 12 recognizes "the right of everyone to the enjoyment of the highest attainable standard of physical and mental health." It provides further that State Parties shall take steps necessary to achieve the full realization of this right, including reducing infant mortality, improving environmental and industrial hygiene, preventing and treating disease, and creating "conditions which would assure to all medical service and medical attention in the event of sickness" (*ICESCR* 1966, Art. 12(2)). This right clearly includes the right to health care, such as immunization services, essential drugs, and emergency medical treatment. But it also includes health-related issues, such as safe water, adequate sanitation, and environmental health (Toebes 1999).

International conventions require State Parties to file periodic reports describing their efforts to comply with the convention's obligations. The *ICESCR* reports are filed with the Committee on Economic, Social and Cultural Rights. With each report the Committee publishes concluding remarks, which indicate the direction of international law developments.

Canada filed its third periodic report to the Committee in 1998. In its concluding observations, the Committee did not comment negatively on health-care services, except with respect to the "significant cuts to services on which people with disabilities rely" and programs for people discharged from psychiatric institutions (Committee on Economic, Social and Cultural Rights 1998, para 36). However, it expressed concern about many aspects of Canada's social programs, including the cuts to social assistance, the restrictions on unemployment insurance, the growing problem of homelessness, and the inadequate protection of women's rights. It drew attention to the adverse consequences for poor people that flowed from the replacement of the Canada Assistance Plan with the Canada Health and Social Transfer (CHST), including the absence of national standards for social assistance programs. Furthermore, it found inexplicable the double standards in the CHST: "[The CHST] did, however, retain national standards in relation to health, thus denying provincial flexibility in one area, while insisting upon it in others [social assistance]. The delegation provided no explanation for this inconsistency" (Committee on Economic, Social, and Cultural Rights 1998, para. 19). Overall, one can conclude that Canada's Medicare program fulfills its international obligations, but its social programs need improvement. Insofar as a right to health includes basic necessities, such as income and shelter, Canada is failing to meet its obligations.

International obligations may influence proposals to reform the existing health-care system. In a number of reports, the Committee asked State Parties to report on whether disparities exist between the public and private sectors in their health-care systems. Furthermore, it has noted that plans to decentralize and privatize health-care services do not relieve a state party from its obligations to promote access to health-care services, especially for poor people (Toebes 1999, 105–106). Thus, if Canadian governments were to privatize health-care services to a significant degree, they may run more afoul of their international obligations.

One issue in international law debates is whether social and economic rights, such as the right to health in Article 12 of the *ICESCR*, should be given the same priority as civil and political rights, such as freedom of expression. Many scholars have argued that international law should be governed by a principle of indivisibility: social and economic rights are indivisible from civil and political rights, and should have the same priority in terms of enforcement (Schabas 1999). Critics of this approach argue that social and economic rights involve different considerations, such as imposing positive obligations on governments, and should not be lumped in with civil and political rights (Richards 1999).

This debate has relevance to the question about the future impact of the *Charter* on the health-care system. If the principle of indivisibility becomes more widely accepted, courts will be more willing to interpret *Charter* rights broadly to include a general right to health, and to issue *Charter* remedies for the enforcement of social rights. Insofar as judicial deference is grounded, at least in part, on acceptance of a distinction between political rights and social rights, a removal of the distinction weakens that particular argument for deference.

V. The *Charter* and Future Developments

This paper addresses the question of the impact of the *Charter* on health-care costs. The case study shows that the number of successful *Charter* challenges since 1982 is not large, and the impact of these decisions, except for the doctors' challenges, has not yet been significant. Most claims have played around the edges of the current health-care system, rather than attacked its foundations, and many court decisions have been sensitive to the dynamics of health-care reform.

One reason that the *Charter's* impact has not been revolutionary is the relative comprehensiveness and accessibility of the Medicare system. A number of basic principles informed the Royal Commission in the 1960s and are currently articulated in the *Canada Health Act*. In particular, the three principles of universality, accessibility, and comprehensiveness can be cast as manifestations of the *Charter* values of equality and protection of human dignity. In this respect, *Charter* rights augment the existing health-care system; to state the obvious, section 15 claims about the scope of coverage do not introduce equality as a foreign concept to the health-care system. However, apparent compatibility between Medicare's principles and *Charter* values does not forestall continued litigation. Since general principles do not mechanically translate into a single set of practical policies (Okma 2002, 46), agreement in principle does not erase sharp disagreement about implementation. Moreover, more litigation can be expected if governments engage in reform measures that are perceived to depart from *Charter* values, or if courts change their views about what are *Charter* values.

Several structural factors will also influence the extent of future *Charter* litigation. First, litigation is expensive. Individuals rarely have sufficient personal resources to initiate a major constitutional challenge. If individuals with complaints about inadequate health services do have money, they are more likely to use it to buy the medical services they need rather than go to court. Moreover, public funding for litigation is not available. The Court Challenges program, which provides limited funding for individuals and groups to launch legal actions, only has power to fund cases that challenge federal laws. Since health care is a matter of provincial responsibility, and provinces make most health policy decisions, most challenges to health-care policies are outside the program's purview. Second, time is an important consideration. Legal actions take a long time to proceed through the judicial system, and the very nature of some health decisions means that many patients cannot effectively use the courts.

These factors, however, have less salience for providers, such as doctors, or for private providers, such as dentists and pharmaceutical companies. With less cost constraints, they may initiate *Charter* litigation as a sword to obtain favourable policy changes, or as a shield to maintain their position. For instance, litigation to strike down the ban on private health insurance uses the *Charter* as a sword to increase private health care. The hypothetical doctors' challenge to employment or capitation contracts would use the *Charter* as a shield to prevent structural changes in physician remuneration. Moreover, *Charter* actions may be initiated as a tactic to pressure governments and influence public debate, even if the likelihood of success in court is low.

Governments could forestall some litigation by using the section 33 override. For those *Charter* cases involving sections 2, and sections 7 to 15, Parliament and provincial legislatures may declare that a law operates notwithstanding those *Charter* rights and freedoms. However, the override is not often used because of the fear of negative political repercussions. Moreover, some *Charter* rights (such as section 6's mobility rights) and the Constitution's fundamental principles fall outside the override's ambit, and governments are unable to immunize themselves from constitutional challenges on these grounds. Governments will have no recourse other than section 1 to justify interference with rights, as they have done successfully with some challenges to date.

One important question involves deciding what constitutes governmental action in the health-care area. Section 32 states that the *Charter* applies to Parliament, the federal government, and the legislatures and governments of each province and territory. Hypothetically, if a government decided to privatize health care entirely—whatever that might mean (Gray 1998, 908)—the *Charter* would no longer govern the health-care system. However, even if this most unlikely scenario were to unfold, the *Charter* will likely not be avoided. The question of what is government action under section 32 is notoriously complex, and it may be quite possible to find sufficient government action to ground *Charter* claims, especially since wholesale privatization does not avoid Canada's obligations under international law. The very point of positive governmental obligations is to require governments to provide particular services. Insofar as *Charter* jurisprudence develops more positive obligations (and *Gosselin* may be a harbinger), privatization options might become more difficult. In any event, the private sector is regulated by statute and the common law. The *Charter* directly regulates the former, and its values regulate the latter.

In considering reforms to the health-care system, governments should take *Charter* values into account. This can be done in a number of ways that not only show respect for constitutional values, but may also diminish the risk of courts striking down health-care policies. These ways are not startling, but are integral to good governance in any policy area. Specifically, policies should be justified with evidence, such as economic studies about the merits and drawbacks of particular changes. In addition, reforms should be publicly justified as furthering important *Charter* values, such as equality, and decision making within the health-care system should be transparent and include procedural safeguards, such as appeals from funding decisions. Space does not permit fuller consideration of implementing these methods, but they are worthy of further study. For instance, a statutory Patients' Bill of Rights may assist courts in elucidating the core requirements of rights in the health-care context. More judicial education about the economics of health-care systems would do no harm. The health-care system is one that every Canadian uses but few know much about, including members of the legal community. If judicial review in a democracy is a dialogue between judges and legislatures, more and better information about the content of the dialogue—in this instance, health-care policy—would only enrich the debate.

VI. Conclusion

There will always be *Charter* litigation seeking to enforce and expand upon constitutional rights as a means of effecting health policy. The dynamic between the *Charter* and the health-care system, or to put the matter more precisely, between judges and health-care officials, is an inescapable component of Canada's health-care system. To date, there have only been a few successful *Charter* challenges to the health-care system, and, with the exception of the British Columbia doctors' cases, their financial impact on the system has not been great. Several fundamental *Charter* values, such as equality and non-discrimination, animate the existing Medicare system. The principles in the *Canada Health Act* fulfill Canada's international obligations with respect to health services, and go a long way toward satisfying the requirements of sections 7 and 15. Courts have shown considerable sensitivity to the dynamics of Canada's health-care system, recognizing the importance of accessible health care for everyone, the unbelievably complex system in place for its delivery, and the need to give governments a wide margin of appreciation. However, the number, type, and likely success of challenges depend on many factors, including the nature of reforms introduced by governments. If governments delist more services or significantly change the mix of public and private sector delivery, they can expect more *Charter* claims from individuals using the *Charter* as a shield to preserve the current system. Alternatively, if governments do not change the system, or if they change in a controversial direction, they will face challenges from people using the *Charter* as a sword to force changes in a different direction. To lessen the impact on health-care costs of the inevitable *Charter* challenges, governments can explicitly take *Charter* values into account in their health-care policies, and justify their decisions with the best available evidence.

Bibliography

Angus, Douglas. 1999. Some Thoughts on Rights and Responsibilities in Healthcare. *National Journal of Constitutional Law* 11, 261–72.

Auton (Guardian ad Litem of) v. *British Columbia (Minister of Health)*. 2000. [2000] B.C.J. No. 1547 (British Columbia Supreme Court).

Baker v. *Canada (Minister of Citizenship and Immigration)*. 1999. (1999) 174 D.L.R. (4th) 193 (Supreme Court of Canada).

Brown v. *British Columbia (Minister of Health)*. 1990. [1990] B.C.J. No. 151 (British Columbia Supreme Court).

Cameron v. *Nova Scotia (Attorney General)*. 1999. (1999) N.S.J. No. 33 (Nova Scotia Supreme Court).

Cameron v. *Nova Scotia (Attorney General)*. 1999a. [1999] N.S.J. No. 297 (Nova Scotia Court of Appeal); leave to appeal to the Supreme Court of Canada denied, 29 June 2000.

Canada Health Act, R.S.C. 1985. c. C-6.

Canadian Egg Marketing Agency v. *Richardson*. 1998. [1998] 3 S.C.R. 157 (Supreme Court of Canada).

Carver, Peter. 2002. A New Director for Mental Health Law: Brian's Law and the Problematic Implications of Community Treatment Orders, in *Health-care Reform and Law in Canada: Meeting the Challenge*, edited by Tim Caulfield and Barbara Von Tigerstrom. Edmonton, University of Alberta Press, p. 187–222.

Chaoulli c. *Québec (Procureur général)*. 2002. [2002] J.Q. n 759 (Cour d'appel du Québec).

Chaoulli c. *Québec (Procureur général)*. 2000. [2000] J.Q. n 479 (Cour supérieure du Québec—Chambre civile).

Chapman, Audrey (ed.). 1994. *Health-care Reform: A Human Rights Approach*. Washington, D.C.: Georgetown University Press.

Committee on Economic, Social and Cultural Rights. 1998. *Concluding Observations on Canada*. UN Doc. E/C.12/1/Add.31.

Costco Wholesale Canada Ltd v. *British Columbia (Board of Examiners in Optometry)*. 1998. (1998) 157 D.L.R. (4th) 725 (British Columbia Supreme Court).

Eldridge v. *British Columbia (Attorney General)*. 1997. [1997] 3 S.C.R. 624 (Supreme Court of Canada).

Flood, Colleen. 1999. Contracting for Health-care Services in the Public Sector. *Canadian Business Law Journal* 31, 175–208.

Gosselin c. *Québec (Procureur général)*. 1999. [1999] J.Q. no. 1365 (Cour d'appel du Québec).

Gray, Gwen. 1998. Access to Medical Care Under Strain: New Pressures in Canada and Australia. *Journal of Health Politics, Policy and Law* 23, 905–47.

Hartt, Stanley and Patrick Monahan. 2002. *The Charter and Health Care: Guaranteeing Timely Access to Health Care for Canadians*. Toronto: C.D. Howe Institute.

Hogg, Peter. 2001. *Constitutional Law of Canada* (2001 Student Edition). Toronto: Carswell.

International Covenant on Economic, Social, and Cultural Rights. 1966. Adopted 16 December 1966, UN Doc. A/6316.

Irshad (Litigation Guardian of) v. *Ontario (Minister of Health)*. 2001. [2001] O.J. No. 648 (Court of Appeal for Ontario).

Irwin Toy v. *Quebec (Attorney General)*. 1989. [1989] 1 S.C.R. 927 (Supreme Court of Canada).

Jackman, Martha. 1995. The Regulation of Private Health Care Under the Canada Health Act and Canadian Charter. *Constitutional Forum* 6(2), 54.

J.C. v. *Forensic Psychiatric Service Commissioner*. 1992. (1992) 65 B.C.L.R. (2d) 386 (British Columbia Supreme Court).

Karr, Andrea. 2000. Section 7 of the Charter: Remedy for Canada's Health-care Crisis? *The Advocate* 58(3)(4), 363–74, 531–41.

Kelly, James. 1999. The Charter of Rights and Freedoms and the Rebalancing of Liberal Constitutionalism in Canada, 1982–1997. *Osgoode Hall Law Journal* 37, 625–95.

Lalonde v. *Ontario (Commission de restructuration des services de santé)*. 2001. [2001] O.J. No. 4767 (Court of Appeal for Ontario).

Law v. *Canada (Minister of Employment and Immigration)*. 1999. [1999] 1 S.C.R. 497 (Supreme Court of Canada).

Leary, Virginia. 1993. Implications of a Right to Health, in *Human Rights in the Twenty-first Century*, edited by K. E. Maloney and P. Maloney. Dordrecht: Martinus Nijhoff, p. 481–93.

Lepofsky, David. 1996-97. A Report Card on the Charter's Guarantee of Equality to Persons with Disabilities after 10 Years—What Progress? What Prospects? *National Journal of Constitutional Law* 7, 263–431.

Lewis, Steven et al. 2000. Ending Waiting-List Mismanagement: Principles and Practice. *Canadian Medical Association Journal* 162(9), 1297–1300.

Manfredi, Christopher and Antonia Maioni. 2002. Courts and Health Policy: Judicial Policy Making and Publicly Funded Health Care in Canada. *Journal of Health Politics, Policy and Law* 27(2), 213–40.

New Brunswick (Minister of Health and Social Services) v. *G.(J.)*. 1999. [1999] 3 S.C.R. 46 (Supreme Court of Canada).

Okma, Kieke. 2002. What Is the Best Public-Private Model for Canadian Health Care? *Policy Matters* 3(6), 1–60.

Ontario Nursing Home Assn. v. *Ontario*. 1990. (1990) 72 D.L.R (4th) 166 (Ontario High Court of Justice).

Ponteix (Town) v. *Saskatchewan*. 1994. [1995] 1 W.W.R. 400 (Saskatchewan Court of Queen's Bench).

R.B. v. *Children's Aid Society of Metropolitan Toronto*. 1995. [1995] 1 S.C.R. 315 (Supreme Court of Canada).

R. v. *Morgentaler*. 1988. [1988] 1 S.C.R. 30 (Supreme Court of Canada).

R. v. Oakes. 1986. [1986] 1 S.C.R. 103 (Supreme Court of Canada).

R. v. Parker. 2000. [2000] O.J. No. 2787 (Court of Appeal for Ontario).

Reference Re Criminal Code, Ss. 193 & 195.1(1)(c). 1990. [1990] 4 W.W.R. 481 (Supreme Court of Canada).

Reference Re Motor Vehicle Act of British Columbia. 1988. [1988] 2 S.C.R. 486 (Supreme Court of Canada).

Re Mia and Medical Services Commission of British Columbia. 1985. (1985) 17 D.L.R. (4th) 385 (British Columbia Supreme Court).

Richards, John. 1999. William Schabas v. Cordelia. *National Journal of Constitutional Law* 11, 247–260.

Rocket v. Royal College of Dental Surgeons of Ontario. 1990. (1990) 71 D.L.R. (4th) 68 (Supreme Court of Canada).

Rodriquez v. British Columbia (Attorney General). 1993. [1993] 3 S.C.R 519 (Supreme Court of Canada).

Rombaut v. New Brunswick (Minister of Health and Community Services). 2001. [2001] N.B.J. No. 243. (New Brunswick Court of Appeal).

Schabas, William. 1999. Freedom From Want: How Can We Make Indivisibility More Than Just a Mere Slogan? *National Journal of Constitutional Law* 11, 189–212.

Schrecker, Ted. 1998. Private Health Care for Canada: North of the Border, an Idea Whose Time Shouldn't Come? *Journal of Law, Medicine & Ethics* 26, 138–48.

Sholzberg-Gray, Sharon. 1999. Accessible Health Care as a Human Right. *National Journal of Constitutional Law* 11(2) 273–91.

Singh and Minister of Employment and Immigration, Re. 1985. (1985) 17 D.L.R. (4th) 422–72. (Supreme Court of Canada).

Stoffman v. Vancouver General Hospital. 1990. [1990] 3 S.C.R. 483. (Supreme Court of Canada).

Toebes, Brigit. 1999. *The Right to Health as a Human Right in International Law.* Antwerp: Intersentia.

Von Tigerstrom, Barbara. 2002. Human Rights and Health-care Reform: A Canadian Perspective, in *Health-care Reform and Law in Canada: Meeting the Challenge,* edited by Tim Caulfield and Barbara von Tigerstrom. Edmonton: University of Alberta Press, p. 157–85.

——. 1999. Equality Rights and the Allocation of Scarce Resources in Health Care: A Comment on Cameron v. Nova Scotia. *Constitutional Forum* 11(1) 30–40.

Waldman v. British Columbia (Medical Services Commission). 1999. [1999] B.C.J. No. 2014 (British Columbia Court of Appeal).

Wellesley Central Hospital v. Ontario (Health Services Restructuring Commission). 1997. [1997] O.J. No. 3645 (Ontario Court of Justice, General Division).

Wilson v. British Columbia (Medical Services Commission). 1988. [1988] B.C.J. No. 1566 (British Columbia Court of Appeal).

Appendix I. Canadian Charter of Rights and Freedoms

Guarantee of Rights and Freedoms
Rights and freedoms in Canada

1. The *Canadian Charter of Rights and Freedoms* guarantees the rights and freedoms set out in it subject only to such reasonable limits prescribed by law as can be demonstrably justified in a free and democratic society.

Mobility Rights
Mobility of citizens

6. (1) Every citizen of Canada has the right to enter, remain in and leave Canada.

    (2) Every citizen of Canada and every person who has the status of a permanent resident of Canada has the right

      a) to move to and take up residence in any province; and

      b) to pursue the gaining of a livelihood in any province.

(3) The rights specified in subsection (2) are subject to

    a) any laws or practices of general application in force in a province other than those that discriminate among persons primarily on the basis of province of present or previous residence; and

    b) any laws providing for reasonable residency requirements as a qualification for the receipt of publicly provided social services.

(4) Subsections (2) and (3) do not preclude any law, program or activity that has as its object the amelioration in a province of conditions of individuals in that province who are socially or economically disadvantaged if the rate of employment in that province is below the rate of employment in Canada.

Legal Rights

Life, liberty and security of person

7. Everyone has the right to life, liberty and security of the person and the right not to be deprived thereof except in accordance with the principles of fundamental justice.

Equality Rights

Equality before and under law and equal protection and benefit of law

15. (1) Every individual is equal before and under the law and has the right to the equal protection and equal benefit of the law without discrimination and, in particular, without discrimination based on race, national or ethnic origin, colour, religion, sex, age or mental or physical disability.

    (2) Subsection (1) does not preclude any law, program or activity that has as its object the amelioration of conditions of disadvantaged individuals or groups including those that are disadvantaged because of race, national or ethnic origin, colour, religion, sex, age or mental or physical disability.

Application of Charter

Application of Charter

32. (1) This Charter applies

    a) to the Parliament and government of Canada in respect of all matters within the authority of Parliament including all matters relating to the Yukon Territory and Northwest Territories; and

    b) to the legislature and government of each province in respect of all matters within the authority of the legislature of each province.

    (2) Notwithstanding subsection (1), section 15 shall not have effect until three years after this section comes into force.

Exception where express declaration

33. (1) Parliament or the legislature of a province may expressly declare in an Act of Parliament or of the legislature, as the case may be, that the Act or a provision thereof shall operate notwithstanding a provision included in section 2 or sections 7 to 15 of this Charter.

    (2) An Act or a provision of an Act in respect of which a declaration made under this section is in effect shall have such operation as it would have but for the provision of this Charter referred to in the declaration.

    (3) A declaration made under subsection (1) shall cease to have effect five years after it comes into force or on such earlier date as may be specified in the declaration.

    (4) Parliament or the legislature of a province may re-enact a declaration made under subsection (1).

    (5) Subsection (3) applies in respect of a re-enactment made under subsection (4).

Appendix II. Table of Cases

Case name and citation	Facts	Argument, right claimed	Analysis	Disposition
Patients—specific treatment				
Brown v. British Columbia (Minister of Health) [1990] BCJ 151 (BC SC)	AIDS patients, drug AZT was placed on Pharmacare plan, which meant that all AIDS patients except those on social assistance or in long-term facilities had to pay for part of the drug's cost.	s.15—discrimination against AIDS patients as compared to other patients, such as cancer patients. s.7: deprivation of right to life, liberty and security of the person.	No violation: the reason for AIDS drugs being on a different plan than cancer drugs has to do with a difference between the drugs, not inequality as contemplated by s.15. No violation: s.7 does not contemplate economic deprivation.	Plaintiffs lost.
Ontario Nursing Home Assn. v. Ontario [1990] OJ 1280 (Ont HCJ)	Plaintiffs challenge the provision of more funding to homes for the aged than for other nursing homes.	s.7: deprivation of right to life, liberty security of the person because better care was available at homes for the aged than at other nursing homes. s.15: discrimination.	No violation: no evidence that plaintiff's was not adequately cared for; s.7 does not entitle person to additional benefits that might enhance plaintiff's life, liberty or security of the person. no violation: type of residence (aged/nursing) not an enumerated or analogous ground.	Plaintiffs lost.
Fernandes v. Manitoba [1992] MJ 279 (Man CA)	F was in hospital but wanted to live in an apartment; if he did, he would need an attendant for 16h/day; Director of Income Security refused F's request for additional allowance.	s.7: life, liberty, security of the person. s.15—discrimination on the basis of disability.	No violation: desire to live someplace in particular is not a right protected by s.7. No violation: no discrimination on the basis of personal characteristics or disability.	Plaintiff lost.
Cameron v. Nova Scotia (Attorney General) [1999] NSJ 297 (NS CA)	Infertile couple, wanted government to pay for fertility treatments.	s.15: infertile people have a disability; denial of payment was substantially different treatment on the basis of disability; found to be discrimination.	Violation, but justified under s.1. Best possible health care with limited financial resources requires flexibility in apportioning social benefits; the violation minimally impaired s.15 right because it denied funding for only two procedures.	Plaintiffs lost.

Case	Facts	Issue	Analysis	Result
Irshad v. Ontario (Minister of Health) [2001] OJ No. 648 (Ont. CA)	Immigrants to Ontario not eligible for medicare; upon reaching a certain immigration status, had to wait 3 months.	s.15—denial of medical coverage on the basis of residency in Ontario.	No violation: residency requirement did not offend dignity; there were alternatives to provincial medical coverage.	Plaintiffs lost.
N (DJ) [Niznik] v. Alberta (Child Welfare Appeal Panel) [1999] AJ 798 (Alta QB)	N's son is autistic; N received some funding for family support, and wanted funding for further therapy and training; Director, Appeal Panel refused.	2.15: discrimination	No violation: no evidence that N was treated differently than other similarly-situated children. N received some therapy at school; special needs were of the type that School Act provided for.	Plaintiffs lost. [overruled by Auton?]
Auton v. British Columbia (Minister of Health) [2000] BCSC 1142 (BC SC)	Parents of autistic children want government to pay for Lovaas behavioural therapy for preschool children; government would not fund until school age because treatment was considered "education," and it was very expensive treatment.	s.15—discrimination: primary health care need of children with autism is early behavioural intervention, a necessary treatment.	Violation: Lovaas was medical treatment; government failed to give children the treatment they needed. Violation not justified under s.1.	Plaintiffs won; court ordered government to pay for Lovaas treatment when doctor recommended it.
Martin v. NS WCB [2000] NSJ 353 (NS CA)	Workplace injury caused chronic pain that caused disability; WCB did not compensate except in limited circumstances; at trial plaintiffs won.	s.15: discrimination against people who suffer chronic pain.	No violation: no evidence that sufferers of chronic pain experienced historical disadvantage or stereotyping; overall purpose of compensation scheme was compensatory.	Plaintiffs lost.
Eldridge v. British Columbia (Attorney General) [1997] 3 SCR 624	Deaf patients wanted government to provide sign language interpretation [SLI] when they communicated with health care providers.	s.15: failure to provide SLI, where necessary for effective communication, is discrimination on the basis of disability.	Violation: discrimination because deaf patients denied equal access to health services available to everyone. Failure to provide SLI was adverse effects discrimination; decision not to fund SLI was not justified under s.1.	Plaintiffs won. Court directed government to administer Medicare legislation in manner consistent with s.1; declaration suspended for 6 months.

RR v. Alberta (Child Welfare Appeal Panel) [2000] AJ 580 (Alta QB)	Rs had 3 children: 2 with spastic hemiplegia, 1 with cerebral palsy; wanted funding for conductive education during school year and at summer camp; Director, Appeal Panel refused; parents knew other children with CP who got funding.	s.15: these children (denied funding) with CP were treated differently from other children with CP (received funding).	No violation: children were subjected to differential treatment, but not on listed or analogous ground; differential treatment was not on the fact of disability, but personal characteristics, specific medical needs and family situation.	Plaintiff lost.
Patients—criminalized treatment				
R. v. Morgentaler [1988] 1 SCR 30	Doctor violated Criminal Code by performing abortions on women who had not obtained certificate from therapeutic abortion committee at an approved hospital; women also guilty of Criminal Code offences.	s.7: breach of life, liberty and security of the person, not in accordance with the principles of fundamental justice.	Violation. State interference with bodily integrity (forcing woman to carry to term; delay and subsequent risks) and state-induced psychological stress (at least in criminal law) is a breach of women's security of the person. Deprivation not in accordance with principles of fundamental justice: defence is illusory, not all hospitals qualify to have a committee; even if they do qualify, having the committee is not mandatory. "Security of the person" includes a right of access to medical treatment for a condition representing a danger to life or health, without fear of criminal sanction.	Court declared the Criminal Code provisions invalid, and of no force and effect.
Rodriguez v. British Columbia (1993) 107 DLR (4th) 342	Plaintiff, who suffered from terminal illness, sought declaration that Criminal Code prohibition on assisting suicide was unconstitutional.	s.7: prohibiting persons from helping plaintiff commit suicide violates plaintiff's security of the person, s.15—violation of equality rights on the ground of physical disability.	No violation of s.7. The security interest was infringed, but the deprivation did not infringe the principles of fundamental justice. S.15—assuming a violation, it was justified under s.1.	Plaintiff lost

Case	Facts	Decision	Result
R. v. Parker [2000] OJ No. 2787 (Ont CA)	P had severe epileptic seizures, conventional medicine did not control condition, but marijuana did; he could not find a legal source so he grew his own; charged with criminal offences of possession and cultivation.	s.7: prohibiting P from using a necessary medication infringed right to security of the person; threat of jail engaged right to liberty.	Violation. Depriving access (via criminal sanction) to medication reasonably required for a medical condition that threatens life or health violates security of the person. Liberty violated by threat of imprisonment; liberty also includes right to make decisions of fundamental importance, including choice of medication. Deprivations violated the principles of natural justice because blanket prohibition did little or nothing to enhance state interest.	Court declared the criminal prohibition of marijuana invalid, and of no force and effect. It suspended the declaration for 12 months, and gave a personal exemption to P.
Hospital restructuring			
Lachine General Hospital v. Quebec (1997) 142 DLR (4th) 659 (Que. CA).	Pursuant to restructuring legislation, several hospitals in the Montreal region were ordered closed, including an English-language hospital.	s.15—closing hospital that primarily served anglophone patients violated equality rights of patients and personnel.	No violation. No discrimination proven; difference in bilingual hospitals before and after closure was minimal.	Plaintiffs lost.
Ponteix (Town) v. Saskatchewan [1995] 1 WWR 400 (Sk. Q.B.)	Pursuant to restructuring legislation, many local hospitals converted to health centres, with reduced emergency/ overnight service. Rural coalition reached agreement with government about such service, which plaintiff alleges was breached.	s.7 and 15—reduced availability of emergency/ overnight service violated security of the person and equality rights.	No violation. Even if Charter applies, it does not require the same standard of health care for all residents, regardless of where they live.	Plaintiffs lost.
Russell v. Ontario [1998] OJ 4116 (Ont. Ct. of Justice)	Ontario Health Services Restructuring Commission ordered Hotel Dieu, a hospital run by nuns, to shut down and transfer its operations to another hospital.	s. 2(a) freedom of religion— plaintiffs, the nuns who run Hotel Dieu, cannot carry out their religious mission to minister to the sick poor.	No violation. Freedom of religion does not entitle anyone to state support for one's religion. Nothing prevents nuns from ministering to the sick poor on that site.	Plaintiffs lost.

Case	Facts	Holding	Result
Wellesley Central Hospital v. Ontario [1997] OJ 3645 (Ont Div. Ct.).	Ontario Health Services Restructuring Commission ordered Wellesley hospital to transfer its services to another hospital, which was administered by a religious order; individual plaintiffs, who were HIV positive homosexuals, objected.	s. 2(a), s.15 — compelling gay men to receive treatment at a hospital administered by a religious order violated freedom of religion, and was discriminatory.	No violation. No evidence that gay men would be compelled to receive treatment at the hospital; no evidence of breach of other Charter rights.	Plaintiffs lost.
SGEU v. Saskatchewan (1997) 145 D.L.R. (4th) 300 (Sk QB); affirmed 149 DLR (4th) 190 (Sk CA).	Hospital restructuring plan would move 20% of SGEU membership to other unions, who would be bargaining agents for these employees.	s.2(d) — mandatory move of some employees to other unions violated freedom of association.	No violation; freedom of association does not include freedom to choose one's bargaining unit.	Plaintiffs lost.
Jewish Hospital of Hope v. Quebec (1997) 139 DLR (4th) 456 (Que. CA).	Pursuant to hospital restructuring legislation, hospital became subject to a regional board of directors.	s.2(d) — freedom of association violated by imposing a regional board of directors.	No violation. Freedom of association does not include a hospital's administrative autonomy.	Plaintiffs lost.
Pembroke Civic Hospital v. Ontario [1997] OJ 3142 (Ont. Ct. Gen.Div); dismissed [1997] OJ 3603 (Ont. CA).	Health Services Restructuring Commission ordered Pembroke Civic Hospital to merge with another one, operated by the Roman Catholic Church.	s.2(a), 7 and 15 — the religious views of RC hospital would influence health care.	No violation. Charter challenge was premature. No evidence that Roman Catholic views were forced on patients, or affected treatment.	Plaintiffs lost.
Lalonde v. Ontario (Health Services Restructuring Commission) [2001] OJ 4767 (Ont CA)	Bilingual hospital provided service in French 24 hours a day; government (HSRC) restructured hospital and limited its services.	s.15: discrimination against the francophone community. Fundamental constitutional principle of protecting minorities violated by HSRC.	No violation: language was not an enumerated or analogous ground. HSRC must respect fundamental constitutional principles. It failed to give serious weight and consideration to the hospital's importance to the francophone community.	Plaintiffs won. Court remitted matter back to Minister (who replaced HSRC) for reconsideration taking into account fundamental constitutional principles.

Doctors/hospital employees—discrimination			
Sniders v. Nova Scotia (1988) 55 DLR (4th) 408 (NS CA)	Plaintiff, a member of a bargaining unit, challenged hospital's mandatory retirement policy.	s.15—age discrimination.	Violation. Mandatory retirement is age discrimination, and cannot be justified under s.1.	Plaintiff won. Court ordered him reinstated as employee.
Stoffman v. Vancouver General Hospital (1990) 76 DLR (4th) 700 (SCC).	Plaintiffs had their admitting privileges terminated when they reached the age of 65, pursuant to the hospital's mandatory retirement policy.	s.15—age discrimination.	Hospital was not covered by Charter. However, even if it was, the s.15 violation was justified under s.1.	Plaintiffs lost.
Jamorski v. Ontario (AG) [1988] OJ 221 (Ont CA)	Plaintiffs were graduates of Polish medical schools, and had passed Canadian exam. They could not get internship because of differential treatment for foreigners; had to pass pre-internship program, which only had 24 places.	s.15: discrimination on the basis of graduating from accredited or non-accredited schools.	No violation: was not differential treatment because grads of accredited vs. non-accredited schools are different, unreasonable to expect that grads of both would be the same; even if there was a violation, it would have been justified under s.1.	Plaintiffs lost. Appeal dismissed.
Doctors—liberty and mobility with respect to practice			
Jaeger v. Quebec (1998) 155 DLR (4th) 599 (Que. CA)	Foreign doctors could obtain license to practice in designated geographic regions, if they stayed in the region for 4 years. Penalty for moving earlier was $50,000/year. Plaintiff doctor, who obtained licence under the program, objected to the penalty.	s.7—requirement to stay in one place for 4 years violated liberty. s.15—policy discriminated against foreign doctors.	No violation. Liberty does not include freedom to practice profession wherever one wishes, without financial penalty. Equality rights not violated by special program that increased opportunities for foreign doctors.	Plaintiff lost.
Kirsten v. College of Physicians and Surgeons [1996] SJ 462 (Sk. QB).	Plaintiff challenged agreement with College to practice in rural Saskatchewan for 5 years, in exchange for license.	s.6—mobility—5-year agreement denied right to move to another province. s.7—liberty.	Assuming that rights were violated, plaintiff waived his Charter rights.	Plaintiff lost.

Case	Facts	Analysis		Outcome
Mia v. British Columbia (Medical Services Commission) (1985) 17 DLR (4th) 385 (BC SC)	M studied and graduated in British Columbia, but interned, did post-graduate training and practiced outside province; British Columbia would not give M a billing number.	s.6: mobility; prima facie right to move to a province for work, and to work anywhere in province. s.7: liberty includes freedom to practice a profession.	Violation: s.6 protects right to practice on a viable economic basis anywhere in province. Liberty in s.7 protects freedom of movement within a province for purpose of pursuing professional practice; breach of principles because policy was arbitrary.	Plaintiff won. Court declared that M entitled to billing number for services rendered anywhere in province.
Wilson v. British Columbia (Medical Services Commission) [1988] BCJ 1566 (BC CA)	Plaintiffs were 6 doctors: 4 graduated from UBC and practised outside British Columbia, 2 were educated outside British Columbia and now subject to British Columbia restrictions; legislation gave MSC power to not grant billing numbers, and, if granted, to restrict numbers to specific area or purpose (e.g., locums).	s.7: freedom to practice profession was so severely restricted that it violated liberty; "liberty" should be interpreted generously to include right to choose an occupation and where to pursue it. s.6: mobility rights infringed by geographic restrictions within province.	Violation: liberty includes right to practice medicine in British Columbia without geographic restriction. Breach of principles of fundamental justice because of procedural unfairness (vague criteria, uncontrolled discretion of MSC) and the manifest unfairness of a scheme in which doctors with restricted numbers were at the mercy of doctors with unrestricted numbers, abuse of the system. Court did not address s.6 arguments.	Plaintiffs won. Court declared that legislation invalid, and of no force and effect.
Waldman v. British Columbia (Medical Service, Commission) [1999] BCJ 2014 (BC CA)	Plaintiffs challenged physician supply management. MSC created a new billing system: if new billers wanted to work in a place that already had enough doctors, they could only bill a maximum of 50% of the normal rate; after 5 years of practice in British Columbia the geographical restriction was lifted; preference was given to BC-educated new doctors.	s.6: mobility rights violated by geographic restrictions. s.15: discrimination on the basis of province of training or residence.	Mobility rights violated by preference to doctors who were trained in British Columbia, or who started studies in British Columbia by a certain date; the remainder of the scheme did not violate s.6. Court of Appeal did not consider s.15; trial judge had held that s.15 not violated because billing system did not discriminate on enumerated or analogous ground.	Plaintiffs won. Court refused to sever invalid provision from valid provisions, and it declared entire scheme invalid.

Case	Facts	Claim	Analysis	Result
Rombaut v. New Brunswick (Minister of Health and Community Services) [2001] NBJ 243 (NB CA)	Plaintiffs challenged physician resource management plan. Doctors practising in New Brunswick before the plan came in were exempted or grandfathered; New Brunswick does not have a medical school, so there is no distinction between new doctors from here or new doctors from away.	s.6 grandfathering provisions are preferential for New Brunswick practitioners. s.15: gender discrimination because system perpetuates the gender imbalance of the status quo. s.7: right to practise with the partners they want and be paid for it.	No violation. A purpose of s.6 is to protect dignity (human rights); there is a preference that would count as discrimination, but it is not on the basis of residency; even if there is a violation it is justifiable under s.1. No violation: system is equally hard on men and women, it does not promote men over women. No violation: s.7 is not concerned with economic deprivation.	Plaintiffs lost.

Practice regulation

Case	Facts	Claim	Analysis	Result
Rocket v. Royal College of Dental Surgeons of Ontario (1990) 71 DLR (4th) 68 (SCC).	Several dentists challenged the rule of their professional association prohibiting advertising.	s. 2(b)—freedom of expression. Ban on advertising violated dentist's expressive freedom.	Violation. Ban prohibits legitimate forms of expression, and cannot be justified under s.1.	Plaintiffs won.
Costco Wholesale Canada Ltd v. British Columbia (1998) 157 DLR 725 (BC SC).	Two optometrists challenged bylaw of Board of Examiners in Optometry, which prohibited optometrists from having business associations with non-optometrists.	s. 2(d)—ban on business associations violated freedom of association.	Violation. Freedom of association includes economic associations. Ban not justified under s.1. Absolute ban not proportionate to objective of maintaining high standards of professionalism.	Plaintiffs won.

Medicare structure

Case	Facts	Claim	Analysis	Result
Chaoulli c. Québec (Procureur Général) [2002] JQ759 (Que. CA).	Plaintiffs challenged Quebec law that prohibited private health insurance for health services covered by Medicare.	s.7—limits on access to the private insurance violates right of security; health care is an important personal decision, and therefore its curtailment infringes liberty right.	No violation. s.7 does not include economic rights. Even if s.7 applies, no violation of principles of fundamental justice. Prohibition aims to safeguard public system of protection of health.	Plaintiffs lost.

23

The Contribution of the Social Economy to Social Policy

Lessons from Quebec*

YVES VAILLANCOURT, FRANÇOIS AUBRY, LOUISE TREMBLAY,
MURIEL KEARNEY, AND LUC THÉRIAULT

> Societies that enable all their citizens to play a full and useful role in the
> social, economic and cultural life of their society will be healthier than those
> where people face insecurity, exclusion and deprivation.
> —World Health Organization, 1998: 9

Introduction

The social economy is definitely an ally to the State if the State's objectives are to improve health and well-being. This paper will argue that the social economy plays an important role in social policy and, consequently, that it has positive impacts on the health and well-being of individuals, families, and communities.

One cannot discuss social policy as a determinant of health and well-being without taking into account the innovative practices of the growing third sector. For over 35 years, thousands of organizations and associations have become convinced that various life conditions constitute social determinants of health and well-being—an idea that has emerged in part from grass-root initiatives. Such initiatives are increasingly involved in a variety of activities related to personal services that have a direct influence on the quality of life of individuals and families.

The contribution of the social economy in restructuring the social policy agenda in Quebec is not unique in North America. What is new in Quebec since 1996 is that social economy is now recognized and supported by certain levels of government, in particular the Quebec government. In other provinces, the reality of the social economy exists, but it is not conceptualized as a third sector of the economy by those involved in these activities. However, things may be changing since interest in the concepts of third sector, voluntary sector or non-profit sector is growing in certain organizations and socio-political and aca-

* This paper is a modified version of a working paper published by the Social Policy Research Unit, Faculty of Social Work, University of Regina, 2003. The authors would like to acknowledge that the research for this chapter has been made possible thank to funding provided by two SSHRC grants (842-2001-0006 and 410-2002-1039).

demic circles.[1] These changes are increasingly apparent since the arrival of Paul Martin as leader of the federal government early in 2004. In fact, the social economy is presented as a government priority in the Speeches from the Throne of February and October 2004. Paul Martin and others in his government have made a commitment "[...] to foster the social economy—the myriad not-for-profit activities and enterprises that harness civic and entrepreneurial energies for community benefit right across Canada" (Speech from the Throne, October 5, 2004: 10–11). Moreover, the 2004–2005 Budget Speech announced an investment of $132 million to support the development of the social economy in Canada. Of this amount, $15 million will be used to promote research on the social economy via the Social Sciences and Humanities Research Council of Canada. This paper is devoted to analyzing the growing contribution of the social economy to social policy. It comprises four parts.

The first part proposes a definition of the social economy and aims at clarifying terms and concepts. We then present our analytical framework followed by an historical look at the relationships between the social economy and health and welfare policy in Quebec.

In the second part, we look at the specific contribution of social economy organizations and enterprises in the realm of social policy. We will begin by underlining the importance of user and worker empowerment in these entities and the positive influence of such empowerment on health and well-being. We will also examine the contribution of social economy organizations and associations in four particular areas of social policy that have grown significantly over the last few years: social housing, early-childhood care, occupational integration, and home care services.

The third part examines the importance of citizen participation in the development of social policy and underlines the contribution of social economy to a more active citizenship.

In the fourth part, we will address the question of a plural economy in which the social economy, through its interactions with the State and the market, can impact positively on the democracy of workplace rules and practices within government and the for-profit sector.

Part I: Definitions and Terminology

Whatever the terms used—*social economy*, non-profit sector, third sector, voluntary sector—the reality that is covered "is deeply rooted in the social, economic, political and cultural history of a society, the conditions in which it emerges and the role that it currently plays will necessarily vary from one province to another" (Vaillancourt and Tremblay, 2002: 164).

In Quebec, the term *social economy* is widely used and refers to a vast array of organizations, mostly non-profit organizations including advocacy groups, voluntary organizations, and other community-based organizations (CBOs), as well as cooperatives and social enterprises.

The term *social economy* is not widely used in the English-speaking countries. It is rarely used in English Canada although some literature acknowledges the term (Quarter, 1992; Quarter et al., 2003; Shragge and Fontan, 2000; Vaillancourt and Tremblay, 2002).

If we were to choose an expression used in the English language literature that better befits our definition, we would, with Taylor (1995: 214) and a certain number of Irish authors (Donnelly-Cox, Donoghue and Taylor, 2001) prefer the term "Voluntary and Community Sector" instead of terms such as "Voluntary Sector" or "Voluntary and Non-profit Sector," which used in English Canada; or "Non-profit Sector," which is frequently used south of the border (Salamon and Anheier, 1998; Salamon et al., 1999). In our view these terms are too limited in their scope: the first one insists on organizations relying mostly on voluntary or unpaid work, while the second and third terms exclude an important part of CBOs made up of social enterprises such as cooperatives. In that respect, our viewpoint is similar to the one expressed by some European social policy and third sector researchers (Evers and Laville, 2004).

Since the middle of the 1990s, the term *social economy* has been widely used in Quebec. At the Economic and Employment Summit of 1996, attended by representatives of the government, business, labour, the women's movement, and community-based organizations, consensus was achieved over a five-element definition of the social economy (Chantier de l'économie sociale, 1996). Social economy organizations produce goods and services with a clear social mission and have these ideal-type characteristics and objectives:

• The mission is services to members and community and not profit oriented;
• Management is independent of government;
• Democratic decision making by workers and/or users;
• People have priority over capital;
• Participation, empowerment, individual and collective responsibility.

The advantage of this designation is that it is inclusive of all types of socially based economic activity namely community-based organizations, cooperatives, and other social enterprises. Although the social economy is not composed only of community-based organizations, these organizations make up the larger part of the social economy sector (Vaillancourt et al., in Raphaël, 2004; Kearney et al., 2004).

Historic recall

Research and observation show that the social economy exists and has existed in Canada and Quebec at least since the nineteenth century and has gradually gained vigour (Lévesque, Girard and Malo, 1999; Vaillancourt and Tremblay, 2002).

Up until the 1960s, in the pre-Welfare State period in Quebec, the social economy was present when vulnerable populations were in need, often through faith-based organizations. Economic growth and new ideas regarding policy brought about a constant increase of the State's implication in all health and welfare related areas. In the 1960s and the 1970s, the Welfare State period was significant in standardizing the supply of social services and ensuring free and accessible health care to the whole population. However many now recognize that the downside of this era was the growing bureaucracy and the centralization of policy-making and service delivery. The economic crisis of the 1980s put a terrible strain on all Western governments facing decreasing revenues and high expenses. Unable to respond adequately to exploding unemployment rates and new social inequities, the Market/State couple seemed to have reached certain limits within health and welfare policy. In some way, this crisis created new opportunities for social economy initiatives in many areas and more specifically in the field of health and welfare. The more recent of such activities are often referred to as the new social economy.

The social economy on the rise

Today social economy organizations play a major role in many spheres of economic and social life, in particular in the following areas:

- Health and social services
- Labour market integration
- Media and information technologies
- Popular education
- Sports and recreation
- Tourism
- Advocacy
- Cultural communities
- Land management
- Environment
- Local and regional development
- Ethical trade

Growing numbers

Notwithstanding its feeble recognition, the social economy is a powerful contributor to job creation in a vast majority of countries, whether they are in the North or in the South. Let us examine the situation in some developed regions of the world.

In the mid-1990s, the European Statistical Agency Eurostat (1997) estimated that 5,254,000 people worked in cooperatives, mutual societies and associations in Europe. Specifically:

- 1,743,000 in cooperatives;
- 226,000 in mutual benefit societies (in the social protection field);
- 3,285,000 in associations.

According to the *Centre interdisciplinaire de recherche et d'information sur les entreprises collectives* (CIRIEC) (1999):

- at the end of the decade, the social economy represented between 6 percent and 7 percent of the European Union labour force (approximately 9 million jobs);
- voluntary work, particularly within associations, represented the equivalent of millions of jobs.

The international study of the John Hopkins University estimated at 7 million the number of employees in the American non-profit sector, which represents 6.9 percent of total employment in the United States. In the 22 countries best covered by the study, the non-profit sector represented approximately 18.8 million jobs and mobilized 28 percent of the population through voluntary work. The importance of the non-profit sector varies substantially from one country to another, but can exceed 10 percent of total employment in some countries like Holland, Ireland and Belgium (Defourny, Develtere, and Fonteneau, 1999).

In Quebec, the social economy represents about 160,000 jobs in 11,000 organizations of which 3,200 are cooperatives. The social economy generates about 7 percent of the province's income (Chantier de l'économie sociale, 2001; Vaillancourt et al. in Raphaël, 2004: 317). Social economy organizations are very present in the health and welfare arena where more than 2,500 organizations are financed by the Department of Health and Social Services alone.

A multipolar versus a bipolar model

Looking at these figures it is clear that the widespread analysis of society articulated around a bipolar State/Market model is not only too simplistic, but it is also erroneous. How can we ignore all these organizations that are neither privately or State owned and operating outside the domestic sphere?

The mainstream trend in Canadian and Quebec literature (be it progressive or conservative) on Health reform is caught up in this bipolar framework. Despite the fact that the third sector is now referred to in the literature with genuine interest and often in a positive fashion, we do not observe a real recognition of the sector as a significant capacity builder to be taken into account in health and well-being policy making. In Canada as in Quebec, the important work of community organizations is still too timidly acknowledged (Gouvernement du Quebec, 1992; Forum national sur la santé, 1997a et 1997b; Commission d'étude sur les services de santé et les services sociaux, 2001; Groupe de travail sur la complémentarité du secteur privé dans la poursuite des objectifs fondamentaux du système de santé au Quebec, 1999; Conseil de la santé et du bien-être, 2002).

Many actors in the public health sector in Quebec, although convinced of the importance of the social determinants of health and well-being such as poverty, housing, education, and employment are, to this day, unable to comprehend fully that the actors of the social economy are key allies especially when non-medical determinants of health and well-being must be taken into account. Consequently, the social economy is still far from full recognition as a potential partner in a new development model.

With a growing number of analysts we find that this dual State/Market framework is unrealistic for it ignores important parts of our social and economic reality such as the social economy, but also the domestic sphere where women, unfortunately, still play the major caring role.

In our work, we regularly put forward the idea that social economy is one pillar of a plural economic development model. Along with Polanyi (2001), we consider that the economy must be envisioned as plural, and must be conceived around three major poles (the market economy, the non-market economy, and the non-monetary economy) and four governing principles that interact with each other and whose relative importance varies in time and place. These economic principles are as follows: market, redistribution, reciprocity, and household management (i.e., home economics). Four sectors of economic activity, each dominated by one of these three poles, can therefore be identified: the market, the State, the social economy, and the domestic sector.

The double nature of social policy

Social policy can be viewed as State and government interventions that foster citizenship and contribute to the well-being of individuals and communities. These policies are distinct from the activities of the market and the domestic spheres:

> Social policy begins where the laws of the market and the virtues of family and domestic solidarity cannot guarantee to individuals and communities the quality of life to which every citizen has a right. (Vaillancourt and Dumais, 2002: 30)

Social policy is a question of well-being **and** citizenship, of financial resources **and** dignity, of income distribution **and** access to services and, most importantly, of **participation or empowerment of people and communities**. Social policy concerns State and government intervention, but not exclusively.

Social policy increasingly implies various interactions between the interventions of the State and those of the social economy, as noted by Laville and Nyssens (2001) and Evers and Laville (2004). These authors emphasize that the history of the Welfare State and that of the non-profit sector are closely intertwined, the two having contributed to the "de-commodification" of social services, including services to senior citizens.

This fact is important if one wants to understand the evolution of social policy. The decrease of the importance of the market and of the family in the sphere of social services and social policy cannot be attributed only to the increase in the role of the public sector. It also stems from an increasing presence of the non-profit sector and a growing recognition of its contribution by the State that manifests itself by a growing cooperation between the State and the non-profit sector (Vaillancourt and Dumais, 2002; Vaillancourt, 2003). However, the improvement of social policy:

> is not a question of having more social economy initiatives. It is the consolidation of a development model based on solidarity and democracy in which social economy contributes to the emergence of an economy that we define, with others, as "authentically plural," which means less dominated by market rules. (Vaillancourt and Dumais, 2002: 363–64)

Historically the interaction of the State with the social economy has contributed widely to the development of social policy (Laville and Nyssens, 2001). Our particular interest with the social economy lies in its capacity to democratize social policy through the double empowerment of workers and users of personal services.

Part II: The Social Economy in the Realm of Social Policy

Social economy organizations are distinctive because of their values and rules. Their approach to health and welfare issues can be of great interest to policy-makers as partners in service delivery and as a model of user, worker, and community empowerment.

Be it through the democratic rules that govern them (one person, one vote), through the values of solidarity, autonomy, reciprocity, and self-determination that inspire them, through the ends that they pursue, through their contribution to social and economic networking, through their capacity to create jobs (paid or voluntary), or through the empowerment of users and workers that they favour, social economy organizations contribute positively to the health and well-being of individuals, families, and communities.

Double empowerment of users and workers

What is particularly interesting in social economy organizations is the possibility offered by their legal attributes to empower users and to democratize work organization and the way services are organized in order to empower workers.

We do not want to infer that for-profit and public sector organizations are by nature not able to empower workers and users or to put forth a democratic work organization, nor do we want to infer that such practices can be found, in a perfect form, in all community-based organizations. However, we believe that community-based organizations and other social economy organizations have a comparative advantage over public and for-profit organizations in this area since their rules and values are better adapted to and favour such practices. In the following sections, we will elaborate on this notion of double empowerment.

Social economy and users' empowerment

Social economy encourages individual and collective empowerment of users of social policy and services. The case of disabled people is particularly enlightening in this area and the work of the *Independent Living Movement* is most conclusive in this regard. In fact, the empowerment of these people as consumers of services was developed through a trend that can substantiate reflection on social policy-making in general.

The Independent Living Movement that started in the U.S. in the late 1960s puts forward the rights of disabled people to live an "ordinary life" as do people without a handicap and insists on treating people with disabilities as citizens (Ramon, 1991). The movement aims at increasing the autonomy of disabled persons in order that they make the decisions that concern them. The philosophy of the Independent Living Movement rapidly became an example for other advocacy groups defending the rights of vulnerable segments of the population: native groups, women's groups, ex-offenders, drug addicts, gay/lesbian rights groups, and welfare rights groups (Fuchs, 1987).

In Canada, the Roeher Institute and the network of Independent Living Resource Centres have contributed to put in place and popularize this approach which has been cited in different federal and Quebec publications since the beginning of the 1980s (Office des personnes handicapées du Quebec, 1984; Federal/Provincial/Territorial Ministers Responsible for Social Services, 1998).

The Independent Living Movement encourages self-management. As Don Fuchs of the University of Manitoba says:

> Disabled people through their experience in being disabled, best know the needs of disabled person: support services should be based on consumer-controlled policies; the focus of services is to change the environment and not the individual; the goal of services is integration into the community; the disabled individual can help him/herself through helping other disabled people. (1987: 193)

When disabled persons take charge of the organization of services at the user end, the empowerment is individual and collective and gives rise to an *identity movement* (Caillouette, 2001; Bélanger, 2002). Disabled persons that join and engage become social actors capable of developing and investing CBOs to defend their interests and influence social policy.

This vision and way of doing is totally different from the old progressive framework of "welfarist" policy reforms that consider users solely in positions at the "receiving end" of social policy. The new approach shatters the traditional structure where the user "demands" and the provider "supplies" social policies. It convenes users and providers to cooperate in a mutual elaboration of supply and demand (Laville, 1992).

Social economy and workers' empowerment

It is today recognized that a certain number of conditions that affect life and work, such as social and economic exclusion, unemployment, and poverty, have a negative impact on the health and well-being of individuals and can lead to lower life expectancy. On the other hand, having a job, doing meaningful work, having a certain amount of autonomy in one's work, and benefiting from varied and rich social relations in the workplace and in the community generally have a positive impact on the health and well-being of individuals and families (Beaulieu et al., 2002; Charbonneau, 2004).

It is generally admitted that work has a complex influence on the health and well-being of men or women whether they have a job or are deprived of one. Although work may have downsides and contradictions, work is a fundamental activity that facilitates time structuring, and creates opportunity for social relations. It consolidates self-esteem, gives access to identity, security, and human contact (Mercier et al., 1999).

Even though it has been demonstrated that these factors play a very important role in the case of people suffering from mental illness, they can also contribute positively to improve the health and well-being of individuals who do not suffer from any specific medical problems.

Moreover, the empowerment of workers is a factor that improves the quality of life in the workplace. The role of workers in the organization of their tasks and democratic practices can help counter Taylorist relations between managers and workers. Anti-democratic relations increase chances of burn out and demotivated personnel. These relations are at the origin of a growing number of health and safety issues in the workplaces of modern societies (Lippel, 1992; Lauzon and Charbonneau, 2001; Charbonneau, 2002). While it is shown that work can have a positive effect on health and well-being, it can also have a negative impact. Must we remember that:

- the number of days of absenteeism due to problems related to mental health tripled from 1992 to 1998 and benefits issued by the Quebec Work Health and Safety Commission (CSST) for these absences rose from 1.5 million dollars to 5.4 million dollars during this period;
- the Mental Health Committee of Quebec estimated that, in 1992, costs related to stress problems in the workplace accounted for 4 million dollars in Quebec (Vézina, 1998); according to insurers, mental illness and situational depression represent the main cause of long-term invalidity claims (Charbonneau, 2004);
- in Quebec, more than one-third of workers absent from work for medical reasons had received a diagnosis related to mental health.

It is generally recognized that work has an influence on the health and well-being of individuals. When, in a workplace, the organization of production relies on the intelligence and the responsibility of workers, these workers will tend to mobilize their imagination, their efforts and their know-how in order to meet production goals. In such a system, work is healthier, profitable and productive:

> Evidence shows that stress at work plays an important role in contributing to the large differences in health, sickness absence and premature death that are related to social status. Several workplace studies in Europe show that

health suffers when people have little opportunity to use their skills, and low authority over decisions.

Having little control over one's work is particularly strongly related to an increased risk of low back pain, sickness absence and cardiovascular disease. (World Health Organization, 1998: 16)

On the other hand, when the organization of production is characterized by an increasing number of controls and regulations, by a reduction of workers' autonomy and freedom, by process fragmentation and standardization, there is a loosening of solidarity and identity ties within the workplace. Such work organization, which values only the increasing effort demanded of workers, depreciates workers' knowledge, know-how and imagination. This type of "dehumanized" organization (Shimon, Lamoureux and Gosselin, 1996) will become "toxic" (Malenfant and Vézina, 1995; Burnonville, 1999; Charbonneau, 2002; 2004) because of the negative impact of such a guilt-driven and destructive work relation on the mental health of workers.

As we emphasized earlier, we do not wish to imply that all social economy organizations are always characterized by perfect worker control over work organization. However, because of their intrinsic characteristics, these organizations tend to be more open to the needs of workers, including their need to participate in the workplace.

In the field of health and welfare, there is a very real possibility of a double empowerment that reconciles user and worker participation (unionized workers, professionals, managers) (Vaillancourt and Jetté, 1997; Jetté et al., 2000; Jetté, Lévesque, and Vaillancourt, 2001).

Let us return to the case of disabled persons. The empowerment of these persons is closely related to the empowerment of workers. Thus, the more workers are empowered in the workplace, the more the workplace will be hospitable and encouraging for the integration of the disabled into the workforce. Also, can we not assume that, when employees working in organizations for the disabled are empowered, they will be more efficient in their efforts to improve the health and well-being of the disabled persons and make them more active citizens? Double empowerment within organizations for the disabled might contribute to ensure that these persons will be supported socially as users and as workers.

The study of the interactions between the third sector and the health and welfare policy shows the presence of a large number of social economy organizations in this field (Vaillancourt, 2002; Vaillancourt and Dumais, 2002). For the last 30 years, they have actively developed many innovative practices in response to increasing social problems. Community-based organizations contribute to the social and occupational integration of youth, single-mothers, physically and mentally disabled persons, the homeless, etc. They operate day-care services for pre-school children, home-care and home support services for the elderly and for persons with temporary or long term disabilities. They manage social housing with or without community support for vulnerable segments of the population.

Let us look more closely at some of these innovative practices in four areas: occupational integration, early childhood day-care services, homecare services, and social housing.

Occupational integration

We have stated previously that having a job is one of the most significant social determinants of health (World Health Organization, 1998; Raphaël, 2004). Work gives structure to one's life and enhances social relations. Following the economic crisis of the early 1980s, unemployment became a critical social and economic issue in Canada that devastated more vulnerable groups of the population such as school drop-outs, single mothers, physically or mentally disabled, and individuals dealing with mental health problems.

Social policy in this area is operationalized through public agencies such as *Emploi-Quebec* that offer programs to promote learning, occupational integration, and employment services.

In reaction to the job crisis and echoing the State policies, many community-based organizations are involved in creating jobs and developing employment services targeted to victims of social exclusion. These new social economy organizations often offer products or deliver services at the local level and provide social services with a different set of skills, objectives, and rules than those of the State or the private, for-profit sector (Larose et al., 2004). In this area, the contribution of community economic development is increasingly acknowledged. For example, the well-known federal-provincial paper *In Unison* explicitly underlines the contribution of community economic development (a component of social economy) to labour market integration of persons with disabilities:

> Opportunities for enhancing the integration and employment of persons with disabilities also could be explored through support for community economic development (CED) and self-employment. CED is an approach to local economic development that combines economic and social goals. (Federal/Provincial/Territorial Ministers Responsible for Social Services, 1998: 24)

In the area of job integration, the case of people with mental health problems in Quebec is interesting. Since 1987, research by *Santé Quebec* indicates that psychological despair and problems related to drug or alcohol addiction have increased. It is estimated that 500,000 people suffer from mental illness in the province—depression, manic depression, and schizophrenia (CSMQ, 1997). These problems are critical for youth, and many of them face major obstacles integrating into the labour force.

For over a decade the Quebec Health and Social Services Department has indicated in its policy objectives the crucial importance of work for people with mental health problems: "[…] integration to a socially productive activity such as work is, among other things, a process toward building an identity, a status, a role and finally a reconciliation with the social sphere that is identified as carrying certain determinants of health." (Charbonneau, 2004).

Accès-Cible (Santé Mentale et Travail) is a good example of a new social economy organization that offers various job integration activities to individuals that have mental health problems. Over the last 14 years, *Accès-Cible* (SMT) welcomed over 800 persons in group workshops, office skill learning, employment services, and professional training practice. Some 60 percent of participants found a job that helped them take better control of their life and health (Dumais, 2001).

As other organizations of the social economy, this innovative practice that stemmed from the community contributes to the well-being of citizens with a different approach than that of public institutions. However their objectives are similar and a partnership between the State and the social economy appears natural and fundamentally constructive.

Despite the positive returns of their efforts, organizations like *Accès-Cible* often deplore the lack of recognition of their role in supporting social policy. To continue to work adequately they require a long-term financial contribution from the government. Social economy initiatives in the fields of health and welfare constitute part of the solution to the crisis of the Welfare State and of the labour market (Vaillancourt, 1999). However this innovative part of the solution cannot act alone. A plural social development model, in our view, is one where society is built upon all the components or pillars aforementioned.

Early childhood day-care services

The social economy model has been determinant in the construction of Quebec's day-care services for pre-school children. Today's universally subsidized program is the result of numerous experimentations and struggles conducted by social movements and community-based organizations since the end of the 1960s (Aubry, 2001). These grassroot groups argued that a locally-run, but centrally financed, day-care structure was the best approach to allow women to pursue professional activities and to ensure that all pre-school children evolve in a healthy and stimulating environment.

In the 1960s and 1970s, "subsidized day-care services were viewed as a social welfare measure and were restricted to underprivileged recipients, unrelated either to a woman's right to work or to educational planning for young children" (Vaillancourt, Aubry, Jetté, and Tremblay, 2002: 38). As the number of women joining the labour force increased, the demand for day-care services also grew substantially. On one hand, the private for-profit sector was active in responding to the needs of parents who could pay for day-care services while on the other hand, civil society established a number of affordable neighbourhood day-care centers based on the social economy model of non-profit and democratic rules.

In 1979, the Quebec Government recognized the principle of collective responsibility for day-care and granted a two dollars per day subsidy for each authorized day-care space. This opened the door to further universalize day-care services.

In the 1980s and 1990s more institutionalization took place in Quebec with the development of spaces and public funding. By then, most of the services were provided by independent non-profit organizations. The 1997 Family Policy constituted a major reform in this field. At that time, the State, confirming its preference for non-profit day-care announced that day-care services would become universally available for a minimal fee of five dollars per day per child to be paid by parents (Vaillancourt, Aubry, Jetté, and Tremblay, 2002: 38).

This innovative program stimulated an increase of day-care spaces from 78,000 in 1998 to 145,000 in 2002. Early childhood day-care centres employ 22,000 people, making it the third larger employer in Quebec outside of the public sector.

The non-profit orientation of these day-care centres is a distinguishing feature of Quebec's program. Another distinctive feature of the system is the control of parents on the board of directors of each community day-care centre. Worker representatives are also present on these boards. The democratic participation of users ensures that the service corresponds to the needs of the children and remains independent from the State. In our view, this empowering environment is a positive determinant of well-being not only for children and parents but also for the entire community.

Concerning health and well-being, it appears that early involvement of pre-school children in day-care programs has a positive impact on their future. The World Health Organization (WHO) notes that "important foundations of adult health are laid in early childhood" (WHO, 1998: 12). The WHO indicates that early-life policy should (among other things) aim to "introduce pre-school programmes not only to improve reading and stimulate cognitive development but also to reduce behaviour problems in childhood and promote educational attainment, occupational chances and healthy behaviour in adulthood" (WHO, 1998: 13). The importance of these programmes is particularly crucial in the case of vulnerable populations.

A consensus now exists that day-care and its costs are not a responsibility of parents alone but of society. The day-care system in Quebec is made up of non-profit organizations providing services in the public interest that are controlled by local stakeholders and financed by the State. This is an eloquent example of social economy principles attaining certain social policy objectives.[2]

Homecare services

The Quebec Government recognizes that remaining in one's natural living environment constitutes a positive factor towards health and well-being (MSSS, 1992). For people experiencing temporary or permanent incapacities, staying at home implies numerous support services to ensure good life conditions. Generally these home support services are provided by public sector actors—*Centres locaux de services communautaires* (CLSC)—and private sector agencies. However social economy actors play a growing role particularly in dispensing homecare services such as home maintenance and meal preparation.

Community-based organizations that are active in domestic services have evolved significantly in recent years. Since 1997, social economy organizations account for a large part of domestic service provision. The sector now consists of 5,500 workers in 103 community-based organizations that offer services to 62,400 clients across the province (Ministère de l'Industrie et du Commerce, 2002: 58). With a non-profit or a cooperative status, these entities operate according to the rules and principles of the social economy, namely democratic management, user and worker empowerment, and priority of people and work over capital. While they generate revenue through billing their clients, they depend largely on State funding. In this context, a 36 million dollar State financial assistance program for domestic help services offers citizens a revenue-linked financial support to pay for domestic services offered by a recognized social economy organization (Ministère de l'Industrie et du Commerce, 2002).

Social economy enterprises in this area provide specific domestic services (light and heavy cleaning and maintenance, non-diet meal preparation, etc.) to an aging population or people with temporary or permanent incapacities. Partnership relations are established with local public sector agencies (CLSCs) in all regions, which ensure exclusivity to social economy domestic help organizations on their territory. Moreover, the CLSC personnel refer clients that require such services.

However, social economy organizations in domestic services, like many social economy organizations, must deal with a certain number of difficulties often related to inadequate funding: manpower shortage, low wages and high turn-over (Ministère de l'Industrie et du Commerce, 2002; Vaillancourt and Jetté, 2001). Nevertheless, the services they offer respond to an increasing need.

For this reason, the State must ensure them an even greater role as partners in this social policy area. The segment of the population over 65 years of age will continue to increase significantly over the next years. Further considerations should be given to the financial commitment the State is ready to make in the domestic service area (Vaillancourt, Aubry, and Jetté, 2003). If the government considers that the home environment is most adequate in view of its health and well-being policy, and if it believes that community-based organizations can ensure quality services in which users and producers have a say, then more resources must be allocated for them to do so.

Social housing

Housing is a major determinant of health and well-being (MSSS, 1992). As Pomeroy (1996: 42) noted: "Health and welfare are connected to the presence of support networks, opportunities to participate, controlling the elements that affect one's life and the ability to stay in a stable community. These elements are closely linked to the housing environment."

Social housing policy is an element of any integrated social policy. In Quebec, the social economy's input in the transformation of social housing policy and practices has been significant.

In the field of housing, three types of actors are involved on the Quebec scene (Vaillancourt and Ducharme, 2001). Firstly, there is the private sector comprised of the owners of rental properties, boarding houses, and apartment buildings. Then, there are the actors related to public institutions such as the Canada Mortgage and Housing Corporation (CMHC), the Société d'habitation du Quebec (SHQ), and the municipal housing offices. Finally, we find the actors of the social economy that we will discuss more fully here. Who are they? There are community-based organizations (CBO) such as advocacy groups, cooperatives and non-profit organizations that are responsible for a growing number of social housing units. There are also associated actors who provide services or community support to vulnerable residents in their own buildings. There are technical resource groups that offer services such as setting up a non-profit organization, helping residents form a cooperative, providing expert advice and skills, etc.

These CBOs are very active in Quebec in the construction of new social housing units and in redefining social practices in this area. Since the 1960s, 49,000 cooperative and non-profit housing units have been created in Quebec. Of the 20,000 public housing units run by the Montreal Municipal Housing organization, some 600, administered by non-profit organizations and cooperatives, provide community support services (Vaillancourt and Ducharme, 2001).

Innovative practices have expanded during the 1990s in Quebec. It is the crisis of the Welfare State that has exposed the limits of the social security system and has forced public servants and CBOs to find new approaches to enhance the quality of life of their recipients. These approaches are reflections of demands made by social movements and responses given by public decision-makers (Vaillancourt and Favreau, 2000).

Social housing with community support is a good example of innovative practices developed by actors of the social economy. Community organizations and cooperatives have been working with the Municipal Housing Office of Montreal to offer support, personal attention and services to their vulnerable groups of residents. These services are intended for semi-independent seniors, people with mental disabilities or psychiatric problems and victims of domestic violence, for example. Among the projects emerging from these new forms of cooperation between the public and third sector, there are eight group homes for young people, eight mental health day centres, many collective kitchens and home care services for seniors (Vaillancourt and Ducharme, 2001).

Another interesting case is the supplier relation between the Municipal Housing Office of Montreal and the Fédération des Organisations d'habitation sans but lucratif (OSBL) de Montréal. In the first year of its creation in 1987, the Housing Office contracted the social economy actors to manage non-profit rooming houses. These housing organizations now administer 192 social housing locations with community support and five non-profit organizations which represent delivery of services to nearly 2,000 housing units in Montreal (Jetté et al., 1998). The community support consists of on-site janitor-supervisors and follow-up visits by community service workers for individuals who have problems of housing instability, substance abuse or mental health, or are HIV-positive. This approach has an impact on the tenants' quality of life. According to Jetté et al. (1998) who studied social housing with community support, there are positive changes in their physical environment (accommodation, neighbourhood, services), their security, their social relations (e.g., friends, family) and, finally their self-esteem.

Social housing with community support is a new practice initiated by actors of the social economy. Empowerment of the users is a fundamental element of this approach. And that, for example, allows low-income and vulnerable people to have a decent home, make their own decisions and assume normal tenant responsibilities (Vaillancourt and Ducharme, 2001; Jetté et al., 1998; Thériault et al., 2001).

Social housing with community support represents:

> a viable alternative to institutionalization in a context of the redefinition of the Welfare State, provided that the people who are marginalized receive the support they need in order to be integrated into society. This entails not only the adoption of a more cross-sectoral approach, but also a reorientation of financial and human resources from the curative toward the preventive. (Jetté et al., 1998: 187)

Part III: Increasing the Role of Civil Society in Public Policy Development

We have seen that the social economy is very present in the field of social policy and can impact positively through the empowerment of users and producers in social economy organizations that are direct service providers. But the positive impact of the social economy on the health and well-being of individuals, families, and communities goes well beyond this. Indeed, it can be argued that the social economy also impacts positively on social policy through the pressure exercised on government by the actors of the social economy in the development of social policy. The mobilization of disabled persons is a good example of this phenomenon that could be qualified as "citizen empowerment."

Disabled persons' associations now stand up for their rights and are recognized as an autonomous social actor capable of provoking social change and influencing social policy. The movement is engaged in a critical discourse with regard to governmental intervention (Vaillancourt and Dumais, 2002b).

Let us consider the example of *In Unison: A Canadian Approach to Disability Issues. A Vision Paper* (Federal/Provincial/Territorial Ministers Responsible for Social Services, 1998), where changes in social policy were determined by the pressure of community organizations that advocate for disabled persons and by the development of alternative services.

Within the framework of inter-provincial and federal-provincial discussions on the Canadian Social Union Initiative (Fortin, St-Hilaire, and Noël, 2003), the question of disabled persons is one of five collective priorities along with the reduction of child poverty. In the area of social integration, the federal government has a new approach that is summarized in the document *In Unison* where the concept of "beneficiary" is replaced by the "participant," and that of "dependency" by "autonomy." The recommended approach gives the person a central position on decisions that concern him or her: the user knows best what he or she needs.

Citizenship, which is central to this approach, refers to "the inclusion of persons with disabilities in all aspects of Canadian society":

> It is the overarching theme that shapes the vision and the building blocks. Full inclusion means that the needs of persons with disabilities are met through generic programs, while additional essential supports are provided to those individuals whose needs cannot be met through generic programs and services. Future reforms will need to ensure that the policies and programs in each building block are consistent with this concept. (Federal/Provincial/Territorial Ministers Responsible for Social Services, 1998: 20)

The social economy can contribute to the development of social policies that encourage the active participation of disabled persons. In this vision, it is important not only to go beyond the welfarist approach but to break the traditional relations between the user and the provider because disabled persons have the capacity to contribute to the planning, the management, and the evaluation of social policies that concern them. In this way, supply and demand for services are constructed jointly (Laville, 1992; 2000).

The example of the empowerment of disabled persons illustrates a collective dimension (Beresford and Holden, 2000) that can be extended to all users of social policy. Users must be viewed as a collective subject as well as an organized social movement. They are actors in the elaboration and analysis of social policy. They must be considered as active participants and partners in the development of social policy (Boucher, 2002).

Focusing on Quebec's experience, we observe frequent influence of grass-root independent organizations on social policy making. In some cases, locally created activities have been nationalized and institutionalized across the province (CLSC). In other cases, the State has chosen to support the services as part of public policy while maintaining the independent governance structure, as is the case for preschool day-care services discussed in the previous section. Thirty years ago, users, parents, and women instigated day-care services locally. In the early childhood child-care network, the users still have control on the orientations of their centre through board participation:

> The growth of day-care services highlights the role of social movements introducing new social practices and in extending these practices to all of society. (Vaillancourt, Aubry, Jetté, and Tremblay, 2002: 37–38)

Through social policy, government has conveyed the principle that early childhood care is a "public good" that can best be organized by user-controlled, community-based organizations rather than by for-profit business or government agencies.

In Quebec, progress in institutionalizing social economy projects has allowed the third sector to gain a measure of recognition alongside the private and public sectors. However, we must be cautious in our assessment. While some government policies support growth in certain areas of the social economy, including child-care centres and household services, other policies, such as the move toward more non-institutional community care, may result in an increased burden for natural helpers, who in the vast majority of cases are women.

Nevertheless, it is important to note that even when the social economy makes breakthroughs at the policy level, the gains remain precarious if the government fails to establish funding policies that enable organizations to strengthen and develop their activities.

Part IV: Interactions between the Social Economy, the Market and the State

The social economy can also have a positive impact on health and well-being through the influence it can exert on democratic practices and organizational innovations in the public and the for-profit private sectors with which it interacts (Vaillancourt, 2003; Vaillancourt, Aubry, and Jetté, 2003).

By advocating the submission of economic relationships to social objectives within its organizations, the social economy contributes to put the economy and the market at the service of society and not the other way around. The recognition of the social economy in our society by the acknowledgement of its representatives, through the growing knowledge of its innovative practices and better and longer term financing from the State will increase influence on for-profit and public sector practices.

In order to optimize its contribution to the acquisition of citizenship for the excluded and the marginalized, the social economy must be audacious in order to influence the market economy by advancing a new paradigm (Lipietz, 2001). Hence, the social economy must:

- promote a model of work organization where the empowerment of users and workers give them control over their environment;
- resist the mainstream management culture and focus on human resources to ensure the success of its organizations.

The sectors of economic activity are not watertight categories. Indeed, they can influence or even transform each other by incorporating the values and practices of other sectors. To the extent that our society recognizes concretely that the social economy contributes to its development, as do the public sector and the market economy, it will be possible to increase linkages between these three sectors. In this manner, innovative practices of the social economy could more easily be transferred to the two other sectors.

Let us give an example, taken from the public low-rent housing field, of such influence of the social economy on the public sector. Until recently, tenants of public low rent housing were not represented on the board of directors of these housing facilities. Since 2000, the Quebec government passed legislation stating that low rent public housing must contribute to the social development of the community and providing that two seats on the board of directors are reserved for tenants' associations. These new requirements stem from democratic practices characteristic of the social economy housing organizations where tenants play an important role. Such practices contribute to the active citizenship of public housing tenants (Vaillancourt and Ducharme, 2002).

But this is not a one-way street. Indeed, if the social economy can influence positively the public and for-profit organizations, the reverse is also true. In Ontario, for example, the decision of the Harris government to open up certain areas of the health and welfare systems to competition between private enterprises and community organizations forced these organizations to reformulate their strategies and to adopt private sector management and assessment models (Leduc Browne and Welch, 2002).

The challenge for the social economy is to transfer the "common cause" philosophy to the public and private economic sectors. How? In the public sector, this means encouraging consultation with the civil society, fostering social investment, etc. In the private sector, it could mean requiring the application of an ethical code that defines the social responsibilities of companies.

Even if social economy organizations develop to meet needs expressed at the local level, the development of a social and solidarity-based economy requires a multi-level strategy that focuses simultaneously on the local, regional, national and international levels. We have learned that changes at the local level can induce major social and economic changes at higher levels that contribute to the health and well-being of individuals and families (Ortiz, 1999).

Conclusion

In our presentation, the role of social policy as a determinant of health and well-being is examined through the specific contribution of the social economy (and its organizations) within the social policy field. We have tried to show that whatever the terms and concepts used—social economy, third sector, non-profit sector, voluntary sector, etc.—they represent a similar reality; that is, the emergence within the civil society of economic activity whose objective is to answer, through citizen participation, needs that cannot be satisfied by the market or the State.

We have tried to demonstrate that within the area of social policy, the social economy can contribute in many ways to the health and well-being of individuals, families, and communities. We have distinguished three original contributions of the social economy.

First, the values at the heart of the social economy and the democratic rules that govern social economy organizations can facilitate the empowerment of users and workers within such organizations that are direct service providers. The Independent Living Movement is an example of such empowerment where users, instead of being considered as passive beneficiaries, become active participants in the decisions that concern them. We have also made the point that the empowerment of workers has positive impacts on the quality of life in the workplace, contributing favourably to their health and well-being.

Second, the actors of the social economy have the capacity to mobilize civil society in order to instigate social policy reform, thus contributing to what can be qualified as "citizen empowerment" or "active citizenship." The implication of users and workers within community-based organizations, the demands of social movements and their capacity to mobilize communities and their members at the local, regional and national levels, can constitute powerful forces in the definition and development of social policy. The developments of early childhood day-care services in Quebec, since the 1970s, and the new family policy put in place in 1997 are examples of such input from the social economy.

Finally, the social economy can contribute to the health and well-being of individuals and families through the positive influence it can exert on the values and practices of the public and for-profit organizations; such as, for example, more democratic forms of governance in the public sector, a governance open to the empowerment of users and workers and to the contribution of local communities and their networks.

Our view of the growing contribution of the social economy, not only in the realm of social policy, but in almost every sphere of economic and social life, is contradictory to the bipolar State/Market model still dominant in most research and political circles notwithstanding the enormous progress of the social economy in many countries and regions during the last twenty years.

In Quebec, the recognition of the contribution of the social economy by the State has made giant steps since the beginning of the 1990s. This is particularly the case in many social policy fields like family policy and preschool day-care services, social housing, homecare services, and occupational integration.

We believe that the recognition of the contribution of the social economy to society is a condition to better social policy reform, since the importance of the non-medical determinants of health and well-being is at the heart of the development of much of the social economy. This is true in Quebec, but in other regions of Canada as well. The actors of the social economy have always insisted that improving living conditions is crucial in order to better the health and well-being of citizens and communities. These living conditions are what we now call social determinants of health and well-being.

In this view, giving the social economy the tools it needs consists in recognizing its contribution, accepting the presence of its representatives in decision-making circles and consultation processes, respecting its independence and improving and increasing its financial support. As an active partner of the State in social policy, the social economy network can offer an innovative contribution to better health and well-being.

Notes

1. See, for example, Quarter, Mook and Richmond (2002) and Banting (2000). See also the Voluntary Sector Initiative website at www.vsi-isbc.ca.
2. Paradoxically, early in 2005, the so called "Québec model of early childhood services" which gives preference to the non-profit sector for the delivery of services seems to be more popular in the minority government of Paul Martin in Ottawa than in the government of Jean Charest in Québec City!

Bibliography

Aubry, F. (2001). *Trente ans déjà: Le mouvement syndical et le développement des services de garde au Quebec.* Confédération des syndicats nationaux et Table ronde pour le développement des ressources humaines du secteur des services de garde, Montréal.

Banting, K.G. (2000). *The Nonprofit Sector in Canada: Roles and Relationships.* Montreal and Kingston, McGill-Queen's University Press.

Beaulieu, A., Morin, P., Provencher, H., and H. Dorvil (2002). "Le travail comme déterminant de la santé pour les personnes utilisatrices des services de santé mentale (notes de recherche)." *Santé mentale au Quebec* 27: 1, 177–93.

Bélanger, P.R. (2002). "La présence des usagers dans les organisations: La relation de service." In Bélanger, P.R. and P. Ughetto (eds), *La dimension de service dans les organisations et les entreprises.* Paris/Montréal: LSCI-CRISES 1-0203.

Beresford, P. and C. Holden (2002). "We have Choices: Globalization and Welfare user Movements." *Disability and Society* 19: 7, 973–89.

Boucher, N. (2002). "Politiques sociales et handicap au Quebec: Une relecture historique de l'interface fédérale-provinciale, 1945–1980." In Vaillancourt, Y., Caillouette, J., and L. Dumais (eds), *Les politiques sociales s'adressant aux personnes ayant des incapacités au Quebec: Histoire, inventaire et éléments de bilan.* Montréal: LAREPPS/ARUC-EC/UQAM.

Burnonville, F. (1999). "Détresse psychologique au travail, syndrome du survivant et usure mentale." *Intervention* 109.

Caillouette, J. (2001). "Pratiques de partenariat, pratiques d'articulation identitaire et mouvement communautaire." *Nouvelles pratiques sociales* 14: 1.

Chantier de l'économie sociale (1996). *Osons la solidarité.* Rapport du groupe de travail sur l'économie sociale, Sommet sur l'économie et l'emploi, Quebec.

Chantier de l'économie sociale (2001). *De nouveau nous osons.* Document de positionnement stratégique, Montréal.

Charbonneau, C. (2002). "Développer l'intégration au travail en santé mentale, une longue marche à travers des obstacles sociopolitiques." *Santé mentale au Quebec* 27: 1.

Charbonneau, C. (2004). *Travail et santé mentale: Perspectives et defies.* Montréal: UQAM/ LAREPPS.

CIRIEC (1999). *Les entreprises et organisations du troisième système: enjeu stratégique pour l'emploi.* Liège.

Comité de la santé mentale du Quebec (CSMQ), rédigé par N. Potvin (1997). *Bilan d'implantation de la politique de santé mentale.* Quebec, ministère de la santé et des services sociaux.

Commission d'étude sur les services de santé et les services sociaux (2001). *Les solutions émergentes—Rapport et recommandations (Rapport Clair).* Quebec.

Conseil de la santé et du bien-être (2002). *Avis pour une stratégie du Quebec en santé. Décider et agir.* Quebec.

Defourny, J., Develtere, P., and B. Fonteneau (eds) (1999). *L'Économie sociale au Nord et au Sud.* Brussels: De Boeck Université.

Demoustier, D. and E. Pezzini (1999). "Économie sociale et création d'emplois dans les pays occidentaux." In Defourny, J., Develtere, P., and B. Fonteneau (eds), *L'Économie sociale au Nord et au Sud.* Brussels: De Boeck Université.

Donnelly-Cox, G., Donoghue, F., and R. Taylor (eds) (2001). "The Third Sector in Ireland, North and South." *Voluntas* 12: 3 (September).

Dumais, L. (2001). *Accès-Cible (SMT) : Monographie d'un organisme d'aide à l'insertion pour les personnes ayant des problèmes de santé mentale.* Montréal: UQAM/LAREPPS.

Esping-Andersen, G. (1999). *Les trois mondes de l'État-providence: Essai sur le capitalisme moderne.* Paris: PUF, coll. Le Lien social.

Evers, A. et J.-L. Laville (eds) (2004). *The Third Sector in Europe.* Cheltenham, UK: Edward Elgar.

Eurostat (1997). *Le secteur coopératif, mutualiste et associatif dans l'Union Européenne.* Luxembourg: Commission européenne.

Federal/Provincial/Territorial Ministers Responsible for Social Services (1998). *In Unison: A Canadian Approach to Disability Issues. A Vision Paper.* Ottawa: Development of Human Resources Canada.

Fortin, S., Noël, A., and F. St-Hilaire (eds.) (2003). *Forging the Canadian Social Union: SUFA and Beyond.* Montreal: Institute for Research on Public Policy.

Forum national sur la santé (1997a). *La santé au Canada: un héritage à faire fructifier: Rapport final.* Ottawa: Forum national sur la santé.

Forum national sur la santé (1997b). *La santé au Canada: un héritage à faire fructifier: Rapports de synthèse et documents de référence.* Ottawa: Forum national sur la santé.

Fuchs, D. (1987). "Breaking Down Barriers: Independent Living Resource Centres for Empowering the Physically Disabled." In Ismael, J. S. and R. J. Thomlison (eds), *Perspectives on Social Services and Social Issues.* Ottawa: Canadian Council of Social Development.

Groupe de travail sur la complémentarité du secteur privé dans la poursuite des objectifs fondamentaux du système public de santé au Quebec (1999). *La complémentarité du secteur privé dans la poursuite des objectifs fondamentaux du système public de santé au Quebec (Rapport Arpin).* Quebec.

Jetté, C., Lévesque, B., Mager, L., and Y. Vaillancourt (2000). *Économie sociale et transformation de l'État-providence dans le domaine de la santé et du bien-être: Une recension des écrits (1990-2000).* Montréal: Presses de l'Université du Quebec.

Jetté, C., Lévesque, B., and Y. Vaillancourt (2001). "The Social Economy and the Future of Health and Welfare in Quebec and Canada." Montréal: UQAM/LAREPPS.

Jetté, C., Thériault, L., Mathieu, R., and Y. Vaillancourt (1998). *Évaluation du logement social avec support communautaire à la Fédération des OSBL d'habitation de Montréal (FOHM).* Montréal: UQAM/LAREPPS.

Kearney, M., Aubry, F., Tremblay, L., and Y. Vaillancourt (2004). *L'économie sociale au Quebec : Le regard d'acteurs sociaux.* Montréal: LAREPPS.

Larose, G., Vaillancourt, Y., Shields, G., and M. Kearney (2004). *Contribution de l'économie sociale au renouvellement des politiques et des pratiques dans le domaine de l'insertion socioéconomique au Quebec, de 1983 à 2003.* Montreal: UQAM/LAREPPS.

Lauzon, G. and C. Charbonneau (with the collaboration of G. Provost) (2001). *Favoriser l'intégration au travail: L'urgence d'agir.* Quebec: Association québécoise pour la réadaptation psychosociale.

Laville, J.-L. (ed.) (2000). *L'économie solidaire: Une perspective internationale,* 2nd edn. Paris: Desclée de Brouwer.

Laville, J.-L. (1992). *Les services de proximité en Europe.* Paris: Syros Alternatives.

Laville, J.-L. and M. Nyssens (eds) (2001). *Les services sociaux entre associations: État et marché. L'aide aux personnes âgées.* Paris: La Découverte/Mauss/Crida.

Leduc Browne, P. and D. Welch. (2002). "In the Shadow of the Market: Ontario's Social Economy in the Age of Neo-liberalism." In Vaillancourt, Y. and L. Tremblay (eds), *Social Economy: Health and Welfare in Four Canadian Provinces.* Montreal/Halifax: Fernwood/LAREPPS.

Lévesque, B., Girard, J.-P., and M.-C. Malo (1999). "L'ancienne et la nouvelle économie sociale: Deux dynamiques, un mouvement : Le cas du Quebec." In Defourny, J., Develtere, P., and B. Fonteneau (1999), *L'Économie sociale au Nord et au Sud.* Brussels: De Boeck Université.

Lipietz, A. (2001). *Rapport sur l'économie sociale et solidaire.* Montréal: UQAM/LAREPPS.

Lippel, K. (1992). *Le stress au travail: L'indemnisation des atteintes à la santé en droit québécois, canadien et américain.* Cowansville, Quebec: Les Éditions Yvon Blais.

Malenfant, R. and M. Vézina (eds) (1995). *Plaisir et souffrance: Dualité de la santé mentale au travail.* Actes du Colloque "Les aspects sociaux et psychologiques de l'organisation du travail." Quebec: ACFAS.

Martin, P. (2004). *Adresse du Premier ministre en réponse au discours du Trône.* 3 February.

Mercier, C., Provost, G., Denis G., and F. Vincelette (1999). *Le développement de l'employabilité et l'intégration au travail pour les personnes ayant des problèmes de santé mentale.* Montréal: Centre de recherche de l'hôpital Douglas.

Ministère de l'Industrie et du Commerce (2002). *Portrait des entreprises en aide domestique.* Quebec: Gouvernement du Quebec.

Ministère de la Santé et des Services sociaux (MSSS) (1992). *La Politique de la santé et du bien-être.* Quebec: Gouvernement du Quebec.

Ministère de la Santé et des Services sociaux (MSSS) (2000). *Plan stratégique 2001–2004.* Quebec: gouvernement du Quebec.

Office des personnes handicapées du Quebec (OPHQ) (1984). *À part ... égale: L'intégration sociale des personnes handicapées : un défi pour tous.* Drummondville: gouvernement du Quebec.

Ortiz, H. (1999). "L'Économie solidaire en Amérique latine." *Inter-Réseaux de l'économie solidaire.* Lettre 3, May–June–July.

Polanyi, K. (2001). *The Great Transformation.* Boston: Beacon Press.

Pomeroy, S. (1996). "Final Comments." In Ken Battle, Veronica Doyle, Dougas Page, Steve Pomeroy, Janet Thomas, eds., *The Role of Housing in Social Policy.* Ottawa: Caledon Institute of Social Policy.

Quarter, J., Mook, L., and Richmond, B. J. (2003). *What Counts: Social Accounting for Nonprofits and Cooperatives.* Upper Saddle River, NJ: Prentice Hall.

Quarter, J. (1992). *Canada's Social Economy: Cooperatives, Non-profits, and other Community Enterprises.* Toronto: Lorimer.

Ramon, S. (ed.) (1991). *Beyond Community Car: Normalisation and Integration Work.* London, Macmillan.

Raphael, D. (ed.) (2004). *Social Determinants of Health: Canadian Perspectives.* Toronto: Canadian Scholars' Press.

Roeher Institute (1993). *Social Well-Being: A Paradigm for Reform.* North York: Roeher Institute.

Salamon, L. and H.K. Anheier (1998). "Le secteur de la société civile, une nouvelle force sociale." *La Revue du MAUSS semestrielle* 11.

Salamon, L., Anheier, H.K., List, R., Toepler, S., Sokolowski, S., and Associatives (eds.) (1999). *Global Civil Society: Dimensions of the Nonprofit Sector.* Baltimore, MD: The John Hopkins Center for Civil Society Studies.

Shimon, L. D., Lamoureux, G., and É. Gosselin (1996). *Psychologie du travail et des organisations.* Boucherville: Gaëtan Morin.

Shragge, E. and J.-M. Fontan (2000). *Social Economy: International Debates and Perspectives.* Montreal: Black Rose Books.

Taylor, M. (1995). "Voluntary Action and the State." In D. Gladstone (ed.), *British Social Welfare. Past, Present and Future.* London, UCL Press.

Thériault, L. Jetté, C., Mathieu, R., and Y. Vaillancourt (2001). *Social Housing with Community Support: A Study of the FOHM Experience.* Ottawa: Caledon Institute of Social Policy.

Vaillancourt, Y. (1999). "Tiers secteur et reconfiguration des politiques sociales." *Nouvelles pratiques sociales* 12: 1, 21–39.

Vaillancourt, Y. (2003). "The Quebec Model in Social Policy and Its Interface with Canada's Social Union." In Fortin, S., Noël, A., and F. St-Hilaire (eds.), *Forging the Canadian Social Union: SUFA and Beyond.* Montreal: Institute for Research on Public Policy.

Vaillancourt, Y. and M.-N. Ducharme (with the collaboration of R. Cohen, C. Roy, and C. Jetté) (2001). *Social Housing—A Key Component of Social Policies in Transformation: The Quebec Experience.* Ottawa: Caledon Institute of Social Policy.

Vaillancourt, Y. and L. Dumais (2002a) "Introduction." In Vaillancourt, Y., Caillouette, J., and L. Dumais (eds), *Les politiques sociales s'adressant aux personnes ayant des incapacités au Quebec: Histoire, inventaire et éléments de bilan.* Montréal: LAREPPS/ARUC-ÉS/UQAM.

Vaillancourt, Y. and L. Dumais (2002b) "Conclusion. Vers un premier bilan à chaud." In Vaillancourt, Y., Caillouette, J., and L. Dumais (eds), *Les politiques sociales s'adressant aux personnes ayant des incapacités au Quebec: Histoire, inventaire et éléments de bilan.* Montréal: LAREPPS/ARUC-ÉS/ UQAM.

Vaillancourt, Y. and L. Favreau (2000). *Le modèle québécois d'économie sociale et solidaire.* Montréal: UQAM/LAREPPS.

Vaillancourt, Y. and C. Jetté (1997). *Vers un nouveau partage de responsabilité dans les services sociaux et de santé: rôles de l'État, du marché, de l'économie sociale et du secteur informel.* Montréal: UQAM/LAREPPS.

Vaillancourt, Y. and C. Jetté (1999a). *Le rôle accru du tiers secteur dans les services à domicile concernant les personnes âgées au Quebec.* Montréal: UQAM/LAREPPS.

Vaillancourt, Y. and C. Jetté (1999b). *L'aide à domicile au Quebec: Relecture de l'histoire et pistes d'action.* Montréal: UQAM/LAREPPS.

Vaillancourt, Y. and C. Jetté (2001). "Quebec: Un rôle croissant des associations dans les services à domicile." In Laville, J.-L. and M. Nyssens (eds), *Les services sociaux entre associations, État et marché. L'aide aux personnes âgées.* Paris: La Découverte/Mauss/Crida.

Vaillancourt, Y. and L. Tremblay (eds) (2002). *Social Economy: Health and Welfare in four Canadian Provinces.* Montreal/Halifax: LAREPPS/Fernwood.

Vaillancourt, Y., Aubry, F., Jetté, C., and L. Tremblay (2002). "Regulation Based on Solidarity: A Fragile Emergence in Quebec." In Y. Vaillancourt and L. Tremblay (eds), *Social Economy: Health and Welfare in Four Canadian Provinces.* Montreal/Halifax: LAREPPS/Fernwood.

Vaillancourt, Y. Aubry, F., D'Amours, M., Jetté, C. Thériault, L., and L. Tremblay (2000). "Social Economy, Health and Welfare: the Specificity of the Quebec Model with the Canadian Context." *Canadian Review of Social Policy* 45–46.

Vaillancourt, Y., Caillouette, J., and L. Dumais (eds) (2002). *Les politiques sociales s'adressant aux personnes ayant des incapacités au Quebec: Histoire, inventaire et éléments de bilan.* Montréal: LAREPPS/ARUC-ÉCONOMIE SOCIALE/UQAM.

Vaillancourt, Y. Aubry, F., and C. Jetté (eds) (2003). *L'économie sociale dans les services à domicile.* Quebec: Presses de l'Université du Quebec.

World Health Organization (WHO) (1998). *Social Determinants of Health: The Solid Facts,* Copenhagen: World Health Organization Regional Office for Europe.

Sources

Babcock, Robert H. "Blood on the Factory Floor: The Workers' Compensation Movement in Canada and the United States" from *Social Welfare Policy in Canada. Historical Readings* ed. Raymond B. Blake and Jeff Keshen, Copp Clark Ltd., 1995: 107–21. Reprinted by permission of the author.

Balcom, Karen. "Scandal and Social Policy: The Ideal Maternity Home and the Evolution of Social Policy in Nova Scotia, 1940–51." *Acadiensis* 31:2 (2002): 3–37. Reprinted by permission of the publisher.

Banting, Keith. "The Social Policy Divide: The Welfare State in Canada and the United States" from *Degrees of Freedom: Canada and the United States in a Changing World* edited by Keith Banting, George Hoberg, and Richard Simeon, McGill-Queen's University Press, 1997: 267–309. Reprinted by permission of the publisher.

Baum, Joel A.C. "The Rise of Chain Nursing Homes in Ontario, 1971–1996." *Social Forces* 78:2 (1999): 543–83. Reprinted by permission of University of North Carolina Press.

Blake, Raymond B. "In the Children's Interest?—Change and Continuity in a Century of Canadian Social Welfare Initiatives for Children." *Journal of Indo-Canadian Studies* 1:1 (2001): 113–37. Reprinted by permission of the author.

Bowen, Dawn S. "'Forward to a Farm': Land Settlement as Unemployment Relief in the 1930s." *Prairie Forum* 20:2 (Fall 1995): 207–29. Reprinted by permission of the publisher.

Carter, Donald. "Employment Benefits for Same Sex Couples: The Expanding Entitlement." *Canadian Public Policy* 24:1 (1998): 108–17. Reprinted by permission of the publisher.

Drover, Glenn. "Tilting Toward Marketization: Reform of the Canadian Pension Plan." *Review of Policy Research* 19:3 (2002): 86–107. Reprinted by permission of Blackwell Publishing Ltd.

Evans, Patricia. "Eroding Canadian Social Welfare: The Mulroney Legacy, 1984–1993." *Social Policy and Administration* 28:2 (1994): 107–19. Reprinted with permission of Blackwell Publishing Ltd.

Greschner, Donna. "How Will the Charter of Rights and Freedoms and Evolving Jurisprudence Affect Health-Care Costs?" from *The Governance of Health Care in Canada: The Romanow Papers*, Volume 2, edited by Tom McIntosh, Pierre Gerlier-Forst, and Gregory Marchildon, U of Toronto P Inc., 2004: 82–124. Reprinted with permission of the publisher.

Guest, Dennis T. "Saving for a Rainy Day: Social Security in Late-Nineteenth-Century and Early-Twentieth-Century Canada" from *The Emergence of Social Security in Canada*, third ed., UBC Press, 1997: 20–39. Reprinted by permission of the publisher.

Hudson, Peter and Sharon Taylor-Henley. "First Nations Child and Family Services, 1982–1992." *Canadian Social Work Review* 12:1 (1995): 72–84. Reprinted by permission of the publisher.

Hunter, Garson and Dionne Miazdyck. "Current Issues Surrounding Poverty and Welfare Programming in Canada: Two Reviews." Social Policy Research Unit, Faculty of Social Work, University of Regina, 2004. Reprinted by permission of the authors.

Keshen, Jeffrey A. From *Saints, Sinners and Soldiers*. UBC Press, 2004: chapter 10. Reprinted by permission of UBC Press.

Lund, Richard. "Income Maintenance, Insurance Principles, and the 'Liberal 1960s': Canada's Unemployment Insurance Program" from *Canada at the Crossroads, the Critical 1960s* ed. Gustav Schmidt and J.L. Granatstein, Universitatsverlag Dr. N. Brocmeyer, 1994: 3–23. Reprinted by permission of the publisher.

Marchildon, Gregory P. "Three Choices for the Future of Medicare," Caledon Institute of Public Policy, April 2004. Reprinted by permission of the publisher.

Prince, Michael J. "Canadian Disability Policy: Still a Hit-and-Miss Affair." *Canadian Journal of Sociology* 29:1 (2004): 59–82.

Rivest, François, Pascal Bossé, Silvu Nedelca, and Alain Simard. "Access to Physician Services in Quebec: Relative Influence of Household Income and Area of Residence." *Canadian Public Policy* 25:4 (1999): 453–79. Reprinted by permission of the publisher.

Struthers, James. "'In the Interests of the Children': Mothers' Allowances and the Origins of Income Security in Ontario" from *The Limits of Affluence: Welfare in Ontario, 1920–1970*, U of Toronto P, 1994: 19–49. Copyright © James Struthers. Reprinted by permission of James Struthers.

Tester, Frank James. "Integrating the Inuit: Social Work Practice in the Eastern Arctic, 1955–1963." *Canadian Social Work Review* 11:2 (1994): 168–83. Reprinted by permission of the publisher.

Tillotson, Shirley. "A New Taxpayer for a New State: Charitable Fundraising and the Origins of the Welfare State" from *The Welfare State in Canada: Past, Present, and Future*, edited by Raymond B. Blake, Penny E. Bryden, and J. Frank Strain, Irwin Publishing, 1997: 138–55. Reprinted by permission of the author.

Vaillancourt, Yves, François Aubry, Louise Tremblay, Muriel Kearney, and Luc Thériault. "The Contribution of the Social Economy to Social Policy: Lessons from Quebec" from a modified version of a working paper published by the Social Policy Research Unit, Faculty of Social Work, University of Regina, 2003. Reprinted by permission of Luc Thériault.

Vigod, B.L. "History According to the Boucher Report: Some Reflections on the State and Social Welfare in Quebec Before the Quiet Revolution" from *The Benevolent State: The Growth of Welfare in Canada*, edited by Allan Moscovitch and Jim Albert, Garamond Press, 1987: 175–86. Copyright © B.L. Vigod. Reprinted by permission of the publisher and the estate of B.L. Vigod.